Gender, Taste, and Material Culture in Britain and North America 1700–1830

Studies in British Art 17

Gender, Taste, and Material Culture in Britain and North America 1700–1830

Edited by John Styles and Amanda Vickery

Published by
The Yale Center for British Art
The Paul Mellon Centre for Studies in British Art

Distributed by
Yale University Press, New Haven & London

Published by

The Yale Center for British Art
P.O. Box 208280
1080 Chapel Street
New Haven, CT 06520-8280
www.yale.edu/ycba

and

The Paul Mellon Centre for Studies in British Art
16 Bedford Square
London WC1B 3JA
United Kingdom
www.paul-mellon-centre.ac.uk

Distributed by

Yale University Press
P.O. Box 209040
302 Temple Street
New Haven, CT 06520-9040
www.yalebooks.com

Volume edited by John Styles and Amanda Vickery
Publication coordinated by Julia Marciari Alexander and Anna Magliaro
at the Yale Center for British Art and Kristin Swan at Yale University Press
Copyedited by Richard Slovak
Index by Indexing Partners, LLC

Designed by Miko McGinty
Set in Garamond by Tina Henderson
Printed in Canada by Friesens

Library of Congress Control Number: 2006932894

ISBN-13: 978-0-300-11659-5
ISBN-10: 0-300-11659-4

A catalogue record for this book is available from the British Library.

10 9 8 7 6 5 4 3 2 1

This is the seventeenth in a series of occasional volumes devoted to studies in British art, published by the Yale Center for British Art and the Paul Mellon Centre for Studies in British Art. It is the first volume to be administered by the Yale Center for British Art, which has assumed the role of lead publisher for the series.

Jacket illustrations: *(front)* Artist unknown, *A Morning Ramble, or The Milliners Shop* (detail), mezzotint with hand color (1782), 13⅞ x 9⅞ in. (35.1 x 24.9 cm), plate. Courtesy of The Lewis Walpole Library, Yale University; *(back)* Ralph Earle, *Elijah Boardman* (detail), oil on canvas (1789), 83 x 51 in. (210.8 x 129.5 cm). The Metropolitan Museum of Art, Bequest of Susan W. Tyler, 1979 (1979.395). Photo: © 1985 The Metropolitan Museum of Art.

Contents

Politics

People

Acknowledgments

THIS COLLECTION OF ESSAYS began life as one of the focused research studies undertaken between 2001 and 2006 by the British Arts and Humanities Research Council (AHRC) Centre for the Study of the Domestic Interior. The Centre was a collaboration among three institutions in London—the Royal College of Art, the Bedford Centre for the History of Women at Royal Holloway, University of London, and the Victoria and Albert Museum. The editors are indebted for financial, organizational, and intellectual support to the AHRC, to the Centre's Management Committee and its Academic Advisory Board, to Centre Director Jeremy Aynsley, to its Research Fellows, and to its administrators. Two of the Centre's Research Fellows worked directly on this project. Karen Harvey played a vital role in its early planning. We hope the final outcome does justice to her insistence on the importance of men. Hannah Greig's role has been indispensable to the whole project. She contributed not just a chapter, but her critical intelligence, her intellectual enthusiasm, her formidable organizational talents, and her command of source materials, both visual and textual. We owe her particular thanks for her incisive reading of the complete manuscript of the book.

This book is a transatlantic collaboration. Though edited in Britain, it has benefited hugely from the generosity of two great American scholarly institutions: The Huntington Library, Art Collections, and Botanical Gardens and the Yale Center for British Art. The Huntington hosted the conference "Gender, Taste and Material Culture in Britain and North America in the Long Eighteenth Century" in May 2004, where most of the chapters in the book were first aired. We owe a great debt to Robert C. Ritchie, W.M. Keck Foundation Director of Research, who in his own work and in his deft leadership of research at The Huntington has consistently supported transatlantic perspectives on eighteenth-century Britain and America. We would like to thank the staff of the Research Division at The Huntington for their sterling support for the conference; Wendy Bellion, Adrian Evans, Adrienne Hood, and Susan Stabile for their papers; and Shelley Bennett, Ann Bermingham, John Brewer, Kathryn Norberg, Felicity Nussbaum, and Carole

Shammas for chairing, comments, and criticisms. In January 2005, the Yale Center for British Art hosted an editorial workshop where the contributors reworked the chapters. We are indebted to YCBA Director Amy Meyers and Head of Research Michael Hatt for their generosity and their infectious intellectual enthusiasm, and to the staff at the YCBA who organized the workshop. Our deliberations there benefited enormously from the presence of a number of scholars who do not appear in the book. We would like to thank Julia Marciari Alexander, Christopher Breward, Edward Cooke, Michael Hatt, Amy Meyers, Alex Nemerov, Morna O'Neill, Jules Prown, Susan Stabile, and Keith Wrightson for their contributions.

To say that a book could not have been completed without the efforts of publishers, copy editors, and designers is an authorial cliché, but in the case of this book it is emphatically true. The book would not have seen the light of day without the hard work, persistence, and patience of Julia Marciari Alexander, who superintended its publication on behalf of the Yale Center for British Art; of Anna Magliaro, who provided invaluable research help with captions and documentation; of Richard Slovak, the book's copy editor; of Miko McGinty, its designer; and of Patricia Fidler and Kristin Swan at Yale University Press.

Introduction

John Styles and Amanda Vickery

HISTORIES OF MATERIAL LIFE have boomed over the last decade. Books about commodities—nutmeg, salt, aniline dyes, cod, porcelain, glass—have repeatedly appeared on best-seller lists.[1] Academic research into fields as far apart as Renaissance art history and twentieth-century urban geography have been transformed by investigations that employ the notion of consumption as their conceptual point of departure.[2] The eighteenth century has been crucial for these new histories of artifacts and their consumption. The idea that Great Britain experienced a consumer revolution in the eighteenth century, leading to the birth of the world's first consumer society, has profoundly affected the way we think about the period.[3] Not surprisingly, historians of eighteenth-century Britain have delighted in these compelling phrases, which identify that century as the era when the modern world began and Britain as its birthplace. Applying these twentieth-century notions to the eighteenth century runs the risk of exaggerating the extent to which the country's material life was transformed, but there is no doubt that major changes in consumption did accompany Britain's emergence in the eighteenth century as Europe's most successful mercantile and manufacturing economy.[4] Britain's North American colonies shared in these developments, not least as key markets for British manufactured goods, with rapidly growing populations that together were about a third the size of England's on the eve of independence in 1776. The British Atlantic empire was, in Timothy Breen's telling phrase, an "Empire of Goods," held together not just by political authority, military force, and a common language, but by a shared material culture constantly nourished by flows of commodities.[5] In declaring independence from that empire, the colonists also had to declare their independence (at least temporarily) from what the Boston radical Samuel Adams derided in 1771 as the "Baubles of Britain."[6]

The things people owned, displayed, and coveted are now prominent in historical interpretations of the eighteenth century, whether in depictions of the English as a polite and commercial people, or in the interweaving of consumer politics and the American Revolution.[7] It has been scholars of eighteenth-century

America, working under the broad multidisciplinary umbrella of material-culture studies, who have brought the greatest conceptual range and sophistication to the cultural interpretation of eighteenth-century artifacts.[8] Gender has been central to these new histories of material life, reflecting scholars' awareness of the long-standing, misogynistic association in Western culture between women and material acquisitions. Nevertheless, basic questions about women, men, and things remain unanswered. This book sets out to address some of these questions. It asks how taste was gendered in the eighteenth-century British Atlantic world and what material things can tell us about it.

GENDER

History has had it in for the female consumer. Since Eve reached for the apple, and so led Adam astray, Western women have been seen as more covetous than men. Classical philosophers and Christian moralists have long associated men with the rational world and women with the material. Western writers inherited Aristotle's contempt for feminine reasoning, and many saw fit to deride women for mindless materialism and uncontrolled love of ostentation. Cleopatra, the Queen of Sheba, Pope's Belinda, Emma Bovary, and George Eliot's Rosamond Vincy are all vain antiheroines obsessed with self-adornment and competitive tinsel. More recently, these misogynistic anxieties about female materialism have focused on shopping. A frivolous desire to "shop till you drop" has been seen as a peculiarly feminine vice. Shopping is considered both a woman's therapy and woman's addictive disease.

Georgian retailers raised shopping to an art form. They employed a range of retail strategies that have often been assumed to have a more recent origin, including advertising, marketing, branding, mail order, dress hire, fashion magazines, fashion dolls, shop design, and window dressing. Moreover, shopping as an enjoyment of spectacle, browsing, lingering, and sauntering long predated the emergence of the Victorian department store. In fact, the word "shopping," used to describe a pleasurable tour of the stores, was an eighteenth-century coinage. It was still a novel piece of slang in 1778, when Fanny Burney used it in her novel *Evelina*, although it described a practice that already had a long history. "We have been *a shopping*, as Mrs. Mirvan calls it, all this morning, to buy silks, caps, gauzes, and so forth."[9] There were as many shops per head in England in 1750 as in the twentieth century.[10] Daniel Defoe delighted in their spread: "I have endeavour'd to make some calculation of the number of shop-keepers in this kingdom, but I find it is not to be done; we may as well count the stars."[11]

Yet such abundance provoked as much anxiety as excitement. Did not God punish vanity and luxury? Luxurious living was believed to have softened and effeminized the Romans, bringing them to their knees before the invading barbarian hordes, so shopping and high living might as easily undermine the greatest empire since Rome. Milliners dressing like the nobility, servants impersonating their masters, ladies scorning the spinning wheel for the shops—where would it end? Bernard Mandeville was typical in his belief that poorer women were driven wild by their desire for inappropriate finery: "The poorest Labourer's Wife in the Parish, who scorns to wear a strong wholesome Frize, as she might, will starve herself and her Husband to purchase a second hand Gown and Petticoat, that cannot do half the Service, because, forsooth, it is more genteel."[12] The poison of fashion was spreading apace. On the road to Oxford in 1781, the curmudgeonly traveler John Byng complained, "I meet milkmaids on the road with the dress and looks of Strand misses."[13] Nor were richer women spared criticism. Tobias Smollett's fictional ladies were often comic caricatures, openly competitive consumers, driving their husbands "at full speed, in the high road to bankruptcy and ruin." In *The Expedition of Humphry Clinker* (1771), Mrs. Baynard, governed by "vanity . . . of a bastard and idiot nature, excited by shew and ostentation," sells the family plate, spends money like water, tours Europe collecting tasteless bric-a brac, and back in England fells the oak trees and destroys the facade of the house for the sake of fashion.[14] Conservatives thought women were sucking men deeper and deeper into a vortex of extravagance, vanity, and dissipation.

However, for all the satire about the folly and featherbrains of female consumers, effective shopping required diligence and discernment. Scholars have noted the skills, expert knowledge, and practical power that women accrued as consumers in eighteenth-, nineteenth-, and early-twentieth-century Britain and North America. In her essay in this volume, Claire Walsh emphasizes the wife's ideological inscription as guardian of the purse strings in eighteenth-century England, and the practical role that even wealthier mistresses played in relentless, hands-on shopping for food and household basics: haggling, testing food for quality, spotting adulteration, deciding when to send servants or shop herself. Mistresses of middling and genteel families stored information on prices and fashions in their diaries and account books. Daughters were trained early to judge bargains and recognize quality.[15] They were not to be fools seduced by sales patter, although the blandishments of silver-tongued shop assistants were proverbial. Moreover, shopworkers were obliged to defer to women, and to indulge their whims—if legal. Elizabeth Owen was tried for shoplifting at the Old Bailey, the principal criminal court for London, in 1748. Playing the role of the difficult customer, she had managed to hide some fabric in her skirt, as the exasperated shop assistant explained:

> The prisoner came into my master's shop to buy some purple and white cotton, I showed her two or three pieces, and she liked none of them; she pointed to this piece and I shewed it to her, and she did not like the piece, she desired to see more; I showed her more, then she desired to see a remnant, which I took down, she desired I would call my mistress; I turned my head to call my mistress, and when I turned my head back again I saw her going out of the shop . . . and something hanging down behind under her clothes.[16]

She was found guilty and sentenced to be transported to America. Elizabeth Owen was clearly a skillful, self-confident shopper, if an inadequate thief.

It was precisely because women were seen to manage the business of everyday shopping that American patriots made such efforts to ensure female cooperation in the colonial boycott of British imports, particularly tea, in the 1760s and 1770s.[17] Similarly, female management of the household petty purse explains why early-nineteenth-century associations of British women found consumer boycotting an ideal political strategy.[18] Antislavery activists expressly targeted women because "in the domestic department they are the chief controllers; they for the most part, provide the articles of family consumption."[19] There is an emerging consensus that women enjoyed some recognized independence as routine consumers.

However, it could be fairly argued that the recent fascination of historians with women and the world of goods has overshadowed the role of eighteenth-century men. Margot Finn cautions that "as the burgeoning literature on women and possession has come to outpace research on male activity in the consumer market, the very richness of this body of scholarship has tended to promote the assumption that the sex of things is predominantly female, the history of gender and consumption in the modern period is primarily a history of women's experiences."[20] Drawing on four English diaries from the eighteenth and early nineteenth centuries—those of a Sussex shopkeeper, two clergymen from Norfolk and Somerset, and an East Yorkshire schoolmaster—Finn documents male consumption of a broad range of goods, from basic to luxurious. She reminds us that men were as highly acquisitive as women and rejects the assumption that women were the primary consumers for the family. Although Finn is surely right to lament historians' neglect of the male consumer (there is some important work on men's clothing but little else),[21] her sources and the situation of her subjects leave questions unanswered: it remains to be seen, for instance, whether the Norfolk parson James Woodforde would have run the grocery accounts had he been in possession of a wife.

It is not our intention in this volume to reinforce the old myth that men produce and women consume. There is no suggestion here that men were Spartan stoics immune to the lure of goods. Georgian retailers who targeted the male consumer as a desirous individual, and not just as the representative of his household, were plentiful. Barbers, tailors, tobacconists, stationers, wine merchants, saddlers, sword cutlers, horse dealers, and makers of coaches, watches, scientific instruments, hats, and wigs, among many others, prospered by attending to the personal needs of bachelors and patriarchs alike. Claire Walsh's essay alerts us to the models of Scottish Highland soldiers standing at attention outside tobacconists' shops and of naval officers guarding scientific instrument shops, proclaiming the unambiguous manliness of the treasures within. Men's ornaments and accoutrements were as varied as women's. "A fool cannot withstand the charms of a toy-shop . . . ," Lord Chesterfield warned his son in 1749; "snuff boxes, watches, heads of canes, etc. are his destruction."[22]

It is an irony that the consumer self-indulgences of eighteenth-century married men so often went unnoticed; the dandy and the fop singled out in satire are almost always young bachelors. Yet a wife's responsibility for basic provisioning exposed her to accusations of vanity, avarice, extravagance, materialism, and even fetishism. Nevertheless, while we should avoid constructing stereotypical male and female consumers, there were important differences between the way men and women consumed.

The sexes shared a common desire to explore the world of goods and to possess things, but they operated in different ways when they went out to acquire them. Claire Walsh argues that in London, women were far more likely to shop conspicuously in groups, whereas male consumers were loners, attracting criticism for their flirtatious lolling at the counter. Linzy Brekke finds that in North America, some men used women and slaves for sartorial displays that they denied themselves. Others embraced fashion in practice even while disdaining it in print. The existence of competing regimes of masculine display is reinforced by the contrast between Brekke's American politicians, who agonized over the degree of display appropriate to a republic, and Hannah Greig's fashionable London noblemen. Entry into, and continued membership of, London's *beau monde* rested on an ability to flaunt the new fashions in clothes, carriages, and reception rooms each season. Outrageous ostentation was *the* defining feature of London's *beau monde.* Lords shared diamonds with their ladies to ensure the necessary glitter.

That male consumers might differ should not surprise us. Even at the level of stereotype, there were competing models of manhood in circulation in eighteenth-century word and image—the rakish libertine, the cosmopolitan polite gentleman, the Christian gentleman, the sensible economical tradesman, the red-blooded butcher, and the brave but truculent sailor, to name some of the most common. All implied different repertoires of goods. And of course men, like women, did not just copy their identity from a book. The case of James Boswell, the son of a

Scottish nobleman, is instructive here. Boswell was only too aware of competing images and archetypes of manhood in mid-eighteenth-century London, from the "man of dignity" to the "pretty gentleman" to the "blackguard," which he acted like theatrical roles when the mood took him, or the situation demanded. He was the "pretty gentleman" in a genteel frock coat when pursuing patronage, and the "blackguard" in dirty breeches and battered army hat when seeking sex with whores on Westminster Bridge.[23] In fact, without the constant burden of proving an unblemished sexual reputation, men had much more freedom than women to slip between roles, and they may have played with goods like props in their performances.

Men, like women, varied in their willingness and desire to engage with the new world of goods, as eighteenth-century inventory data on the different propensities of English farmers, craftspeople, professionals, merchants, and gentry to acquire new kinds of goods make clear. As consumers, farmers were substantially less inclined to innovate than craftspeople, preferring to plow profits back into stock and to spend on a wider array of familiar commodities such as pewter and linens. By contrast, lesser traders and craftspeople had more varied domestic goods and far more of the new East Asian imports.[24] The contrast in consumption patterns reminds us that the ability to consume is not synonymous with a propensity to consume. The availability of new goods and the existence of a surplus to buy them were not in themselves sufficient to ensure that they were bought.

The extent of a man's own engagement and expertise as a consumer might affect the consumer expression of the women in his household. Amanda Vickery's comparison of three surviving sets of his and hers accounts for husbands and wives from the English landed gentry reveals that the most adventurous individual consumer, the wealthy Abraham Grimes of Coton Hall in Warwickshire, was the husband who accorded his wife the least financial room for maneuver. Grimes was obsessed with the gadgets and novelties of the 1780s. Unusually, he bought a Bramah water closet (patented in 1778) and Argand lamps (patented in 1784), as well as a regulator stove, an array of Wedgwood earthenware, and plated silver candlesticks and tea urns. He was an archetypal early adopter of consumer innovations, and his wife was outshone.[25]

The way spouses carved up their shopping lists did vary from couple to couple. When the London schoolmaster William Ramsden and his wife, Bessy, fulfilled the commissions of a cousin from the north of England in 1765, it was Bessy Ramsden who bought the "Gowns, Caps, Ruffles and such like female Accoutrements," while her husband was accountable "for the Wafers, Paper & Pocket Book." Undoubtedly, men considered themselves skillful consumers of particular types of commodity. After all, it would be remarkable if a schoolmaster had not been able to judge the quality of stationery. But the remarkably uxorious William Ramsden was unusual among husbands in going to market to purchase humdrum groceries. Individual variations notwithstanding, while a wife's consumption was predominantly repetitive and mundane, a husband's consumption was by contrast characteristically occasional and impulsive, or expensive and dynastic.[26]

Looking at the consumption of men and women in tandem offsets a tendency in the more celebratory accounts of consumer behavior to glorify the individual economic actor, wrenching him or her from the context of household and family. We should not forget the lessons of the history of poverty—that the consumption of one almost always affects or responds to the consumption of the others who are closest. Individual consumers rarely operate in a vacuum. The neglect of the household as a unit of consumption is especially odd for a century when family and household loomed so large as lived experience, organizational category, and ideological trope. Indeed, as Jonathan White's essay shows, it was in the course of the eighteenth century that patrician thinkers first conceptualized the plebeian household as an accounting unit and differentiated the behavior of the men and women within it as consumers. Jan de Vries has urged researchers to look behind the myth of patriarchy, whereby the household speaks with one voice (and that voice the master's), to get a sense of the choices made *within* households about market participation.[27]

Vickery's study of his and hers account books represents just such an attempt to unlock the black box of the household. It reveals a deep-seated notion about what women and men should control. The idea of female responsibility varied from marriage to marriage in what it embraced at its fullest, but at its most circumscribed the female dispensation still covered personal dress, the clothing and education of children, especially girls, and the provision of the family's personal linen. Married gentlemen were able to rise above daily dealings with the grocer and the butcher only because their wives handled these tedious accounts for them. The explicit contract recorded in 1758 by Mary Delany, then wife of the Dean of Down in Ireland, is suggestive of a division of labor recognized in most propertied households: "The Dean has now settled my allowance for housekeeping at six hundred a-year, which I receive quarterly, and out of that pay everything but the men's wages, the liveries, the stables, wine cellar and garden, furniture and all repairs."[28] Comparable research into American accounts and letters suggests a similar division of labor in French Louisiana in the 1750s, in colonial Philadelphia, and among Quakers in Rhode Island in the early republic.[29] Wives and daughters were unlikely to trespass on the masculine preserves of horse furniture and port; nor did men bother with linens.

Business records confirm that men dominated the purchase of high-status, expensive luxury goods. Few business historians have bothered with a gender breakdown of the eighteenth-century consumer market, but research on the ledgers of the London art dealer Arthur Pond,[30] the Derby porcelain factory,[31] and the London silversmiths Parker and Wakelin[32] reveals the broad patterns of male and female formal patronage of the luxury trades in Britain. Stark male dominance of luxury spending emerges in all three cases. Women do not figure as prominent patrons and collectors in their own right at the top end of the market. The satirists may have believed that female customers were spending a fortune on shiny gewgaws, but shop ledgers do not bear this out.

Of course, ledgers conceal as much as they reveal; they tell us who formally paid and represented the family, not necessarily who truly chose.[33] Kate Retford's essay in this volume shows that the noblewoman Caroline Fox was primarily responsible for commissioning new paintings in the gallery at Holland House, in the London suburbs, in the early 1760s and for the way they were hung, but you would never know this from the family account books or the bills of the artist Joshua Reynolds, for whom the family sat. Nor are ledgers from Philadelphia, the New England seaports, or rural Virginia bristling with women's transactions.[34] Ann Smart Martin's essay wrestles with the problem of how to interpret row upon row of men's names in rural shopkeepers' accounts in the American South. In Virginia, as in most of the English-speaking world, married women were not accountable for their debts. She concludes that a woman's decisions in the shop often lie concealed behind her husband's name in the ledger. Sometimes, as a late-eighteenth-century shop ledger from Penmorfa in North Wales reveals, they were concealed from the husband as well. The ledger includes repeated entries for purchases on men's credit by wives or maidservants that use phrases such as "handkerchief . . . wife, not to tell" or "hat 11s. 6d., to tell 8s." Evidently, the purchase or its real cost was not to be divulged to the man of the house.[35]

Shop credit was ubiquitous in eighteenth-century retailing. As a consequence, we must rid ourselves of the modern idea of a retail transaction in which an independent, resource-rich individual pops into a shop, makes a selection, hands over currency or uses bank credit, and strolls out with the purchase. In the eighteenth century, the person who selected the goods, the person who went to the shop to collect them, the person who met the shopkeeper to settle the account, and the person who handed over cash in settlement were often different people. From first glance to final payment, the whole transaction could last months, even years. Ellen Hartigan-O'Connor's essay makes it clear how fundamentally the consumer choices of householders in the towns of Newport, Rhode Island, and Charleston, South Carolina, were structured by their access to credit and performed via proxies, sometimes friends and kin at a distance, but often slaves and servants. Shopping, far from being the ultimate in economic individualism, was a collaborative act depending on shared knowledge. Moreover, as John Styles emphasizes in his analysis of London lodgings, many of the things that poorer people used, treated, and spoke of as their own were provided to them by others, on terms that restricted their ability to choose.

Moving from acquisition to possession, recent research has revealed the deep psychic investment some women made in the world of goods. Lancashire merchant's wife Elizabeth Shackleton, Massachusetts pioneer Hannah Barnard, Shropshire spinster Katharine Plymley, aristocratic tourist Elizabeth Berkeley Somerset, and the fourth Duchess of Beaufort, among many others, can be seen using possessions as props in self-fashioning, some creating an assemblage that came close to a self-portrait—a picture that could be shown off, rearranged, or hidden as circumstances demanded. Indeed, Johanna Dahn argues that the connoisseur and courtier Mary Delany, the twice-widowed niece of a nobleman, self-consciously crafted an "objectscape" in china to testify to the cultured female community that she did so much to nurture.[36] Women could use objects to convey a multitude of meanings, from fashion, taste, and style to wealth and status, history and lineage, and from science, education, political allegiance, and religious conviction to personality, relationships, memory, and mortality.[37] Material culture emerges as an arena for the expression of considerable female eloquence and creativity.

Is the fact that wealthy women could use objects in this way evidence for a distinct and separate female aesthetic sphere in the home? Ideas about gender, space, and the home have been central to many recent interpretations of eighteenth-century culture. A persistent tradition arising out of British and American women's history emphasizes a process of female incarceration in a separate domestic sphere sometime in the later eighteenth or early nineteenth century (chronologies vary) and sees all aesthetic endeavor in a domestic setting as mere gilding on the cage.[38] The idea that the home was a feminized refuge insulated from the social, cultural, and political world is not one that finds support here. It would have perplexed anyone in eighteenth-century Britain and North America with pretensions to politeness or enlightenment.[39] Indeed, the creation of tiny intimate rooms for quiet reflection and seclusion within domestic interiors was a response to the overwhelming publicity, bustle, traffic, and commotion of eighteenth-century households.[40] The essays by Karen Lipsedge and Robert Blair St. George both re-create the importance of the closet for reading, writing, reflection, and the defense of the boundaries of the self. For the novelist Samuel Richardson's heroine Clarissa Harlowe, a closet was a psychological necessity, the stronghold of her self-command, not a prison. It is worth remembering that Clarissa's closet locked on the inside, and it was for her to decide when to draw the curtain on the internal window. Privacy in this interpretation is a hard-won privilege, not a badge of subjection.

The great late-seventeenth-century houses demonstrated a high formality, usually offering the visitor an enfilade—a parade of state rooms—which enforced status and was impossible to short-circuit. Mark Girouard charts the rise from the 1720s of what he calls "the social house," where the enfilade was replaced by an elegant circle of rooms arranged around a central staircase.[41] These were all communal rooms for entertaining, and they ran into one another. By the late eighteenth century, the social rooms began to be situated on the ground floor with easier access to the garden. Meanwhile, servants were gradually relegated from central areas to the attics and separate annexes. This fashionable transition has been said to embody greater "privacy and intimacy," making homes at once more "habitable and human" for the employing classes.[42]

In both Britain and North America, it was the conventions of decorum that dictated how newly built houses for the fashionable and genteel were laid out. Architectural textbooks maintained that surroundings should directly reflect status. Isaac Ware advised aspiring architects in 1756, "There are apartments in which dignity, others in which neatness, and others in which shew are to be consulted."[43] After the differentiations of rank, the strongest architectural distinction lay not between masculinity and femininity, nor precisely between public and private, but between formality and informality, rooms for "convenience" and rooms "for shew."

Of course, the internal arrangements of older, less fashionable houses did not always reflect the set conventions of the textbooks. Propertied households contained servants or slaves, and often apprentices or dependent kin as well. They were constantly expanding and contracting, so fixed internal arrangements must have been the exception. Convenience and show were registered in different ways. Lancashire merchant's wife Elizabeth Shackleton distinguished between best and common dining paraphernalia. It was the props themselves that registered formality, not necessarily the room. Genteel letters reveal that the same interior spaces could be more or less public, more or less formal, according to the time of day, the arrangement of furniture and tableware, the level of ceremony, and the status and number of guests.[44] Vast numbers of houses accommodated a workshop, a commercial space, or live-in tenants. Indeed, as Styles's essay points out, the lodger, that archetype of urban life, had to make do in one or two rooms, often eating elsewhere, and registering ceremony with a few tea wares or a decorative bed covering chosen by the landlady. Polite ceremony was a goal, not a description of daily life, for most people.

Decorum contained within it the possibility that men's and women's apartments might be decorated differently. "For a noble hall nothing is so well as stucco; for a parlour, wainscot seems properest; and for the apartments of a lady hangings."[45] Architectural historians note an increasing specialization of spaces, with the rise of the masculinized dining room and the feminized drawing room. As the gender associations of certain rooms became more fixed in theory, a decorative vocabulary that expressed differences emerged. When Mary Delany stayed at Cornbury in Oxfordshire in 1746, the guest rooms were decorated in a deliberate his and hers idiom. Mr. Delany's apartment was "hung with flowered paper of a grotesque pattern, the colouring lively and the pattern bold and handsome," whereas hers was a lighter affair "hung with the finest paper of flowers and all sorts of birds."[46] Among the richest innovators, the dressing room emerged as an intimate informal reception room for ladies, and it became a metonym for close female companionship and an exquisite enlightened feminine sensibility. It was in the dressing room that noblewomen experimented with exquisite and exotic decoration, such as painted wallpaper, japanned furniture, and chinoiserie in general.[47] The third edition of Thomas Chippendale's *The Gentleman and Cabinet-Maker's Director*, in 1762, included "Nine Designs of Chairs after the Chinese Manner . . . very proper for a Lady's Dressing-Room: especially if it is hung with India Paper."[48]

Formally at least, gentlemen seem to have led expensive schemes for domestic redecoration, yet many commentators paid lip service to the superiorities and sensitivities of female taste. Moreover, readers of eighteenth-century novels might assume that interior decoration was an utterly female affair, while letters and diaries support a view of developed stylistic preferences among female leaders of fashion. Misogynistic eighteenth-century commentators such as John Byng, the heir to a noble English family, were apt to identify certain kinds of domestic decorative scheme as evidence of female agency:

> The parlour was (ill) furnish'd in the modern taste, with French chairs, festoon'd curtains, and puffed bell ropes; this and his keeping in bed informed me that the gentleman was not master of his own house.[49]

Yet the essays by Amy H. Henderson, Amanda Vickery, and Bernard L. Herman suggest that, in practice, differences between male and female taste were not the principal influence on the way domestic spaces were decorated and furnished. We should be wary of assuming an automatic correlation between female spaces and a "feminine" style of decoration. Claire Walsh reminds us that the New Exchange, one of late-seventeenth-century London's premier shopping galleries, was seen as a feminized space because of the feminine goods it sold and its popularity with women. Its decoration, however, emphasized grandeur and high living, not femininity as opposed to masculinity.

It is clear that certain objects, like certain rooms, could be constructed as "masculine" or "feminine" in character. In a stage play of 1730, the caddish Gainlove rejects Lady Science and marries her daughter instead, because, he insists, "the Dressing-Room, not the Study, is the Lady's Province and a Woman makes as ridiculous a Figure, poring over Globes, or thro' a Telescope, as a Man would with a Pair of *Preservers* mending Lace."[50] Manufacturers were well aware that some products were bought predominantly by men or by women. For example, a book of patterns for printed cottons, circulated by a print works in the north of England about 1780, assumed a female clientele, noting that "when any Lady sends for a Sight of the Book, it is entreated she will give Orders that it be Returned immediately."[51] The rise of advertisements and other kinds of printed commercial propaganda provided manufacturers with new opportunities to manipulate gender as a marketing tool. From the middle of the eighteenth century, London cabinetmakers, led by Thomas Chippendale, started to publish books of designs for furniture. Compiling these books required that the different pieces of furniture be categorized in ways that made sense to their readers and attracted them. The principal categories that the cabinetmakers employed were functional and stylistic, but "lady's" and "gentleman's" soon came to be used to differentiate certain specific types of furniture, principally writing tables, desks, and dressing tables.[52]

There has been important research on the gender associations of particular eighteenth-century objects and commodities, but china and tea have received disproportionate attention to date. For Elizabeth Kowaleski-Wallace, the tea table was first and foremost the "place where the upper-class female body was disciplined to participate in a narcissistic display of availability."[53] But commodities believed to have had a feminine quality, such as tea, china, novels, silks, printed cottons, and haberdashery, were not necessarily the preserve of women, although their widespread use by men did not dislodge their feminine associations. Indeed, a certain feminine allure may have added to their deliciousness for male consumers.

A closely related issue is the content and meaning of male and female collecting. There are few comparisons of men's and women's collecting habits in eighteenth-century America and Britain. Nevertheless, stereotyped assumptions prevail that men were collectors and women curators or preservers of objects. Kate Retford's essay on family picture galleries complicates the distinction between collector and curator. Custodianship was the raison d'être of a landed dynasty, and protecting dusty heirlooms an inescapable duty for both men and women. Yet women could be as deft as men in arranging a distinctive and speaking history in these objects. The principles of patrilineage and patriarchy inevitably dominated the narrative of noble galleries, as duke followed duke and earl followed earl. However, they could also register the connections, titles, land, and wealth transferred into the family through marriage, underscoring the importance of women to the dynasty. Henrietta Cavendish, for example, widow of the second Earl of

Oxford, reorganized two hundred portraits at her country mansion, Welbeck Abbey, with paintings of her own ancestors in the majority. As Horace Walpole, the connoisseur and son of a prime minister, reported in 1756, her collection primarily commemorated "all the great families from which she descended, and which centred in her."[54] As she had formed the collection for posterity, she would not be marginalized.

Retford suggests that in crafting an assemblage of objects, women and men might have had different stories to tell. Of course, almost all women lacked the resources to collect on the scale of men of equivalent rank, and the role of curator of everyday domestic objects rarely fell to men. Women's account books and pocket diaries substantiate an ongoing and relentless responsibility for the upkeep of household utensils, linen, and small furniture. But the value of "collectibles" also lay in the eyes of the beholder. Many were adept at using even mundane objects to pass messages down through time. Anxious to provide her estranged daughter with a sense of the history of her mother's family, Lancashire governess Ellen Weeton sent a bundle of humble heirlooms, cataloguing their associations:

> The green ribbon is part of a box-full my mother (your grand-mother Weeton) once had; they were taken in a prize which my father captured during the American war. . . . I am thus minute, my Mary, that you may know something of the history of your mother's family. . . . The piece of patchwork is out of an old Quilt I made above 20 years ago. . . . The Hexagon in the middle was a shred of our best bed hangings; they were Chintz, from the East Indies, which my father brought home with him from one of his voyages.[55]

Handed down from generation to generation in this way, objects could sustain a specifically matrilineal family history. In 1756, in a letter intended for her daughter Mary, the English gentlewoman Ann Dewes insisted that "the old china cup with the gilt cover and saucer, that has a setting in gold belonging to it, Mary must have, and give it to *her daughter* if she has one, if not to one of her brother's *daughters*, as it has gone from *daughter* to *daughter* these *three hundred years*!"[56] Laurel Thatcher Ulrich observes similar female lineage marked in goods in the descent of a carved cupboard, a sampler in wood, from mother to daughter in eighteenth-century Massachusetts.[57]

Most women lacked the opportunities enjoyed by the wealthy to construct a domestic objectscape replete with choice, costly items. But domestic possessions did not have to be expensive or stereotypically feminine to be the objects of female expertise, knowledge, and emotional investment. Greater female knowledge of the objects in the domestic interior is one suggestive conclusion of Styles's recovery of the role of the landlady in London's booming rental market. A similar conclusion about gendered knowledge has been drawn by Mary Beth Norton from a comparison of compensation claims made by loyalist men and women exiled during the American Revolution. Although the men consistently placed a precise valuation on their house and land, very few of the women were able to do so. By contrast, men submitted inadequate inventories of household goods such as furniture, tableware, and kitchen utensils, while the women could produce minute accounts. A New York woman wrote with regret of "a fine large new stove"; a Rhode Islander called attention to the closets in her "large new dwelling house." Norton concludes that "to men, furniture, dishes and clothing could be easily lumped together under general headings; to women such possessions had to be carefully enumerated and described."[58] The contrasting lists submitted by men and women suggest not only discrete fields of knowledge, but different material priorities.[59]

TASTE

Taste was a key word in the cultural landscape of the eighteenth-century English-speaking world. "Of all our favourite Words lately," noted one London publication in 1747, "none has been more in Vogue, nor so long held its Esteem, as that of TASTE."[60] Despite its popularity, taste was a slippery, indeterminate concept. Then, as now, it embraced a number of overlapping meanings, but it was the issue of proper aesthetic judgment that filled the pages of the treatises on taste which multiplied in the course of the century. In an intellectual climate where wealth and virtue were constantly juxtaposed as implacable opponents, the notion of taste became the vehicle for an intense debate about aesthetic discernment. Ever-increasing luxury was thought to jeopardize social hierarchy, public morality, military might, and economic efficiency. In a burgeoning commercial society, how could standards of beauty be established when judgment was clouded by the effeminizing lure of excess?

In the struggle to ensure that commerce served to refine rather than to corrupt, establishing those standards became a crucial weapon. Refining taste was an especially important priority for those who endeavored to defend the newly emerging category of the fine or elegant arts. Poetry, painting, music, architecture, sculpture, the theater: all were marketed by a new breed of cultural entrepreneur as commodities to be bought and sold.[61] The notion of taste provided a defense against the accusation that the commercial market in culture simply pandered to the baser lusts of whoever could afford to pay, with no regard to aesthetic value, personal morality, or the national good. Taste offered disinterested discernment as a corrective to the crude gratification of the appetites. Those anxious to employ it in this way struggled to keep its use conceptually precise and socially exclusive. Joshua Reynolds was reluctantly prepared to admit dress to the realm of taste in his *Discourses*, but only with the qualification that it "is certainly one of the lowest subjects to which this word is applied."[62] Yet, as critics and satirists delighted in pointing out, the "poor, prostituted Word TASTE" had become fashionable.[63] "Every utensil almost has now pretensions, very frequently ill founded, to taste," complained Frederick Robinson in London to his brother the British ambassador in Madrid in 1778.[64] As taste became ubiquitous, its power to enforce distinctions was leached away.

> Taste is at present the darling idol of the polite world, and the world of letters; and, indeed, seems to be considered as the quintessence of almost all the arts and sciences. The fine ladies and gentlemen dress with Taste; the architects, whether *Gothic* or *Chinese*, build with Taste; the painters paint with Taste; critics read with Taste; and in short, fiddlers, players, singers, dancers, and mechanics themselves, are all the sons and daughters of Taste. Yet in this amazing super-abundancy of Taste, few can say what it really is, or what the word itself signifies.[65]

Nevertheless, taste survived the critics' censure and the satirists' ridicule. "Good taste"—what it was, who had it, who should judge it, which things partook of it—remained an obsession of the genteel classes, not just in Britain, but across the eighteenth-century English-speaking world. The anxiety it provoked and the corresponding hunger for reassurance could induce a certain weariness in those who had to serve the genteel. Francis Place, the radical London tailor, complained that his business required him to make himself "acceptable to coxcombs, to please their whims, to have no opinion of my own, but to take especial care that my customers should be pleased with theirs. It was all matter of taste; that is of folly and caprice."[66]

There is a certain irony in the pervasiveness of the notion of good taste in the Anglo-American world, because systematic use of the word "taste"—*goût*—to signify aesthetic discernment had emerged in later-seventeenth-century France. In France, this use of the word was rooted in the literary battle between the ancients and the moderns. Taste stood for modern as opposed to classical learning, an assertive yet elegant courtly culture, and real, though limited, cultural opportunities for elite women.[67] In eighteenth-century Britain and North America, the word came to have entirely different associations, grounded in the critique of luxury. The idea that luxury was a fundamental danger to society derived from a civic humanism rooted in the republican political thought of ancient Rome. In this intellectual tradition, luxury was deplored as effeminizing. Its dangers were as much courtly and French as commercial and opulent.

Published defenses of aesthetic discernment against the threat of luxury, from Joseph Addison to Joshua Reynolds and beyond, focused on how proper norms of taste should be derived. Some of these defenses, such as those offered by the third Earl of Shaftesbury early in the eighteenth century, were narrowly masculine, not to say misogynistic, and austerely patrician. For Shaftesbury, civic duty required that the temptations of the consumer luxuries he termed "lady-fancies" be met with stoic disregard.[68] Similar views continued to be expressed on both sides of the Atlantic until the end of the century, often by writers far removed from Shaftesbury's elevated social background.[69] In 1795, the imprisoned English republican John Thelwall was still lambasting luxury's "gaudy visions," arguing that liberty could flourish only in "virtuous Poverty."[70] But increasingly during the eighteenth century, as Robert Jones has pointed out, British writers on taste came to endow women with a distinctive aptitude for regulating claims to culture and refinement in a commercial society. Virtuous women, by making consumer choices that were moderate and reasonable, could moralize commercial society, protecting it from its own depravity.[71] Most of these published efforts to construct standards of taste shared a focus on the capacities that people brought to their judgments, rather than the intrinsic properties of the things they judged. Many entailed distinctions between different kinds of people—connoisseur and fop, the refined and the vulgar, men and women. Objects such as tea tables or coaches were often invoked, but usually they served as little more than illustrative props to familiar arguments, deployed in ways that were both stereotypical and repetitive.

A different approach emerges if we turn, as we repeatedly do in the essays in this book, to the voices of individuals debating their choices of material things. It is predominantly the voices of the genteel—the wealthy and the educated, both men and women—that survive. We find them self-consciously struggling to exercise good taste. However, as Amanda Vickery's essay shows, in practice they debated taste not so much in the terminology of luxury and virtue, but rather in the language of decorum. Their struggle to exercise good taste became a struggle to arrive at material choices that were socially appropriate, avoiding those that were unseemly. This was a discourse of self-restraint and occasionally anxiety, far removed from the uninhibited hedonism that historians have sometimes associated with an eighteenth-century consumer revolution. Decorum required at least a nominal acceptance of prevailing social distinctions and hierarchies. The rule of decorum decreed that different forms of conduct were appropriate to different stations in life, according to social rank, age, sex, or occupation. Inappropriate diversions from the rule of decorum were criticized as indecorous. Amazonian assertiveness in women, effeminacy in men, extreme vivacity in the elderly, excessive dignity in children were all breaches of the rule of decorum. Maintenance of established hierarchies was its explicit goal, although decorum could also guide the upwardly socially mobile in how to advance inconspicuously. Yet decorum was philosophically more all-encompassing than simply knowing one's place. It married perfectly with eighteenth-century aesthetics. Music, literature, and painting, as well as architecture and design, shared the language of harmony, proportion, and order. Indeed, taste was often described as an innate sense of decorum. Decorum also expressed a vision of social harmony and cohesion (however traditional). Above all, decorum was the keystone of the code of manners that came to be known as politeness. The reach of politeness was wide, from judges to journeymen.[72] Polite men and women would hardly pursue a reputation for flouting decorum.

Those who applied the rule of decorum to mundane material things in the eighteenth century rarely offered any systematic reflections on what they were doing. Its origins lay in classical thought. In England between the fourteenth and sixteenth centuries, it had been embodied in sumptuary laws, mainly controlling dress. By the eighteenth century, however, it no longer had much legal backing. General sumptuary legislation had expired in England in 1604 and was not renewed, despite frequent requests.[73] In America, such legislation was enforced in Massachusetts for much of the seventeenth century, but laws of this kind in the eighteenth century applied only to slaves in parts of the South.[74] The everyday notions of decorum that prevailed in the eighteenth century may have been influenced by recent restatements of the idea, such as John Locke's notion of good breeding: "a due and free Composure of Language, Looks, Motion, Posture, Place, etc., suited to Persons and Occasions."[75] Alternatively, they may have drawn on older ideas of Protestant civility, which emphasized temperance and decency. Yet, with a few exceptions such as the Quakers and the Methodists, an explicitly religious language was rarely used, in contrast to the way Victorian discussions of taste were sometimes conducted.[76] Nevertheless, decorum carried considerable moral weight and the capacity for powerful moral censure, of the kind familiar from the English radical William Cobbett's assault on "the piano-fortes, and the parlour-bells and the carpets" that he offered as proof the new-fashioned English farmers of the Napoleonic era had material ideas above their station.[77]

It is the published works of writers concerned with establishing norms of good taste that have been a principal focus of recent studies of taste in the eighteenth-century English-speaking world.[78] The essays in this book address taste in these normative terms, but they devote more attention to taste as a sociological and an economic category. Economists use the word "taste" to describe those consumer preferences that cannot be explained by price. Similarly, sociologists from Thorstein Veblen to Pierre Bourdieu and beyond have employed the word to map the aesthetic, cultural, and consumer preferences of different people, groups, nations, and epochs.[79] But they have been more willing than economists to explore the explanatory potential of social, geographical, and chronological differences in taste, employing notions such as Veblen's conspicuous consumption and Bourdieu's cultural capital. Recent historians of the eighteenth-century English-speaking world have followed suit. Neil McKendrick famously identified the desire of the British middle classes to emulate the taste of the aristocratic elite as the motor of the British Industrial Revolution.[80] Historians of slavery have found much evidence for a distinctive and nuanced African set of tastes among slaves in the American South.[81] For David Porter, the Chinese taste appealed to elite Englishwomen, because it offered an alternative aesthetic to a masculine neoclassical orthodoxy.[82] Peter Borsay and Dror Wahrman argue that a national society was created in eighteenth-century England by provincial elites who aped London taste and consequently failed to nurture distinctive regional tastes.[83] As these examples suggest, studies of consumer and cultural preferences in the eighteenth century have ranged well beyond the hierarchical, class distinctions that drove work in the older sociological tradition exemplified by Veblen and Bourdieu. Distinctions of nation, region, gender, and, especially in America, race have been explored in addition to those of class.

We should bear in mind that these economic and sociological usages of the word "taste" were already familiar in the eighteenth-century English-speaking world. Phrases such as "the Taste of the last Century," "French taste," "female taste," and "the taste of the common people" were regularly used to categorize people's preferences, including their material preferences.[84] Moreover, such phrases often embodied eighteenth-century assumptions about social and economic processes, which modern historians have enthusiastically adopted as explanations. It was a commonplace of eighteenth-century social thought that exposure to the tastes of others could stimulate emulation. Eighteenth-century businessmen shared this belief and exploited the fact that the power to influence taste was distributed unequally. Some, such as the potter Josiah Wedgwood, devoted considerable effort to cultivating the patronage of those who led taste—the royal court and the nobility, architects and connoisseurs. Wedgwood termed these people the "Legislators in Taste" and regarded their patronage as crucial in driving improvements in the manufacturing arts.[85] But they were not the only people to whose taste Wedgwood deferred. He was convinced that the fortunes of his pottery also turned on women's taste. To monitor it, he relied on his wife. "I speak from experience in Female taste," he wrote to his partner Thomas Bentley, "without which I should have made but a poor figure amongst my Potts; not one of which of any consequence is finished without the Approbation of my Sally."[86]

We should remember, however, that eighteenth-century categorizations of people and their tastes rarely offered disinterested descriptions. On the contrary, they often entailed normative judgments, drawing on the language employed in the debates over good taste. The deficiencies of some taste groups were lambasted, while the virtues of others were extolled. Thus, dress in "the taste of the last century" was dismissed as "old-fashioned," gardens in "the French taste" were pronounced "wretched," male manners were judged in need of "the refining of female taste," and the "taste of the common people" was deplored as vulnerable to "low humour, buffoonery, and other various amusements."[87] Taste was a heavily loaded word in most of its eighteenth-century uses. This emerges in British discussions of American taste in the years after the War of Independence. The Earl of Sheffield adopted a technical, objective tone in his 1784 *Observations on the Commerce of the American States* to express the view that "to suit the American taste," metal wares had to unite "the solid and the useful with the showy and elegant."[88] Others were less dispassionate. Several British commentators were dismayed to discover the canker of luxury at the heart of the new republic. The anonymous author of *The European Traveller in America* (1785) was horrified to find republican frugality and simplicity corrupted by fashion. "I readily confess the idea I had formed of America in this respect was imaginary. When I left my native country . . . I fancied the American taste too noble and philosophic to be endangered by any thing in its nature so perfectly empty."[89] Isaac Weld, an Irish gentleman traveling in the 1790s in the recently settled area to the south of Lake Ontario, had lower expectations, writing that "in the true American taste the greatest pains were taking to diminish, and, indeed, to shut out all the beauties of the prospect."[90]

The eighteenth century has sometimes been characterized as a century of taste.[91] Insofar as the essays in this book endorse that characterization, they aim to redirect our attention away from the philosophical debates about correct taste in treatise and pamphlet, toward the way tastes were identified, mapped, articulated, and judged in the many, overlapping taste communities that constituted the eighteenth-century English-speaking world. This is not to deny the influence of the published eighteenth-century treatises on taste, nor the fact that certain kinds of people, such as those Wedgwood identified as the legislators in taste, enjoyed disproportionate power to order, regulate, and police it. Taste was undoubtedly about power—the power of the metropolitan over the provincial, of men over women, of mistresses over slaves, of landladies over tenants, of shopkeepers over customers (and vice versa). Nevertheless, as Bernard L. Herman's essay warns us, too often scholars have focused narrowly on the emulation of the tastes of the elite by those lower down the social scale.

Emulation depended on choice. Yet throughout the British Atlantic world, many of the things poorer people used came to them through nonmarket, semi-market, or indirect mechanisms, which to different degrees limited their ability to choose. After all, one-fifth of the population of the mainland North American colonies on the eve of the Revolution were slaves, and many more, in both America and Britain, were menial servants, apprentices, parish paupers, soldiers, sailors, or children, whose choices as consumers were subject to the authority of others. A servant girl might periodically blow her wages on a silk hat or a printed cotton gown at the annual village fair, but the food she ate day after day, the bed she slept on night after night, and the soap that cleaned her clothes month after month were chosen by her mistress. Moreover, when plebeian consumers did exercise choice, they sometimes resisted the tastes and fashions of the elite and the metropolis, as the buckle maker James Gee discovered when he arrived in Walsall, in the English Midlands, from Dublin looking for work in the 1760s, wearing a cocked hat that was smart by Dublin standards. He was reluctantly obliged to conform to what he called "the custom of the place" and wear a round hat with a brim that flapped down over the face.[92] Nevertheless, it is true that whole new categories of goods, such as muslins, tea wares, watches, and cotton counterpanes, first were acquired by the rich and the fashionable and only subsequently trickled down into the receptive hands of plebeian men and women. But this was rarely just a matter of the poor emulating the taste of the rich—"the mill girl who wanted to dress like a duchess," as Neil McKendrick puts it.[93] We should beware of reproducing eighteenth-century snobberies by portraying such behavior as an attempt at emulation that inevitably ended up getting it wrong. It is important to remember that as new types of objects moved through the social hierarchy, they changed. They were made from different materials, they joined different assemblages of goods, they were used in different ways, and they acquired different meanings.

Tastes did not attach limpet-like to things in ways that were uniform and immutable. As John Styles has argued, when young, English plebeian women bought cheap silks and muslins that aped the fashions of the wealthy, as they often did, it was not to wear at the balls and assemblies frequented by the genteel, but at the fairs and the hirings, the parish feasts and the harvest homes, that featured so prominently in the customary festive calendar. These popular festivities often provoked elite hostility as inducements to profligacy, drunkenness, and immorality, for the reasons discussed by Jonathan White.[94] Hence the emphasis in this book on the way tastes were embedded in eighteenth-century practices, relationships, and words. The essays repeatedly ask who participated in shaping different tastes, how they did it, and what it meant to them. They find answers not just among the metropolitan leaders of fashion, but in the sales patter of urban shopkeepers, the work of slaves running errands, matrimonial conversations about wallpaper, and landladies' purchases of secondhand furniture.

MATERIAL CULTURE

The use of the term "material culture" in the title of this book signals its intention to treat the relationship between people and objects seriously. The origins of the term lie in nineteenth-century anthropology, but more recently it has been embraced, particularly in the United States, by archaeologists, historians, decorative arts scholars, and folklife specialists. As Ann Smart Martin and J. Ritchie Garrison have shown in their recent survey, material culture, conceived in a broad, multidisciplinary way, has proved an exceptionally fruitful framework for understanding colonial and early national America.[95] Interpreting the formative era in American history through its material remains has provoked intense debate, both conceptual and methodological, about the role of objects in the study of the historical past. Archaeologists who study prehistoric cultures have, of course, little choice but to investigate them through their material remains. Those who study artifacts from periods for which substantial textual sources survive have to decide how to establish a dialogue between the evidence provided by objects and the evidence provided by texts. Some have treated material evidence as an adjunct to text-based history; others have argued for the superiority of material over textual evidence for studying the illiterate majorities that characterized most historical societies; others again have made a case for according empirical precedence to material evidence over textual evidence.[96] But all those who adopt a material-culture framework share a commitment to thinking about the social and cultural work performed by artifacts.

It is a shortcoming of recent studies by social and economic historians of eighteenth-century consumption, especially in Britain, that they give relatively little consideration to the materiality of the artifacts they address. In their eagerness to identify the origins of a consumer society in eighteenth-century Britain, many historians have simply reiterated the exaggerated claims about new products peddled by entrepreneurs, or the horrified reactions of moralists confronted by objects they regarded as seductive fripperies and worthless gewgaws.[97] Other, less colorful studies have treated objects principally as units to be counted. It is from painstaking quantitative work on the domestic goods listed in inventories that some of the most dramatic recent findings have emerged.[98] Such work has been essential for mapping the diffusion of new products, but, as is so often the case with quantitative work, the benefits of counting have become available only when the enormous diversity of instances studied have been reduced to a limited number of general categories—chairs, tables, clocks, silver, earthenware. In the process, the materiality of the actual objects is bypassed and with it our ability to grasp how objects impinged physically on those who handled them, altered them, put them to work, positioned them alongside other objects, cleaned them, or simply gazed longingly at them.[99] Curiously, recent work in the history of art has sometimes shared this reluctance to engage with the materiality of the objects studied, reflecting a concern to emphasize historical context in opposition to the connoisseur's focus on the art object associated with an older, more conservative art history.

The essays in this book are not the products of single-minded object-based research, grounded primarily in material evidence. It is hard to imagine how they could be in the case of essays like those by Jonathan White on economic writers' ideas about the plebeian household, or by John Styles on objects in plebeian interiors that no longer survive. But each of the essays focuses on objects and the variety of interactions that people sustained with them. They share the assumption that objects enable the social world to happen, rendering narratives concrete. Key issues are what objects did—especially how they came to embody and project human agency—what they meant, and how they were used, categorized, and represented.[100] The essays address these issues in a variety of ways. Some, like Ann Smart Martin's, emphasize the talismanic power of objects to evoke desire; others, like Hannah Greig's, Amy H. Henderson's, and Kate Retford's, the capacity of objects to articulate human networks across space and across time. Some, like Linzy Brekke's, highlight the ways in which objects were implicated in the performance of social or political roles; others, like Claire Walsh's, the ergonomics of objects and spaces.[101] All question the assumption that objects had a single, transparent meaning. Objects emerge as ambiguous and multivalent, their significance dependent on particular uses and particular contexts. And each of the essays devotes special attention to the ways objects could be gendered—to the capacity of things to create, sustain, or articulate gendered identities and tastes—at the same time that they question whether any objects are gendered per se.

BRITAIN AND NORTH AMERICA

This book juxtaposes studies of gender, taste, and material culture in eighteenth-century Britain and eighteenth-century North America. Such a juxtaposition poses more of an intellectual challenge than might be at first be imagined. For much of the period, long stretches of the Atlantic seaboard of North America were British colonies, with large populations of British descent. Yet despite the recent emphasis in eighteenth-century studies on the need for an Atlantic perspective, communication between those who study eighteenth-century British North America and eighteenth-century Britain is not always as effective as it might be. There are major gaps and mismatches between the current historiographies of the two sides of the British Atlantic, perhaps particularly so in the study of material culture.

This is partly because of the legacy of American exceptionalism in aspects of the historiography of early America. The search for national explanations of cultural forms was prominent in early American history for the first two-thirds of the twentieth century, and it was reflected in a concern to identify the origins of cultural and stylistic characteristics that were distinctively American. The authentically American was the main theme; British imports and influences were the counterpoint. In the study of material life, the emphasis was on identifying distinctively American craft traditions in fields such as silver and furniture, as well as the vernacular, the self-sufficient, the homespun. More recently, although an interest in what was distinctive about America remains, it is no longer organized around a single, monolithic notion of what was American. The cultural and material integration of the British Atlantic world has become central to the way early Americanists approach their subject. Notably, James Deetz and Jack Greene have argued, in rather different ways, that American culture, including material culture, underwent a process of anglicization (or re-anglicization) in the course of the eighteenth century.[102] According to Deetz, "On the eve of the American Revolution, Americans were more English than they had been in the past since the first years of the colonies."[103] Timothy Breen has proposed that without the colonies' saturation in British goods and the reaction it provoked, the American Revolution would have been impossible.[104] Indeed, the anglicization thesis has become so pervasive that some historians have felt the need to ask what was colonial about colonial America.[105] Yet scholars working on eighteenth-century British culture have displayed little awareness of these developments, nor have they considered how they might change the way they think about the imperial metropolis. David Armitage's recent bold assertion that "we are all Atlanticists now" is for the moment more a call to arms than an established fact.[106]

But the gaps and mismatches between American and British historiographies of eighteenth-century material life also reflect the absence of a distinct academic field in Britain to play the role that material-culture studies have performed for the history of seventeenth- and eighteenth-century North America. Historical archaeology, the history of vernacular architecture, and folklife studies—all of which have helped mold material-culture studies in America—have been less prominent in Britain. There have been no departments of British studies in British universities to provide the institutional setting for studies of material life offered by American studies departments in the United States. In Britain, as in America, studies of the decorative arts and extant furnished interiors have been conducted, by and large, outside the academy. The most important source for the recent interest in eighteenth-century material culture in Britain is the rise of the history of consumption. The way that eighteenth-century material culture tends to be treated in British scholarship reflects this origin. There is wonderful work on who owned goods and on how artifacts were applauded or disparaged, promoted and sold, but major issues for Americanists, such as foodways, house forms, and domestic self-sufficiency, have been almost entirely ignored in British academic circles, until very recently. And there is certainly no big book for Britain on eighteenth-century people and objects that has captured the popular imagination—the equivalent of, say, Laurel Thatcher Ulrich's *The Age of Homespun*.[107]

Even where the concerns of those who study the two opposite shores of the eighteenth-century Atlantic coincide, the same topics are often treated in different ways. For example, the rise of a culture of gentility or politeness in the eighteenth century has been a key concept for new approaches to material things, especially important for Deetz's argument for a re-anglicization of American life in the period. Yet studies of eighteenth-century America have often associated gentility with increasing inequality, while the emphasis in Britain has recently been more on the inclusiveness of its appeal, extending from the nobility at the top to sections of the laboring poor at the bottom.[108] The disparity remains surprising, because what is at issue is essentially the same cultural phenomenon in closely related cultural settings.

This book sets out to address some of these transatlantic mismatches and contradictions. The essays treat the British Atlantic world as a series of material provinces, each with its distinctive features but each looking (in one way or another) to London as its metropolis. These material provinces not only included the different North American colonies and regions of England, which are the main focus of attention here, but extended to Wales, Scotland, Ireland, the West Indies, and beyond.[109] At the same time, the essays endeavor to be precise about what was distinctive to Britain and what was distinctive to North America. Some differences were striking. James Horn's comparison of the inventories of Chesapeake planters and English country dwellers at the start of the eighteenth century alerted us some time ago to the fact that, in the Chesapeake, furnishings were extraordinarily sparse and dwellings small and flimsy compared with their English equivalents.[110] Hannah Greig's essay in this collection highlights the self-conscious splendor of London's *beau monde*, with which even the wealthiest among colonial America's merchants and planters could not compete. Colonial ostentation was closer to that displayed by the wealthy rural gentry and the urban elites of provincial England. Extremes of poverty and wealth among the white American population appear to have been less marked than in England. And, of course, plantation slavery did not exist in the British Isles. In addition, some of the essays consider the thorny issues raised by the persistence in America of a strongly anglicized material culture, beyond the Revolution into the early national period.[111] What role were material things expected to play in the formation of a national taste in the new republic? Were they to embody a distinctive national style, as was to be the case in many new European nations later in the nineteenth century, or was national identity at this earlier period less a matter of how things looked and more a matter of where they were made?[112]

FORMAT

Many of the essays in this book consider gender, taste, and material culture in the context of the domestic interior. This orientation toward the domestic reflects the book's origins in one of the focused research studies undertaken by the British Arts and Humanities Research Council (AHRC) Centre for the Study of the Domestic Interior between 2001 and 2006. The Centre was a collaboration among three partner institutions in London—the Royal College of Art, the Bedford Centre for the History of Women at Royal Holloway, University of London, and the Victoria and Albert Museum. Its purpose was to develop new histories of the home, its contents, and its representation. The book addresses that task by analyzing gender, taste, and material culture in their domestic settings; in addition, it steps outside the home to ask corresponding questions about dress and retailing.[113] The book is also a transatlantic collaboration. This is not just a matter of the subjects of the essays, or the residence of the contributors. Though edited in Britain, it has benefited hugely from two opportunities to present and discuss the chapters in the United States, the first at The Huntington and the second at the Yale Center for British Art.

As well as providing a geographical comparison of Britain and North America, the book aspires to be multidisciplinary—to consider the ways in which issues of gender, taste, and material culture have been handled across a number of academic disciplines. It embraces intellectual history, social history, cultural history, art history, architectural history, literary history, design history, and material-culture history. The book does not attempt to be rigidly comparative, with matched chapters from each discipline, or chapters on the same topic dealing with both Britain and America. But together, the essays are intended to provide a broad comparative overview of the field. To this end, they are grouped into four thematic sections. Each of these sections juxtaposes essays dealing principally with North

America and essays dealing principally with Britain. The first theme is Spaces, which considers objects and the spaces in which they were located. The second is Shopping, which deals with the practices and attitudes associated with acquiring goods. Third is Politics, which assesses the role of material things in political, economic, and social debate. Fourth is People, which focuses on the relationships between particular kinds of artifacts and particular kinds of people.

The organization of the essays into thematic sections should not obscure what they have in common. They share a critical engagement with theoretical debates around gender and things. They also share a commitment to empirical research. They champion the use of empirical sources unfamiliar in the study of material life, such as pamphlets on the English poor laws and the records of criminal trials. At the same time, they use familiar sources, such as ledgers and business letters, in new ways, attending to the language employed and people who are absent. The essays repeatedly draw our attention to the ways in which things, people, and ideas moved within and between places. They show that letters, proxy shoppers, and shiploads of goods all helped shape taste at a distance, but not always in ways consistent with the established notions of authority and subordination, of core and periphery, that were supposed to order relationships within the household as well as within the empire. The essays uncouple the links between acquisition, possession, and ownership. They suggest that the point of acquisition in the shop, where the emphasis was most likely to be on display and spectacle, was not necessarily the defining moment in the life cycle of an object. Repeatedly, they find objects acquiring meanings, and often specifically gendered meanings, through memorializing, dispersal, and persistence—in other words, through their capacity to manipulate time.[114] Above all, the essays share a conviction that in the eighteenth-century British Atlantic world, everyday things were powerful. Mundane artifacts such as silk ribbons and woolen coats, cotton counterpanes and trellis wallpapers, were capable of evoking wonder or provoking anxiety, of forging identities across space and time or fracturing them. In the process, they provoked profound ethical questions that were, in part, questions about the proper relationship between masculine and feminine, women and men.[115]

In writing this introduction, we have benefited from ideas contributed by our fellow authors and all those who debated these essays at The Huntington and the Yale Center for British Art, especially John Brewer, Edward Cooke, Michael Hatt, Alex Nemerov, and Jules Prown. We would also like to thank Susan Juster, Giorgio Riello, and Frank Trentmann. We owe a special debt of gratitude to Hannah Greig for her many contributions to shaping this introduction and to Christopher Breward for a masterly summing-up of the essays presented at the Yale Center for British Art, from which we have drawn shamelessly.

1. Giles Milton, *Nathaniel's Nutmeg: How One Man's Courage Changed the Course of History* (London: Hodder & Stoughton, 1999); Mark Kurlansky, *Salt: A World History* (New York: Walker, 2002); Simon Garfield, *Mauve: How One Man Invented a Colour That Changed the World* (London: Faber and Faber, 2000); Kurlansky, *Cod: A Biography of the Fish That Changed the World* (London: Cape, 1998); Janet Gleeson, *The Arcanum: The Extraordinary True Story of the Invention of European Porcelain* (London: Bantam, 1998); Alan Macfarlane and Gerry Martin, *The Glass Bathyscaphe* (London: Profile, 2002).
2. For a discussion of the turn to consumption in a variety of disciplines, see Daniel Miller, *Acknowledging Consumption: A Review of New Studies* (London: Routledge, 1995).
3. For numerous examples, see John Brewer and Roy Porter, eds., *Consumption and the World of Goods: Consumption and Society in the Seventeenth and Eighteenth Centuries* (London: Routledge, 1993). For important examples of the broader influence of this idea in very different fields, see Richard Goldthwaite, *Wealth and the Demand for Art in Italy, 1300–1600* (Baltimore: Johns Hopkins Univ. Press, 1993), 253, and Don Slater, *Consumer Culture and Modernity* (Cambridge, UK: Polity Press, 1997), chap. 1.
4. For critiques of the application of phrases such as consumer revolution and consumer society to eighteenth-century Britain, see John Styles, "Manufacture, Consumption and Design in Eighteenth-Century England," in Brewer and Porter, *Consumption and the World of Goods*, 527–54; John Brewer, "The Error of Our Ways: Historians and the Birth of Consumer Society," ESRC/AHRC Cultures of Consumption Research Programme, Working Paper 12, June 2004, www.consume.bbk.ac.uk; and Frank Trentmann and Vanessa Taylor, "From Users to Consumers: Water Politics in Nineteenth-Century London," in *The Making of the Consumer*, ed. Frank Trentmann (Oxford: Berg, 2006), 53–79.
5. See T. H. Breen, "An Empire of Goods: The Anglicization of Colonial America, 1690–1776," *Journal of British Studies* 25, no. 4 (Oct. 1986): 467–99.
6. Samuel Adams to Arthur Lee, 31 Oct. 1771, in *The Writings of Samuel Adams*, ed. Harry Alonzo Cushing, 4 vols. (New York: G. P. Putnam's Sons, 1904–8), 2:267.
7. Paul Langford, *A Polite and Commercial People: England 1727–1783* (Oxford: Oxford Univ. Press, 1994); T. H. Breen, *The Marketplace of Revolution: How Consumer Politics Shaped American Independence* (Oxford: Oxford Univ. Press, 2004).
8. For an excellent overview, see Ann Smart Martin and J. Ritchie Garrison, "Shaping the Field: The Multidisciplinary Perspectives of Material Culture," in *American Material Culture: The Shape of the Field*, ed. Ann Smart Martin and J. Ritchie Garrison (Winterthur, DE: Henry Francis du Pont Winterthur Museum, 1997), 1–36. For a collection of key essays in the field, see Robert Blair St. George, ed., *Material Life in America, 1600–1860* (Boston: Northeastern Univ. Press, 1988).
9. Frances Burney, *Evelina; Or The History Of A Young Lady's Entrance Into The World* (1778; Oxford: Oxford Univ. Press, 1992), 27.
10. Lorna H. Mui and Hoh-cheung Mui, *Shops and Shopkeeping in Eighteenth-Century England* (London and Montreal: Routledge and McGill-Queen's Univ. Press, 1989), 44–45.
11. Daniel Defoe, *The Complete English Tradesman*, 2nd ed. (London: Printed for Charles Rivington, 1727), 329.
12. Bernard Mandeville, *The Fable of the Bees; or, Private Vices Publick Benefits* (London: J. Roberts, 1714), 105.
13. John Beresford, ed., *The Torrington Diaries, containing the Tours through England and Wales of the Hon John Byng (later fifth viscount Torrington)* (London: Eyre and Spottiswood, 1934), 1:6.
14. Tobias Smollett, *The Expedition of Humphry Clinker*, 3 vols. (London: Printed for W. Johnston and B. Collins, 1771), 3:140, 126.
15. Amanda Vickery, *The Gentleman's Daughter: Women's Lives in Georgian England* (New Haven and London: Yale Univ. Press, 1998), 133–34, 147–49, 151, 164–68.
16. Old Bailey Proceedings Online (www.oldbaileyonline.org, 11 Nov. 2005), Feb. 1748, trial of Elizabeth Owen (t17480224-14).
17. Mary Beth Norton, *Liberty's Daughters: The Revolutionary Experience of American Women, 1750–1800* (Toronto: Little, Brown & Co., 1980), 157–63.
18. Claire Midgley, "Women Anti-Slavery Campaigners in Britain" (PhD diss., Univ. of Kent, 1989), chap. 2. Perhaps most famously, the early-nineteenth-century women's antislavery societies agreed to forgo slave-

grown sugar. The tactic lived on in the Chartist women's exclusive dealing campaign, which involved boycotting retailers who refused to support the Chartist movement, and the female boycott of feathers from endangered birds in late Victorian department stores.

19. Elizabeth Heyrick, *An Appeal to the Hearts and Consciences of British Women* (Leicester: A. Cockshaw, 1828), 4, 6.
20. Margot Finn, "Men's Things: Masculine Possession in the Consumer Revolution," *Social History* 25, no. 2 (May 2000): 133–55. The problem is also raised by Victoria de Grazia in the introduction to *The Sex of Things: Gender and Consumption in Historical Perspective*, ed. Victoria de Grazia and Ellen Furlough (Berkeley: Univ. of California Press, 1996), 1: "If women figure not only as the proverbial shoppers, the ur-decorators, the perennial custodians of the bric-a-brac of daily life but also as objects of exchange and consumption, what then can be inferred about the relationship of man, males, and masculinity to the world of commodities?"
21. See David Kuchta, *The Three-Piece Suit and Modern Masculinity: England 1550–1850* (Berkeley: Univ. of California Press, 2002); Christopher Breward, *The Hidden Consumer: Masculinities, Fashion, and City Life, 1860–1914* (Manchester: Manchester Univ. Press, 1999); and Catherine Horwood, *Keeping Up Appearances: Fashion and Class between the Wars* (Stroud, UK: Sutton, 2005), a study that gives equal attention to men's and women's dress. For a fascinating glimpse of masculine passion for mechanical goods, especially bicycles, see Lesley Whitworth, "Shop and Shopfloor: Men's Sense of Belonging in 1930s Coventry," in *Making & Unmaking: Creative and Critical Practice in a Designed World; Selected Proceedings Design History Society Annual Conference 2000*, ed. Tim Putnam and others (Portsmouth, UK: DHS / Univ. of Portsmouth, 2000), and "Men Changing Allegiance: From Workshop to Shopper in 1930s Coventry," in *History and Change: Selected Conference Proceedings*, ed. Anu Lahtinen and Kirsi Vainio-Korhonen (Helsinki: SKS / Finnish Literature Society, 2004).
22. David Roberts, *Lord Chesterfield: Letters* (Oxford: Oxford Univ. Press, 1992), 132.
23. Philip Carter, "James Boswell's Manliness," in *English Masculinities, 1660–1800*, ed. Tim Hitchcock and Michele Cohen (London: Longman, 1999), 111–30. See also Carter, *Men and the Emergence of Polite Society, Britain, 1660–1800* (London: Longman, 2001).
24. Lorna Weatherill, *Consumer Behaviour and Material Culture in Britain, 1660–1760* (London: Routledge, 1988); Mark Overton and others, *Production and Consumption in English Households, 1600–1750* (London: Routledge, 2004), chap. 7.
25. See Amanda Vickery, "His and Hers: Gender, Consumption and Household Accounting in Eighteenth-Century England," in *The Art of Survival: Essays in Honor of Olwen Hufton*, ed. Lyndal Roper and Ruth Harris (Past and Present Supplements, Oxford Univ. Press Journals, 2006).
26. Vickery, *Gentleman's Daughter*, 166–68.
27. Jan de Vries, "Between Purchasing Power and the World of Goods: Understanding the Household Economy in Early Modern Europe," in Brewer and Porter, *Consumption and the World of Goods*, 118.
28. Lady Llanover, ed., *The Autobiography and Correspondence of Mary Granville, Mrs Delany*, 6 vols. (London: Richard Bentley, 1861–62), 3:530.
29. The comparison of the Robinson family accounts and the accounts of Abigail Robinson in Rhode Island between 1794 and 1806 suggests that "like most families of middling and well to do circumstances the Robinsons divided the duties of household management roughly by gender." The women hired and managed servants, cared for children, and provided and maintained food and clothing, while the menfolk orchestrated financial transactions concerning land and inheritance. See Ellen Hartigan O'Connor, "Abigail's Accounts: Economy and Affection in the Early Republic," *Journal of Women's History* 17 (2005): 39. The correspondence of Chevalier de Pradel, a Limousin who settled in eighteenth-century Louisiana, "shows that he was responsible for all orders placed in France, while his wife is mentioned shopping in New Orleans. It was Pradel who placed the actual order for his wife's taffeta summer gown, which was an expensive and substantial purchase. But it was she who was responsible for the more mundane clothing matters, as witnessed by her return to the plantation to see to her grown son's clothes." S. K. White, "This Gown Was Much Admired and Made Many Ladies Jealous: Fashion and the Forging of Elite Identities in French

Colonial New Orleans," in *George Washington's South*, ed. T. Harvey and G. O'Brien (Gainesville: Univ. Press of Florida, 2004), 86–118. See also Karin Wulf, *Not All Wives: Women of Colonial Philadelphia* (Ithaca, NY: Cornell Univ. Press, 2000), chap. 3.

30. Louise Lippincott examined the records of Arthur Pond, the London painter and art dealer, and discovered that three-quarters of his customers were men, one-quarter women—and all of them wealthy or noble. However, the average individual expenditure of the female customers was in most cases lower than that of men of the same rank; only two women spent more than £50, and none exceeded £100. L. Lippincott, *Selling Art in Georgian London: The Rise of Arthur Pond* (New Haven and London: Yale Univ. Press, 1983), 66–69.

31. Judith Anderson's analysis of visitors and sales at the Derby porcelain showroom in the 1790s finds that although women were numerically superior as visitors in the season and bought odd pieces of tableware or full tea sets, most of their purchases were less than 10 guineas in value. By contrast, men were more likely to purchase dessert or dinner services costing between 30 and 100 guineas, as well as large ornamental vases. J. A. Anderson, "Derby Porcelain and the Early English Fine Ceramic Industry, c. 1750–1830" (PhD diss., Univ. of Leicester, 2002).

32. Helen Clifford's study of the London silversmiths Parker and Wakelin reveals that female customers were in a distinct minority. Only 37 of the 321 clients in the 1766–70 ledger were female: two "Countesses," seven "Ladys," twenty-two "Mrs," and six "Miss." Only 3 women out of the 37 made large orders for investment goods such as entire tea services or gold and precious stone jewelry. Most of Parker and Wakelin's female customers bought smaller, less expensive items, such as individual pieces of tea ware, snuffboxes, and paste and silver jewelry. Helen Clifford, *Silver in London: The Parker and Wakelin Partnership, 1760–1776* (New Haven and London: Yale Univ. Press, 2004), 138.

33. Clifford is well aware of this, as she concludes that "although the number of women appearing in Parker and Wakelin's accounts is small, and their purchases in their own names modest, their true consumer power and influence is hidden behind the names of their fathers, husbands, brothers, sons and lovers. . . . Wealthy ladies advised their husbands, brothers and fathers on the purchase of the silverware." Clifford, *Silver in London*, 140.

34. See Carole Shammas, "The Female Social Structure of Philadelphia in 1775," *Pennsylvania Magazine of History and Biography* 107, no. 1 (1983): 73–76, and Elaine Forman Crane, *Ebb Tide in New England: Women, Seaports, and Social Change, 1630–1800* (Boston: Northeastern Univ. Press, 1998), 131–32.

35. Penmorfa, Caernarvon, shop ledger, c. 1788–c. 1803, fol. 4, account of Harry Evan of Tyddynfilin, 14 May 1792, and fol. 13, account of William Evans of Wern, 15 Aug. 1793, MS 82, Dept. of MSS, University College of North Wales, Bangor.

36. Johanna Dahn, "Mrs Delany and Ceramics in the Objectscape," *Interpreting Ceramics* 1 (2000), http://www.uwic.ac.uk/ICRC/issue001/, 30 Sept. 2005.

37. For a micro study of the practices and attitudes of one consumer based on diaries, letters, account books, and ledgers, see Amanda Vickery, "Women and the World of Goods: A Lancashire Consumer and Her Possessions, 1751–1781," in Brewer and Porter, *Consumption and the World of Goods*, 274–301. For a compelling reconstruction of the potential connotations of one piece of furniture, see Laurel Thatcher Ulrich, "Hannah Barnard's Cupboard: Female Property and Identity in Eighteenth-Century New England," in *Through a Glass Darkly: Reflections on Personal Identity in Early America*, ed. Ronald Hoffman, Mechel Sobel, and Fredrika Teute (Chapel Hill: Univ. of North Carolina Press, 1997), 238–73. On the intertwining of gender, politics, religion, consumption, and aesthetics, see Johanna Dahn, "Women and Taste: A Case Study of Katharine Plymley (1758–1829)" (PhD diss., Univ. of Aberystwyth, 2001); Dahn, "Material Culture, Abolitionism, and Dissenting Discourse (1791–1830): The Simplicity of a Quaker but Not Their Language" (conference paper at "Women and Material Culture, 1660–1830," Univ. of Southampton and Chawton House Library, 14–15 July 2004); Maura Henry, "Keeping Up with the Beauforts: Consuming Passions," *Harvard Magazine* (Sept.–Oct. 1997); and Marcia Pointon, *Strategies for Showing: Women, Possession and Representation in English Visual Culture, 1665–1800* (Oxford: Oxford Univ. Press, 1997). One of the earliest attempts, based on inventory data, to wrestle with the differences between male and female materialism is Lorna Weatherill, "A Possession of One's Own: Women and Consumer Behaviour in England, 1660–1740,"

Journal of British Studies 25 (1986): 131–56. On the language of bequests, see Maxine Berg, "Women's Consumption and the Industrial Classes of Eighteenth-Century England," *Journal of Social History* 30 (1996): 415–34.

38. Older criticisms of these interpretations include Linda Kerber, "Separate Spheres, Female Worlds, Woman's Place: The Rhetoric of Women's History," *Journal of American History* 75, no. 1 (1988): 9–39, and Amanda Vickery, "Golden Age to Separate Spheres: A Review of the Categories and Chronologies of English Women's History," *Historical Journal* 36, no. 2 (1993): 383–414. More recently, there has been a reconsideration of the analytical utility of the public/private binary in women's history; see the articles in *Journal of Women's History* 15, nos. 1 and 2 (2003).
39. On polite sociability at home, see Vickery, *Gentleman's Daughter*, chap. 7. Historians of American visiting have used their material deliberately to question the public/private dichotomy so widely deployed in women's studies and to posit the existence of an intermediate social sphere. See Karen V. Hansen, *A Very Social Time: Crafting Community in Antebellum New England* (Berkeley: Univ. of California Press, 1996). On the politicization of domestic life, see Kathryn Gleadle, "British Women and Radical Politics in the Late Nonconformist Enlightenment, 1780–1830," in *Women, Privilege and Power: British Politics, 1750 to the Present*, ed. A. Vickery (Stanford: Stanford Univ. Press, 2001), 123–51.
40. On the struggle to find privacy and keep secrets in the upper ranks, see Linda Pollock, "Living on the Stage of the World: The Concept of Privacy among the Elite of Early Modern England," in *Rethinking Social History: English Society, 1570–1920*, ed. Adrian Wilson (Manchester: Manchester Univ. Press, 1993), 78–96. And if concealment was difficult for the elite, it was near impossible for middling Londoners; see Tim Meldrum, *Domestic Service and Gender, 1660–1750: Life and Work in the London Household* (Harlow, UK: Longman, 2000), 68–127. On architectural responses, see John Bold, "Privacy and the Plan," in *English Architecture Public and Private: Essays for Kerry Downes*, ed. John Bold and Edward Chaney (London: Hambledon, 1993), 107–15, and Anne Laurence, "The Closet Disclosed: The Ambiguous Privacy of Women's Closets in Seventeenth-Century England" (unpublished paper, 2004).
41. Mark Girouard, *Life in the English Country House: A Social and Architectural History* (Harmondsworth, UK: Penguin, 1978).
42. Colin Cunningham, "'An Italian House Is My Lady': Some Aspects of the Definition of Women's Role in the Architecture of Robert Adam," in *Femininity and Masculinity in Eighteenth-Century Art and Culture*, ed. Gill Perry and Michael Rossington (Manchester: Manchester Univ. Press, 1994), 63.
43. "Of the three kinds of [wall coverings], the grandest is that in stucco; the neatest that in wainscot, and the most gaudy that in hangings"; Isaac Ware, *A Complete Body of Architecture* (London: T. Osborne and J. Shipton, 1756), 469.
44. Vickery, *Gentleman's Daughter*, 195–223.
45. Ware, *Complete Body of Architecture*, 470.
46. Llanover, *Mrs Delany*, 2:441. For more reflections on gender and style, see Cunningham, "An Italian House Is My Lady," 63–77.
47. John Cornforth, *Early Georgian Interiors* (New Haven and London: Yale Univ. Press, 2004), 208, 253.
48. See, for example, Thomas Chippendale, *The Gentleman and Cabinet-Maker's Director*, 3rd ed. (London: Printed for the author, 1762), plates 26, 27, and 28.
49. Beresford, *Torrington Diaries*, 1:24.
50. James Miller, *The Humours of Oxford* (Dublin: Powell, 1730), 82. For a gloss, see Patricia Fara, *Pandora's Breeches: Women, Science and Power in the Enlightenment* (London: Pimlico, 2004), 11. We thank Patricia Fara for pointing out this dichotomy.
51. Victoria and Albert Museum, *Catalogue of a Loan Exhibition of English Chintz* (London: Her Majesty's Stationery Office, 1960), 13.
52. For an early example, see Chippendale, *Gentleman and Cabinet-Maker's Director*, plates 51, "A Dressing-Table for a Lady," and 116, "A Writing-Table and Bookcase for a Lady."
53. See Elizabeth Kowaleski-Wallace, "Women, China and Consumer Culture in Eighteenth-Century England," *Eighteenth-Century Studies* 29 (1995–96): 165; Kowaleski-Wallace, *Consuming Subjects: Women, Shopping,*

and Business in the Eighteenth Century (New York: Columbia Univ. Press, 1997); Sarah Richards, *Eighteenth-Century Ceramics: Producers for a Civilised Society* (Manchester: Manchester Univ. Press, 1999); and Dahn, "Mrs Delany and Ceramics in the Objectscape."

54. Horace Walpole to Richard Bentley, Aug. 1756, in *Horace Walpole's Correspondence*, ed. W. S. Lewis, W. H. Smith, and G. L. Lam, 48 vols. (London: Oxford Univ. Press; New Haven: Yale Univ. Press, 1937–83), 35:271.
55. Edward Hall, ed., *Miss Weeton: Journal of a Governess*, 2 vols. (London: Oxford Univ. Press, 1939), 2:325.
56. Llanover, *Mrs Delany*, 3:633.
57. Ulrich, "Hannah Barnard's Cupboard."
58. M. B. Norton, "Eighteenth-Century American Women in Peace and War: The Case of the Loyalists," *William and Mary Quarterly*, 3rd ser., 33 (1976): 397. See also Norton, *Liberty's Daughters*, 396–97.
59. This is something that is also suggested by the distinctive mix of goods stolen by female thieves. See Lynn MacKay, "Why They Stole: Women in the Old Bailey, 1779–1789," *Journal of Social History* 32 (1999): 623–39.
60. Henry Stonecastle, *The Universal Spectator*, 4 vols. (London: Printed for A. Ward, 1747), 3:46–47.
61. John Brewer, *The Pleasures of the Imagination: English Culture in the Eighteenth Century* (London: HarperCollins, 1997).
62. Sir Joshua Reynolds, *The Works of Sir Joshua Reynolds, Knight*, 3 vols. (London: Printed for T. Cadell, Jun. and W. Davies, 1798), 1:231.
63. John Gilbert Cooper, *Letters Concerning Taste* (London: Printed for R. and J. Dodsley, 1755), 62.
64. Frederick Robinson, Whitehall, to Thomas Robinson, second Baron Grantham, Madrid, 4 May 1778, Wrest Park Papers, Bedfordshire Record Office, L30/14/333/91.
65. George Coleman, *The Connoisseur, By Mr. Town, Critic and Censor-General*, 3rd ed., 4 vols. (London: Printed for R. Baldwin, 1757–60), 4:121.
66. Mary Thrale, ed., *The Autobiography of Francis Place* (Cambridge: Cambridge Univ. Press, 1972), 216.
67. Michael Moriarty, *Taste and Ideology in Seventeenth-Century France* (Cambridge: Cambridge Univ. Press, 1988).
68. Anthony Ashley Cooper, third Earl of Shaftesbury, *Characteristics of Men, Manners, Opinions, Times, etc.*, 3 vols. (London: Printed [by J. J. Tourneisen] for J. J. Tourneisen; and J. L. Legrand, 1790), 1:269.
69. For American examples prior to the Revolution, see Breen, *Marketplace of Revolution*, 172–82. For British examples from the later eighteenth century, see Gregory Claeys, "The Origins of the Rights of Labor: Republicanism, Commerce, and the Construction of Modern Social Theory in Britain, 1796–1805," *Journal of Modern History* 66 (1994): 249–90.
70. John Thelwall, *Poems Written in Close Confinement in the Tower and Newgate under a Charge of High Treason* (London: Printed for the author, and sold by J. Ridgway, H. D. Symonds, and D. I. Eaton, 1795), 3.
71. Robert W. Jones, *Gender and the Formation of Taste in Eighteenth-Century Britain: The Analysis of Beauty* (Cambridge: Cambridge Univ. Press, 1998).
72. Lawrence Klein, "Politeness and the Interpretation of the British Eighteenth Century," *The Historical Journal* 45 (2002): 869–98, and Klein, "Politeness for Plebes: Some Social Identities in Early Eighteenth-Century England," in *The Consumption of Culture, 1600–1800: Image, Object, Text*, ed. Ann Bermingham and John Brewer (London: Routledge, 1995).
73. N. B. Harte, "State Control of Dress and Social Change in Pre-Industrial England," in *Trade, Government and Economy in Pre-Industrial England*, ed. D. C. Coleman and A. H. John (London: Weidenfeld and Nicolson, 1976), 132–65.
74. John Faucheraud Grimke, *The Public Laws of the State of South-Carolina* (Philadelphia: R. Aitken & Son, 1790), 137, "An Act for the better Ordering and Governing Negroes and other Slaves in this Province, 1740," XL, "*Be it enacted*, That no owner or proprietor of any negro slave or other slave (except livery-men and boys) shall permit or suffer such negro or other slave, to have or wear any sort of apparel whatsoever, finer, other, or of greater value than negro cloth, duffels, kerseys, oznabrigs, blue linen, check linen or coarse garlix, or calicoes, checked cottons, or Scots plaids."
75. John Locke, *Some Thoughts Concerning Education*, 9th ed. (London: Printed for A. Bettesworth and C. Hitch, 1732), 118.

76. For Quakers, see Emma Lapsanky and Anne Verplanck, *Quaker Aesthetics: Reflections on a Quaker Ethic in American Design and Consumption, 1720–1920* (Philadelphia: Univ. of Pennsylvania Press, 2002); for Methodists, see Edwina Ehrman, *Dressed Neat and Plain: The Clothing of John Wesley and His Teaching on Dress* (London: John Wesley's House and the Museum of Methodism, 2003).

77. Quoted in Ian Dyck, *William Cobbett and Rural Popular Culture* (Cambridge: Cambridge Univ. Press, 1992), 62.

78. For examples, see Jones, *Gender and the Formation of Taste*, and George Dickie, *The Century of Taste: The Philosophical Odyssey of Taste in the Eighteenth Century* (New York and Oxford: Oxford Univ. Press, 1996).

79. Thorstein Veblen, *The Theory of the Leisure Class: An Economic Study in the Evolution of Institutions* (New York: Huebsch, 1899), especially chap. 6, "Pecuniary Canons of Taste"; Pierre Bourdieu, *Distinction: A Social Critique of the Judgment of Taste*, trans. Richard Nice (Cambridge, MA: Harvard Univ. Press, 1984). For a useful overview of recent sociological work in this idiom and a prospectus for future research that parallels some of the issues taken up in this book, see Mark Harvey and others, *Between Demand & Consumption: A Framework for Research*, ESRC Centre for Research on Innovation and Competition, Discussion Paper no. 40 (Manchester: Univ. of Manchester, Centre for Research on Innovation and Competition, 2001).

80. Neil McKendrick, "The Consumer Revolution of Eighteenth-Century England," in *The Birth of a Consumer Society: The Commercialization of Eighteenth-Century England*, ed. Neil McKendrick, John Brewer, and J. H. Plumb (London: Europa, 1982).

81. Shane White and Graham White, *Stylin': African American Expressive Culture from Its Beginnings to the Zoot Suit* (Ithaca, NY: Cornell Univ. Press, 1998); Philip D. Morgan, *Slave Counterpoint: Black Culture in the Eighteenth-Century Chesapeake and Lowcountry* (Chapel Hill: Univ. of North Carolina Press, 1998); Michael Angelo Gomez, *Exchanging Our Country Marks: The Transformation of African Identities in the Colonial and Antebellum South* (Chapel Hill: Univ. of North Carolina Press, 1998).

82. D. L. Porter, "Monstrous Beauty: Eighteenth-Century Fashion and the Aesthetics of the Chinese Taste," *Eighteenth-Century Life* 26 (2002): 395–411.

83. Peter Borsay, "The London Connection: Cultural Diffusion and the Eighteenth-Century Provincial Town," *The London Journal* 19 (1994): 21–35; Dror Wahrman, "National Society, Communal Culture," *Social History* 17 (1992): 43–72.

84. For examples, see Anon., *The Complete Letter-Writer: or, Polite English Secretary* (London: Stanley Crowder & Co.; Henry Woodgate, 1758), 227; William Bingley, *A Tour round North Wales, performed during the Summer of 1798*, 2 vols. (London: E. Williams, 1800), 2:5; Hannah More, *Essays on Various Subjects, principally designed for Young Ladies* (London: J. Wilkie; T. Cadell, 1778), 13; and Anon., *An Inquiry into the Management of the Poor, and our usual Polity respecting the Common People* (London: Printed for Benjamin White, 1767), 23.

85. [Josiah Wedgwood and Thomas Bentley], *A Catalogue of Cameos, Intaglios, Medals, Busts, Small Statues, and Bas-reliefs*, 2nd ed. (London: Sold by Cadel, Robson, and Parker, printseller, 1774), 1. See also Neil McKendrick, "Josiah Wedgwood and the Commercialisation of the Potteries," in McKendrick, Brewer, and Plumb, *Birth of a Consumer Society*.

86. Josiah Wedgwood to Thomas Bentley, undated, referable to 1776–77, in *The Life of Josiah Wedgwood*, by Eliza Meteyard (London: Hurst & Blackett, 1865), 2:156.

87. See note 84.

88. John Holroyd, Earl of Sheffield, *Observations on the Commerce of the American States* (London: Printed for J. Debrett, 1784), 34.

89. Anon., *The European Traveller in America. Contained in three letters to his friend, in London* (Hartford, CT: Hudson & Goodwin, 1785), 22.

90. Isaac Weld, *Travels through the States of North America, and the Provinces of Upper and Lower Canada, during the Years 1795, 1796, and 1797* (London: Printed for John Stockdale, 1799), 435.

91. See, for example, Dickie, *Century of Taste*.

92. Walsall Local History Centre, "The Life and Times of James Gee of Walsall, 1746–1827" (unpaginated typescript, chap. 4).

93. Neil McKendrick, "Home Demand and Economic Growth: A New View of the Role of Women and

Children in the Industrial Revolution," in *Historical Perspectives: Studies in English Thought and Society in Honour of J. H.Plumb*, ed. Neil McKendrick (London: Europa, 1974), 209.

94. John Styles, "Custom or Consumption? Plebeian Fashion in Eighteenth-Century England," in *Luxury in the Eighteenth Century: Debates, Desires and Delectable Goods*, ed. Maxine Berg and Elizabeth Eger (London: Palgrave Macmillan, 2003), 103–15. For similar elite concerns in America about holiday clothes and insubordination among slaves and poor whites, see Breen, *Marketplace of Revolution*, 165.

95. Martin and Garrison, "Shaping the Field," 1–36.

96. For these debates, see Martin and Garrison, "Shaping the Field," 1–20. For a powerful statement of the primacy of material evidence, see Henry Glassie, "Meaningful Things and Appropriate Myths: The Artefact's Place in American Studies," in St. George, *Material Life in America*, 63–92. For a rare recent overview of these issues in a British context, see Marilyn Palmer and Peter Neaverson, *The Textile Industry of South-West England. A Social Archeology* (Stroud, UK: Tempus, 2005), 11–14.

97. See, for example, Neil McKendrick, "The Commercialisation of Fashion," in McKendrick, Brewer, and Plumb, *Birth of a Consumer Society*.

98. For examples, see Weatherill, *Consumer Behaviour and Material Culture*; Peter Earle, *The Making of the English Middle Class: Business, Society and Family Life in London, 1660–1730* (London: Methuen, 1989), especially chap. 10; and Carole Shammas, *The Pre-Industrial Consumer in England and America* (Oxford: Clarendon Press, 1990).

99. For a discussion of this issue, see John Styles, "Product Innovation in Early Modern London," *Past and Present* 168 (2000): 124–69.

100. The issue of objects and agency is one that has become prominent in the sociology of science and technology, in particular in the debates around actor network theory. See John Law and John Hassard, *Actor Network and After* (Oxford: Blackwell, 1999). For an exciting historical application of these ideas, see Paul Glennie and Nigel Thrift, "The Spaces of Clock Times," in *The Social in Question: New Bearings in History and the Social Sciences*, ed. P. Joyce (London: Routledge, 2002), 151–74.

101. And in doing so, they draw on a range of innovative recent work concerned with the performative and conversational capacities of objects. For a challenging overview of the problems, see Dell Upton, "Form and User: Style, Mode, Fashion, and the Artifact," in *Living in a Material World: Canadian and American Approaches to Material Culture*, ed. Gerald L. Pocius (St. John's, Newfoundland: Institute of Social and Economic Research, 1991). For the application to objects of the notions of expression and performance, see Robert Blair St. George, *Conversing by Signs: Poetics of Implication in Colonial New England Culture* (Chapel Hill: Univ. of North Carolina Press, 1998), introduction. For ergonomics, see Mimi Hellman, "Furniture, Sociability, and the Work of Leisure in Eighteenth-Century France," *Eighteenth-Century Studies* 32, no. 4 (1999): 415–45.

102. James Deetz, *In Small Things Forgotten: The Archaeology of Early American Life* (New York: Anchor Press, 1977); Jack P. Greene, *Pursuits of Happiness: The Social Development of Early Modern British Colonies and the Formation of American Culture* (Chapel Hill: Univ. of North Carolina Press, 1988).

103. Deetz, *In Small Things Forgotten*, 38.

104. Breen, *Marketplace of Revolution*, especially 299.

105. See, for example, Michael Warner, "What's Colonial about Colonial America?" in *Possible Pasts: Becoming Colonial in Early America*, ed. Robert Blair St. George (Ithaca, NY: Cornell Univ. Press, 2000), 49–70.

106. David Armitage and Michael J. Braddick, eds., *The British Atlantic World, 1500–1800* (Basingstoke, UK, and New York: Palgrave Macmillan, 2002), 11.

107. Laurel Thatcher Ulrich, *The Age of Homespun: Objects and Stories in the Creation of an American Myth* (New York: Alfred A. Knopf, 2001).

108. For America, see Richard L. Bushman, *The Refinement of America: Persons, Houses, Cities* (New York: Alfred A. Knopf, 1992); for England, see Klein, "Politeness and the Interpretation of the British Eighteenth Century," and Klein, "Politeness for Plebes."

109. For examples, see Stana Nenadic, "Middle-Rank Consumers and Domestic Culture in Edinburgh and Glasgow 1720–1840," *Past and Present* 145 (1994): 122–56; Toby Barnard, *Making the Grand Figure: Lives*

and Possessions in Ireland, 1641–1770 (New Haven and London: Yale Univ. Press, 2004); and Amin Jaffer, *Furniture from British India and Ceylon: A Catalogue of the Collections in the Victoria and Albert Museum and the Peabody Essex Museum* (London: V&A Publications, 2001).

110. James Horn, *Adapting to a New World: English Society in the Seventeenth-Century Chesapeake* (Chapel Hill: Univ. of North Carolina Press, 1994), chap. 7.

111. P. P. Hill, *French Perceptions of the Early American Republic, 1783–1793* (Philadelphia: American Philosophical Society, 1988), reveals French disappointment at the continuing devotion to British goods in the new republic. For reflections on this issue, see also St. George, *Conversing by Signs*, 12.

112. As was the case in late-eighteenth-century Ireland; see Sarah Foster, "Buying Irish: Consumer Nationalism in Eighteenth-Century Dublin," *History Today* 47 (1997): 44–51.

113. For a thoughtful assessment of another juxtaposition of eighteenth-century furnishing and fashion, in an exhibition at The Metropolitan Museum of Art, New York, see Peter McNeil, "Exhibition Review: *Dangerous Liaisons: Fashion and Furniture in the Eighteenth Century*," *Fashion Theory* 9 (2005): 477–86.

114. For a useful discussion of these issues, see M. Kwint, C. Breward, and J. Aynsley, eds., *Material Memories: Design and Evocation* (London: Berg, 1999), introduction.

115. For ethical issues in debates about consumption in the eighteenth century and since, see Matthew Hilton, "The Legacy of Luxury: Moralities of Consumption since the Eighteenth Century," *Journal of Consumer Culture* 4 (2004).

Spaces

Tabletop Conversations: Material Culture and Everyday Life in the Eighteenth-Century Atlantic World

Bernard L. Herman

THE TEA TABLE, upended, spills its contents to the floor. Teacups plunge to their catastrophic fate, and the ceremony of sociability crashes to a conclusion. A fallen woman—a country girl led into a life of sex for hire in London—shatters the propriety of the moment. Her body and country origins counter the assertion of tasteful urban femininity; the upended table concretizes her transgressions (fig. 1).

The magistrate enters the room, warrant in hand, deputies at the ready. The woman perches on her bed in a chamber notable for its disarray and dirtiness. A maidservant of dubious character bends in a parodic curtsy, teapot poised. We can almost hear her knees crack. A turned stool serves as makeshift tea table. Laid with the requisite objects, it violates the boundaries of polite society as surely as if it were overturned (fig. 2).

She sags. Draped in white, evocative of the habit of virtue it belies, of the funeral shroud it portends, Moll, unconscious, departs this world. Joined stool is fallen, tea things broken, tabletop conversations concluded. The harlot's progress is mapped by the objects that, set in play, are enacted, sustaining too little, revealing too much (fig. 3).

Encoffined, her dead presence occasions the paradox of mourners intent on life. Celebrants in death's domain, they flirt, connive. Her coffin lid, askew, doubles as tabletop; a young woman, her breasts barely contained within her bodice, peers at the corpse. The conversation of dishes continues. Wine glasses clink, and their contents slosh and spill; a fork brushed from its plate hangs precariously, threatening to drop into the coffin (fig. 4). Even in her shroud, Moll animates and complicates the world of things: ambiguous, situational, unstable. She has been consumed by the sequence of tables that maps her history.

William Hogarth, an artist whose work graced dwellings on both sides of the Atlantic, positions these tables at the center of the action, anchoring and organizing the moment that whirls around each. Every table captures the viewer's eye, freezes our attention, accelerates our ability to grasp, to understand, to narrate.[1]

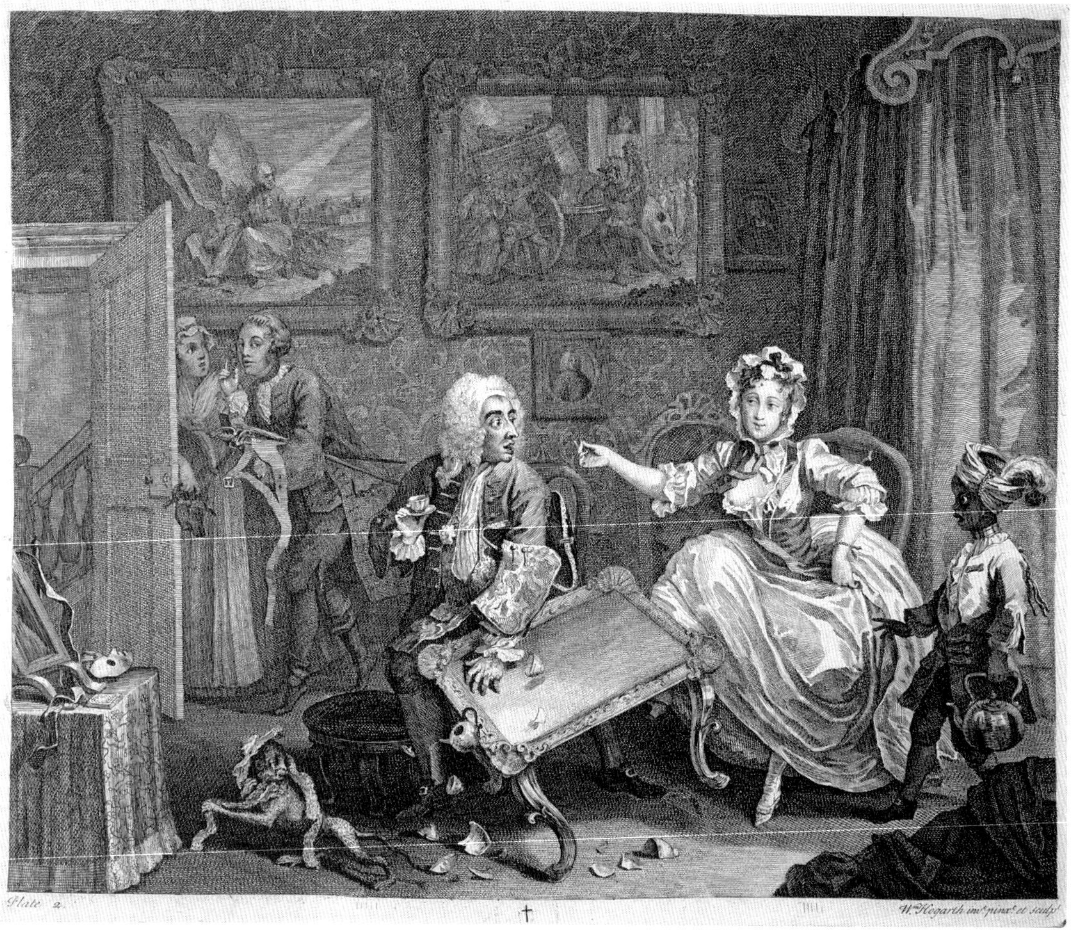

1. William Hogarth, *The Harlot's Progress*, plate 2, engraving (1732), 11⅞ x 14⅝ in. (30 x 37 cm), from *The Original and Genuine Works of William Hogarth* (London: Baldwin, Cradock, and Joy, 1820–21). Yale Center for British Art, Paul Mellon Collection. Photo: Richard Caspole, Yale Center for British Art.

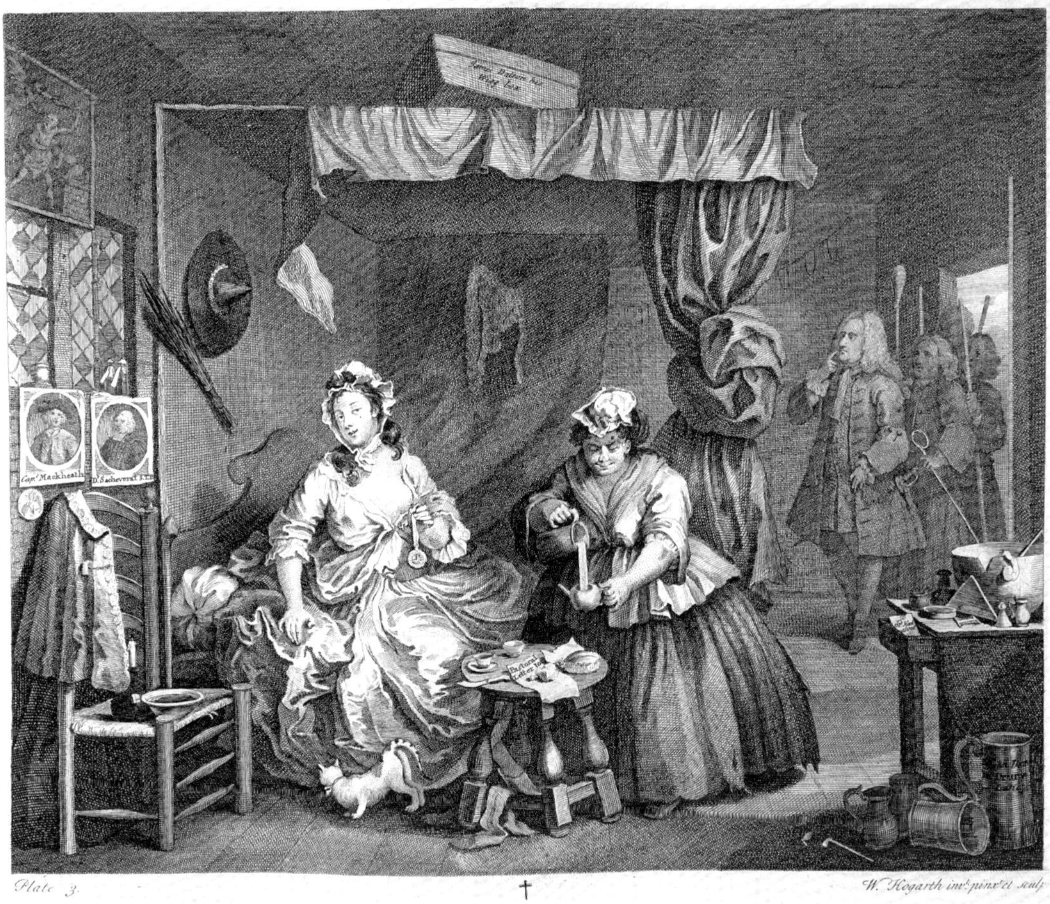

2. William Hogarth, *The Harlot's Progress*, plate 3, engraving (1732), 11⅞ x 14⅝ in. (30.2 x 37 cm), from *The Original and Genuine Works of William Hogarth* (London: Baldwin, Cradock, and Joy, 1820–21). Yale Center for British Art, Paul Mellon Collection. Photo: Richard Caspole, Yale Center for British Art.

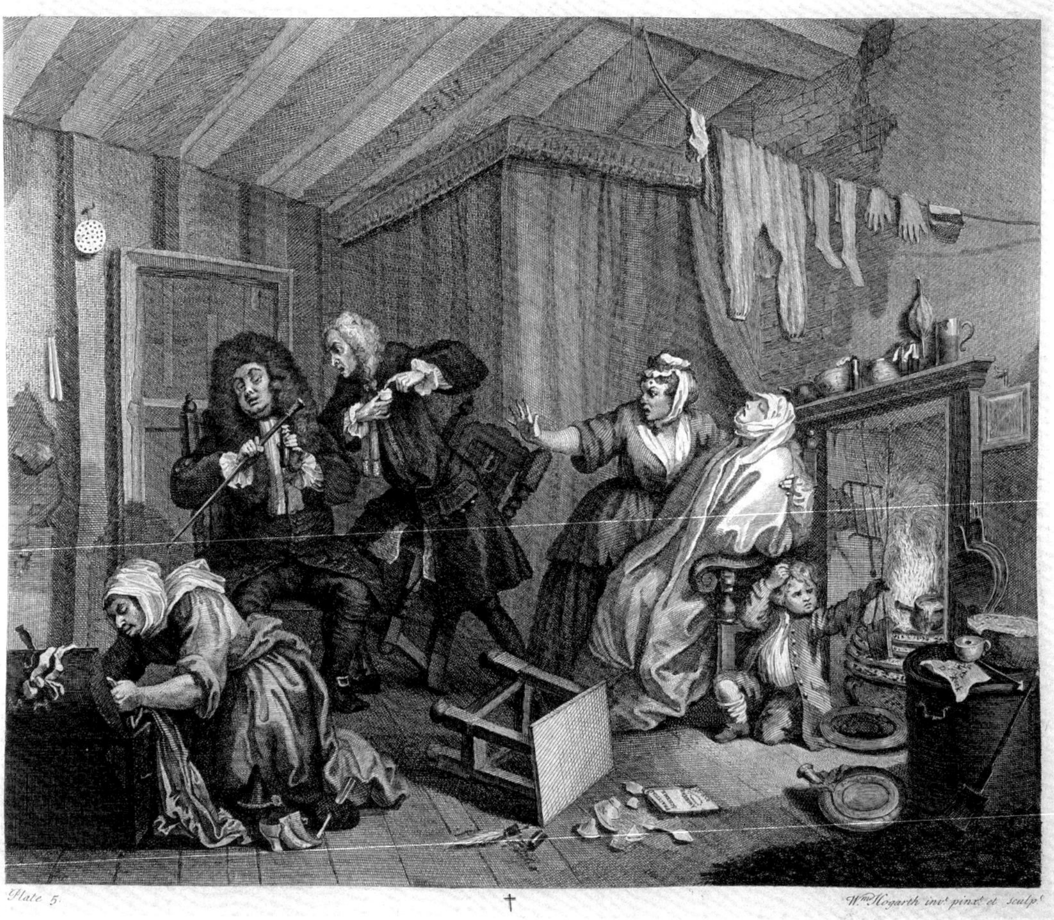

3. William Hogarth, *The Harlot's Progress*, plate 5, engraving (1732), 12 x 14⅝ in. (30.5 x 37 cm), from *The Original and Genuine Works of William Hogarth* (London: Baldwin, Cradock, and Joy, 1820–21). Yale Center for British Art, Paul Mellon Collection. Photo: Richard Caspole, Yale Center for British Art.

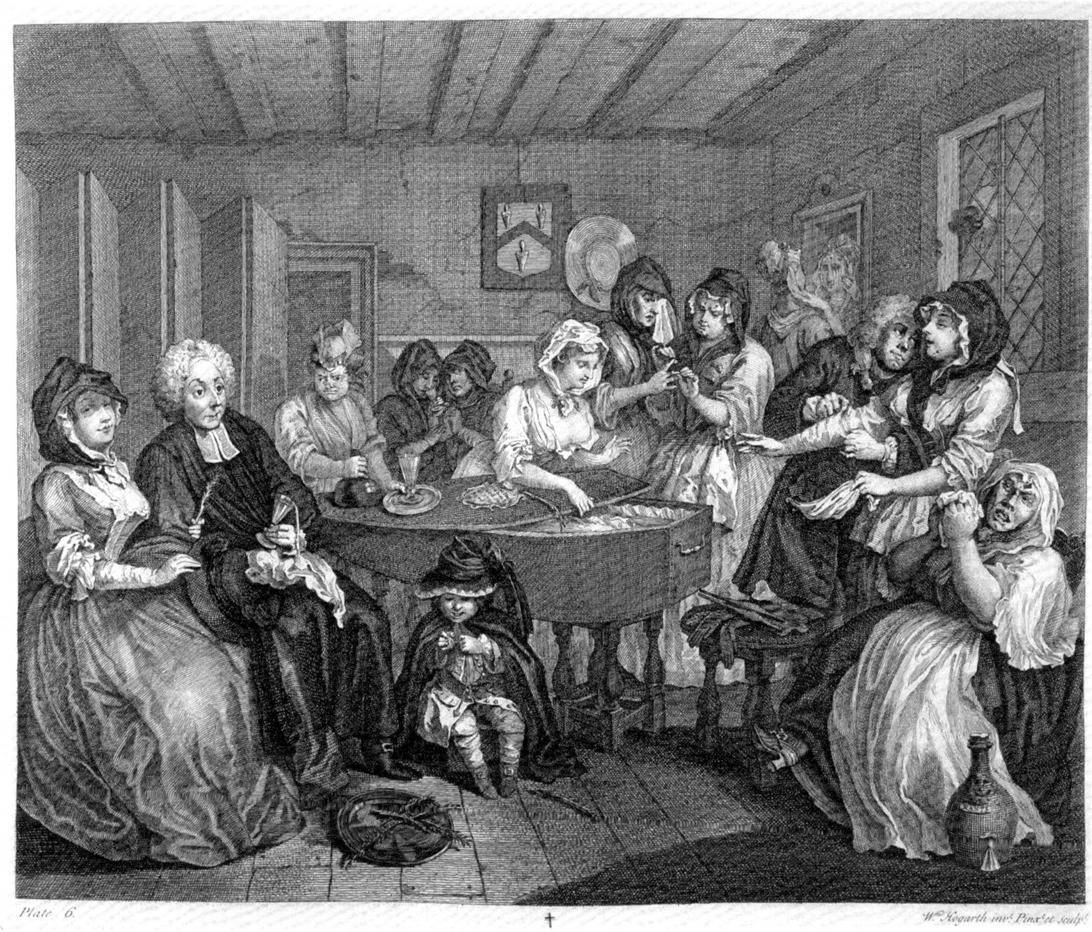

4. William Hogarth, *The Harlot's Progress*, plate 6, engraving (1732), 11⅞ x 14⅞ in. (30.2 x 37.7 cm), from *The Original and Genuine Works of William Hogarth* (London: Baldwin, Cradock, and Joy, 1820–21). Yale Center for British Art, Paul Mellon Collection. Photo: Richard Caspole, Yale Center for British Art.

Tabletop conversations evoke a world of relationships in which objects and behaviors intersect around outward show and the material culture of sociability.[2] Tabletops, metaphoric fields of social play, strategically enabled assertions of self as actor, witness, and judge through the deployment of objects and the ability to enact their rituals. Studies that explore the emergence of an eighteenth-century culture of taste, sociability, and gentility typically proceed from an implied position that society as a whole moved inexorably, albeit unevenly, in a particular direction that embraced the substance and symbolic implications of those rituals.[3] The collective sense of the objects that furnished those practices typically refers back to debates on the origins of consumer society. Historians have ably tracked the dramatic rise in the availability and affordability of commodities ranging from ceramics and foodstuffs to furniture and housing in both urban and rural settings. Their explorations and the statistical and anecdotal data that support their arguments plot an increasingly vigorous presence of an urban "middling sort" drawn from the ranks of successful artisans, shopkeepers, and merchants.[4]

For all we have learned about the material world of eighteenth-century cities, however, we continue to have a tenuous grasp on urban life as lived experience, as having the substance of its many, many occasions.[5] Two forces shape this lacuna. First, the desire to find pattern in human action sustains a distrust of individual stories in more than an illustrative role. Although the work of cultural historians looking at topics as varied as heresy trials, the regulation of royal forests, portraiture, and underground print culture has garnered attention, it has generally failed to reshape the larger disciplines of which it is a part. Second, these same studies, even as they demonstrate the ways in which individuals constructed their own worlds, reify deeply embedded notions of power. They tend to be written from a position that holds them hostage to dominant methodological, theoretical, and critical ideologies. Even the language of resistance and transgression emerges from an acceptance of authority and community as driving engines in the eighteenth-century Atlantic world.[6]

The question—at least the one raised here—that bedevils material culture and social and cultural history is how we formulate an approach that lets us renegotiate the weight of categories such as taste and gender and come at them from a different perspective, one that is in some measure free of the defining construction of a dominant culture. This dilemma is not the exclusive concern of material-culture studies, but also runs through the diverse methodologies it employs. Current feminist critiques, for example, concern themselves with the necessity for shifting debate away from deeply engrained binary approaches.[7] An answer, it seems, resides in a sense of the situational and the conversational and the ways we locate and map the agency of objects and their attendant ambiguities. Events take place; therefore, place matters. But how does it matter? What are its textures? And how do we render the material world symbolically scrutable and sensible on multiple interconnecting levels?

Two problematic terms haunt this exploration into the material culture of the eighteenth-century Atlantic world: "taste" and "gender." But of the two, taste holds the central position at the start of this conversation. Taste—good and bad, individual and collective—is a "form, style, or manner" for the demonstration of "a sense of beauty, excellence, fitness, [and] propriety."[8] The sticking words here include "beauty," with the implication of aesthetic value; "excellence," with the presumption of hierarchical values; "fitness," with the notion of comportment and inclusive and exclusive social relationships; and "propriety," conveying a sense of balance and etiquette. Taste can be read as a system of social and cultural values focused in the eighteenth century on regularity, hierarchy, order, and standardization, all materially grounded in and made visible through architecture and an astonishing range of artifacts and social behaviors. Taste also functions as a coded material and performative language strategically employed in a process of self-identification along lines of both affinity and difference. In this sense, taste serves as an instrument that simultaneously privileges processes of social cohesion and social distinction. Taste in this context informs material and visual representations of power.[9]

We accept taste as a contested intellectual property—a body of academically grounded aesthetic knowledge ostensibly owned by an educated, sophisticated, and cosmopolitan few, but always at risk of being appropriated into the world of the hoi polloi.[10] Performance—the ways in which individuals enact objects and establish themselves in relationship to other individuals, communities, and the material worlds they inhabit—reconciles the tensions that surround the idea of taste. We grasp taste and the many contexts it superintends through the buildings that people designed and built, the objects and images with which they furnished private and public spaces, and the myriad ways they acted on those objects and in those spaces in a continuous construction of everyday experience. Although the evocation of the everyday often stands in as a synonym for the demotic, the quotidian, the vernacular, the term entails more specific and nuanced connotations. In his meditation on walking in the city, Michel de Certeau introduces the notion of "pedestrian speech acts" defined by three processes: "appropriation of the topographical system on the part of the pedestrian," "a spatial acting out of place," and the implication of "relations among differentiated positions."[11]

The idea of everyday life presented here refers specifically to the many ways in which people project, perceive, understand, and narrate themselves in the material worlds they inhabit. The distinction is between place as locus and space as the enlivening of place.[12] The spatial imagination in this context is not about the ways in which picture space is conceived (though that is certainly part of a more expansive argument), but the strategies through which individuals and communities inhabited their material worlds, real and imagined. The social imagination can be summarized within the framework of two parallel and interconnected concerns. First, there is Charles Taylor's formulation of the social imaginary: "the ways people imagine their social existence, how they fit together with others, how things go on between them and their fellows, the expectations that are normally met, and the deeper normative notions and images that underlie these expectations."[13] Significantly, the social imaginary "is not a set of ideas," but a process. It is what enables the practices of society, through making sense of them, and it is "the coming to be of certain social forms," for example, public spheres.[14] Second, Dell Upton, addressing the notion of everydayness, synthesizes the intersection of place and process around "habitus," defined as "the nexus of spaces and times that repeatedly trigger bodily habits and cultural memories."[15] Habitus is recursive in nature, a process dependent on "the repetition and routine of everyday life." And, like the social imaginary, habitus is cultural process—but a process that we see visible only in its practices and artifacts. This chapter seeks to recover a sense of habitus and the social imaginary in the material world.[16]

Object-driven questions about taste and gender define the scope of this collection of essays. How, for example, might ordinary houses have manifested individual and collective tastes that may have been gendered in distinctive ways? Within the interpretation of demotic housing, the steps toward resolving this question require an understanding first of dwellings, second of their furnishings, and third of their practice. Given the fact that the kinds of archival research and fieldwork required for broad generalizations remains largely unrealized, we move forward, of necessity, by example and with the understanding that the goal of this discussion is to locate where answers might reside. The urban houses of Deptford (an early London suburb west of Greenwich, on the south bank of the River Thames) and Philadelphia (with an emphasis on Elfreth's Alley and its environs, located in the oldest part of the city, near the Delaware River waterfront) provide those examples (figs. 5, 6). Both places grew dramatically through the long eighteenth century, and both were homes to populations of minor merchants, artisans, shopkeepers, and the host of occupational groups and households that we think of as composing the middling sort. Some possessed money, but very few could be considered wealthy. Nevertheless, they vigorously constructed, communicated, and even caricatured status through the acquisition, display, deployment, and performance of objects in everyday life.

First, the house—and here I emphasize the house as an envelope and focus on its interior arrangements. In Deptford, the four most common types of houses

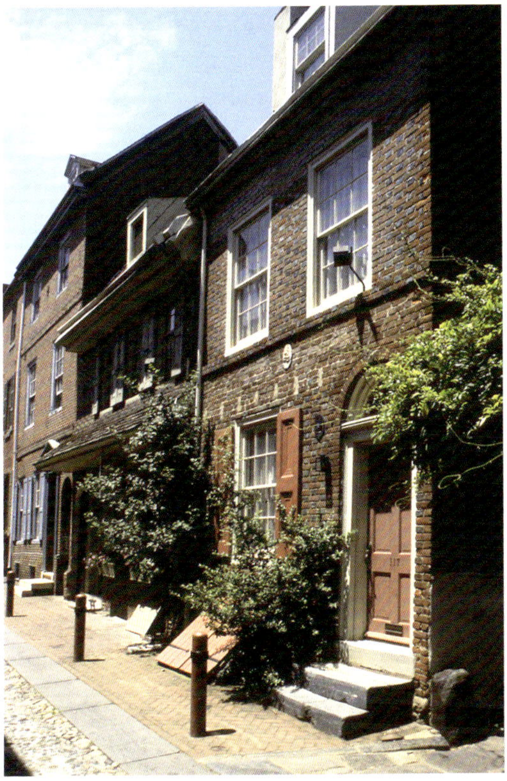

5. View in Elfreth's Alley, Philadelphia. Photo: Bernard L. Herman.

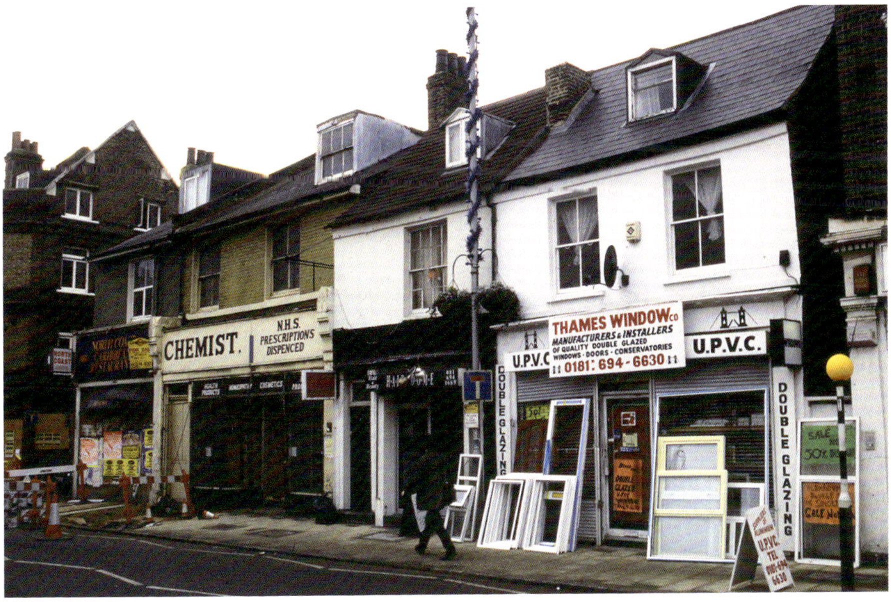

6. View in Deptford High Street, Deptford, London. Photo: Bernard L. Herman.

ranged from dwellings one room in plan, and two to three stories in height, to variations on a four-room arrangement that included an entry and passage, parlor, dining room, and chamber on the ground floor.[17] Multistoried one-room houses built in brick and frame appeared both in the commercial thoroughfare of Deptford High Street and in smaller lanes such as Tanners Hill. Somewhat larger were dwellings two rooms in plan, often with a shop and back kitchen on the ground floor and parlor and chambers above. Significantly, the common larger houses followed two very different alternatives. Still standing in Deptford High Street, but also known to have lined the many side streets that fed into the town center, were a class of houses two and three stories in height, with their plans organized around a central chimney that effectively divided the house into front and back spaces accessible via a passage that contained the stairs. Finally, Deptford builders erected finer houses, such as those in Albury Street, based on the idea of an unheated formal entry and stair hall and chimneys built into the gable walls. Most often, these houses were two rooms in depth, but site conditions and personal desires occasionally gave rise to variations that were double-fronted and a single room deep. Houses of this last sort were common currency throughout eighteenth-century London, from Spitalfields in the east to Chelsea in the west—so common, in fact, that they have blinded us to the variety of London's housing stock as it evolved from the late seventeenth century through the 1700s.[18]

The interior finishes in Deptford houses were consistent regardless of plan. Paneled walls were standard in houses of all sorts, as were a succession of classical and neoclassical chimneypieces (fig. 7). Houses with open stairs emphasized their sculptural qualities, with turned balusters that typically ascended through the house in a hierarchy of interior finishes (fig. 8). Construction, too, was relatively standard, although the custom of carrying home "chips"—surplus timber from Deptford's royal dockyards—produced some distinctive framing solutions.

Eighteenth-century Philadelphia houses reflect something of the same range of options in plan, construction, and interior finishes as the houses of Deptford. Two- and three-story dwellings containing a single room on a floor were common throughout the city and its suburbs—and remained a favored solution for the development of tenement courts into the mid-nineteenth century. Similarly, Philadelphians erected residences two rooms in depth, with gable chimneys. Houses two rooms deep, with formal entries and stair halls (often contained in a separate "piazza"), were common stock for Philadelphia's more well-to-do householders (fig. 9). The rising popularity of the Philadelphia "piazza" toward the end of the eighteenth century architecturally documents the increasing desire to isolate the public and private, refined and coarse, functions of the house. There were also significant differences from Deptford houses. Center-chimney dwellings of the

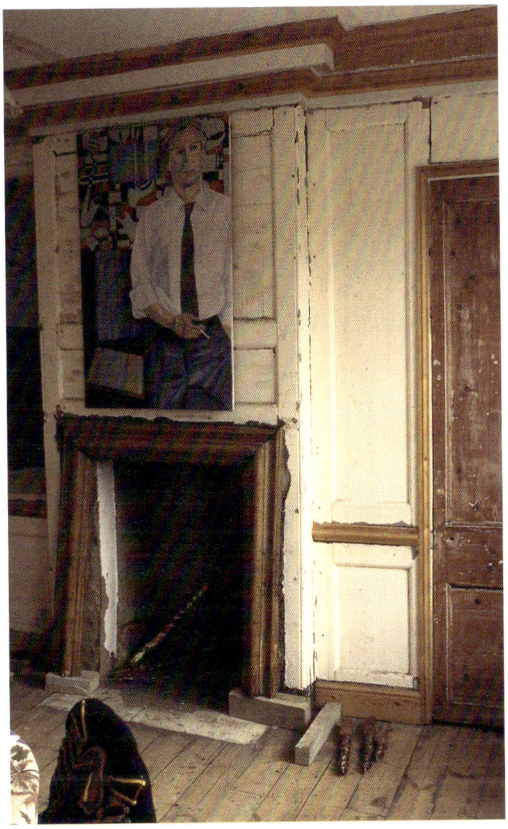

7. Fireplace paneling, ground floor, Albury Street, Deptford, London, 1720s. Photo: Bernard L. Herman.

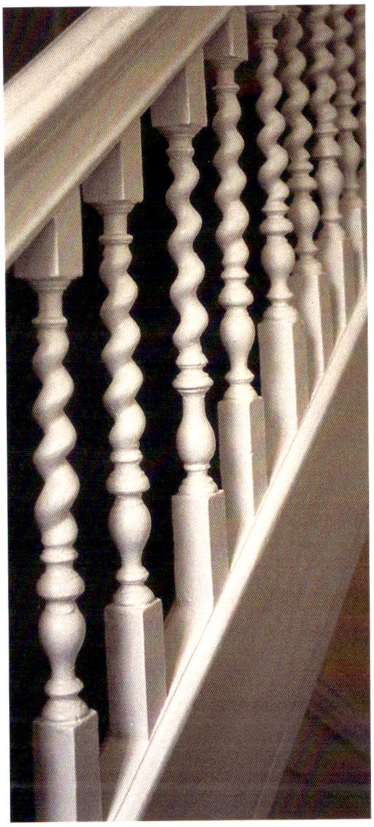

8. Stair, Albury Street, Deptford, London, 1720s. Photo: Bernard L. Herman.

sort built in Deptford High Street do not appear to have been part of the Philadelphia lexicon. And a favored house plan in Philadelphia, which consisted of a large front room and small kitchen ell, failed to make an appearance in Deptford's streetscapes. The extant houses of Elfreth's Alley erected from the late 1720s through the 1830s epitomize the range of Philadelphia's middling dwellings.

Compact in plan, eighteenth-century Elfreth's Alley houses contained a sufficient number of rooms for an effective cultivation of distinct polite and domestic work spaces within the dwelling. Without exception, these house also incorporated architectural elements that communicated hierarchies of interior spaces, with the "best" rooms outfitted with more elaborate trim and "lesser" spaces left less adorned. The three houses that Thomas Patterson built between 1757 and 1762, for example, each consisted of two rooms on each floor, with a paneled front room overlooking the street and a smaller, less finished kitchen ell. While the

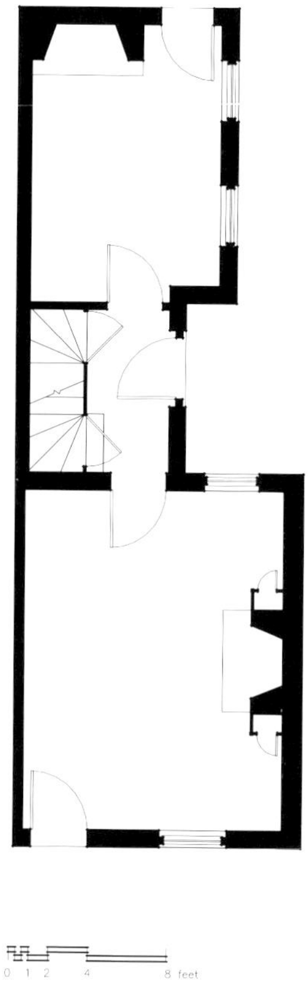

9. Piazza-plan house, Elfreth's Alley, Philadelphia, early nineteenth century. Plan: Jeff Klee.

upper-story front chamber in each house incorporated paneling similar to the room below, it tended to be slightly less elaborate in its design and the quality of its moldings. A quality of functional ambiguity, however, characterized the use of ornament to convey impressions of hierarchy and purpose. Identically finished ground-floor rooms facing the street served as both shops and parlors at varying points in their residential lives (fig. 10).[19] And like Deptford houses, Philadelphia dwellings drew on local conventions tempered by international styles. Mid-eighteenth-century interiors utilized raised paneling, molded fireplace surrounds, and variations on ogee and quarter round moldings for cornices and door and window surrounds. Variation tended to occur by degree; for example, wealthier builders were more likely to install elaborate paneling that might feature carved chimney-pieces or decorative stair trim. Speculative or bespoke, Philadelphia interiors, like those in Deptford houses, engaged material conversations that simultaneously promoted distinctions and cultivated common ground.

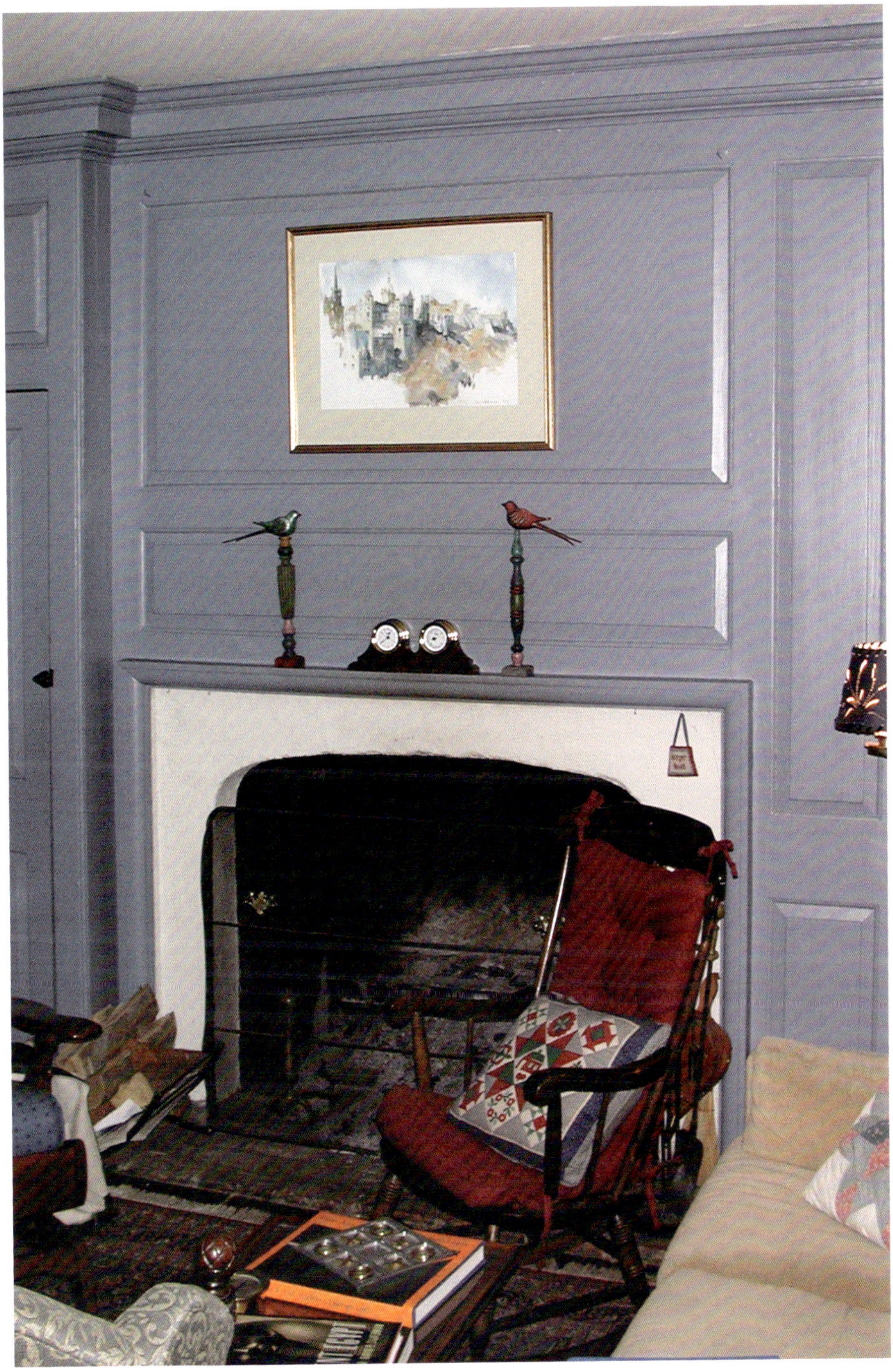

10. Ground-floor interior, Thomas Patterson house, Elfreth's Alley, Philadelphia, 1757–62. Photo: Bernard L. Herman.

Regarding the furnishings, the conversational quality of the interior spaces comes into bolder relief when we look at parlor furnishings recorded in Deptford and Philadelphia inventories. The eleven room-by-room Philadelphia inventories taken from 1730 to 1733 record a nearly identical constellation of parlor objects, without regard for house plans. They also all list male decedents. Each parlor possessed at least two tables; where details were noted, these tables lent themselves to dining or the tabletop behaviors surrounding drinking, conversing, toasting, and other forms of sociability. Two parlors, however, contained tea tables associated with behaviors that we tend to categorize of as more feminine, more refined, and more intimate. If parlor tables lent themselves to the performance of the rituals of sociability, other parlor objects identify complementary forms of social knowledge. Clocks kept time; books and desks marked literacy and commerce; maps and mantel ornaments signified tasteful display; mirrors lightened rooms and reflected the images of occupants back on themselves.

The inventory for Elizabeth Ham, though not a room-by-room listing, tentatively suggests that men shared expressive strategies with women of comparable social and economic standing. Her parlor contained the requisite escritoire (writing desk with space for books), clock, tables (though no tea table), and looking glass. Sociability, time, literacy, display—all behaviors enacted in the material world spoke to sensibilities steeped in an intensifying engagement with the expression of social inclusiveness and exclusiveness, ordered society, and the material forms of regularity implicated in the residential architecture of the city. These forms of engagement, however, did not come easily, but occasioned considerable anxiety about the very stability of society in its many parts.[20]

Deptford parlors were much the same. Seven room-by-room inventories taken between 1725 and 1735 record parlors there. Significantly, each of the Deptford parlors contained a predictable complement of tables, but, unlike Philadelphia, all but one held a tea table. Clocks were rare in Deptford parlors, but art was a common fixture. India pictures, an "alabaster image," and China figures evoke a sense of literacy based in the ability to read visual and material culture—in particular, the material culture that linked Deptfordians to the larger world of empire. Thus, ship models, a weatherglass, and birdcages complemented books and pictures in a heightened culture of reading that textualized tavern signs and carved doorways, such as those in Albury Street that were enriched with cherubs clasping drafting tools and unfurled scrolls of paper (fig. 11). Deptford parlors remind us that people in motion populated the eighteenth-century seaports of the Atlantic world. Inventories for two of the male decedents note that they died at sea, far from home. The evidence that their widows arranged and managed their houses is clear, as is the implication that taste in its familial contexts was often companionate and

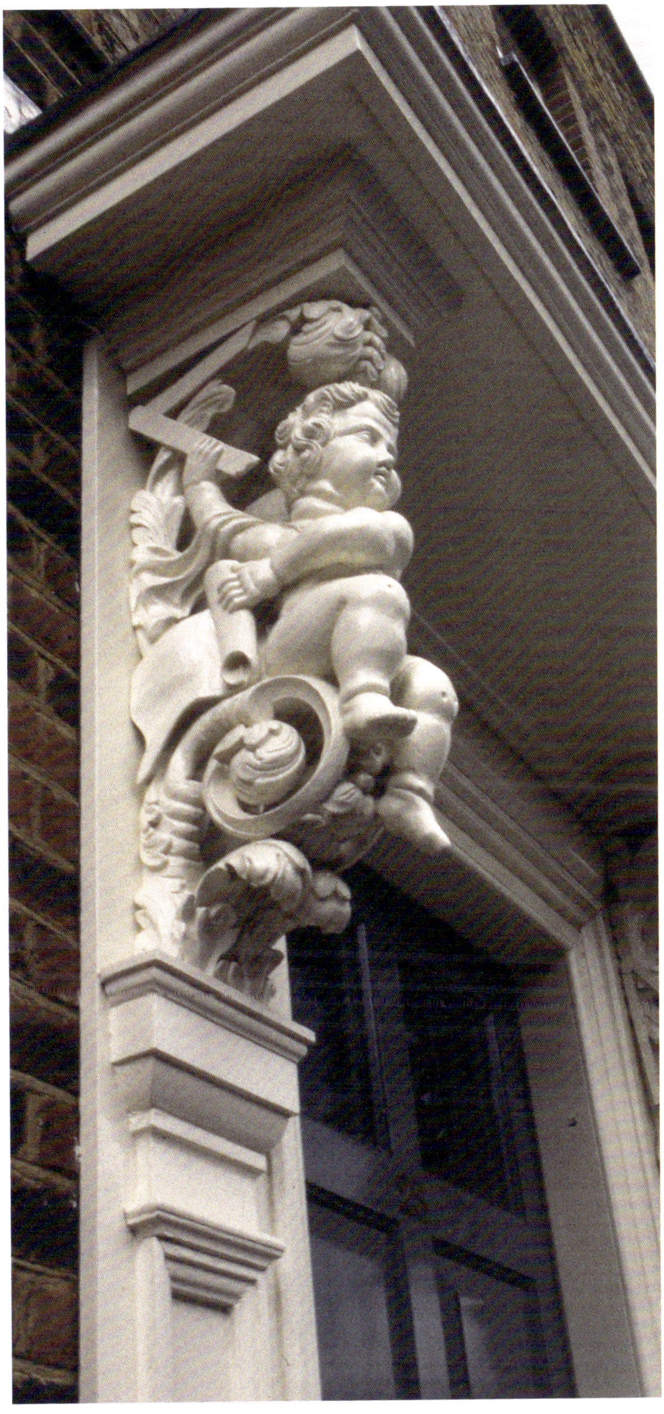

11. Doorcase, Albury Street, Deptford, early eighteenth century. Photo: Bernard L. Herman.

corporate. In the quest for gendered identities expressed in the material culture of the home—especially the eighteenth-century home—we tend to forget the conjugal practice of everyday life.

Buildings and objects furnish the praxis of taste in the world of the everyday. What can we deduce from these two building communities about taste and gender in eighteenth-century urban domestic houses? At the most basic level, buildings reflected taste as a strategy for social cohesion and difference. The practice of everyday life brings us to a central point in this brief exploration: the proposition that taste manifests itself through praxis, and that the practice of taste is always situational and strategic. When we look at the dynamic practice of taste in the context of the cultures in each of these places, we find visual differences that synthesize local practice and polite ideas around fragmented but shared desires for economic and social expression. The ethos for advancement, however, lay not necessarily in a desire to emulate elite affectations, but in the very nature of the competitive and acquisitive culture of trade that defined the eighteenth-century Atlantic world. Given significant physical distances, strong local cultures, and movement of individuals of all classes in and out of cities, there was a deep need for a visual and material lingua franca that communicated effectively in local and international contexts. Taste worked as a strategy that lent itself to situational deployment in the slippery world of eighteenth-century urban demotic culture.

The most popular houses erected in Elfreth's Alley in Philadelphia through the mid-1700s, as we have seen, stood two stories in height and consisted in plan of a single main room on the ground floor, supplemented with a service space provided by a smaller kitchen ell. Built of brick, often laid in glazed-header Flemish bond, and provided with sheltering pent eaves between the ground floor and upper story, these houses seem to have little to do with academic formulations of taste. Mary Smith and Sarah Melton operated their mantua (dressmaking) shop in a house of this type.[21] Small but well finished, the interior featured paneled fireplace walls with paneled chimney closets, along with cyma-molded mantel shelves and ceiling cornices. The house tells only part of the story. An inventory of the possessions of Mary Smith and Sarah Melton yields a sense of how these houses were furnished and occupied. Taken in 1766, the inventory describes the modest household of two women with aspirations to economic and social independence. The ground-floor front room served as their parlor, furnished with a walnut oval table, tea table, and stand. A "large" oval table, listed with six rush-bottom chairs, likely served as a dining table. Tea wares included a dozen cups and saucers, six silver teaspoons, and a pair of silver sugar tongs; the dining service consisted of six china plates and a half-dozen knives and forks, stored in a box in the adjoining kitchen. A mirror and a "glass framed" picture hung on the wall. The contents of the kitchen stood in sharp contrast to the furnishings of sociability (objects for tea, dining, and conversation) in the parlor. As with most kitchens, the major furnishings comprised two worktables and a dough trough. Fireplace tools, "pott-racks," a gridiron, pots, kettles, and other cooking implements littered the area around the hearth. Dishes of pewter and earthenware were good enough for everyday meals.

The upper rooms of Mary Smith's and Sarah Melton's house served as sleeping chambers. Each woman rested in her own bed, but they seem to have shared their old "case of drawers" and a dressing box. Tumblers and glasses on the table and curtains in the windows record rooms that were more private in character. Two aspects of the upper-story furnishings stand out. First, given the women's occupation as dressmakers, the natural light in the room, and its place in the overall plan, the kitchen chamber may have been where Smith and Melton practiced their trade. In the overall scheme of their house, the clientele may well have been received and fitted in the ground-floor front room, but the actual work of fabricating garments was likely undertaken upstairs in the kitchen chamber. Second, the chambers lacked the sort of furnishings associated with sociability and image—all of those objects were clearly concentrated in the ground-floor front room. The desire for privacy, however, was probably not the primary motivation for this furnishing scheme. The concentration of the highest-quality furniture in the best and most public room of the house put the dressmakers' best image forward, and in that act it inspired the confidence of their clients, a class of women who could afford the cost of a fine gown.[22]

At the close of the eighteenth century, the outward expression of taste, particularly drawing on classical referents, within and on the houses of Elfreth's Alley was increasingly visible. Owners pried old doorcases from their openings and sawed off their unfashionable pent eaves (fig. 12). In their stead, they installed exactly the same pedimented doorcases that they saw affixed to the entries of the new dwellings erected in the street and throughout the city. Interior woodwork now featured chimneypieces with engaged pilasters supporting neoclassical entablatures, overmantels with crossettes, and cupboards for the display of stylish and valued objects. The personal possessions that furnished Elfreth's Alley households in the second half of the eighteenth century are almost formulaic in the array of objects and surfaces. Esther Meyer (widow of potter Matthis Meyer), for example, owned a tea table, pictures on the walls, drinking glasses, chairs, and tables, all objects that provided surfaces and forms suitable for the assertion of her taste in the context of her urban world.[23]

Barney and Phebe Schumo's engagement with taste and fashion stands out for its poignancy.[24] At the turn of the nineteenth century, Barney Schumo operated a turner's shop in Elfreth's Alley and lived with his wife and children in one of the older houses across the street. Their residence, nearly identical to the former house

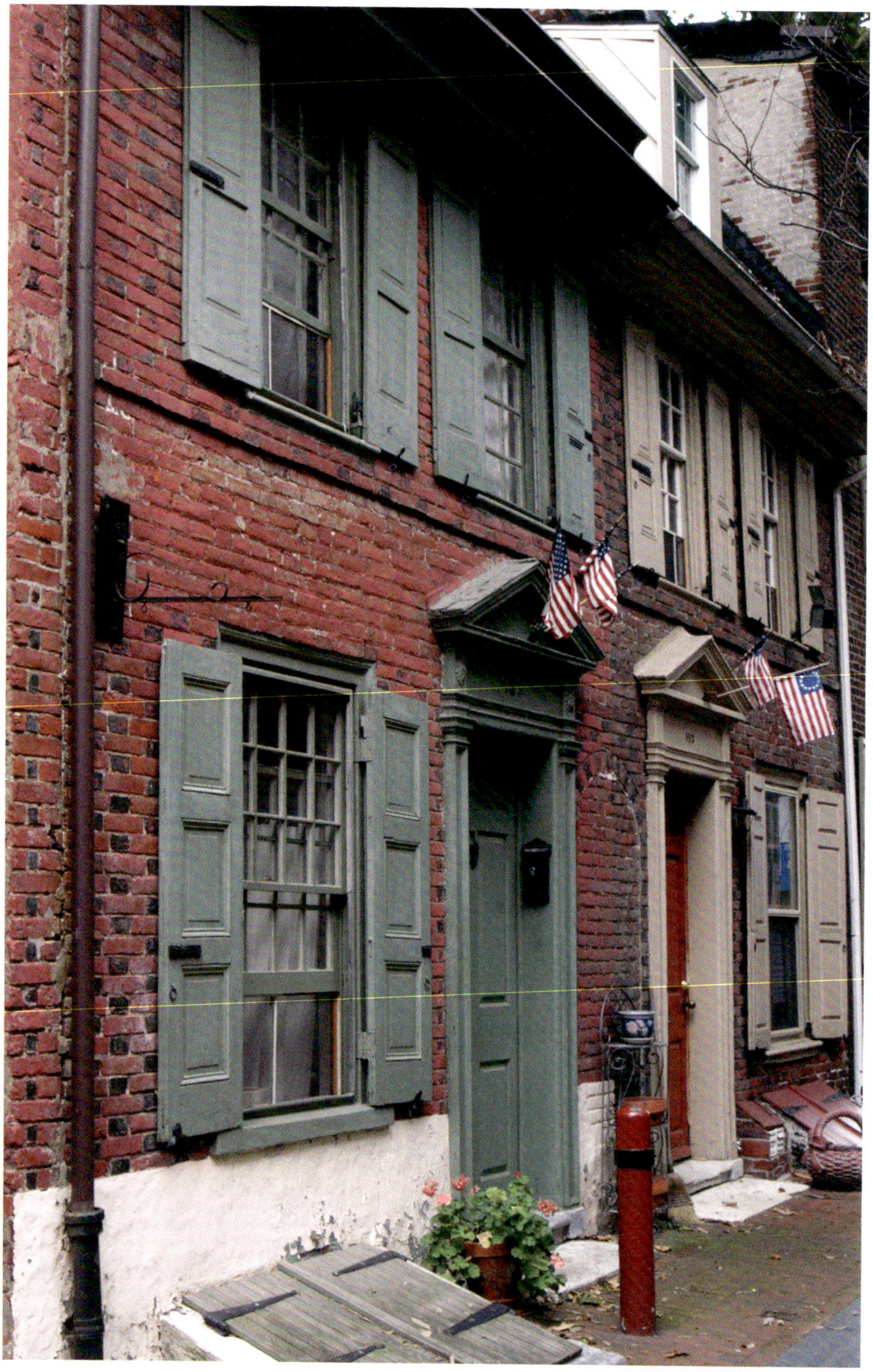

12. Replaced doorcases, Elfreth's Alley, Philadelphia, c. 1800. Photo: Bernard L. Herman.

of Mary Smith and Sarah Melton, had already been modernized with a new neoclassical doorway in 1815 when the Schumos decided to pull down the turner's shop and build themselves a new house. Their new residence, complete with its modern cellar kitchen, articulated a hierarchy of interior spaces with architectural elements in the form of pilasters, composition ornament, and runs of ogee molding quoting neoclassical fashion. It clearly stretched the family's financial resources to the limit. When Barney Schumo died a year later, his will directed that the widowed Phebe and their children retreat to their old house across the way, and that the new dwelling—the grandest in the street—be rented or sold to satisfy outstanding debts.

The lesson taken from this parable, in the context of the consumption of signs, is that the ability to signify failure is as present as the capacity to commemorate success. The textures of taste provided an outward means to represent and give meaning to personal fortunes—and misfortunes—through a broadly understood common visual and material language. It was not the wholesale consumption of taste that made this possible, but the enactment of certain forms of behavior linked to semiotically charged objects. The paneled doorway on the Schumos' old house proved to be an empty gesture in more than one way. Not only did it mark the threshold across which Phebe and the orphans beat their retreat, it also promised interior finishes, and by extension sensibilities, that were absent. More to the point of this discussion, though, is the observation that taste in the material world of eighteenth-century Philadelphia and beyond was not about objects, but about how objects enabled conversations and performances in the material world.

The dwellings of Barney and Phebe Schumo and of Mary Smith and Sarah Melton provide one context for a consideration of taste (an abstraction demonstrable only through performance and the objects that sustain it) as a visual language constituted as much by its individual terms and their deployment as by a larger, coherent, ideologically rooted system of utterance. What we see in several Deptford inventories, however, is an intersection of work, taste, social position and aspiration, and gendered identities. We gleaned a kernel of this nexus of forces in the house of mantua makers Mary Smith and Sarah Melton, where the two women employed objects that signified their possession of the social knowledge necessary to satisfy the taste of their clients. The same constellation of work and taste appears in Deptford in the estates of Rebecca Weekes and Elizabeth and Joshua Bennett.

Rebecca Weekes and Rebecca Bell operated a school in the second-floor front room of Weekes's two-story house.[25] As teachers, Weekes and Bell advanced a curriculum that instilled both an awareness of and an ability to engage polite and tasteful behaviors. Weekes's inventory documents the ways in which her curriculum was gendered toward the refinement of girls and young women. In addition to the complement of benches and stools for students, the schoolroom was furnished with an image of "Qn Anne in her Robes in Phillagree in a frame w/ a Glass before it," a flower piece in shellwork, and ornamental embroidery. Shellwork and embroidery represented mainstays of curricula that advanced social identities tied to certain forms of labor that produced, reproduced, and displayed feminine social competencies.[26] Girls from Deptford's artisan and trading community were enrolled by their parents and guardians with the intention of equipping them with skills that could demonstrate the students' possession of taste. The skills taught were gendered in the sense that they were directed toward a homosocial student body.

Rebecca Weekes's display of her abilities extended through her house. The most public room in the house, the ground-floor room below the schoolroom, held the makings for embroidery, a teaboard, and china on the mantel—three categories linked to the production, display, and performance of taste. Although a coat of arms in "phillagree" hung in her best chamber and sewing implements were found in her garret chamber, the objects that most forcefully communicated the production and consumption of taste were situated where they were most visible: in the schoolroom—the source of Weekes's livelihood—and the ground-floor front room, which served as her parlor and the stage on which she displayed her own competencies to prospective students and their families as well as to her friends and intimates.

The connection between gender, work, and taste takes on a different cast in the inventory of Elizabeth and Joshua Bennett's house.[27] Joshua, a Deptford shipwright, predeceased Elizabeth, who continued to live in the couple's dwelling. The taste that the Bennetts brought to bear in their material world was less prescriptive than Rebecca Weekes's, but it was still linked to a strategy that connected the family's material successes to decorative display. The Bennetts crammed their parlor with objects that recalled Joshua Bennett's world of work. A painting of a ship on the stocks, ten paintings of ships at sea, and a glass case enshrining a model of a rigged ship aestheticized, miniaturized, and commemorated his work through the display of tasteful objects in the couple's best room. A collection of seven punch bowls, twenty-two china plates, fifteen jelly glasses, fourteen blue-and-white china cups, ten wine glasses, and ivory-handled cutlery defined a room where the objects of taste and attendant sociable behaviors surely constrained behavior by virtue of numbers and fragility. Add to this assemblage the seven canaries in seven cages that Elizabeth maintained. Seated at the mahogany claw-foot table in one of the seven "matted" chairs that furnished the Bennetts' parlor, a visitor could easily become overwhelmed, even deafened, by the sort of tasteful display ridiculed by "polite" society and lampooned by contemporary satirists.[28]

But that is the point of taste in its demotic and quotidian contexts. The aestheticized celebration of Joshua Bennett's life in the dockyard and the display of Rebecca Weekes's instructional capabilities engaged taste not as a monolithic top-down construction. Rather, taste emerges as a process that enabled the expression of sensibilities linking them to the economic and social contexts in which they lived. Their world of taste was cultivated not through acts of imitation and confrontation, but acts of conversation. The same concerns with the demonstration of a sense of beauty, excellence, fitness, and propriety that we associate with elites animated their worlds. Rebecca Weekes, Joshua and Elizabeth Bennett, and their neighbors in eighteenth-century Deptford, along with Mary Smith, Sarah Melton, and Barney and Phebe Schumo in Philadelphia, colonized polite behaviors in visible ways. In the process, they provoked anxiety in an elite society eager to consolidate and protect its own identities.

Finally, we tend to construct our interpretations of objects around their perceived instrumentality—the purposes they serve ranging from the performance of everyday work to their role in the communication and facilitation of social relationships. As a rule, we have been reasonably successful in the exploration of how objects function. Material culture, however, also invites a poetics of taste that privileges ambiguity over certainty and tempers instrumentality with lyricism. Objects of all sorts call attention to themselves, often in aesthetic terms, and in that gesture direct our attention to the instrumental—what things mean. This poetic resides in the play between language and performance and the instabilities of meaning in the unsteady world of eighteenth-century urban society. What things meant depended on the perceptions of audience and actors in shared and infinitely mutable contexts. Where people stood in relationship to one another and the objects around them shaped the expressive content of the material world. Ambiguity admits and reconciles the uncertainties of taste.

This essay benefited greatly from discussions and conversations at the 2004 Huntington and AHRC Centre for the Study of the Domestic Interior conference on "Gender, Taste and Material Culture in Britain and North America in the Long Eighteenth Century." Special thanks go to Amanda Vickery, John Styles, Eric Slauter, Susan Stabile, Fredrika Teute, John Bold, Peter Guillery, and David Shields for their comments as I revised this essay.

1. Jenny Uglow, *Hogarth: A Life and a World* (New York: Farrar, Straus, and Giroux, 1997), 191–213.
2. John Brewer, *The Pleasures of the Imagination: English Culture in the Eighteenth Century* (London: HarperCollins, 1997); David S. Shields, *Civil Tongues and Polite Letters in British America* (Chapel Hill: Univ. of North Carolina Press for the Institute of Early American History and Culture, 1997); Susan M. Stabile, *Memory's Daughters: The Material Culture of Remembrance in Eighteenth-Century America* (Ithaca, NY: Cornell Univ. Press, 2004), 149–62.

3. Peter Borsay, *The English Urban Renaissance: Culture and Society in the Provincial Town, 1660–1770* (Oxford: Clarendon Press, 1989); Richard L. Bushman, *The Refinement of America: Persons, Houses, Cities* (New York: Alfred A. Knopf, 1992).
4. Ann Smart Martin, "Makers, Buyers, and Users: Consumerism as a Material Culture Framework," *Winterthur Portfolio* 28, nos. 2/3 (1993): 141–57; Cary Carson, "The Consumer Revolution in Colonial British America: Why Demand?" in *Of Consuming Interests: The Style of Life in the Eighteenth Century*, ed. Cary Carson, Ronald Hoffman, and Peter J. Albert (Charlottesville: Univ. of Virginia Press for the United States Capitol Historical Society, 1994), 483–697.
5. A key exception is the cumulative work of Dell Upton: see "The City as Material Culture," in *The Art and Mystery of Historical Archaeology*, ed. Mary C. Beaudry and Ann Yentsch (Boca Raton, FL: CRC Press, 1992), 51–74; "Another City: The Urban Cultural Landscape in the Early Republic," in *Everyday Life in the Early Republic*, ed. Catherine E. Hutchins (Winterthur, DE: Henry Francis du Pont Winterthur Museum, 1994), 61–117; and "Architecture in Everyday Life," *New Literary History* 33, no. 4 (Autumn 2002): 707–23.
6. E. P. Thompson, *Whigs and Hunters: The Origin of the Black Act* (New York: Pantheon Books, 1975); Carlo Ginzburg, *The Cheese and the Worms: The Cosmos of a Sixteenth-Century Miller* (New York: Penguin, 1982; original Italian ed., 1976); Robert Darnton, *The Great Cat Massacre and Other Episodes in French Cultural History* (New York: Vintage, 1984); Peter Stallybrass and Allon White, *The Poetics and Politics of Transgression* (Ithaca, NY: Cornell Univ. Press, 1986); Gillian Rose, *Feminism and Geography: The Limits of Geographical Knowledge* (Minneapolis: Univ. of Minnesota, 1993), 86–112.
7. See Elizabeth Grosz, *Volatile Bodies: Toward a Corporeal Feminism* (Bloomington: Indiana Univ. Press, 1994), 19–24.
8. *Webster's New World Dictionary of the American Language: College Edition* (Cleveland and New York: World Publishing, 1966 ed.), s.v. "taste."
9. Basil Bernstein, *Class, Codes, and Control: Theoretical Studies Towards a Sociology of Language* (New York: Schocken Books, 1975), 125–30; Dell Upton, *Holy Things and Profane: Anglican Churches in Colonial Virginia* (New York: Architectural History Foundation, 1986), 101–2.
10. See, for example, W. Kenrick, "The Cit's Country Box, 1757," in *The Poetical Works of Robert Lloyd, A.M.* (London: T. Evans, 1774), 2:41–46.
11. Michel de Certeau, *The Practice of Everyday Life*, trans. Steven Rendall (Berkeley: Univ. of California Press, 1984), 97–98.
12. De Certeau, *Practice of Everyday Life*, 117–18.
13. Charles Taylor, *Modern Social Imaginaries* (Durham, NC: Duke Univ. Press, 2004), 23.
14. Taylor, *Modern Social Imaginaries*, 2.
15. Upton, "Architecture in Everyday Life," 720.
16. Barbara G. Carson, *Ambitious Appetites: Dining, Behavior, and Patterns of Consumption in Federal Washington* (Washington, DC: American Institute of Architects Press, 1990); Anne Yentsch, "Minimum Vessel Lists as Evidence of Change in Folk and Courtly Foodways," *Historical Archaeology* 24, no. 3 (1990): 29; Guy Debord, *Society of the Spectacle*, trans. Donald Nicholson Smith (New York: Zone Books, 1995), 104–6.
17. The architectural character of Deptford houses is summarized in Peter Guillery and Bernard Herman, "Deptford Houses," *Vernacular Architecture* 30 (1999): 58–84. An overview of the houses of Elfreth's Alley, along with their individual histories, has been compiled in the research files of the Elfreth's Alley Association, Philadelphia. For plans of smaller London houses, including those found in Deptford, see Peter Guillery, *The Small House in Eighteenth-Century London: A Social and Architectural History* (New Haven and London: Yale Univ. Press for the Paul Mellon Centre for Studies in British Art, 2004).
18. A. F. Kelsall, "The London House Plan in the Later 17th Century," *Post-Medieval Archaeology* 8 (1974): 80–91; Elizabeth McKellar, "The City and the Country: The London Vernacular in the Late Seventeenth Century and Early Eighteenth Century," in *Georgian Vernacular*, ed. Neil Burton (London: The Georgian Group, 1996), 10–18; Guillery, *Small House in Eighteenth-Century London*, 39–77. For discussions on spatial practices and values encoded in house plans, see Matthew Johnson, *Housing Culture: Traditional Architecture in an English Landscape* (Washington, DC: Smithsonian Institution Press, 1993), 44–105;

Julienne Hanson, *Decoding Homes and Houses* (Cambridge: Cambridge Univ. Press, 1998), 56–79; and Bernard Herman, "Space in the Early American City," *Journal of the Early Republic* 24 (Summer 2004): 319–26. Johnson's approach is foreshadowed in Henry Glassie, *Folk Housing in Middle Virginia: A Structural Analysis of Historic Artifacts* (Knoxville: Univ. of Tennessee Press, 1975).

19. Research files for 110, 112, and 114 Elfreth's Alley, Elfreth's Alley Association.
20. On the idea of implication, see Robert Blair St. George, *Conversing by Signs: Poetics of Implication in Colonial New England Culture* (Chapel Hill: Univ. of North Carolina Press, 1998), 6–7. St. George's "poetics of implication" resonate with Susan Stewart's discussion of "haunted" works and "lyric possession" in *Poetry and the Fate of the Senses* (Chicago: Univ. of Chicago Press, 2002), 116–17.
21. Research files for 126 Elfreth's Alley, Elfreth's Alley Association.
22. For the distinction between public and private rooms in English inventories, see Lorna Weatherill, *Consumer Behaviour and Material Culture in Britain, 1660–1760* (London: Routledge, 1988), 9.
23. Research files for 119 Elfreth's Alley, Elfreth's Alley Association.
24. Research files for 125 and 130 Elfreth's Alley, Elfreth's Alley Association.
25. Inventory for Rebecca Weekes, late of Deptford Strand, PRO 29/215, PROB 3.
26. Jennifer Van Horn, *Samplers, Social Capital, and the Formation of Feminine Identities: The Embroidery Work of Leah Galligher and Her Students, Lancaster, Pennsylvania, 1798–1802* (master's thesis, Newark, DE: Univ. of Delaware, 2002).
27. Inventory for Elizabeth Bennett, late of St. Nicholas, Deptford, PRO 42/93, PROB 3.
28. See, for example, Draper Hill, *Mr. Gillray the Caricaturist* (London: Phaidon, 1965), plates 134, 136, 138; John Wardroper, *The Caricatures of George Cruikshank* (London: Gordon Fraser, 1977), 73; and Jerold J. Savory, *Thomas Rowlandson's Doctor Syntax Drawings: An Introduction and Guide for Collectors* (London: Cygnus Arts, 1997).

Lodging at the Old Bailey: Lodgings and Their Furnishing in Eighteenth-Century London

John Styles

IN APRIL 1799, Susannah Priest appeared at the Old Bailey, the principal criminal court for London, charged with breaking and entering at the house of Elias Isaacs in Little Essex Street, Whitechapel.[1] The court was told that one evening, about a month earlier, Priest had broken open the window shutters of a ground-floor room in Isaacs's house, pulled up the sash, and climbed in. But the room was not in Isaacs's possession. He rented it ready-furnished to Lydia Harcourt—or, more probably, his wife did the renting, as it was she who appeared in court to identify the missing property. Harcourt testified that she had gone out for the evening, securing the shutters with a black-handled fork and locking the door. When she returned between 10 and 11 P.M., she "found nothing in the room but three chairs, a table, a pair of white stockings and a bedstead." Susannah Priest had carried off the rest of the contents, which belonged partly to the landlord and partly to his tenant.

Apart from a cheap wooden trunk, the stolen goods belonging to Lydia Harcourt consisted entirely of clothing: a man's waistcoat, a silk bonnet, a muslin cap, half a yard of ribbon, a silk sash, and a fan. Together they were valued at 3s. 9d. Along with the clothes she stood up in and the pair of white stockings that Susannah Priest left in the room, this list of goods probably represents the best part of Harcourt's possessions.[2] Far more valuable at £2 6s., but equally familiar to Harcourt as an intimate part of her material world, were the other goods Priest stole from her room: a feather bed (what we would call a mattress) valued at 30s., a pair of sheets valued at 10s., two blankets valued at 2s., a coverlid (bedspread) valued at 2s., and a bolster valued at 2s. Along with the table, the three chairs, and the bedstead, these were the principal items of furniture that Harcourt rented along with the room.

The Susannah Priest case is an unusual one, because it involved the theft of property belonging both to a landlord and to his tenant, but for precisely that reason it alerts us to three significant questions for histories of material life. First, what kind of things did working people own or have the use of? Second, what was the balance in their material lives between things they acquired themselves and things provided for them by others? Third, when things were provided for them by others, who made the choices and how did considerations of price, suitability, and taste shape their decisions? Each of these questions touches on two key, linked issues in recent histories of eighteenth-century consumption: choice and agency.

In studying eighteenth-century consumption, historians have tended to assume there was a general growth in consumption, characterized by an increase in individuals' capacity and desire to choose. Often studies have simply asserted a progressive expansion in the available range of goods and services from which choices might be made and in the willingness of certain sections of the population to exercise those choices as independent consumers. They have then proceeded to devote a great deal of attention to social mechanisms, such as emulation and distinction, that might explain why people engaged with these opportunities, as well as to the cultural anxieties they unleashed, especially in the debates over luxury. Less attention has been devoted to the growth of consumption itself. It has proved difficult to provide satisfactory answers to essentially economic questions about changes in people's ability to consume, or their preferences as consumers. Addressing these questions requires measurement of the relationship between incomes and prices, along with a mapping of desires and tastes as realized through patterns of acquisition.

Within the small group of studies focusing on the activities of the poorer half of the population as consumers, there has been particular disagreement. The view that plebeian men and women in the eighteenth century enjoyed limited but expanding choices as consumers is pitted against the argument that they enjoyed next to no choice, earning too little to provide access to anything more than the barest of necessities and often making do with what was chosen for them by their social superiors, in the form of charity or payment in kind.[3] I have argued elsewhere that, at least as far as their clothing is concerned, plebeian men and women performed a more active role as consumers in eighteenth-century England than the pessimists admit.[4] Nevertheless, it remains the case that many of the things they used, treated, and spoke of as their own were provided to them by others through nonmarket, semi-market, or indirect mechanisms, on terms that restricted their ability to choose.[5] Goods were highly diverse in the ways they reached plebeian consumers. Plebeian consumers were often involuntary consumers.

On the March evening when Lydia Harcourt's lodging was stripped, she owned enough clothes to leave a number of her choicer and more expensive accessories—her silk hat, her fan, her muslin cap, her silk sash—at home. But her home was a rented room whose furnishings—the bed on which she lay, the chair on which she sat, the table at which she ate—were chosen by the couple who rented her the furnished lodging, and it is important to stress that the furnishings were almost certainly worth considerably more than the clothing she owned. This is not to say that Harcourt exercised no influence over the way her room was furnished. Her rented furnishings were of a range and, presumably, of a quality consistent with the rent she paid. Owners and tenants certainly had notions of what was appropriate: "She had the front garret, there was a bedstead in it, and bedding, chairs and table, and every thing that is common in a lodging," one landlord told the court in 1793.[6] But whereas Harcourt's clothing suggests a capacity to choose, to duplicate, and to differentiate, her furniture indicates a far more restricted set of options dictated by the workings of the market in furnished rooms and, specifically, by the landladies who provided them.

Although Lydia Harcourt's evidence at the trial provides only a snapshot of a day in the material life of a single woman in the East End of London, it serves to show how, in that life, different kinds of relationships with material things coexisted in ways that problemize notions of eighteenth-century consumption as a terrain of ever-expanding individual choice. As a consumer, Harcourt's relationship with the furnishings of her rented room was indirect, even involuntary. She may have chosen to rent the room, but its furniture was supplied and selected by her landlord and landlady. This indirect relationship with intimate material things was one that was familiar to eighteenth-century working men and women. Apprentices and servants slept on their employers' bedding and ate their employers' food; paupers resident in the parish workhouse relied on parochial officials to provide them with food and shelter, warmth and light; common soldiers, naval seamen, and liveried servants wore clothes supplied by their superiors. The things used by working people came to them through a variety of channels over which they exercised widely differing degrees of control. For plebeian consumers especially, we need to ask not simply what they owned, but what they had in their possession and how it came to them. In other words, we need to explore the diversity of means by which they sustained an engagement with things. In doing so, we must beware of assuming that the things they chose were necessarily superior or preferable to the things they were provided.

Yet often it is difficult to know exactly what was provided. In the case of working men and women like Lydia Harcourt who rented lodgings in London, we know next to nothing about how their rooms were actually furnished.[7] Much of our factual knowledge about life in furnished lodgings in eighteenth-century London has come from the memoirs of wealthy tenants such as the Scottish gentleman James Boswell or the visiting German pastor Carl Philipp Moritz.[8] By contrast, it is only the very meanest London lodgings that can be readily identified in paintings and engravings. Eighteenth-century visual images of London domestic interiors are largely fictional and virtually never specify the type of tenure. Only when an artist employs the confined space of a garret or broken-down sticks of furniture to signal the impoverished circumstances of a failed poet or a common prostitute do we know that what is being portrayed is probably a furnished lodging (figs. 13, 14, 15). A rare exception is the second plate of William Hogarth's *Harlot's Progress*, in which Moll Hackabout is portrayed in the sumptuous lodging provided by her Jewish protector (see fig. 1).

We do know that most Londoners lived in rented accommodations and that, in a city of high rents, very large numbers of people, both rich and poor, lived in lodging rooms, many of them furnished. The precise extent of multiple occupancy is difficult to establish. An estimate based on the 1692 poll-tax returns for the City of London suggests that nearly half the houses contained subsidiary lodger households. An estimate from the subsequent decade for the metropolitan area as a whole puts the proportion of divided houses at only 10 percent.[9] Even at the lower estimate, tens of thousands of Londoners, especially poorer ones, would have lived in rented lodgings. Yet what little has been written on the furnishings of London domestic interiors has often assumed that residents chose and owned the objects they lived with. The eighteenth century saw the population of London nearly double, a vast amount of new house building be undertaken, and the domestic furnishings of wealthier households undergo radical changes in kind, in materials, and in style—from tankard to teapot, from walnut to mahogany, from pewter to creamware. How were the residences and modes of domestic life of the poorer majority of London's population affected by these developments? Who made the decisions about how they should be furnished?

The Susannah Priest case alerts us to the potential, but also to some of the limitations, of the printed records of the trials at the Old Bailey as a source for addressing these questions. Studies of the things acquired and used by eighteenth-century Londoners (as elsewhere) have relied heavily on postmortem inventories, which survive in huge numbers for the period 1550–1740.[10] Inventories have proved an invaluable and flexible source for studies of changing patterns of consumption, bringing a welcome precision to debates about changes in the ownership of goods.[11] Nevertheless, they suffer from severe limitations. Their numbers and quality decline after the mid-eighteenth century, their social reach is limited to the wealthier half of the population, and they employ stilted descriptive language. If detailed inventories survived in any numbers for Middlesex in 1799, the year of Susannah Priest's trial (which they do not), they might have included the likes of the landlord Elias Isaacs, although there would be little in such an inventory to prove that the furnishings of Lydia Harcourt's room were for the use of his lodger. But it is most unlikely that Harcourt's meager possessions would ever have been inventoried. The tens of thousands of printed trial transcripts that survive for the Old

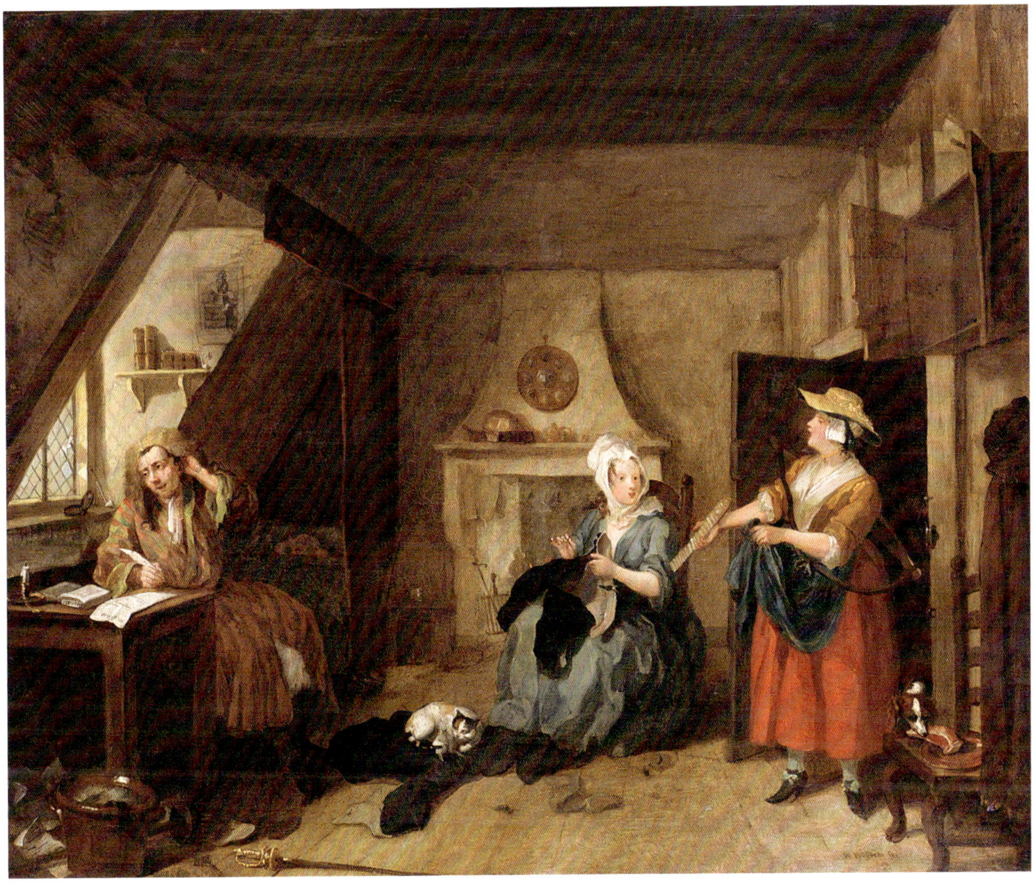

13. William Hogarth, *The Distressed Poet*, oil on canvas (1736), 25 x 30⅞ in. (63.5 x 78.4 cm). Birmingham Museums & Art Gallery.

Bailey from the late seventeenth century, mostly involving the illegal appropriation of property, offer an alternative perspective on the ownership of goods. It is a perspective that is wider in both its social reach and in the information it provides about the ways artifacts were used. At the same time, it is a perspective that is more limited in scope than inventories. Inventories attempt a listing of the owner's movable goods; the goods listed in criminal trials reflect the highly selective activity of those who stole.

The Old Bailey trials provide evidence about the way rented lodgings were furnished because an act of 1691 (3 W. & M., c. 9) made the appropriation of furniture out of a furnished lodging with intent to defraud the owner a felony.[12] From the 1730s, a large number of such cases were tried at the Old Bailey, providing

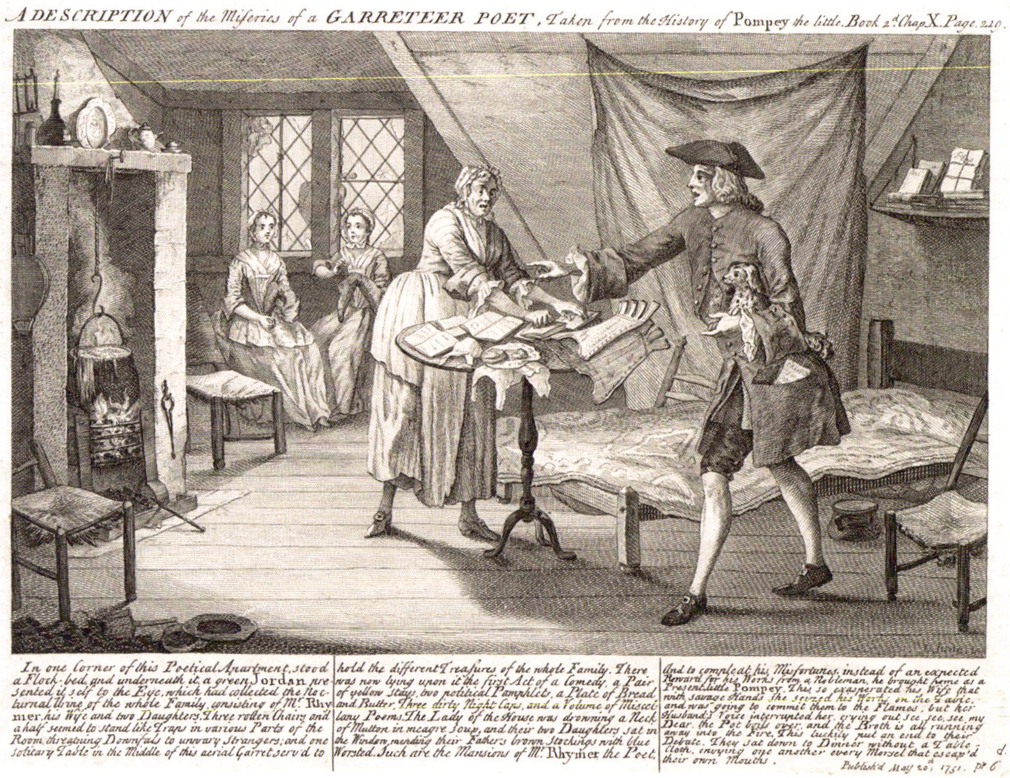

14. Artist unknown, *A Description of the Miseries of a Garreteer Poet*, engraving (1751), 6⅛ x 10⅜ in. (15.4 x 26.2 cm), from *The History of Pompey the Little: Or the Life and Adventures of a Lap Dog*, by Francis Coventry (London, 1751). Courtesy of The Lewis Walpole Library, Yale University.

unmatched evidence about the way hundreds of lodgings were furnished. The printed records of these cases offer descriptions of the stolen furnishings, drawn from the indictments against the accused and the evidence given in court.[13] Many cases also provide valuations of the furnishings, information about the occupations of landlord and tenant, details of the rooms and the rent, and particulars of how the goods were disposed. This chapter is based principally on searches in Old Bailey Proceedings Online for prosecutions under the 1691 act in two decades—the 1750s and the 1790s—using two sets of keywords: "furnished" and "lodging room."[14] The searches generated 265 cases under the 1691 act, involving 1,682 stolen objects.

The list of stolen furnishings in an Old Bailey indictment did not, of course, include every item of furniture that had been provided for the tenant's use. The furnishings listed in the indictment had gone through a two-stage process of selection, first by the lodger, who took some, but rarely all, of the owner's goods, and

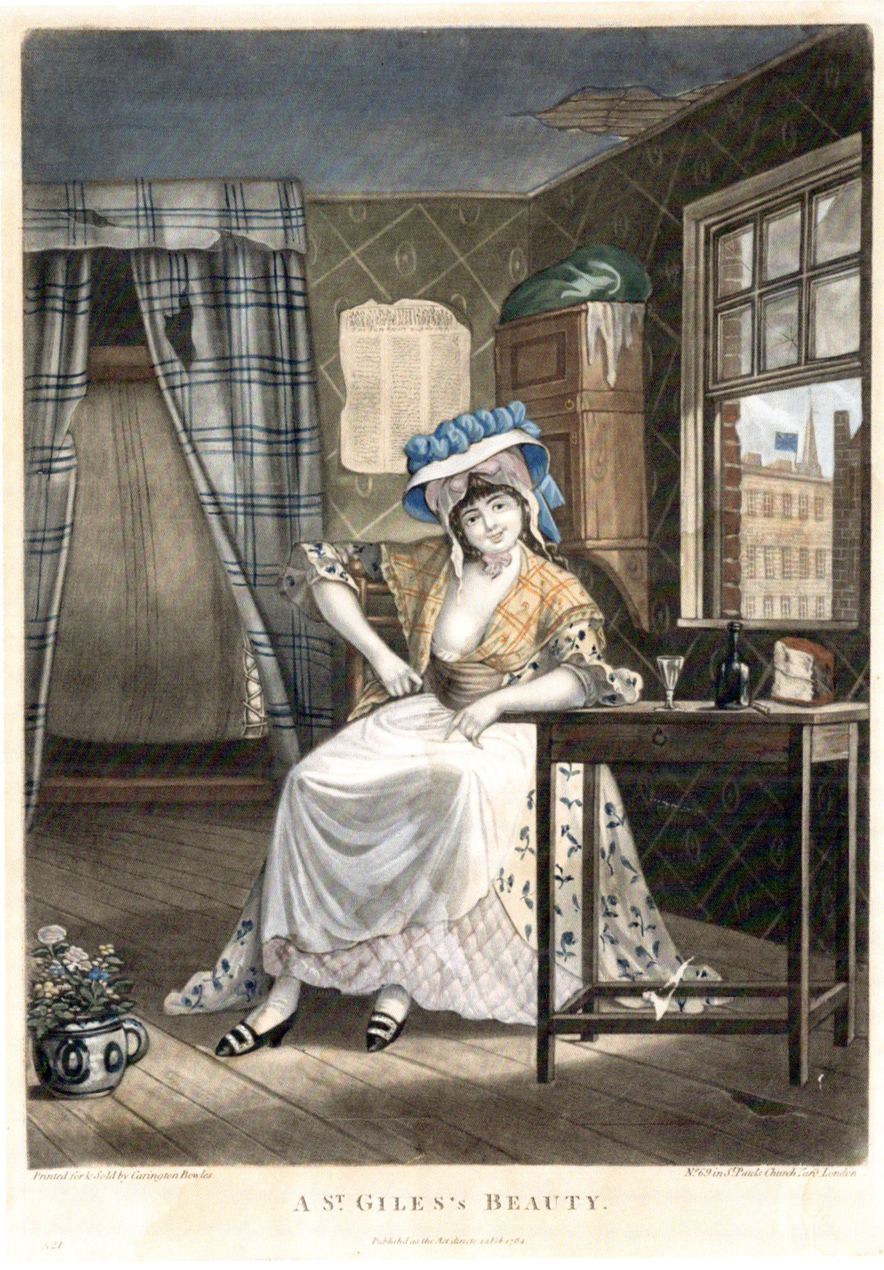

15. Artist unknown, *A St. Giles's Beauty*, mezzotint with hand color (1784), 12⅞ x 9¾ in. (32.7 x 24.8 cm), image. Courtesy of The Lewis Walpole Library, Yale University.

second by the owner and the court clerk who, between them, drew up the indictment. A number of considerations seem to have influenced lodgers in deciding which goods to take. It was important that they be portable. Tables and chairs hardly figure at all among the stolen goods. The need for concealment also encouraged lodgers to take less bulky items. Sarah Jones was discovered with a "sheet concealed under her petticoats."[15] But a wish to conceal could also militate against the theft of such things as covers and hangings, which might be used to hide the fact that other things were missing. Martha Bridle noticed that her tenant had stolen a sheet and a bolster only when she "went to the bed and turned down the coverlid."[16] The need to avoid detection could discourage lodgers from taking things that were showy or distinctive and therefore easy to trace, even if they were valuable. But the value of the goods was crucial. Almost all the lodgers tried at the Old Bailey attempted to realize a cash sum in exchange for the goods, either by pawn or by sale. Hence the rarity in the indictments of low-value objects such as earthenware pots and cups, even though some landlords and landladies did provide them.[17] Lodgers who rented rooms with the intention of stealing their contents may have focused on more expensive lodgings and the more valuable items.

The overwhelming majority of the things taken were pawned.[18] Indeed, defendants often claimed that they had been given permission to pawn the goods. "The Prosecutrix gave me leave to pawn them upon my promising to pay her 10 s.," declared Sarah White in 1752. She received some support from the pawnbroker, who testified that "the prisoner brought these things to me to pawn at several times, the first time was in April, the last in September."[19] Henry Crabtree told the court in 1756, "My wife died and left me five children, my poverty was great, and it was a very hard winter. I went to borrow a shilling of the prosecutor's wife, and she gave me liberty to pawn these things."[20] One witness went so far as to state that "it is a usual thing to pawn these things and get them out again."[21] A significant proportion of these cases probably represent, therefore, unresolved disputes between lodging keeper and tenant over borrowing or payment of rent (although there were others where this is unlikely to have been the case, because the theft followed so quickly on the let).[22] Tenancy emerges as a multifaceted relationship of mutual obligation involving more than just accommodations.

The second stage in the process of selection that produced the lists of furnishings we find in the Old Bailey indictments involved the owner and the court clerk as, between them, they drew up the indictment. Poorer landlords might not prosecute at all, although in a number of cases prosecution may have been necessary to force a pawnbroker to return the goods without payment.[23] Generally, only those goods that had been found or retrieved were included. Things of small value might be ignored. "Not half the things are in the indictment," complained a landlady in 1793.[24] Valuations in the indictments tended to be slightly higher than the values put on the goods by the pawnbrokers who had taken them in as pledges, but they were largely secondhand values.[25]

What are the implications of this two-stage process of selection for using the Old Bailey cases to explore the furnishing of lodgings in eighteenth-century London? Most importantly, it means that they can tell us little about larger pieces of wooden furniture, or about items of small value. It also means that they do not necessarily include all the portable objects that were worth taking. Depending on the circumstances, it might have been the more anonymous and mundane objects that appeared in the indictment, or the more distinctive and valuable. In aggregate, the Old Bailey cases can tell us what was present in lodging rooms, but we have to be cautious in using them to establish what was absent. And there is reason to believe that the cheapest, least-furnished lodgings are underrepresented.

Most of the 265 Old Bailey cases involved relatively inexpensive lodgings and lodgers drawn from among the working population. In only 8 out of 99 cases where the rent is recorded did it exceed 7s. a week. Those 8 cases involved tenants who passed themselves off to their landladies as respectable, or at least affluent, and rented more than one room. In 6 of these 8 cases, they rented the whole of a first floor (the American second floor, the most prestigious and expensive floor in a London house) for between 21s. and 32s. a week. In almost all the other cases, the lodging consisted of a single furnished room. Their rents ranged from 1s. to 7s. a week, with an average of 2s. 10d., although rents for these cheaper lodgings at less than 7s. a week were higher in the 1790s (average 3s.) than in the 1750s (average 2s. 3d.) and more frequently reported (67 cases compared with 27).[26] Rents were usually quoted on a weekly basis, but one of two women who rented a room for 2s. a week (they paid 1s. a week each) on the first floor of a house in George Street, Spitalfields, in 1790 described it as "a two-penny lodging," the colloquial term for the cheapest and most basic kind of furnished accommodations, which could be rented for 2d. a day.[27] The cheaper single lodging rooms in the sample tended to be garrets or back rooms; the more expensive ones were the often larger rooms at the front of the house. Cellars are conspicuous by their absence.

Nearly two-thirds of the lodgers were female and single, one-fifth were men on their own, and the rest were (or at least presented themselves as) married couples. Unfortunately, the printed Old Bailey proceedings provide little information about their occupations. The sixteen men whose occupations were noted were mainly laboring men or craftsmen; two were in clerical jobs.[28] The women's occupations are even more obscure, although they included a charwoman, an old-clothes seller, and a fish seller, while a few were said by witnesses to be prostitutes. Of those identified as single women, thirty-four were unmarried and twenty-two were widows. In the 1790s, ages were recorded for many of those convicted. The average age of the twenty-five women was thirty-three, although two-thirds of them were younger. The seven men were older, with an average age of forty-four.

The occupations of landlords and landladies are a little less obscure. The thirty-seven landlords whose occupations are stated seem to have been more consistently involved in trades as masters than their tenants. Sometimes they combined their trade with keeping a separate house that was let as lodgings.[29] Seven landlords and landladies described themselves as lodging-house keepers.[30] But the most striking feature of these cases is the prominence of women—single women, widows, wives, daughters, servants—in managing the actual letting of the lodgings and the preparation and servicing of the rooms. Women, mainly widows, constituted only 15 percent of owners, but it was a wife or a daughter who arranged the let in nearly two-thirds of the cases where a man is named as the owner.[31] And it was the women of the house who managed the rooms once they were let. Not all lodging rooms were serviced. Some owners reported that after letting the room, they never entered it and hardly ever saw or heard the tenant. Many tenants had their own room key and kept their rooms locked. But in the case of those rooms that were serviced, it was women who did the work.[32]

What is never stated explicitly, in the cases in which the court was told that a wife or a daughter took responsibility for the day-to-day letting and running of the lodgings, is whether she chose the furnishings that, under the law, were the property of her husband or father. But sometimes it is clear from the man's ignorance of the stolen furnishings that the woman of the house must have done the furnishing. In 1795, Parthenia Webb stated in court, "I live at Dartmouth-row, Westminster; I live along with my father, he is a housekeeper. On the 17th of November, that woman took our lodging. Q[uestion]. What business is your father? - He is a carpenter by business, he keeps a broker's shop. . . . Q[uestion]. Where is your father? - He knows nothing at all about the property, he leaves it all entirely to me, he would not know them if he was to see them."[33] And, of course, the woman of the house often had a hand not simply in the selection and upkeep of the furnishings, but also in their making. Mary Bunyan, the wife of a Spitalfields cooper, declared to the court in 1793 that "it is part of a mattrass, and part is gone; they have taken the inside out: I know it to be part of my mattrass, because I made part of it and I stuffed it with fine flocks."[34]

How were these lodgings furnished? A 1767 pamphlet on the inadequacy of the wages paid to London clerks in public offices suggested that for a rent of 2s. 6d. a week (slightly less than the average rent in the Old Bailey cases from the 1750s), a single clerk would get a furnished room in one of the "dirtiest and meanest Parts of the Town," containing

> a Half-Tester Bedstead, with brown Linsey-Woolsey Furniture, a Bed and bolster, half Flocks, half Feathers, a green glazed Chamber-pot, a small Wainscot Table, two old Chairs with Cane Backs and Bottoms, a small Looking-glass 6 inches by 4 in a Deal Frame painted red and black, a red Linsey-Woolsey Window-Curtain, an old Iron Stove, Poker, Shovel, Tongs and Fender, an Iron Candlestick mounted with Brass, a Tin Extinguisher, a wooden Wash-hands Bowl, a Quart Bottle for Water, a Tin Pint Pot, a Tin Pepper-box, a Vial for Vinegar and a Stone white Tea cup for Salt. Also two large Prints cut in Wood and coloured, framed with Deal, but not glazed, viz. 1. "Hogarth's Gate of Calais, or The Roast Beef of Old England." 2. "Queen Esther and King Ahasuerus".[35]

Allowing for the fact that the theft cases rarely include large pieces of joined furniture such as bedsteads, tables, and chairs, or smaller things of little financial value like prints, earthenware chamber pots, and stoneware teacups, the Old Bailey cases from the 1750s suggest that the 1767 list was broadly representative (table 1).

But the pessimistic interpretation of the furnishings in the pamphlet was overdone. In the Old Bailey cases from the 1750s, the quality of items named in the pamphlet was often better, or at least more diverse, than the pamphleteer allowed. Eleven beds were described as "feather," only one as "feather and flock," and none as just "flock." All the candlesticks for which the material was given were brass. Twice as many curtains were made from harrateen, worsted, wool, or linen as from linsey-woolsey. Pots were overwhelmingly made from copper, iron, and brass; only one was tin. Other furnishings mentioned repeatedly in the Old Bailey cases are not mentioned at all in the pamphlet. They include quilts and counterpanes, coverlids and rugs, saucepans and frying pans, plates and teakettles, all stolen in numbers from the cheaper lodgings. None of these were obvious necessities, yet they were not confined to the more expensive lodgings, which were distinguished by such items as mahogany waiters (trays), silver spoons, and diaper napkins. A silk quilt was stolen from a 1s. lodging. Looking glasses, quilts, teakettles, pewter plates, and feather beds were stolen from 2s. 6d. lodgings—exactly the same rent as the lodging described in the pamphlet. Indeed, with an average value of 6s 9d., looking glasses were the second most valuable category of goods stolen, exceeded only by the bed itself, but they were also one of the more frequently stolen items.

Comparison of the pamphlet and the Old Bailey cases suggests, therefore, that modest rented rooms in mid-eighteenth-century London sustained a level of furnishing that, though hardly elaborate, could embrace some of the more ambitious material aspirations of their tenants: their desire to drink tea at home (teakettles), to monitor their personal appearance (looking glasses), and to prettify their rooms

TABLE 1. The dozen most frequently mentioned types of objects in the 142 Old Bailey charges for theft from furnished lodgings, 1750–59

Objects	*Number*	*Number and % of charges with object*
1. Sheets	213	111 (78%)
2. Blankets	114	75 (53%)
3. Cooking equipment (pans, pots, kettles, trivets)	77	47 (33%)
4. Pillows and bolsters	62	38 (27%)
5. Curtaining (bed and window curtains, valances, tester cloths, head cloths)	52	21 (15%)
6. Fire equipment (bellows, fenders, tongs, shovels, pokers, grates)	51	31 (22%)
7. Pillow and bolster cases	45	27 (19%)
8. Candlesticks	38	26 (18%)
9. Bed coverings (quilts, coverlids, counterpanes, bed rugs)	37	35 (25%)
10. Teakettles	29	29 (20%)
11. Tableware (plates, dishes, trenchers, basins)	29	14 (10%)
12. Looking glasses	28	27 (19%)

Note: Most charges included more than one kind of stolen item.

Source: Old Bailey Proceedings Online, 23 June 2005.

(bed and window curtains, quilts, and counterpanes). Of course, these goods had a functional appeal—drinking tea at home could save money, as could shaving at home in front of the mirror, while quilts and counterpanes conserved warmth in bed, especially in beds without full curtaining. Nevertheless, they were hardly necessities. Their absence in descriptions of the bare interiors of the most squalid garret rooms is striking.

If we turn to the Old Bailey cases from the 1790s, this impression of an approach to furnishing weekly lodgings that acknowledged the material aspirations, albeit modest, of tenants is reinforced. The dozen most frequently mentioned stolen furnishings were not radically different from those in the 1750s (table 2). Teakettles and looking

TABLE 2. The dozen most frequently mentioned types of objects in the 123 Old Bailey charges for theft from furnished lodgings, 1790–99

Objects	*Number*	*Number and % of charges with object*
1. Sheets	192	97 (79%)
2. Blankets	87	56 (46%)
3. Curtaining (bed and window curtains, valances, testers, head cloths, bed furniture, bed hangings)	73	33 (27%)
4. Pillows and bolsters	70	44 (36%)
5. Bed coverings (quilts, coverlids, counterpanes, bed rugs)	47	42 (34%)
6. Smoothing irons	39	32 (26%)
7. Cooking equipment (pans, pots, kettles, stoves, grid irons, trivets, boilers)	38	27 (22%)
8. Pillow and bolster cases	37	24 (18%)
9. Fire equipment (bellows, fenders, tongs, shovels, pokers, fire irons)	30	15 (12%)
10. Teakettles	27	27 (22%)
11. Beds (i.e., mattresses)	23	20 (16%)
12. Looking glasses	20	19 (15%)

Note: Most charges included more than one kind of stolen item.

Source: Old Bailey Proceedings Online, 23 June 2005.

glasses again figure prominently, although we have more descriptive detail by this period. For example, among the looking glasses in 2s. and 3s. lodgings were some with gilt, mahogany, or walnut frames. But what is most striking is how a number of the more frequently stolen decorative items supplied by landlords had changed since the 1750s to reflect wider changes in availability and taste. Two categories of textiles will serve to make the point: first, bed and window curtains; second, bed coverings.

In the 1750s, the curtains for beds and windows mentioned in the Old Bailey cases were almost all made from either linen or woolen materials: linsey-woolsey, pure linen, harrateen (a worsted), or other kinds of worsted. They could be decorative as well as functional items—colors of blue and green are mentioned. There was only one mention of a cotton curtain. By the 1790s, linsey-woolsey curtains had virtually disappeared from the Old Bailey cases. There were more than twice as many curtains made from cotton as from worsted, linen, or harrateen, reflecting the growing availability of cotton fabrics. If the valuations in the indictments are to be believed, this shift to cotton was not a consequence of cotton curtains being cheaper than the alternatives. In the 1790s, cotton curtains in lodgings under 7s. a week were valued at 1s. 6d. to 3s. 6d. Worsted, harrateen, and linsey-woolsey curtains in the 1750s had been valued at 1s. to 2s. 6d.; in the 1790s, they were valued at 1s. to 2s. The appeal of cotton, here as in many of its other uses, reflected not its price but its appearance—its ability to display colorful printed patterns in fast colors that could be kept clean and attractive by washing.

A similar pattern emerges for bed coverings. In the Old Bailey cases in the 1750s, two-thirds of bed coverings were quilts, made from linen, cotton, woolen cloth, or silk. By the 1790s, quilts (sixteen mentioned) had been superseded by counterpanes (twenty). In the 1750s, there had been only three counterpanes, made from wool and linen. By the 1790s, three-quarters of them were cotton. As with the changes in curtains, the shift away from quilts made from a variety of materials to counterpanes made from cotton reflected changes in taste as much as price and functionality. By the 1790s, average quilt values had risen slightly from their 1750s level, but they were lower than those of cotton counterpanes, even in the lodgings under 7s. a week. The white cotton counterpane, woven in distinctive tufted decorative patterns, was one of the great domestic furnishing success stories of the late eighteenth century. It brought prosperity to the fancy weavers of Bolton, Lancashire, and an appearance of

TABLE 3. Old Bailey cases mentioning counterpanes made from cotton materials, 1710–99

	All cases	*Cases of theft from furnished lodgings*
1710–19	0	0
1720–29	0	0
1730–39	0	0
1740–49	1	0
1750–59	2	0
1760–69	5	1
1770–79	21	2
1780–89	53	7
1790–99	43	16

Source: Old Bailey Proceedings Online, 23 June 2005.

TABLE 4. Old Bailey cases mentioning bed or window curtains made from cotton materials, 1710–99

	All cases	*Cases of theft from furnished lodgings*
1710–19	0	0
1720–29	0	0
1730–39	1	0
1740–49	1	0
1750–59	2	1
1760–69	0	0
1770–79	2	0
1780–89	9	2
1790–99	25	7

Source: Old Bailey Proceedings Online, 23 June 2005. NB: This table is based on a narrower range of search criteria than tables 1 and 2, resulting in a smaller number of thefts from lodgings.

crisp, decorative cleanliness to beds, including many of those in furnished lodgings. Again, it was appearance, not price, that gave the cotton counterpane its appeal.

The fact that the owners of mundane furnished lodgings began to provide their tenants with these decorative and relatively expensive cotton furnishings demonstrates that they could be responsive to changes in prevailing taste on their tenants' behalf. Comparison of the furnished-lodging cases with other Old Bailey cases involving these goods demonstrates that landladies and landlords were following closely on the heels of those who bought the same things for their own use (tables 3 and 4). Moreover, this dynamism was not something that emerged only in the second half of the eighteenth century. Teakettles were prominent among the things stolen from furnished lodgings in the 1750s. Unknown before the later years of the seventeenth century, there are no references to them in the printed Old Bailey records before the 1710s. Thereafter, they are mentioned at the Old Bailey ever more frequently as they became a familiar feature of middling households.[36] Owners of furnished lodgings followed this trend (table 5). They provided teakettles to their tenants in increasing numbers between the 1730s and the 1750s, responding to wider changes in consumer taste, just as they would with other new furnishings in the later decades of the eighteenth century.

It is not the argument of this chapter that the presence of these relatively new kinds of objects made modest lodgings fashionable. Among the stolen furnishings mentioned in the Old Bailey cases were items that were cheap and threadbare, old

TABLE 5. Old Bailey cases mentioning teakettles, 1700–1759

	All cases	*Cases of theft from furnished lodgings*
1700–1709	0	0
1710–19	3	0
1720–29	10	0
1730–39	28	3
1740–49	48	8
1750–59	81	29

Source: Old Bailey Proceedings Online, 23 June 2005.

and shabby. They included some of the newer types of objects. A cotton counterpane stolen from a Clerkenwell lodging in 1797 was four years old and had "a mark of a bit of wax." Catherine Higginson, the wife of a Clare Market grocer and cheesemonger, identified a looking glass stolen in 1794 from the room she let for 3s. 9d. a week by the "crack at the corner."[37] Indeed, there is every reason to believe that, like many of the furnishings owned by modest householders, the domestic objects landlords and landladies supplied to their tenants were often reused, recycled, or secondhand. It is likely that they included items from the sales of unredeemed pledges mounted by the very pawnbrokers their tenants visited to dispose of the furnishings they had purloined. Secondhand dealers could certainly fit out lodgings. Sarah Mitchell, who kept a broker's shop in Shoreditch, identified a young woman who had stolen the contents of a furnished room, saying that "she brought them to me for sale; I have known her many years, living in the neighbourhood; I have furnished rooms for her mother."[38]

Nor is it the argument of this chapter that every tenant of a furnished lodging enjoyed the use of objects such as teakettles, cotton curtains, or cotton counterpanes that reflected recent changes in taste. Many of the poorest languished in conditions of extreme squalor. In 1798, the living quarters of Henry Gilbert, a journeyman coach-harness maker, consisted of "only a part of a bed on the second floor" of a house in Silk-street, Cripplegate, which he had to share with all comers.[39] Only slightly better were the furnishings of a young apothecary in 1787, who lodged for 10d. a week "in a garret, no fire place nor window in it, only a sky light; he slept on a sliding board upon a bit of a bed; he had two blankets, and a rug, like what they throw over the horses."[40]

Nevertheless, the generality of lodgings encountered in the Old Bailey cases were not so squalid. At an average rent of between 2s. and 3s. a week, a rental that eighteenth-century commentators suggest was typical, they were the abodes of working men and women. They were furnished modestly, but nevertheless according to a rough-and-ready set of conventions that were neither static nor driven simply by cost. As we have seen, these conventions could accommodate innovations reflecting broader changes in taste among the more affluent sections of London's population. Not all lodgings at this level of rent benefited from these innovations, but a good number did, indeed probably more than appear in the Old Bailey cases, given the ways in which the goods listed in the trials were selected. And because lodgers moved frequently, surprisingly large numbers of them may have been exposed to new tastes in furnishing.[41]

Indirect consumers could therefore be dynamic consumers. Tenants enjoyed these innovations in taste courtesy of their landladies, but whether they were initiated by landlady or tenant remains unclear. Landladies may have responded to the preferences revealed by tenants who chose lodgings according to the quality of their furnishings. But the choices available to tenants were between furnishing schemes predetermined by landladies, not between individual items of furniture. Alternatively, landladies may have anticipated the material aspirations of prospective tenants, drawing on a knowledge of wider changes in taste acquired in shops, in acquaintances' houses, and (always a crucial point of reference for any business) in lodgings run by their competitors across the city. And, of course, some changes in taste were inescapable, as goods embodying outmoded tastes became impossible to obtain. When the London sister of a Bedfordshire rector tried to buy him a new brass pot in 1759, she could find only a copper one. "I hope you was not displeased at your copper pot, for a brass one is now quite out of date," she explained. "They make none, for nobody asks for them."[42]

What is clear is that these landladies, though generally far from wealthy, commanded superior resources to most of their tenants, especially the young, single women encountered in so many of the Old Bailey cases, whose own limited and hard-won capital was often tied up in clothes. Lodging offered tenants a way of putting the more abundant capital and credit of householders to work to secure themselves access not just to accommodations, but often to newer kinds of domestic objects that reflected changing tastes and modes of living. Objects in the prevailing taste were attuned not just to tenants' desire to be up-to-date, but also to their need to generate cash at the pawnbrokers. The lives of the working poor were precarious and unpredictable. Just as female servants sometimes mobilized their masters' credit to acquire costly printed gowns and silk hats, so poor tenants in furnished lodgings drew on their landladies' resources to secure possession of copper teakettles, walnut-framed looking glasses, and white cotton counterpanes.[43] For those with meager incomes, few assets, and poor credit, relationships of inequality, subordination, and dependence could provide—at a price—opportunities to possess material things that would otherwise have been unattainable.[44]

The author would like to thank John Beattie, Hannah Greig, Vanessa Harding, Bernard Herman, Tim Hitchcock, Michael Lobban, Kathryn Norberg, Giorgio Riello, Amanda Vickery, and Keith Wrightson for suggestions and references.

1. Old Bailey Proceedings Online (www.oldbaileyonline.org, 23 June 2005, hereafter OBP), April 1799, trial of Susannah Priest (t17990403-30).
2. However, she must have owned other things, especially things of small value, that remain unknown to us. In other cases where a lodger's possessions were stolen, they consisted of a box, clothing, and sometimes money; for examples, see OBP, Feb. 1797, John Smith (t17970215-30); April 1798, Moses Knott (t17980418-73); and Feb. 1798, Alexander Elder (t17930220-61).
3. For a pessimistic assessment of the implications of payment in kind and hand-me-downs for economic growth, see Ben Fine and Ellen Leopold, "Consumerism and the Industrial Revolution," *Social History* 15 (1990): 169. The same argument is restated in Ben Fine and Ellen Leopold, *The World of Consumption* (London and New York: Routledge, 1993), 123–30. Similar lines of reasoning are developed in John Rule, *The Labouring Classes in Early Industrial England, 1750–1850* (London: Longman, 1986), 67; Pat Hudson, *The Industrial Revolution* (London: Arnold, 1992), 178; and Carole Shammas, *The Pre-Industrial Consumer in England and America* (Oxford: Clarendon Press, 1990), 210–14.
4. See John Styles, "Involuntary Consumers? The Eighteenth-Century Servant and Her Clothes," *Textile History* 33, no. 1 (2002): 9–21, and Styles, "Custom or Consumption? Plebeian Fashion in Eighteenth-Century England," in *Luxury in the Eighteenth Century: Debates, Desires and Delectable Goods*, ed. Maxine Berg and Elizabeth Eger (London: Palgrave Macmillan, 2003), 103–15.
5. For a lodger's use of the phrase "my bed," see OBP, April 1798, Moses Knott (t17980418-73). In 1793, a lodger was said to have justified disposing of the contents of her lodging because she was "the mistress of the room," OBP, May 1793, John Beane (t17930529-41).
6. OBP, Dec. 1793, Susannah Emery (t17931204-48); see also June 1793, Jane Taylor (t17930626-45).
7. Indeed, our understanding of these matters has progressed little beyond Dorothy George's excellent discussion, first published in 1925; see Dorothy George, *London Life in the Eighteenth Century* (London: Kegan Paul, 1925), especially 94–105. For more recent treatments of the subject, see Dan Cruickshank and Neil Burton, *Life in the Georgian City* (London: Viking, 1990), 60–63; Alison C. Kay, "A Little Enterprise of Her Own: Lodging-house Keeping and the Accommodation Business in Nineteenth-Century London," *London Journal* 28 (2003): 41–53; and Peter Guillery, *The Small House in Eighteenth-Century London: A Social and Architectural History* (New Haven and London: Yale Univ. Press for the Paul Mellon Centre for Studies in British Art, 2004), especially chaps. 1, 2, and 3.
8. Frederick A. Pottle, ed., *Boswell's London Journal, 1762–1763* (New Haven: Yale Univ. Press, 1950), 50, 58–59; Carl Philip Moritz, *Journeys of a German in England in 1782* (London: Jonathan Cape, 1965), 27–28. For the use of these memoirs to illustrate life in lodgings, see Cruikshank and Burton, *Life in the Georgian City*, 60–63.
9. Craig Spence, *London in the 1690s: A Social Atlas* (London: Centre for Metropolitan History, Institute of Historical Research, Univ. of London, 2000), 90; Guillery, *Small House in Eighteenth-Century London*, 34–35.
10. See Lorna Weatherill, *Consumer Behaviour and Material Culture in Britain, 1660–1760* (London: Routledge, 1988), and Peter Earle, *The Making of the English Middle Class: Business, Society and Family Life in London, 1660–1730* (London: Methuen, 1989).
11. For the most sophisticated recent quantitative analysis of British consumption patterns based on probate

inventories, see Mark Overton and others, *Production and Consumption in English Households, 1600–1750* (London: Routledge, 2004).

12. For new criminal legislation at this period, see John Beattie, *Policing and Punishment in London, 1660–1750: Urban Crime and the Limits of Terror* (Oxford: Oxford Univ. Press, 2001), 314–38.
13. It should be noted, however, that the descriptions of the stolen goods found in the printed trials tend to be less full than those found in the original manuscript indictments. The advantage of the printed trials is that they provide far more circumstantial evidence than the surviving manuscript trial records and, using Old Bailey Proceedings Online, can be searched far more efficiently. The quality of the information provided in the printed trials declines after 1800, when it becomes rare for the charge against the accused to include the materials from which the stolen goods were made.
14. OBP, keyword search, date range: 1750s and 1790s.
15. OBP, June 1758, Sarah Jones (t17580628-29),
16. OBP, Sept. 1794, Henrietta Banks (t17940917-104).
17. OBP, Feb. 1791, George Smith (t17910216-36).
18. Surviving account books and inventories for London pawnbrokers suggest that household furnishings often formed a significant minority of their pledges. For a set of a pawnbroker's accounts including furnishings among the pledged goods, see Public Record Office (hereafter PRO), C 110/134: Chancery Masters Exhibits, Pawnbroker's account books, London, 1822–34. For examples of eighteenth-century pawnbrokers' inventories including furnishings, see Guildhall Library Archives, MS 9174/46: inventory of Joseph Gun, St. Brides, London, pawnbroker, 1727; PRO, PROB 3/47/5: Prerogative Court of Canterbury inventories, Ann Cooper, St. Anne's Westminster, widow, 1748; PROB 3/49/28, Elizabeth Shipley, St. Ann, Middlesex, widow, 1750.
19. OBP, Dec. 1752, Sarah White (t17521206-1).
20. OBP, June 1756, Henry Crabtree (t17560603-11); see also April 1790, William Morse (t17900424-90).
21. OBP, Oct. 1793, Thomas Dempsey (t17931030-31).
22. For a broader discussion of this issue, see Lynn MacKay, "Why They Stole: Women in the Old Bailey, 1779–1789," *Journal of Social History* 32 (1999): 623–39.
23. See OBP, Feb. 1743, Jane Winnell (t17430223-12), in which it was noted that the pawnbroker agreed to return the goods despite an acquittal, and OBP, May 1790, John Taylor (t17900526-47), in which "the pawnbroker delivered the sheets to me without any money; he said he would have no more trouble about it."
24. OBP, Feb. 1793, Mary Jones (t17930220-78). Some charges in the printed trials, especially in the 1750s, listed three or four items and then simply concluded the list with the words "and other things."
25. See OBP, May 1755, Thomas Cooper (t17550515-21).
26. Rents paid by overseers of the poor for cottages in rural Oxfordshire in the 1790s varied between 7d. and 1s. a week: Edward Newbold, "The Geography of Poor Relief Expenditure in Late Eighteenth-Century and Early Nineteenth-Century Rural Oxfordshire" (DPhil diss., Univ. of Oxford, 1995), 228–29.
27. OBP, Feb. 1790, Mary Dightman (t17900224-47).
28. Their occupations were street seller, waterside worker, watchmaker, painter (3), carter, carpenter, mason, watchman, soldier, sailor (2), house broker, tax official, and banker's clerk.
29. See, for example, OBP, Sept. 1797, Sarah Lenore (t17970920-38).
30. For example, John Hickson, who in 1798 began his evidence to the court, "I keep a lodging house, No. 1, Robinhood-Court, Shoe-lane, in the parish of St. Andrew," OBP, Feb. 1798, Ann Ganley (t17980214-64).
31. A total of 65 out of 108 cases where the circumstances of the let are detailed.
32. For examples, see OBP, Feb. 1749, Francis Throgmorton (t17490222-35); Sept. 1753, Ann Humphreys (t17530906-10); May 1754, James Lee (t17540530-24); and June 1758, Sarah Jones (t17580628-29).
33. OBP, Jan. 1795, Elizabeth Dickson (t17950114-29); see also July 1756, Eleanor Fletcher (t17560714-4), and Dec. 1793, Susannah Emery (t17931204-48).
34. OBP, May 1793, John Beane (t17930529-41); see also April 1795, Catharine Fairchild (t17950416-55), and Oct. 1796, Margaret Anderson (t17961026-7).
35. Anon., *Considerations on the Expediency of Raising, at this Time of General Dearth, the Wages of Servants that are not Domestic; particularly, Clerks in Public Offices* (London, 1767), 10, 6–7.

36. The trend is consistent with the growing numbers of hot-drink utensils appearing in middling London probate inventories during the early eighteenth century; see Weatherill, *Consumer Behaviour and Material Culture*, 88.
37. OBP, Dec. 1797, Peter Catapodi (t17971206-35), and April 1794, Margaret Brown (t17940430-102); see also May 1793, John Beane (t17930529-41); Sept. 1794, Henrietta Banks (t17940917-104); and Sept. 1796, Henry Levy (t17960914-32).
38. OBP, Sept. 1799, William York and Charlotte Jennings (t17990911-46).
39. OBP, April 1798, Moses Knott (t17980418-73).
40. OBP, July 1787, John Elliot (t17870711-41).
41. It is impossible to establish the duration of a typical tenancy from the Old Bailey cases, because by definition they ended prematurely in the events that brought the cases to court, but few lasted longer than six months.
42. F. J. Manning, ed., *The Williamson Letters, 1748–1765*, vol. 34 (Bedford: Bedfordshire Historical Record Society Publications, 1953), 49. Christian Williamson ("Tidy"), London, to her brother Edmond ("Mun") Williamson, rector of Millbrook, Bedfordshire, 8 Dec. 1759.
43. For servants, see Styles, "Involuntary Consumers?"
44. The key word here is "possess," indicating a degree of control that went beyond the intimate contact with otherwise unattainable goods available to domestic servants and apprentices in the houses of their employers. For a discussion of reciprocal but unequal relationships in gifting and credit, see Margot Finn, *The Character of Credit: Personal Debt in English Culture* (Cambridge: Cambridge Univ. Press, 2003), 76–105.

Reading Spaces in Eighteenth-Century New England

Robert Blair St. George

In 1748, Anthony Stoddard, a Boston, Massachusetts, cooper turned merchant, died with a total estate valued at over £16,000. Much of his wealth lay in rental properties, shares in vessels, and stock in an active trade as a coastal shipping agent. His house, in the port town's fashionable King Street, was large by the standards of the day, valued at an impressive £6,000, including both his domestic possessions and a "warehouse chamber"—suggesting that Stoddard based some of his mercantile operations from his private dwelling. Consider, however, the list of the rooms his house contained, as cited in his probate inventory made the same year:

> Front room, back room, closets in lower back room, easterly back chamber, great chamber, west lower chamber, great chamber closet, west back lower chamber, west lower chamber closet, shop, east upper back chamber, Cellar under kitchen, cellar under west lower room, back kitchen, garden, kitchen, west chamber, west chamber over shop, warehouse chamber, Simeons Lodgings, Sugar Closet, Front upper loft, Upper back loft, stairway, Front room closet, front garrett, front room closet, back garrett.[1]

What are we to make of this extensive range of interior spaces? How are we to offer an interpretive reading of these rooms? Surely some of these room designations refer to the directional layout of Boston's houses, on deep town lots with relatively narrow street fronts; "back room" and "front room"—and their corresponding chambers—in the plan of Thomas and Rebecca Smith's house suggest as much (fig. 16). We can also link aspects of Stoddard's house to the fact that some rooms—likely the shop (with "west chamber over shop" and, to the east, perhaps the "warehouse chamber," once again)—are close to the public way. The presence of a "back kitchen" juxtaposed with a "garden" points to the presence of either a completely detached rear kitchen, similar to the one behind the house that brazier John Holyoke bought from Joseph Webb in 1734, or a back kitchen joined to the main structure by a gallery, as shown in the plan of a property purchased by Ann

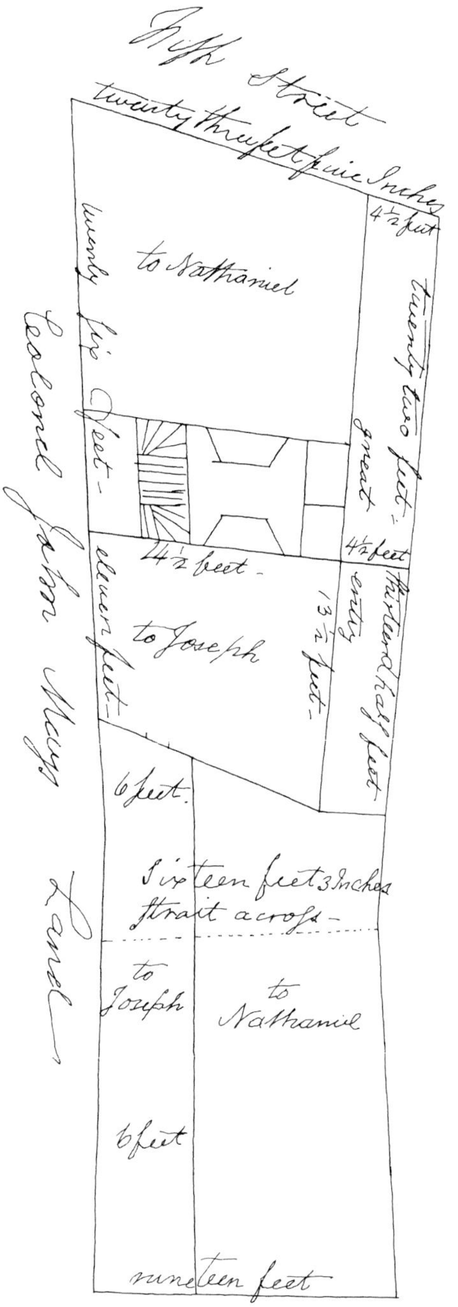

16. Plan of house of Thomas and Rebecca Smith, pre-1670; survey of house taken in 1803. Courtesy of the Massachusetts Historical Society, Boston. Drawing: Robert Blair St. George.

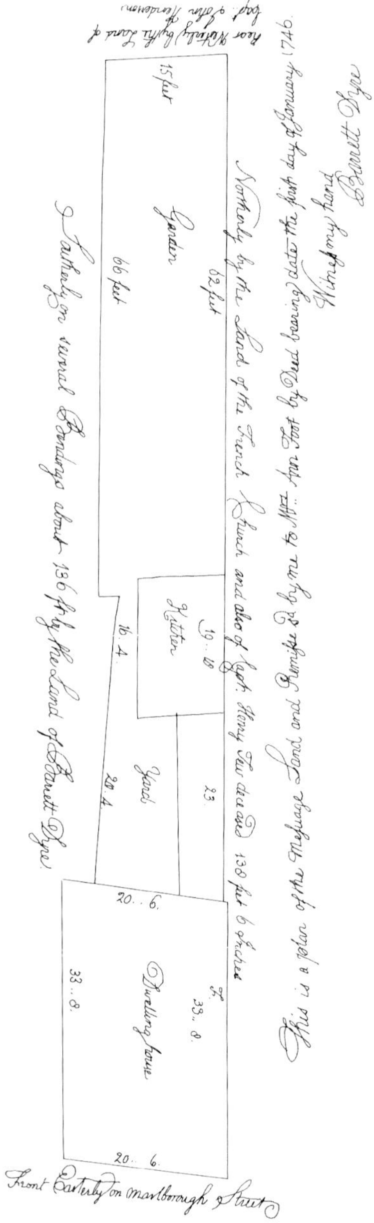

17. Survey of house with detached rear kitchen and connecting gallery or shed, purchased by Ann Foot, Marlborough Street, Boston, 1746. Suffolk County Deeds, Suffolk County Courthouse, Boston. Drawing: Robert Blair St. George.

Foot in 1746 (fig. 17). Perhaps Stoddard's African slave, Simeon, lived in the upper floor of such an outkitchen, and the "sugar closet" may have been carved somehow out of that space; another configuration is also possible, in which Simeon's lodging and the sugar closet may have been located in the warehouse chamber, since they appear in series with it in the document. Finally, we can maintain with confidence that the lofts, also termed cocklofts in English records as well as earlier Boston documents, refer to upper front and rear garrets, formed when boarding is placed along the collar beams that tie together the principal rafter couplings; lofts were used for a variety of storage functions, including grain or corn, old but not yet discarded household goods, and miscellaneous "lumber."[2]

Some spaces, however, resist easy reading; as Bernard L. Herman's essay in this volume readily attests, house plans and the quotidian social life they defined were in states of continual experimentation during the long eighteenth century, and therefore even small spaces might be highly varied in their use and location. In particular, what are seven closets (taking, for the moment, the "closets in the back room" to mean only two) doing in a wealthy merchant's likely Georgian house? To this closet confusion we can add a few more examples from the inventory of Boston merchant Nathanial Cunningham, taken just nine months after Stoddard's. His rooms included, among others, the following: "Great Parlour, Closett of Great Parlour, Entrance of the Front Door, Little Parlour, Closet of the Little Parlour, upon the Great Stairs, upper chamber closet, Kitchen, Kitchen chamber closet," and "closet upon the Back stairs." From the prominent reference to "the Great Stairs," it seems that Cunningham's Boston residence was a neo-Palladian design, with the back stairs likely reserved for servants. But his five closets—including one likely occupying part of the middle landing of the back stairs—are harder to explain in terms of relative size and placement.[3] The difficulties presented by these two inventories of the late 1740s affected eighteenth-century women and men as they immersed themselves in the visceral materiality of quotidian existence. In an age of nascent domestic performance and rituals of enlightened pleasure, how does one establish and then anchor an object-subject position that is at once denotatively social and connotatively fictive? How, indeed, can we begin the larger project of sketching a gendered social imaginary of eighteenth-century Anglo-America?

As the philosopher Charles Taylor has argued, a social imaginary is more than merely the "intellectual schema" that citizens may contemplate when they reflect on their social life, their generative and adaptive strategies for gaining individual or group advantage, in a more or less disengaged or reflexive manner. Instead, a social imaginary consists of the myriad ways that people "imagine their social existence, how they fit together with others, how things go on between them and their fellows, the expectations that are normally met, and the deeper normative notions and images that underlie these expectations." For Taylor, there are critical distinctions between a social imaginary and social theory. One is that the imaginary has vernacular currency and develops historically; it is not, like "theory," the property of an initiated and small minority. Therefore, the imaginary is identical to the "common understanding that makes possible common practices and a widely shared sense of legitimacy," particularly political legitimacy. But more useful for historical purposes is Taylor's other observation, that such commonality is expressed not in theoretical terms but in the appreciable representations that are "carried in images, stories, and legends."[4] In other words, attained legitimacy—in politics, culture, and gender—depends on the pragmatics of vernacular language, material signs, and the externalization of experimental selves in the domestic spaces dedicated to sustained reading and writing. It depends less on the shared content of these images and texts than on the widely disseminated techniques of opening and comprehending specific texts, rituals, and spaces.[5] As this essay suggests, the social imaginary emergent in eighteenth-century society depended on four vernacular strategies: (1) *contingency* (meanings that are context-dependent), (2) *ambiguity* (an inability to fix relative meanings of a specific event or set of actions), (3) *implication* (chains of metaphoric reference that inform or index intertextual assemblages), and (4) *supposition* (unverifiable claims on truth as a means of resisting ambiguity about people, language, law, and religion).

We can take an initial step toward the clarification of the social imaginary of eighteenth-century New England by exploring those spaces that people used for the rapidly yet unevenly privatizing practice of reading. Or, to phrase it differently, as technologies advanced for collapsing the illusory disjunction of word versus thing, how were spaces themselves narrativized as people continually redefined them through their material reading practices? The question warrants a quick survey of where people kept books in their domestic interiors. But first, a trio of warnings: (1) room-by-room estate inventories may offer key clues, but they share predictable biases of gender (they radically underreport women decedents) and social station (they overreport merchants, magistrates, and ministers); (2) inventories that anchor books in room settings fail to account for the wonderful portability of books and the unpredictability of where—and in what postures—they might have been read (anyone who has glanced at Andre Kertesz's *On Reading* will recognize the ethnographic difficulty);[6] and (3) inventories may specify the room where books were kept, but they tantalizingly fail to offer titles. For example, in the "Dining Room" of merchant William Clark's house in Boston's North End, he had "Sundry Bookes as p[er] Catalogue" worth over £105 in 1742, while his fellow trader John Boydell had "a p[a]rcell of Bookes & Catalogue" worth almost £60 in his "office" (likely a counting room) two years earlier. Similarly, William Skinner had "in the Library . . . a collection of Books & Pamphlets" appraised at £40. Other estate listings offer more detail. In 1747, Boston merchant James Pemberton kept books in his upstairs "chamber" that listed such steady sellers as sermons by Increase and Cotton Mather and "Chauncy's Seasonable Thoughts" (Boston, 1742), along with "Quarles Emblems" (London, 1635) and "Doolittle on Earthquakes" (Boston, 1755). Pemberton's chamber books also included a "*History of Virginia*" (likely John Smith's), "Robinson Crusoe 2 vols.," "The Turkish Spy 5th vol.," and "a Bundle of Pamphlets."[7] Of course, we cannot be certain if Skinner's "Library" resembled any of the small but well-appointed private English libraries that gave "aspirant local gentry," as James Raven has argued, a technique "to outdistance established neighbours in buying yards of literature to decorate their homes and give visible weight to claims of ranks."[8]

Nevertheless, Pemberton's library demonstrates the continuing popularity of such steady sellers as religious books, prescriptive tracts, and volumes on domestic government. Edward Gray, a Boston rope maker, had "Henry on the Sacramt. 5s" in his "Front Room" in 1740; James Bownd, a leather-breeches maker, had in his "Lower Roome" in 1752 an "Old Quarto Bible considerable Part gone," "a large Folio Vo. Of Mr. Bunyan's Works," and "5 small Family Books." And Sarah Bennett, a Boston widow, kept in her "Lower Room" in October 1742 precisely this sort of material: "1 vol. Body Divinity 80/," "Watt's Lyrick Poems 15/," "D[itt]o. Hymns 5/," and "20 Sacramental Discourses 12/." The ongoing readership of pious works on religion and regulation warrants attention, in part because these often-read-aloud texts provided the substrate of critical self-examination upon which popular fiction, travel literature, and the novel construct an alternate world of silently read moral action and experimental character. In 1751, Mary Bennett (no relation to Sarah) left a library containing Cotton Mather's *Magnalia*, "Dr. Cotton Mather's Life, Jonathan Edwards's *Thoughts on Religion*," and *Pamela* and *The Life and Death of Tom Thumb*.[9]

Works of popular fiction and novels appear with growing frequency in New England in the 1740s and 1750s, and they rapidly increase in availability between 1760 and 1775. There are many sources that figure into the always-incomplete research on transformations of reading and readers: here, newspapers, auction catalogues, sermons, records of circulating social libraries in Boston, Newport, and Braintree in Massachusetts and Madison, Lyme, and Stonington in Connecticut, booksellers' broadsides, and diaries augment the flyblown scraps of probate inventory references. The titles seem far removed from the sermons of the Mathers, Foxcroft, or Chauncy: *Moll Flanders, Pamela, Clarissa, Grandison, Vicar of Wakefield, Shamela, Tom Jones, Roderick Random, Tristram Shandy*—the list of canonical novels continues unabated. So, too, extends the popular embrace of less-recognized fiction, or so Boston bookseller John Mein believed when he included these titles in his circulating library list of 1765: "Matrimony, a Novel by Sebbeare, containing a series of interesting Adventures," "The Entertaining Novels of Mrs. Jane Barker," and "Instructive Novels, translated from the Spanish by Shelton." This last volume included such gripping tales as "Two Damsels, Lady Bentivoglio, generous Lover, Forces of Blood, Spanish Lady, jealous Husband, [and] Cervantes' Life." Mein was likely following the market demand for such titles evinced the previous year when bookseller Andrew Barclay posted a broadside announcing the availability of *Parish Girl, Robin Redbreast, Hocus Pocus, Joe Miller's Jest, Laugh and be Fat,* and *London Jests.*[10]

Whether they read works by Samuel Richardson, Henry Fielding, or Oliver Goldsmith, or the pulp fiction collated in penny pamphlets—and many people devoured works from both traditions—what stands out by the early 1750s is the intensifying engagement of readers in the moral assessment of and identification with characters through their experiential or "empirical" actions. In her essay in this volume, Karen Lipsedge guides us through a nuanced reading of the reception to *Clarissa; or, The History of a Young Lady* in England; the same novel had a remarkable impact in New England. Initially published in 1747–48, *Clarissa* likely made the Atlantic crossing almost immediately, although tracking the actual ownership or circulation of the book remains elusive. The 1765 circulating library of Mein in Boston cites "Clarissa Harlow 8 vols, 'comprehending the most important concerns of private life' (London 1764 edition)," for which it charged a borrower's fee of £2 2s. The same year in New Haven, Connecticut, Benedict Arnold (when he was still a bookseller) had a copy of "Clarissa" for sale that he had lately imported from New York.[11]

But oblique proof that the first edition of the novel was indeed circulating much earlier in New England emerges in February 1753, when the Reverend Aaron Burr, a minister in Newark, New Jersey, wrote a letter to Sarah Prince in Boston concerning his wife's severe fever. Sarah, the daughter of Boston clergyman Thomas Prince, was the closest girlhood friend of his wife, Esther Edward Burr, herself the daughter of minister Jonathan Edwards and thus reared in Northampton, Massachusetts. Burr explains his wife's current illness by writing to Sarah Prince, "Your dear Burrissa, my best beloved—has been confined with a lingering Fever for about 2 Months."[12] In her response, Prince versifies her sense of inadequacy to express sympathy equal to her love for Esther:

> Was I possest of that fine art,
> Which chaste Urania does impart;
> I wou'd in gentle number tell,
> What graces in Burrisa dwell.

But oh! My genius is not form'd,
In pleasing lines by friendship warm'd;
For while I strive her worth to paint,
My thoughts prove low my language faint.[13]

In each case, these letters reveal that Esther Burr, at least by age twenty-one, had taken on the character of Clarissa by referring to herself as Burrissa. The following year, after her health had stabilized, Esther reported on two additional texts. In November 1754, she reports, "Mr Burr has got a new thing of Miss Joans's putting out. The title is *Miscellanies in Prose and Verse.* She has a turn for poetry, is quite lively in some places, but in other that which I wonder at. She has some fine strokes on friendship which shews a turn for, but no turn for relegion [*sic*]. I believe her to be a Deist in principle. What a pity!" As the daughter and the wife of a minister, Esther brought to her reading a consistently high level of religious critique. She watches for distinctions between Old Light orthodoxy and New Light theology—or in New Jersey, between Old Form and New Form Presbyterianism—and at times reveals an interest in observing the preaching style and sermonic authority of local preachers. In her correspondence with Sarah, she was similarly probing in what books and fashions were popular in Boston. On 12 November 1754, she thanked Sarah for her last missive, admitting, "I am much pleased with the passage you quote out of Sir Charles Grandson that says the Character of a friend, the greatest that can be given, or to that purpose."[14]

That Burrissa praises her friend for a passage on the quality of friendship that Sarah had lifted from Richardson's last novel (brand-new in 1753–54) should come as no surprise. Indeed, Esther and Sarah's upbringing in the families of leading clergymen helped to define their particular brand of both literary praise and critique; their reading was entirely contingent on their accumulated experiences and rare level of female education. As they read *Clarissa,* for instance, their emphasis no doubt fell on the virtue, riches, honor, and proper role of women in an economy that saw through all things matrimonial to a larger, framing sphere of consolidated fortunes and the politics of control over families, land, and labor. For this reason, the embrace of *Clarissa* could bring tears and extremes of emotional engagement for even the most disciplined women. When Lady Bradshaigh, the wife of a Lancashire baronet and a valued correspondent of Samuel Richardson, revealed to him her reaction to *Clarissa,* she stressed its transformative effects: "When alone in Agonies would I lay down the book, take it up again, walk about the Room, let Fall a flood of Tears, wipe my Eyes, read again, perhaps not three Lines." Here, the reader, alone in the intimate protection of domestic privacy, has the autonomy to risk merging herself with the sad adventures of the book's title character. But wait: after one last attempt, she must "throw away the book crying out Excuse me good Mr Richardson, I cannot go on."[15] For both Esther Burr and Lady Bradshaigh, control over the domestic setting led them to identify with the emotional confinement of the novel's character and action. As Ian Watt and Cynthia Griffin Wolff observed long ago, the critical embrace of novels by women was continuous with and even extended a Puritan emphasis on self-examination, introspection, and the transcendent power of Christian friendship.[16] And so, sitting in an upstairs bedchamber of her center-chimney house in Newark, Esther obtained a loan copy of Richardson's first novel, *Pamela; or, Virtue Rewarded* (1741), and began reading on 10 March 1755.

More popular than *Clarissa* in New England and more widely circulated, *Pamela* appears in Boston probate inventories in the early 1750s. Mary Bennett owned "Pamela in 4 Vollums," appraised at £1 6s. 8d., in 1751. The very next year, Boston bookseller Daniel Gookin carried "2 Setts Pamela," each in four volumes and selling for 11s. 4d.; in 1754, Boston shopkeeper Jotham Maverick had "Pamela in 4 Vols" available for 16s. in "ye Front Lower Room" of his house. A 1762 edition of the four-volume set was in Mein's circulating library in 1765, available for a £1 borrowing charge. As late as 1772, Cox and Berry included "Pamela, or Virtue rewarded, 4 Vol.," as well as a French edition of only two volumes.[17] Thus, *Pamela* was being read widely and could be purchased as well as borrowed from circulating libraries. By picking it up, Esther was surrounded by fellow fans of Richardson's initial claim on literary taste. We also have some insight into *how* she read it.

Writing to Sarah Prince, Esther at first compares it unfavorably to *Clarissa*, which she had read prior to early 1753:

> Eve[ning]. I have borrowed Pamela and am reading it now. I fancy I sha'nt like it so well as I did Clarissa, but prejudice must have its weight.
>
> I remember you said that in your opinion it did not equel her. Your judgment my dear has a very great influence on mine.[18]

Still, Esther must have relished the read; by the very next evening, she indicates that she is halfway through the first volume—and now sees only Mr. B's evil ways:

> Eve. Pray my dear how could Pamela forgive Mr. B. all his Devilish conduct so as to consent to marry him? Sertainly this does not well agree with so much virtue and piety. Nay I think it a very great defect in the performance, and then is'n't it seting up Riches and honnour as the great essentials of happiness in a married state? Perhaps I am two rash in my judgment for I have not read it half out tho' I have enough to see the Devil in the Man.[19]

By day three of her evening reading, 12 March, she is visibly upset:

> I am quite angry with Mr. [Richardson]. He has degraded our sex most horribly, to go and represent such virtue as Pamela, falling in love with Mr. B. in the midst of such foul and abominable actions. I could never pardon him if he had not made it up in Clarissia. I gu[e]ss he found his mistake, so took care to mend the first opportunity."[20]

Thus positioned partway through the novel, Esther had to break off for a few weeks, as other tasks intervened. She visited the sick and comforted her poor neighbors; household chores demanded attention. Saturday, 15 March: "So very busy that I cant get time to write." After a brief hiatus, Esther returned to *Pamela* on 8 April 1755:

> Today I have [been] reading an account of Mr B. s going after the *Coun[tess]* of ———. This appears very strange to me considering the [title] of the Book, which is, *Virtue Rewarded*—I could not by ju[st] stomach to allow it that title before, for he was a sad fello[w] to be sure, had one Child, *bastard*, and did his indevour to get many more as it seems by *Lady Davers*, and his own confession two—but I don't know—I have a poor judgme[n]t of my own. . . . In my humble opinion *Riches*, and *honour*, are set up two much—can Money reward virtue? And besides Mr Bs being a *libertine* he was a *dreadfull high-spirited Man, impatient of Contradiction* as he says of himself—*Pamela* had a task of it, with all Mr Bs good qual[i]ties. She was as much afraid of him as of a Lyon—If the author had [le]ft it to me to have intitled the Books, I think I should hav[e] chose *Virtue tryed*, instead of *rewarded*—In that af[fai]r of the Contess he was vastly to blame, and would no dou[bt] have kept with her some part of his time at least, as his [wife?] if he had not been prevented just when he was.[21]

What stands out in these passages—in which Esther Burr attempts to come to terms with marriage, property, and the shifting, meager sentimentalities of the man, as "Devilish," "a sad fello[w]," "a *libertine*," and "a *dreadfull high-spirited Man, impatient of Contradiction*"—is how fully she is bringing her own gendered experiences and critical capacities to the challenging task of reading all the ambiguities of *Pamela* in the bedchamber of her house. First, the schedule of her reading was at times erratic and always fragmentary, cut through at occasional and unpredicted intervals of domestic labor, child-rearing, and the duties of a ministerial wife. On this score, Esther's experience corresponds closely to the "intermittent" pattern—of mixing reading and labor, as well as interrupting novels with other literary genres—that Naomi Tadmor has observed in the reading practices of Thomas and Peggy Turner in East Hoathly, Kent, in England.[22] Esther feels alternately betrayed by Richardson and then, perhaps, merely critical of his subtitle's apparent inaccuracy.

For Esther, reading an epistolary novel like *Pamela* had direct relevance for the collaborative project she and Sarah Prince were undertaking. They were writing to one another not merely to stay in touch; they saved their letters, mailed out packets of copies, and numbered each letter. On 18 November 1755, Esther worried that she was missing some of Sarah's letters in the sequence. "I just now received your kind dear No. 17, but where are Nos. 15 and 16?" Esther wondered. "I have nithe[r] of 'em, unless that little line that had dated October 13 be one of them, and that is not Numbered. There is missing from Page 274 to Page 314." With the exchange of correspondence in *Clarissa* as a likely model, Sarah and Esther were consciously assembling—but with no desire to publish it in mind—an epistolary novel of religious piety, marital loneliness, and the lively sociability of female culture in the Atlantic world. While Sarah and Esther were coconspirators in their epistolary novel in the making, their circuit of friends and correspondents included a handful of other well-placed young women in eastern Massachusetts. Using Fidelia now as her preferred pseudonym, Esther wrote to Sarah in late January 1756, worried by the thought that she might never see them all again:

> Pleas to give my most Respectfull regards to your Honored Papa and Mamma. And my kindest regards to all the Sisterhood—I will mention their names because it may be the last opportunity I may ever have to do it—First Marina because she is married—Costancia who I love as one of your best friends—Confidenta as another—Laura as a good Christian and a friend to all such—Simpathia for her name tho' I don't know her—Leomira as a promissing young Lady and has many amiable quallities—and Julia I love for two many things to be mentioned in a Letter—You my friend I shall Love for-ever—pray for me till you hear again.

Trust of the sort missing in the calculating world of misrepresentation of *Pamela* was mollified by the existence of her "Sisterhood" of friends in mid-eighteenth-century New England. Friendship with other women was key to Esther's life, as she had written to Sarah back in October 1754: "I have not one Sister I can write to so freely as to you the Sister of my heart."[23]

What also resonated with Esther's life—even as her epistolary efforts and her sisterhood of friends provided an opening away from it—was reading about domestic spaces in *Pamela* that suggested withdrawal and isolation from the social world. While her husband was gone from home in October 1754, Esther had felt the house as a kind of solitary confinement. "I feel something gloomy," she admitted, "but endeavour not to give it way. . . . All solitary! Our house seems so still. I am alone, almost afraid to step about [the] house for fear of [mak]ing a disturbance."[24] So when she read of Pamela's being similarly imprisoned in the house of Mr. B—one of Richardson's many uses of architectural scaffolding to support characters—there was prompt empathy with her fictive alter ego. "About Eight at Night," Pamela describes, "we enter'd the Court-yard of this handsome, large, old, and lonely Mansion, that looks made for solitude and Mischief, as I thought, by its Appearance, with all its brown nodding Horrors of lofty Elms and Pines about it: And here, said I to myself, I fear, is to be the Scene of my Pain, unless God protect me, who is all-sufficient."[25] Confinement struck a nerve in polite Boston readers, for whom enclosed and constricted domestic properties, often on small, irregularly shaped town lots or, like the estate of William Webster in 1720, subdivided into distinct courtyards, were surprisingly common (fig. 18).

The problems of gendered confinement—of public merchants and praying ministers choosing a closeted moment, of housebound women for whom such isolation might seem like a sentence to solitary confinement (especially during long winters)—led to a reading of those two spaces of intimacy where the autonomous self is rescued and liberated to read and write: the bedchamber and the closet. Bedchambers, like the one in which Esther Burr read and wrote, were principally to be found "above stairs," and they were used not only for sleeping but also for the reception and polite entertainment of guests of a status equal to that of the householder; bedchambers were also enumerated on occasion in single-story houses, in which case they shared a wall with the principal hall or kitchen. As we have seen, closets are elaborated in houses in eighteenth-century New England and also are fictive spaces in which reading took place. Thus, the fictional Pamela retreats to her closet to read, to write letters, and to pray: "So I looked into the closets; and kneeled down in my own, as I used to do, to say my prayers, and this with my under clothes in my hand." Her closet seems to be a small room—possibly an "inner room" partitioned from the bedchamber she shares with Mrs. Jewkes, and surely descended from the "inner room" that had split more intimate social activities apart from both the multipurpose old hall and bedchambers since the mid-sixteenth century.[26] It seems to have been a space that both allowed and contained the restrained eroticism of praying with one's underclothing held in one's hand. Yet for women busy with visitors and too demanding a household entertainment schedule, the closet's confinement could be alternately figured as a haven from a heartless society.

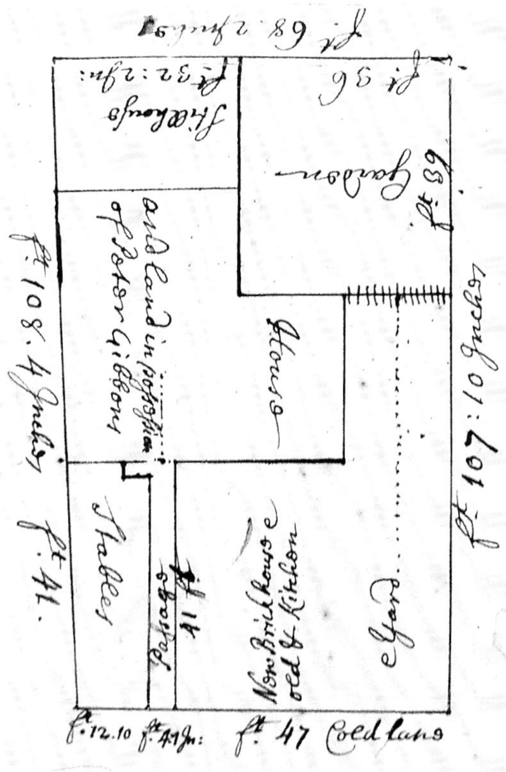

18. Plan of enclosed estate of William Webster, Cold Lane, Boston, 1720. Suffolk County Deeds, Suffolk County Courthouse, Boston. Photo: Robert Blair St. George.

But as readers tried to vicariously enter the ambiguities of Pamela's (or Clarissa's) closet with their heroine, what other images and associations flooded forth? Prayer, preparation, devotion, study: the closet was a space long familiar to New England clergy and laity alike as a small, private room used for ritual castigation, apologia, and regeneration, for which textual justification appeared in the Bible. As daughters of ministers, both Esther and Sarah would have recognized Joel 2:16—"let the bridegroom go forth of his chamber, and the bride out of her closet"—and encountered its gendered association with preparation for marriage, similar to a 1530 citation of a "closet for a lady to make her redy." Part of what made confinement tolerable for Esther was that, while her role as a minister's wife always brought out what she termed her "best self"—the pious handmaiden of the Lord and helpmate to her husband—immersing herself in Pamela and her intimate correspondents articulated what she called "my other self," the self that threw off the patriarchal order and interceded with feminine, mutual nurture and fictive lives lifted from the "distractions" of novels. Strictly devotional use of the closet—cited in Cotton Mather's diary on numerous occasions, and perhaps visually revealed in

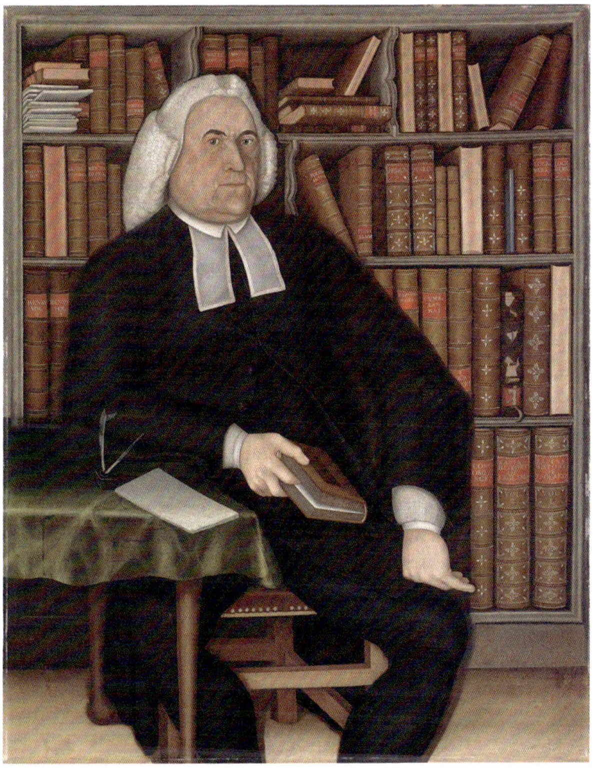

19. Winthrop Chandler, *Reverend Ebenezer Devotion*, oil on canvas (1770), 55 x 44 in. (139.7 x 111.8 cm). Brookline Historical Society, Brookline, Massachusetts. Courtesy of Museum of Fine Arts, Boston. Photography © 2006 Museum of Fine Arts, Boston.

Winthrop Chandler's 1770 portrait of the Reverend Ebenezer Devotion of Brookline (fig. 19)—derives from Christ's instructions to his disciples in Matthew 6:6: "But thou, when thou prayest, enter into thy closet, and when thou has shut thy door, pray to thy Father, which is in secret; and thy Father which seeth in secret shall reward thee openly." Ministers saw the closet and study as synonyms, the space appropriate for a working library. The 1652 inventory of the Reverend John Cotton in Boston shows that this room contained "The Liberary of bookes as valued in the will by himself though cost much more . . . £150," as well "1 presse desk & chest" valued at 20s.[27] A drawing from about 1835 of the Reverend Thomas Hooker's house in Hartford states that his "study" occupied the small chamber located in the projecting "porch" of the structure (fig. 20).

In this case, Hooker's closet or study was in the same position as a reference to "In ye porch chamber . . . bookes" in the 1658 inventory of merchant John Coggan. On a plan of Boston merchant Benjamin Backway's premises, made in 1702 (fig. 21), a projecting two-story entry tower bears the label "Closet or *porch*." So instead of being linked solely to the bedchamber, the closet was in this instance connected with the study and the porch. But what did merchants actually *do* in

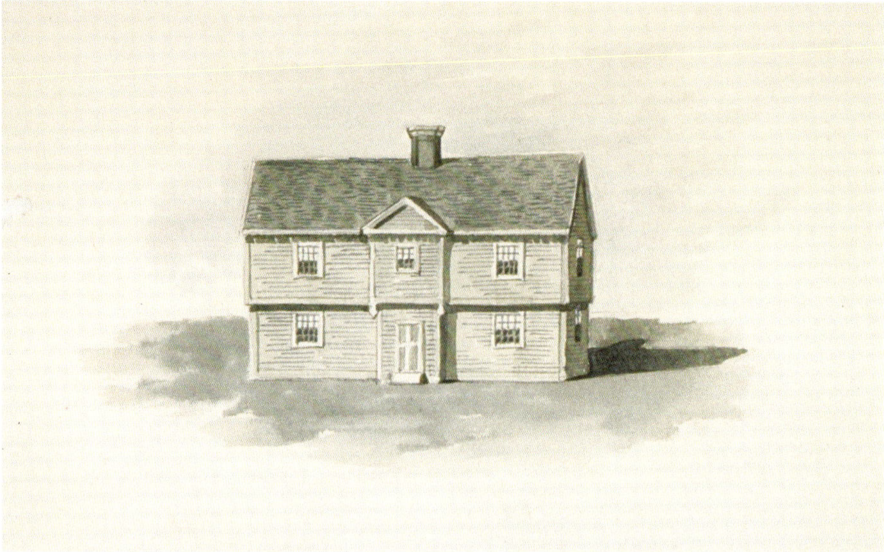

20. John Warner Barber, *Thomas Hooker House, Hartford*, graphite, ink, and wash on paper (c. 1835). The Connecticut Historical Society, Hartford.

their closets? They read books and prayed. When local merchant Richard Smith of North Kingstown, Rhode Island, died in 1692, his house contained three closets. His inventory taken in May 1692 described them in detail. A "little Clossett" in the second story of his house, next to the "Kitchen Chamber" in the rear of the structure, contained "Shoes and some lumber" valued at £2. In another upstairs "Clossett," likely partitioned from the "Hall Chamber," lay "one pr. of brass andirons on[e] Jack and other things" worth £3. Immediately below, in the hall, was the only downstairs closet. Surviving evidence suggests that this space opened into the rear wall of the hall but was actually partitioned into a small sleeping room located in the range of rear service rooms (fig. 22). In this final "Clossett," trader Smith kept "Sundry Books & other things," appraised at £5.[28]

But merchants also kept accounts and displayed collections of prized or rare objects in their closets. A drawing of the "Ende of the Clossette" that Robert Smythson executed in the early 1620s, described in the files of the Royal Institute of British Architects as "Designs for a closet, apparently to be used as a business room," shows a framed wall panel in which are set two compartments marked "For Incke," three boxes "For Loose Papers," and three slanted surfaces marked "Deske" (fig. 23). In the section drawing, no seating adjacent to the writing surfaces is shown, indicating that this merchant's closet was likely a workroom. Closets also held specialized objects, such as the "15: peeces of Earthen ware" kept "In a little

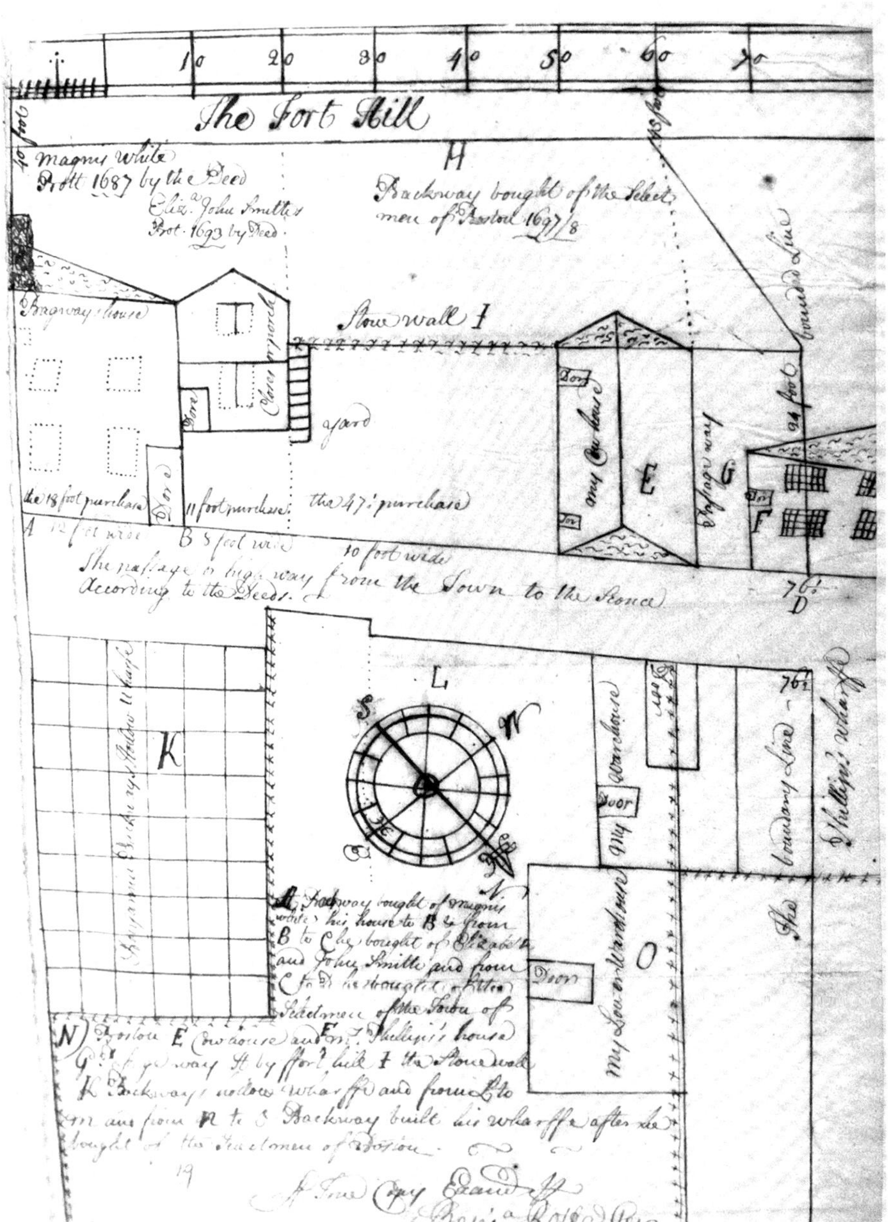

21. Plan of merchant Benjamin Backway's premises, Boston, 1702. Suffolk County Deeds, Suffolk County Courthouse, Boston. Photo: Robert Blair St. George.

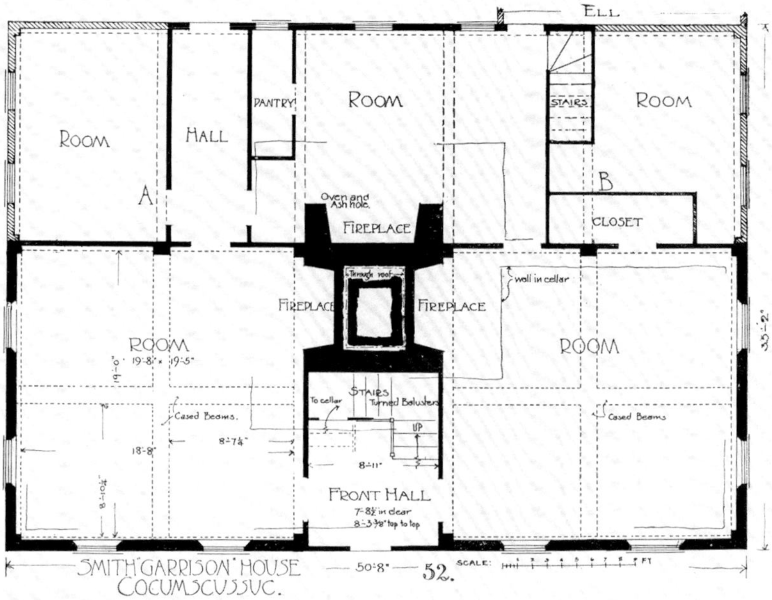

22. Plan of Richard Smith's house, North Kingstown, Rhode Island, before 1692, from *Early Rhode Island Houses: An Historical and Architectural Study*, by Norman M. Isham and Albert F. Brown (Providence, RI: Preston & Rounds, 1895), plate 52. Photo: Courtesy Historic New England (Society for the Preservation of New England Antiquities).

Clossett adjoining" the "little Parlor" of merchant Antipas Boyce in 1669.[29] "In a little clossett, within this chamber"—in other words, "In the Hall Chamber"—of Charlestown merchant John Ellyott, Jr., "there are glasses."[30] In John Boydell's "closet" in 1740 were painted portraits of the town's notables, "Judge Sewall Judge Byfield & Judge Auchmuty's Pictures £30," images of secular judgment consistent with the closet's function as a cabinet of God's providence through prayer. A final reference to prized objects being "confined" to closets returns us to merchant Nathaniel Cunningham's estate inventory of 1748/49. Arranged in the "Closet of the Little Parlour" were "1 large China Woman," "2 Allabaster Parrotts," and "1 Dutch Picture in a Laxered Frame."[31] Closets of the gentry—shadowed in style by the ones in which Pamela and Clarissa stole away to write and read with furtive commitment—had more elaborated and varied uses than the prayer closets of local clergy or the closet-counting rooms of small merchants such as Richard Smith.

One final type of closet is strikingly similar to our current use of the term—meaning a small, built-in area for the storage of clothing and miscellaneous house-

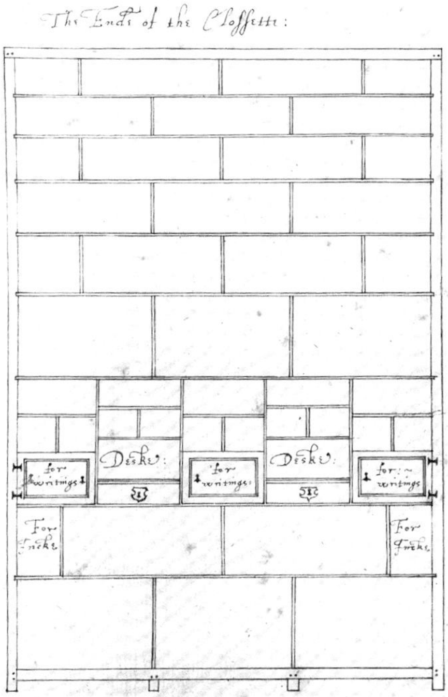

23. Robert Smythson, *The Ende of the Clossette,* c. 1620–25. Photo: RIBA Library Drawings Collection.

hold items. By the late seventeenth century, this kind of closet had already made its appearance in the rural English countryside. One of the first documented small closets (though still perhaps large enough for "closeted" prayer) at the vernacular level was built at Yew Tree Farm in Salmesbury, Lancashire. A substantially but very small stone house, it was built with no parlor. But in the hall chamber, two small closets were built into either side of the end chimney stack, with each one being lit by a small glass window. Architectural historian Maurice Barley wrote that "the closets upstairs" at Yew Tree, "each with a small window[,] are a new and widespread feature of the age." By 1729, when a contract was drawn for the rebuilding of a farmhouse in nearby Gosberton, the installation of small closets flanking both downstairs and upstairs chimneys was common. According to the agreement, carpenter John Proudlove was "To make a Chimney in each of the Low: Rooms and Closets on each Side of the said Chimneys," and then "To build two Chambers over the said Low: Rooms and to make a Chimney in each Chamber with Closets on each side of the Chimneys."[32] The client, Christopher Clayton, was a local merchant keen to store small goods in his chimney closets, or perhaps place books of accounts in a small, lit room that he could keep under lock and key. By 1700 in London, the use of small closets, still termed "cupboards," appeared in an illustration in the short treatise on bricklayer's work that James Moxon added to the earlier but incomplete compilation of trade descriptions, *Mechanick Exercises: Or, The Doctrine of handy-works*, by his father, Joseph Moxon (fig. 24). In British North America, the use of small but varied closet spaces appeared between 1720 and the mid-1770s. In many instances, these closets were built into whatever space remained left over once the staircase and chimneys had been constructed. They fit easily on either side of chimneys in double-pile houses in London and Boston alike. In 1773, a contract drawn for a double house divided into two tenant properties indicates the common location of closets (fig. 25). According to the builder's contract that accompanied the plan, "All the rooms in each tenement to have 2 closets in each, except the front room on the second floor of each tenement which are to have one closet." These small spaces, engineered by clever carpenters into cramped quarters in town and country alike, accounted for a majority of closets that eighteenth-century householders used and knew.[33]

The closets of transatlantic merchants, allied as they were to older traditions of the secured medieval countinghouse, were in debt as well to aristocratic uses of the closet as a much larger domestic space that could encompass the functions of small reception room, preparatory or dressing room, or a transition room between one's chamber and the garden outside. James Brydges, the future Duke of Chandos,

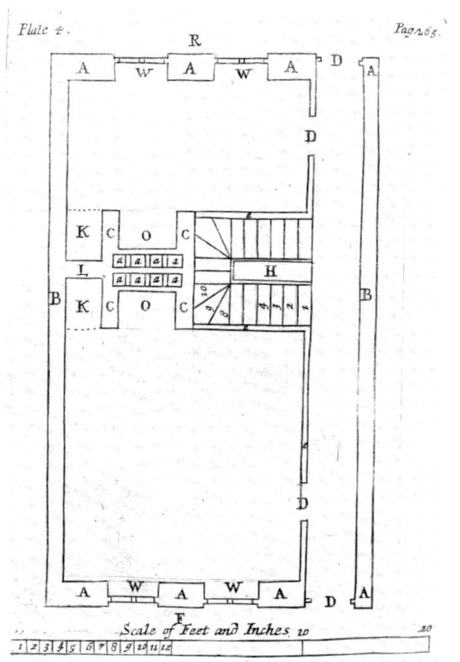

24. Plan of central-chimney-plan house, plate 4 from *Mechanick Exercises: Or, The Doctrine of handy-works*, by Joseph Moxon (London, 1703). Courtesy The Winterthur Library: Printed Book and Periodical Collection. This illustration, showing two rooms separated by a chimney stack (O) flanked by two "closetts" (cupboards) (K), accompanied *The doctrine of handy-works applied to the art of bricklayers-works*, which James Moxon first added in 1700 to his father's earlier publication.

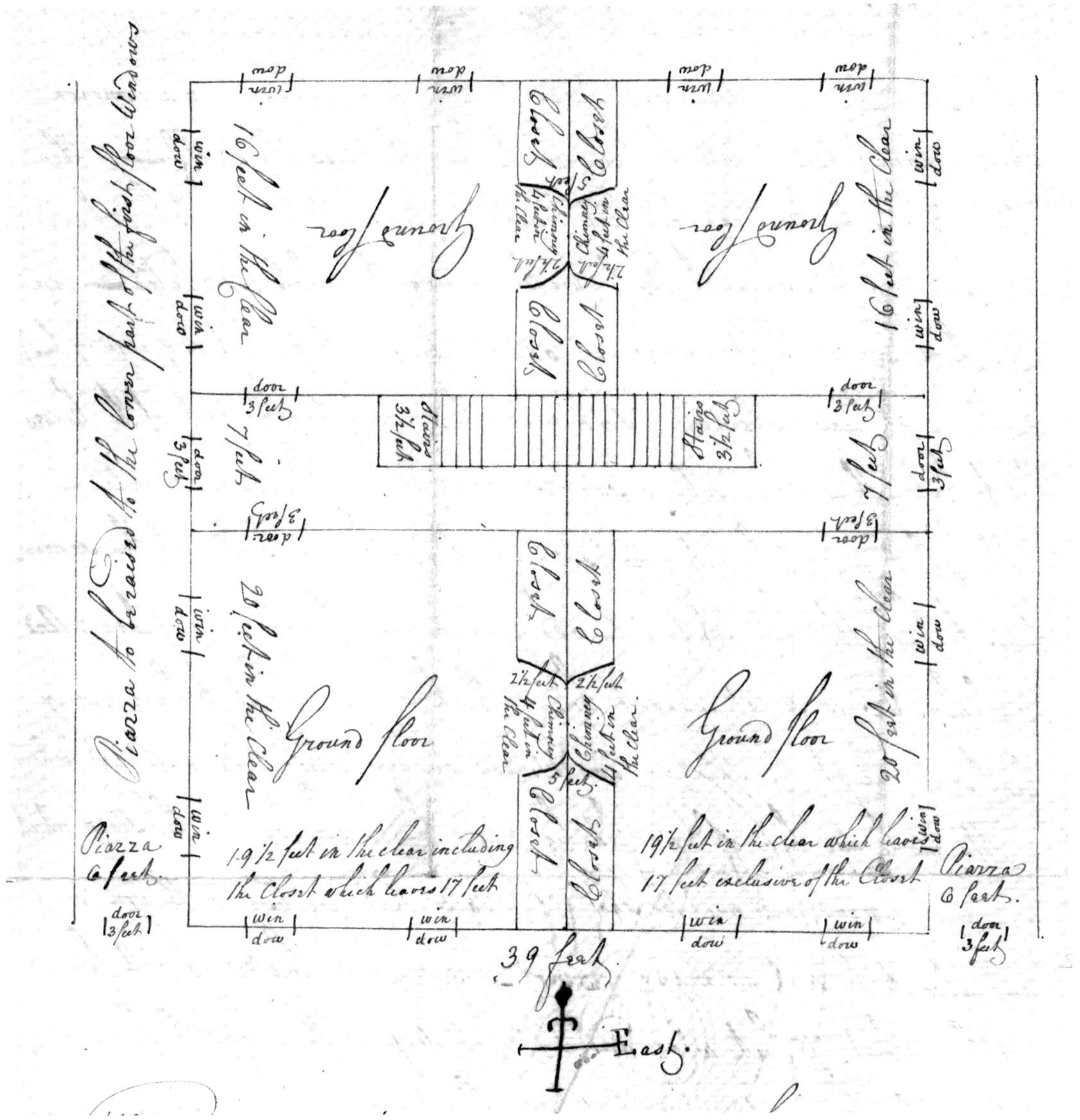

25. Jackson and Higginson, plan for a tenement house, 1773. Caleb Davis Papers, Massachusetts Historical Society, Boston. Courtesy of the Massachusetts Historical Society.

reported that when he returned to his rented residence in St. James's Square, London, on 22 June 1697, "I found ye joynor at work making a door out of my closet into ye garden." Four days later, he added that "ye mason came to put up a chimney piece in my closet," thus ensuring that it would comfortable year-round. In short order, the same closet was painted and fitted up with curtains. In 1719, Brydges, by then the duke, bought the largest house in St. James's Square from the disgraced Jacobite Duke of Ormond. In 1725, his principal closet there measured thirteen feet wide by eleven and one-half feet deep, or about 150 square feet (almost as large as Esther Burr's entire bedchamber). It had blue damask curtains and such furniture as "A large red japan'd bureo" and "A red japan'd card table wth doors and drawers and top lined wth green velvet." It also was decorated with "A chimney glass in a guilt frame"—perhaps better for the duke to admire himself in, as he slipped into "a large bathing tub and steps a great square copper over the same."[34] Merchants thus saw the closet as an opportunity for mixing the business of profit with the dense symbolism of distant metropolitan social advance. Theirs was an instrumental gentility.

With devotion to both profits and prophets, preparation for ritual purifications in both church and "bathing tub," and, for readers of *Pamela* and *Clarissa*, self-transformation all at stake in the "closet"—which is only at certain rare moments the specifically feminine gendered space Richardson exploited—and with so many different locations in the house, contents, and activities at stake as well, we must ask: do these places and occasions have in anything at all in common? Do these small, preparatory rooms implicate other closeted spaces? Perhaps here we encounter the full force of contingency, ambiguity, and those different understandings of an identical place that implication serves to link at the level of metaphor. Thus, to reduce the dense overlay of confined masculinist and open, epistolary feminist readings of the closet may be unnecessary. After all, the Duke of Chandos took a bath in his closet. Boston merchant Anthony Stoddard counted or prayed or stored sugar in his. Pamela and Clarissa used the closet to confine their hearts, while Sarah Prince and Esther Burr opened theirs up. One element common to these implicated spaces may be that in the protected, "private" space of the closet, preparations for public exchange took place—for commodities and social position (merchants), for one self in place of another (Pamela as she moves from a position of moral compromise to triumph in attaining gentle status), of this mortal life for an eternal one (ministers preparing for what they termed the "Great Exchange" of resurrection), and of moral calculus amid the collection of commodities as a possible disease (Brydges). Indeed, "preparation" is a word with multiple meanings in eighteenth-century closet culture; preparation as a process links the body (as in bathing and dressing), society (entertaining, intimate reception, personal retreat and exhaustion), and spirit (prayer, conversion, salvation).

As characters such as Pamela or Clarissa occupy these fictive spaces, however, they also find books in the household spaces they occupy. In Richardson's novels, reading happens continually, as in the cruel and then critically supportive reading aloud of Pamela's private letters by Mr. B, or the endless recitation of private correspondence by Clarissa. The place of reading in the construction of the social imaginary of an eighteenth-century household, however, figures more centrally in the domestic life mapped in Oliver Goldsmith's *The Vicar of Wakefield* (1766), a novel that Boston bookseller Robert Bell had for sale or auction in July 1770. One scene from the novel will suffice for many: Primrose objects to his wife's concern that reading (of the wrong kind) might be injurious to their daughter Olivia, who "is very well skilled in controversy."

> "Why, my dear, what controversy can she have read?" cried I. "It does not occur to me that I ever put such books into her hands: you certainly over-rate her merit." "Indeed, pappa," replied Olivia, "she does not. I have read a great deal of controversy. I have read the disputes between Thwackum and Square; the controversy between Robinson Crusoe and Friday the savage; and I am now employed in reading the controversy in Religious courtship."— "Very well," cried I, "that's a good girl, I find you perfectly qualified for making converts, and so go help your mother to make the gooseberry-pie."[35]

In books that Olivia reads in her bedchamber (the closet per se is not employed), there is hilarious commentary on the "controversies," with Goldsmith letting Olivia take a quick slap at Daniel Defoe even while the patriarch counters his daughter's voracious reading by having her assist her mother in preparing dessert, setting the stereotype of gendered labor into parodic high relief. The moral vision remains conservative, of course, since such "controversies" might distract Olivia—hence, Primrose's dark supposition concerning the commoditization of beauty itself. "'What signifies beauty, Mr. Thornhill?' he ponders, 'or what signifies all the virtue, and all the qualifications in the world, in this age of self-interest? It is not, what is she? but what has she? is all the cry.'"[36] The implied rebuttal to his supposition is in fact darker still: if Olivia does not possess the material commodities of attraction, another young woman will simply be substituted in her place in the local marriage market.

The dangers posed by dangerous books, especially novels that might distract pious young women like Olivia from living a virtuous life, were recognized in New England as well. The same critique of reading "useless books" was common especially in the houses of the Massachusetts clergy. Consider the effort undertaken by the Reverend Ebenezer Turrell of Medford to put together a fitting tribute to his deceased wife, Jane, "chiefly collected from her own Manuscripts." Her father, the Reverend Benjamin Colman, claims, "At *nine* or *ten* (if not before) she was able to write." In early 1722 (when she was thirteen years of age), Jane had an "awakening" and wrote to her father, "I often mourn the Loss of that *Time* I have spent in reading useless Books, which I am sensible had been better improv'd in working out my *Souls Salvation*." Her father replied that these are the "pangs" of the "New Birth. . . . You mourn the time spent in reading *useless Books*; you do well, I am glad you see the Emptiness and Folly of them: Mr. Turrell has a Library for you to be repairing to, let him put proper and profitable Books into your Hand." After she had put down "useless" reading, Jane Turrell wrote to her sister in 1727, "Oh, *My Dear*, let me beg of you not to spend any part of your precious Time in reading *Romances* or idle *Poems*, which tend only to raise false *Ideas* and impure Images in the mind, and leave a vile Tincture upon it."[37]

Reading spaces in eighteenth-century New England, then, cut into different levels of the relationship between word and thing. People inhabit houses that are in imaginatively completed through houses of fiction; the reading spaces in houses demand reading about spaces in novels in which reading happens. Material objects and narrative strategies are thus mutually constitutive; there are strings that tie things to texts, and then lash texts back onto and into things. One final instance of this narrative materiality or "languaged thingness" will suffice, this one a novelized parody of gendered fashion. In Lady Mary Walker's 1778 novel, *The Munster Village*, she comically describes the attempt by women to turn the tables of architectural control on their husbands: "A love of play, and building, are the characteristics of this age," Walker observes. "Our sex imitates the other as far as they can in the former—and having no *terra firma* for the latter, and not contented with the ancient custom of castle-building"—no doubt because of its moated, ruinous, and confining qualities—instead "erect fabrics on their heads three stories high. The rage of building is so great, that nothing can check their ardour in it, although it has been the ruin of many individuals; and there are at present (it is said) fifteen hundred uninhabited houses in the two parishes of St. Mary le-Bone and Pancras."[38] At the same time, women in the British North American colonies affected the same high-hair, "fabric on their heads" fashion. Just after the Battle of Bunker Hill in the summer of 1775, a print appeared that lampooned the catastrophic loss of Joseph Warren's militia. Entitled *Bunker Hill, or America's Headdress*, the image reprises the battle, this time with circles of tents, tottering figures, and, supporting the whole, the British navy firing from the harbor, showing that a woman could support a narrative of the lost encounter, perhaps, better than any veterans of the skirmish.[39]

This print is at once an object and a narrative; the narrative is objectified. Because it assumes agency in debates on fashion and politics, however, the print also is a narrative subject in its own right. In Esther Burr's precise readings of *Pamela*, she domesticates a circulating commodity so fully to her own being that the narrative is subjectified in a similar manner, which in turn becomes the necessary precondition for the epistolary novel that she and Sarah Prince are assembling from the fragments of fashion, faith, and family they live through. Yet these same qualities—especially that of seeing in one text or space a range of possible strategies for use—may also be wrenched across the line of gender labor and, in a shift of content and register, be a means of understanding the ways that men behaved in their closeted confinement, as always an appropriation of feminine tactic of relative autonomy. By exploring dimensions of reading spaces in eighteenth-century New England, we can begin charting the social imaginary of the everyday life they shaped. To be sure, gender is a key element, but it remains so as a frame with entirely contingent meanings. What may be a masculine space for one set of interactions may be appropriated as a feminine domain for another. Closets make this exchange visible, while confinement completes its emotional circuitry.

Thus, the existence of entirely distinct spheres of action for men and women may yield to a cultural cartography of places where regimes of male and female values came into sustained contact. As I have outlined in this essay, we may approach a gendered social imaginary more from the specific interpretive techniques appropriated in reading spaces than from the nominal content matter of reading per se. By emphasizing, in series, contingency, ambiguity, implication, and supposition, it is possible to imagine both reading and spaces as practices that shaped vernacular legitimacy in eighteenth-century New England society.

1. Suffolk County Probate Records, Massachusetts Archives, Boston (hereafter SCPR), 41:160–75 new pagination (hereafter np).
2. On Boston urban house forms, the interpretation of its experimental qualities, and the Webb house plan, see Robert Blair St. George, "Afterthoughts on Material Life in America, 1600–1860: Household Space in Boston, 1670–1730," *Winterthur Portfolio* 32, no. 1 (Spring 1997): 1–38.
3. SCPR, 42:155–64 np, taken 6 Feb. 1748/49, Total Estate Value (hereafter TEV): £6,095 5s. 6d.
4. Charles Taylor, *Modern Social Imaginaries* (Durham, NC: Duke Univ. Press, 2004), 23–24.
5. This emphasis on the techniques of reading an imaginary, by emphasizing semiotic processes, is distinct from the suggestion that "communities are to be distinguished, not by their falseness/genuineness, but by the *style* in which they are imagined"; Benedict Anderson, *Imagined Communities: Reflections on the Origin and Spread of Nationalism*, 2nd ed. (London: Verso, 1991), 6, emphasis added.
6. For photographs of individuals reading in a variety of poses that stress the complete portability of books and the radical decontextualization of reading, see Andre Kertesz, *On Reading* (New York: Penguin, 1982).
7. SCPR, 36:206–9 np (Clark); 35:176–80 np (Boydell); 57:272–75 np (Skinner); 39:497–505 np (Pemberton).
8. James Raven, "From Promotion to Proscription: Arrangements for Reading and Eighteenth-Century

Libraries," in *The Practice and Representation of Reading in England*, ed. James Raven, Helen Small, and Naomi Tadmor (Cambridge: Cambridge Univ. Press, 1996), 190.

9. SCPR, 35:306–7 np (Gray); 46:70 np (Bownd); 36:209–12 np (S. Bennett), TEV: £948 7s. 6d.; 46:456–73 np (M. Bennett), taken 11–14 Sept. 1751, TEV: £880 2s. 6d.

10. John Mein, *A Catalogue of Mein's Circulating Library* (Boston, 1765), 4–42, and Charles K. Bolton, "Circulating Libraries in Boston, 1765–1865," *Publications of the Colonial Society of Massachusetts* 11 (1906–7): 197–201. Mein's library may be viewed as part of the expansion of circulating libraries in the eighteenth century; see Hilda M. Hamlyn, "Eighteenth-Century Circulating Libraries in England," *The Library*, 5th ser., 1, nos. 3–4 (Dec. 1946–March 1947): 197–222, and Ian Fergus, "Eighteenth-Century Readers in Provincial England: The Customers of Samuel Clay's Circulating Library and Bookshop in Warwick, 1770–72," *Papers of the Bibliographic Society of America* 78, no. 2 (1984): 155–213. The southern Connecticut social library is discussed in Silvia Garrard Roberts Lowrey, "A History of Libraries in Madison (East Guilford), Connecticut" (MA thesis, no. 547, Southern Connecticut State Univ., April 1963); started in the mid-1730s, this local library had 222 titles in a list made in 1760. The Braintree library is suggested in the 1775 inventory of James Thayer, a Braintree blacksmith, which cites "His Right in a Library 12s." SCPR, 76:152 np, TEV: £755 6s. 8d. For additional material on the expansion of the book trade and publication in the English West Midlands to inform Fergus's study, see *Working Papers for an Historical Directory of the West Midlands Book Trade to 1850*, no. 1: to 1779, ed. P. B. Freshwater (Birmingham: Birmingham Bibliographic Society, 1975). See also Robert B. Winans, "The Growth of a Novel-Reading Public in Late Eighteenth-Century America," *Early American Literature* 9, no. 3 (Winter 1975): 267–75.

11. Mein, *Catalogue*, 4; "Benedict Arnold, Has Just Imported (via New-York) and sells at his Store in New Haven . . ." (New Haven, 1765), broadside.

12. Aaron Burr to Sarah Prince, 8 Feb. 1753, in *The Journal of Esther Edwards Burr, 1754–1757*, ed. Carol F. Karlsen and Laurie Crumpacker (New Haven and London: Yale Univ. Press, 1984), 279.

13. Sarah Prince to Aaron Burr, 27 March 1753, in Karlsen and Crumpacker, *Journal of Esther Burr*, 282.

14. Entries of 11 and 12 Nov. 1754, in Karlsen and Crumpacker, *Journal of Esther Burr*, 62.

15. Lady Bradshaigh, quoted in Charlotte Sussman, "Women's Private Reading and Political Action, 1649–1838," in *Radicalism in British Literary Culture, 1650–1830: From Revolution to Revolution*, ed. Timothy Morton and Nigel Smith (Cambridge and New York: Cambridge Univ. Press, 2002), 144.

16. Ian Watt, *The Rise of the Novel: Studies in Defoe, Richardson, and Fielding* (Berkeley: Univ. of California Press, 1957), 74–76, 84–85, and Cynthia Griffin Wolff, *Samuel Richardson and the Eighteenth-Century Puritan Character* (Hamden, CT: Archon Books, 1972), 58–73 (on *Pamela*), 74–173 (on *Clarissa*). See also Patricia Meyer Spacks, *Privacy: Concealing the Eighteenth-Century Self* (Chicago: Univ. of Chicago Press, 2003), 27–54, 115–39. This essay takes for granted the displacement of the "private reader" into distinct and multivalent reading and writing practices, some novel, many pervasively continuous with early techniques of orality.

17. SCPR, 46:456–73 np (M. Bennett); 46:4–13 np (Gookin), proved 11 Feb. 1752; 49:307–8 np (Maverick), proved 10 May 1754. Mein, *Catalogue*, 4; *A Catalogue of a very large assortment of the most esteemed Books in Every Branch of Polite Literature, arts and Sciences . . . which are to be sold by Cox & Berry at their store in King-Street, Boston* (Boston: Cox & Berry, 1772), 21.

18. Entry of 10 March 1755, in Karlsen and Crumpacker, *Journal of Esther Burr*, 98.

19. Entry of 11 March 1755, in Karlsen and Crumpacker, *Journal of Esther Burr*, 98.

20. Entry of 12 March 1755, in Karlsen and Crumpacker, *Journal of Esther Burr*, 99.

21. Entry of 8 April 1755, in Karlsen and Crumpacker, *Journal of Esther Burr*, 107.

22. Naomi Tadmor, "'In the even my wife read to me': Women, Reading, and Household Life in the Eighteenth Century," in Raven, Small, and Tadmor, *Practice and Representation of Reading in England*, 166–68.

23. Entries of 18 Nov. 1755, 22 Jan. 1756, and 11 Oct. 1754, in Karlsen and Crumpacker, *Journal of Esther Burr*, 167, 184, 53. See also Lucia Bergamasco, "Amitié, Amour et Spiritualité dans la Nouvelle-Angleterre du XVIIIe Siècle: L'expérience d'Esther Burr et de Sarah Prince," *Annales ESC* 41, no. 2 (March–April 1986): 295–323.

24. Entry of 1 Oct. 1754, in Karlsen and Crumpacker, *Journal of Esther Burr*, 52.
25. Samuel Richardson, *Pamela*, 1:138, quoted in Warren Harding Smith, *Architecture in English Fiction*, Yale Studies in English (New Haven: Yale Univ. Press, 1934), 43:65–66.
26. Richardson, *Pamela*, 1:240, 293.
27. *The Compact Edition of the Oxford English Dictionary*, 2 vols. (Oxford: Oxford Univ. Press, 1971), vol. 1 (A–O), C, 519; SCPR, 2:67–70 old pagination (hereafter op) (Cotton), proven in court 26 Jan. 1652.
28. SCPR, 3:111 np (Coggan), taken 20 July 1658; 13:32 np (Smith), taken 3 May 1692, TEV: £1159 15s. On Smith's house and its plan, see John Hutchins Cady, "Cocumscussoc," *Old-Time New England* 39, no. 3 (Jan. 1949): 61–70.
29. For the Royal Institute of British Architects citation, see http://www.greatbuildings.com/cgi-bin/rllk?http://www.greatbuildings.com/cgibin/riba_search.cgi?searchdata1=Robert+Smythson. SCPR, 5:178 op (Boyce).
30. Middlesex County Probate Records, Middlesex County Courthouse, East Cambridge, Massachusetts, 3:204, taken 9 Feb. 1668.
31. SCPR, 35:176–80 np (Boydell); 42:157 np (Cunningham).
32. Maurice Barley, *The English Farmhouse and Cottage* (London: Routledge and Kegan Paul, 1961), 231–32, 255, 272.
33. On small London houses and the James Moxon plan, see Peter Guillery, *The Small House in Eighteenth-Century London: A Social and Architectural History* (New Haven and London: Yale Univ. Press for the Paul Mellon Centre for Studies in British Art, 2004), 59 (fig. 41), 63 (fig. 44), 64–65. Contract for 1773 tenement house, Caleb Davis Papers, 1684–1826, Massachusetts Historical Society, Boston, MS no. N-1096. The use of closets next to chimneys is also clear in two eighteenth-century houses in Deerfield; see J. Ritchie Garrison, *Landscape and Material Life in Franklin County, Massachusetts, 1770–1860* (Knoxville: Univ. of Tennessee Press, 1991), 159, fig. 7:8 (Joseph Stebbins house, 1772), 164, fig. 7:13 (Thomas Williams house, 1748–75). See also the small closets next to the chimney stacks in the three-room Samuel Nicholson house, Elsinboro Township, Salem County, New Jersey, 1752, in *Everyday Architecture of the Mid-Atlantic: Looking at Buildings and Landscapes*, by Gabrielle Lanier and Bernard L. Herman (Baltimore: John Hopkins Univ. Press, 1997), 22 (fig. 2.7B).
34. The Huntington, Stowe Manuscripts, vol. 26 (vols. 1–2), James Brydges, 1st Duke of Chandos, Journal, 1697–1702; vol. 83, James Brydges, 1st Duke of Chandos, Inventories, 1725 inventory of Chandos House, St. James's Square. I am indebted to Hannah Greig for these references.
35. Oliver Goldsmith, *The Vicar of Wakefield*, ed. Stephen Coote (London, 1766; New York: Penguin, 1982), 62.
36. Goldsmith, *Vicar of Wakefield*, 101.
37. Ebenezer Turrell, *Memoirs on the Life and Death of the Pious and Ingeneous Mrs. Jane Turrell* [Boston, 1735], 62, 87, 95.
38. Lady Mary Walker, *The Munster Village*, 2 vols. (London, 1778), 2:106, quoted in Smith, *Architecture in English Fiction*, 48.
39. Kate Haulman, "A Short History of the High Roll," *Common-Place* 2, no. 1 (Oct. 2001), at: http://common-place.dreamhost.com//vol-02/no-01/lessons/index.shtmlhas.

"Enter into Thy Closet": Women, Closet Culture, and the Eighteenth-Century English Novel

Karen Lipsedge

Literary historians from Ian Watt to Christina Marsden Gillis concur that the novels of the mid-eighteenth-century English writer Samuel Richardson convey to the reader a clear impression of inhabited living spaces.[1] Rooms are not barren places, whose sole function is to provide an architectural backdrop for the action. Instead, rooms in Richardson's novels are represented as named sites, each with its own specific function and decorative style, as well as with a spatial atmosphere that is almost as tangible as the characters who occupy it.

So the immediate question that comes to mind is, where does the reader's "vivid sense of location" come from? It is not from a detailed account of the decorative style of the interior. "Sustained description, particularly where it relates to interiors, is extremely rare in Richardson's writing." Nor does it derive solely from the attention that Richardson pays to character and "the minutiae of emotions and attitudes."[2] Instead, as Francis Jeffrey describes in his 1804 account of Richardson's epistolary method, the reader's vivid impression of an inhabited living space is based on the degree to which Richardson engages the reader:

> With Richardson, we slip, invisible, into the domestic privacy of his characters, and hear and see every thing that is said and done amongst them, whether it be interesting or otherwise, and whether it gratify our curiosity or disappoint it. . . . We feel for [them] as for our private friends and acquaintances, with whose whole situation we are familiar.[3]

On reading Richardson's novels, then, the reader does not remain an outsider, or a bystander who observes the narrative from afar. Instead, he or she glides into the "domestic privacy" of Richardson's protagonists.

As Watt has observed, the term "domestic privacy" is significant. It does not refer just to the "private experience" of the characters, but also to their domestic interiors—that is, the houses in which they live and the ways in which they inhabit them.[4] The term also emphasizes a key constituent of Richardson's narrative method. In earlier forms of prose fiction, characters are depicted as "general human types" who act out conventional plots, in a nonspecific time and place.[5] During the course of the first half of the eighteenth century, however, attention began to shift from the "essentials" to the "accidental details."[6] Substantial detail is imparted not only about the characters—their sentiments, modes of behavior, and attire—but also about their homes. The two are intimately related, for unlike earlier types of prose fiction, by the mid-eighteenth century the novel had begun to situate characters firmly in domestic space.

It is the intimate relationship Richardson establishes between characters and domestic space in his novels that distinguishes him from his contemporaries. This does not mean we should overlook Daniel Defoe. As Watt notes, Defoe is undoubtedly one of the first British writers to "visualiz[e] the whole of his narrative, as though it occurred in an actual physical environment." The descriptions of milieu, particular objects, and aspects of architectural structure are vivid—but intermittent. Nevertheless, even this occasional attention to minute detail "supplements the continual implication of the narrative" and makes the reader attach characters such as Roxana and Crusoe "more completely to their setting."[7]

Yet the presence of emblematically concrete detail in Defoe's novels does not by itself enable the reader to "slip, invisible, into the domestic privacy of [the] characters." For a reader to have this level of intimate knowledge, the direction of the narrative also needs to be inward and subjective, focusing on the domestic life of the interior and the private experience of the characters inhabiting it. It is this "re-orientation of narrative perspective" that enables Richardson to construct connected visual interiors, in which both the architectural spaces and the objects within them have a psychological, social, and narrative importance.[8] Presented to the reader in a series of a letters, these connected interior spaces and the objects within them give the reader a greater understanding of the residents.[9] It is also this "re-orientation of narrative perspective" that distinguishes Richardson from Defoe. As Anna Laetitia Barbauld explained in 1804, although both Defoe and Richardson are "accurate describers, minute and circumstantial, the minuteness of Defoe was more employed about things, and that of Richardson about persons and things."[10]

What sets Richardson apart from contemporary novelists, therefore, is the amount of attention he devotes to "persons and things" and the relationship he establishes between them. Consequently, an understanding of what constitutes the characters' domestic privacy is essential for an appreciation of his novels, for the reader can have a full understanding of the protagonists only by knowing these interiors. Watt notes that "the delineation of the domestic life and the private experience of the characters who belong to it . . . go together—we get inside their minds as well as inside their houses."[11] To put it another way, it is only by entering their houses that we can penetrate their minds.

To further explicate how the reader penetrates a character's mind by entering into that character's domestic interior, along with what this means for Richardson's novels, this chapter focuses on Richardson's second novel, *Clarissa*, and on its representation of heroine Clarissa Harlowe's private closet. To highlight the relationship between the fictional and the "real," the chapter begins with an account of the social significance and function of the eighteenth-century private closet. Consideration of the location, function, the objects stored within it, and its increasing significance to women reveals why privacy and the freedom of access to a private room are so essential for Clarissa's survival in Harlowe Place, her ancestral country house. Furthermore, an assessment of the private closet's decorative style, use, and social significance also indicates why, contrary to current opinion, Clarissa's private closet does not remain a blank space. Instead, given access to it almost as frequently as Clarissa herself, the reader becomes as familiar with Clarissa as she is with her small, secluded, private room.

The first question that needs to be addressed is, what constituted the eighteenth-century private closet?

> But thou, when thou prayest, enter into thy closet, and when thou hast shut thy door, pray to thy Father which is in secret; and thy Father which seeth in secret shall reward thee openly.[12]

In the King James Version of the Bible, the term "closet" is employed to denote an inner sanctuary for the soul. Enclosed and separate, this sanctuary is represented as a secret, private room. In the above passage from Matthew, it is evident that privacy and enclosure are also a requisite for deliverance, since only the individual who prays in private is rewarded openly by God. Yet by the eighteenth century, privacy and enclosure were also conceived of as essential for the transformation of self. During this period, a secular idea—upheld by women in particular—of retreating into a private domestic closet enabled the woman to retreat into herself.

The secular notion of the private closet as a "workshop of the mind, a laboratory of the soul," was commonplace, as is supported by the increased provision of a private closet for young members of the family, servants, and, in particular, women.[13] The increased provision of private closets can, of course, also be explained with reference to the structural changes to the domestic interior. During the early eighteenth century, the function of the country house began to change. "No longer a place of work as it had been in the Middle Ages," it became a site of new forms of sociability.[14] Small groups of guests invited to "at homes" would arrive at intervals throughout the morning and afternoon for tea and polite conversation. Meanwhile, in the evening, more formal assemblies were held, during which guests would engage in one or two activities.

In the eighteenth century, however, the country house was not just a social place. It was also what Sir John Vanbrugh referred to as a "private Habitation": a home in which the owner and his family could enjoy time together.[15] The *Oxford English Dictionary* defines "privacy" as "the state or condition of being withdrawn from the society of others," and "privacies" as "private or retired places; private apartments; places of retreat."[16] The inhabitants' desire to have a private domestic space "withdrawn from others" did not begin in the eighteenth century, of course. As early as the late sixteenth century, and increasingly in the seventeenth century, writers on both architecture and conduct were articulating the growing demand for privacy and convenience within the domestic interior.[17] But the increased demand for domestic privacy from the seventeenth to the mid-eighteenth century was fueled by the changing shape of English Protestantism, "with its emphasis on private reading, introspection and thought."[18] Witold Rybczynski has observed that "the desire for a room of one's own was not simply a matter of personal privacy. It demonstrated the growing awareness of individuality—of a growing inner life—and the need to express this individuality in physical ways."[19]

Equally significant was the increase in leisure and literacy of women of the middling class in the early to mid-eighteenth century.[20] An increase in leisure time and an ability to read gave women more opportunity to pursue those pastimes that had previously been predominantly male activities, such as reading and writing letters. Since the private closet was the only truly private room in the domestic interior, it was the ideal place in which to perform these solitary and personal types of activity.

Naomi Tadmor has argued that during the eighteenth century, the practice of reading in the domestic interior was not always a solitary private experience; often it was also a sociable one.[21] Yet, as underlined by Robert Blair St. George's references, in his essay in this volume, to Esther Edwards Burr's private reading experiences, a private room of one's own that facilitated solitary reading and writing was a domestic possession highly cherished at this time, especially by women.[22] In a letter to Miss Westcombe, Samuel Richardson contrasts the social rooms, in which one is bombarded with "Goose-like Gabble-Gabble-Gabble," to her closet, which he writes is "the modest [Lady's] paradise."[23] The private closets that appear in Richardson's three novels often exemplify this idyllic quality: they are all separate, self-transformative spaces that enable the heroines to escape temporarily from their domestic environments into the secret, intimate world of their inner consciousness and their familiar letters.

Thus, the increased provision of private domestic closets in the early to mid-eighteenth century can be explained with reference to three key factors: structural changes to the domestic interior, the changing shape of English Protestantism, and the increase in leisure and literacy among women of the middling class. The combination of these factors resulted in the emergence of what J. Paul Hunter refers to as a "kind of closet culture," in which "the habits of privacy and solitude" became more widespread.[24]

By the first half of the eighteenth century, the middling-class interior was usually furnished with more than one type of closet. Yet, as Sir Roger Pratt makes clear in his architectural manual of 1660, it was only the principal bedchambers located upstairs (on the British first floor) that "must each of them have a closet" adjacent to them.[25] Furthermore, the upstairs closets alone were conceived of as truly private space. Naturally, the size of each private closet, the types of materials employed to decorate it, and the objects stored within it would have varied according to the social status of the occupant. The private closet belonging to a servant, for example, was often only a sparsely furnished "nook or loft."[26] Conversely, the one belonging to the owner of the house was usually a light closet, fronted by its own lockable door. If the closet was fronted by a sash door, then it was also likely to be provided with internally drawn curtain.[27] Meanwhile, the interior of this type of private closet was generally furnished with a small corner fireplace, a small window, and, perhaps most important, a writing desk and a standish (a stand for writing materials).

Regardless of differences in size and mode of decoration, all these private closets then shared the same quality: they were "owned" spaces, whose location away from the main domestic arena signified the right of each individual to have a separate, private place of his or her own. As Hunter observes, "However small or inauspicious, it was 'owned' by an individual, a space apart where the self was externalized, recognized, and certified."[28]

The notion of a personalized space, whose particular furnishings and decorative style should be as unique as the user's heart and soul, is exemplified by the small private closet constructed for the Countess of Dysart at Ham House, near Richmond in Surrey, in the 1670s.[29] Located at the end of the enfilade next to the large White Closet, a room for entertainment, the countess's private closet was not a room that announced its presence. Instead, secreted behind a "jib-door" and covered with a "white sarsnet . . . Curtaine," this small closet was a private and secluded room for more solitary, religious, and intellectual activities.[30] The decorative style of the furnishings and their location within the private closet further emphasized the room's sacred character, while also accentuating the differences between the private closet and the adjacent White Closet. For example, in one corner of her private closet there was a "scriptore and frame of walnut tree," as well as "two cases of Shelves for bookes, Japanned," where she kept her "Bible with ye book of Common Prayer."[31] Meanwhile, hanging on the wall in front of the scriptore (writing desk) were four pictures with gilded frames, each depicting religious themes. On this particular wall, the countess is also believed to have hung a number of family portraits, including a miniature portrait of her mother, "Catherine Bruce, Countess of Dysart, contained in an ebony case." According to the 1683 inventory, there were approximately nineteen other pictures in this private closet. Yet it was only the religious and sentimental pictures that the countess hung above her scriptore and around her cases of shelves for books. Gathered together in this one corner, these pictures would have accentuated the distinctly religious character of this part of her private closet.

As a wealthy woman who followed all the latest fashions, the Countess of Dysart had a private closet that was also furnished with a variety of exquisite articles of japanned and gilded furniture, some made especially for her, such as the "Japan'd backstooles with Cane bottomes."[32] But the luxurious nature of the fabrics and furnishings selected for the countess's private closet should not suggest that it was anything other than a truly private space. Nor should the amount of attention to decor imply that it could not be perceived as a sacred space. What was important was the types of objects and furnishings selected, as well as how they were arranged in the room. As Edward Wetenhall reiterates throughout his devotional manual, *Enter into thy Closet: Or, a Method and Order for Private Devotion,* even a private closet as opulent as that of the Countess of Dysart, if it is treated with reverence, "fitted up," and organized appropriately, can be "after a sort separate or sacred, a certain secret Chappel for my self." Once within the private closet, the individual, distracted by neither worldly objects nor "vain" company, can look "inwards"[33] and "converse" honestly with his or her "subtle heart."[34]

The individual's right to have a separate, private place of her own "appears to have been generally accepted by the early eighteenth century," as the number of manuals that were written exclusively for the owner of a private closet demonstrates.[35] Nevertheless, contemporary commentators also expressed concern about "misuses of private space and time," especially by the young and by women.[36] After all, as a room "where neither men's eye, nor ear can reach them,"[37] the private closet offered the individual a secret place of her own, in which she could "titillate [herself] with novels" and engage in clandestine romances.[38] The notion of the private closet as a "locus of liberation and licence" is often exploited by novelists of the period.[39] In Henry Fielding's *Tom Jones* (1749), for instance, the gamekeeper's daughter Molly Seagrim conceives of her "mock" closet in her "garret" (an "enclosed little hole" that she created by "nail[ing] up an old rug against the rafters of the house") as the best place to secrete philosopher Square.[40] In Frances Sheridan's *Memoirs of Miss Sidney Bidulph* (1761), while Sidney is staying at Mr. Ware's house, he assumes that he has the right to come into "a closet where I was reading, and there in the warmest manner declared him my lover." As Sidney recounts, the fact that the closet is in Mr. Ware's house does not mean he has the right to enter it without her permission. To do so, she tells Mr. Ware, is a "cruel insult."[41]

Thus, by the early eighteenth century, the private closet had assumed a dual identity: it was an external symbol of the individual's right to privacy and "a secret world . . . [protected] from adult scrutiny."[42] It is the way in which the private closet can be read as both secret world and external symbol, as well as the consequences of that dual identity, that Richardson explores in *Clarissa.*

Richardson represents the Harlowes as "relatively newly established . . . extensive landowners" who are desperate to display their status as "country gentlemen," and he encourages the reader to assume that they have "fitted up" their country house, Harlowe Place, in modish, polite English Palladian style.[43] Set almost exclusively within the boundary walls of Harlowe Place, most of the action in the first two volumes of *Clarissa* takes place in one of the four "rooms" that Clarissa owns. The two that receive the least attention are her external "rooms": her dairy house and her ivy summerhouse. It might seem curious to refer to these as rooms. Yet Samuel Johnson's *Dictionary* definition of the "summer-house" as "an apartment in [the] garden" indicates that at this time, these two garden buildings were conceived of as rooms "out-of-doors."[44]

Clarissa conceives of her ivy summerhouse, located in a secluded tranquil area at the back of the Harlowes' formal "Dutch" garden, as a relatively private place for working, reading, writing, and drawing, like her lesser parlor (251). Meanwhile, Clarissa's dairy house, situated on the estate bequeathed to her by her grandfather just prior to the start of the novel, has a dual function. Like her historical contemporaries, Clarissa uses her dairy house, which is "fitted up" to her own taste, as an intimate reception room. It is also a successful domestic enterprise that Clarissa runs almost single-handed (41). Both external "rooms" are architectural symbols of Clarissa's independence; in addition, the dairy house testifies to her dexterity and self-sufficiency. Located on an estate that the Harlowes regard as their property, meant for her brother, Clarissa's dairy house is also a public sign of her "flagrant disregard" of the Harlowes' "ideas of patriarchal possession."[45]

Not surprisingly, perhaps, it is the dairy house that is the first of Clarissa's architectural spaces to be repossessed by the other Harlowes. The loss of her dairy house is the first stage in their attempt to delimit her access to space and to reduce Clarissa to a "small compass" (96). But that loss also signals the start of her exclusion from the family. The Harlowes' desire to exclude Clarissa is reinforced by their subsequent repossession of her lesser parlor, an action that is combined with their banning Clarissa from her parents' presence and from the main communal areas: the ground floor and the parlors. Thus, by Letter 22, Clarissa—"shunned" like one of Defoe's plague victims "as a person infected" (116)—has only one "internal" room of her own: her private closet, which is adjacent to her bedchamber upstairs.

Despite the significance of her private closet, of all the architectural spaces referred to in the first two volumes of *Clarissa,* it is this small room that Richardson seems most reluctant to describe in detail. Unlike the dairy house and ivy summerhouse, there are not, for example, any helpful footnotes explaining the private closet's decorative style, or even its exact location. Interestingly, Richardson does not show a similar reluctance to describe the closets in his two other novels. In *Pamela,* for instance, he not only gives an account of the location and contents of Pamela's dressing room–cum–closet at the Bedfordshire estate, but also describes Mr. B's rather ornate closet, as well as Mrs. Jervis's closet in her chamber.[46] He pays an equal amount of attention to the closets in *Sir Charles Grandison.* For example, at Grandison Hall, Sir Charles has a closet for his curiosities that is decorated in a style similar to Horace Walpole's at Strawberry Hill. Meanwhile, for Clementina della Porretta, a devout Italian Catholic, her closet is a confessional space where she holds a "conference" with Sir Charles. As her melancholy begins to "lay hold of her heart," Clementina's closet is also the private space in which she most frequently "closete[s]" herself.[47]

Contrary to current opinion, however, Clarissa's private closet is not "invisible."[48] In fact, from the series of clues that Richardson scatters at intervals throughout the first two volumes of the novel, the reader is able to ascertain that the closet is located "up" stairs and can be reached from within her apartment. It also soon becomes apparent that Clarissa's closet is not an empty receptacle. As Anna Howe, her best friend, records in her account (after the heroine's death) of Clarissa's daily routine, "her first three morning hours," and any extra hours she might have, "were generally passed . . . in her closet-duties" (that is, her private study and prayer) and her "epistolary amusements" (1470). Richardson draws attention to the objects with which her closet, employed as a place for private study, devotion, and letter writing, is furnished: namely, her "escritoire," her "pens," "ink and paper," and her religious books, including Lewis Bayley's *Practice of Piety* and a *Thomas á Kempis* (561). It is also possible to determine the layout of Clarissa's private closet. In contrast to the manner in which "the Beauteous *Philautia*" organizes her "Dressing-room"–cum–"Chappel," Clarissa would not have her "Prayer-Book" lying next to her "Paint" in her private closet.[49] Instead, like the Countess of Dysart, those items that Clarissa uses to perform her "closet-work" would be set apart from her "worldly objects," in a space reserved for her religious duties.

Thus, despite a lack of detailed description, Clarissa's private closet does not remain a blank space. By revealing occasional snippets of information, in particular about how Clarissa uses and furnishes her private closet, Richardson makes it evident that its function and decorative style are similar to those of her "real" contemporaries. As the Harlowes become more determined to crush her will, it also becomes evident that her private closet serves as a built refuge, where she is protected from their physical and emotional torments and can regain her sense of self. Furthermore, Richardson's revelations about how Clarissa uses and furnishes her private closet enable the reader, from as early as Letter 4, to enter into this small private room, for these objects are not just functional items. As tools that Clarissa alone employs and, more importantly, as furniture that contain her letters—her recorded self—these objects are all symbols of Clarissa: "veritable organs of the secret psychological life."[50] It is in Letter 53 that the reader becomes fully aware of just how essential the private closet is for Clarissa's physical and psychological survival within Harlowe Place.

At this point in the novel, Clarissa—still refusing to marry the odious Mr. Solmes, her family's choice for a husband—has been ordered to "strictly . . . confine [herself] to [her] chamber." Meanwhile, the Harlowes constantly invade that chamber, transferring upstairs the battlefield that they created downstairs (197–99). In the final section of Letter 53, it is her sister Bella who storms into Clarissa's chamber. "All in a flame," Bella starts "tapping" and "beating" Clarissa (228). "Almost foaming with passion," Bella then turns her attention from Clarissa's body and her chamber to the downstairs domain, challenging Clarissa to inform their parents that she refuses to go to her uncle Anthony's "moated house." Initially, Clarissa intends to take up her sister's "invitation," and so, eager to have direct communication with her parents, she "[posts] towards the stairs." But as soon as Bella reminds her sister of the reality of the downstairs—that is, the presence of her brother—Clarissa "[shrinks] back" from the chamber door, the stairs, the ground floor, and her family, silently retiring to her private closet (229). She knows that despite the presence of her parents, she will suffer the same persecution from her brother James downstairs that she is currently enduring from her sister upstairs. "Attacked within her own chamber," Clarissa's only option "is to move further within, towards her" closet: her one safe place.[51]

Although Clarissa's retreat to her private closet prevents her from having direct contact with her parents, I would suggest that it does not signify her defeat. Instead, her withdrawal to her private closet signals her awareness that this little room is her own safe place in which, removed from all of the Harlowes, she can be protected from unwanted invaders. Clarissa's flight inward, toward her private closet, is therefore the most logical—almost natural—solution.

> Why don't you go! Why don't you go, miss—following me to my closet, whither I retired with my heart full, and pulled the sash-door after me; and could no longer hold in my tears.
>
> Nor would I answer one word to her repeated aggravations and demands upon me to open my door (for the key was on the inside) nor so much as turn my head towards her, as she looked through the glass at me. And at last, which vexed her to the heart, I drew the silk curtain that she should not see me, and down she went, muttering all the way. (228–29)

On closing her door, Clarissa is securely removed from her chamber and Bella's uncontrolled passion. She is now enframed within her own private, clearly demarcated architectural space and is finally able to release her tears. However, this preliminary image of Clarissa, seated weeping in her closed private closet, does not form the focus of this closet description. Enclosed within her own room, this is the first time that instead of being excluded, Clarissa has become the excluder.

Thus, after only a momentary pause, Clarissa—as if suddenly acknowledging this novel inversion of their roles—turns her attention to Bella and starts to taunt her with relish. Observing that "the key was on the inside," she begins by locking her closet door. She then turns her head away from Bella, reinforcing her intention to neither go downstairs "nor . . . answer one word to her repeated aggravations and demands upon me to open my door." By locking her private closet door, Clarissa is both physically excluding Bella and flaunting her ability to possess, control, and mediate her own space, despite the Harlowes.

Clarissa's self-control over her private closet is immediately reinforced when she draws the "silk curtain." Frustrated, but nonetheless still determined to find a way in which to invade Clarissa's private closet, Bella begins to look through the sash door's uncovered glass. Yet, as adept at the game of closet irritation as Bella is at "scolding-bouts," Clarissa merely turns her head and, with calm precision, "drew the silk curtain so that she should not see me" (192). As previously indicated, the presence of a curtain to cover a closet's sash door was relatively commonplace. The color and length of the curtain often varied, but its function was always the same: to obscure what was taking place within the closet. Like the door key, the curtain served as a barrier, reinforcing the notion of the closet as a secret private place, belonging to one person alone.

Once Clarissa has drawn the curtain, Bella, defeated and "vexed . . . to the heart," finally leaves Clarissa, her closet, and her chamber; humiliated, she returns downstairs, "muttering all the way." As for Clarissa, completely cocooned as if in her own miniature "moated house," she can barely contain her sense of glee. It is this image of empowerment and triumph, rather than of loss and suffering, that concludes the description of the private closet.

Thus far, this chapter has focused on the physical and psychological protection that Clarissa's private closet proffers her. Yet one also needs to consider the private closet's functional properties, as a room in which Clarissa performs her "closet-duties" and her letter writing. As critics such as Cynthia Griffin Wolff have noted, Clarissa's letters, like the spiritual diaries belonging to her Puritan ancestors, provide her with an honest account of her life, her spiritual and emotional state.[52] But while acknowledging the parallel between Clarissa's letters and the spiritual diaries belonging to her Puritan ancestors, it is important to remember that these are not diary entries and Clarissa is not a diarist. She is a correspondent. "Confined like a prisoner to narrow and disgraceful limits" as she is, Clarissa's ability to correspond with Anna Howe—her friend, her "sister" (55)—is central to her survival within Harlowe Place. By being able to "convers[e] with . . . [Anna]—by *letter*, when [she] cannot in *person*" and share the secrets of her heart, Clarissa is able, even if only metaphorically, to transgress the architectural boundaries that divide them, and to invite Anna—and, with her, the reader—into her private closet (53). Thus, unlike the spiritual diary keeper or her fictional predecessor Pamela, who by writing for themselves are marked by their "spatial and temporal isolation," Clarissa, the correspondent, is not alone.[53]

Yet accepting that Clarissa's letters are a means of communication with the world outside Harlowe Place, as well as a tool for self-knowledge and self-preservation, means conceding that in order to provide an accurate image of her private closet, one also needs to consider it in relation to the Harlowes. As a room in which she discovers spiritual, psychological, and, via her letters to Anna, physical liberation, Clarissa's private closet is a sacred place. But it is not the private closet's religious function that concerns the Harlowes. Instead, the activity within it that causes the Harlowes the most concern is the correspondence that Clarissa continues with Lovelace, despite her family's ban on all letter writing, in Letter 24.

Curiously, the Harlowes do not make the connection between Clarissa's private closet and her secret letter writing until the end of volume 2. This is not to suggest that they are unaware of the "pen and ink" that she stores within her closet, or of her passion for letter writing. With her physically confined to the peripheries of the house like an "alien" or a "slave" (281), however, the Harlowes are convinced that they have successfully severed all of Clarissa's modes of communication and hence the source of her power. But in Letter 78, after the failure of the courtship scene between Clarissa and Mr. Solmes, the focus of the Harlowes' attention suddenly shifts from the exterior, and the routes that the completed letter takes, toward the domestic interior and the locus in which the letters are created—that is, Clarissa's private closet. At this point, her closet assumes a dual quality: it becomes an external symbol of Clarissa's defiance and the source of her power. It is also at this point that the Harlowes realize the only way to eradicate the power with which the private closet imbues her is to invade and destroy it. Their aim now is to violate Clarissa's privacy and tear her physically from her literary projects.

The Harlowes' first invasion of Clarissa's closet takes place immediately after the courtship scene. During this "closet searching," she is forced to remain within the lesser parlor (313). Finally let back inside her chamber, Clarissa discovers the extent of the Harlowes' search. They have not restricted themselves to her closet alone but have searched all of her chamber. Everything has been exposed: her books have been rifled through, and her clothes have been unfolded. Where order and coherence once reigned, the Harlowes have introduced confusion and disarray.

As obsessive in their "strange searching" and their looting and pillaging as the Harlowes are in their "baiting" and tormenting, this new activity becomes a daily, sometimes twice-daily, occurrence; it even replaces their weekly church visit (362). Warned that her "pen and ink . . . would not be long in [her] power," Clarissa "instantly [deposits] . . . some in her ivy summerhouse" (320). But the knowledge that she has "managed to get away some of her papers" (319), and that she still has access to her own "private pen" (341), ink, and a few sheets of paper, does not eradicate the extreme emotional pain that Clarissa suffers as her private closet is invaded and defiled. As everything within the closet is part of her being, she knows that each of these losses will result in the reduction of self. Thus, as Clarissa is "stripped" of her "heaps and stores," she is rendered vulnerable and exposed (322). Furthermore, as her private closet, like the house itself, becomes a "topsy-turvy" place, Clarissa becomes "disordered"; she writes to Anna:

> All is in a hurry below-stairs. Betty is in and out like a spy. Something is working, I know not what. I am really a good deal disordered in body as well as mind. Indeed I am quite heart-sick! (328)

This disturbing image of a young woman being physically and mentally crushed by the weight of her family's cruelty evokes the intimate relationship that Richardson establishes between domestic rooms and the body. He uses the domestic interior, and in this particular instance the private closet, as a reflection of the state of Clarissa's mind and body. The "confusion" and physical disorder in the quotation above underline that her private closet is more than just a writing place. Clarissa's access to her private closet, as a small, separate room in which she discovers spiritual, psychological, and physical liberation, is the means by which she manages to survive both her "confinement" and the relentless cruelty that she suffers. Thus, an assault on her private closet is an assault on her as well.

It is not surprising that of all the domestic rooms referred to in both *Clarissa* and the earlier *Pamela*, it is the private closet that is represented as the most valuable one to the two heroines. In *Sir Charles Grandison*, his final novel, Richardson also underlines the significance of the private closet's value to the two women Grandison contemplates marrying: Harriet Byron and Clementina della Porretta. By the end of Richardson's first and last novels, however, none of the closets referred to are represented as exclusive sites for one member of the family alone. Instead, they are all depicted as places that can be shared with others. For example, Grandison, aware that Harriet Byron is concerned she will have to sacrifice her privacy and her identity once she marries him, presents her with her own private closet. Harriet repays him for his sensitivity and his understanding by "compliment[ing] him with a place in my closet."[54] Conversely, in *Clarissa*, an individual's right to privacy and to her own identity is constantly challenged. At the Harlowes' estate, rooms are not just perceived of as architectural spaces. They are also possessions: valuable objects that the "principals" bestow on and withdraw from members of the family, in proportion to the level of those members' duty and obedience.

By failing to marry Mr. Solmes, Clarissa has lost her right to a room of her own. Dispossessed of her dairy house, her lesser parlor, and her private closet, she learns that nowhere within the Harlowes' house is inviolable; no room is sacred. Even her "isolated" ivy summerhouse, located at the back of the formal garden, quickly transforms from a place of refuge to a place of danger. At the end of volume 2, Clarissa is forced to take "the rash step" of leaving "her father's house" with her suitor Lovelace (365).

It is no coincidence that Clarissa returns to Harlowe Place in a coffin. In fact, Clarissa's coffin is her ultimate closet. Beautifully "fitted up" in her own taste, her coffin—what she refers to as her "palace" and her "house"—is an external symbol of its owner (1306, 1273). Placed inside her coffin on top of a table in the center of her lesser parlor, with her family gathered around her, Clarissa has finally resumed her position in the heart of Harlowe Place. Eternally protected, she has gained "spiritual and spatial" triumph.[55] She now has complete control not only over her own self, but over Lovelace and the Harlowes as well. But in her spiritual and spatial triumph, Clarissa is alone. Unable to bear the anguish of looking at her coffin, each member of her family hurriedly walks away from both it and her lesser parlor. This image of each of the Harlowes fleeing from Clarissa's coffin underlines the function of domestic rooms in Richardson's novels.

In all three of his novels, Richardson uses the private closet to highlight each of the heroines' need for an architectural place of her own, as well as for a family who respects their daughter's right to it. Retreating into the private closet is a necessary, devotional act. For Clarissa, retreating into her private closet is also the only way for her to maintain her inner self: her soul. By employing an inward and subjective narrative, which focuses on both the domestic life of the interior and the private experience of the characters inhabiting it, Richardson enables the reader to "slip invisible" into the most private of spaces—that is, Clarissa's private closet. Once inside, the reader has unlimited access to her private letters and to her soul.

1. See Ian Watt, *The Rise of the Novel: Studies in Defoe, Richardson, and Fielding* (London: Chatto & Windus, 1987), and Christina Marsden Gillis, *The Paradox of Privacy: Epistolary Form in "Clarissa"* (Gainesville: Univ. Press of Florida, 1984). Richardson published three novels, all hugely successful: *Pamela* (1740), *Clarissa* (1747–48), and *Sir Charles Grandison* (1753–54). For the editions used for this essay, see notes 27, 46, and 47.
2. Philippa Tristram, *Living Space in Fact and Fiction* (London: Routledge, 1989), 229.
3. Francis Jeffrey, "Edinburgh Review" (Oct. 1804), in *Contributions to the Edinburgh Review*, ed. Francis Jeffrey, 4 vols. (London: Longman, Brown, Green and Longmans, 1844), 1:321–22.
4. Watt, *Rise of the Novel*, 175.
5. Watt, *Rise of the Novel*, 15.
6. Cynthia Wall, "A Geography of Georgian Narrative Space," in *Georgian Geographies: Essays on Space, Place and Landscape in the Eighteenth Century*, ed. Miles Ogborn and Charles W. J. Withers (Manchester: Manchester Univ. Press, 2004), 115.
7. Watt, *Rise of the Novel*, 26. Defoe's *Robinson Crusoe* was first published in 1719 and his *Roxana* in 1724.
8. Watt, *Rise of the Novel*, 175.
9. Wall, "Geography of Georgian Narrative Space," 115–17.
10. Anna Laetitia Barbauld, "Life," prefixed to *Correspondence of Samuel Richardson* (London: Richard Phillips, 1804), 1:xx, in Watt, *Rise of the Novel*, 175–76.
11. Watt, *Rise of the Novel*, 175.
12. Matthew 6:6.
13. E. J. Clery, *The Feminization Debate in Eighteenth-Century England: Literature, Commerce and Luxury* (London: Palgrave Macmillan, 2004), 136.
14. Charles Saumarez Smith, *Eighteenth-Century Decoration: Design and the Domestic Interior in England* (London: Weidenfeld and Nicholson, 1993), 83.
15. G. Webb and B. Dobrée, eds., *The Complete Works of Sir John Vanbrugh*, 4 vols. (London: Nonesuch Press, 1928), 4:45.
16. As Jennifer D. Melville indicates, the terms "privacy," "privacies," and "private" were interchangeable with the words "separateness" and "secrecy" in late-seventeenth-century inventories. See Jennifer D. Melville, "The Use and Organisation of Domestic Space in Late Seventeenth-Century London" (PhD diss., Univ. of Cambridge, 1999), 148–49.
17. See John Bold, "Privacy and the Plan," in *English Architecture Public and Private: Essays for Kerry Downes*, ed. John Bold and Edward Chaney (London: Hambledon, 1993), 108–9. See also R. T. Gunther, ed., *The Architecture of Sir Roger Pratt* (Oxford: Printed by J. Johnson for the author at the Univ. Press, 1928), 27–28.
18. Naomi Tadmor, "'In the even my wife read to me': Women, Reading, and Household Life in the Eighteenth Century," in *The Practice and Representation of Reading in England*, ed. James Raven, Helen Small, and Naomi Tadmor (Cambridge: Cambridge Univ. Press, 1996), 163.
19. Witold Rybczynski, *Home: A Short History of an Idea* (London: Heinemann, 1988), 110.
20. Watt, *Rise of the Novel*, 189.

21. Tadmor, "'In the even my wife read to me,'" 162–74.

22. For examples of Esther's experiences in reading *Pamela* and *Clarissa,* see Carol F. Karlsen and Laurie Crumpacker, eds., *The Journal of Esther Edwards Burr, 1754–1757* (New Haven and London: Yale Univ. Press, 1984), 98–102, 105–8.

23. Samuel Richardson to Sophia Westcombe, 15 Sept. 1746, in *Selected Letters of Samuel Richardson,* ed. John Carroll (Oxford: Clarendon Press, 1964), 68.

24. John Paul Hunter, *Before Novels: The Cultural Contexts of Eighteenth-Century English Fiction* (New York and London: W. W. Norton, 1990), 157.

25. Gunther, *Architecture of Sir Roger Pratt,* 27.

26. In view of the closet size of her "real" contemporaries, the fictional Pamela's provision of what she refers to as "*my* closet in Mr B's Lincolnshire house" is highly significant. It is an architectural reflector of her transitional state from maid to mistress.

27. As "light closet" suggests, this is another name for a closet that was provided with a window and "was agreeable to inhabit." Dan Cruickshank and Neil Burton, *Life in the Georgian City* (London: Viking, 1990), 59. For details of Clarissa's "light" and "dark closets" adjacent to her bedroom at Mrs. Sinclair's house, see Samuel Richardson, *Clarissa; or, The History of a Young Lady,* ed. Angus Ross (Harmondsworth, UK: Penguin, 1985), 470, 676. Ross's text follows that of the first edition, 7 vols. (1747–48). Unless otherwise indicated, all of my quotations from *Clarissa* refer to Ross's edition, and page references appear parenthetically in the main body of the text.

28. Hunter, *Before Novels,* 157.

29. Unlike most contemporary closets, the countess's private closet was not located upstairs close to her bedchamber, but downstairs next to the duke's bedroom. For a detailed explanation of the reason this curious arrangement existed at Ham House, see Peter Thornton and Maurice Tomlin, "The Furniture and Decoration of Ham House," *Furniture History* 16 (1980): 36.

30. Thornton and Tomlin, "Ham House," 80, inventory of 1679.

31. Thornton and Tomlin, "Ham House," 84, inventories of 1679 and 1684; 85, inventory of 1677.

32. Thornton and Tomlin, "Ham House," 83, inventory of 1683.

33. Edward Wetenhall, *Enter into thy Closet: Or, a Method and Order for Private Devotion* (London: John Martyn, 1676), 12, 56.

34. "Meditations," appended to Elizabeth Mascall, *Remnants of Life: With Letters of Her Relatives and Friends,* ed. A. W. Matthews (London: Printed by the author, 1902), no page reference given, in Gillis, *Paradox of Privacy,* 41.

35. John Paul Hunter, "The World as Stage and Closet," in *British Theatre and the Other Arts, 1660–1800,* ed. Shirley Strum Kenny (London: Associated Univ. Presses, 1984), 282.

36. Hunter, "World as Stage and Closet," 282.

37. Wetenhall, *Enter into thy Closet,* 12.

38. Hunter, "World as Stage and Closet," 282.

39. Watt, *Rise of the Novel,* 187.

40. Henry Fielding, *Tom Jones,* ed. John Bender and Simon Stern (Oxford: Oxford Univ. Press, 1996), 197–98.

41. Frances Sheridan, *Memoirs of Miss Sidney Bidulph,* ed. Patricia Koster (Oxford and New York: Oxford Univ. Press 1995), 398–99.

42. Hunter, *Before Novels,* 158.

43. Angus Ross, introduction to Richardson, *Clarissa,* 20–22.

44. Samuel Johnson, *A Dictionary of English Language . . .* (London: Printed by W. Strahan, for J. and P. Knapton [etc.], 1755).

45. Cynthia Wall, "Gendering Rooms: Domestic Architecture and Literary Acts," *Eighteenth-Century Fiction* 5 (1993): 361.

46. Richardson, *Pamela; or, Virtue Rewarded* (London: J. M. Dent, 1914), 1:22, 65, 70.

47. Richardson, *The History of Sir Charles Grandison,* ed. Jocelyn Harris (Oxford: Oxford Univ. Press, 1986), 2:249, 125.

48. Gillis, *Paradox of Privacy*, 28.

49. *Spectator*, no. 79, 31 May 1711, in *The Spectator*, ed. Donald F. Bond, 5 vols. (Oxford: Clarendon Press, 1965), 1:340.

50. Gaston Bachelard, *The Poetics of Space*, trans. Maria Jolas (Boston: Beacon Press, 1994), 78.

51. Gillis, *Paradox of Privacy*, 34.

52. Cynthia Griffin Wolff, *Samuel Richardson and the Eighteenth-Century Puritan Character* (Hamden, CT: Archon Books, 1972), 17, 32.

53. Gillis, *Paradox of Privacy*, 122.

54. Richardson, *Sir Charles Grandison*, 7:270, 311. See also *Pamela*, 1:323.

55. Wall, "Gendering Rooms," 362.

Shopping

Collaborative Consumption and the Politics of Choice in Early American Port Cities

Ellen Hartigan-O'Connor

IN 1824, Ann Eleanor Vanrhyn, a shopkeeper in Charleston, South Carolina, tried one last time to collect on a long-unpaid debt. The defendant in her lawsuit, Christian Breithaupt, was married to a former customer of Vanrhyn's from the turn of the century. Under the law of coverture, Breithaupt was liable for his wife's debts. The problem for Vanrhyn was that at the time of her purchases, Mrs. Breithaupt had been married to a Colonel Senf, and it was to this (now-dead) man's name that the goods were charged. As was typical in a suit over book debt, Vanrhyn copied Colonel Senf's accounts out of her daybook for the court. But she added a notation system that classified each purchase as

> got by & for Mrs. Senf herself
> Delivered to Col. Senf for Mrs. Senf
> got by and for Col. Senf himself[1]

Her unusual annotations of the account suggest her thoughts about shopping, material life, and gender. Most clearly, she felt that being in the store and making purchasing decisions conferred economic responsibility on Mrs. Senf. Although the account was under the colonel's name, Mrs. Senf made 71 out of 118 separate shopping trips; by Vanrhyn's reckoning, Mrs. Senf was directly responsible for half of the debt. Her classification of the colonel's purchases reveals that Vanrhyn considered certain kinds of objects to be ultimately within Mrs. Senf's purview. Colonel Senf's cigars and epaulets were easily categorized as "for" him. But when the colonel collected spices, groceries, or tableware, Vanrhyn marked them as really "for" Mrs. Senf and, knowing or guessing that she had chosen and would use these goods, expected her to pay for them. Dissatisfied with the legal system's understanding of economic responsibility, the shopkeeper tried to give female agency and management of goods their due.

Vanrhyn's account alerts us to a central fact of shopping in eighteenth-century America and Britain—that it was conducted very often by proxy.[2] The extensive involvement of disparate proxies meant that acquiring goods depended on networks of individuals. Not only did husbands collect goods for wives and vice versa, but all manner of local and far-flung contacts were pressed into service. Servants and slaves selected fabric for their mistresses; cousins in distant cities hunted down books and apples. Once the selection had been made, payment was likewise arranged through economic networks. Women bought tea and charged it to a neighbor's account. Brothers used the credit established through a sister's spinning to pay for their tobacco. Finally, delivery was embedded in a mixed context of gifts, loans, and favors. In a red trunk that the slave Jack carried from Charlestonian Eliza Pinckney to her daughter, Pinckney reported, "is limes, 2 Osnaberg aprons, and your Pavalions, with some book musling which Tom will be obliged to you to have made into C[ollar] Bands."[3] Far from representing the ultimate in economic individuality, then, shopping was a collaborative act that depended on shared knowledge.

Scholars have recognized shopping as "social" in various senses of the word, but the significance of collaboration and mediation has received less attention.[4] Historians of colonial North America have focused on the social meanings of goods acquired through shopping. Owning similar objects, they argue, helped create a social and even political "sensus communis" among consumers with shared tastes.[5] Although they disagree about whether the connections forged by owning the same teacup ultimately unified or divided the American colonies along class lines, scholars have focused on illuminating an object-based "language of goods," further promoted by a flourishing print culture that fostered emulation.[6] If ownership of goods has been presented as social and frequently emulative, shopping for goods has been characterized in recent studies as transformingly individualistic. Faced with more goods and greater variety, Richard Bushman and Timothy Breen have argued, American consumers in the late eighteenth century gained unprecedented economic and psychological confidence. The previously subordinate could assert their own opinions and needs in the shop and on the street, encouraged by the "strikingly egalitarian" nature of a market in which "anyone with money could purchase what he or she desired."[7]

In the eighteenth and early nineteenth centuries, however, even "having money" for purchases depended on the goodwill and cooperative involvement of others, a fact that challenges both emulation and individualism as consumer paradigms. Choice took place in a context of collaboration, which could be creative or oppressive, as it incorporated individuals of strikingly different economic and social standing. We still know very little about the effect of this context on choice. Who participated in shopping networks, and on what terms? Did collaboration expand or constrain people's material lives? Whose preferences mattered when intermediaries were sent to make selections, and how did the "language of goods" mutate in the process? Scholars of eighteenth-century English credit practices have demonstrated the importance of dependent relationships and social intermediaries to an emerging commercial economy. They argue that these credit relationships, in turn, shaped popular ideas about human character and autonomy.[8] Eighteenth-century shopping also existed through dependent ties. In the real activities of intermediaries and collaborators, egalitarianism plays little part; instead, the inflection of consumer knowledge through ideas about fashion, identity, gender, class, and economy shaped material life.

One relationship not documented in Vanrhyn's account is that between mistress and slave, although families like the Senfs frequently used enslaved people to evaluate and obtain goods at local stores and marketplaces. In the 1790s, when the Senf debt was first contracted, an enslaved proxy would have caused little comment. But in 1824, white Charlestonians could no longer overlook the perils of entrusting an enslaved person with money and mobility. Two years earlier, the arrest, trial, and execution of former Charleston slave Denmark Vesey and his followers for an alleged conspiracy exposed just these dangers; many of the accused had acted as proxies in the stores and workshops of Charleston.[9] Looking at shopping through the lens of collaboration shows us the poor and enslaved as people who created credit through their work, took economic license, and parlayed errands into matters of life and death. The Vesey case highlights what was at stake in enlisting the labor of dependents to acquire goods. It also reminds us how local experience shaped the boundaries of trust for intermediaries, debtors, and all kinds of collaborators. By considering collaborative shopping practices in the port cities of Newport, Rhode Island, and Charleston, South Carolina, we can see how these dangers were managed.

WHOSE MONEY? THE ECONOMICS OF CHOICE

Vanrhyn's accounting experiment addressed a problem that still vexes historians: in a market of credit, coverture, and collaboration, whom do we hold responsible for economic decisions? Obtaining goods in this period was rarely a simple matter of an independent shopper making a choice and handing over cash. Although merchants and shopkeepers of all kinds craved cash payments and were willing to offer discounts to secure them, most purchases in the eighteenth century were made on credit, and a credit-based system fundamentally shaped what it meant to shop, from the merchants who first imported the goods, across the distribution system, to the person who brought them home. A minority of the overall population had the independence, financial reputation, and wealth to obtain accounts of their own. They paid for the privilege with anxious vigilance over their public credit or suffered the consequences.[10] For the rest, mediated access to credit—through a husband, neighbor, or master—was the rule. As Vanrhyn recognized in her ultimately unsuccessful attempt to get the Senfs to pay their bills, the financial power behind a shopper's selection was often not directly in the hands of the person across the store counter.

To understand the relationship between economic power and consumer choice, it is important to untangle the diverse transactions falling under the category of third-party credit. There were two sorts of shoppers exercising mediated access to credit in urban shops. The first were proxies, who selected goods at the request of someone else. Proxies could be kin, friends, or servants—anyone with the time and access to goods. The second sort of shopper was choosing for herself but drawing on someone else's credit to pay for her purchases. In each case, credit relationships shaped the degree of autonomy and the parameters of choice for the individuals who went to the shops. While proxies were constrained by the desires of the individual who requested the item, credit users had to answer only for the cost.

Accounts from Newport shopkeeper Sarah Rumreil's customers of the 1760s suggest how the financial power of shared credit was allocated. For example, more than ten people purchased or received goods on Captain Peter Simon's account, including slaves, family members, and townswomen.[11] The Simon household delegated shopping tasks to proxies based on the size and importance of the purchase. When Mrs. Simon needed handkerchiefs or pins, she sent one of her servants, slaves, or children. But when she wanted twenty-six yards of Holland cloth, she went to the store herself to ensure that the quality was worth £130. Her purchases were marked by higher-quality goods and high overall price. With rare exceptions, the Simon family sent slaves and servants to make regular, low-value purchases and reserved larger purchases of finer articles to the mistress of the house. Their shopping patterns suggest that proxies were useful for general provisioning, but certain classes of expensive goods required the direct involvement of the mistress of the house because their selection was more financially significant. Since fine fabrics were most often used for clothing, it was also culturally important to make the "right" choice (fig. 26).

Other families delegated shopping tasks more freely to their slaves and their children. Robert Crooke's account with Rumreil demonstrates a broader credit network that enabled more than twenty individuals to receive goods charged to him.[12] Crooke and his daughter came to the store from time to time, but two of his enslaved workers, "Caty," and "Sayer," did most of the household shopping, and one or the other usually visited the shop several times each month, as Rumreil's notes "dld Caty" and "pr. Sayer" indicate. Caty and Sayer were entrusted with

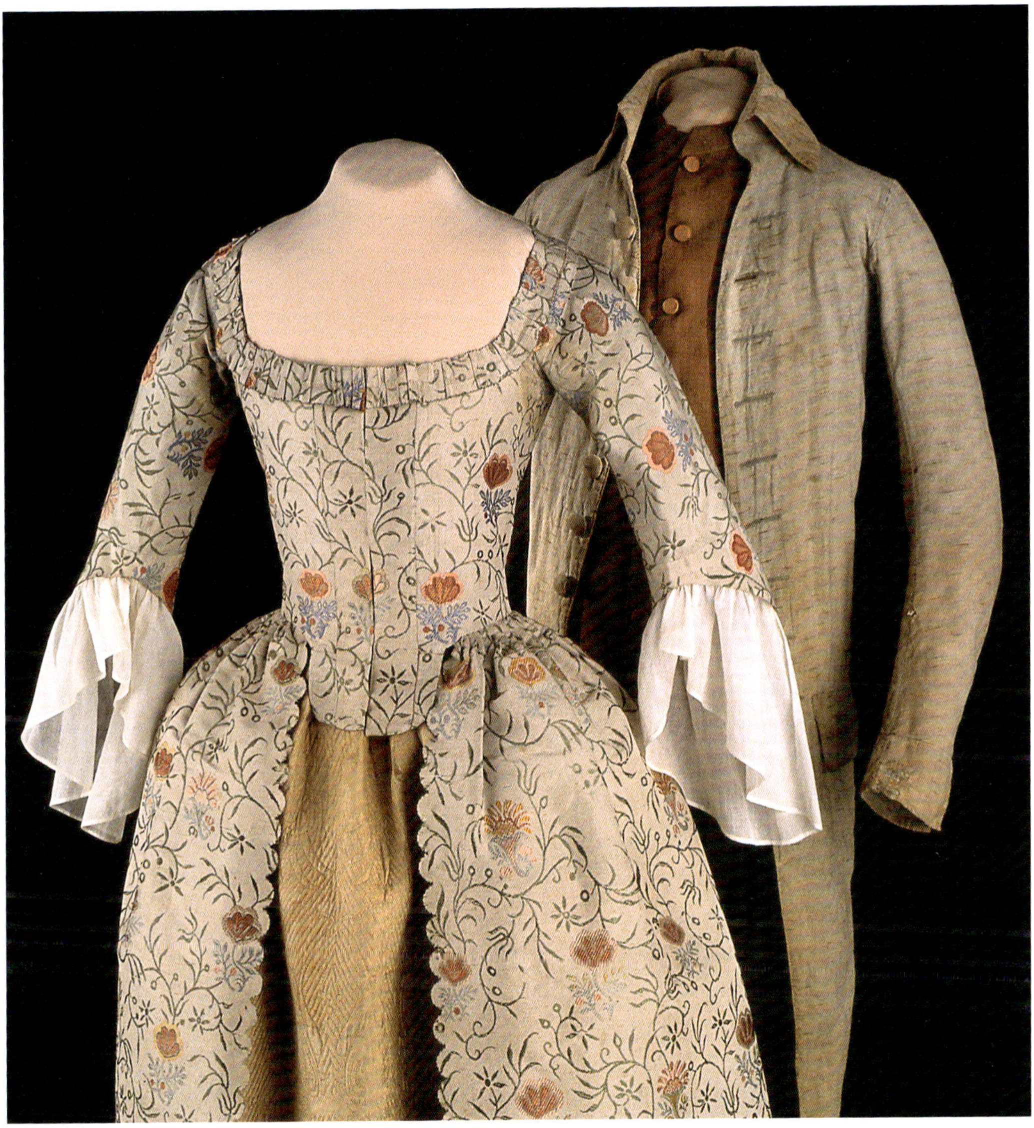

26. Brocaded silk gown, Spitalfields, England, textile, worn in Rhode Island, 1726–28, remade c. 1775, silk brocaded with silk (sleeve ruffles are twentieth-century reproductions), Colonial Williamsburg Costume Collection, 1951-150, 1; petticoat, Rhode Island, c. 1750, silk quilted on wool backing, Colonial Williamsburg Costume Collection, 1951-150, 2; coat, Virginia, c. 1780, homespun and cotton mixed with wool, Colonial Williamsburg Costume Collection, 1964-174A; waistcoat, America, c. 1780, wool lined with linen, Colonial Williamsburg Costume Collection, 1952-113. The Colonial Williamsburg Foundation. American clothing combined imported and domestic fabrics. Women prolonged the use of valuable fabrics by taking clothing apart and remaking it as styles changed.

purchasing yards of fabric, dozens of buttons, and multiple skeins of thread. Caty twice picked up earrings and once an ivory fan, which at £24 and £11, respectively, were among the most expensive individual items on the account. Overall, this household treated shopping as a transaction that could be managed by white or black members, free or slave, who possessed judgment and reliability. Familiarity with Crooke's mercantile business may have given all household members the required skills associated with shopping.

Like all proxies, Caty and Sayer acted as the economic agents of the people they shopped for. From a legal point of view, what mattered was the identity of the account holder. When Rumreil's patience wore out, she sued Robert Crooke to recover the cost of their selections. Since acquisition, selection, and payment were separate processes in eighteenth-century shopping, the economic power that proxies wielded within the shop did not translate directly to other kinds of social power. The earrings Caty collected would not adorn her ears and testify to her discernment to outsiders. Similarly, when the wealthy Ann Simons unpinned a note worth $10 from her friend Mary Singleton's letter and carried it into a Charleston shop to buy fabric and ribbon for Singleton, she flexed financial power only by proxy and did not improve her own wardrobe in the transaction.[13]

The non-proxy names receiving credit on the Simon and Crooke accounts represent another kind of mediated access to material culture. These men and women entered Rumreil's shop empty-handed and left with goods or money charged to account holders Simon or Crooke. Those who obtained goods (as opposed to money) tended to be women, and the range of their social positions is evident from the way they are named: from "Nigra" to "D. Reeds Dautr." to "Amey Peirce" to "Mrs. Pollen." For these shoppers, some of whom undoubtedly worked for their creditors, Simon and Crooke were the intermediaries who transformed them into Rumreil's customers. This transformation enabled them to select fabric, notions, and groceries of the same sort that Crooke and Simon used in their own households. As John Styles found among English servants in the same period, their very dependency in the marketplace facilitated consumer choice by providing access to credit and, therefore, fashionable goods.[14] People who lacked dependent ties also lacked this avenue to acquiring goods.

Free married women, by definition, had this double-edged relationship to consumer credit, since they, like Vanrhyn's customer Mrs. Senf, were legally unable to contract debts of their own. In spite of their legal disabilities, such women regularly made credit purchases, exploiting the common-law provision of the "law of necessaries," which gave a woman the right to buy certain goods without her husband's express consent, even if the couple were separated.[15] In practice, shopkeepers had little incentive to question or limit the purchasing freedom of married or enslaved women, provided the shopkeepers knew that a husband or owner was good for the debt. Husbands in failing marriages therefore resorted to public advertisements warning shopkeepers, tradespeople, and merchants not to credit their wives on the family account.[16]

The individuals who received money (notes or cash) from Sarah Rumreil on the Crooke and Simon accounts were mainly free men. In some senses, the cash they carried out of the shop was liberating, since it was a movable form of money that shoppers could take from supplier to supplier.[17] In contrast with credit accounts that remained on the books until reckoning day, cash payments could more easily elude the surveillance of a tightfisted father or overbearing master.[18] But in many ways, the use of cash mirrored the social and economic liabilities of its carriers. Details of transactions preserved in account books and court evidence make clear that the place of cash in a person's life was shaped by income and social position. A poor woman with no credit connections had to save up the small sum of cash when she wanted to purchase a pair of shoes or a half pound of tea. A woman with the resources to grind chocolate or spin candlewick could initiate regular transactions in goods, punctuated with an occasional cash payment. A wealthier widow or businesswoman used long-term credit to run up larger debits before arranging a reckoning, employing partial infusions of cash to mollify an impatient shopkeeper enough to allow further credit purchases. Mrs. Jackson was on her third visit to Ann Smith's shop in Charleston and trying to make her most expensive purchase (a cloak worth almost £4) when she finally paid the shopkeeper 20s. "on the Cloak" (fig. 27).[19]

These financial practices had emotional and social implications for shoppers. When selecting items for their home or table, poor shoppers felt the connection between object and price most directly, not only because they had less money to spare, but because they were granted less latitude in paying their bills. Among the middling-class and wealthy customers, cost was a matter of long-term budgeting rather than immediate negotiation. These customers usually did not select and pay on the same day; there were trips for choosing and trips for reckoning. Regular patrons in this group could keep an eye out for a specific style or price. Even where cash played a larger role in daily shopping, as it seems to have in Charleston as compared to Newport, payment practices reflected the position of the shopper more than the intrinsic qualities of the medium. Scattered receipts and account-book fragments suggest that the well-to-do preferred to run up a number of credits before paying in full for their purchases with cash.[20] For example, Henry Muckenfuss's female customers typically paid "cash in full" several months after their purchases, a practice that did not change according to the relative size of their balances.[21]

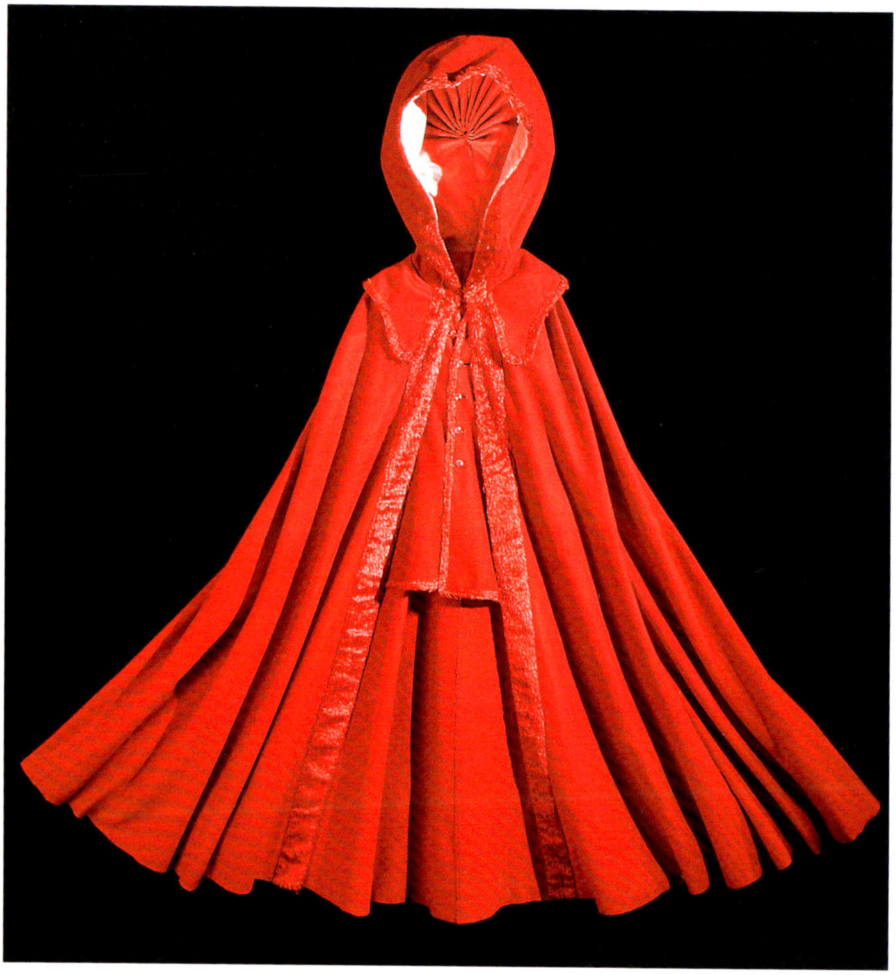

27. Red cloak, Britain or America, worn in New York, 1775–1810, wool broadcloth trimmed with wool shag and silk-covered buttons, from the collection of Mrs. Cora Ginsburg, Colonial Williamsburg Costume Collection, 1989-402. The Colonial Williamsburg Foundation.

Consumer choice was channeled through these different economies. Newporter Jabez Carpenter sold thousands of pounds of "sundries" to customers from the 1740s to the 1760s, but this had less to do with a shared sense of what made calico pretty or shoes durable, and more to do with the fact that he accepted goods and work, such as Mary Dumoy's knitted mittens, as a form of payment. His credit ties in the community further extended his pool of customers. The sales of thread, pins, and tape that he made to Sarah Martain, for example, were completed because of credits that Francis Honyman had with Carpenter and extended to cover Martain's costs.[22] Men and women without accounts of their own had to shop where their connections permitted. Their ability to exhibit their own taste preferences—whether calculated in comparison shopping or honed in discussions with other shoppers—was both facilitated and constrained by the credit economy.

WHOSE CHOICES? THE LIMITS OF AUTONOMY

If economic connections limited where people shopped, social and cultural ties constrained what they shopped for. In a gesture typical of well-connected port residents, Philadelphian Mary Robinson Morton sent her sister Abigail a package in 1817 with two kinds of fabric and a note encouraging her to make a choice between them "as freely as if thou made it in a shop. I would not give a pin to influence thy decision."[23] Her analogy was based on the idea that selections made in a shop were not beholden to personal obligation or a desire to please anyone but oneself. Her comments appear to confirm historians' celebrations of choice. The rest of her letter, however, qualified that consumer freedom, as Morton guided her sister into making a skilled, informed choice: "The Senshaw is the largist pattern, & the prittier colour—the persian will probably wear better, & neither will look smarter than a nice bengal, after a little wear, & will be pleasanter for hot weather." The freedom of shopping as Morton understood it was not the thrill of frivolous indulgence, but the liberty to act on one's own judgment—a capacity formed in a community of consumers.

The elites of American port cities documented the values of this consumer community at length in their letters. They championed practicality ("pleasanter for hot weather") as well as beauty ("prittier," "smarter"), were triumphant in locating bargains, and presented themselves as tenacious and prudent "economists." Mary Rotch commented approvingly that the handkerchiefs Ruth Hadwin had procured for her in Newport "are indeed very cheap for so good a quality" (fig. 28).[24] The "language of goods" that they spoke connected them both to the fashionable trends of Europe and to the venerable values of colonial housewifery, binding the authors together in a society of savvy shoppers. Their words exposed the shared considerations and calculations that defined "taste" in material goods specific to their rank.[25] For these consumers, the process as well as the final product of shopping constructed genteel identities as peers policed one another's purchases. In fact, given the small, mundane items frequently discussed, the process of shopping and the ties it confirmed could be more important than the goods alone.[26]

This model of shopping choice, which stresses the interplay among acts of selecting goods, acquiring goods, discussing goods, and the development of taste,

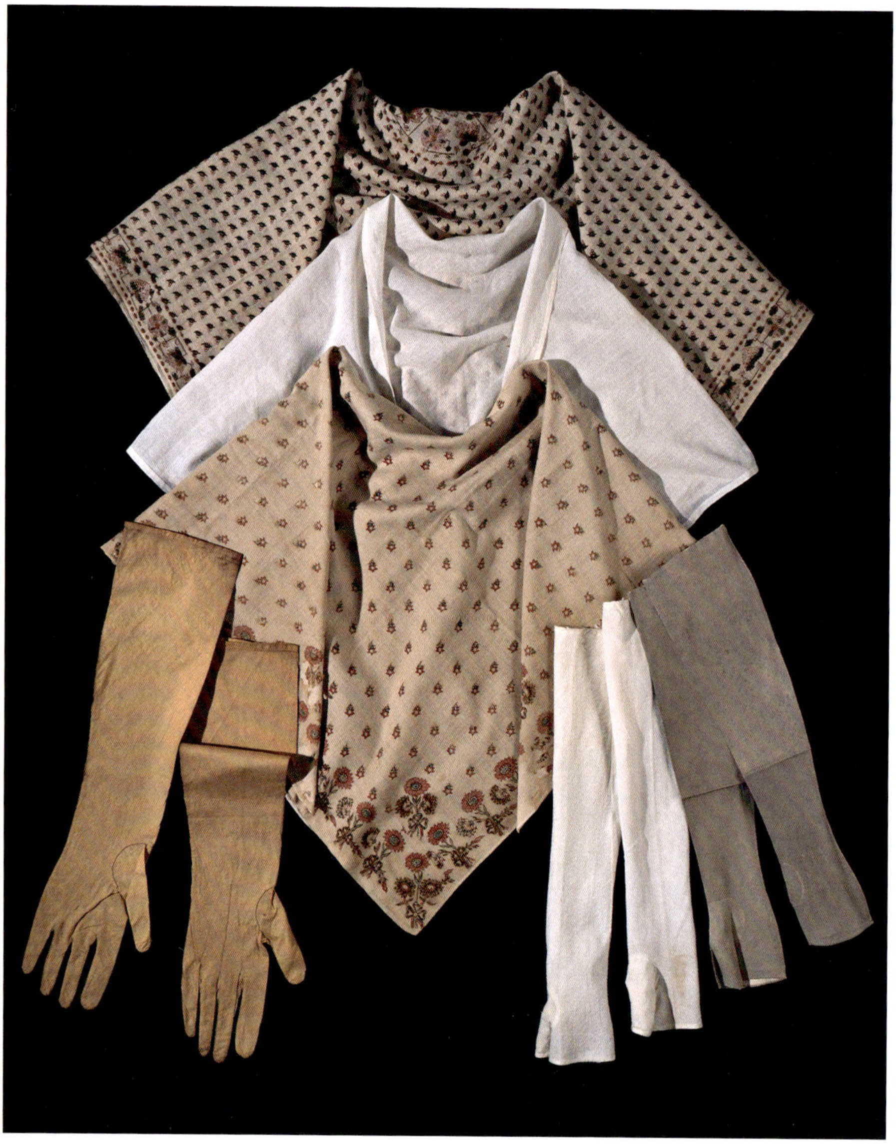

28. Neck and arm coverings (from the top): printed kerchief, America or Britain, 1800–1825, block-printed cotton, bequest of Grace Hartshorn Westerfield, Colonial Williamsburg Costume Collection, G1974-377; white kerchief, Pennsylvania or Delaware, 1780–1810, cotton, gift of Frances Matthews, Colonial Williamsburg Costume Collection, G1983-303; floral kerchief, America or Britain, 1795–1810, block-printed cotton, bequest of Grace Hartshorn Westerfield, Colonial Williamsburg Costume Collection, G1974-376; yellow gloves, Britain or America, 1780–1840, cotton sewn with silk, Colonial Williamsburg Costume Collection, 1986-206; white mitts, America, c. 1800, cotton dimity, gift of Titi Halle, Colonial Williamsburg Costume Collection, G2000-20; gray mitts, Britain, c. 1800, leather, Colonial Williamsburg Costume Collection, 1991-445. The Colonial Williamsburg Foundation. Rotch and Hadwin would have worn kerchiefs to fill in the necklines of low-cut gowns as well as to protect themselves from sun and cold.

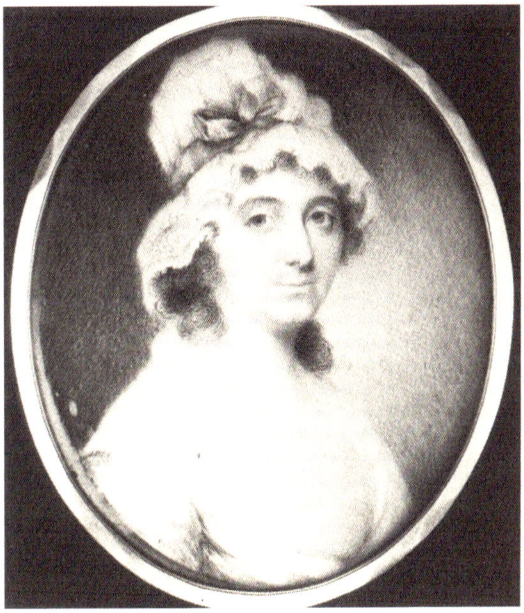

29. Attributed to Walter Robertson, ivory miniature of Harriott Pinckney Horry, c. 1790s. Photograph, taken before the accidental destruction of the miniature, from *The Letterbook of Eliza Lucas Pinckney: 1739–1762*, ed. Elise Pinckney (Chapel Hill: Univ. of North Carolina Press, 1972). From the Collections of the South Carolina Historical Society. In this portrait, Horry is dressed in the light, gauzy fabrics popular in the Early Republic period.

is more accurate than that of the liberated solo shopper. But how did the ubiquitous servant and slave proxies fit in? These individuals were indispensable in the crafting of a rich elite material life. The Morton household's "our Bella" spent days with a swatch in hand looking for a match in Philadelphia stores. The Pinckneys' "old Mary" promised cash to merchant after merchant in an effort to obtain the best price for gauze.[27] Were they merely the agents of their owners' desires, "conceived of as aspects of their master's capacities and abilities," as eighteenth-century legal and political thought understood them?[28]

Mistresses imparted some consumer knowledge to their servants and slaves for practical purposes, hoping to indoctrinate them with a particular sense of "taste." They also relied on the capacities of those they owned and employed. Eliza Pinckney described the process of finding fabric for her daughter Harriott Horry (fig. 29) in 1775 as follows:

> Jones sent me word a few days after I came to town that the stores had been serched and he could not get a bit of fine washing pavilion Gause any where; I afterwards sent old Mary with directions not to miss a store, and to let them know it was Cash, and after two or three days serch she got me some coarse stuff. . . . I sent her to Cape (I am glad you mentiond him) and have got 40 yards of fine Pavilion washing gause; 'tis more than your quantity but they wont cut it and it will do to mend it. It is 15s. per yd.[29]

Several things are striking about her depiction. First is the number of proxies and their geographic and social distance from the person who wanted the goods. Second is the alternation between direction and discretion. Pinckney gave precise directions to Mary about how to bargain. But she also reported that the slave was on her own searching for "two or three days." Harriott Horry did not initially dictate the quality, price, or preferred shop, because shopping required that the chooser be entrusted with some powers of selection. Newporter Robert Crooke's female slaves Caty and Sayer, for example, made their own judgments when purchasing items from Sarah Rumreil's shop.[30] The sheer volume of their work tells us that while Caty may have been sent to pick up a certain pair of earrings her mistress had selected earlier, there could not be such oversight of every yard of ribbon she brought home. Elites in their correspondence indirectly acknowledged that their servants and slaves were entrusted with this kind of economic decision making.

To read every "per yr Negro woman" entry in an account book as the footprint of a mere errand girl for elite consumption would be to misconstrue the social context of shopping. Scholars of informal slave economies have devised ways to read absences and indirect evidence in elite sources, and shopping fits well into their complex models of relationships between masters and slaves.[31] Literate women did not always note the degree to which their consumer expertise was shared with servants, slaves, and poor neighbors, but they seldom complained about miscommunication with these individuals. Masters and mistresses recognized individuality and specialized knowledge among those who worked for them, whether it was in a skilled trade or the "business" of shopping. At the same time, enslaved people could shape mundane errands, from conveying messages to selecting calico, to suit their own purposes.

Urban slaves were encouraged to understand consumer language for the benefit of their owners—indeed, this knowledge made consumer networks in port cities possible—but were not expected to act on the other kinds of desires satisfied by shopping. "Choice," for them, was supposed to be the direct application of training, not the free expression of opinion. "Taste" was supposed to consist of discrete forms of knowledge, not personal preferences. Enslaved people who violated these expectations created a dilemma that seems to have been particularly acute in Charleston, where slaves constituted half the population. In that city, enslaved people who purchased clothes or accessories with their own money were immediately suspected of theft. Whites criticized slaves who dressed in bright, fashionable colors, and one late-eighteenth-century newspaper report even suggested that "authorized persons are going about this city for the purpose of depriving negroes of their clothes."[32] When Jane Ball said to "tell Binah [her slave in town] send me some Black Ribbon wide & narrow," she did not intend for her slave to trim her own jackets according to current styles.[33] It is likely, though, that regular exposure to the values and judgments of shopping networks influenced enslaved consumers' material lives. Bella ducked out on Frances Pinckney one evening in March 1781 in a gown of a red and white calico and a blue calimanco striped coat, topping her outfit with a muslin cap adorned with just such a black ribbon.[34]

Enslaved people realized the potential for self-fashioning that economic autonomy and consumer knowledge provided, and they were particularly attuned to the role of clothing in declaring or masking identity. Charlestonian Anne McKernan announced that her slave Hannah "had on when she went off a blue woolen spencer, a homespun frock, and a humhums apron. She may however change her dress, as she has many acquaintances in the city who would no doubt lend her clothes" (fig. 30).[35] McKernan's announcement suggests that Hannah's clothing could be the difference between freedom and capture. Masters and mistresses envisioned proxy shopping as a limited gesture of agency; enslaved people sought to use that moment of trust to improve their own lives, transforming the meaning of proxy agency.

Place was also vital to how the poor and enslaved used commercial connections to shape their own material lives. While some slaves, like white servants, received old cast-off clothing in styles and fabrics originally suited to their masters and mistresses, enslaved men and women on plantations and small farms received drab, ill-fitting clothing. Merchants and store owners in Charleston advertised "negro cloth"—a coarse fabric bought for this purpose and sold in bulk. Unlike other fabrics, which were named for their contents (linsey-woolsey), durability (everlasting), or appearance (luster), this was named specifically for the group of people who were supposed to be dressed in it.[36] Over time, slave clothing in the South became more uniform, and enslaved men and women from the countryside could expect their attire to be an announcement of their status. When Bella was accosted at Ponpon and removed to the Charleston workhouse, she was dressed in the typical garb of "a white negro cloth gown and oxnabrug petticoat."[37] Given this identification of clothing and its wearer's status, many urban slaves used their own earnings—as well as strategic thefts—to enhance their material lives, most notably in clothing. These enslaved Charlestonians were not seeking to disguise themselves, but rather to proclaim themselves part of a fashionable culture, simultaneously presenting to whites "a challenge to their exclusive claim to the symbols of civilization" (fig. 31).[38]

Newporters did not sell or use "negro cloth." Stores and homes stocked coarse, sturdy fabrics that could be used for slaves', servants', or laborers' clothing, but black people were not linked by name to a fabric reserved to them. Unlike Charleston, Newport did not service many large plantations in need of slave clothing in

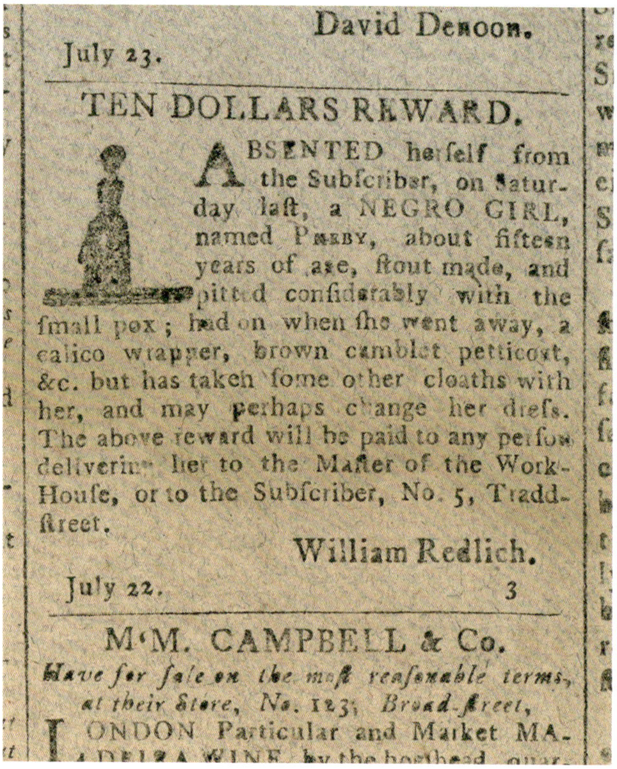
David Denoon.

July 23.

TEN DOLLARS REWARD.

ABSENTED herself from the Subscriber, on Saturday last, a NEGRO GIRL, named Peggy, about fifteen years of age, stout made, and pitted considerably with the small pox; had on when she went away, a calico wrapper, brown camblet petticoat, &c. but has taken some other cloaths with her, and may perhaps change her dress. The above reward will be paid to any person delivering her to the Master of the Work-House, or to the Subscriber, No. 5, Tradd-street.

William Redlich.

July 22. 3

M'M. CAMPBELL & Co.

Have for sale on the most reasonable terms, at their Store, No. 123, Broad-street,

LONDON Particular and Market MA-

30. Notice, [Charleston] *City Gazette and Daily Advertiser*, 23 July 1800. Courtesy of the University of Texas Libraries, University of Texas at Austin. Printers used stock images of runaway slaves in their notices that reflected the gender of the escapee. The clothing depicted in these stock images changed over time, as styles of clothing worn by enslaved people changed.

southern Rhode Island, and so the imported fabric was not in great demand. The contrast between the appearance of rural and urban slaves who interacted on the streets of Newport may not have been as stark as in Charleston. Certainly the presence of enslaved Newporters did not unsettle the white population enough to complain about it in court or in newspaper editorials. Whatever measures enslaved people took in Newport to express their individuality through clothing were not seen as a threat to the social order in the way they were in the southern city. Nor was clothing likely to be the ticket to escape. Enslaved women in Newport were far less likely to run away; not only were their options fewer, but their presence was more conspicuous due to their smaller numbers. Changing clothes alone would not sufficiently conceal them.

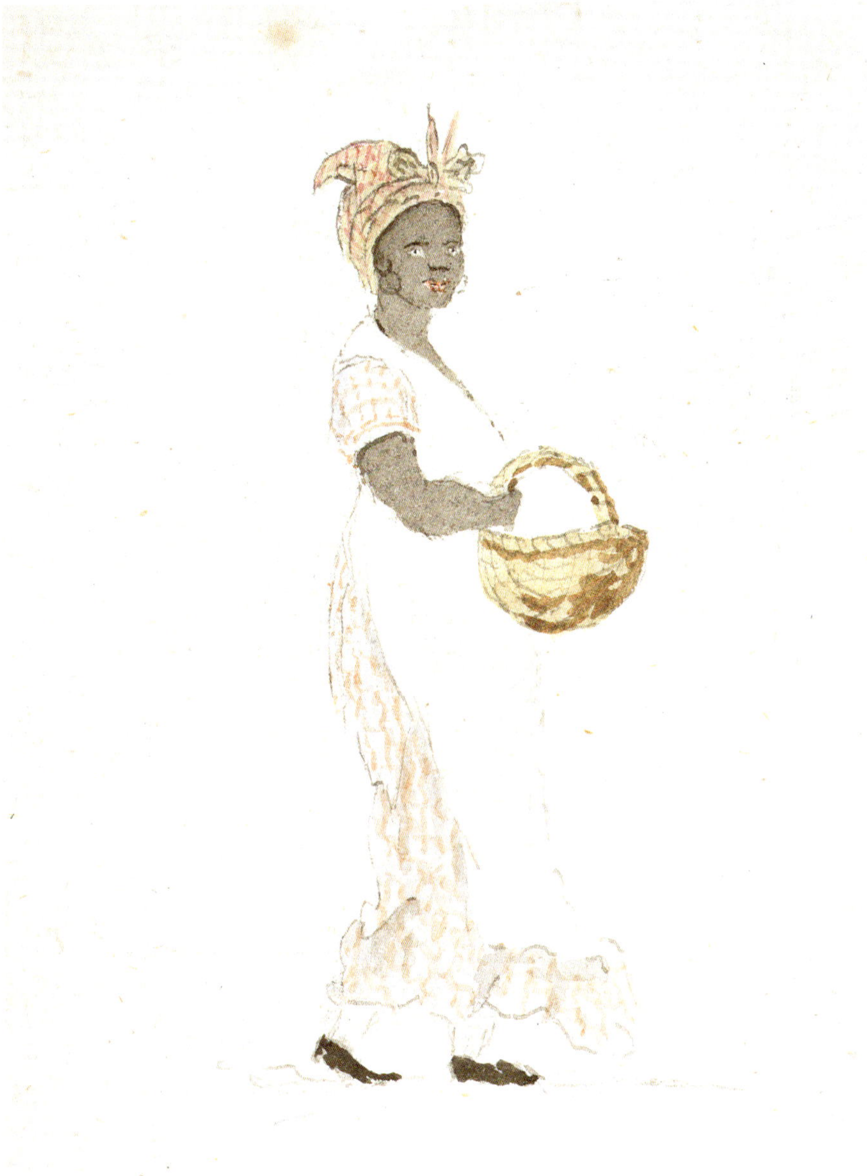

31. J. S. Glennie, *Slave Girl Going to Market,* journal (c. 1815). Andre De Coppet Collection, Manuscripts Division, Department of Rare Books and Special Collections, Princeton University Library. The cut of this woman's dress and apron are in a style free women also would have worn. Her head wrap and earrings reflect African cultural influences and a personal assertion of taste.

Instead, they, like poor women in both cities, employed consumer knowledge for symbolic or often meager economic reward. Drawn into consumer networks as intermediaries and through reciprocal obligations, poorer free women's participation in the consumer "language of goods" was more equivocal than their well-to-do neighbors'. Poor women's skills in "economy" had higher stakes than those who sought affirmation of their thriftiness from discerning friends. Newport and Charleston had almshouses, workhouses, and hospitals, but the free poor typically received "outdoor relief" from town or church overseers, either directly or through a designated caretaker, so that money had to be stretched by means of careful budgeting, charity, and additional earnings.[39] Unable to purchase or store goods in large quantities, poor women could not take advantage of bulk discounts and instead had to mete out income in small increments, which influenced not only what they bought, but what the purchase meant to them.

Not every consumer found satisfaction and self-expression through shopping. Newporter Mary Dumoy bought her sugar, coffee, and flour a few shillings at a time, which placed her ahead of many fellow residents, but she was not necessarily exercising a liberating choice by visiting Jabez Carpenter's store once a week.[40] Consumers who could skillfully balance their needs and desires found shopping to be a pleasurable endorsement of their place in the urban economy. Those whose financial resources always came up short against the price of refinement needed to look elsewhere for self-worth and satisfaction.[41] Poor and enslaved customers found shopping socially embedded while not necessarily socially rewarding. What different ranks could share was a sense of the value that their own skill added to the process of selection.

The social character of shopping meant greater vulnerability for some shoppers in the store itself. Old Mary, the slave who was sold fabric that Eliza Pinckney dismissed as "coarse stuff," was surely not alone in failing to receive adequate "education" from a storekeeper. Rural shoppers, awed by the array of goods, could be intimidated by a brusque proprietor.[42] Mobile city populations and high turnover in the competitive urban marketplace meant that customers were frequently confronted with new, unknown shopkeepers. To reassure insecure shoppers, at least one Newport businesswoman promised that "the most unexperienced in the different Qualities of Goods, shall be charged not a Farthing more than the most knowing" (fig. 32).[43] On the other hand, the social nature of shopping also checked the power of the purveyor. Since so many consumption decisions were made outside the shop, in the context of a network of consumers, shoppers had ample opportunity to compare prices and confer over quality with those who shared their interest.

Ideas about gender, in addition to those about race and rank, increasingly constrained shopping choices in perception and practice. The growth and specialization

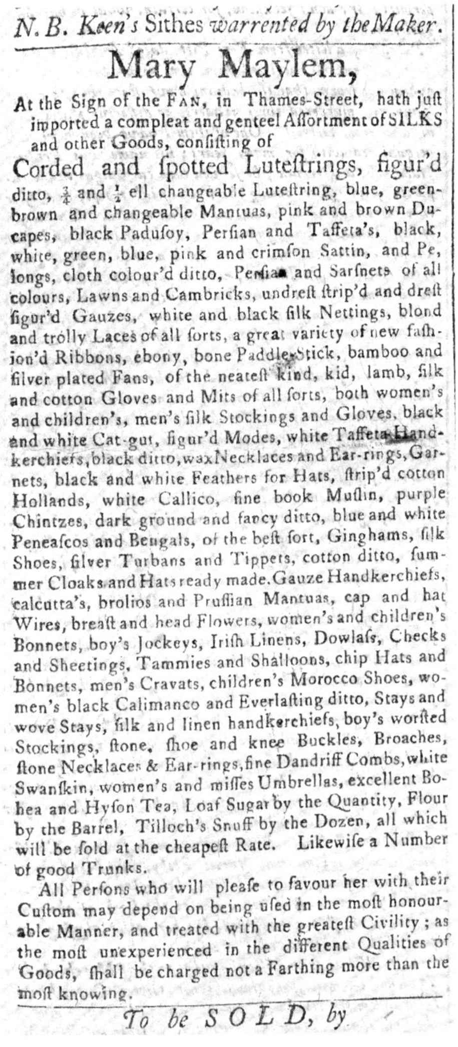

N. B. Keen's Sithes *warrented by the Maker.*

Mary Maylem,

At the Sign of the Fan, in Thames-Street, hath juſt imported a compleat and genteel Aſſortment of SILKS and other Goods, conſiſting of

Corded and ſpotted Luteſtrings, figur'd ditto, $\frac{3}{4}$ and $\frac{1}{2}$ ell changeable Luteſtring, blue, green-brown and changeable Mantuas, pink and brown Du-capes, black Paduſoy, Perſian and Taffeta's, black, white, green, blue, pink and crimſon Sattin, and Pe, longs, cloth colour'd ditto, Perſian and Sarſnets of all colours, Lawns and Cambricks, undreſt ſtrip'd and dreſt figur'd Gauzes, white and black ſilk Nettings, blond and trolly Laces of all ſorts, a great variety of new faſh-ion'd Ribbons, ebony, bone Paddle-Stick, bamboo and ſilver plated Fans, of the neateſt kind, kid, lamb, ſilk and cotton Gloves and Mits of all ſorts, both women's and children's, men's ſilk Stockings and Gloves, black and white Cat-gut, figur'd Modes, white Taffeta Hand-kerchiefs, black ditto, wax Necklaces and Ear-rings, Gar-nets, black and white Feathers for Hats, ſtrip'd cotton Hollands, white Callico, fine book Muſlin, purple Chintzes, dark ground and fancy ditto, blue and white Peneaſcos and Bengals, of the beſt ſort, Ginghams, ſilk Shoes, ſilver Turbans and Tippets, cotton ditto, ſum-mer Cloaks and Hats ready made. Gauze Handkerchiefs, calcutta's, brolios and Pruſſian Mantuas, cap and hat Wires, breaſt and head Flowers, women's and children's Bonnets, boy's Jockeys, Iriſh Linens, Dowlaſs, Checks and Sheetings, Tammies and Shalloons, chip Hats and Bonnets, men's Cravats, children's Morocco Shoes, wo-men's black Calimanco and Everlaſting ditto, Stays and wove Stays, ſilk and linen handkerchiefs, boy's worſted Stockings, ſtone, ſhoe and knee Buckles, Broaches, ſtone Necklaces & Ear-rings, fine Dandriff Combs, white Swanſkin, women's and miſſes Umbrellas, excellent Bo-hea and Hyſon Tea, Loaf Sugar by the Quantity, Flour by the Barrel, Tilloch's Snuff by the Dozen, all which will be ſold at the cheapeſt Rate. Likewiſe a Number of good Trunks.

All Perſons who will pleaſe to favour her with their Cuſtom may depend on being uſed in the moſt honour-able Manner, and treated with the greateſt Civility; as the moſt unexperienced in the different Qualities of Goods, ſhall be charged not a Farthing more than the moſt knowing.

To be SOLD, by

32. Mary Maylem advertisement, *Newport Mercury*, 2 May–9 May 1768. Courtesy the Rhode Island Historical Society (RHi X3 7896). In addition to reassuring insecure shoppers, Mary Maylem's advertisement highlights the expansion and elaboration of choices offered in imported cloth, clothing, and accessories.

of Charleston shops at the turn of the nineteenth century intensified the association of each gender with specific goods and led to a discourse among elites suggesting that shopping skill had a gendered dimension. As the variety of goods and the population increased, retail shops proliferated and the goods and personal dynamics in these venues took on a more gendered shape. Advertisements imagined a clientele divided by gender-specific interests, calling out from the pages with news "IMPORTANT TO THE LADIES!" and promising that discerning Englishwomen, not the male proprietors, had overseen the selection of fashionable goods.[44] The division of interests was repeated in the letters of wealthy Charleston families.

During the American Revolution, the wealthy Harriott Horry looked for tents, ink, bearskins, and "whatever else you think my Situation requires" for her brother.[45] By the early nineteenth century, this kind of proxy pragmatism is less evident. On his Jamaican plantation, Oliver Hering depended on a supply of seed rice from his sister Mary Middleton in Charleston, sending her plants and fruit trees in return. When she wrote to him in England for boots and shoes, however, he reported, "Your commissions . . . is forwarded through my Mother to Kitty."[46]

Gendered discourse was more muted in Newport. Occasionally, a milliner might entreat "the Ladies of Newport" to patronize her shop, but most proprietors urged as wide a section of the population as possible to "Strike, While the Iron is Hot!!!"[47] Newport families expected men and women to be ready in a pinch to apply their best judgment to imported goods. Husbands, brothers, sons, and other men were drawn in to participate in the hunt for goods. Consider the letter from a woman to her brother that asserted, "Amy enclosed 4/ this currency for Molly to purchase a pair of gloves for Polly Hazzard but as she is not in town I wish thou would desire Billy Thurston to get them she wants french kid, of a light purple color" (fig. 33). Sisters and female relations might be the first choice when a woman was looking for a new pair of gloves, but a male acquaintance could also be pressed into service and could be trusted to make judgments about the size ("desire him to remember that she has a very large hand and arm") and color ("if he cannot get a light purple, a lead or any other handsome neat color will please her").[48] The retail environment of a particular place shaped not only the practical experience of shoppers, but also local understandings about where shopping fit into ideas about gender and family.

Legal practice endorsed gendered limits to consumer choice. The "law of necessaries," which supported a married woman's role as consumer, added a qualitative limit to her purchases over and above the financial constraints that all shoppers faced. Authorized only as far as those items "suitable to [her husband's] rank and fortune," her selections were legally restricted to a group of objects deemed appropriate by the community that upheld the law.[49] Her dependent status placed her choices under this scrutiny, but it was community ideas about gender and rank that defined the limits. In his 1816 treatise, American legal scholar Tapping Reeve wrote that a husband was required "to fulfil the contract of his wife, when it is such an one as wives in her rank of life usually purchase. . . . If, however, she were to purchase a ship or yoke of oxen, no such presumption would arise, for wives do not usually purchase ships or oxen."[50]

Did enslaved or servant proxies bear the presumed prejudices of gender? On the one hand, enslaved women were decried for the same kinds of marketing and dressing crimes that free women were singled out for, namely, ostentatious and

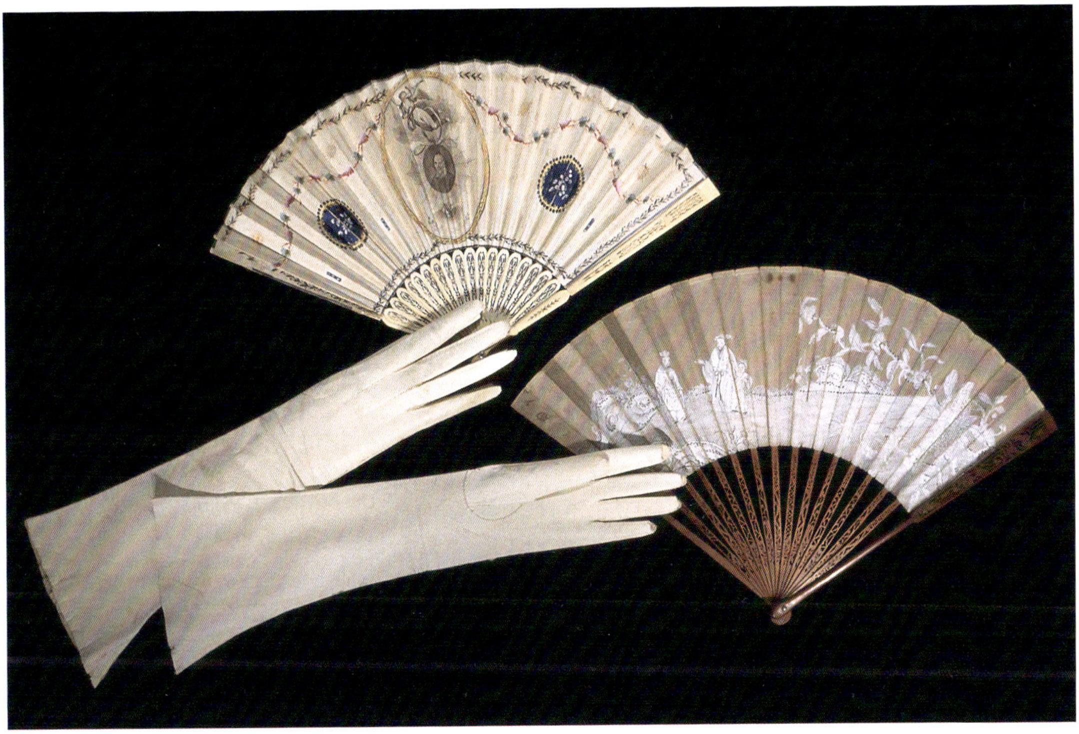

33. Imported accessories (left to right): gloves, Britain, worn in New York, 1775–1800, leather, gift of Mrs. Cora Ginsburg, Colonial Williamsburg Costume Collection, G1990-8; fan, Britain, used in Virginia, 1780–1820, bone, sequins, engraved and painted paper, Colonial Williamsburg Costume Collection, 1978-90; fan, China, used in Philadelphia, 1770, bamboo, painted and silvered paper, gift of Mrs. Beatrix Rumford, Colonial Williamsburg Costume Collection, G1980-238. The Colonial Williamsburg Foundation.

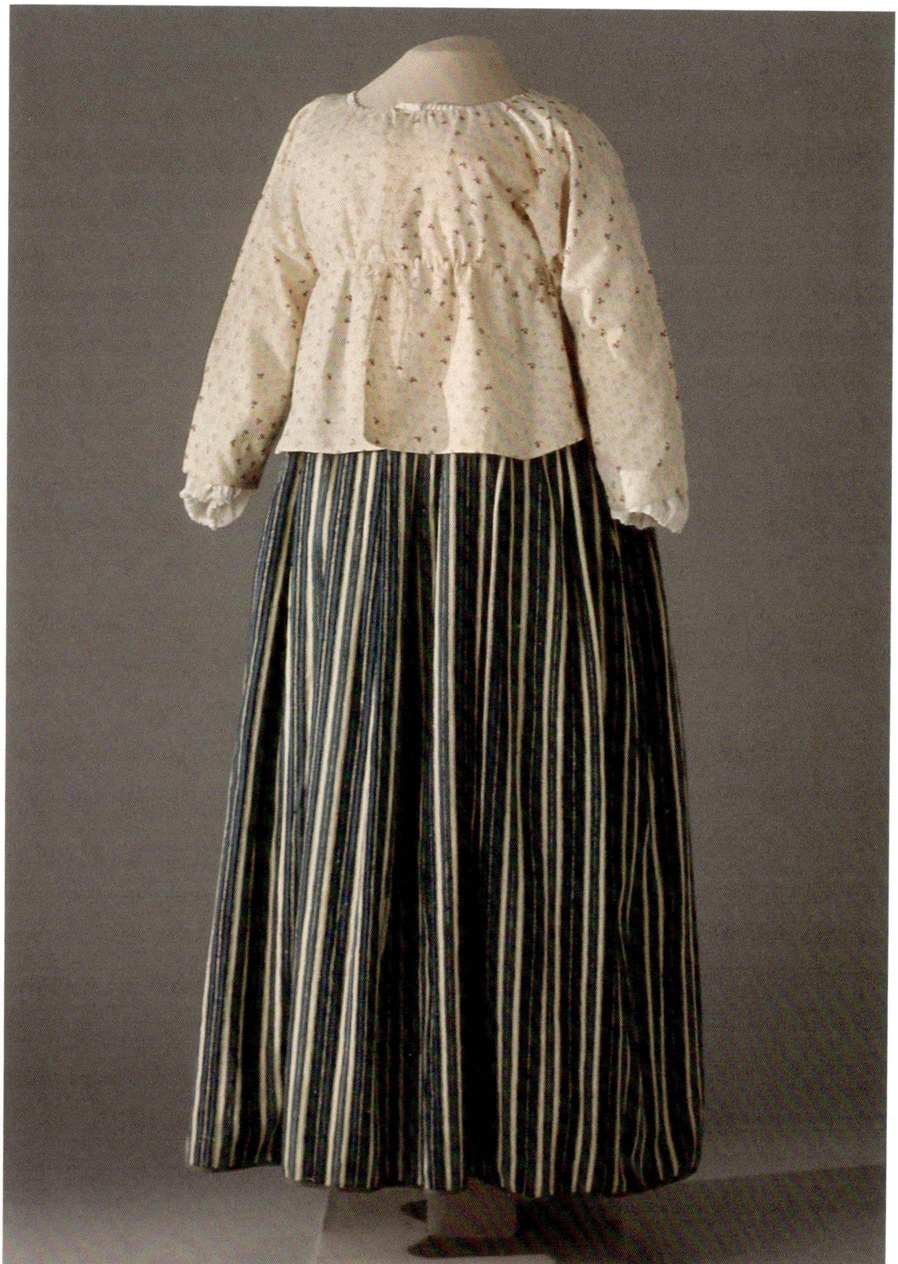

34. Short gown, America, 1800–1820, roller-printed cotton, Colonial Williamsburg Costume Collection, 1996-95 (white shift seen underneath is a twentieth-century reproduction); petticoat, New England or Britain, 1770–1820, linen-wool with wool hem binding and linen waistband, Colonial Williamsburg Costume Collection, 1991-444. The Colonial Williamsburg Foundation. Working women's clothing was much plainer but incorporated imported goods and changing fashionable silhouettes.

expensive clothing, obtained through pushy bargaining tactics. Their gender placed a particular stamp on their material lives as shoppers. For example, while "Job" bought leather breeches on Ruth Thurston's account, "Pheebe" bought four yards of ribbon.[51] On the other hand, as with free proxies, sometimes a customer entrusted the best available person, regardless of gender. Peter Simon's family sent their "Negro Boy" or "Toney" most often to collect the thread, needles, and smallish lengths of cloth that the household required. There seems to have been no presumption for them that a male slave would be less competent to obtain goods associated with female clothing manufacture. This family limited the overall discretion of its proxies, making the particular identity of the person choosing the goods less important. For others, proxies brought particular attributes and skills to the process of shopping, skills honed in the daily work of obtaining and processing goods. Those elite women who singled out servant proxies for commendation identified women. Mary Morton boasted that her servant "is a very good hand at the business. . . . I believe she has searched every probable store in town" (fig. 34).[52]

We typically think of a consumer's power in her community coming from the ability to exercise choice—to purchase one thing rather than another, to save here and spend there by balancing internal factors such as desire, need, and knowledge with external ones like availability and price. Advice writers in the eighteenth and nineteenth centuries, as well as the urban Americans who read them, valued the skills of discernment, budgeting, and evaluation associated with choice. This well-documented culture of consumer choice has prompted historians to theorize that it served as the soil in which new real political choices took root.[53]

Yet the ubiquity of intermediaries and the importance of credit illustrate the paradox of consumer choice in a world of collaborative shopping. At one level, just as "independence" for free white men was produced by the labor of white women and slaves, so, too, was "choice" for free white men and wealthy women produced by the shopping labors of the women and men who made up the web of any consumer's network.[54] Although white women particularly prided themselves on consumer savvy, they relied on the consumer knowledge of enslaved women and men to seek out bargains and locate rare materials. Shopping for goods was a fundamentally social act that bore the stamp of social inequities and prejudices. Men and women who shopped were producing a collaborative form of consumer knowledge about goods that can be labeled "taste," but this was knowledge to be selectively used according to gender, race, and rank. Since shopping networks included bonds formed by affection and those formed by violence and compulsion, consumer selections were shaped as much by things one could not choose as by the free exercise of will.

Acknowledging that discourses of consumption were shared across divisions of race and class does not slight the inequalities that existed in late colonial and early national urban society. An enslaved servant and a free son used the consumer knowledge honed in proxy shopping to different ends when outfitting themselves. They fashioned their preferences by putting together knowledge about goods and prices with a sense of how the item would work in their daily social life.[55] The market brought people together, economically and socially, but the consumer act of selecting shirt fabric, for example, could translate into starkly different meanings.

The evidence of credit networking and proxy shopping points toward a collaborative model of economic and material life more generally. Economic activity involved many more levels of society than is apparent at first glance, encompassing servants, slaves, and children as significant household consumers. Their prominent place highlights the ambiguities of agency in material life and the unruly dispersion of the power of choice.

1. The first category counted for the majority of purchases ($673.25); the next two were fairly evenly divided ($308.53 and $332.35, respectively). Charleston Court of Common Pleas (CCP) Summary Process Rolls, 1824 04749a, 1824. She was suing only to recover money from the first two categories. Original spellings have been retained.
2. See the essays by John Styles, Claire Walsh, and Ann Smart Martin in this volume, although their definition of proxy shopping is not always precisely the same as that employed here.
3. Elise Pinckney, ed., "Letters of Eliza Lucas Pinckney, 1768–1782," *South Carolina Historical Magazine* 76, no. 3 (July 1975): 152.
4. Studies that explore the social dimensions of shopping include T. H. Breen, "An Empire of Goods: The Anglicization of Colonial America, 1690–1776," *Journal of British Studies* 25, no. 4 (Oct. 1986): 467–99; Ann Smart Martin, "Buying into the World of Goods: Eighteenth-Century Consumerism and the Retail Trade from London to the Virginia Frontier" (PhD diss., College of William and Mary, 1993), 306–31; Richard L. Bushman, "Shopping and Advertising in Colonial America," in *Of Consuming Interests: The Style of Life in the Eighteenth Century*, ed. Cary Carson, Ronald Hoffman, and Peter J. Albert (Charlottesville: Univ. of Virginia Press for the United States Capitol Historical Society, 1994), 233–51; Elizabeth Kowaleski-Wallace, *Consuming Subjects: Women, Shopping, and Business in the Eighteenth Century* (New York: Columbia Univ. Press, 1997); Daniel Miller, *A Theory of Shopping* (Ithaca, NY: Cornell Univ. Press, 1998), 35; Amanda Vickery, *The Gentleman's Daughter: Women's Lives in Georgian England* (New Haven and London: Yale Univ. Press, 1998), 162–72; and Stacy Helmbrecht-Wilson, "'Went a Shopping': Elite and Middling Women as Consumers in Massachusetts, 1790–1830" (PhD diss., Boston Univ., 1999), chap. 2.
5. David S. Shields, *Civil Tongues and Polite Letters in British America* (Chapel Hill: Univ. of North Carolina Press, 1997), 111.
6. T. H. Breen has argued that purchasing tea, for example, fostered visible links among disparate colonists on the eve of the American Revolution; see Breen, "'Baubles of Britain': The American and Consumer Revolutions of the Eighteenth Century," *Past and Present* 119 (May 1988): 81–84. Cary Carson has argued that the most important affinities were transatlantic; see Carson, "The Consumer Revolution in Colonial British America: Why Demand?" in Carson, Hoffman, and Albert, *Of Consuming Interests*, 502. Phyllis Whitman Hunter makes a

similar point in *Purchasing Identity in the Atlantic World: Massachusetts Merchants, 1670–1780* (Ithaca, NY: Cornell Univ. Press, 2001), including 9. For studies stressing emulation that highlight its potential for self-formation and other social uses, see Richard L. Bushman, *The Refinement of America: Persons, Houses, Cities* (New York: Alfred A. Knopf, 1992), 406, and Ann Smart Martin, "The Role of Pewter as Missing Artifact: Consumer Attitudes toward Tablewares in Late Eighteenth-Century Virginia," *Historical Archaeology* 23, no. 2 (1989): 1–27.

7. T. H. Breen, *The Marketplace of Revolution: How Consumer Politics Shaped American Independence* (New York: Oxford Univ. Press, 2004), 24–25.

8. See Craig Muldrew, *The Economy of Obligation: The Culture of Credit and Social Relations in Early Modern England* (New York: St. Martin's Press, 1998), and Margot Finn, *The Character of Credit: Personal Debt in English Culture, 1740–1914* (Cambridge and New York: Cambridge Univ. Press, 2003).

9. Douglas R. Egerton, *He Shall Go Out Free: The Lives of Denmark Vesey* (Lanham, MD: Rowman & Littlefield, 2004), chap. 3.

10. Bruce Mann, *Republic of Debtors: Bankruptcy in the Age of American Independence* (Cambridge, MA: Harvard Univ. Press, 2002), chap. 4.

11. Newport Court of Common Pleas (NPCCP), Nov. 1768 term, no. 281.

12. NPCCP, Nov. 1763 term, no. 193.

13. Ann Simons to Mary Singleton, 25 April 1809, Singleton Family Papers, Southern Historical Collection, Wilson Library, University of North Carolina, no. 668, box 1, folder 4.

14. John Styles, "Custom or Consumption? Plebeian Fashion in Eighteenth-Century England," in *Luxury in the Eighteenth Century: Debates, Desires and Delectable Goods*, ed. Maxine Berg and Elizabeth Eger (London: Palgrave Macmillan, 2003), 103–15. NPCCP, Nov. 1768 term, no. 281; NPCCP, Nov. 1763 term, no. 193.

15. Margot Finn, "Women, Consumption, and Coverture in England, c. 1760–1860," *The Historical Journal* 39, no. 3 (Sept. 1996): 709. See also Craig Muldrew, "'A Mutual Assent of Her Mind'? Women, Debt Litigation, and Contract in Early Modern England," *History Workshop Journal*, no. 55 (2003): 47–71. South Carolina permitted free married women to operate as "femes sole" traders under certain circumstances; see Mary Roberts Parramore, "'For Her Sole and Separate Use': Feme Sole Trader Status in Early South Carolina" (master's thesis, Univ. of South Carolina, 1991).

16. Godfrey Wenwood claimed that his wife, Mary, planned to spend freely on his credit and therefore warned Newporters, "I am determined not to pay any debts of her contracting after the date hereof: I also take this method to forbid all persons, who are indebted to me, paying her any thing on my account for the future." *Newport Mercury*, 22 Aug. 1774. Sarah Leavitt discusses runaway-wife advertisements in Rhode Island in "'She Hath Left My Bed and Board': Runaway Wives in Rhode Island, 1790–1810," *Rhode Island History* 58, no. 3 (Aug. 2000): 91–104.

17. Cornelia Hughes Dayton and Deborah Rosen discuss the changing gender profile of credit arrangements in Dayton, *Women Before the Bar: Gender, Law, and Society in Connecticut, 1639–1789* (Chapel Hill: Univ. of North Carolina Press, 1995), chap. 2, and Rosen, *Courts and Commerce: Gender, Law, and the Market Economy in Colonial New York* (Columbus: Ohio State Univ. Press, 1997). Credit users themselves could send proxies, as is suggested in the way Charleston merchant James Sharpe emphasized that a charge to Patrick Clark's account for sundries was "pd. William Jones at his desire, and in his presence." South Carolina Court of Common Pleas (SCCCP), 1759, 47b 28a.

18. Linda Sturtz, *Within Her Power: Propertied Women in Colonial Virginia* (New York: Routledge, 2002), 122–23.

19. Charleston CCP Summary Process Rolls, 1800 044a, 1800. For examples of poorer women's methods, see the accounts of Nurs Huddy and Abigail Sanford in the pages of Jabez Carpenter's ledger. Nurs Huddy bought a pair of women's shoes in the fall of 1755 for £4 12s. and twenty days later paid the cash in full, her only transaction recorded with Carpenter. Abigail Sanford's purchases were periodically adjusted by "a ballance due in my [Carpenter's] favour." Jabez Carpenter ledger, 1755–72, Newport Historical Society, 111; 13, 136, 246, 258, 319, 351.

20. See, for example, Mrs. Ball to Ann Savage, Account Book, John Ball, Sr., Papers, Rare Book, Manuscript, and Special Collections Library, Duke University, box 1, folder 9.

21. Mary Shields purchased just $3.72 worth of rice, currants, vinegar, and sugar over the course of a year but brought cash to the shop only in late December. Muckenfuss's largest female customer, Jane Strawberry, made purchases six times in a year and paid in two lump sums totaling $201.10. Henry Muckenfuss Daybook, 1810, South Caroliniana Library.
22. Carpenter ledger, 21, 103, 147; 29, 142, 205, 270. For additional extended examples, see Aaron Lopez, "Taylors and Spinners" book, 1769–74 (no. 767), Newport Historical Society.
23. Mary Robinson Morton to Abigail Robinson, 10 July 1817, Robinson Papers, New England Women and Their Families in the 18th and 19th Centuries: Personal Papers, Letters, and Diaries, series b: selections from the Newport Historical Society (Bethesda, MD: LexisNexis Academic & Library Solutions, 2000), microfilm (hereafter Robinson Papers), reel 14.
24. MR [Mary Rotch, New Bedford] to Ruth Hadwin, Newport, 3 April 1806, Williams Papers, New England Women and Their Families in the 18th and 19th Centuries: Personal Papers, Letters, and Diaries, series b: selections from the Newport Historical Society (Bethesda, MD: LexisNexis Academic & Library Solutions, 2000), microfilm, item 44, reel 19.
25. Pierre Bourdieu theorizes a class-based construction of taste in *Distinction: A Social Critique of the Judgment of Taste*, trans. Richard Nice (Cambridge, MA: Harvard Univ. Press, 1984).
26. See Claire Walsh's essay in this volume for an extensive discussion of this phenomenon among Englishwomen.
27. Mary Robinson Morton, Philadelphia, to Sarah Robinson, Newport, 22 Oct. 1794, Robinson Papers, reel 14; Pinckney, "Letters," 151.
28. Carolyn Steedman, "The Servant's Labour: The Business of Life, England, 1760–1820," *Social History* 29, no. 1 (Feb. 2004): 2.
29. Pinckney, "Letters," 151.
30. NPCCP, Nov. 1763 term, no. 193.
31. Betty Wood, *Women's Work, Men's Work: The Informal Slave Economies of Lowcountry Georgia* (Athens: Univ. of Georgia Press, 1995); Philip D. Morgan, *Slave Counterpoint: Black Culture in the Eighteenth-Century Chesapeake & Lowcountry* (Chapel Hill: Univ. of North Carolina Press, 1998), 318–26; Robert Olwell, *Masters, Slaves, and Subjects: The Culture of Power in the South Carolina Low Country, 1740–1790* (Ithaca, NY: Cornell Univ. Press, 1998), chap. 4; Walter Johnson, *Soul by Soul: Life Inside the Slave Market* (Cambridge, MA: Harvard Univ. Press, 1999), chap. 6.
32. Morgan, *Slave Counterpoint*, 601; for property owning among slaves, see Morgan, *Slave Counterpoint*, 374–76; *City Gazette*, 2 Sept. 1793, quoted in Philip Morgan, "Black Life in Eighteenth-Century Charleston," *Perspectives in American History*, n.s. 1 (1984): 203. Gail Gibson stresses the simple clothing that Charleston slaves were allotted by law and custom in "Costume and Fashion in Charleston, 1769–1782," *South Carolina Historical Magazine* 82, no. 3 (July 1981): 233. In the nineteenth century, Betty Wood argues, criticisms of female slave marketeers' clothing were linked to white claims that these women were prostitutes. See Wood, "'White Society' and the 'Informal' Slave Economies of Lowcountry Georgia, c. 1763–1830," *Slavery and Abolition* 11, no. 3 (December 1990): 320–21.
33. Jane Ball to Isaac Ball, 19 Aug. 1803, Ball Family Papers, South Caroliniana Library, box 1, folder 24.
34. *The Royal Gazette*, 24 March–28 March 1781. See also Ann Smart Martin's discussion of ribbons in her essay in this volume.
35. *City Gazette and Commercial Daily Advertiser*, 30 March 1815.
36. For descriptions of fabrics, see the "dictionary" section included in Florence M. Montgomery, *Textiles in America, 1650–1870* (New York: W. W. Norton, 1984), 141–377.
37. *South Carolina Gazette*, 1 March–8 March 1760.
38. Ira Berlin, *Many Thousands Gone: The First Two Centuries of Slavery in North America* (Cambridge, MA: Belknap Press of Harvard Univ. Press, 1998), 160. Linda Baumgarten, "'Clothes for the People': Slave Clothing in Early Virginia," *Journal of Early Southern Decorative Arts* (Nov. 1988): 43, emphasizes the homogeneity of slave clothing. Morgan, *Slave Counterpoint*, 126–33 and 598–99, also discusses ways that enslaved people modified clothing to suit their own purposes.

39. For example, in 1788, the Newport Town Council granted two poor women, Susannah Sims and Mrs. Hasted, 5s. each per week to support themselves; Town Council Notes, 1784–1794, no. 2013, 4 Feb. 1788, Newport Historical Society. For discussions of Newport poor relief, see Lynne Withey, *Urban Growth in Colonial Rhode Island: Newport and Providence in the Eighteenth Century* (Albany: State Univ. of New York Press, 1984), 56–71, and Elaine Forman Crane, *A Dependent People: Newport, Rhode Island in the Revolutionary Era* (New York: Fordham Univ. Press, 1992), 63–68; for Charleston, see Stephen Edward Wiberly, Jr., "Four Cities: Public Poor Relief in Urban America" (PhD diss., Yale Univ., 1975); Barbara Ulmer, "Benevolence in Colonial Charleston," in *The Proceedings of the South Carolina Historical Association, 1980* (Aiken: South Carolina Historical Association, 1980), 1–12; Walter Fraser, Jr., "Controlling the Poor in Colonial Charles Town," in *Proceedings of the South Carolina Historical Association*, 13–30; Barbara L. Bellows, *Benevolence among Slaveholders: Assisting the Poor in Charleston, 1670–1860* (Baton Rouge: Louisiana State Univ. Press, 1993).
40. Carpenter ledger, 21.
41. For two different interpretations of the democratic elements of the link between proliferating material goods and gentility, refinement, and status, see Elaine Forman Crane, *Ebb Tide in New England: Women, Seaports, and Social Change, 1630–1800* (Boston: Northeastern Univ. Press, 1998), 136, and Bushman, *Refinement of America*, 409–13.
42. See the examples discussed by Ann Smart Martin in her essay in this volume.
43. *Newport Mercury*, 2 May–9 May 1768.
44. *City Gazette and Commercial Daily Advertiser*, 20 Nov. 1816.
45. Thomas Pinckney to Harriott Horry, 5 Oct. 1777, in "Letters of Thomas Pinckney, 1775–1780," ed. Jack L. Cross, *South Carolina Historical Magazine* 58, no. 3 (July 1957): 145.
46. Oliver Hering to Mary Middleton, 8 March and 19 June 1801, Hering Family Papers, South Carolina Historical Society, 24/63/13.
47. *Newport Mercury*, 4 May 1805; *Newport Mercury*, 4 March 1820.
48. A[bigail] Robinson to her brother [Rowland Robinson], 12 Nov. 1786, Robinson Papers, reel 1.
49. Finn, "Women, Consumption, and Coverture," 709.
50. Quoted in Linda Kerber, *No Constitutional Right to Be Ladies: Women and the Obligations of Citizenship* (New York: Hill and Wang, 1998), 14. One hundred years later, the courts were still struggling to adjudicate the credit relationship among husbands, wives, and retailers. See William Leach, *Land of Desire: Merchants, Power, and the Rise of a New American Culture* (New York: Pantheon Books, 1993), 128–30.
51. Carpenter ledger, 201. For perceptions of enslaved women in the marketplace, see Olwell, *Masters, Slaves, and Subjects*, 166–78, and Wood, *Women's Work, Men's Work*, 91–92, 144–45.
52. Mary Robinson Morton to Sarah Robinson, 22 Oct. 1794, Robinson Papers, reel 14.
53. Breen, "Empire of Goods," 489. Some examples of advice books that discussed shopping (and went through many reprintings) are Mrs. [Hester] Chapone, *Letters on the Improvement of the Mind, Addressed to a Young Lady* (Hagers-Town, MD: Printed by William D. Bell for Gabriel Nourse, 1815); William Kenrick, *The Whole Duty of Woman: or, an unfallible Guide to the Fair Sex* (London: Printed for T. Read, 1737); and [Ann] Taylor, *Practical Hints to Young Females, on the Duties of a Wife, Mother, and a Mistress of a Family* (Boston: Wells and Lilly, 1816).
54. For a detailed study of the "production" of independence in South Carolina, see Stephanie McCurry, *Masters of Small Worlds: Yeoman Households, Gender Relations, and the Political Culture of the Antebellum South Carolina Low Country* (New York: Oxford Univ. Press, 1995), chap. 2.
55. Pierre Bourdieu believes that individuals make "a choice of the necessary," as defined by both function and other people's expectations of what they should have. I am arguing that in the context of late-eighteenth- and early-nineteenth-century proxy shopping, there was more strategic borrowing of information. Bourdieu, *Distinction*, chap. 7.

Shops, Shopping, and the Art of Decision Making in Eighteenth-Century England

Claire Walsh

INTRODUCTION

FOR A LONG TIME, the subject of eighteenth-century retailing remained practically unresearched, while the belief was held that both retailing and shopping really began only in the nineteenth century. However, over the last decade or so, new source-based research has been carried out in this neglected field, sparked initially by the growing interest in consumption. There have been explorations of the numbers and distribution of shops,[1] provincial retailing,[2] shop design,[3] and itinerant retailing[4] in the period, coinciding with increasing work on retailing in the medieval period[5] and in early-modern Europe and colonial North America.[6] This wealth of new, primary research has been vital for a greater understanding of consumption before the industrial revolution and for recontextualizing the development of retailing and consumption across time. Clarifying the nature of pre-nineteenth-century retailing has revised some of the key assumptions about the innovatory and revolutionary impact of later retail techniques, the "professionalisation of retailing," the manipulative power of advertising, and the "birth of shopping," as well as their impact on consumers. Retailing before the industrial revolution had previously been dismissed as "primitive," but historians are now seeking not simply to highlight evidence of sophisticated marketing, display, and sales strategies as far back as the sixteenth century and earlier, but to understand the appropriateness of these strategies in the social, cultural, and economic context of their time.[7] Neil McKendrick's idea that the late eighteenth century saw the emergence of a consumer society has been rejected in favor of a depiction of slow expansion in consumption and retailing over many centuries (certainly beginning before the mid-seventeenth century).[8] The aim now is to recognize the complexity, skill, and innovation of early-modern retailing and to locate the shopping practices particular to the period in their own context, rather than paint them as immature forerunners of later archetypes. The question of gender has always been a central issue in the study of shops and shopping, because of the long-standing association of women with fashion and with purchases for the home, but as yet the exploration of the actual practices of shopping and the unpicking of the myths that connect women inherently with shopping and obscure male shopping has only just begun.[9]

THE APPEARANCE OF SHOPS

In the early-modern period in England, shops existed alongside other forms of retailing, such as auctions, markets, and the vast range of itinerant retailing, but increasingly—albeit very gradually, with the decline in the numbers and importance of markets from the fourteenth century onward—they became the most numerous form of retail outlet.[10] Shops could take many forms and sizes, ranging from wooden shacks (known as bulks) with let-down counters and lockup fronts, to stone or brick buildings with many rooms (including showrooms) or on many floors, to the front rooms of houses converted simply by enlarging the domestic

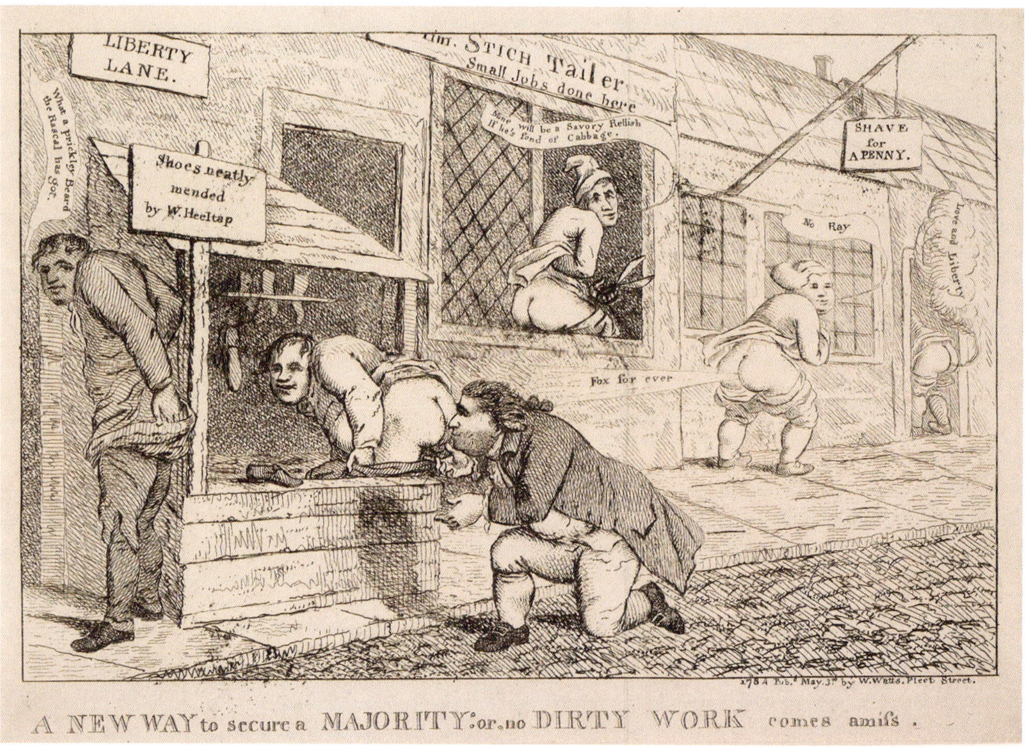

35. Artist unknown, *A New Way to Secure a Majority*, uncolored etching (c. 1784). © The Trustees of the British Museum.

window (fig. 35).[11] The display of goods and window dressing were crucial components of shopkeepers' retail strategies, and the pleasure and attention of looking was a central part of eighteenth-century shopping. Glazed windows were not necessary for effective selling; goods were hung across the open aperture or displayed on the window board. Racks, hooks, display boards, and cases were used inside to show goods to their best advantage.[12] When glazed sash windows began to come into widespread domestic use in the seventeenth century, they were quickly taken up by some shopkeepers; over time, glazing techniques and pane size increased, with most shops eventually following the glazing trend.[13] Displays in glazed shop windows with suitable object types made the most of the small-pane format, with select items placed behind each pane, which framed them individually and drew attention to them amid a patchwork miscellany of goods (fig. 36). Glazing bars focused the consumer's gaze, but window shopping was a matter of practical information gathering as well as a pleasure.

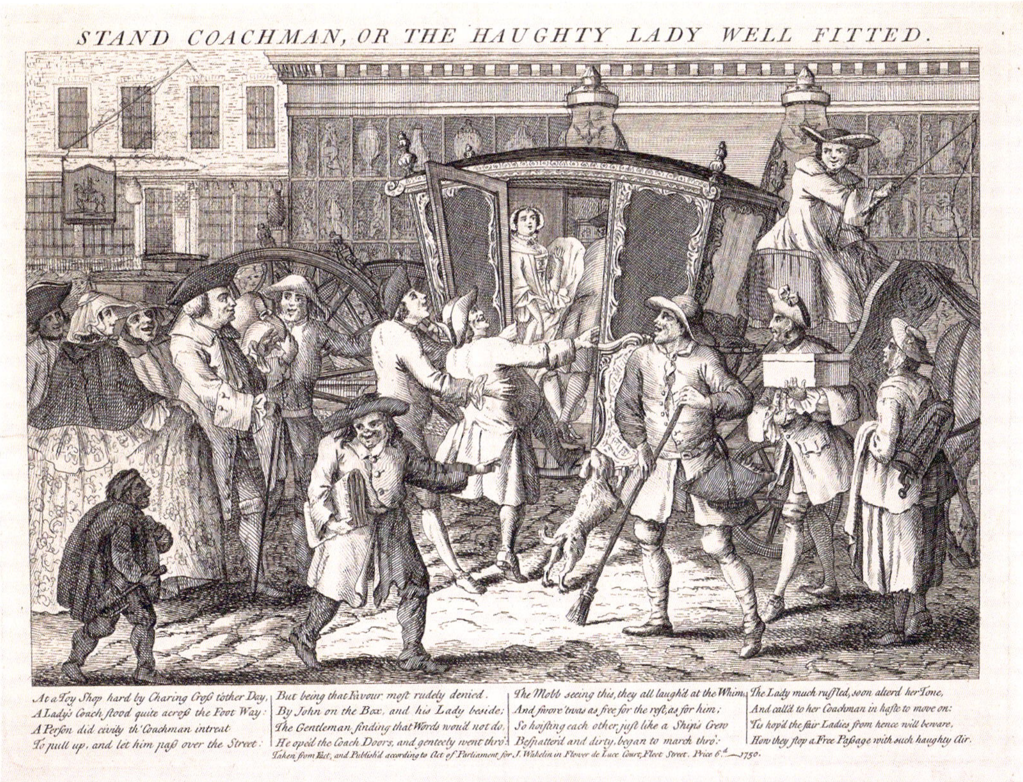

36. Artist unknown, *Stand Coachman, or the Haughty Lady Well Fitted*, uncolored etching (1750), showing Deard's Toy Shop. © The Trustees of the British Museum.

It is important to establish that the majority of shops in the early-modern period were not workshops into which a counter had been placed. Although some working tradesmen did sell from their workshops, shopkeepers' inventories show that the vast majority of retail shops were a distinct and separate area specialized for the activity of selling and kept away from the dirt and noise of manufacturing.[14]

Shopkeepers with some capital to invest or very expensive wares to sell could fit their shops out in very comfortable, fashionable, or showy manners. Upholstered seating, cushions, mirrors, sconces, candlesticks, velvet-lined drawers, tea tables (and the provision of tea and small beer), and prints on the walls are traceable in London and provincial shopkeepers' inventories. A reconstruction based on the inventories for Martha Braithwaite's shop in London, taken in 1746, provides a good impression of the interior decoration of a goldsmith's shop in the first half of the eighteenth century (fig. 37).[15] The fore shop was a typical size and shape for shops of the period. The decorative features listed (pillars, arches, glass, moldings, gilded cornice) fit in well with nonspecific representations of goldsmiths' shops on trade cards, shop plans, and other written evidence (fig. 38). It was just these elements that Jean André Rouquet, a French visitor to London in 1755, stated were "productive of an air of wealth and elegance."[16] The responsiveness of shops to domestic aesthetics of the elite can be confirmed in places such as Josiah Wedgwood's late-eighteenth-century premises in Greek Street, London, where color schemes and display arrangements were couched in a domestic rendition of the neoclassical taste.[17] Shops that chose to invest in this way must have rung the changes in infinite variations geared to different segments of the market. Such reverberations between shop and consumer enabled shops to make new tastes more established, identifiable, and reproducible.

Elite shopping zones developed in physical conjunction with other elite leisure and entertainment venues, such as assembly halls, theaters, promenades, and milk bars, and such sites of personal and material exhibition were mutually reinforcing.[18] Shops sometimes held "exhibitions," blurring the lines between these and their own displays.[19] Decorative elements, such as arches, screens, and moldings, that echoed (or, in smaller shops, suggested) grand architectural gestures of wealthy private homes or the public splendor of assembly halls and pleasure gardens thereby created shop interiors that were dramatic, fashionable, market specific, and desirable to be seen in (fig. 39). But these grand interiors would be ripped out and replaced frequently, as were the fronts of shops, according to the latest fashion trends.[20]

The architecture and layout of shops played with their inherent appeal: the seduction of goods. The interior arrangements not only facilitated access to goods, but also were used to assist the imaginative grasp of goods and their social, cultural, and fashionable contexts, through the porosity of the shop fronts (whether

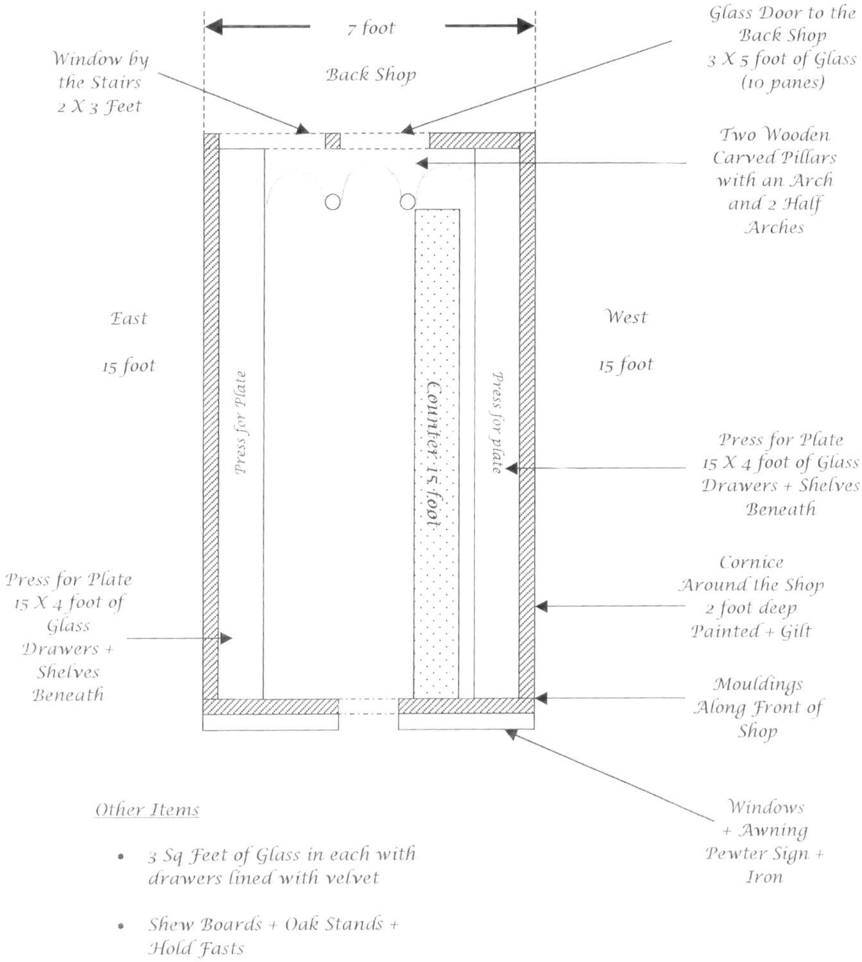

37. *Reconstructed Plan of George and Martha Braithwaite's Goldsmith's Shop*, based on Chancery Masters Exhibits C105/5, Part I (1746). The National Archives, London. Drawing: Claire Walsh.

glazed or unglazed); the fluidity of space created by the removal of interior walls and the introduction of arches, mirrors, and internal windows; and the ethos of service underpinned by long counters, comfortable seating, and intimate and domestically styled back shops or parlors.[21] Above all, the ability to provide visual, conversational, and relational social and cultural references around goods produced environments that eroticized the everyday.

The pleasure and allure of shops were reflected in social comment that connected the world of the shop and the world of the theater: for example, the *Female*

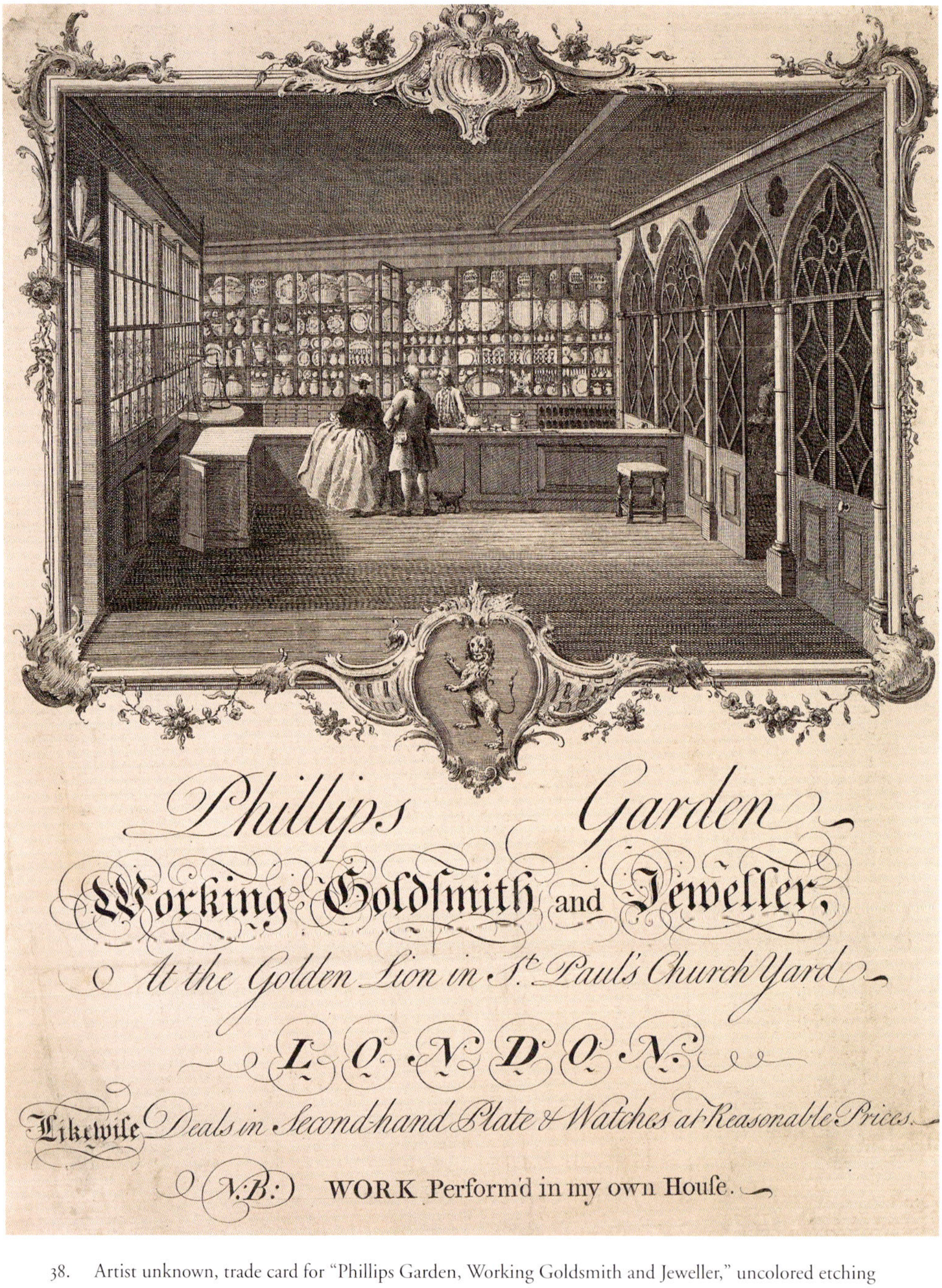

38. Artist unknown, trade card for "Phillips Garden, Working Goldsmith and Jeweller," uncolored etching (1750s). © The Trustees of the British Museum.

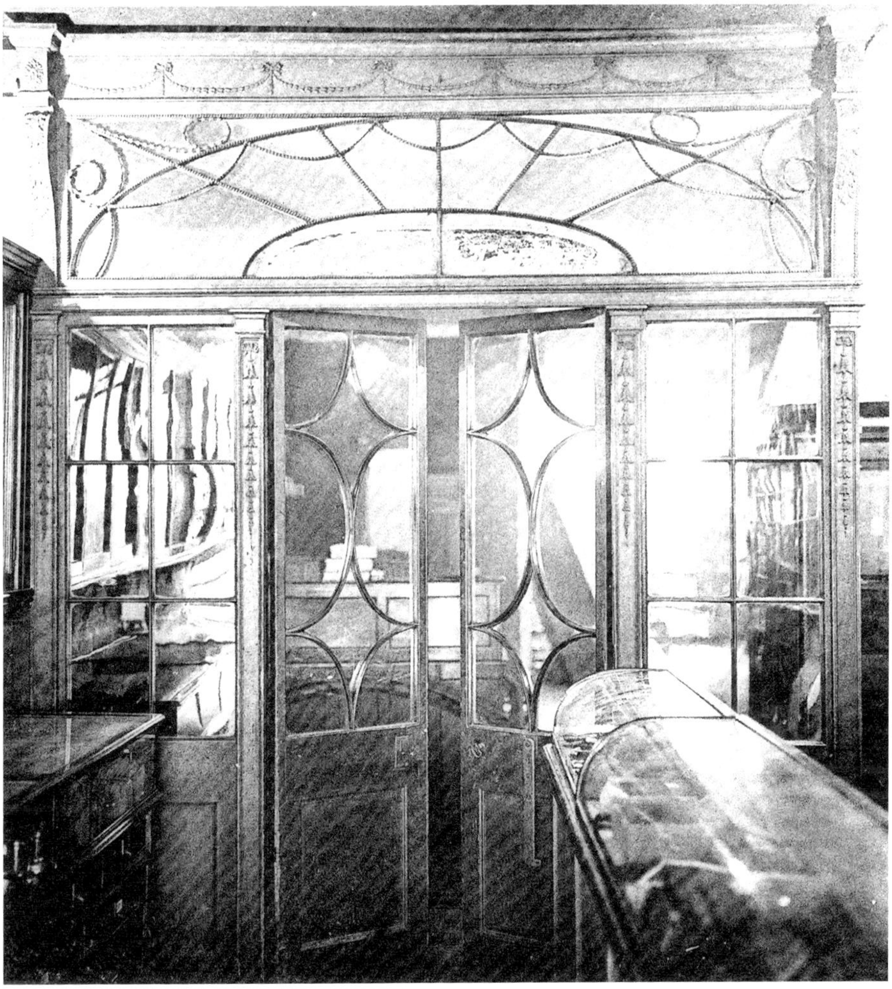

39. Artist unknown, neoclassical shop screen inside Freibourg & Treyer, Tobacconists, Haymarket, London (1780s), photograph from 1940s. © The Trustees of the British Museum.

Tatler of 1709 described the drapers' shops on Ludgate Hill in the City of London as "perfect gilded theatres," and trade cards could present shops as the stage sets on which the fashionable shopper would perform (see fig. 49).[22] The talismanic power of shops had been in existence for centuries, as much through the aesthetic charge of the goods sold as through any particular setting, but more shopkeepers were now able and willing to create a comfortable and sociable experience for a greater range of customers who could access a greater range of goods at affordable prices. The increasing efficiency, pleasure, comfort, and theatricality of shopping molded it as a social art that succeeded by process—simply going shopping became an activity in itself, independent of the goal of acquisition.

Creating a pleasurable environment and exploiting the sociability of shopping did not have to be dependent on high levels of investment or gilded columns; it could also be achieved through a domestic and intimate setting. Once created, the pleasurable shopping environment became not only a manipulative strategy but a social space colonized and owned by the shop's customers (fig. 40). All shops depended on strong connotations of efficient shopkeeping through tightly packed, well-structured storage in the form of boxes, racks, parcels, and nests of drawers.[23] This suggested an extensive, well-managed stock, good supply contacts and origins, and quality that could be vouched for—all crucial to consumers in a period when supply could be irregular, goods were not standardized, and cash flow was problematic. Such visual cues underpinned professional reputation.

The introduction of domestic fittings and furnishings into shops may suggest appeals to female customers, but "feminization" of the retail space does not necessarily depend on intimations of domesticity.[24] The New Exchange, situated on the Strand and one of several London shopping galleries, was at its height of popularity in the late seventeenth century. It was perceived as a feminized space because it sold goods related to women and because so many women shopped there, but the decoration of the gallery, in fact, emphasized grandeur and high living far more than it did domestic security, or femininity as opposed to masculinity. By contrast, the shopping gallery at Westminster Hall, adjacent to the Houses of Parliament, was a "masculinized" site, dominated by men because of its proximity to the law courts and Parliament and its sale of books, shirts, and stationery, although the design and decoration of the building were resonant of royalty and the grandeur of Gothic antiquity rather than any specific masculinity. Neither establishment excluded either gender.[25]

The prominent display of goods was a more reliable signal of gender bias—bulky, gender-specific items such as coats, jackets, hooped petticoats, and bustles hanging from the ceilings, shelves, and doorways of shops (fig. 41). Models of Scottish Highland soldiers outside tobacconists' shops and naval officers outside shops selling scientific instruments would have signaled to women that these were male environments. Most drapers stocked a range of cloth and served both male and female customers, so prominently displayed bustles or hoops would have signaled to men that this particular draper's shop concentrated on female-oriented cloths and other goods. Male customers would enter such shops if they wanted to buy female goods, though it is possible that some men, depending on their sensibilities, would have been deterred by the need to duck under a bustle to enter a shop. But these men were not excluded from shopping elsewhere, and the novelist Samuel Richardson saw such sensibilities as affectations.[26] The gendering of shops

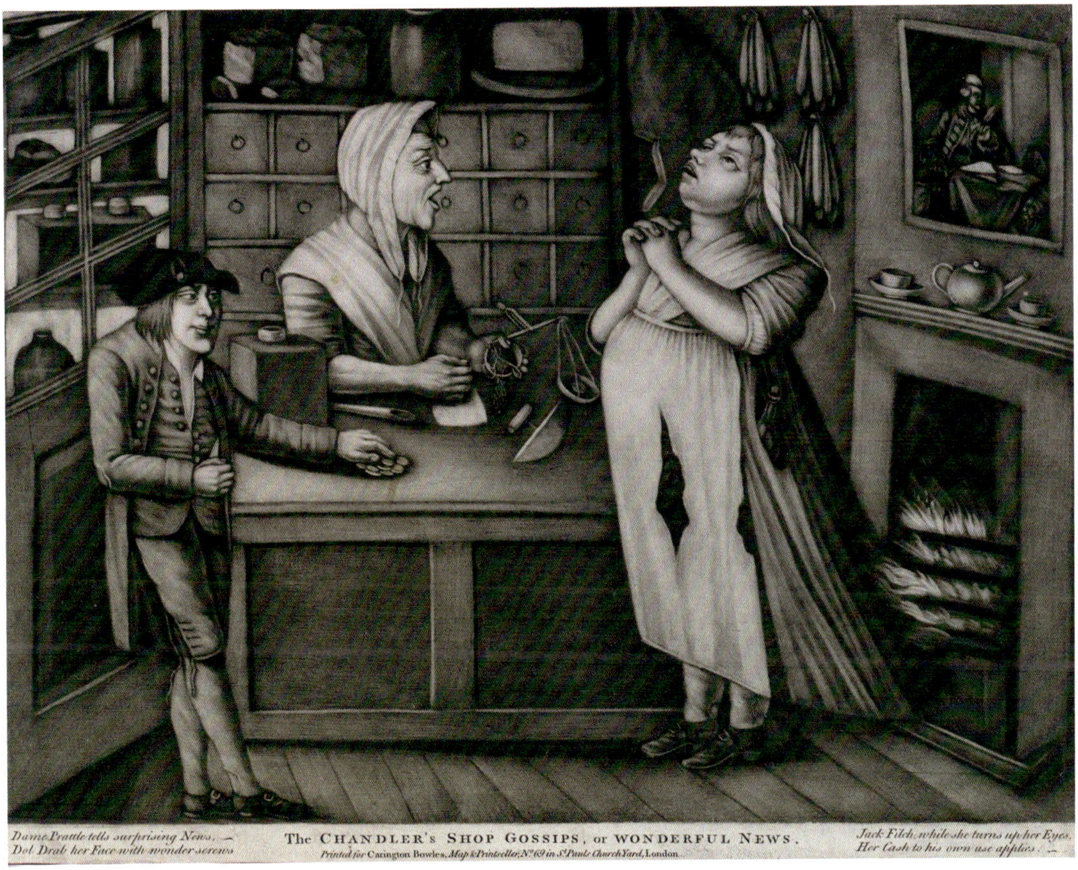

40. Artist unknown, *The Chandler's Shop Gossips, or Wonderful News,* mezzotint (c. 1770). The Colonial Williamsburg Foundation.

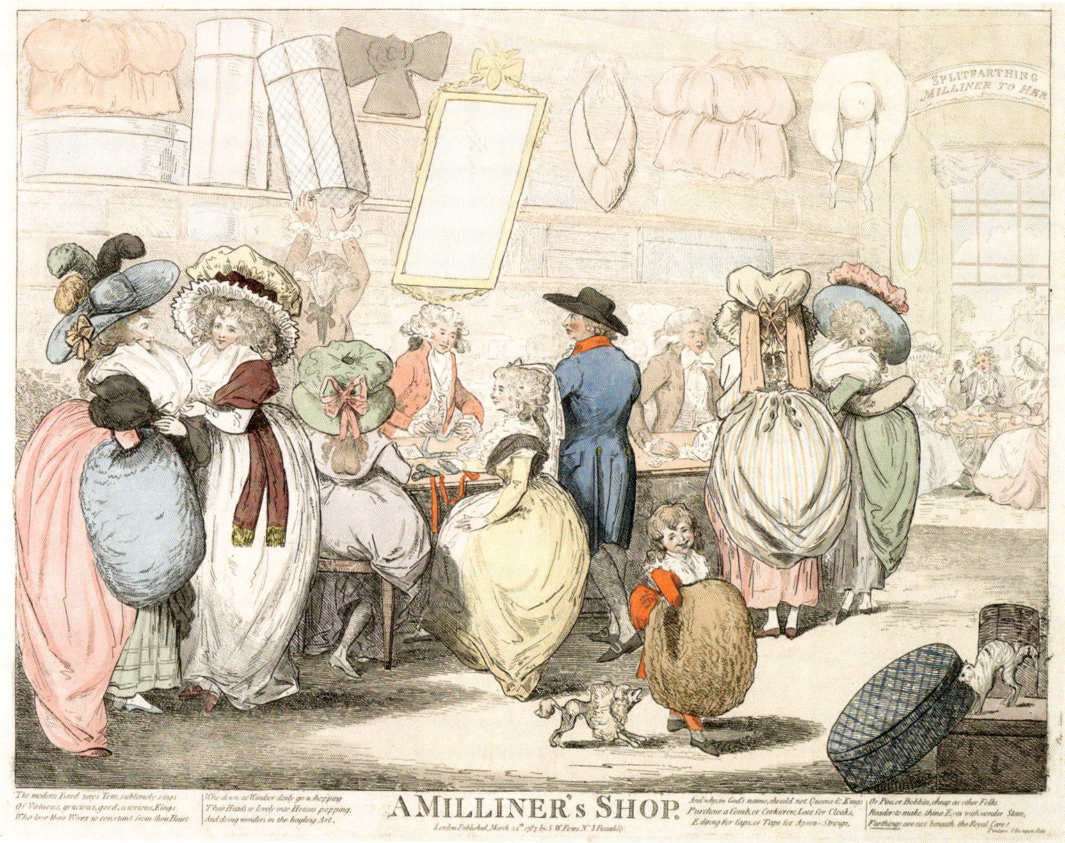

41. Artist unknown, *A Milliner's Shop or Splittfarthing's the Milliner's*, etching with hand color (1789), 14½ x 19¾ in. (36.8 x 50 cm). Courtesy of The Lewis Walpole Library, Yale University.

through the prominent positioning of clearly gendered goods was not necessarily aimed at, or read as, excluding the other sex. Lace and ribbons streaming from milliners' doorways and across windows (fig. 42) signaled to female customers a feminine environment in which to purchase—and to male customers, a feminine environment that they might appropriately enter for purchases or for dalliance with the female staff.

Part of the pleasure and appeal of shopping must have been the erotic encounter of the opposite (or attractive) sex provided within a formalized (and thus safe) setting, with its physical barriers of doors and counters, its public exposure through open or glazed windows and easy access to the street, its hints of intimacy through private conversation or admittance to the back shop, and the standardized behavioral etiquette and conversational exchange of shopping. Shops

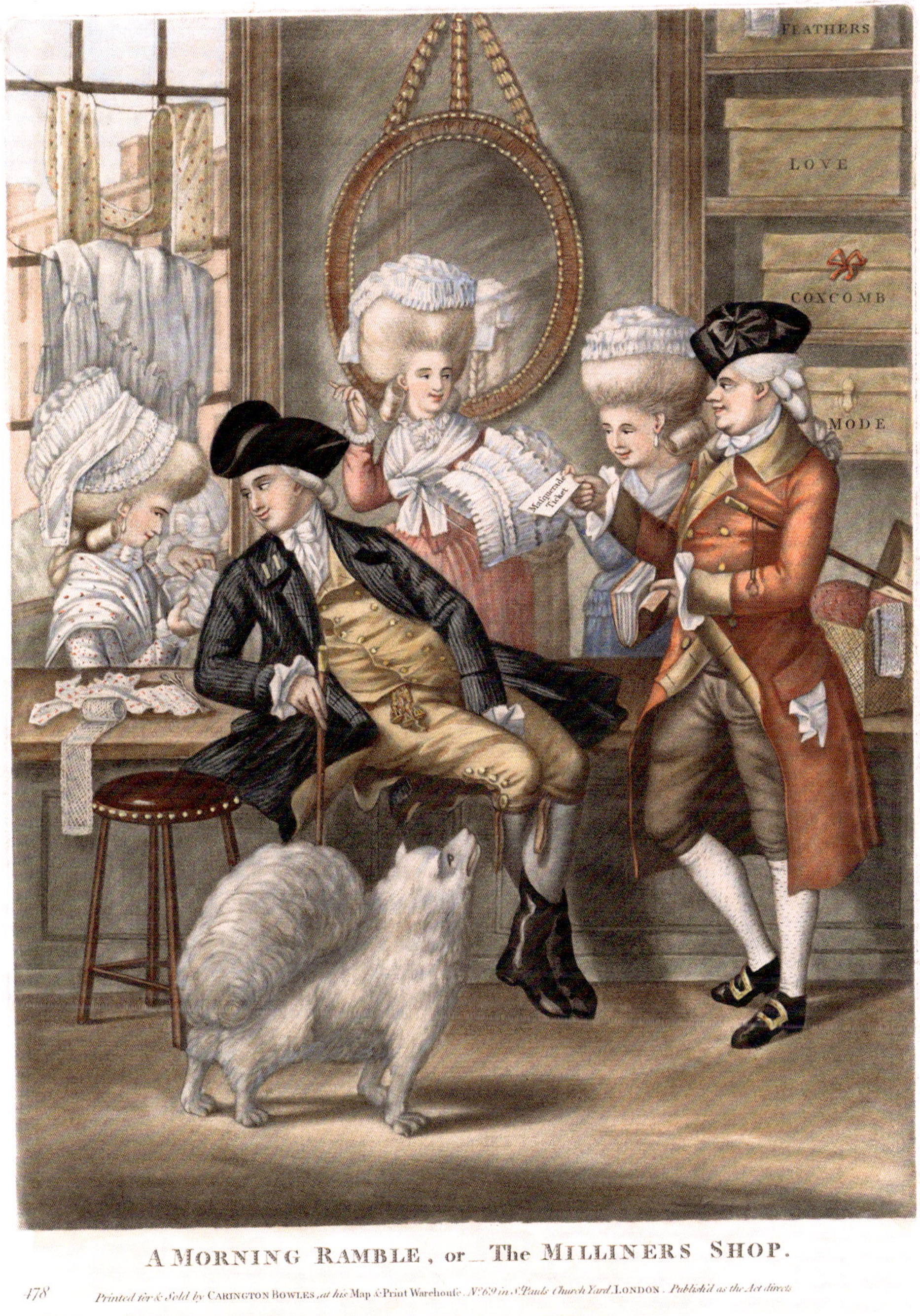

42. Artist unknown, *A Morning Ramble, or The Milliners Shop*, mezzotint with hand color (1782), 13⅞ x 9⅞ in. (35.1 x 24.9 cm), plate. Courtesy of The Lewis Walpole Library, Yale University.

were the sites of licit and illicit meetings between male and female customers in both the arts and practice.[27] Caricatures of customers' flirtations with shop staff applied to both genders, and flirtation by shop staff was well known as a (sometimes aggressive) sales strategy (see fig. 42).[28] Harry Peckham, visiting the shops at the Palais de Justice in Paris in 1772, reversed the trope that female sales staff must also have their bodies on sale for male customers, commenting that "a man must have more than legal impudence to run the gauntlet through such a number of chattering females."[29]

The gendering of retail environments was thus a complex matter, with multiple and not necessarily set readings. The gendering of a retail environment was the result of a confluence of factors: types of goods, customer use, location, sales strategy, and retailers' reinforcing signals.

GENDER AND SHOPPING

Turning from the sites of shopping to its practice, we can take a broader perspective that relates purchasing to the home and to social networks, rather than relying on the simple linear connection usually made between retail strategies and consumer behavior. The limited but revealing range of surviving diaries, letters, advice manuals, and shopping lists allows shopping in the seventeenth and eighteenth centuries to emerge as a sophisticated, multiskilled activity that involved complex decision making, the ability to deal with retail manipulation, and the application of thrift and good judgment.[30] There is plenty of evidence to show that even the middling sort went out shopping themselves in the eighteenth century to buy food and household basics, rather than sending their servants or having the tradesman or shopkeeper call at their home.[31] Good shopping involved shopping around, comparing prices, haggling down prices, developing good relationships with retailers, and searching out quality or a bargain, as much for foodstuffs as for anything else, and it was feared that servants would not apply themselves sufficiently in the task.[32] Shopping in the period involved the purchase of all kinds of things—food, clothing, furniture, basic household items, secondhand goods, as well as the so-called fashionable "luxuries" of the period—and visits to shops were also often for the reconditioning, repair, and refashioning of goods.[33] Eighteenth-century shopping was enjoyable, important to get right, and such a thoroughly accepted convention that George III and his family were caricatured in 1789 at "Splittfarthing's the Milliner's" (see fig. 41).

Shopping was associated with women in the period, because women bore the brunt of shopping for the household and were particularly burdened with shopping for foodstuffs on a daily basis. They therefore shopped more frequently than men did, and their skills and application, as Ann Smart Martin shows in her essay in this volume, were vital economically, socially, and culturally. Women also socialized differently when shopping, being more likely to shop in groups with other women, which made their shopping more publicly visible.[34]

Women took responsibility for the complex decision making about the spread of resources for managing the household and keeping the store cupboard stocked.[35] To them fell the constant burden, in an age without preservatives, pesticides, or refrigeration, to consider the freshness and quality of food that was inevitably damaged, about to go off, or had already perished. Shopping for food was *not* a simpler form of shopping, but one requiring fine judgment and the application of particular skills—sniffing, pinching, and tasting to choose, not from a standardized range, but from the best of a bad bunch. To test the freshness of a chicken, for example, the housewife had to be prepared to "try the Legs, and Hands, or Springs, at the Bone that comes out in the middle of the fleshy Part, by putting in your Finger, and smelling to it; for there it first taints."[36] Mistresses of households encountered more tedium, repetition, and responsibility in shopping than men did.

The discourse of the period in England characterized shopping as a female activity: for example, in a poem by Jonathan Swift, when the rain comes down on a London street, then "To shops in Crowds the daggled Females fly / Pretend to cheapen Goods, but nothing buy."[37] Despite this association of shopping with women, diaries and letters show how men constantly made purchases both for themselves and others. Men had both the opportunity to shop and the need—whether they were acquiring objects of male material culture, such as globes, guns, books, scientific instruments, and waistcoats, or were sent to make purchases decided on by their wives.[38]

There is plenty of evidence to show that men took as much pleasure in shopping as women did. The seventeenth-century diarist Samuel Pepys referred to "buying a few baubles to while away time" at the New Exchange;[39] in the eighteenth century, Horace Walpole, when he had the chance to go shopping every day, exclaimed, "And is there greater happiness?"[40] Men engaged in both the pleasurable and the skilled aspects of shopping. They do not seem to have been any less efficient at shopping or less interested in it than women, and they spent as much time comparing and contrasting and shopping around. Walpole, when buying a coat for his friend George Montagu, nephew of the Earl of Halifax, dealt with the complex, interwoven issues of cut, price, styling, quality, wear, and the right supplier, and he was willing to deal with tedious repeat visits. He wrote to Montagu in 1766:

> I have chose your coat . . . but I have fixed nothing about the lace. Barret had none of gauze, but what were as broad as the Irish Channel. Your tailor found a very reputable one at another place, but I would not determine rashly; it will be two or three and twenty shillings the yard - you might have a very substantial real lace, and that would wear like your old buffet [foot-stool], for twenty. the second order of gauzes are frippery, none above twelve shillings, and those tarnished, for the species is out of fashion. You will have time to sit in judgement upon these important points.[41]

Recognizing the fact that men were active shoppers, and that their shopping was more frequently personally pleasurable than women's, allows men to be positioned as active components in the discussion of increasing consumption in the eighteenth century, with their own interest in a male material culture, as well as in the world of goods more generally.[42] The criteria that theorists have used to condemn women's consumerism—fantasy, identity building, individual-based shopping, and voyeurism—might, in fact, be seen to be better ascribed to men. The key emphasis here, however, is that the sexes shared a common desire to explore the world of goods and to possess things, but they operated in different ways when they went out to acquire them.

Gender differences also emerge in the way shopping was criticized in the period. Criticisms of the frivolity and acquisitiveness of women, found in texts on luxury or consumption, have constantly been applied to shopping as well. It is often assumed that a condemnation of consumption means a condemnation of shopping, and this premise has dominated the study of other periods as well. However, from research into eighteenth-century texts that refer specifically to shopping rather than to consumption, it emerges that they did not in fact criticize shopping per se, but particular shopping behaviors.[43]

In these texts, women were criticized for being rowdy when out shopping, especially in large, pushy, groups, an image reinforced by satirical prints (fig. 43). Female shoppers were criticized for exhibiting poor taste, showing rudeness to shop staff, damaging goods by rummaging through them, and having poor shopping skills, such as not haggling the price down low enough, wasting shopkeepers' time by getting them to unpack a large amount of stock and then buying little or nothing, and vacillating rather than demonstrating incisive decision making.[44] A fictional shopkeeper of 1724 was made to lament satirically that "they tumble over my Goods, and deafen me with a Round of Questions, 'till, having found nothing in my shop, *to their Fancy*, as they call, they toss themselves again into their Coaches, and *drive on the Persecution*, to the Terror and Disturbance of most of the honest shopkeepers, from one End of the Town, to the other."[45]

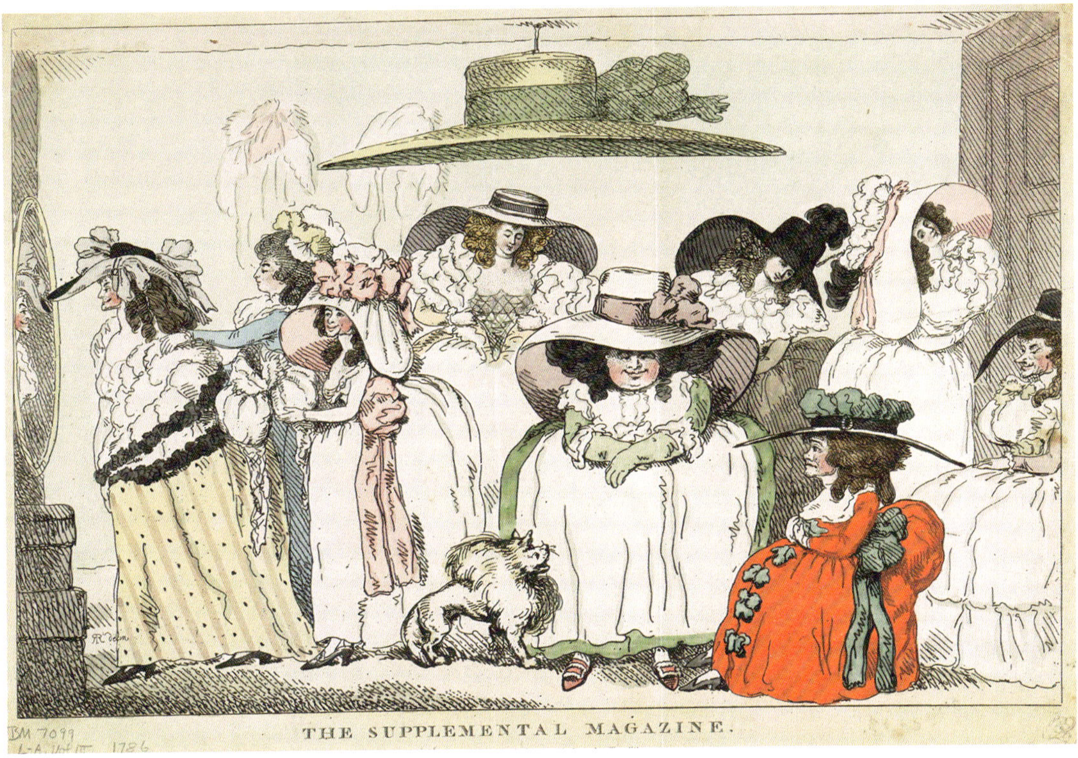

43. Artist unknown, *The Supplemental Magazine*, etching with stipple hand color (1786), 11 x 17⅛ in. (27.9 x 43.4 cm), image. Courtesy of The Lewis Walpole Library, Yale University.

This rowdy shopping behavior is contrasted with the dignity of properly performed shopping, in which shoppers are sensible, fashionably dressed, and, of course, buy English goods—depicted, for example, in *Pride's Exchange Broke Up* of 1703:

> Four modest Ladies, and Two pretty Girls,
> Bedeckt with Lockets, Chains of Gold and Pearls,
> And clad in English Silks, they made a stay,
> To see the greedy Vultures take their Prey.[46]

Neither pleasure, fashionability, nor consumption itself were perceived as the problem in shopping, but rather a lack of dignity, the wasting of others' time and resources, and an absence of personal restraint, all of which might lead to excess and familial and national ruin (the common themes of the contemporary debate on luxury).

Anxiety about loss of control over purchasing habits or frenzied shopping may have been partially fueled by the high public visibility of female shoppers and by the need of the mistress of a household to seize with speed and incisiveness the best buy in a world of varying, non-standardized, and unbranded goods as well as a finite supply of edible foodstuffs. Ostentatious displays of shop goods in the street added to the picture: besides window displays, goods might be piled up in baskets or (more elegantly) exhibited in glass showcases on the pavement in front of the shop, or textiles might be arranged to flow from door frames or upper windows. Robert Owen, the factory owner and social reformer, described the air of frenzy created at the fast-selling, low-class drapers Flint & Palmer, on Old London Bridge, where he worked as a young man from 1785 to 1786:

> Not much time was allowed for bargaining, a price being fixed for everything, and, compared with other houses, cheap. If any demur was made, or much hesitation, the article asked for was withdrawn, and, as the shop was generally full from morning till late in the evening, another customer was attended to.[47]

The allure of shopping and consumers' captivation by it were also highly visible. Diarists recorded impulse purchases, an eye for a bargain was constantly noted (with approval) in letters and diaries, and the term "bargain hunter" stems from at least the 1790s.[48] However, a personal and proper concern with thrift, which figures highly in shoppers' letters and which was socially commended, did not make itself evident in the way that the enjoyment and energy of women's shopping did.

It is noteworthy, in light of our modern-day association of shopping with women and the disassociation of men from shopping, that the eighteenth-century texts also criticized men for poor shopping in exactly the same way that they criticized women: for using up shopkeepers' time without buying, for tumbling and damaging goods, and for showing poor haggling skills.[49]

Nevertheless, subtle gender distinctions encroach. Men were not characterized as a noisy, threatening, overwhelming presence in shops in the way that women shoppers were, and the male shopper often wasted the female shopkeeper's time because he was sexually attracted to her, spending far too much time "loll[ing]" upon her counter (see fig. 42).[50] In an issue of *Spectator*, a female shop assistant is made to complain, "And here is one who makes me once or twice a Week tumble over all my Goods, and then owns it was only a Gallantry to see me act with these pretty Hands; then lays out three Pence in a little Ribband for his Wristbands."[51] Viewed as a discourse, these comments about male shopping reinforced conventions about positive male sexual energy and disassociated them from a frenzied desire for goods. In these texts, the (heterosexual) male shoppers are focused on the shop assistants, while female tumblers are focused on the goods themselves. Men lose control over sex; women (and the fop) lose control in their desire for things. But the problem, as far as the eighteenth-century discourse put it, was the loss of control. Bad shopping behavior in both men and women was decried as leading to the same thing: potential harm to the economy.

So, despite the association of women with shopping, there was no anxiety about male shopping in and of itself. The discourse on male shopping did not distance masculinity from the activity of shopping, merely from a feminine approach to it. And the texts criticizing the shortcomings of male shopping provided a rationale that enabled men to shop without compromising their gender identity, as their shortcoming was their virility. The discourse constructs the avidly shopping man as following the instincts that make him male, as opposed to the instincts that make women female. In practice, men displayed as much of a love of goods as women ("I find I cannot live without Stosch's intaglia of the gladiator").[52] An important result of the way the discourse was constructed, however, was that both men and women could shop without a sense of an overarching stricture on their behavior, and without a need to hide or disguise their personal shopping.

It seems that in the eighteenth century, even though shopping was perceived as feminized in terms of physical space and as a social and cultural activity, men were not deterred from shopping, either practically or ideologically. Men negotiated this feminization practically by abdicating to women the responsibility for much day-to-day shopping and by shopping for male items in shops that were perhaps more overtly masculinized, clubbish, and exclusive than feminized shops. They may have viewed some feminized retail areas as opportunities for heterosexual sociability, while avoiding those that were too intimidatingly female. Ideologically, they negotiated the feminization of shopping by producing discourses that distinguished between male and female motivations in shopping, stressing their distance particularly from fashion and material excess, and that devalued the expressiveness and physical presence of women shopping, promoting subdued behavior as a model for correct female shopping. Such discourses made clear that while the retail environment was in the main a female arena, rowdy or excessive female pleasure and sociability in it could be characterized as idle, disorderly, and financially dangerous. In contrast, similar male pleasure and sociability were unconnected, on the level of discourse, with the arena of the shop. The value of women's role in consumption and the critical skills of shopping are, unsurprisingly, not acknowledged. In terms of a moral discourse, neither men nor women were reproached for shopping and spending, but they were censured for the spendthrift or economically detrimental ways they might shop and spend.

While men were as proficient at shopping as women, in the discourse of the period, women were attributed with superior sensitivities toward taste, and in surviving diaries and letters, women *are* requested to help men shop. When Madame Du Deffand in Paris wanted Horace Walpole to buy some silk and six "beautiful fans" as presents, she insisted that he "call on some woman of taste."[53] And in 1759, Lord Kildare wrote from London to his wife in Ireland, "I went to Lady Harrington; and beg'd that she would be so good as choose you a birthday gown, which she has undertaken."[54] But the assistance of women in these matters of taste and shopping was applied when buying objects of exclusively female material culture—things intended to be used by women and with a high "feminine" decorative element (such as fans and dress trimmings). This suggests that for a particular range of goods thought to be distinctively feminine, women were best skilled in both selecting and buying them. The reverse was also true, however: men were more familiar with, and thus more expert in selecting, goods that formed part of their world of concerns—guns, tobacco, saddlery, and the like. When Walpole's male friends asked him to buy something for them, he shopped himself, and they told him: "I am sure of your good choice."[55] When Elizabeth Pepys wanted a pair of globes, it was her husband, Samuel, who went to Moxon's, the maker of scientific instruments, to make the purchase—browsing, looking around Moxon's house as well as shop, and drawing on his connection with Moxon and on male patterns of sociability in ways that would not have been open to Elizabeth.[56]

Certain goods required extensive knowledge that could be gained only through familiarity and actual use (and never more so than in periods without branding or standardization). If these goods related to a particular gender, then control was in the hands of that gender, and the other gender was excluded from the knowledge needed to select and buy them. Knowledge encompassed suppliers, prices, innovations, styling, and cultural and social inflections related to that object group. As the world of goods grew (and, particularly in the nineteenth century, as the gendered styling of objects by manufacturers increased), so did this gendered category, and at the same time the flexibility of shoppers to be able to cross these gendered boundaries decreased. Control is a double-edged sword, however: shopping for women, as always, has been compounded by their greater knowledge of the needs of the home, which then also positions them as the shoppers with the greater burden of mundane household shopping.

SHOPPING AS SOCIAL INTERACTION

Shopping in the period was not only a visually based practice, but also a tactile and verbal one. Eighteenth-century shoppers handled and examined goods, compared and contrasted them, gathered information, and discussed qualities and provenance with shop staff and, most of all, with their shopping companions. The conversations of shopping were as important as the looking and the physical activity of shopping, but only a small portion of the conversations that related to purchase decisions took place in the shop. Shopkeepers inserted themselves into the felted fabric of taste making in their discussions with customers, their attempts to influence decision making, their selection of stock and communication with manufacturers, and the information they passed along to consumers about the purchase patterns of other groups. But objects played a role as symbols of belonging in social networks between people, and it was these networks that formed the bedrock of decision making about purchases. Shop windows and shopkeepers informed, facilitated, and interjected (if at crucial moments), but they did not underpin the purchase decision. The majority of the thinking about goods—where to buy, what was relevant, and how taste should be construed in this individual's particular circumstances—constituted a part of a shared social intercourse and a broad cultural and social network.

A consumer's social network was the most significant influence on her shopping behavior. Elizabeth Purefoy, the widowed mother of a Buckinghamshire landed gentleman, wrote in 1738 to a London ironmonger, Mr. Belchier: "A gentleman & gentlewoman who came to our house liked your candlestick (with a Tin thing to hide the candle) so well that they would have each of them one. So I desire you will send two."[57] Consumers used their hands-on experience of goods in the homes of others to check whether products worked well, whether they looked right in certain settings, whether they wore well, or to fight down prices. Elizabeth Purefoy wrote to the grocer, Mr. Wilson, on the matter of sugar: "I hope you will let mee have a better pennyworth [bargain] than the last, for my neighbours had a better sugar at that price."[58] Lady Mary Wortley Montagu wrote to her sister in 1721 asking her to spend three guineas for her, "one of which I beg you would lay out in the same narrow minunet [mignonette, a fine lace] that you sent [Mrs.] Murray, and send it me by the fi[rst] Oppertunity for the use of my Daughter."[59] In this circumstance, both the decision to buy and the purchase were organized and carried out without the recipient even entering a shop. Making a purchase decision was never a single-moment event, and even impulse purchases were socially situated.[60]

When considering how people made their purchase decisions and what criteria they used, it is important to recognize how much they were able to engage firsthand with the actual goods they were considering by personally handling them. This could take place in other people's homes or inside the shop; consumers did not depend on an image or description one step removed. This is why shopkeepers exploited tactile engagement with goods to the full, playing with excitement and anticipation by revealing goods in elaborate sequences and encouraging a thorough handling of goods that induced a momentary sensation of ownership.

While opinions and ideas were formed in social interaction, the practice of shopping itself was also not an isolated event. Shopping was more often than not carried out with friends, family, or socially important acquaintances rather than alone, and these shopping partners' ideas, tastes, opinions, and influences all came into play—not only on a shopping trip, but in the whole discussion about what and whether to buy.

People in the period also spent a lot of time shopping *for* others. This can be termed "proxy shopping," to make a distinction between two slightly differing practices. The term "proxy shopping" is used here to define shopping carried out for someone by family, friends, or socially significant contacts, in order to distinguish this from "correspondence shopping"—that carried out by agents, bankers, servants, or tradespeople.[61] Proxy shoppers had to devote the same time, effort, and consideration as they might in shopping for themselves, in a way that could never be expected of servants or agents. The proxy shopper, in particular, had to think herself or himself into the skin of the person commissioning a purchase, intimately understanding that person's likes, dislikes, and requirements, and a good proxy shopper also was a highly valued social connection. The shopper had to understand taste and the degree of fashionability to which the commissioner wished to go. George Montagu wrote to Horace Walpole in Paris asking him to "lay me out a little money in matters you know are to my fancy."[62] Proxy shopping was so important that at times the shopping relationship was more valuable than the goods that were bought, the acts of requesting and responding being the cement that sealed and nurtured the relationship.[63]

Certainly for eighteenth-century elites, but possibly also for other strata of society, it seems to have been usual for friends and family of a particular circle to review the progress of a particular purchase as a group—during as well as after the selection process. Examples or "patterns," or a range of ready finished goods, were brought home for examination and selection, the members of the group offering their opinions on taste, craftsmanship, and suppliers as a form of quality control.[64] The Parisian socialite Madame Du Deffand continuously bowed to "la décision générale,"[65] and even when Walpole went to the trouble of finding a "woman of taste" to buy fans and silk for Du Deffand's mother, the group opinion of the success of the purchase was fed back to him that while the fans were found pretty, the silk had found criticism.[66] A little lower down the social scale, Fanny Boscawen, an admiral's wife, wrote to her husband of her newly furnished "bow-window room": "Everybody commends each separate, but dislike them together and maintain I must have coloured linen to my coloured paper."[67] In an age anxiously concerned with propriety and solvency, family or peer-group review was there, practically or symbolically, as an effective restraint on excess. Ironically, of course, the social network was also the crucible of desire.

Again, such review processes were not discussions of goods in the abstract, but were made with the object at hand, so that quality of workmanship or styling could be discussed in relation to the form of that actual object, its function, price, domestic setting, and related objects. Therefore, discussions of beauty, taste, and fashion did not operate in a void but in relation to specific objects, varying with every selection or purchase. Fashion and taste were marshaled within the working dynamics of everyday life—what was available at a particular time and place, at a certain price, for certain needs, and with particular uses and qualities. The purchase of the Duke and Duchess of Leinster's taffeta for Carlton House in Ireland in 1759 was subjected to review by a string of family members in London, with the duchess's sister writing: "The taffeta is I think pretty; I have seen prettier. I like my own better, but that was the prettiest among many we saw, except one on a white ground, of which there was only a small quantity to be had."[68]

Letters requesting proxy or correspondence shopping are revealing about purchasing criteria. Judgments that shoppers were expected to make, even at the highest social levels, revolved constantly around the issues of fitness to purpose and propriety, function, wear, price, and quality: "I don't care how plain my Barometer is so as it be strong & durable because it is for travelling, & if one of 18s is as durable as one of a guinea I had as soon have ye 18s one."[69] Color, taste, pattern, or "fashion" are rarely mentioned, and sometimes they are dismissed ("as to the ffancy of ye pattern I leave that to you"), while alternatives and compromises were made explicit.[70]

These omissions are not because taste was unimportant, but perhaps because it was so dependent on a shared knowledge of what was appropriate. As Hannah Greig shows in her essay in this volume, taste was not necessarily about modishness or the latest style. The constant reiteration of the values of fitness, function, price, and quality reminds us that no matter how crucial the elusive element of taste or fashion was to a purchase, it did not operate independently of these other criteria, which in turn were determined by their social context. Madame Du Deffand's mother herself felt that the fans Walpole had bought were not particularly beautiful; however, she placed this outcome within a practical economic context, replying, "But it's my own fault for not having laid out enough money."[71] Through the examination of shopping as a practice, we discover the options that people had to operate within, and decide how to lead, their lives. Shopping in all its myriad forms was a process for this to happen—it was the drawstring connecting consumer, goods, and social relations.

CONCLUSION

Over the course of several hundred years, consumers came to purchase more finished goods rather than semifinished ones or the raw materials for making goods at home, and increasingly they purchased affordable new items rather than secondhand goods. New shopping skills were not needed to cope with this change—shoppers had been used to purchasing finished goods for centuries, but now they spent more time comparing and contrasting finished articles (rather than selecting raw materials), as well as developing their knowledge about these goods and their respective qualities. As the choice of finished goods increased, consumers' options to experiment also would have increased, and more time might have been spent in decision making and shopping than in making things at home. Consumers now would have more time and effort invested in categorizing the different types and ranges of finished goods, and the efficient management of the household would depend more often on skills in shopping than on abilities in making items.

This development over time represents a change in the mental focus of shopping. It moved from assessing how the materials purchased would function in the production or finishing process to uncovering the full range of finished items, considering how they compared with one another, and selecting the best possible options to serve the home from among these. Consumers increasingly looked for what could be found in the shops to elaborate their ideas of how to fill their homes and load their tables. The scope of the desired outcome had changed. Shopping became more often a process of seeking out the best from the range of goods on offer, after spending time finding out what that range was, rather than finishing off to best advantage what one already possessed. The parameters of what might constitute a suitable item for the home had become enlarged and set by the search and the choice available in the shops, rather than limited to what was achievable in the home. This process of seeking out the best or choosing among ranges of options would have acted as a spur to the refinement of ideas about goods for the home.[72]

In this essay, shopping is considered as a whole experience, or as a complex of procedures, whereby a variety of practices leads to ideas and opinions, rather than the other way around. This makes more sense than the focus of historians of the nineteenth century on responses to the single external stimulus of advertising, or shop display, or on monolithic notions of fashion and emulation. This attention to shopping as a social, situated practice helps us to position men as well as women as active consumers in a period of expanding consumer choice, and to move away from the typical condemnatory association of femininity and shopping. Identifying how sociability in shops, gender strategies of some shops, and the gendered nature of some shopping operated in the period helps us understand how shops fitted into the process of the selection of goods, which began and ended not in the shop but in the home, as well as among the social networks of consumer groups.

I am very grateful to the Economic and Social Research Council for awarding me a postdoctoral fellowship for the period during which this essay was written.

1. See Lorna H. Mui and Hoh-cheung Mui, *Shops and Shopkeeping in Eighteenth-Century England* (London and Montreal: Routledge and McGill-Queen's Univ. Press, 1989), and Nancy Cox, *The Complete Tradesman: A Study of Retailing, 1550–1820* (Aldershot: Ashgate, 2000).
2. See L. B. Barley and M. W. Barley, "Lincolnshire Shopkeepers in the Sixteenth and Seventeenth Century," *Lincolnshire Historian* 2 (1962): 7–21; Trevor Fawcett, "Bath's Georgian Warehouses," *Costume* 26 (1992): 32–39; Dianne Collins, "Primitive or Not? Fixed Shop Retailing before the Industrial Revolution," *Journal of Regional and Local Studies* 13, no. 1 (Summer 1993): 4–22; John Benson and Gareth Shaw, eds., *The Retailing Industry*, part B, *The Early Modern Period* (London: I. B. Tauris, 1999); Cox, *Complete Tradesman*; H. Berry, "Polite Consumption: Shopping in Eighteenth-Century England," *Transactions of the Royal Historical Society* 12 (2002): 375–94.
3. Claire Walsh, "Shop Design and the Display of Goods in Eighteenth-Century London," *Journal of Design History* 8, no. 3 (1995), repr. in Benson and Shaw, *Retailing Industry*; Walsh, "The Newness of the Department Store: A View from the Eighteenth Century," in *Cathedrals of Consumption: The European Department Store, 1850–1939*, ed. Geoffrey Crossick and Serge Jaumain (Aldershot: Ashgate, 1999).
4. See Margaret Spufford, *The Great Reclothing of Rural England: Petty Chapmen and their Wares in the Seventeenth Century* (London: Hambledon Press, 1984); Beverly Lemire, "Peddling Fashion: Salesmen, Pawnbrokers, Taylors, Thieves and the Second-hand Clothes Trade in England, c. 1700–1800," *Textile History* 22 (1991): 67–82; and Lemire, "Peddlers, Charlatans and Alewives: Plebeian Commercial Circuits in English Daily Life, c. 1600–1800," in *Buyers, Sellers and Salesmanship in Medieval and Early-Modern Europe*, ed. Bruno Blondé and others (Turnhout, Belgium: Brepols, 2006).
5. See Derek Keene, "Shops and Shopping in Medieval London," in *British Archaeological Association Conference Transactions for the Year 1984*, vol. 10, *Medieval Art, Architecture and Archaeology in London*, ed. Lindy Grant (London: British Archaeological Association, 1990), and John Schofield and Alan Vince, *Medieval Towns* (Leicester: Leicester Univ. Press, 1994).
6. See Ann Smart Martin, "Commercial Space as Consumption Arena: Retail Stores in Early Virginia," in *People, Power, Places*, ed. Sally McMurry and Annmarie Adams, vol. 8 of *Perspectives in Vernacular Architecture* (Knoxville: Univ. of Tennessee Press, 2000), 201–18; Evelyn Welch, *Shopping in the Renaissance: Consumer Cultures in Italy, 1400–1600* (New Haven and London: Yale Univ. Press, 2005); Blondé and others, *Buyers, Sellers and Salesmanship*; and Martin's essay in this volume.
7. Among early attempts to uncover retail marketing strategies in the eighteenth century, see Claire Walsh, "Shop Design and the Display of Goods in the Eighteenth Century" (MA diss., V&A / Royal College of

Art, 1993), and Walsh, "Shop Design and the Display of Goods in Eighteenth-Century London." For greater contextualization of retailing and retail strategies in early periods, see Keene, "Shops and Shopping in Medieval London"; Cox, *Complete Tradesman*; Richard Britnell, "Markets and Fairs in Medieval and Early-Modern England," in Blondé and others, *Buyers, Sellers and Salesmanship*; Walsh, *Shops and Shopping in Early-Modern England* (forthcoming).

8. Neil McKendrick, John Brewer, and J. H. Plumb, eds., *The Birth of a Consumer Society: The Commercialization of Eighteenth-Century England* (London: Europa, 1982). For a revision of McKendrick's revolution thesis, see John Styles, "Manufacturing, Consumption and Design in Eighteenth-Century England," in *Consumption and the World of Goods: Consumption and Society in the Seventeenth and Eighteenth Centuries*, ed. John Brewer and Roy Porter (London: Routledge, 1993).

9. See Amanda Vickery, *The Gentleman's Daughter: Women's Lives in Georgian England*, (New Haven and London: Yale Univ. Press, 1998); Margot Finn, "Men's Things: Masculine Possession in the Consumer Revolution," *Social History* 25, no. 2 (May 2000); Claire Walsh, "Shopping in Early-Modern London, c. 1660–1800" (PhD thesis, European Univ. Institute, Florence, 2001); Walsh, *Shops and Shopping in Early-Modern England*; and Vickery's essay in this volume.

10. Mui and Mui, *Shops and Shopkeeping*, introduction. For the relative position of markets, see Britnell, "Markets and Fairs."

11. The earliest reference to showrooms comes from the *Oxford English Dictionary*, s.v. "showrooms," R Cocks, Diary, 2 Jan. 1617. On bulks, see Walsh, *Shops and Shopping in Early-Modern England*, chap. 2. On conversions from houses, see Keene, "Shops and Shopping in Medieval London," and Kathryn Morrison, *English Shops and Shopping: An Architectural History* (New Haven and London: Yale Univ. Press, 2004).

12. Walsh, "Shop Design" (1993), chap. 2 and appendices.

13. See Walsh, "Shop Design" (1993), chap. 1; H. Louw, "The Rise of the Metal Window during the Early Industrial Period in Britain c. 1750–1830," *Construction History* 3 (1987); and Louw, "Window-glass Making in Britain c. 1660–c. 1860 and Its Architectural Impact," *Construction History* 7 (1991).

14. This is clear from the study of retailers' probate inventories. For London, these were taken from the Orphans Court, Corporation of London Records Office, List C of Working Trades, 1695–1732, and from Probate 31, The National Archives, London, for the period 1742–90; see Walsh, "Shop Design" (1993), chap. 2 and appendices. For provincial retailers' inventories, see Cox, *Complete Tradesman*.

15. George Braithwaite, The National Archives, London, Chancery Masters Exhibits C105/5, Part I.

16. Jean André Rouquet, *The Present State of the Arts in England* (1755), quoted in Bernard Denvir, *The Eighteenth Century: Art, Design and Society, 1689–1789* (London and New York: Longman, 1988), 44.

17. Una des Fontaines, "Portland House: Wedgwood's London Showrooms 1774–94," *Proceedings of the Wedgwood Society*, 2:136–48

18. See Walsh, *Shops and Shopping in Early-Modern England*, chap. 2, and Peter Borsay, *The English Urban Renaissance: Culture and Society in the Provincial Town, 1660–1770* (Oxford: Clarendon Press, 1989).

19. A good example is Wedgwood, especially his exhibition of the "Frog Sevice"; see Malcolm Baker, "A Rage for Exhibitions: The Display and Viewing of Wedgwood's Frog Service," in *The Genius of Wedgwood*, ed. Hilary Young (London: Victoria & Albert Museum, 1995), 118–33.

20. Changes in internal structure over time can be seen clearly in amendments made to floor plans on shop leases; see Comptroller City Land Deeds, Corporation of London Records Office, for example, James Price's shop on Cheapside, 1746–47.

21. Evidence from inventories in the Orphans Court, Corporation of London Records Office, and Probate 31, The National Archives; shop lease plans, Comptroller City Land Deeds, Corporation of London Records Office; and shoplifting cases at the Old Bailey, Proceedings of the Old Bailey, London, 1674 to 1834.

22. *Female Tatler*, no. 9, 25–27 July 1709.

23. There was an increase in the number of formal display fittings in shops throughout the century, observable from an analysis of inventories in the Orphans Court, Corporation of London Records Office, and Probate 31, The National Archives.

24. In the literature on nineteenth-century retailing, emphasis has been placed on the way department stores

echoed the features of the secure middle-class home as a means of establishing the retail landscape as a safe space for women, in line with separate spheres thinking that women were safe in, and associated with, the domestic: "the fantasy world of escape from dull domesticity was also, in another way, a second home." Rachel Bowlby, *Just Looking: Consumer Culture in Dreiser, Gissing and Zola* (London and New York: Methuen, 1985), 4.

25. On the New Exchange and Westminster Hall, see Walsh, "Shopping in Early-Modern London," chap. 2, and Claire Walsh, "Social Meaning and Social Space in the Shopping Galleries of Early-Modern London," in *A Nation of Shopkeepers: A History of Retailing in Britain, 1550–2000*, ed. John Benson and Laura Ugolini (London: I. B. Tauris, 2003).

26. Samuel Richardson to George Cheyne, 31 Aug. 1741, referring to *Tatler*, no. 143, 9 March 1710, in *Selected Letters of Samuel Richardson*, ed. John Carroll (Oxford: Clarendon Press, 1964), 47. Men seemed to have been in no way deterred from entering the New Exchange despite its clear association with women, and guidebooks of the period encouraged male tourists to visit the gallery as part of their experience of London; see Walsh, "Shopping in Early-Modern London," chap. 2.

27. The New Exchange shopping gallery had a reputation as meeting place, and it was used in plays as a setting for sexual intrigue; see Sir George Etherege, *The Man of Mode; or Sir Fopling Flutter* (1676), in *The Plays of Sir George Etherege*, ed. Michael Cordner (Cambridge: Cambridge Univ. Press, 1982), act 3, scene 3. For shops as safe zones for heterosexual encounters, see, for example, Eliza Haywood, *The History of Miss Betsy Thoughtless* (1751), 3:47–48.

28. For customer flirtations, see *Spectator*, no. 155, 28 Aug. 1712 (by men) and the *Times* (London), 1 Aug. 1786 (by women). As a sales strategy, flirtation and sexual intimidation had operated at least since the medieval period; see Derek Keene, "Shops and Shopping in Medieval London," 41.

29. Harry Peckham, *The Tour of Holland, Dutch Brabant, The Austrian Netherlands, and Part of France* (London: Printed for G. Kearsly, 1772), 140.

30. See Walsh, "Shopping in Early-Modern London," chap. 1, and Walsh, *Shops and Shopping in Early-Modern England*, chap. 5.

31. For example, Fanny Boscawen, an admiral's wife, wrote from Hatchlands to her husband in London on 28 Dec. 1756, asking him to bring "half a firkin of good salt butter and a gallon of spirits"; Fanny Boscawen, *Admiral's Wife: Being the Life and Letters of the Hon. Mrs Edward Boscawen from 1719–1761*, ed. Cecil Aspinall-Oglander (London: Longmans, Green, 1940), 246.

32. See Walsh, "Shopping in Early-Modern London," chap. 4, and Walsh, *Shops and Shopping in Early-Modern England*, chap. 11.

33. The concept of these "fashionable luxuries" is given considerable significance, but it is sometimes ill defined by historians; for example, see Maxine Berg and Helen Clifford, eds., *Consumers and Luxury: Consumer Culture in Europe, 1650–1850* (Manchester: Manchester Univ. Press, 1999), introduction. For more precise outlines of these goods, see Lorna Weatherill, *Consumer Behaviour and Material Culture in Britain, 1660–1760* (London: Routledge, 1988); Styles, "Manufacturing, Consumption and Design"; Cox, *Complete Tradesman*; and John Styles, "Product Innovation in Early Modern London," *Past and Present* 168 (2000): 124–69.

34. See Walsh, "Shopping in Early-Modern London," chap. 3, and Walsh, *Shops and Shopping in Early-Modern England*, chap. 6.

35. See Vickery, *Gentleman's Daughter*, chap. 4, and Olwen Hufton, *The Prospect Before Her: A History of Women in Western Europe, 1500–1800* (London: HarperCollins, 1995), 163–72.

36. *The Accomplish'd Housewife; or the Gentlewoman's Companion* (London: J. Newbery, 1745), 157.

37. Jonathan Swift, "A Description of a City Shower," *Tatler*, no. 238, 17 Oct. 1710.

38. See the introduction to this volume.

39. Samuel Pepys, diary entry, 26 Nov. 1666, in *The Diary of Samuel Pepys*, ed. R. C. Latham and W. Mathews (London: Bell & Hyman, 1983).

40. Horace Walpole to Lady Mary Coke, 4 Jan. 1766, in *The Yale Edition of Horace Walpole's Correspondence*, ed. Wilmarth Sheldon Lewis (New Haven: Yale Univ. Press, 1937–83), 31:93.

41. Walpole to George Montagu, 16 April 1761, in *Horace Walpole's Correspondence*, 9:258.
42. As Amanda Vickery has shown, male shopping was more frequently more interesting and personally creative than was women's; Vickery, *Gentleman's Daughter*, 166–68.
43. Key texts include *Female Tatler*, no. 9, 25–27 July 1709; *Female Tatler*, no. 67, 7 Dec. 1709; *Female Tatler*, no. 110, 27 March 1710; *Tatler*, no. 151, 28 March 1710; *Spectator*, no. 155, 28 Aug. 1711; *Spectator*, no. 336, 26 March 1712; *Spectator*, no. 454, 11 Aug. 1712; *Plain Dealer*, 28 Dec. 1724.
44. See, for example, *Pride's Exchange Broke Up* (London, 1703); *Tatler*, no. 238, 17 Oct. 1710; *Spectator*, no. 336, 26 March 1712; *Spectator*, no. 454, 11 Aug. 1712; Daniel Defoe, *The Complete English Tradesman*, 2nd ed. (London: Printed for Charles Rivington, 1727), 60–61.
45. *Plain Dealer*, 28 Dec. 1724.
46. *Pride's Exchange Broke Up*.
47. Robert Owen, *The Life of Robert Owen Written by Himself* (London: C. Knight, 1971), 19.
48. For impulse purchases, see Pepys, diary entries, 13 Feb. 1660 and 1 Jan. 1662, in *Diary*; for bargain shopping, see Mary Delany, 30 Oct. 1732, in *The Autobiography and Correspondence of Mary Granville, Mrs Delany*, ed. Lady Llanover, 6 vols. (London: Richard Bentley, 1861–62), 1:389; and for "bargain hunters," see James Lackington, *Memoirs of the First 45 Years* (1795), 128.
49. See, for example, *Spectator*, no. 155, 28 Aug. 1711, and *Spectator*, no. 454, 11 Aug. 1712.
50. *Spectator*, no. 155, 28 Aug. 1711.
51. *Spectator*, no. 155, 28 Aug. 1711.
52. Walpole to Horace Mann, 26 Nov. 1741, in *Horace Walpole's Correspondence*, 17:212–13.
53. ". . . adressez-vous à quelque femme de goût." Mme Du Deffand to Walpole, 1 Feb. 1771, in *Horace Walpole's Correspondence*, 5:20.
54. This was a gown for the queen's birthday celebrations. Lord Kildare, London, to Emily, Duchess of Leinster, 28 April 1759, in *Correspondence of Emily, Duchess of Leinster, 1731–1814*, ed. B. Fitzgerald (Dublin: Irish Manuscripts Commission, 1949), 1:69.
55. Horace Mann to Walpole, 27 March 1762, in *Horace Walpole's Correspondence*, 22:20.
56. Samuel Pepys, diary entry, 8 Sept. 1666, in *Diary*.
57. Elizabeth Purefoy to Mr. Belchier, letter 293, 3 Dec. 1738, in *Purefoy Letters, 1735–1753*, ed. G. Eland (London: Sidgwick and Jackson, 1931).
58. Purefoy to Mr. Wilson, letter 105, 21 Dec. 1746, in *Purefoy Letters*.
59. Lady Mary Wortley Montagu to her sister, Lady Mar, c. 11 Aug. 1721, in *The Complete Letters of Lady Mary Wortley Montagu*, ed. R. Halsband (Oxford: Clarendon Press, 1965), 2:10–11.
60. Daniel Miller, *A Theory of Shopping* (Ithaca, NY: Cornell Univ. Press, 1998).
61. The terms "correspondence shopping" and "proxy shopping" have been used before, but without this distinction; see, for example, Anne Buck, *Dress in Eighteenth-Century England* (London: B. T. Batsford, 1979). For more on these types of shopping, see Claire Walsh, "Shopping as a Skilled Practice in Early-Modern England," in Blondé and others, *Buyers, Sellers and Salesmanship*.
62. George Montagu to Walpole, Paris, 27 Aug. 1769, in *Horace Walpole's Correspondence*, 10:285–86.
63. One excellent example is the friendship between Horace Mann and Horace Walpole; see Walsh, "Shopping in Early-Modern London," chap. 1.
64. For example, Walpole, Paris, to Conway, 30 July 1771, addendum on 31 July, in *Horace Walpole's Correspondence*, 39:145–46.
65. For example, Mme Du Defand to Walpole, 8 April 1776, addendum on 10 April, in *Horace Walpole's Correspondence*, 6:302. This approach seems not to have been a result of Madame Du Deffand's blindness, as her usual terminology when referring to actions that must have been performed for her by others, such as reading, was to use the first person.
66. Mme Du Deffand to Walpole, 27 Feb. 1771, in *Horace Walpole's Correspondence*, 5:32.
67. Fanny Boscawen was reluctant to let her friends see her room in the making, because of the power of such peer-group censure. Boscawen, *Admiral's Wife*, 72–73. See also Jane Austen, *Jane Austen's Letters to Her Sister Cassandra and Others*, ed. R. W. Chapman (Oxford: Clarendon Press, 1932), 82.

68. Caroline Fox, London, to Emily, Duchess of Leinster, June 1759, in *Correspondence of Emily, Duchess of Leinster*, 1:233.

69. Henry Purefoy to George Sterrop, letter 185, 14 June 1752, in *Purefoy Letters*.

70. Elizabeth Purefoy on chintz for curtains; Elizabeth Purefoy, letter 201, 17 Dec. 1746, and letter 172, 20 Aug. 1738, in *Purefoy Letters*. For an example of alternatives, see Lady Montagu, 25 Dec. 1722, in *Complete Letters*, 2:21.

71. ". . . mais c'est ma faute de n'avoir pas voulu y mettre plus d'argent." Mme de Choiseul to Mme Du Deffand, 3 March 1771, in *Correspondance complète de Mme du Deffand*, ed. L.-C.-J. de Beaupoil (Paris: Michel Lévy frères, 1866), S-A i. 354.

72. For more on this idea of ranges of options for consumers within product brackets, see Styles, "Product Innovation in Early Modern London," 124–69, and Marina Bianchi, ed., *The Active Consumer: Novelty and Surprise in Consumer Choice* (London: Routledge, 1998), introduction.

What turns people into shoppers? Why do people buy particular things? Ultimately, how can we understand human desire for material objects? All of these questions were already being asked in the eighteenth century, as people navigated changes regarding material goods. Historians have written extensively about new forms and scales of consumption in the eighteenth and early nineteenth centuries. Those who have asked questions about consumers and their motivations most often focus on metropolitan areas and issues of social class. Perhaps historians have been loath to worry about the mundane things that concerned small-town merchants, like a "good pennyworth" or "the freshness of merchandise." Studying consumer behavior in more rural places and examining the evolution of petty exchange systems have lagged behind the study of larger economic questions.[3]

This volume helps address another curiously neglected area. Western society links shopping and women as natural practice; after all, literary sources are rife with tales of women who shop—and, most often, not very well. Yet a precisely gendered behavioral account of consumption in the colonial and early national periods of American history remains to be written. The lack of easily read or manipulated evidence means that women are somctimes simply dropped into an undifferentiated household designation. Several essays in this volume explore the household as a locus of consumption, but shopping remains, quite simply, a quotidian activity about which we understand too little. We do not know enough about agency (who controlled access to resources and initiated purchase choice), authority (who was the final arbiter in consumption decisions), or action (who physically moved about the landscape to acquire goods).[4]

Combining these two areas of interest highlights rural women as active economic players. In the rural American South in the eighteenth century, women were part of a petty economy that moved small foodstuffs and home-produced goods from plantations into the regional circuits of exchange that provisioned towns and distributed imported European household goods. Women had control of cash earned from the sale of items considered to be of their own production. In turn, they were the target market for a large portion of even a general merchant's stock. These women were not afraid of market relationships. For many, greater productivity meant the ability to buy more things. Raising chickens and selling eggs might bring a new ribbon or apron, a creamware plate or more tea.

This essay offers three interpretive handles for thinking about gendered consumption. First, it looks at the point of purchase. It examines the relationships between merchants and customers; between women and their husbands, fathers, or lovers; and, as important, between customers and objects. The point of purchase was always a triangulation between merchant, customer, and object, but women's consumption decisions often contained an additional element—male relatives who might contest their freedom to choose. The second section examines the question, who controls the decision? by asking who had power over the money and by searching for what eighteenth-century women called their "little purse to themselves."[5] The final section looks for women who were in the store but seem to be missing from the documentary record because of standard accounting practices. It also addresses the linked issue of proxy shopping, whereby women might acquire things without choosing them in person. Together, these three components can paint at least a partial picture of women's interaction with consumer society.

RELATIONSHIPS: AGENTS, INFLUENCES, AND ACTIONS

The act of purchase is a performative moment that can reveal the unstable relations of merchant, customer, and consumer good. Sarah Kemble Knight was a wealthy merchant's daughter who traveled from Boston to New York in 1704, and her commentary is trenchant. Knight's description of a "tall country fellow" making a purchase is, like the portrayal of other characters in her journal, a bit of a comic sketch, yet nonetheless it is worth quoting at some length:

> He advanc't to the middle of the Room, makes an Awkward Nodd, and spitting a great deal of Aromatick Tincture, he gave a scrape with his shovel like shoo, leaving a small shovel full of dirt on the floor, made a full stop, Hugging his own pretty Body with his hands under his arms, Stood staring rown'd him like a Catt let out of a Basket. At last, . . . he opened his mouth and said, have you any Ribenen for Hatbands to sell I pray. The Questions and Answers about the pay being past, the Ribin is bro't and opened. Bumpkin Simpers, cryes[,] its confounded Gay I vow; and beckoning to the door, in comes Jone Tawdry, dropping about 50 curtsies, and stands by him. hee shows her the Ribin. *Law You*, sais shee, *its right Gent*, do You take it, *tis dreadfully pretty*. Then she enquires *have You any hood silk I pray*? wh[ich] being brought and bought. *Have you any thred silk to sew it wth* says shee, wh[ich] being accomodated with they Departed.

Knight observed that when poor country folk entered the store building, they generally stood "a great while speechless and sometimes don't say a word til they are askt what they want." She attributed this to the "Awe they stand in of the merchants." This awe originated in and testified to a relation of power: customers were often indebted "and must take what they [the merchants] bring [out to the counter] without Liberty to choose for themselves."[6] Yet Knight, the merchant's daughter, had little sympathy for these consumers, for they too often made the merchant wait for his pay.

Knight's words on rural shopping starkly illustrate the relationship between merchant and poor ordinary customer. Note the absolute discomfort, gestures of humility, body language, wonder at the beauty of ribbons, even how "Jone Tawdry" was forced to wait outside until her husband beckoned her. The control of the merchant continued even after she entered the store. Did she have the choice of all ribbons, or did he preselect those he thought she could afford—or deserved?

This scene can be contrasted with experiences of the more well-to-do. In his diary, Virginian planter Landon Carter recorded a shopping trip that his twenty-four-year-old daughter Lucy made in 1775. On Saturday, 23 October, he drily wrote, "Lucy as usual is much in want of necessaries." She had planned to go to one store, but when told by another person about a better selection elsewhere, she went there instead. Her father had given her $7 to spend, and she returned in time for dinner with a fan, some ribbons, and "several such prodigious nothings," costing much more than that amount. But Landon Carter's credit was good in any store, and she could spend freely. As her father put it, "I am trusted and that is her comfort."[7]

Here the power relationship between merchant and female customer is reversed. If one merchant treated Jone Tawdry with disdain, another was complaisant and deferential to a social superior. Because Lucy Carter was the daughter of one of the wealthiest men in Virginia, her business was welcome. Both Lucy Carter and Jone Tawdry purchased ribbons, but the ways that merchants treated them and their personal comfort in the world of goods present a stark contrast. Lucy no doubt did not stand stock-still or wide-eyed in the shopping environment; she had far finer things at home. While shopping was an enjoyable activity that got her out of the house and gave her fashionable things, she may not have taken the same intense pleasure as Jone Tawdry at their color and visual appeal, nor felt as great a thrill at their ownership.

Elizabeth Hog's acquisition story was preserved in the Augusta County, Virginia, court records when she gave a deposition in 1765 about incorrect billing for a ribbon. Three years earlier, she had been with a nineteen-year-old friend, Priscilla Christian, on the occasion of the first fair held in Staunton, Virginia. Elizabeth's testimony paints a vivid scene in which a more modern form of trade—an entry of goods in an account as a debt—comes squarely up against a customary, old-fashioned obligation.

Priscilla was a merchant's daughter, Elizabeth the daughter of a wealthy planter and local leader. Priscilla asked if Elizabeth would go with her to Mr.

Crow's store, across from the courthouse, to get a fairing (an inexpensive tribute or gift purchased or presented at fairs). Elizabeth demurred, but Thomas Crow, standing on the doorstep of his brother's store, soon waved his hand to beckon the girls to come over. At about the same time, his sister-in-law called to him. As he passed by the girls, Priscilla asked him if he was going to give them a fairing. "Stay till I come back," he replied. Inside the store, Priscilla made the same demand of Joseph Bell, "who was then within the counter." He made no reply for some time. At last, he took from the shelves "two pieces, or bolts, of ribbon" and told her to take her choice, which she did. After he cut off a yard and gave it to her, he gave one to Elizabeth too, at Priscilla's request. Soon after, Priscilla asked if he would not give them each a fairing for Thomas Crow, and he did so. This was clearly a good day's work for a persistent girl like Priscilla.

Later, however, Elizabeth went to pay off her account with William Crow, and "on hearing the articles read over with which she stood charged," she was surprised to find a yard of ribbon included. She objected, stating that she had never bought a yard of ribbon in the store—but it was charged to her along with a yard of linen that she had bought from Bell. She told Crow that Bell was wrong to have charged her, as he had made a present of a ribbon to her and Priscilla. This led to the court case, with Crow the plaintiff and Bell the defendant.[8]

The notion of a fairing is important—it is one of those economic scenarios in which custom trumped capitalism. While it can signify the object itself—the thing is a fairing—the word also signified a particular gift as a form of courtship, potentially the first of a number of ever more expensive presents that was a customary binding or promise of marriage. Hence the painting by George Morland titled *Valentines Day, The Fairing* (fig. 44). Morland's choice of title links the fairing and courtship completely. The young man looks back at his love, who holds a blue ribbon that he has just bestowed upon her. The ribbon is the desire.[9]

Each of the women in these stories is linked to ribbons. Most bought them for themselves, a relatively inexpensive treat to update a wardrobe or entwine the body or hair. Unlike the simple ties with which we wrap packages, these ribbons could be quite complex, and colors, sizes, ornamentation, and materials were quickly changing indices of fashion. For some, merely wearing any ribbon was an emblem of fashionable excess. The diary of Ann Cooper Whitall, an eighteenth-century Quaker, mourned, "Oh the fashions and running into them." The young men were already wearing their hats up behind, "and next it's likely to be a ribbon to tie their hair behind." She continued to wail that "the girls in Pennsylvania have their necks set off with a black ribbon, a sorrowful sight indeed!"[10] Even tying a black ribbon around one's neck was important. Portraits are filled with such beribboned subjects; for example, see a portrait of Martha Washington in 1782 (fig. 45).

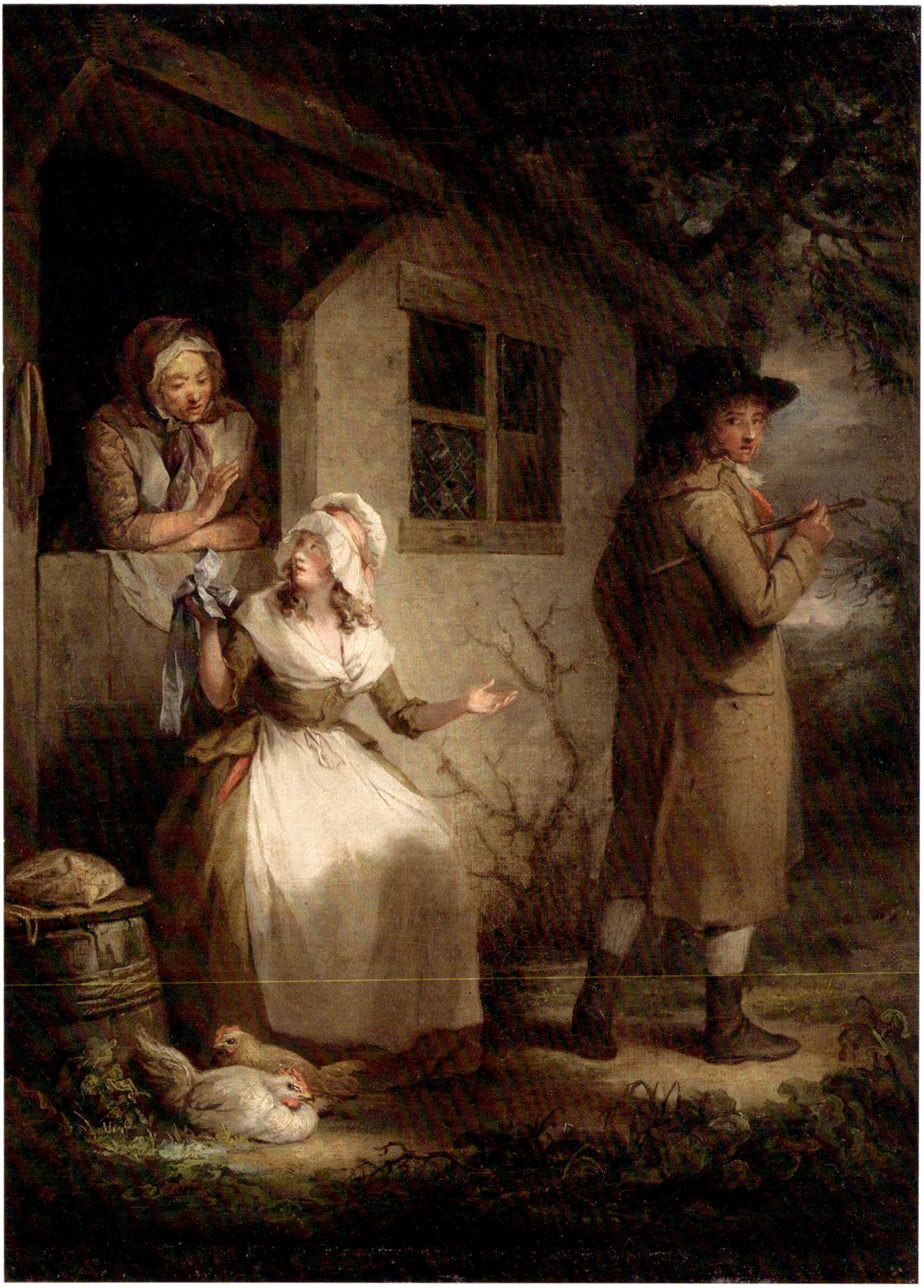

44. George Morland, *Valentines Day, The Fairing,* oil on canvas (1787), 18 x 13½ in. (45.7 x 34.3 cm). V&A Images / Victoria and Albert Museum.

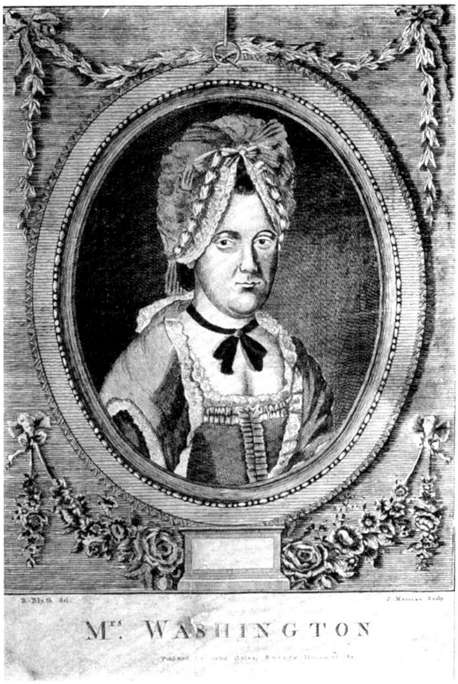

45. J. Norman after a drawing by B. Blyth, *Mrs. Washington*, engraving (1782), 13½ x 9⅜ in. (34.1 x 23.8 cm). Courtesy Winterthur Museum, Garden, and Library.

In another example related to the purchase of a ribbon, Richard Stith's slave Suckey bought a looking glass and a ribbon at John Hook's store at New London, Virginia, in February 1774. Hook was a Scottish tobacco factor (broker) and storekeeper, and New London was a booming small market town in the backcountry of Virginia that in 1772 had four merchants, including Hook, competing with one another for customers (a similar situation, perhaps, to Sam Walton's 1940s rural American town). Suckey's purchases totaled 3s. 9d. —a third of which was for the ribbon—and she paid for part of her purchase with four pounds of cotton. Unlike the written descriptions of purchases, we have no sense from the entry in Hook's ledger of the larger scene or the other people involved at the point of acquisition.[11] A key missing man is Suckey's owner, Richard Stith, who by law should have approved his slave's purchase; Suckey was most likely a slave in his house. As for the missing physical setting, it can be filled in from architectural plans of the store (fig. 46).

The architecture and interior finishing of rural Virginia stores tell us more about the ways in which social class and consumption intersected. Most stores resembled domestic spaces more than specialized commercial environs. The most notable feature was a counter that bisected the space and separated customer from merchant. Behind the merchant was a wall of goods in multiple shelves and holes.

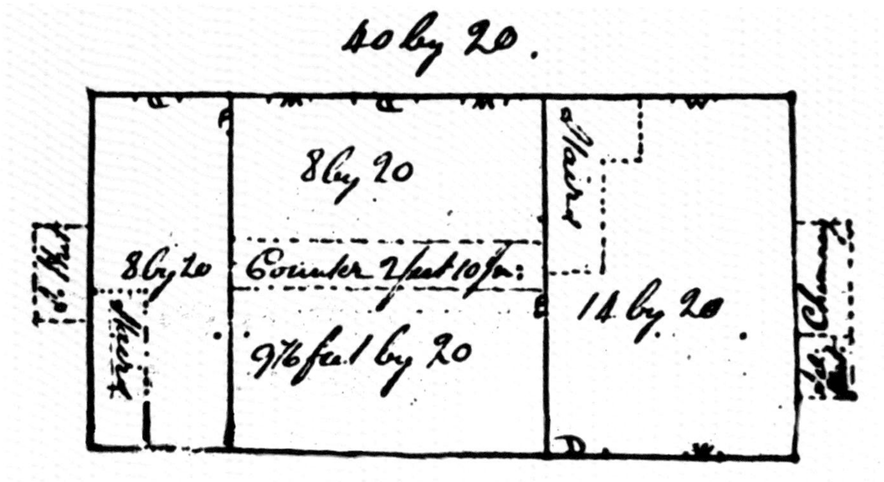

46. Plan of John Hook's store, New London, Virginia (undated, probably 1771), original location unknown, microfilm copy. John Hook Papers, Rare Books and Manuscript and Special Collections Library, Duke University.

We can imagine Suckey entering the door, crossing through the thin February light, and reaching the counter, where the world of goods was arrayed before her. Was she, like Jone Tawdry, in awe of the space, the goods, and the merchant?

Although built in a domestic vocabulary, these stores were larger and more refined than nearly everyone's home in the locality, with interior finishes such as chair rails, plaster, and paint. To many Virginians, the store may have seemed commodious, well-lit, and exciting. But Richard Stith's and Lucy Carter's homes were far finer. How did Stith's slave Suckey experience the world of goods in John Hook's store? She probably moved between a more luxurious world of goods at Stith's home and a far simpler and more desperate world down the path, in the quarters where the slaves lived.[12]

All of these scenarios embody the theme of triangulation between merchants, customers, and objects. All contain a story of shopping. But whose choice and whose tastes did these purchases ultimately reflect? My strategy in beginning my argument with these transactions is to point out that any discussion of larger economic issues and changes immediately comes back to particular people, relationships, and desires. Social position mattered. Ribbons mattered too. Analysis of them takes us to multiple meanings and relationships, some filled with the excitement of fashionable firsts or sexual entanglement. But they also show us how often, when we study women's consumption in the eighteenth-century Atlantic world, we find a man.

In summary, each of these eighteenth-century scenarios pairs a material object with an acquisition. Some suggest a single moment of negotiation involving merchant, customer, and object, as well as prompt questions about choice and price. Some encode relationships between women and their fathers, brothers, or lovers. Some offer evidence of uses: a ribbon to band a hat, to weave through hair, to hang a mirror. Finally, each is a gendered analysis of material culture. Following the ribbon's trail raises questions not only about women, but also about how this simple object was part of a relationship with men. In any case, ribbons—whether moderate or extravagant—were consummately *desirable* things with *value*.

LITTLE PURSES TO THEMSELVES: WOMEN AND THE HOUSEHOLD BLACK BOX

There is still much to learn about the relationship of women to the world of goods and particularly to the acquisition of things through their own agency. Jone Tawdry and Lucy Carter made their own choice of ribbons—inexpensive "prodigious nothings"—or at least made a choice bounded by what was available. But the question, who has choice? is often far more difficult to answer. Who owns? can at least be addressed from common law and the ways that custom buttressed or diverged from it. The question, who decides? leaves little written trail for study. Yet it brings to the surface a complex set of issues about the relationships between men and women, social practices of acceptable and expected behavior, and ways that culturally created boundaries could be pierced. On the one hand are ideas of patriarchy and paternalism, in which authority seems invested in male heads of household. On the other hand are terms such as good wives, deputy husbands, and companionate marriages, which imply a more cooperative relationship between spouses.[13]

Buried within these ideas about relationships are assumptions about appropriate behaviors for the successful functioning of the family in promoting wealth and social standing and in passing property on to heirs. Jan de Vries has pointed to the thorny problem of how the household economy functioned. A patriarchal model assigns a single source of preference: the male head of household dictates how family labor is maximized and consumer choices made. But assigning the man of the house such unilateral control is not consistent with the evidence of women's contributions to the eighteenth-century household economy and the massive purchases of women's commodities. De Vries suggests a more complex model of a cooperative unit—"a realm of altruism"—that guided relationships within the household to a greater maximum utility. Put more simply, de Vries calls on us to unlock the black box of the household in order to get a sense of the choices about market participation made *within* it.[14] This would throw light on the dramatic tensions between authority, ownership, choice, and decision that were present within households. One contemporary observer of America noted that the husband was "still the master upon whatever the monied concerns depend." That power was the crux of the marital relation, and "however much the wife is adored or valued she feels the dependence in this which regulates her conduct." He hastened to add that "still the husband thinks he must be kind and he endeavors to render her life happy."[15]

Beginning marriage meant entering into a new set of economic relations. Women were expected to provide cooperation and assistance in their husband's affairs, the degree and kind calibrated to any number of factors, including wealth, education, and personal circumstance. Thus, when the Virginia lawyer William Wirt announced his engagement, a good friend congratulated him on taking a "helpmate."[16] Elizabeth Wirt's help included actively managing household economic affairs throughout her marriage, an experience that prepared her for a future widowhood of financial ruin and rescue. While she was proud to keep the business accounts, few women were so trained. Nonetheless, informal bookkeeping is seen in the jottings and notes found in women's commonplace books, pocketbooks, journals, and other forms of writing.

Women could step in as needed in many ways. Because the planter Landon Carter had no wife in 1770, his daughter Lucy actively attended to her father's business and went to stores to lay out tobacco and arrange the delivery of cotton and osnaburg for slave clothing.[17] A Virginia merchant described the household system that he devised when ill: he gave his wife "what little money I had to pay out occasional claims and to put in a little ticket [a bill notation] of the amounts paid and to whom."[18] Not only was his wife now serving as deputy accountant; she had been invested with financial authority.

For the less well-to-do, being a helpmate often meant actively working to bring home income or resources. Overseers' wives commonly spun and wove, made butter, or sold eggs.[19] The Scottish tutor John Harrower urged the overseer on a neighboring Virginia plantation to marry the woman he had already spent several nights with, because she would be able to save him money through her own efforts. "One in his Business," opined Harrower, "cou'd afford to live better married, than a man in any Other Business whatever." His wife could make, at small expense, a great many articles in his house, articles that "run away with a deale of money from him when he went to the store."[20]

These are but a few examples of the myriad, flexible ways in which women had connections to and experience with the workings of cash economies and consumer goods. Control of some portion of resources was important, as is delightfully shown in an eighteenth-century English chapbook encounter between the proverbial honest John and his fiancée, Kate. John looks ahead to their marriage by imagining a booming poultry yard, whose increase would send her to market. She asks him squarely who would control "the money made of these odd things?" In the story, the young man replies amiably that she understands "the way of a farmer's wife already, for they had rather have a little purse to themselves, than the knowledge of five hundred pounds of their husbands."[21] The wives wanted freedom of choice.

Producing surplus items in the domestic economy was one way to pay taxes, tithes, and rent, to buy salt and tools—indeed, to cover all the everyday costs of the most mythical of "self-sufficient" farms. But the key point here is more dramatic. Production designed to earn petty cash in the neighborhood economy had a purpose beyond the everyday expenses of the farm. For many women, it was producing as a means of consuming. Products for sale, such as hens and chickens, were resources that a woman could control to provide choices in purchases of consumer goods. That motivation is highlighted in the records of some agricultural women who trafficked in hens and retail things themselves. The plantation mistress Jane Frances Walker Page, for example, may have chosen to forgo her own poultry yard and pay her slaves for fowl and eggs. Paying slaves for produce was not unusual in eighteenth-century Virginia. But she was unusual because she also used small quantities of retail goods such as thread to barter with slaves for products made in their homes. This woman was the center of a large web of domestic economy. She traded and bought from slaves, overseers' wives, and other women in the community, and she traded and bought in the larger Atlantic world of goods.[22] This system was not the bucolic world of rural sharing; these items were accorded a cash value.

Many women were active economic agents who managed poultry for profit. It is in that sense that we can interpret Lewis Miller's sketch of Mrs. Kelly in rural York, Pennsylvania, in 1807 (fig. 47). Miller created a sketchbook filled with delightful sketches of daily life and average rural men and women. His sketches are specific to his town and more particularly his German neighbors, but they also stand for early-nineteenth-century rural life in general.

One scene shows Mrs. Kelly painting chickens in different colors "for amusement," with the black woman "Old Fillis" helping by holding down a bird's wings. Were the two women simply expressing their artistic ideas to enliven dull days? Or were they painting chickens to mark them as *particular* chickens? Writing about the extensive system of antebellum African-American property ownership, Dylan Penningroth has noted that "sometimes neighborhood understanding had to be helped along" by marking and branding hogs, cows, and horses. When kept by different people in close quarters, even poultry was closely watched, with nightly counting and keen observation. Slaves negotiated a kind of accounting that was understood

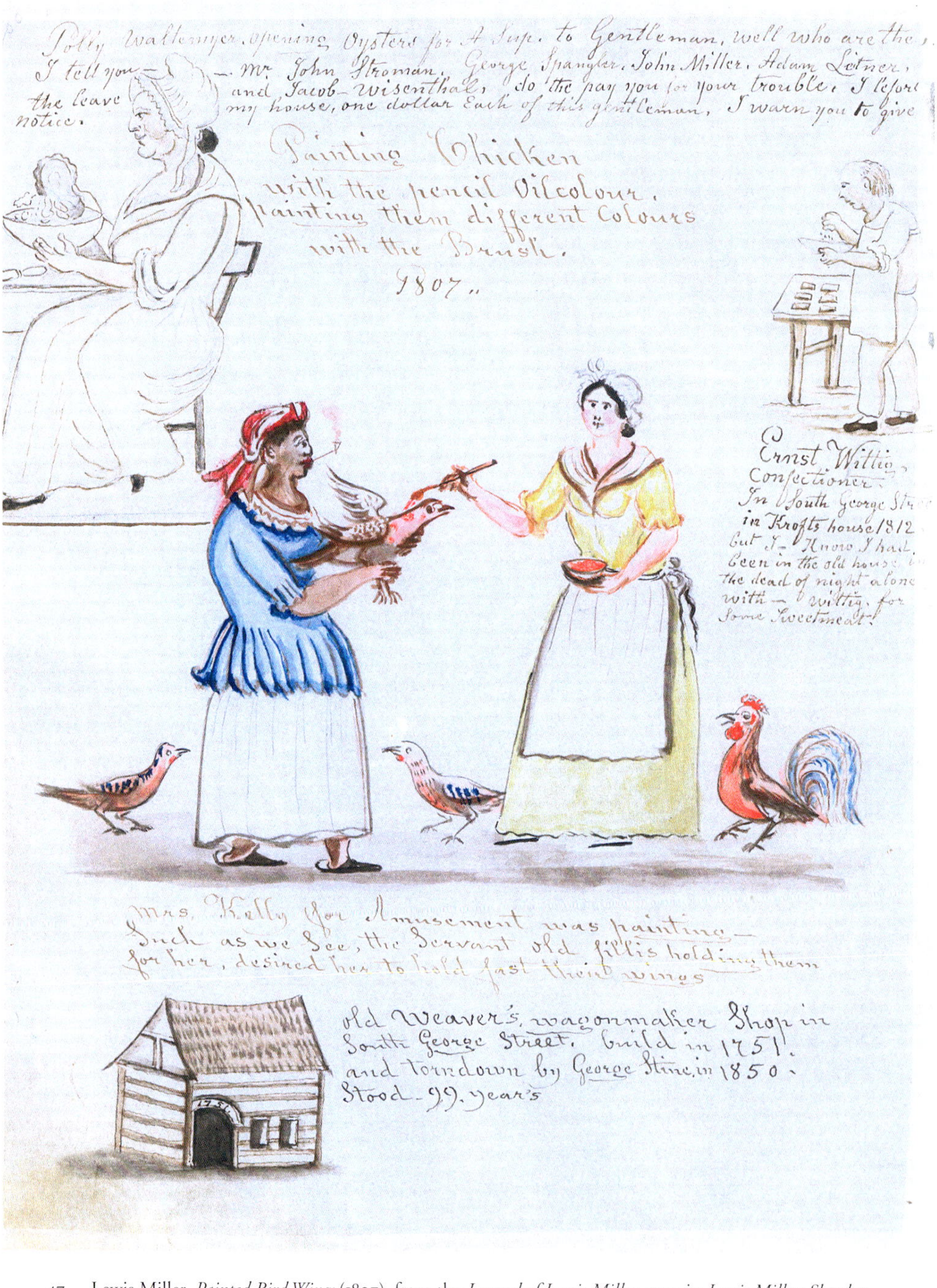

47. Lewis Miller, *Painted Bird Wings* (1807), from the *Journal of Lewis Miller*, repr. in *Lewis Miller: Sketches and Chronicles: The Reflections of a Nineteenth Century Pennsylvania German Folk Artist*, 54. From the Collection of the York County Heritage Trust, York, PA.

by all.[23] In that light, were Mrs. Kelly and Old Fillis engaged in putting their small economy of selling eggs and chickens on a careful business footing?

Virginia store records introduce us to women like Mrs. Kelly. Lucy Bailey used four grown hens and a dozen chickens to purchase a pewter dish in August 1772. Sarah Tisdale chose ribbon, a wax necklace, and expensive fabrics such as muslin, silk gauze, and chintz, totaling over £4, and paid on her balance with 30.5 yards of Virginia cotton cloth, at 2s. a yard. Lucy Bailey brought the products of her poultry yard, Sarah Tisdale the products of her efforts at her spinning wheel and loom. Both women used these few items to purchase a modicum of economic freedom in the world of goods.[24]

Sarah Tisdale's work, trading home-produced textiles for fancier imported ones, is just the kind of behavior that Laurel Ulrich has documented in eighteenth-century Maine, over five hundred miles to the north. Ulrich's evidence, drawn from a diary, brilliantly illuminates how in rural New England, as in rural Virginia, women and men had discrete responsibilities and obligations, as well as how numerous neighborhood systems of exchange bypassed more institutional economic avenues. She also cites a merchant's letter suggesting that women had certain "perquisites" that were clearly their own to barter or sell, and that stocking certain items would induce them to center their exchanges on his store.[25]

Hens and ribbons, therefore, can slowly be drawn into the continuum of the everyday world of women and their economic activity as producers and consumers. But several paradoxes are immediately apparent. First, several historians of colonial Virginia find little evidence of women in retail stores in colonial Virginia. Rhys Isaac, for example, bluntly writes that "women—even widows who controlled property—did not, it seems, go into stores to make purchases." As a continuation of his argument that the world outside the home was a male landscape, Isaac presents eighteenth-century Virginia stores as places "where men gathered, drank, swore, and even boxed."[26] At the same time, literary scholars such as Elizabeth Kowaleski-Wallace have drawn on Henry Fielding and other English authors to argue that shopping in the eighteenth century became constructed as a gendered behavior: business was for men, and it was thus natural that it be orderly and systematic; women, on the other hand, were inconstant, weak, and profligate spenders who could not resist the bedazzlement of things and the smooth, seductive words of shopkeepers.[27]

Did weak and silly women have to shy past fighting boxers to be seduced by merchants in colonial Virginia? If so, this seems at odds with the ample evidence that shopping was often a serious and time-consuming duty, a utilitarian activity that required searching for value (a "good pennyworth"), building relationships (shopping for relatives and friends, as well as sustaining credit with the merchant), even cementing business cooperation (wives of factors shopping for wives of planters).

FINDING THE MISSING: WEBS OF CASH AND CREDIT

How do we account for these divergent views of women and shopping in eighteenth-century Virginia? Much turns on the kinds of records studied. Opening a ledger for a store in the rural South shows row upon row of men's names, their purchases, and their payments. Women's names are difficult to find. Does that mean that women were not in stores? The accounts of sales mislead the historian's eye because they are records of the extension of credit, usually in the form of goods and petty cash, and its payment, usually in the form of crops (tobacco, corn, wheat) or other items of value. The books are not complete records of sales or retailers' activities. The name on the account does not explain who chose what to purchase, nor does it reveal who was at the store. Under Virginia law, married women were not accountable for their debts; their husbands were. To grant credit to a woman in her own name would leave the merchant without his most significant method of debt recovery. Consequently, female purchasers at these stores most often stood metaphorically behind the names of their heads of household.

Some merchants kept account books in ways that make it easier for historians to locate women. One such merchant was John Hook, whom we have already encountered selling a ribbon to the slave Suckey. Hook always carefully recorded when a person other than the account holder made a purchase. To the right of account names, he jotted a name or relation following the word "per." These notations might be "per spouse" or "per daughter," and so we can place women other than account holders in the store on a given day. Not all merchants were so precise, but this practice is consistent with Hook's careful, litigious nature. He recorded specific proof in case a debt was questioned.[28]

The data revealing women's purchases at Hook's store include parts of large daybooks and complete smaller ledgers from his stores in the burgeoning Virginia town center of New London, an associated "country" store, and later, after he relocated, his business on a busy rural road. Few women's accounts in their own names are found in these records. Although the numbers fluctuated slightly in different stores and times, women held only 5 percent of the accounts at these stores. But if we add the female customers who were recorded as playing a part in consumer purchases to those who were legally indebted for them, we triple the number of women we can place in Hook's stores.[29]

Even so, adding a few more women to those we can identify as having been present in the store does not fully recapture their importance to the trade. Several merchants specifically noted that women had a critical role in consumer decisions. While writing to a supplier, one Maryland merchant acknowledged, "You know the influence of the Wives upon their Husbands, and it is but a trifle that wins 'em over," adding that "they must be taken notice of."[30] Trying to untangle the forms of "the influence of the Wives upon their Husbands" is nearly impossible, but John Hook recognized the special consumer desires of women and their potential to improve business in the backcountry. In a letter to one of his suppliers, he urged the sending of more fashionable items—"espetially for women"—even to the rural backcountry.[31] He shrewdly observed that when men traveled to have their tobacco inspected or their court business settled, women often asked them to make purchases. Rather than make the wrong choice, Hook claimed, these men willingly forgot their errand and returned home empty-handed. If men were given lists of goods, particularly textiles, to acquire for wives or daughters in bigger market towns, it could be difficult business. Certainly they could personally see and acquire such things, but their choices may not have been easy. While many elite men had great knowledge of grades and qualities of cloth, they seemed to defer to their wives when it came to news of the current fashion, the kind of detail that often came from female friends and relatives. Ever the good businessman, Hook saw that he could capture a ready market of female customers if he could stock these items locally.

Virginia gentry women who ordered from England went even further in proxy shopping. Some extended their female network of information and choice by entreating the wives of their husband's English tobacco factors for help. Rebecca Chamberlayne expressed her thanks to Mrs. Norton for the selection of a petticoat ordered through her husband's agent, John Norton and Sons. Similarly, Mrs. Downman was anxious that the factor's wife or daughters choose her "a half-yard Spanish purple poplin shot with yellow" as well as cotton. Mrs. Campbell helped in the choice of an elaborate brocade gown for Henry Fitzhugh's daughter. When William Lee moved to England to become an agent, he shrewdly coupled nearly every solicitation for a new Virginia patron's tobacco with the soothing promise that "Mrs. Lee will be attentive in the choice of anything." Perhaps Lee had been on the other side of proxy shopping and saw its problems. Although part of this wish for female supervision came from a desire to prevent unscrupulous shopkeepers from sending shoddy merchandise, it also reflected Virginia women's reliance on other women's knowledge of taste and fashion for effective proxy shopping.[32]

The merchants were clear: women were important to trade and could actually increase business volume. The evidence of orders and sales builds the case. Textiles and notions were the staples of sewing for dress and home, itself a highly gendered activity. Fine notions and trimmings for women's attire were much in demand. The chatter of storekeepers rose to a dull roar when their partners did not supply them with these and other goods considered necessary for the trade, especially inexpensive textiles for everyday household use and clothing.

What did women buy? Their purchases were overwhelmingly items we associate with women and the domestic economy. Nearly two-thirds of women's purchases were fabrics, sewing items, and clothing. In contrast, that category made up only half of the purchases of men, although this partly reflects the far greater range of items that men purchased. Women took home 40 percent of fine lawns (a fabric often used for shirts, aprons, and handkerchiefs), chintzes (fine printed cottons), and duroys (lightweight worsteds). The same was true of fabrics for household use: for example, women made 40 percent of all purchases of ticking, a multipurpose coarse linen and check used for furniture covering and bed hangings as well as clothing.[33]

This is not to say that women were the primary purchasers of textiles; men were. Men carried home most of the ribbons, textiles, thread, beads, pins, and needles, even though they undoubtedly carried them home to women whose names remain hidden in these accounts. And it was overwhelmingly men who purchased the coarser textiles that were the standard uniform of enslaved or laboring people—osnaburg in the earlier period and cotton by the beginning of the nineteenth century.

The patterns of female and male purchasing confirm Hook's early claim to his partner about female preferences. Few of the women who shopped by themselves went home with multiuse, plain, coarse textiles. Rather, they sought the more fashionable cloth that they would prefer to inspect personally. Women did have higher *frequencies* of purchase for certain items than men, rich or poor. If we examine the account books for 1771, these included items that reflect a greater interest in self and fashion (ribbons and looking glasses), the "new groceries" (sugar and tea), and improved styles of eating (cutlery).

The more we learn about the webs of economic connection—institutional, neighborhood, and family—in which women were intertwined, the more we begin to see how these intimate relations were based on cash rather than book debt. Because women were often barred from the more formal economic system of indebtedness, we have grounds for thinking they were more likely to use cash. Hence, the final clue to the presence of women in stores can be found on the mysteriously silent pages of cash sales. A common feature in many account books, they are perhaps the entries of least interest to most scholars, because they simply list sales and not the identity of the purchaser. There is good reason to think, however, that they are linked to missing women.

A single page from Hook's 1773 account, listing forty-four items sold for cash, reveals how those purchases were consistent with wider patterns of women's purchases. First, more than half of the goods were related to textiles and sewing. Finer textiles, such as calico, diaper, lawn, and gauze, and black beads for decoration predominated. Other items that were bought included goods to produce textiles, such as indigo or cotton cards, and those required for cooking and eating, such as knives and forks, mugs, tin pans, a pewter dish, and a funnel. The purchase of two copies of a religious book and medicine might also suggest a female purchase; both fit customary female roles as caretakers of soul and body.[34]

Certainly not all cash customers were women, but the profile of cash sales matches the pattern of women's purchases that can be established in other sources. Moreover, we know that cash sales were a part of the store trade that traditional credit ledgers did not encode. The use of cash allowed women to make purchases without establishing credit relations. Where did they get the cash? Perhaps from their own "little purse," as well as a protean local economy that had opportunities for economic actors of all kinds.

A CHAIN OF FLOWERS AND GIRLS: WOMEN ON THE MOVE

In all, stores were points on the landscape that linked women to merchants, their families, and men—not necessarily relatives—in multiple ways. It is useful, finally, to think about consumerism and shopping in terms of physical movement (separation) and social gathering (clustering). Sam Walton's mid-twentieth-century market town had several stores that competed within just one urban center. Landon Carter complained that his daughter knew where all the best ribbons were on sale, and that shop was not run by the merchant to whom he regularly sold his tobacco.

The words of one young woman's diary tell us much about family visits to stores and provide details about who traveled and what kind of visits they were. Frances Baylor Hill, daughter of a well-heeled plantation-owning family in King and Queen County, Virginia, filled her days with sewing, visiting, riding out, and walking with other young people, many of them women. She described a visit to the store in 1797 as a family affair:

> Papa, Mama Patsy, & myself went to Walkerton dealing Mama got Betsy & Patsy muslinetts got needles thread I got a handkerchief for myself & one for Sister Nancy, saw 4 or 5 gentlemen in the store staid there about two hours[35]

The store experience for Frances Baylor Hill was one that nicely fits the pattern observed in John Hook's accounts. Different family members participated, and the women acquired textiles and clothing. Frances shopped for herself and others, but her family did not simply go shopping. They went "dealing" and spent a long time in the store premises doing it. The same was true on other days, as when Frances stopped by Len Tunstall's store to "speak to Old Betty."[36] Nevertheless, men in the store may have outnumbered women, and few of those women were likely to have had an account in their own names.

Stores akin to Hook's emerge from Frances Baylor Hill's diary as centers for community life, not just sites for provisioning. Certainly men may have boxed one another there, as cited by Rhys Isaac; that is also the kind of drama and entertainment experienced at the fair, another key aspect of community life. Why did Sam Walton trumpet his mid-twentieth-century use of ice-cream or popcorn machines? They were social attractions that brought an experience of pleasure and carnival, familiar from community festivities such as the visit of a circus.

Stores linked families in multiple ways. In some account entries, we can see a mixture of things purchased for the household and for specific family members. We do not know why Hook recorded that William Pollard's wife bought a "silk handkerchief *for son*," but that detail added to the account helps break open the black box of the household.[37] Along with her son's handkerchief, Mrs. Pollard went home with wrapping and powder (probably for a male household member's gun), a bottle of mustard, needles, new clothier's cards, calico, and a necklace. Thus, a single person carried things to different members of the family.

What is most tantalizing is that so many younger women—identified by the appellation "Miss" or "per daughter"—traveled to stores. Richard Callaway was one of the earliest settlers in the area and a trustee of New London when the town was formed in 1761. His daughter Anne visited Hook's store a decade later, purchasing a patch of chintz and a yard of green leather on her father's account.[38] Katie Thomason and Betsy Jones both appeared at Hook's Hail's Ford store on 17 January 1799. Their acquisitions suggest quite different errands: Betsy Jones purchased whisky, brandy, and a quart bottle on her father's account; Katie Thomason bought handkerchiefs and pins, fine fabrics such as taste and muslin, even a scarlet cloak. She charged them to both her father's and her brother's accounts.[39] These girls were traveling to the store together, seemingly without parental supervision.[40]

Cathy Hellier's analysis of visits and social travel confirms what the accounts and diaries have indicated so far. She finds that young women traveled in pairs, groups, or sometimes singly accompanied by a servant. Older teens and unmarried women in their young twenties seemed to have had greater mobility than did those still in school (sixteen or younger).[41] As the nineteenth century progressed, the idea that shopping could be a form of leisure, of celebration, or of recreation for young women reached full formation. By 1836, seventeen-year-old Eliza Barksdale would write of a day's visit by the three "Miss Marshalls" to the home she shared with nine siblings in Charlotte County, Virginia. The girls trooped down to Captain Williamson's store "to look at his new goods" and were treated with "candy, plunbs and Almonds." They all walked in the evening to an ivy cliff, gathered bouquets of flowers, and then proceeded along the street, "one before the other, about two yards apart, making a string of seven ladies including a servant."[42]

The delights of a large group of girls tumbling down to look at new store goods, being treated with candy by a merchant, gathering flowers, and strolling in a long chain through the streets (slave included), no doubt laughing with glee, captures what was both old and new in rural Virginia. They were briefly free of paternal authority, but chaperoned by a slave. These outings were rural pleasures that linked girls and the world of goods in ways that were very different from genteel tea tables. A central element of both these experiences, nonetheless, was acquiring tea or ribbons at the retail store, where, in the course of the early nineteenth century, women were to become ever more familiar and welcome.

The plantation economy, petty economy, informal economy—all are names that scholars have given that ebullient set of economic relations below the horizon of the "official" mercantile exchange of raw products for finished goods within the British imperial system. Women kept the household books and the accounts "on tick"; they counted chickens and combed cotton. Then perhaps they went to the store.

Have we opened the black box of household consumption? Yes, at least a crack. Women come out from behind their husband's and father's accounts and choose their own goods. They move more freely across the landscape. They control their own little purse. They pay with cash. They buy finer textiles. In so doing, they become the link between rural and urban, local and Atlantic, British and global.

This essay has benefited greatly from intensive discussion at meetings at The Huntington and the Yale Center for British Art. I thank those institutions for their foresight in nurturing such projects. In particular, I owe much to John Styles, Amanda Vickery, and Claire Walsh for their stimulating ideas about shopping and consumer goods at those sessions. My student Emily Pfotenhauer has been a remarkably fine reader, and I thank her for all her insights. John Styles alerted me to the visual play of "fairings" and suggested the Morland painting. The essay grows out of a larger project that forms the basis of my book *Buying into the World of Goods: Early Consumers in the Virginia Backcountry* (Baltimore, 2007).

1. Sam Walton with John Huey, *Sam Walton: Made in America, My Story* (New York: Doubleday, 1992), 174–75.
2. A parcel of broadcloth was a "good pennyworth" sent to William Allason. Walker and Company, Glasgow, to Allason, 26 Sept. 1759, William Allason Letter Book, Business Records Collection, Library of Virginia, microfilm, Colonial Williamsburg Foundation.
3. While the literature on eighteenth-century consumerism is massive, three important works nicely frame consumerism with shopping or consumer choice: Neil McKendrick, John Brewer, and J. H. Plumb, eds., *The Birth of a Consumer Society: The Commercialization of Eighteenth-Century England* (Bloomington: Indiana

Univ. Press, 1982); Carole Shammas, *The Pre-Industrial Consumer in England and America* (Oxford: Clarendon Press, 1990); and T. H. Breen, *The Marketplace of Revolution: How Consumer Politics Shaped American Independence* (Oxford: Oxford Univ. Press, 2004).

4. See, for example, Joan M. Jensen, "Cloth, Butter and Boarders: Women's Household Production for the Market," in *History of Women in the United States: Historical Articles on Women's Lives and Activities*, vol. 4, *Domestic Ideology and Domestic Work*, pt. 1, ed. Nancy Cott (New York: K. G. Sauer, 1992), 264–90. Two important studies that take on the role of women as consumers, albeit in England, are Lorna Weatherill, "A Possession of One's Own: Women and Consumer Behavior in England, 1660–1740," *Journal of British Studies* 25 (1986): 131–56, and Amanda Vickery, "Women and the World of Goods: A Lancashire Consumer and Her Possessions, 1751–1781," in *Consumption and the World of Goods: Consumption and Society in the Seventeenth and Eighteenth Centuries*, ed. John Brewer and Roy Porter (London: Routledge, 1993), 274–301.

5. Anon., *A dialogue between honest John & loving Kate. With their contrivance for marriage, and way to get a livelihood: part the second* (Wotton-under-Edge, UK: J. Bence, 1780), 13.

6. Sarah Kemble Knight, "The Journal of Madam Knight," in *Journeys in New Worlds: Early American Women's Narratives*, ed. Sargeant Bush (Madison: Univ. of Wisconsin Press, 1990), 105–6. Although Knight's disdain here is clear—and no doubt colors her perception—the rest of her journal is a precise recording of real events, and there is no reason to suspect that she did not witness such a scene.

7. Jack P. Greene, ed., *The Diary of Colonel Landon Carter of Sabine Hall, 1752–1778* (Charlottesville: Univ. Press of Virginia, 1965), 2:950.

8. *Crow v. Bell*, Oct. 1765, Augusta County Court Judgements, deposition of Elizabeth Hog, 18 Oct. 1765, in *Chronicles of the Scotch-Irish Settlement in Virginia: Extracted from the Original Court Records of Augusta County, 1745–1800*, by Lyman Chalkley (Mary S. Lockwood, 1912; repr., Baltimore: Genealogical Publishing Co., 1965), 1:491–92.

9. Diana O'Hara, *Courtship and Constraint: Rethinking the Making of Marriage in Tudor England* (Manchester: Manchester Univ. Press, 2000), 67–68.

10. Ann Cooper Whitall, "Diary of Ann Cooper Whitall," Oct. 1761, in *John M. Whitall: The Story of His Life* (Philadelphia: privately published, 1879), 8.

11. Account, Richard Stith's Suckey, 14 Feb. 1774, unidentified mercantile ledger (probably Falling River), 1773–75, 15. Most of the activities in the unidentified mercantile ledger were posted from the Daybook, Falling River, Bedford County, 1772–76, hence the attribution. John Hook Papers, Rare Book, Manuscript, and Special Collections Library, Duke University (hereafter DU).

12. For store architecture, see Ann Smart Martin, "Commercial Space as Consumption Arena: Retail Stores in Early Virginia," in *People, Power, Places*, ed. Sally McMurry and Annmarie Adams, vol. 8 of *Perspectives in Vernacular Architecture* (Knoxville: Univ. of Tennessee Press, 2000), 201–18. Camille Wells discusses common house size in "The Planter's Prospect: Houses, Outbuildings, and Rural Landscapes in Eighteenth-Century Virginia," *Winterthur Portfolio* 28, no. 1 (1993): 1–31. For an examination of owners' houses and enslaved people's quarters, see Dell Upton, "White and Black Landscapes in Eighteenth-Century Virginia," in *Material Life in America, 1600–1860*, ed. Robert Blair St. George (Boston: Northeastern Univ. Press, 1988).

13. Some of the works that were helpful to me in their use of these ideas and conflicting ideals are Kathleen M. Brown, *Good Wives, Nancy Wenches and Anxious Patriarchs: Gender, Race, and Power in Colonial Virginia* (Chapel Hill: Univ. of North Carolina Press, 1996); Anya Jabour, *Marriage in the Early Republic: Elizabeth and William Wirt and the Companionate Ideal* (Baltimore: Johns Hopkins Univ. Press, 1998); and Jeanne Boydston, *Home and Work: Housework, Wages, and the Ideology of Labor in the Early Republic* (New York: Oxford Univ. Press, 1990).

14. Jan de Vries, "Between Purchasing Power and the World of Goods: Understanding the Household Economy in Early Modern Europe," in Brewer and Porter, *Consumption and the World of Goods*, 118.

15. "Narrative of the Travels of a Scotsman from Glasgow," manuscript, 1821–24, vol. 1, Manuscript Collection, New-York Historical Society, fol. 43.

16. Jabour, *Marriage in the Early Republic*, 23.

17. Greene, *Diary of Colonel Landon Carter*, 443–44, 523.

18. David Ross to Robert Richardson, Jan. 1813, David Ross Letter Book, Library of Virginia.

19. For a discussion of the multiple ways that food moved through a local economy, see Lorena S. Walsh, Ann Smart Martin, and Joanne Bowen, "Provisioning Early American Towns: The Chesapeake; A Multidisciplinary Case Study" (final report to the National Endowment for the Humanities, Grant RO-226 43-93, Colonial Williamsburg Foundation, 1997).

20. Edward Miles Riley, ed., *The Journal of John Harrower: An Indentured Servant in the Colony of Virginia, 1773–1776* (New York: Holt, Rinehart, and Winston, 1963), 138.

21. *A dialogue between honest John & loving Kate*, 12–13. My thanks to Linda Sturtz for allowing me to read and comment on her manuscript copy of *Within Her Power: Propertied Women in Colonial Virginia* (New York: Routledge, 2002).

22. Jane Francis Walker Page and Jane Byrd Nelson Walker Commonplace Book, manuscript, Virginia Historical Society. Amy Karen Rider has written an outstanding analysis of the manuscript; see Rider, "The Castle Hill Commonplace Book and the Plantation Mistress's World, 1802–1845" (senior honor's thesis, Princeton Univ., 1997).

23. Dylan C. Penningroth, *African American Property and Community in the Nineteenth-Century South* (Chapel Hill: Univ. of North Carolina Press, 2003), 95–96.

24. Account, Lucy Bailey, 21 Aug. 1772, unidentified mercantile ledger (Falling River), 1773–75, 10, Hook Papers, DU; account, Sarah Tisdale, purchases, 13 Aug. and 9 Dec. 1772, payment, 13 Aug., Daybook, 1772–76, Falling River, Bedford County, 21, Hook Papers, DU.

25. Laurel Thatcher Ulrich, "Martha Ballard and Her Girls: Women's Work in Eighteenth-Century Maine," in *Work and Labor in Early America*, ed. Stephen Innes (Chapel Hill: Univ. of North Carolina Press, 1988), 84–86.

26. Rhys Isaac, *The Transformation of Virginia, 1740–1790* (Chapel Hill: Univ. of North Carolina Press, 1982), 57. Isaac was not alone in his gendered assessment of store activity where shopping is seen as a male world. Carole Shammas thought there was little room for women in consumption decisions, because legal restrictions and inheritance patterns disenfranchised women; see Shammas, *The Pre-Industrial Consumer in England and America*, 269. Allan Kulikoff argued that stores were bastions of male presence, and even female account holders sent sons or other men to pick up items at the store; see Kulikoff, *Tobacco and Slaves: The Development of Southern Cultures in the Chesapeake, 1680–1800* (Chapel Hill: Univ. of North Carolina Press, 1986), 225.

27. Elizabeth Kowaleski-Wallace, *Consuming Subjects: Women, Shopping, and Business in the Eighteenth Century* (New York: Columbia Univ. Press, 1997).

28. The accounts studied here record the business of John Hook in New London and then Hail's Ford, Virginia, both in the southern foothills of the Blue Ridge. Papers relating to Hook's business are scattered in a half-dozen repositories. The account books analyzed from the early 1770s are in the John Hook Papers, Rare Book, Manuscript, and Special Collections Library, DU. The latest account analyzed (1799) is held at the Gertrude Caster Mann Room, Franklin County Public Library, Rocky Mount, Virginia. The notations related to women in his stores include all 218 purchases listed "per" spouse, daughter, and other named women, for a total of £54 29s. Female account holders alone made 77 purchases totaling £19 45s.

29. The method of adding purchases made by women annotated by "per" spouse, daughter, or other named woman shows how many women were active consumers through the credit of a man. Female account holders made 77 purchases and payments in the 1771 daybook, totaling £19. Women associated through a man's account similarly accounted for 218 transactions, totaling £54. Later books had similar ratios. In the 1799 daybook, for example, female-headed accounts listed 13 purchases and payments; men's accounts associated with women numbered 39 such transactions.

30. Quoted in Lois Green Carr and Lorena Walsh, "Changing Lifestyles and Consumer Behavior in the Colonial Chesapeake," in *Of Consuming Desires: The Style of Life in the Eighteenth Century*, ed. Ronald Hoffman and Cary Carson (Charlottesville: Univ. Press of Virginia, 1994), 110.

31. John Hook to William Donald, New London, 9 Dec. 1766, Hook Letter Book, 1763–1772, Library of Virginia.

32. For Mrs. Chamberlayne's thanks, see Chamberlayne to John Norton and Sons, 28 July 1770, John Norton and Sons Papers, Colonial Williamsburg Foundation. For Mrs. Downman's request for help from Mrs. Athawes or her daughters, see Raleigh Downman to Edward and Samuel Athawes, 31 March 1776, Downman Letter Book, Library of Congress, microfilm, Colonial Williamsburg Foundation. For Mrs. Campbell's help, see Fitzhugh to Jno. Stewart and Campbell, 28 Jan. 1771, Fitzhugh Letter Book, DU. For Lee's promise, see William Lee to George W. Fairfax, 19 Jan. 1770, William Lee Letter Book, 1769–1771, microfilm, Colonial Williamsburg Foundation.
33. Ann Smart Martin, "Buying into the World of Goods: Eighteenth-Century Consumerism and the Retail Trade from London to the Virginia Frontier" (PhD diss., College of William and Mary, 1993), 307.
34. Noted as "Fisher's Cate'ms," the book was Edward Fisher, *The Marrow of Modern Divinity* (Glasgow: Printed by John Bryce, 1766).
35. William K. Bottorff and Roy C. Flannagan, ed., "The Diary of Frances Baylor Hill of Hillsborough, King and Queen County, Virginia (1797)," special issue, *Early American Literature Newsletter* (Winter 1967): 33.
36. Bottorff and Flannagan, "Diary of Frances Baylor Hill," 23, 40.
37. Account, William Pollard, 30 Nov. 1771, New London Daybook, 1771–72, Hook Papers, DU.
38. Account, Richard Callaway, New London Daybook, 7 Dec. 1771, 75, Hook Papers, DU.
39. Account, John Thomason, and account, Thomas James (brother) and John Jones, 17 Jan. 1799, Mercantile Ledger, Hail's Ford, Franklin County, 15, John Hook Materials, Gertrude Castor Mann Room, Franklin County Public Library, Rocky Mount, Virginia. Young women charging purchases to their father's accounts can also be found in William Allason's store in Falmouth, Virginia. Mary Ann Knight visited the store five times in 1770, often with her brothers, but she maintained her own account. Her purchases were for small niceties such as a teapot, a snuffbox, a black ribbon, and a pair of leather gloves. Her biggest purchase was eight yards of fine calico, at 7s. a yard, and her debts in two years were more than £8. She paid for most of her calico in cash, and her father made another payment in the fall of the following year. We know little about the Knights except that they owned their own house—probably placing them in comfortable ranks—but nowhere does Mary Ann appear in the official records of Stafford County. See Allason Ledger 1, Oct. 1769–1772, Library of Virginia, and Ann Smart Martin, "Textiles and Clothing at Eighteenth-Century Virginia Stores" (paper presented at the "Third Textile History Conference," North Andover, MA, 21–23 Sept. 1990).
40. Alexis de Tocqueville was the most famous observer to note, in 1831, that in America "paternal discipline is very relaxed and the conjugal tie very strict"; *Democracy in America* (New York: Vintage Books, 1945), 2:213.
41. Cathy Hellier, "The Adolescence of Gentry Girls in Late Eighteenth-Century Virginia" (paper presented at the "Southern Association of Women's Historians Conference," Memphis, TN, 1994). My thanks to Hellier for her help with this larger idea of visiting and other documentary references to girls visiting stores.
42. Eliza Barksdale Lavalette Diary, 1836–37, MSS, Virginia Historical Society.

"Neat and Not Too Showey": Words and Wallpaper in Regency England

Amanda Vickery

In August 1799, Dr. Thomas Ferris of the Deanery, Battle, in Sussex, wrote to the London wallpaper and decorating firm Trollope and Sons, having seen some paper at the architect-designed mansion of a local friend:

> I saw the other Day at our Friend Mr Pigous some very pretty papers your Man was putting up and Mrs Pigou recommended me to your HOUSE. I am in want of a paper for a very small Room which must be paper'd immediately. . . . Pray . . . send a few of the cheapest patterns proper for Halls staircases; & Passages for a Parsonage House I care nothing about fashion if they are neat & clean.[1]

The letter is suggestive about taste, personal preferences, and consumer choice. Ferris was influenced by the consumption of his friends, the Pigous, but it was the wife, Mrs. Pigou, who seemed to be the mistress of the facts of the commission. Mr. Ferris privileged the pretty, the neat, and the clean over the modish, and he was concerned to decorate in keeping with the solid dimensions but modest pretensions of a Sussex deanery. Perhaps it did not become a dean to advertise too keen an interest in fashion, however developed his aesthetic appreciation. This is but one letter among hundreds transcribed in the letter book of Trollope and Sons between June 1797 and May 1808. The letters provide a rare insight into the desires and anxieties of a group of consumers and the vocabulary they employed to voice their wishes and their concerns. Indeed, in aggregate, the letters offer a lexicon of the working language of consumer taste.

Taste was a key word in the cultural landscape of eighteenth-century England. Yet despite its wide currency, taste was a vague, indeterminate concept. "The Term taste," reflected Edmund Burke, "like all other figurative terms, is not extremely accurate . . . and it is therefore liable to uncertainty and confusion."[2] Philosophers invoked the sovereign importance of taste, but none nailed down its elements in ways that helped ordinary consumers to make their choices. Similarly, while many historians have wrestled with the extensive debates about taste that preoccupied the likes of Alexander Pope, David Hume, and Joshua Reynolds, no one has asked what taste might have actually meant for the perplexed consumer. Research efforts have concentrated on one of the obsessions of the genre: luxury. Waves of anxiety about the moral, political, social, and economic consequences of new wealth swept through print in the 1690s, in the 1750s, and again in the 1780s in the wake of the loss of the American colonies. The Presbyterian Scot Tobias Smollett put the case with characteristic comic exaggeration in 1771:

> Clerks and factors from the East Indies, loaded with the spoil of plundered provinces; planters, negro drivers, and hucksters, from our American plantations, enriched they know not how; agents, commissaries and contractors, who have fattened in two successive wars, on the blood of the nation; usurers, brokers and jobbers of every kind; men of low birth and no breeding, have suddenly translated into a state of affluence, unknown to former ages; and no wonder that their brains should be intoxicated with pride, vanity and presumption. Knowing no other criterion of greatness, but the ostentation of wealth, they discharge their affluence without taste or conduct, through every channel of the most absurd extravagance.[3]

Concern about immoral profusion and meaningless glitter was still not a spent force in the early 1800s. How *could* wealth be reconciled with virtue? One popular answer was through the operation of taste. Philosophical treatises on aesthetics, moral diatribes, fiction, and graphic satire all circled around the question of good taste and bad taste, and they often invoked objects—from chinoiserie, porcelain, and Venetian windows to French silks, coaches, and liveries—as props in their arguments. However, there was rarely any attempt to differentiate between, for example, tasteful and tasteless porcelain. Nor have historians examined how consumers brought "good taste" to bear in the marketplace. This would require less attention to the philosophical arguments for and against particular norms of taste, and more to the preferences that different kinds of people exhibited. The beauty of the Trollope letter book lies in the insights it gives into how a range of people, from the pen-pushing bureaucrat to the marchioness, appreciated and discussed the same material: wallpaper.

Histories of wallpaper chronicle the rise of this new wall "furniture" over roughly a century. The earliest known example of English patterned wallpaper dates from 1509, but it was in the later seventeenth century that wallpaper came into significant use, as an alternative to tapestry and other textile hangings.[4] Wallpaper established a foothold in the corners of the house most associated with the individual in undress—the dressing room, the bedroom, and the closet. Lady Carlow, the wife of an Irish viscount, was doing up "a small room above stairs for my sanctum sanctorum" in 1782 and rejoiced in the modest cost: "I have got a very pretty white spotted paper with a glazed ground for fourpence a yard (so it won't ruin me), and a festoon of roses in orange colour and green to go round the top."[5] By the early nineteenth century, wallpaper was fashionable in its own right, in use in the best rooms in the grandest houses. Although costly and sophisticated papers were available, it was the affordability of paper that struck commentators most forcibly, bringing redecoration within reach of a much wider public and promising renewal with spanking-fresh paper.[6]

Why should we be interested in wallpaper? Is it not beneath the notice of a historian? "Wallpaper has long been considered the poor relation of the decorative arts," Gill Saunders concludes, "fragile, ephemeral, easy to replace."[7] Wallpaper's career was essentially one of pretense, imitating other materials including wood, stucco, masonry, murals, tapestry hangings, and textiles such as silk, chintz, and velvet. Deception, illusion, ephemerality, and veneer were the literary connotations of wallpaper for the Victorians. Wallpapering became a device for revealing a dishonest concern with surface—perhaps even a false heart.[8] As Saunders tartly notes, wallpaper "has never quite thrown off the taint that comes from faking it."[9] To its critics, wallpaper was cheap in the worst sense: it lacked integrity. However, what could be read as a flashy veneer could also convey wholesome domesticity on a budget.

In the eighteenth century, wallpaper was rarely expected to be an investment for a lifetime; rather, it was embraced as a decoration that, if not quite transitory, was regarded as relatively impermanent. Martha Dodson of Cookham, in Berkshire, the elderly widow of a wealthy tin-plate worker, had rooms papered in 1748, 1749, 1753, 1758, and 1760. The paper for her chamber cost £1 15s., and seven pieces of chintz paper for another room cost £1 13s.—not dirt cheap, but more affordable than the alternatives.[10] Indeed, wallpaper curators estimate that it was possible to buy eleven yards of paper for the cost of a yard of damask.[11] Slapping up wallpaper was one way to make yourself quickly at home, even in lodgings, while landladies resorted to Trollope again and again to freshen up a let.

The effects of paper could be startling. Wallpaper could utterly transform the look of a room for a fraction of the cost of textiles, stucco, or wainscoting. Indeed, one could argue that just as ribbons, lace, and handkerchiefs allowed women to refashion a garment without spending a fortune,[12] so wallpaper offered an economical domestic renovation, bringing experiment and fashion within reach of genteel and middling householders. Highly decorative in terms of both color and ornament, and often bought repeatedly by the same person, wallpaper required a developed aesthetic vocabulary to describe its visual qualities. Wallpaper thus reveals how "taste" was articulated in practice by a broad and articulate consumer public.

Trollope and Sons was based in London, the center of the British wallpaper industry. Launching his company in 1778, Trollope made his reputation in exotic paper, especially Chinese painted paper, but by 1800, when he retired, the firm's stock-in-trade was printed patterns, colored to order. At the turn of the nineteenth century, Trollope and Sons served a wide, heterogeneous market. In 1830, the company became paper hangers to George IV, and in 1842 to Queen Victoria. However, during the period of the letter book, 1797–1808, the royal warrant was not yet on the horizon, and titled patrons could be listed on the fingers of two hands.[13] Trollope's papers were not as chic as those produced by rival London firms Bromwich (later Isherwood and Bradley), which supplied Chippendale and Horace Walpole, and the massive Harwood & Company. The bulk of Trollope's customers were drawn from the ranks of provincial gentility—clerics, doctors, lawyers, small gentry, and merchants across the southern counties of England—and from the fashionable and mighty upper-middle market in London. Based in Westminster, Trollope and Sons served both town and city, papering for the likes of banker Thomas Baring as he rose from city countinghouse to a baronetcy and a smart West End address. Yet the firm also catered to squadrons of London's senior civil servants and commercial managers—papering the offices and apartments of the bureaucrats of the Customs House, General Post Office, the Penny Post Office, the Sun Fire Office, and Doctor's Commons, though it failed in its attempt to get a foot in the door of the Mint. Trollope and Sons had standing relationships with a handful of professional decorators, but also with several landlords and especially landladies in the booming London rental sector. The London trade dominated the letter book, but Trollope and Sons sent papers nationwide to Cheshire, Cumberland, Yorkshire, Staffordshire, Lincolnshire, Huntingdonshire, Devon, Dorset, Somerset, Wiltshire, Buckinghamshire, Bedfordshire, Essex, Suffolk, Surrey, Kent, and Hampshire, as well as Dublin. The company even shipped boxes of paper to army officers at the Cape of Good Hope, though it had no direct trade with the Americas.

What was the gender breakdown among Trollope's private customers? Unsurprisingly, men outnumbered women in the order letters. In the entries in the letter book for 1798, for instance, of a total of forty-three customers and their agents, thirty-four were male, while only seven correspondents were female and two other female customers were represented by upholsterers. Thus, women accounted for only 21 percent of correspondents. There are numerous single women in the letter book, yet married men customarily represented their wives and families. Nevertheless, several women besides landladies led the ordering process, and while it is not always clear whether they were married or widowed, their aesthetic confidence cannot be in doubt. For example, Lady Charlotte Smith, the wife of a member of Parliament, was an exacting customer, blunt in her dealings with her tradesman: "Lady Charlotte cannot say that she likes any of the patterns that Mr Trollope has enclosed."[14] Assertiveness about workmanship was not confined to the titled ladies. Mrs. Hale of Jermyn Street, Westminster, was crisp in 1804:

> Mrs Hale expected Mr Trollope woud have called on her for the payment of his small account when she intended to shew him the staircase which was so very badly done that something must be tried this summer for it is not fit to be seen.[15]

Even where the correspondence was led by a husband, female choices, or at the very least a final female veto, do surface. The Reverend Charles Johnson of Bath had to return his papers "because Mrs Johnson does not like the one w[ha]t I chose for her bedroom therefore will trouble you to send down a dozen more of the newest patterns. . . ."[16] Several letters imply the conjugal cooperation that underlay decorative choices.[17] Certainly eighteenth-century trade cards for wallpaper retailers, advertising well-appointed shops, show women either in groups or coupled with men, examining varieties of paper (figs. 48, 49). Choosing wallpaper *à deux* may even have symbolized marital harmony.

Since Trollope and Sons decorated lodgings, offices, parsonages, and cottages, the firm's letter book is an invaluable source for a discussion of mundane patterns and the middle market —a useful counter to the distortions of surviving museum collections of wallpaper, which inevitably favor the fine, the costly, and the unique.[18] Unfortunately, there is no accompanying book of patterns, or even one-off samples, to demonstrate precisely what a customer meant by a neat and pretty trellis pattern, or for that matter a French red or a bright blue. There is no sample book to rival that of, say, Cowtan twenty years later.[19] What the Trollope letter book offers is an entrée into a whole lexicon of terms.

The analysis that follows explores the factors affecting Trollope customers' choice of particular paper. For example, to what extent were there conventions about which patterns and colors were most appropriate for different rooms? What emerges is a powerful sense of decorum and fitness to context: paper should be proper for its place and situation. Neat, cheap, fashionable, beautiful, pretty, handsome, smart, showy, and gaudy are the words that Trollope customers used in judging the papers. But where did this everyday aesthetic vocabulary come from?

What led consumers to the doors of Trollope and Sons? It was rare for letter writers to map out the path that had brought them to the company. Most got

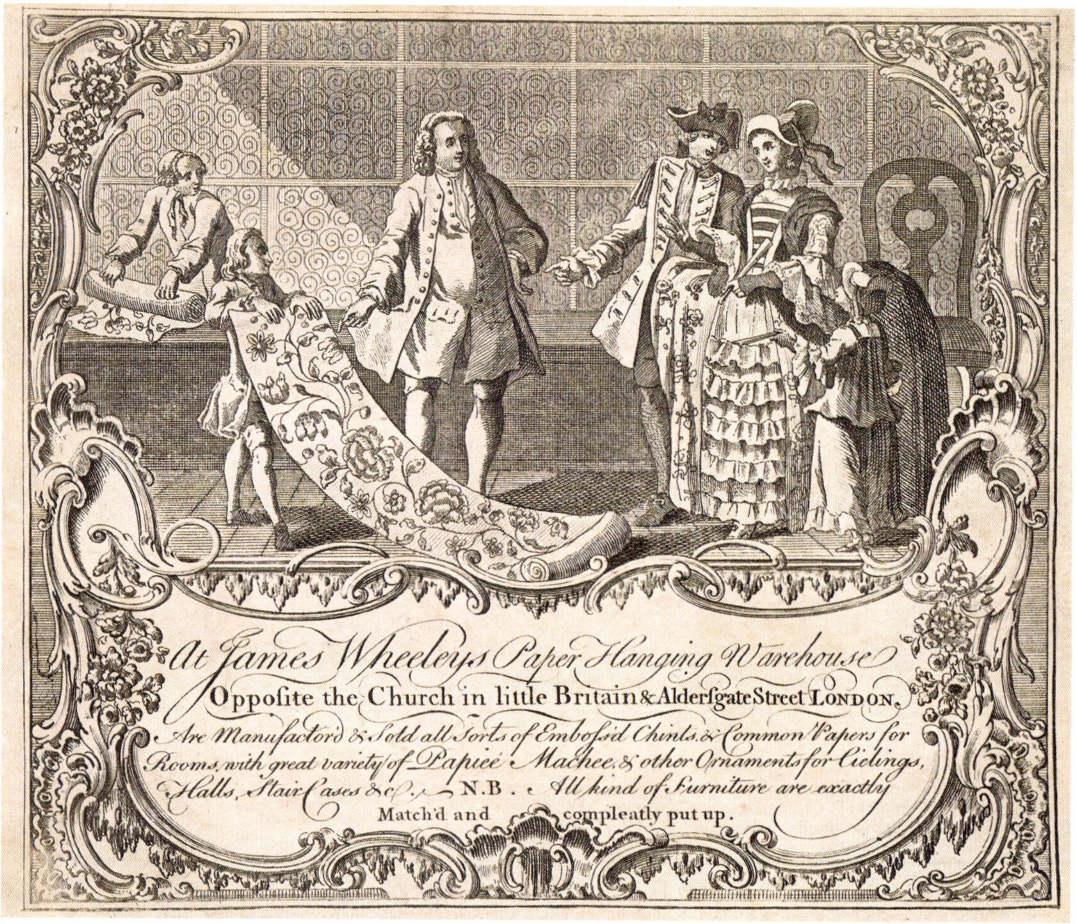

48. Artist unknown, trade card for "James Wheeleys Paper Hanging Warehouse Opposite the Church in little Britain & Aldersgate Street, London," where "All kind of Furniture are exactly Match'd," uncolored etching (c. 1754). © The Trustees of the British Museum.

straight down to the nitty-gritty of ordering wallpaper without revealing why they had chosen that over other decorations, or Trollope over other manufacturers. However, a personal recommendation or a viewing of Trollope's wallpaper in situ, or both, were the commonest reasons committed to paper. Sir Thomas Anson of palatial Shugborough in Staffordshire aborted an order in 1803 when he discovered that another nobleman had something newer and better from a different supplier.[20] Trollope's customers had a lively appreciation of the decorations of their acquaintances.

The most consistent factor shaping the customers' choice of paper was total decor. Indeed, as wallpaper was markedly cheaper than the textiles that accompanied

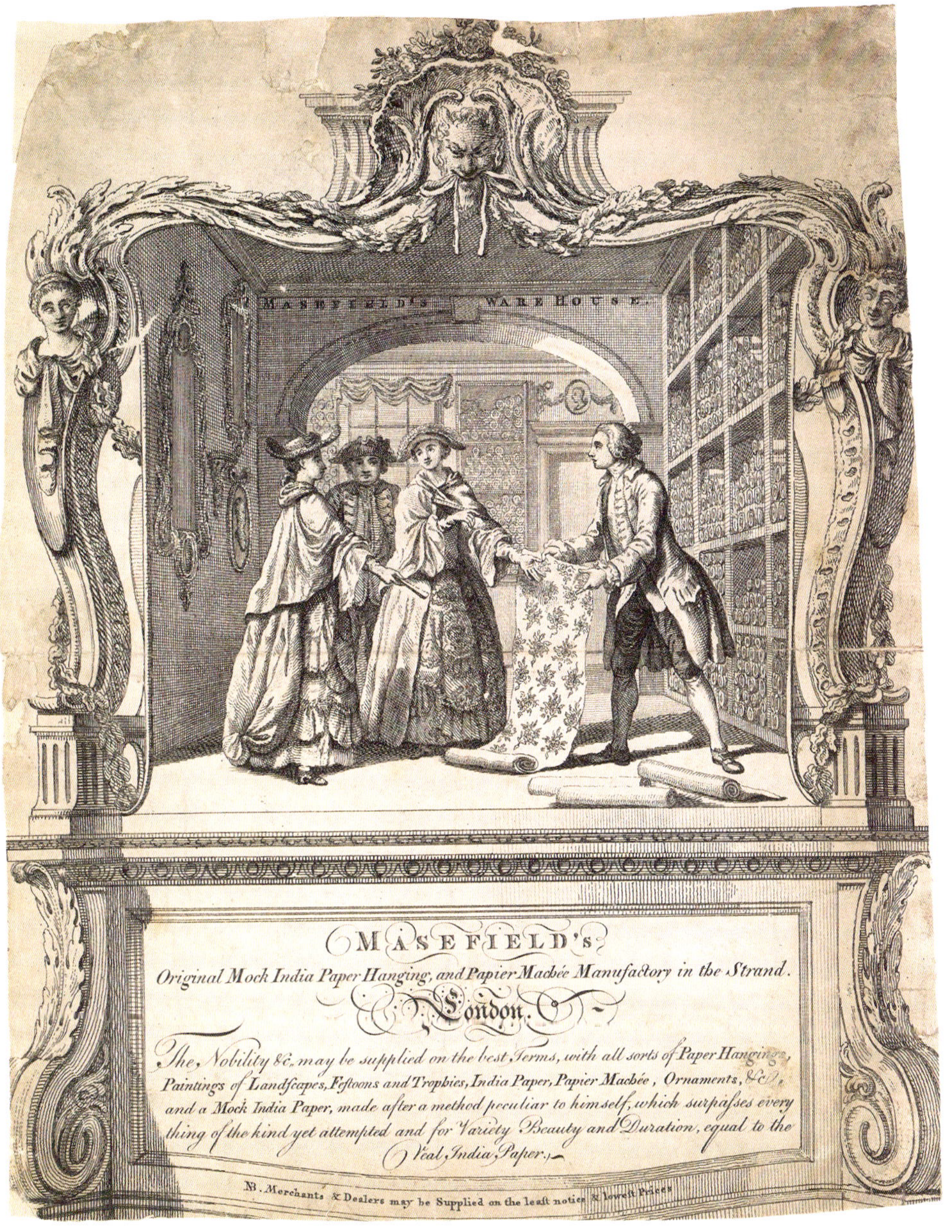

49. Artist unknown, trade card for "[Richard] Masefield's . . . Manufactory in the Strand, London," uncolored etching (c. 1760). © The Trustees of the British Museum.

it, customers expected the paper to be specially colored to correspond. The ability to produce wallpapers to match fabrics was a key selling point. James Wheeley's paper-hanging warehouse advertised in 1754, "All kind of Furniture are exactly Match'd" (see fig. 48).[21] An overarching decorative scheme dictated choice for the most imperious customers. A horror of mismatched decor shrieks from the letter book. Lady Lumm of Cheltenham was incensed when she heard from her housekeeper that Trollope's men had mixed up the hanging, such that everything clashed.

> You must have made a great Mistake in having put up the Crimson and white border in the back room which was only intended to match the curtains and furniture in the front Room; and the Curtains in the back room being yellow I proposed having the border of the paper in the back room something of yellow and black. . . . I am quite vex'd at this Mistake; as it will make the back room frightful . . . you do not know how vexd I am at the Mistake.[22]

Mistaken, mistaken, three times mistaken. There was no question here that the clash was vexing. Paper was expected to marry with curtains and other hangings, upholstery, and even the color of wood, though the "match" was a similarity of hue, not juxtaposition with a contrasting, complementary, or a coordinated color.[23]

Color was the salient feature of wallpaper. Without accompanying samples, it is impossible to know exactly what shade a customer had in mind when using a term such as "crimson." In color theory, Isaac Newton's seven-color spectrum was displaced in about 1800 by a six-color system of the three primary colors (red, yellow, blue) and their complementaries (green, violet, orange); in practice, however, color names could cover a variety of shades.[24] Trollope and his customers may even have been at odds about what a particular color name signified. In 1807, Mrs. Marryat ordered a "border done in a rose color" and was unimpressed when she was sent "a dark crimson."[25] Still, it is clear that a good color was both visually appealing and permanent. What use was an exquisite "pompadour," often a silvery lilac-pink, if it faded?

Whether French gray, brown, green, buff, stone, lilac, straw yellow, or rose pink, the precise color was crucial to the effect in the eyes of Trollope's customers. Moreover, there were quality distinctions to be made within a single color. As the Stricklands wrote in 1799, "We have settled to have the Room done in a plain French Grey, of the best shade."[26] Complaints about the wrong color are scattered throughout the letter book. In August 1805, a Miss Walvo of Weybridge protested about her hall papers that "hers is a darker grey on a pale grey the paper sent a darker blue on a pale grey the Border is still more Different & she cannot possibly make use of any of them." So determined was she to prove her point that she "pinned to a piece of the paper the half of the only bit she has remaining of the original of her Hall paper to prove to Mr Trollope how widely they differ."[27]

Choice of color varied by taste, in dialogue with fashion, and, importantly, according to the room and the light. Consumers' awareness of the symbolism of certain colors is hard to gauge, but in any case there was no universal authority to which they might refer. In late-seventeenth-century color hierarchies, derived from heraldry, red was the principal color. In conventional symbolism, red was associated with the god Mars, represented fire, and was allied with nobility, dignity, and state. Indeed, the state apartments in royal palaces were done in crimson until the reign of George IV. Red drapery in paintings signified justice, virtue, and defense, according to a ladies' art manual in 1777.[28] However, among Trollope's customers there was very little call for red. Perhaps it was a desire for aristocratic panache that led Sir Thomas Anson to order white scrolls on a crimson ground for the drawing rooms of his Staffordshire pile in 1803, specifying that "you will be exact in the colour of the Ground that it may be a rich red & to match the bits of tassel I gave you."[29] With crimson walls, deep red upholstery, and likely festoon curtains, the effect must have mirrored the grand staterooms of the early Georgians. But Anson was unusual among Trollope's customers; no one else ordered red on this scale. Red was known to absorb the light, requiring costly candlepower to show its beauties, so practicality may have warned off the majority.

Green was associated with Venus and came second in the received color hierarchies derived from heraldry, but it was often thought more pleasing than red as a setting for furniture and was probably easier to live with. Green's associations with love and pleasure may have particularly recommended it for bedrooms. In drapery, green signified hope.[30] Further, paintings in gilt frames were thought to look good against green.[31] Among Trollope's correspondents, green was mentioned more than any other color requested for bedrooms, parlors, drawing rooms, breakfast rooms, dining rooms, and billiard rooms. Green must have already claimed a therapeutic reputation, as a Mr. Pryor of the Foreign Office wanted pea green for his rooms in Whitehall in 1800, on account of "his eyes being bad."[32] "I like green" was an entirely safe remark for a Regency consumer to make.

Blue came third in traditional color hierarchies; labeled the color of Jupiter and the Virgin, it signified pity and sincerity. In drapery, it indicated faith and love.[33] The discovery of Prussian blue in the 1700s hastened its use in paint and dye, and by the 1730s, blue had become a feature of fashionable interiors. However, among Trollope's customers, blue paper was less popular than green and even yellow for family rooms, though it was occasionally used for drawing rooms. "Common blue papers" were used for passages, servants' halls, the inside of cupboards, and under-papering. It was offcuts of blue paper that the aptly named civil servant Mr. Feeling of the General Post Office requested when his little girl was ailing, instructing the company to "send by the Bearer any old useless pieces of Borders of papers & particularly any of a Blue pattern to amuse his little Daughter who is very ill and has expressed a desire for them."[34] In grander settings, blue did appear as an accent to gray, yellow, red, and even occasionally orange.

Yellow was not mentioned in heraldry and appears to stand outside the formal hierarchies that governed the language of early Georgian interior decoration. Yellow branded cowards, traitors, heretics, and Jews in early-modern Europe. Yellow drapery signified jealousy, though yellow was the color of Hymen, the Greek god of marriage, so it also denoted marriage in some contexts. Yellow showed no contrast to gilt frames, and references to yellow rooms before 1740 are rare.[35] However, yellow was an exalted color in imperial China, and the craze for chinoiserie must have increased its glamour. Yellow was certainly a popular choice among Trollope's correspondents by the 1790s, coloring the papers for drawing rooms (in darker hues), bedrooms (in lighter), and dressing rooms.

So much for color. As for patterns, what were Trollope's leading designs? Like most manufacturers, the company supplied marbled, plain, and glazed colored papers, as well as flock. The most frequently cited pattern was the trellis (occasionally "lattice"), which came in larger and smaller designs, in pink and white, blue and white, green and white, and green and buff (fig. 50). Trellis was seen as unaffected in look, suiting a modest room in town or country, though it may have had a particular affinity with the idea of "the cottage," a house form that had achieved remarkable popularity by 1800.

Floral designs included Trollope's geranium, convolvulus, and lily, but of these the geranium far outstripped the rest in popularity (fig. 51). Strikingly, all were non-native blooms, so wallpaper brought the exotic garden indoors, domesticated within an urban terrace. Leaf and acorn patterns were also favorites (fig. 52). Stripes, vertical ribbons, waves, and pillars were featured, as were small figures, spots, dots, and dashes on lighter grounds. Intricate patterns, "full of work"—what we might term "busy"—had their supporters, as did so-called "lively" papers.[36] Rock, stone, and brick patterns were requested for staircases. Architectural devices included scrolls, Etruscan borders, and Gothic arches. Were there conventions about appropriate patterns and colors? Trollope's customers abided by the established convention that "rooms for convenience" and "rooms for shew" were hung differently.[37] Halls, entrances, and passages were often papered in stones and other neutrals, a device to ensure that strong effect was reserved for the grander rooms. Simpler patterns suited bedrooms, dressing rooms, attics, garrets, servants' rooms, small parlors, passages, and the like, but drawing rooms and dining rooms, which

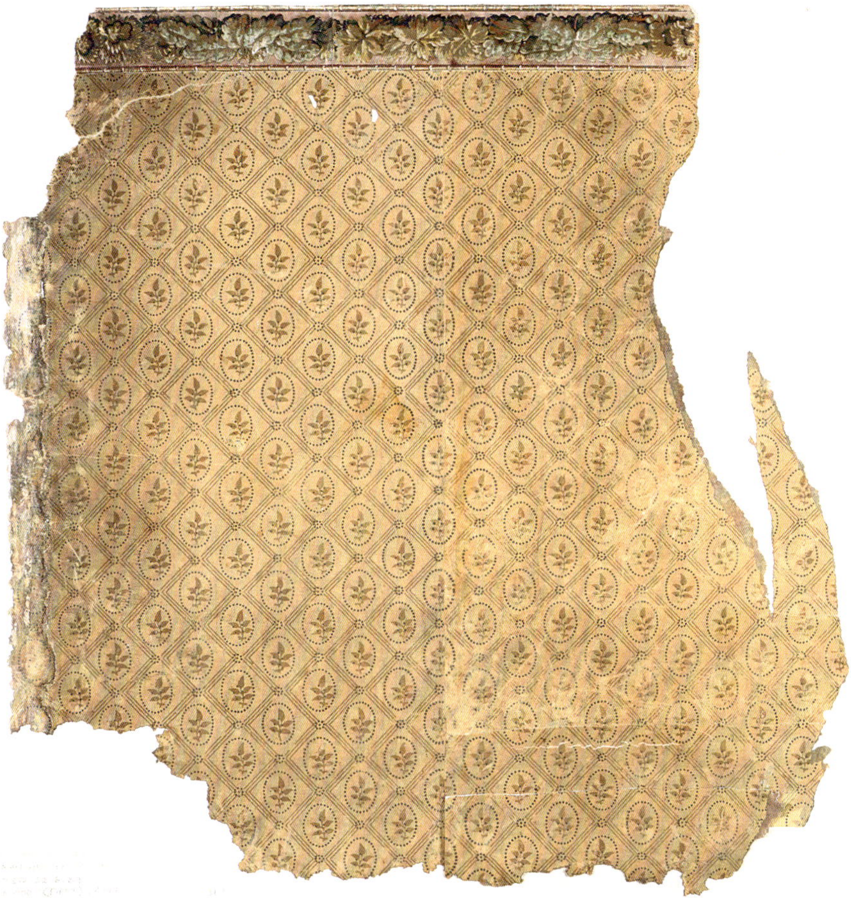

50. Trellis wallpaper and foliate border from the ground-floor front room of 50 Manchester Street, Marylebone, London, block printed (c. 1800). © English Heritage Photographic Library.

saw the most social traffic, required impressive papers. Lady Lumm ordered grand crimson and yellow papers for her formal rooms, but she expected to economize elsewhere: "I hope you will put the very cheapest paper in the room joining the hall, and in the Little Room over the Kitchen."[38]

An obsession with decorum and fitness to context suffuses the Trollope letter book: paper should be suitable for its setting. Customers almost invariably specified the rooms for which they were ordering—"a small bedroom," "a light north room," and so on—and mentioned dominant features such as low ceilings or restricted light, stressing the architectural context ("a small parsonage") and situation ("in the country"). Large designs were believed inappropriate, even oppressive, in small rooms. Lady Charlotte Smith looked for unobtrusive designs for her Chelmsford

51. Geranium-leaf wallpaper and chain border from the ground-floor front room of 48 Manchester Street, Marylebone, London, block printed (c. 1790). © English Heritage Photographic Library. Photo: Jeremy Richards.

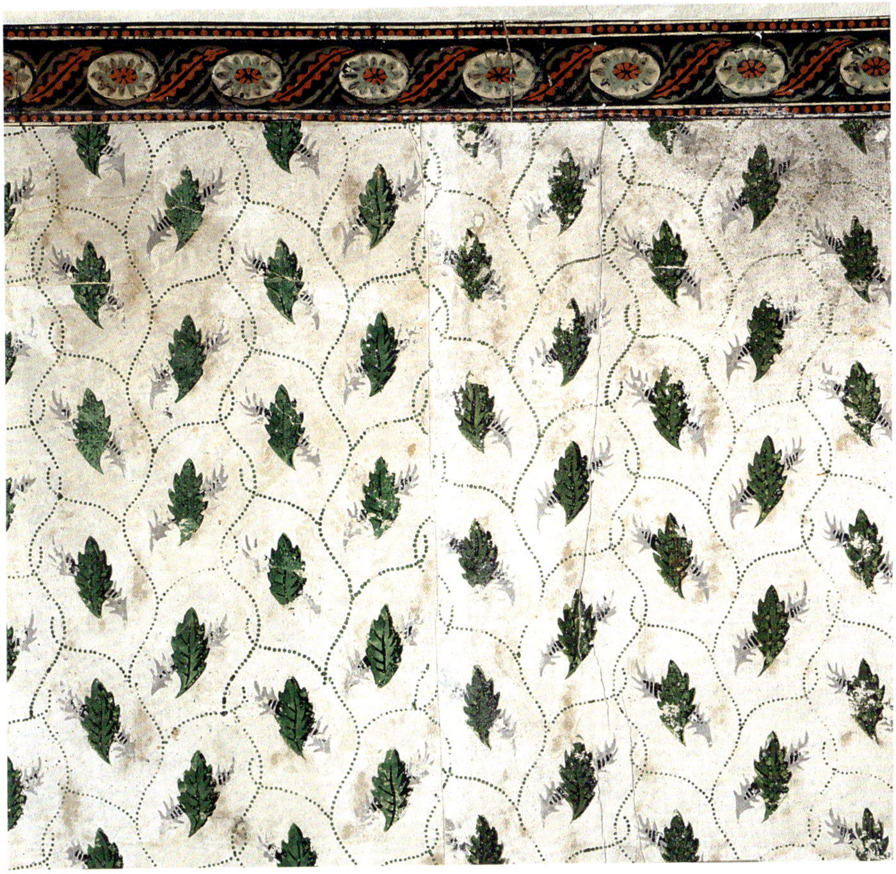

52. Oak-leaf wallpaper and neoclassical border from the ground-floor front room of 50 Manchester Street, Marylebone, London, block printed (c. 1795). © English Heritage Photographic Library. Photo: Jeremy Richards.

nursery, "something neat & genteel & a pattern that does not dazzle the Eyes either in grey blew or yellow as it is a North room which is sunny. She likes green. . . ."[39]

A commitment to decorum was shared by the rich and titled, who did not expect magnificence in all their rooms. Sir Samuel Fludyer, son of an immensely rich London merchant, wanted "patterns of very common papers for Garrets."[40] When Sir John Dyke of Lullingston Castle, Kent, ordered "patterns of green & white papers with proper borders fit for a common sitting room in the country," he was insistent that Trollope "not send anything that is fine as that will not answer for a room that is very low pitched."[41] Majestic designs looked absurd outside grand apartments. Fine paper would not answer in a common room, even if that room belonged to a baronet.

Neatness was a favorite attribute of a wallpaper pattern; it had been positively associated with wallpaper from the first. Wallpaper was commended in 1699 as making "the houses of the more ordinary look neat."[42] In his dictionary, Samuel Johnson defined "neat" as "elegant, but without dignity."[43] For Trollope's customers, neat papers tended to have small patterns and conveyed a lack of ostentation. William Ellis was an old man who disliked change. He had not had his green dining room in Ware, Hertfordshire, redecorated for years, but on recovering from eighteen months of illness, he found repairs forced on him, which "put me quite out of sorts." Reluctantly, he requested new borders, "not too Expensive about 2¼ or 2½ inches wide neat and not too showey."[44] Neat papers were found at the cheaper end of the spectrum. However, "cheap and neat" was a world away from "cheap and nasty" in effect. From the cleric who avowed, "I care nothing about fashion if they are neat & clean," to Lady Charlotte Smith's desire for "something neat & genteel," it is plain that "neatness" connoted propriety.[45] The neoclassical vogue ensured that the neat could be linked with the modern. In 1798, a William Evans of Wimbourne, Dorset, requested an "assortment of Patterns of Papers the best & most modern for a neat Drawing Room."[46]

Cheapness was often the deciding factor in an order. A Mrs. Bonar refused to settle an order in 1799 that she found "extravagantly dear done."[47] Landlords invariably insisted on cheapness in a paper, but private customers often specified that they wanted to see the less expensive patterns, or the common papers, especially for the less formal areas of the house. A small group of customers requested old patterns because they had become attached to the familiar, or to make good their worn patches.[48]

None of which is to say that Trollope's customers disavowed fashion in furnishings. Yet "fashionable" was an umbrella term, which could mean both a loose conformity to prevailing modes and the more demanding definition of possessing the latest model each season. An anxious concern not to be too far adrift of fashion motivated many, rather than a craving to set the modes. The Dowager Countess Poulett ordered extra borders for her drawing room, bedroom, and dressing room at Lyme Regis, "as I am told everyone does the corners now."[49] Some sought reassurance that their choices were fashionable enough. Mrs. Burt of Malling, Kent, confessed she "does not know if the one she has chosen is very fashionable and begs Mr Trollope will send her word whether it is usual to cut out the borders as formerly or whether it is more the custom to leave the edge and for satisfaction sake whether it is tolerably new."[50]

A handful of customers demanded the *dernier cri*, asking for up-to-the-minute patterns barely dry from the printer. Sir Thomas Anson of Shugborough was piqued to hear that Lord Gwydwr had some new French papers at his mansion in

Whitehall, and he worried that his own choice was passé, as "it has been much in use & will not look so new as I could wish."[51] Novelty was his sine qua non in a wall covering, and he was not to be outdone.

A vocabulary of beauty was applied to wallpaper. A desire for "pretty" papers and patterns was widespread. Prettiness was defined as beauty without majesty, stateliness, grandeur, or dignity. The use of the term ("pretty border suitable to a small room," "pretty for a small parlour") suggests that prettiness was an attribute of modest, unassuming papers, conveying an impression of charming, graceful, dainty, but unpretentious decoration. "Smart" was used only once as an adjective in the Trollope correspondence, and in this instance it carried social as well as aesthetic connotations. When Sir John Dyke requested nothing too fine for his common sitting room in the country, what he received was just too ordinary after all. None of the patterns would do, so he applied again for new ones in whites, and "something of a smarter kind than those he sent."[52] There was clearly such a thing as too common for a baronet. "Beautiful" or "handsome" conveyed something altogether more splendid and assertive. "Handsome" had a long-established association with wallpaper,[53] and it was a quality expected of dining rooms.[54] To Trollope's customers, these adjectives indicated the grander end of the stocks. However, there must have been a risk that "handsome" could be interpreted as flashy, since Guchard, an upholsterer who was a regular customer of Trollope's, was careful to specify in 1798 "some patterns of handsome Papers not gaudy" for a London room seventeen feet high.[55] With its associations of overly bright tastelessness, "gaudy" is rarely a term of praise today. But there were earlier positive understandings of splendor, color, and show, coexisting with the negative.[56] Yet none of Trollope's customers used the term with approval; indeed, gaudy epitomized what many sought to avoid. By 1800, florid taste and pompous ostentation were the entrenched associations of gaudy. Thomas Baring sought in 1800 "to chose from the least rich & Gaudy patterns" for his drawing room and bedrooms in the country.[57] Even those with a taste for show and a mighty pretty glitter never admitted the word "gaudy," though surely what was splendid, handsome, and fine to some eyes was loud and tinsel to others.

Where did this aesthetic vocabulary come from? The most striking finding is the extent to which wallpaper consumers adhered to the classical rule of decorum. Decorum held that there were fundamental divisions in society (rank, age, sex, occupation) and that different forms of conduct were appropriate to each. Unsurprisingly, a gentleman's clothes, accoutrements, houses, and furnishings were supposed to be suitable to his rank. Elegance and magnificence in architecture, dignity and splendor in furnishings, were expected of those of birth, title, and wealth. By extension, fine papers in small rooms of families with no fortune would be a flagrant breach of decorum. Thomas Sheraton's *Cabinet Dictionary* of 1803 still preached the ancient view that surroundings should mirror status, that "when any gentleman is so vain and ambitious as to order the furnishing of his house in a style superior to his fortune and rank it will be prudent in an upholsterer, by some gentle hints, to direct his choice to a more moderate plan."[58] Yet even whispers about toning down a scheme were unnecessary among Trollope's customers, so deep was the antipathy to indecorous show. Wallpaper shored up social and spatial hierarchies, the innate appreciation of which was a proof of taste.

The opposite of showy excess was neatness. Neatness was an utterly positive quality, with many nuances of meaning. Indeed, "neat" emerges as a Georgian key word of unexpectedly wide social purchase, which could be applied to towns, houses, objects, personal appearance, and even events. Today, the leading meaning of "neat" is tidy, well-ordered, and trim. However, the most immediate definition for Georgian consumers was more demandingly architectural: "neat" conveyed a simple elegance of form, finely made and proportioned, free from unnecessary embellishments. Neatness often connoted a spare elegance in keeping with Palladian or neoclassical architectural ideals. In its emphasis on regularity, proportion, and simplicity, "neat" sat comfortably with classical vocabularies of decorum and harmony familiar from courtesy literature and polite periodicals. Neatness was a recognized manner of decoration for social groups or rooms that made claims to taste but not ostentatious grandeur. Isaac Ware advised aspiring architects in 1756, "There are apartments in which dignity, others in which neatness, and others in which shew are to be consulted."[59] Elegance on a budget and in compact settings should be fittingly neat.

Neatness also connoted a regularity of form and well-executed integrity of design in objects. Neat things were well contrived, cleverly put together, and smoothly finished. Carpets, stove grates, china, kitchen utensils, prints, upholstery, house carvings, tables, chests of drawers, desks, bookcases, looking glasses, barometers, and other furnishings were all advertised as "neat," "very neat," "neatly done," "neatly finished," or "in the neatest and most modern taste" in the pages of the *Leeds Intelligencer* and *Leeds Mercury*.[60]

Beyond restrained elegance, neatness also demonstrated wholesome cleanliness and propriety. Neat wallpaper expressed decency and good housekeeping, largely because wallpaper was believed to be clean—though what constituted cleanliness for the Georgians is a little obscure. Trade manuals warn of insects breeding behind old wall hangings and of noxious smells,[61] so presumably fresh papers were an attempt to keep the vermin, grease, and nastiness at bay. New paper may even have been the architectural equivalent of spotless personal linen, which even on an unwashed body exemplified inner cleanliness, self-respect, and respectability.

"Neat" was used in its more familiar senses of tidy and trim in relation to dress. When deployed by witnesses at the Old Bailey, the main criminal court for London, "neat" underscored social credit. The dress of a credible member of the public was invariably "neat and clean," and trust was extended on that basis. Neatness could connote a simple smartness, or elegance stopping short of fashion and extra adornment, or a respectable plainness of attire.[62] Neatness radiated a certain moral assertiveness in its very restraint. The Quakers led the most public retreat from finery and show, thereby becoming a byword for sartorial self-control. When Jane Farrin, an Essex yeoman's wife, bespoke a stuff gown of her daughter in the 1750s, she requested a "neat quakers couler," clarifying, "I would not have very dark nor yet gaudey."[63] Gaudy was also anathema to John Wesley, who preached the virtues of simplicity to his Methodist followers, though he endorsed the use of dress to reinforce social position. Wesley prohibited any fabrics that were "gay, glistering, showy," or of "glaring colour," but urged neatness and cleanliness as a reflection of the inner moral state. For Wesley, neatness and cleanliness in person, clothes, and house testified to industry and modesty. "Neat but not gaudy" expressed the self-righteous self-restraint of serious Anglicanism and Protestant dissent.[64]

As the opposite of gaudy show, and deeply linked to wholesomeness, cleanliness, and decent respectability, neatness had a potentially wide social purchase. Beyond the reach of polite consumerism, neatness embodied an ethical rejection of extravagance. Luxury's "gaudy visions" were denounced by the imprisoned English republican John Thelwall, who argued in 1795 that liberty could take root only in "virtuous poverty."[65] The radical tailor Francis Place, looking back on his happiness in the city lodgings that he had taken with his wife in the 1790s, concluded that "our little furniture was good enough for our circumstances and the room was especially neat and clean." "Our neat place" exuded domestic virtue—the fitting home of a self-disciplined, radical young couple.[66] Neat, not gaudy, had become a badge of sober radicalism.

To what extent did taste in wallpaper differ by gender? Decorum contains within it the possibility that decorations would be different for women's and men's rooms. Indeed, wall hangings had long been recommended for ladies' rooms, and fanciful Chinese wallpaper seems to have taken hold in ladies' dressing rooms. Ladies were praised for their skill in creating print rooms, arranging collage on existing papers, and freshening up old papers with paint and new borders. "I have seen great taste exemplified by ladies in this mode of ornamenting apartments," allowed John Pincot, a Hackney colorman, in 1811.[67] Letters and diaries suggest that wallpaper itself could be seen as expressive of femininity, prettiness, and joie de vivre.

Surprisingly, perhaps, the Trollope letter book is neutral on what we might call the gendering of interiors. No explicit link was ever made between men and women as a sex and particular styles or colors of wallpaper. There is not a single reference to light, pretty papers proper for ladies' rooms, or bold, handsome patterns suitable for men's, nor is there any explicit suggestion that dining rooms had a masculine character and drawing rooms a feminine one, as might be expected from the scholarly literature—though this is not to say that certain associations were not taken for granted.[68]

Men and women seem to have shared an aesthetic understanding and vocabulary. Nevertheless, the forthright confidence with which women expressed their preferences in wallpaper is significant, given that we know that men dominated the purchase of luxurious decorative goods such as silver, pictures, and substantial china. Only 37 of the 321 clients in the 1766–70 ledger of the London silversmiths Parker and Wakelin were female, about 12 percent.[69] So although female consumers of wallpaper were in a minority, 21 percent, of Trollope's customers, their numbers were consistent with those associated with the purchase of other costly decorative items—more than silver, but about the same as paintings and china. However, in contrast with silver records, we may simply be seeing the differences between a ledger and a letter book in capturing the language of female choices. Of course, the letter book itself is not a record of all transactions. By its nature, a letter book must overrepresent repeat orders, customers at a distance, those dissatisfied with their orders, and those having difficulty paying. Nevertheless, the letter book illuminates female monitoring of the conduct of decorative work in the home. Female responsibility for the smooth running of a household justified many a complaint.[70]

Certainly, women had some say in the semipermanent furnishing of the house, long before the rise of a Victorian interior-decorating literature aimed at the ladies. It may also be that the similarities between wallpaper and textiles, long an area of female expertise, empowered women to assert their opinions. Female adeptness at describing the pattern and color of textiles is apparent in letters from at least the late seventeenth century. When, in 1747, Mrs. Delany described a silk of purple flowers and white feathers "on a pale deer-coloured figured ground" as "extremely pretty and very modest," she could easily have been describing wallpaper.[71] That the vocabulary used to appreciate wallpaper drew on an older language related to textiles is unsurprising, since wallpaper patterns had so much in common with the silks and chintz that they imitated. Trellis was featured as much on chintz as on Trollope's wallpaper in the 1790s.

This essay began with an interest in objects, and it has found its way back to language. Yet what Trollope and Sons' letter book can tell us about the terms of everyday aesthetic discrimination is exceptional. In examining the language of the letters, we discover the categories and criteria that informed the domestic aesthetic judgments of a broadly constituted consumer public. These are not the categories and criteria of the classical orders that permeate the architectural treatises, nor do they exhibit the dense classical allusion that surfaces repeatedly in the philosophical debates about taste. What these categories and criteria do draw from those philosophical debates is a deep, moralizing suspicion of the outward signs of luxury—the rich, the gaudy, the showy. It is striking that almost all of Trollope's customers, from the plutocrat to the country parson, shared this suspicion, though one suspects that the degree of ostentation they were actually prepared to embrace varied considerably in practice. But in addition, they were adept at applying their everyday language of aesthetic discrimination in very precise ways to the particular visual characteristics of the wallpapers—their colors and their patterns. In these letters, the ancient contest between luxury and virtue is refought on the terrain of trellis, stripe, and ribbon, in ways that draw on a long-standing set of assumptions about domestic decorum. This language could be generalized beyond wallpaper, to textiles, clothing, furniture, china, even food.[72] Middling, genteel, and cosmopolitan English consumers, both male and female, had a rich everyday lexicon with which to conceptualize their choices, be they handsome, elegant, and beautiful, or unshowy, pretty, and neat.

For advice on wallpaper, I am obliged to Liz Miller and Treve Rosoman. For critical readings and trenchant criticisms, I am grateful to Christopher Breward, Michele Cohen, Edwina Ehrman, Amy Meyers, Charlotte Mitchell, John Mullan, Giorgio Riello, and John Styles. I am especially indebted to Hannah Greig for her lively critical engagement, research assistance, eye for visual evidence, and skill with a digital camera. Versions of this essay have been presented at the Yale Center for British Art, the Warren Center at Harvard University, the University of East Anglia, and the "Georgian Interiors Conference" at the Victoria and Albert Museum in Nov. 2005. I benefited enormously from comments and questions at all four events. Finally, I thank the London Metropolitan Archives for permission to quote from the Trollope letter book.

1. Trollope and Sons, letter book, London Metropolitan Archives (hereafter LMA), B/TRL/09, fol. 107.
2. Edmund Burke, *A Philosophical Enquiry into the Origin of our Ideas of the Sublime and Beautiful* (London: J. Dodsley, 1759), 4. Burke also stated: "We find people in their disputes continually appealing to certain tests and standards which are allowed on all sides, and are supposed to be established in our common nature. But there is not the same obvious concurrence in any uniform or settled principles which relate to Taste. It is even commonly supposed that this delicate and aerial faculty, which seems too volatile to endure even the chains of definition, cannot be properly tried by any text, nor regulated by any standard"; Burke, *Philosophical Enquiry*, 2.
3. Tobias Smollett, *The Expedition of Humphry Clinker* (1771; London: Oxford Univ. Press, 1884), 36–37.
4. E. A. Entwistle, *A Literary History of Wallpaper* (London: B. T. Batsford, 1960); R. Hills, *A Short History of Paper Making in Britain, 1488–1988* (London: Athlone Press, 1988); Treve Rosoman, *London Wallpapers: Their Manufacture and Use, 1690–1840* (London: English Heritage, 1992); Gill Saunders, *Wallpaper in Interior Decoration* (London: V&A Publications, 2002).
5. A. C. Clark, ed., *Gleanings from an Old Portfolio Containing Some Correspondence between Lady Louisa Stuart and Her Sister, Caroline, Countess of Portarlington* (Edinburgh: privately printed for David Douglas, 1895), 1:185.

6. However, some dispute the affordability of wallpaper. James Ayres suggests that wallpaper was confined to the first- and second-rate houses at fashionable Bath, based on provenanced examples in The Building of Bath Museum, Bath; Ayres, *Domestic Interiors: The British Tradition, 1500–1850* (New Haven and London: Yale Univ. Press, 2003), 165, 242. Nevertheless, the evidence of the Leeds newspapers, account books nationwide, and the Trollope letter book itself indicates that this is too pessimistic an assessment of the dissemination of paper.
7. Saunders, *Wallpaper*, 7.
8. The shallow stepmother Mrs. Gibson cannot wait to repaper Molly's room and thus obliterate the relics of her happier girlhood; Elizabeth Gaskell, *Wives and Daughters* (1866; Oxford: Oxford Univ. Press, 1987), 189. Similarly, brash Sergeant Troy wants to rip out the oak wainscot and paper Bathsheba's venerable old farmhouse; Thomas Hardy, *Far from the Madding Crowd* (1874; Oxford: Everyman's Library, 1991), 295.
9. Saunders, *Wallpaper*, 7.
10. Museum of London, account book of Mrs. Martha Dodson, 1746–65. For advice on Dodson and her social context, I am especially grateful to Edwina Ehrman of the Museum of London. See Ehrman, "Dressing Well in Old Age: The Clothing Accounts of Martha Dodson, 1746–1765," *Costume* (forthcoming).
11. Personal communication from Treve Rosoman, English Heritage, London.
12. See John Styles, "Involuntary Consumers? The Eighteenth-Century Servant and Her Clothes," *Textile History* 33, no. 1 (2002): 14.
13. The company had a sprinkling of titled customers, including the Marchioness of Exeter, Burghley House, Lincolnshire; Sir Thomas Anson, Shugborough, Staffordshire; Lord Cholmondley, Vale Royal, Cheshire; Lady Dyke, Lullingstone Castle, Kent; the Chutes of the Vyne, Hampshire; the Dowager Countess Poulett of Lyme Regis; Lady Lumm of Cheltenham; and Lady Fludyer of Lincolnshire.
14. LMA, B/Trl/09, fols. 254, 266.
15. LMA, B/Trl/09, fol. 290.
16. LMA, B/Trl/09, fol. 451.
17. For example, see LMA, B/Trl/09, fols. 323, 3.
18. This is Gill Saunders's conclusion based on the collection she knows best, at the Victoria and Albert Museum; see Saunders, *Wallpaper*, 9. However, more modest papers are preserved by English Heritage, London, and the Whitworth Art Gallery, University of Manchester.
19. Cowtan Archive, Department of Word and Image, Victoria and Albert Museum.
20. LMA, B/Trl/09, fols. 246–47.
21. Similarly, Messrs. Hargrave and Plowman, Paperstainers, promised, "Furniture neatly matched to colours, both in papers and in borders"; *Leeds Intelligencer*, 24 April 1787.
22. LMA, B/Trl/09, fol. 345.
23. Matching schemes were favored in later-eighteenth-century Paris too; see Annik Pardailhe-Galabrun, *The Birth of Intimacy: Privacy and Domestic Life in Early Modern Paris* (Cambridge, UK: Polity Press, 1991), 172.
24. See John Gage, *Colour in Turner: Poetry and Truth* (London: Studio Vista, 1969); Ian Bristow, *Architectural Colour in British Interiors, 1615–1840* (New Haven and London: Yale Univ. Press, 1996); S. Lowengard, "Colours and Colour Making in the Eighteenth Century," in *Consumers and Luxury: Consumer Culture in Europe, 1650–1850*, ed. Maxine Berg and Helen Clifford (Manchester: Manchester Univ. Press, 1999), 103–17.
25. LMA, B/Trl/09, fol. 423.
26. LMA, B/Trl/09, fol. 91.
27. LMA, B/Trl/09, fol. 332.
28. John Cornforth, *Early Georgian Interiors* (New Haven and London: Yale Univ. Press, 2004), 119; Hannah Robertson, *The Young Ladies School of Art*, 4th ed. (York: Printed at the New Printing-Office, in Coppergate, for Mrs. Robinson, 1777), 25.
29. LMA, B/Trl/09, fol. 261.
30. Robertson, *Young Ladies School of Art*, 25.
31. Mary Delany had her "English room" painted "a sort of olive . . . for the sake of my pictures" in 1744; Lady Llanover, ed., *The Autobiography and Correspondence of Mary Granville, Mrs Delany*, 6 vols. (London:

Richard Bentley, 1861–62), 2:330. For other examples, see Cornforth, *Early Georgian Interiors*, 120. Green was still the fashionable backdrop for pictures in the 1800s; LMA, B/Trl/09, fol. 324.

32. LMA, B/Trl/09, fol. 163.
33. Robertson, *The Young Ladies School of Art*, 25.
34. LMA, B/Trl/09, fol. 403. The French agreed. Annik Pardailhe-Galabrun finds that red and green were predominant in Parisian decoration and upholstery under Louis XIV and Louis XV, but green increasingly became seen as the softer and more restful color; see Pardailhe-Galabrun, *Birth of Intimacy*, 171. She points out that the *Encyclopédie* described green as just the right mixture of clear and somber to please and strengthen the sight instead of weakening it or troubling it. It claimed that painters had a green cloth hung near the place where they work, on which to throw their glance from time to time, to relieve them of the fatigue caused by the brightness of the colors.
35. Robertson, *Young Ladies School of Art*, 25; Cornforth, *Interiors*, 121; I. H. Evans, *Brewer's Dictionary of Phrase and Fable* (London: Cassell, 1990), 256.
36. LMA, B/Trl/09, fol. 38.
37. Isaac Ware, *A Complete Body of Architecture* (London: T. Osborne and J. Shipton, 1756), 432.
38. LMA, B/Trl/09, fols. 232–33.
39. LMA, B/Trl/09, fol. 266.
40. LMA, B/Trl/09, fol. 256.
41. LMA, B/Trl/09, fol. 452.
42. John Houghton, *Collection for Improvement of Husbandry & Trade*, no. 356 (1699), cited in Entwistle, *Literary History*, 13.
43. Samuel Johnson, *A Dictionary of English Language* . . . (London: Printed by W. Strahan, for J. and P. Knapton [etc.], 1755), s.v. "neat."
44. LMA, B/Trl/09, fol. 367.
45. LMA, B/Trl/09, fol. 107.
46. LMA, B/Trl/09, fol. 21.
47. LMA, B/Trl/09, fol. 88.
48. LMA, B/Trl/09, fols. 213, 368.
49. LMA, B/Trl/09, fol. 123.
50. LMA, B/Trl/09, fol. 296.
51. LMA, B/Trl/09, fols. 246–47.
52. LMA, B/Trl/09, fol. 453.
53. For example, the Golden Lyon Inn in Leeds advertised bedchambers "newly hung with handsome papers" in 1763; *Leeds Intelligencer*, 22 March 1763. Inns and later hotels may have been decorated with bolder patterns than customers could live with every day; Saunders, *Wallpaper*, 18. On the gorgeous, almost tawdry papers found in a Cambridge inn, see Colin Cunningham, "Taste of a Tavern Keeper," *Country Life*, 24 Nov. 1994, 54–55.
54. Ware, *Complete Body of Architecture*, 431.
55. LMA, B/Trl/09, fol. 64.
56. Johnson, *Dictionary*, vol. 1, s.v. "gaudy." Nor did "gaudy" have any negative meaning for Isaac Ware in 1756: "Of the three kinds of [wall coverings], the grandest is that in stucco; the neatest that in wainscot, and the most gaudy that in hangings"; Ware, *Complete Body of Architecture*, 469.
57. LMA, B/Trl/09, fol. 137.
58. Thomas Sheraton, *The Cabinet Dictionary* (London: Printed by W. Smith . . . and sold by W. Row, 1803), 215–16.
59. Ware, *Complete Body of Architecture*, 469. A fictional apartment to let, furnished with "only half a Dozen Cane Chairs, and some Paper Hangings," could nevertheless be approved. "Every thing was neat and elegant; and tho' the Apartment small, it was extremely convenient and well contrived"; *The School of Woman: Or Memoirs of Constantia Address'd to the Duchess of* ****, by the author of *The School of Man* (London: Printed for J. Robinson, 1753), 204. Mary Orlebar of the Bedfordshire gentry described her ideal country-

house retreat in a poem of 1753 as "small, not elegant, though neat"; James Collett-White, ed., *Bedfordshire Historical Miscellany: Essays in Honour of Patricia Bell,* Publications of the Bedfordshire Historical Record Society, vol. 72 (1993), 136. Elizabeth Montagu commended an elegance that stopped short of grandeur for its character of neatness, writing that "easy chairs & soft couches within doors, offer to you the most luxurious repose, fine pictures, pretty hangings & a character of neatness make the whole as pleasing a habitation as ever I saw, she enjoys all that riches can give but what appertains to grandeur & magnificence & pomp, which are rather encumbrances than the pleasures of wealth"; Elizabeth Montagu, Sandleford, to Sarah Scott, 28 Sept. 1753, The Huntington, MO 5737.

60. For example, *Leeds Intelligencer*, 3 May 1763.
61. John Pincot, *Treatise on the Practical Part of Coach & House Painting* (London: J. Bailey for John Pincot, 1811), 6, 19.
62. For example, in middle age in the 1800s, Ellen Weeton adopted "a neat, plain style of dress" consistent with her straitened finances and status as an unmarried governess; *Miss Weeton's Journal of a Governess*, vol. 1, 1807–11 (London: Oxford Univ. Press, H. Milford, 1936), 33, 253, 122.
63. Jane Farrin to Mrs. Mary White [Poll], n.d., Essex Record Office, Chelmsford, D/Dzg 33.
64. John Wesley, *Advice to the People called Methodists, with Regard to Dress* (London: John Paramore, 1780), 5. See also the brief, but suggestive, Edwina Ehrman, *Dressed Neat and Plain: The Clothing of John Wesley and His Teaching on Dress* (London: John Wesley's House and the Museum of Methodism, 2003). In fact, "neat but not gaudy" became something of a British catchphrase in the eighteenth century. Samuel Wesley, the father of John Wesley, pontificated that "style is the dress of thought; a modest dress. Neat but not gaudy, will true critics please"; Samuel Wesley, *An Epistle to a Friend, concerning Poetry* (London: Printed for Charles Harper, 1700).
65. John Thelwall, *Poems Written in Close Confinement in the Tower and Newgate under a Charge of High Treason* (London: Printed for the author, and sold by J. Ridgway, H. D. Symonds, and D. I. Eaton, 1795), 3.
66. Mary Thale, ed., *The Autobiography of Francis Place (1771–1854)* (Cambridge: Cambridge Univ. Press, 1972), 124–25.
67. Ware, *Complete Body of Architecture*, 470; Cornforth, *Georgian Interiors*, 208; Pincot, *House Painting*, 20.
68. On the basis of such sources as the Cowtan Archive, Department of Word and Image, Victoria and Albert Museum, Gill Saunders argues that the conventions became more fixed as the nineteenth century progressed; Saunders, *Wallpaper*, 16.
69. Helen Clifford, *Silver in London: The Parker and Wakelin Partnership, 1760–1776* (New Haven and London: Yale Univ. Press, 2004), 138.
70. LMA, B/Trl/09, fol. 86; see also fols. 11, 249.
71. Llanover, *Mrs Delany*, 2:447.
72. English cookery books often described dishes as "pretty" or "elegant"; see Hilary Young, *English Porcelain 1745–95: Its Makers, Design, Marketing and Consumption* (London: V&A Publications, 1999), 182.

Politics

"To Make a Figure": Clothing and the Politics of Male Identity in Eighteenth-Century America

Linzy Brekke

On 29 January 1789, President-elect George Washington asked his friend General Henry Knox to procure some "American Broad Cloths" advertised in the *New York Daily Advertiser.* Washington trusted that Knox, soon to be his secretary of war, was as capable of acquiring fabric from New York as he had been in obtaining artillery from Fort Ticonderoga during the American Revolution. But local broadcloth manufacture was still in its infancy, and Washington, the experimental sheep farmer, was very particular about his wool. He directed Knox carefully: "As to the colour, I shall leave it altogether to your taste; only observing that if the cloth should not really be very fine, then (in my Judgement) some colour mixed in grain might be preferable to an indifferent (stained) dye." Washington ordered cloth for his wife, Martha, as well, requesting "as much of what is called London Smoke as will make her a riding habit," and querying, "Could they be had from Hartford in Connecticut where I perceive a Manufactory of them is established."[1] Washington's decision to wear American cloth was a shrewd political calculation as well as a gesture of support for local manufacturing. It linked nationalism and politics with clothing and style.

This linkage, though not new in the West, artfully materialized broader changes in transatlantic culture. The concept of gentility profoundly shaped eighteenth-century European and American polite conduct, sociability, and material culture. In an age of revolutions on both sides of the Atlantic Ocean, political developments in turn began to change the meaning of goods and the practice of gentility. In the pre-Revolutionary period, American consumption of British manufactured goods might have helped to forge "a national consciousness," but when opposition to boycotts fell off after the Revolutionary War, speaking through and with those objects became more like a Tower of Babel than "a shared language of consumption."[2] Economic recession and a rising tide of cheap manufactured goods flooding the American marketplace renewed controversies over European imports and the ideological and political systems they represented—only in the 1780s, the issue was not the repeal of taxes or parliamentary coercion, but the viability and identity of a fledgling nation.[3] In a colonial context, Birmingham buckles, Manchester velvet, and London hats had connected proud provincials to a far-flung empire, but those same goods now threatened to undermine the gains of war and the tumultuous process of nation building after independence. If the "baubles of Britain" had once brought a nation together, they now threatened to tear it apart.[4]

Officials like Knox and Washington shared a concern for the pitiful state of American textile manufacturing. Knox, in fact, was corresponding privately with a major shareholder in a Hartford mill, Jeremiah Wadsworth, who sought Knox's advice on how to encourage federal officials to support his venture. The two concurred that the image of federal officials wearing Hartford cloth would at once "set the fashion" for American-made textiles. But patriotism ran aground on the shoals of taste, and Knox was forced to admit that Hartford's cloth was inferior to imports, complaining to Washington, "You will be disappointed with their fineness, it being about the quality of second english cloth."[5] They hardly had time to quibble over quality concerns, since Connecticut broadcloth of any kind was difficult to come by. Weeks after Washington's letter to him, Knox nervously informed the president-elect that "the cloths have not yet arrived although expected by the first wind."[6] With the inauguration looming in April, Knox was frantic to procure the cloth and find a silversmith to fabricate "federal buttons"—large silver buttons engraved with an eagle, which Washington wanted for his coat. Several yards of material were finally sent to Mount Vernon, his Virginia home, on 19 February, with Knox's note inside: "I forward you by the stage . . . 13 1/2 yards of 3/4 Wide bottle green cloth of the Hartford manufacture. I would there were more of it for your and Mrs. Washington's purposes but it was all of the color which came—The greys & the dark browns were too mean and coarse either for you or Mrs. W."[7] Washington politely accepted the cloth but continued to lobby Hartford for alternatives.

We do not know what became of Washington's "Bottle Green" textiles or Martha Washington's "London Smoke" riding habit. Despite the fame of the wearers, these objects have not survived. At the eleventh hour, on 30 March, Washington was relieved by a hand-delivered package of "cloth and buttons," which he exclaimed "really do credit to the manufactures of this Country." There still lacked enough eagle buttons to trim the coat in the manner Washington wished, however; it was not until he arrived in New York, amid great fanfare, that the buttons

OPPOSITE: 53. Brown wool coat and breeches, Hartford, Connecticut, 1789. Courtesy of Mount Vernon Ladies' Association. Photo: Gavin Ashworth. George Washington wore this dark brown woolen suit, manufactured in Connecticut, to his first inauguration, in 1789. The suit was embellished with large silver buttons bearing engraved eagles, fabricated especially for the occasion.

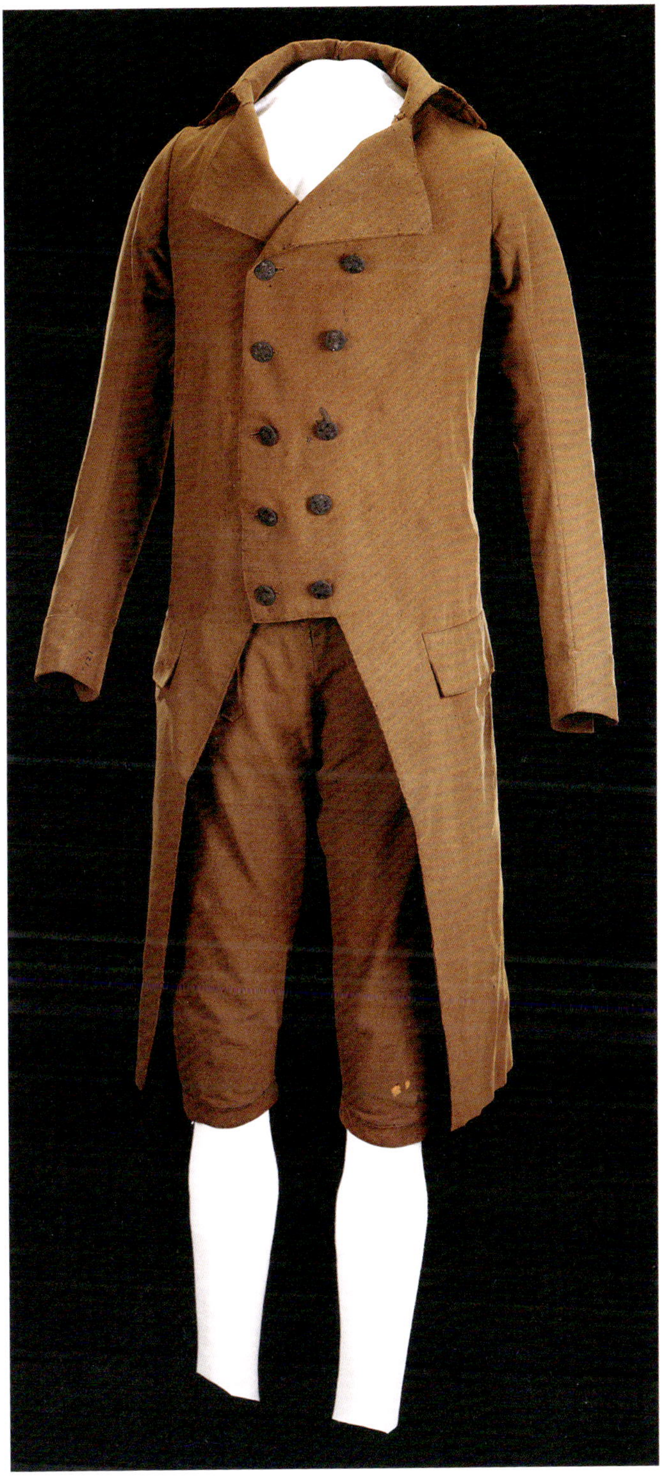

were finally procured and hurriedly sewn on. Surprisingly, the suit Washington wore to his inauguration on 30 April 1789 was made from the material Knox had rejected, the "mean and coarse" dark brown cloth (fig. 53).[8] At the most significant political event in the new nation's history, Washington appeared in a second-rate suit, opting for modesty and local manufacture over grandeur and fine imports.

The significance of his choice extends beyond one man's personal preference for brown over green, or coarse over fine cloth. For a host of elite Anglo-American men shared Washington's shifting and conflicted attitude toward material display. Letters, diaries, and accounts reveal that men's knowledge of clothing and fashion was far more substantial than they cared to admit, and it meant more, both personally and politically, than subsequent historians have recognized. The anxious selection of cloth, concern over appearance, nervous letters to friends for advice on what to wear—all were as important in men's lives as they were in women's. Together, they reveal the fraught relationship between masculinity and fashion in early national America.

By the mid-eighteenth century, Anglo-American elite males had begun to articulate an increasingly tense, ambivalent, and political relationship to dress. They felt anxious in their clothes and in their skin, incapable of demonstrating the "ineffable grace and ease" that was supposed to be the sine qua non of gentility. Certain conversational and sartorial practices became construed as "unmanly," for betraying alternately Anglophile, Francophile, effeminate, corrupt, or slovenly tendencies that suggested either a disregard for politeness or a Jacobin agenda to upset social hierarchy. Genteel men were hard-pressed to balance disparate definitions of manliness, which, as one article laid out, called for a complicated combination of "modesty and boldness, of loquacity and taciturnity, of freedom and reserve, and of every other quality *that degree* which is useful or commendable, but whose extremes are either criminal or ridiculous."[9] The wrong quantity of any of these traits could damage a man's reputation, render him unfit for public office, and threaten his place in polite society.[10]

Recent historical scholarship has explored the relationship of material culture to the creation of an American national consciousness, the influence of refinement, and the formation of industrial capitalism; however, its relationship to the politics of gender remains obscure.[11] The historical and scholarly feminization of consumer culture, shopping, and fashion has hidden from view the way goods, particularly clothing, figured in the lives of men in the second half of the eighteenth century. The disassociation of men from fashion and the body was not natural but coerced and historically constructed. Eighteenth-century magazines and newspapers in America, as in England, criticized men as well as women for their interest in fashion and overattention to dress, a fact that has been lost to subsequent readers.[12] The endurance of the "great renunciation" thesis in fashion history has not helped matters.[13] According to this view, men on both sides of the Atlantic began to eschew sumptuous clothing in the eighteenth century in favor of "inconspicuous consumption," adopting a proto-business suit, a simpler, more sober, and more uniform style of dress. New scholarship has challenged this argument, demonstrating that although men's dress became more restrained over the course of the period, its subtleties and signifiers multiplied, opening a vast and complex arena for the expression and contestation of male political, class, and gender identities.[14]

Male consumers differed from female consumers both in the way they acquired goods and in the kinds of goods they acquired, but the boundaries of these practices were structured ideologically and practically in relationship to women and other household dependents. Under pressure to "avoid ostentation," some elite men came to rely on women and slaves to provide the color, pomp, and pageantry they denied themselves. Others, whose account books and letters reveal that they embraced fashion in practice, nonetheless disdained it in print and conversation. Federalists scoffed at conspicuous disavowals of dress and emblems of prestige, viewing such gestures as political posturing for the "mob" and insisting that these were necessary symbols to consolidate and express power.[15] Embedded in arguments over wigs, dress swords, and whether to walk or ride in a coach lay questions about manliness as well as nationalism. And like the politics of the period, there was little consensus about which position signified the pure, manly patriot. Bodily and material performances took place then, within contending frameworks of masculinity, proffering several variations of republican manhood, not just one. It is precisely the richness of these variations that allows us to historicize and contextualize discrete moments in time when elite men worked out how to "make a figure," as they called it, in late-eighteenth-century America.[16]

Writing in his diary in October 1759, John Adams anguished over his conduct. He often turned to his diary to express himself freely about women, reprove his awkward social behavior, and vent his spleen. That the young lawyer and future president was as likely to vent in person as in writing is testified to by his alternatively cantankerous and angst-ridden recollections: "I talk to Mr. Wibirt about the Decline of Learning, tell him, I know no young fellow who promises to make a figure . . . ask 'when will a Genius rise, that will shave his Beard, or let it grow rather than sink himself in a Cell, in order to make a figure.' I talk to Parson Smith about despising Gay dress, grand Buildings, great Estates, fame &c." Adams desperately desired the "fame" and trappings of worldly success, but he castigated himself for such feelings in his diary: "All this is Affectation and Ostentation. Affectation of Learning, Virtue and Wisdom, which I have not." In composing his

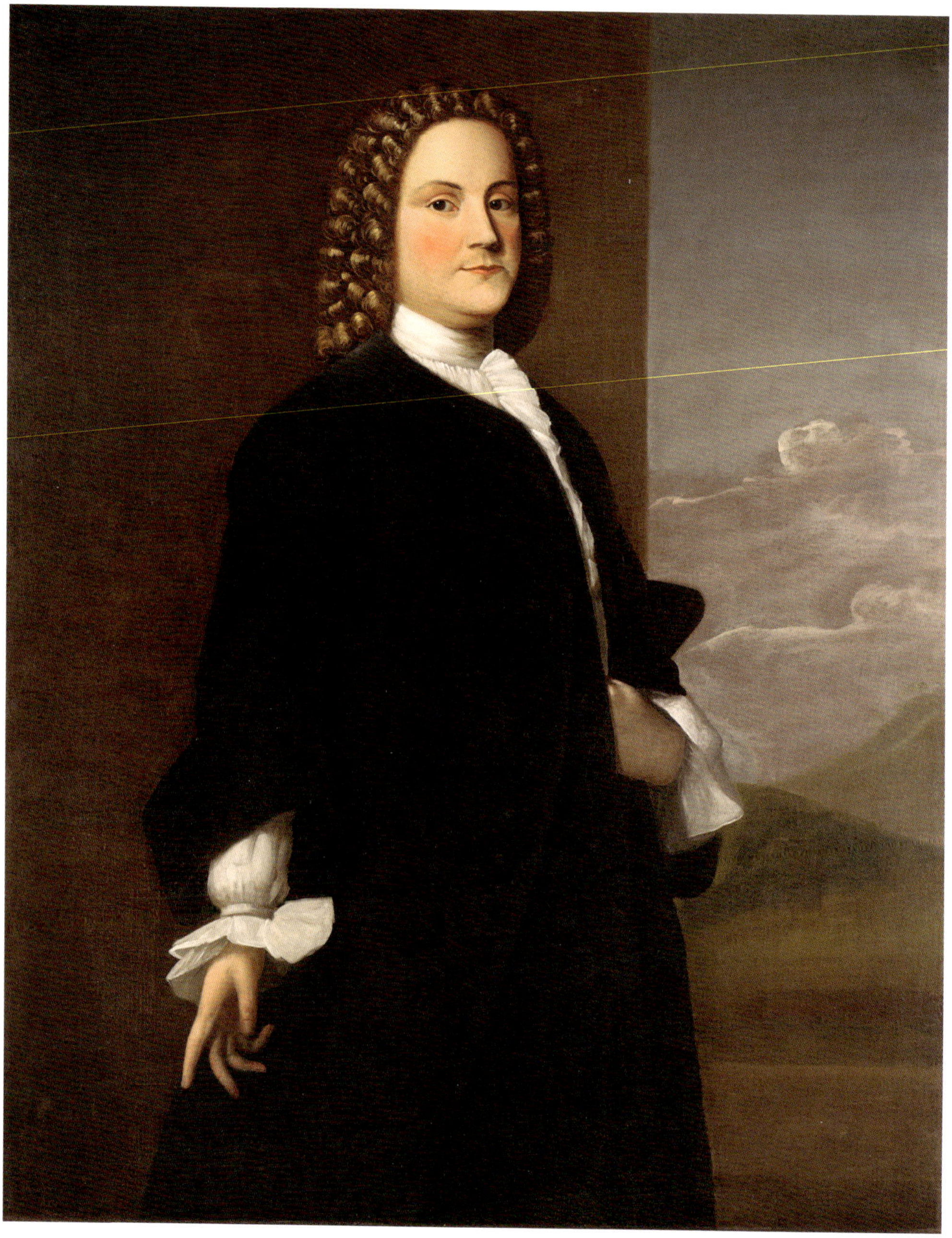

54. Robert Feke, *Benjamin Franklin*, oil on canvas (c. 1746), 50 x 40¼ in. (127 x 102 cm). Courtesy of the Harvard University Portrait Collection, Bequest of Dr. John Collins Warren, 1856 (H47). © 2004 President and Fellows of Harvard College. Photo: Katya Kallsen. By 1746, Franklin was a successful printer and a wealthy man but had not yet earned an international reputation. In this early portrait, he strikes a stiffly genteel pose, donning a tightly curled wig and a shirt with ruffles at throat and wrist to shore up and promote his wealth and politeness.

diary, he tried to compose himself, writing that he wished he could be content "with what will satisfy the real Wants of Nature." He saw other men his age settling down to law practice, eschewing amusement for study, and tried valiantly to do the same. Adams used the daily diary as a tool to inculcate self-discipline, to teach himself industry and economy—the essential components of masculine identity. He wrote: "Let no girl, no Gun, no Cards, no flutes, no Violins, no Dress, no tobacco, no Laziness decoy you from your Books."[17]

Similarly, in his *Autobiography*, Benjamin Franklin (fig. 54) recalled that during his early career, "credit and character" were best secured by projecting an appearance of "industry and frugality." To that end, he claimed that he "drest plainly" and blamed his wife, Deborah, for the introduction of luxury into his family.[18] Franklin's performance of frugality suggests the ideological importance of industry and economy to contemporary masculinity, as well as the role that women played as purported foils to these values. But when his Market Street home in Philadelphia was robbed in February 1739 by a tall Irishman named William Lloyd, Franklin offered a 30s. reward for the return of valuable household goods. The stolen items included "an half worn Sagathy Coat lin'd with Silk, four fine homespun Sheets, a fine Holland shirt ruffled at the Hands and Bosom, a pair of black broadcloth Breeches new seated and lined with leather, two pair of good worsted Stockings . . . [and] a coarse Cambrick Handkerchief, mark'd with a F in red silk." No evidence exists that he ever recovered these items or that, in the intervening years, Franklin lived as plainly as he advocated. The next time his house was robbed, thieves targeted his wife's wardrobe. The items "feloniously taken away" included "a double necklace of gold beads, a woman's long scarlet cloak, almost new, with a double cape, a woman's gown of printed cotton, of the sort called brocade print, very remarkable, the ground dark, with large red roses, and other large red and yellow flowers, and smaller blue and white flowers, with many green leaves, a pair of woman's stays, covered with white tabby before, and dove-colour'd tabby behind."[19] Franklin had purchased these "remarkable" items for Deborah in Philadelphia and London. Homespun sheets and patched breeches embodied the frugality and plainness that Franklin idealized; however, the bright "F in red silk" on his otherwise "coarse Cambrick Handkerchief" and the floral cloth he had selected for Deborah embodied a sense of material refinement that marauding neighbors recognized clearly enough to have sacked his house twice in more than a decade. Adams's and Franklin's battles with the simultaneously alluring and repulsive facets of sociability and consumer culture were to be lifelong, but they point to the ways in which elites, long before the Seven Years War, the Stamp Act, or the American Revolution, politicized consumption and constructed a sober masculinity at odds with the culture of genteel society.

In his first known letter, written in 1762 from Virginia, the teenage Thomas Jefferson (fig. 55) described himself as alienated and persecuted by his peers: "I am now in a house surrounded by my enemies, who take counsel together against my soul." These enemies also included rats that had eaten his "pocketbook and silk garters" and rain that had destroyed his watch. Learning was Jefferson's only consolation, and a small one at that. He wrote, "The old fellows say we must read to gain knowledge; and gain knowledge to make us happy and admired," but he had his doubts that his studies would ensure social success. "The man who powders most, parfumes most, embroiders most, and talks most nonsense," he complained, "is most admired." In another letter, Jefferson warned that "if this letter was to fall into the hands of some of our gay acquaintance, your correspondent and his solemn notions would probably be the objects of a great deal of mirth and raillery."[20] Social insecurity and the fear of failure kept Jefferson marginalized from polite society; he internalized that marginalization into derision.

By European standards, lesser gentry like Jefferson and professionals like Adams and Franklin were hardly "elite," but in their own societies they traveled in the kinds of polite and polished circles of men and women who built fine houses, imported tableware from China and Europe, and wore expensive, imported clothing. Yet figures such as Adams, Franklin, and Jefferson began to imagine themselves as men apart. Education and ambition played no small role in this intellectual construct, for they conceived of themselves as bookish men for whom the study of law, the history of ancient republics, and the idealized practice of politics stood in stark contrast to the superficial social graces practiced by many of their peers. In mid-eighteenth-century America, they struggled to conceive of a framework, either masculine or intellectual, in which they could comfortably reconcile elite material practices with vigorous, studious manhood. They handled this cognitive dissonance by socially participating in their culture while intellectually and politically disavowing the morality of its material expressions.[21] Such equipoise allowed these men to be in the elite but not of it; this masculine moral high ground, staked out at the beginning of their careers, would lend them important political legitimacy later on.

But men's responses were not forged entirely in the mind. While there can be little doubt that transatlantic currents of Whig philosophy and opposition-party politics broadly influenced masculinist critiques of material practices as aristocratic and corrupt, they were also profoundly personal.[22] Both Jefferson and Adams frequently felt socially inadequate when compared to their male peers, and they were uncomfortable speaking and interacting with women and men more polished than they. It is in these specific contexts where they were most likely to abjure card playing and fine clothing and furniture. Adams complained, as much about himself as

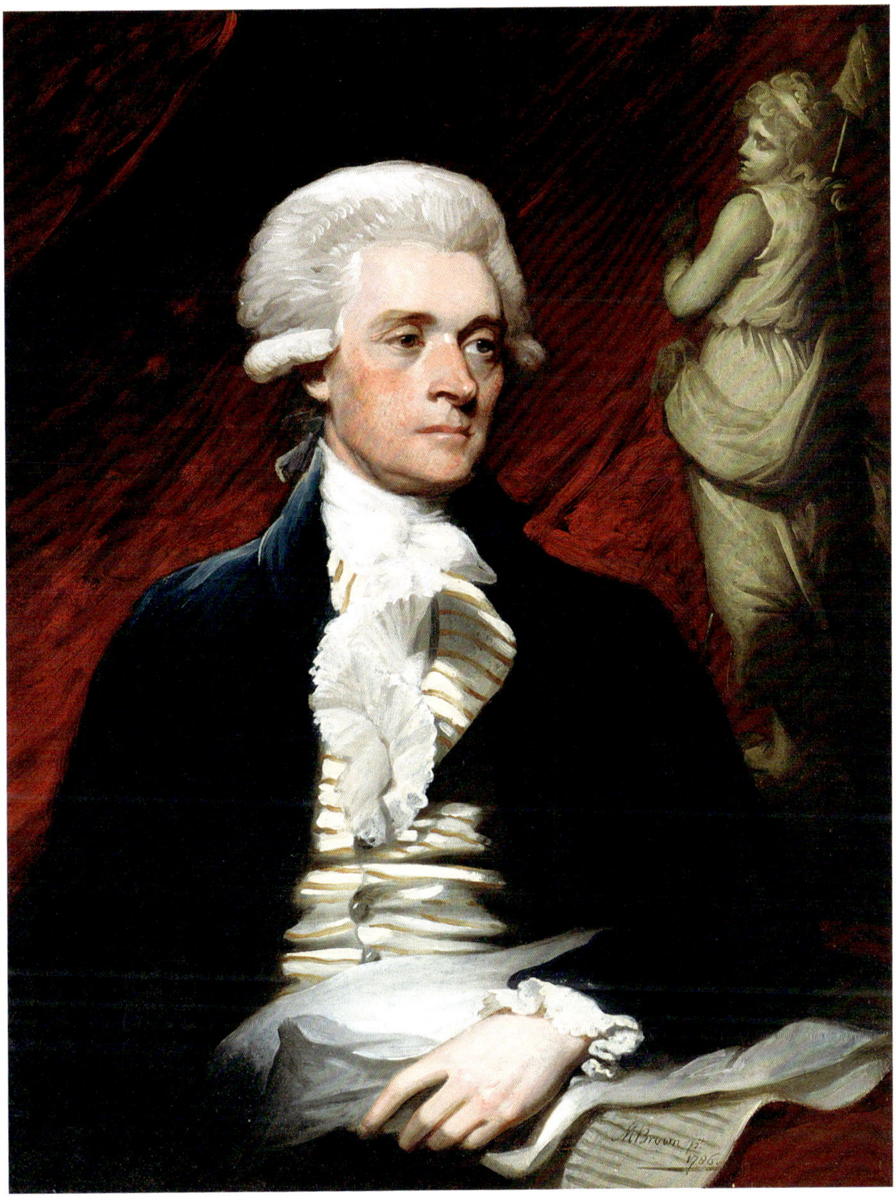

55. Mather Brown, *Portrait of Thomas Jefferson,* oil on canvas (1786), $35\frac{7}{8}$ x $28\frac{1}{8}$ in. (91 x 71.4 cm). National Portrait Gallery, Smithsonian Institution, Bequest of Charles Francis Adams. In Europe, Jefferson struggled to adopt the courtly dress and mien necessary to charm loans from King Louis XVI. Here, he mixes a less formal frock coat with a fashionable striped silk waistcoat and elaborately ruffled shirt and cravat. Brown's portrait betrays Jefferson's ruddy complexion as well as his physical awkwardness.

the age he lived in: "It is a silly Affectation for modern statesmen to Act or descant upon Ancient Principles of Morals and Civility. The Beauty of Virtue, The Love of ones Country, a sense of Liberty, a Feeling for our Fellow Men, are Ideas that the Brains of Men now a Days can not contemplate." Instead, gentlemen were judged by "the Love of Cards and Horse Races, a Taste in Dress, Musick, and Dancing," activities in which Adams did not excel. He preferred "ancient principles of morality and civility," romanticized as a realm in which he might shine. Rejecting "Dress, Musick, and Dancing" was a way to protect oneself against failure and the social criticism of "all who have Power to abuse us."[23]

In 1766, Adams described a social encounter in his diary that reflected the way personal insecurities fueled ambivalence regarding materialism: "Dined at Mr. William Coopers with Messrs. Cushing, Story, and John Boylstone. Cushing, silent and sly as usual. Story I dont know what. Cooper and Boylstone principal Talkers. Boylstone, affecting a Phylosophical Indifference about Dress, Furniture, Entertainments &c., laughed at the affectation of nicely distinguishing Tastes." Elite men pointedly critiqued one another; Adams, who had slowly begun to acquire property, furniture, and clothing and to learn haltingly to "talk fashion" while courting a wife, was put off guard by Boylston's derision of "the great Expences for Furniture, as Nick Boylstones Carpetts, Tables, Chairs, Glasses, Beds &c. which Cooper said were the richest in N. America." Boylston argued that objects of "the highest Taste and newest Fashion" were ephemeral and wasteful, and that they "would soon flatten and grow old." Better men, he suggested, preferred more substantive, intellectual subjects, such as natural history and geography, which centered on manly scientific observation. Adams hotly countered that such topics were as much a part of "fashion" as anything else: "Is not this Nicety of Feeling . . . of the same Nature with the Delicacy of Tastes, and the Curiosity about Furniture just before exploded?"[24]

That Adams was correct hardly mattered. He felt that Boylston had been the better speaker and got the better of him, illustrating how dangerous "talking fashion" might be. Since fashions changed rapidly, men who learned to exercise taste and converse with their peers about consumer goods might be ridiculed rather than applauded. Taste required risk and uncertainty; this made American men who were already critical of manners and material goods as a measure of social leadership even more so. Elite men like Jefferson and Adams never eschewed genteel dress altogether; to have done so would mark them as "singular," in the period's parlance, a level of individual idiosyncrasy that posed an even greater affront than foppery. But their relationship to dress would remain strained for the rest of their lives.

The chaotic political events of the 1760s and 1770s, with repeated nonimportation and nonconsumption movements, further complicated Americans' relationship to material goods. Since the 1763 British Acts of Trade and Navigation had decreed that colonists could buy only goods from Britain or its colonies and were prohibited from producing products that competed with British industries, almost all elite men's outer garments came from overseas. The Virginia nonimportation resolutions carefully specified "woolen and worsted stuffs of all sorts of more than 2s. sterling per yard, broadcloths of more than 8s. sterling per yard, hats, boots and watches," so that men as well as women, and both the more affluent and the lower sort, would suffer the clothing shortage in common cause.[25] But elite men were expected to lead by example.[26] Adams wrote to his wife, Abigail, that "General Washington setts a fine Example" by abstaining from wine and other imported articles. For Adams, "Simplicity of Dress, and Diet" went hand in hand with republicanism.[27] Sartorial restraint, he claimed, was easy, for dress, furniture, and houses were "Bagatelles, introduced, by Time and Luxury in Exchange for the great Qualities and hardy manly Virtues of the human Heart."[28]

But the realities of genteel status were not so simply shed. Not one year after the Virginia nonimportation resolutions, Jefferson sent a commission to London merchants for silk stockings, to be filled as soon as the political crisis had been resolved.[29] While Adams was a diplomat in France, he seethed about his negative image in the press, complaining, "They make fine Work of me—awkward Figure—uncouth dress—no Address—No Character." Given Adams's repeated disdain of outward show, we might think that he embraced these descriptors as a proud republican; he did not, angrily denouncing his detractors as "all false." In France, he had few qualms about purchasing clothing for himself and filling commissions for his immediate family in the midst of war; he fulfilled Abigail's requests for silk mittens, muslin, and figured lawn, which she defended by arguing, "A little of what you call frippery is very necessary towards looking like the rest of the world."[30] Appearances had to be maintained, despite the Revolution and Adams's stated disavowal of "dress." He portrayed himself as a reluctant consumer, but Abigail depended on his proxy purchases to participate in fashion culture and maintain her family's position in polite society.

Of all the founders, Franklin best understood and manipulated the power of dress. When he traveled to Europe to plead the colonial cause, he wore clothing appropriate to the occasion. In France, he donned "a Bag Wig"; in England in 1774, he chose "a full dress suit of spotted Manchester velvet." Manchester velvet was made from cotton, conveying the look of velvet "without the ostentation and expense of true silk velvet." But cotton velvet does not reflect light and give off the same sheen as silk velvet. Although he balanced an aesthetic of understatement with suitable taste and attire, Franklin claimed that he *felt* ridiculous. "Only think what a figure I make!" he wrote a correspondent.[31] When he was not acting in an official capacity, he felt safe making different kinds of clothing choices and in fact became

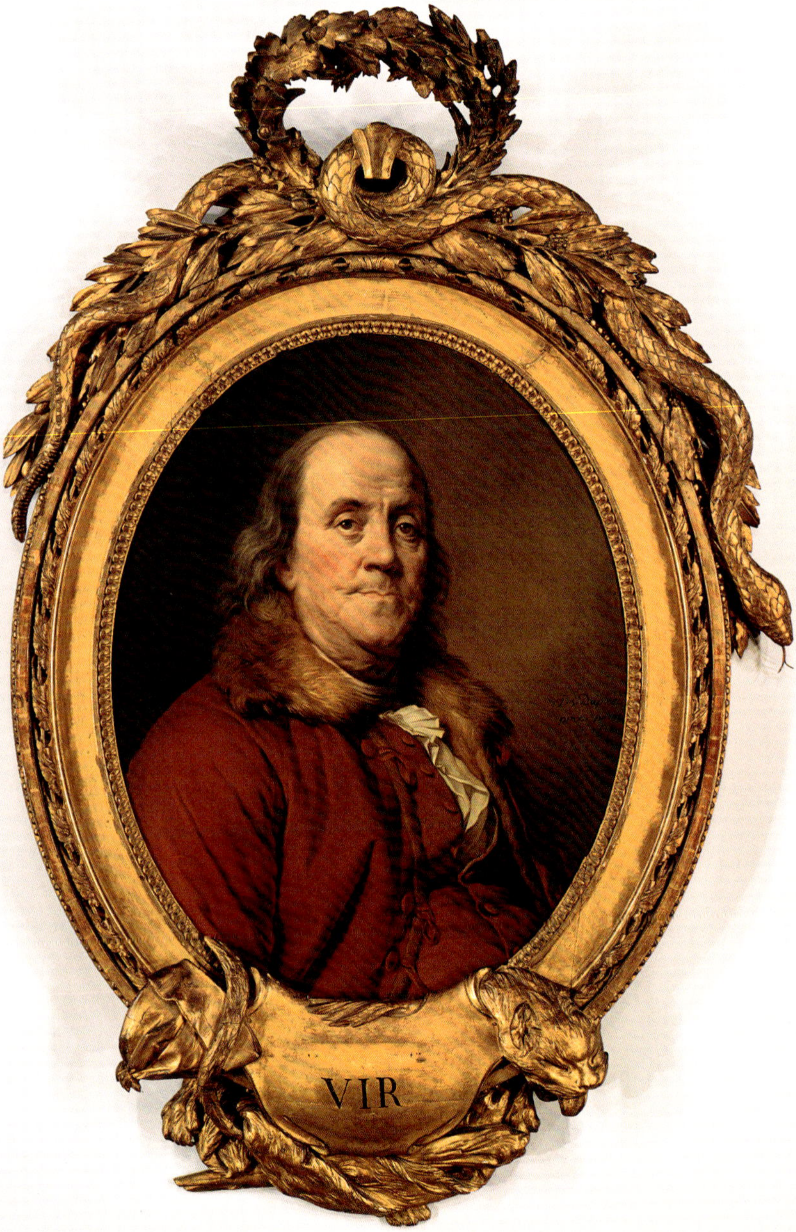

56. Joseph Siffred Duplessis, *Benjamin Franklin*, oil on canvas (1778), oval, 28½ x 23 in. (72.4 x 58.4 cm). The Metropolitan Museum of Art, Friedsam Collection, Bequest of Michael Friedsam, 1931 (32.100.132). Photo: © 1981 The Metropolitan Museum of Art. The rustic American as elder statesman: in the 1770s, Franklin began to wear his hair unpowdered and untied, along with fur-trimmed, loose-fitting frock coats. Age and illness played a part in this sartorial construction, but Franklin vaunted his rusticity as a badge of American authenticity and superiority.

famous for his casual style (fig. 56). Franklin relished contrasting himself, "plainly dress'd, wearing my thin gray strait hair," with "the Powder'd Heads of Paris!"[32]

This sartorial pose partook of the republican political strategy of assuming the role of rustic supplicant in order to garner French financial aid. But Franklin's status as a preeminent scientist, *philosophe*, and diplomat lent his pose social power; it became not just one American man's look but a quintessential American look. Before and during the Revolution, men remained ambivalent, adopting varying modes of genteel dress—some more formal, high style, and "conspicuous" than others. Franklin's model cast American masculinity as rusticity, positioned in contrast to foppish French powder and British tailored formality. The imperial crisis with Britain had led American colonists to see consumer activity as politically powerful, and this realization became a critical link in the long chain of events that led to revolution. In turn, the renunciation of goods, the struggles of war, and the process of nation building ushered in new imperatives for male behavior.[33]

Postwar political and economic struggles brought these streams of change into direct confrontation. Specie flooded out of the new states as consumers turned to their former British suppliers for cloth again. This resumption of colonial dependency was unseemly, and the public called for "patriotic" leaders who would wear "homespun" American cloth (ironically, often the production of slaves), eschew ceremony that would require lavish expense, and renew sumptuary legislation to halt the influx of British goods.[34] Religious leaders, public officials, and newspaper writers fully expected elites to lead these reforms. In an election-day sermon, the Reverend Joseph Lyman of Connecticut argued, "We might have expected effectual laws to discourage excesses, by which the citizens are so certainly degraded to a state of servility and dependence." But more important were the "examples of men in power, and families of fashion and affluence," who chose the "productions of our own country, to commodities received from abroad."[35] These writers and public officials assumed a top-down approach to fashion reform. Although style did not always move that way, late-eighteenth-century Americans shared a broad assumption that ordinary people "would naturally emulate their leaders in lifestyle, manners, and dress."[36]

Elites were to lead fashion reform by voluntarily eschewing imported clothing they could well afford, while state and federal governments enacted tariffs that would tax the goods out of reach for everyone else. Clothing materialized political and social conflicts many had thought resolved at the end of the war. Many raised their voices to oppose high tariffs on imports as an illegal assault on property and a halt to the material progress of American civilization.[37] Opponents of state interference in the marketplace did not agree that republicanism needed to be rustic and unrefined. They supported manufacturing initiatives, so that fine-grade cloth could be domestically produced, and assumed that political power and social power, including expressions of status through material goods, went hand in hand.

Material culture shaped the contours of political debate as well as the men who debated politics. Congressional delegates fought about everything from which taverns and townhouses to sleep in, to whether to walk or ride to work, how many and what kind of horses were appropriate for a representative's carriage, the titles of government officials, their dress, and, lastly, the crucial question of governmental salaries—which might make all other questions moot. Benjamin Huntington of Connecticut, serving in the Continental Congress in the 1780s, witnessed these battles firsthand and recorded them in letters home to his wife, Anne. Before a national capital was selected, delegates first gathered in Princeton, New Jersey, a provincial outpost that many representatives opposed. Huntington often found himself alone in Princeton, because other delegates felt "under Necessity to go to Philadelphia once or Twice a fortnight to Breath in Polite Air. The Country so badly agrees with those sublime & delicate Constitutions that it is to be feared that many of them will Contract a Rusticity that Can never be wholly purged off." He wrote, "Men of taste" kept their wives in Philadelphia while they took "genteel" lodgings in New Jersey, visiting the city whenever Congress recessed. By this arrangement, congressional representatives were compelled to maintain two households, with a level of dress and equipage that strained a government salary. Huntington complained, "I am Spending Money very fast . . . & it is a Mortifying Consideration that my Cash is Spent for no better Purposes, but the Great & General Concerns of a Nation must be attended to and the Fashions & Customs of the World are such as Require it to be done with Expence." He grumbled about the financial pressures of "fashion" but filled his letters to Anne with pages of details on Philadelphia fashions, noting in 1783 that women there were sporting "Men's Beaver Hats with a Large Tye of Gauze like a Sash or Mourning Wead about the Crown . . . which makes a very Daring Appearance." We do not have surviving objects of what Huntington purchased or wore, but his wife wrote him in the summer of 1788, begging him to "come home in September and wear your own Cloaths," suggesting that his congressional clothing might be out of place in provincial Connecticut.[38]

Huntington's experience highlights the way in which, in the contentiousness of republican political culture, dress shaped as well as signified partisan loyalty as political institutions and power structures became solidified. Men in government took copious notes during the ratification debates of the Constitution, interspersing sartorial observations with questions concerning suffrage, taxes, and the power of the executive branch. Senator William Maclay of Pennsylvania worried that his plain clothes, awkward social demeanor, and objections to ceremony and etiquette in the federal government made him many political enemies. His diary is a testament to the intertwining of the personal and the political as well as the depth of male insecurities. When two representatives called on him late one evening in 1790, he met them "in deshabille" and later worried that he looked awkward and "below par," a sign of weakness Maclay feared would have deleterious consequences for him on the Senate floor.[39]

Maclay gave as good as he got. When Thomas Jefferson returned from France and joined the cabinet in New York, Maclay described how his appearance directly undercut his political authority, writing: "Jefferson is a slender man has rather the Air of Stiffness in his Manner. His cloaths seem too small for him. His Whole figure has a loose shackling Air . . . & nothing of that firm collected deportment which I expected would dignify the presence of a Secretary or Minister."[40] Many critics felt that Jefferson's newfound devotion to "republican simplicity" went too far. Writing the history of the early republic, Henry Adams echoed Maclay's sentiments, pointing out that "Jefferson . . . seemed to regard his peculiar style of dress as a matter of political importance, while the Federalist newspapers never ceased ridiculing the corduroy small-clothes, red-plush waistcoat, and sharp-toed boots with which he expressed his contempt for fashion."[41]

A host of material details were scrutinized for their significance. Since, as Beverly Lemire has pointed out, the cost of a garment resulted mostly from the fineness of the cloth, it was "fabric that placed one in the forefront of fashion, or among the passé."[42] The use or rejection of lace, the weave and texture of cloth in a suit—such physical signifiers shaped men's political sympathies as well as betrayed them. Although George Washington, Thomas Jefferson, and other representatives from the South outfitted their slaves with elaborate livery, including fine scarlet cloth, silver trimming, and livery lace, Washington's personal secretary David Humphreys was admonished to "lay aside" the French embroidery on *his* jacket as unmanly. John Adams, too, was reprimanded in the late 1780s for the European cut and fineness of his clothing and for frequently appearing in an elaborate carriage. Other representatives and the public complained about the monarchist tendencies that such personal habits betrayed.[43] Adams was incensed over such criticism, since he had felt coerced into buying European clothes in the first place while a foreign minister. Now, "republican fashion," which seemed to him a contradiction in terms, sought to coerce him in the opposite direction. Republican simplicity was a gendered imperative, an ideological posture, as well as a fashion, devised like other fashions, with its own sartorial and political signifiers. It stigmatized and feminized such goods as lace by consigning them to women and African-American household slaves.

The language of politics and the language of dress informed each other and became intertwined. Thomas Dwight, a Massachusetts state senator, wrote letters from Boston to his wife in Springfield, eighty miles to the west, replete with information on what styles, colors, and fabrics were worn by men and women in the city. Yet he worried that he appeared a "petit maitre" for noticing and describing clothing in such detail.[44] Dwight often complained about the pace of change and the bewildering nature of the styles he observed, writing in 1796 of the new Empire style of gown: "It is a lamentable consideration that the Sex have lost so important a part of their bodies [i.e., their waists], but it cannot be helped for Fashion like Robespierre and Marat deals havoc and destruction without ever assigning a reason to any tribunal."[45] Political writers assailed fashion as a form of arbitrary power that connoted absolutism, corruption, and abrogation of individual freedom, concepts that should elicit opposition in would-be republicans.

Male elites did not seem to recognize that their attempts to modify the material landscape of power led them not to reject fashion altogether, as they imagined, but rather, to replace one fashion orthodoxy with another. Public officials and society leaders reformed fashion through their public performances, political debates in the House and Senate, and taxation policies regarding imported clothing. But fashion re-formed them too, remaking masculinity in the process. Utilizing the press, political writers told threatening stories that highlighted and stigmatized certain forms of male fashionability. For example, *The Philadelphiad*, an inexpensive broadside, narrated a story involving an altercation between "Jack Tensel," an ostensibly wealthy and modish young man, and "Tom Tug," a seaman "tar." Tom, seeing Jack strolling the wharf of an unnamed seaport town, accosts him and forces him to take his clothes off: "Strip! Was the word, and Jack must here comply / Poor fine dress'd gentleman! Observe him cry / while mirthful Tom and comrades laugh to see / Half-naked Jack appear in true degree: / His fine lace ruffles to his finger ends / From half bleach'd sheeting thin and raw depends; / Nor in his waistcoat backs of any kind; / His green silk breeches grafted blue behind, / with all his trappings of a piece with these, / Behind a fright, before designed to please."[46] This story, strongly reminiscent of pre-Revolutionary tar-and-feathering rituals, pits working seamen against would-be gentlemen in a contest over masculine sartorial politics. The seamen here invert the social hierarchy, whereby they become true republicans; industrious and physically robust, they expose the hypocrisy and unmanliness beneath the veneer of gentility.

Another narrative, "A Dialogue in the purgatory of Maccaronies," chronicles two waywardly genteel young men, "Will Toilet" and "Sir Bobby Button," and the ways in which British clothing had corrupted American manhood. In this story, political leadership and social pressure were brought to bear to delineate and shame effeminate consumers to alter fashion. "It was my glory, the whole business of my life," American Will says to British Bobby, "to imitate you, so far as a citizen of a dull simple republic can resemble the splendid grandee of a rich and highly polished monarchy." Will's preoccupation with fashion diminished his capacity for patriotism, he avers: "The number of scutcheon buttons on my coat, was of more importance to me than the confederation of the thirteen states. Republican liberty I detested, as levelling the most elegant beau with a leather-aproned mechanic."[47] Material details such as the point and heel on a pair of men's shoes, the severity of cut and tailoring on a waistcoat, and, especially, the tightness of a man's breeches were read as signs of effeminacy and subversion. Like the science of physiognomy so in vogue at the end of the eighteenth century, the material characteristics of goods were correlated to personality traits such as venality, greed, or Tory political affiliation. Spitalfields silk waistcoats softened men's *amor patriae*, rendering them fit tools for corruption.

The parable of British Bobby and American Will exposes a set of interlocking ideas about consumption and personal display. Will blames his presence in Macaroni purgatory on political economy and cultural reform, stating that "if the civilization of my country had advanced in the rapid progress of 1785, and 1786," a man's fashionable appearance might have paved the way for personal and professional success, "but a curse on the pedantic philosophers, declaimers, and would-be politicians who stopt it. . . . Our first rate macaronies fell into contempt, and were laughed at, even by the women." The press encouraged gendered shaming of foppish men and lauded public figures who reformed fashion by wearing homespun and sober colors. These actions provoked a dramatic response on the part of the protagonist: when Will discovered that "Washington and some others in the new Congress dressed in homespun, I thought it high time for me to leave a stupid savage country and accordingly made my exit by a dose of laudanum."[48] The metaphor of suicide here was intentional and significant, for it frequently served as the "resolution" in seduction novels of the period for women who had irrevocably lost their virtue. Will's story resonated with readers for whom national identity was as much material as political and required dramatic (or melodramatic) breaks with the past. If that meant social death to men who chose colorful and imported high-style clothing, as this story suggests, so be it.

In many aspects of late-eighteenth-century sartorial politics, George Washington emerged as a central—albeit contradictory—figure. We have seen, from his assiduous efforts to procure American-made clothing for his inauguration, how keenly Washington understood the importance of dress to masculinity and power. Jeremiah Wadsworth, the business partner in the Hartford Woolen Manufactory where Washington sent for his suit, aggressively advertised on behalf of the company, touting its production of "Congress Brown" and "Hartford Grey" broadcloth. The entrepreneur and Connecticut congressman's use of nationalistic nomenclature and heavy-handed promotion brought his productions to the attention of political men all over the country. Many singled Washington out as an example of a man who embodied patriotism, but others read his clothes, and by extension his personal character and politics, in a much different light.

Ironically, for all of Knox's and Washington's concern about the second-rate quality of American cloth, Washington's suit was universally mistaken for fine imported woolen cloth, arousing a storm of controversy. The brown suit that he actually wore—the one Knox had rejected—was admiringly described by the *Gazette of the United States*: "The President of the United States . . . appeared dressed in a complete suit of homespun cloaths; but the cloth was of so fine a Fabric, and so Handsomely finished, it was universally mistaken for a foreign manufactured superfine cloth."[49] The *Gazette*, a Federalist organ, had to effect artful damage control with this carefully worded feature, for Washington and his secretary had failed to notify the public that they had gone to such trouble to acquire cloth from a local source—a public-relations mistake that became apparent when editorials excoriated him for his foreign appearance at the single most important political event in the history of the young nation. The *Pennsylvania Gazette* editorialized: "As an indulgence in a single vice must prevent a man from being deemed really virtuous, so ought a perseverance in a line of conduct, detrimental to national happiness, to preclude him from the name of a patriot." The paper acknowledged Washington's past service but argued: "When we see a citizen, who has frequently exposed his life in the cause of freedom, dressed in manufactures of foreign nations, have we not reason to suppose, that either he does not understand the welfare of his country or that he totally disregards it?" Its readers resented listening to orations about patriotic behavior "when we behold the orator [Washington] contradicting his arguments by his practices? Almost every article which he wears is repugnant to his words."[50] Washington's choice of clothing rendered him an erstwhile patriot and questionable leader, suggesting he was not so different a George than the one that had ruled before him.

Washington exacerbated these tensions by wearing not only the dubious "Congress Brown" suit to the public portion of the inauguration, but also a pale cream silk suit with large ornamented buttons to the subsequent social events (fig. 57)—perceived as a two-faced gesture. This led the public (and other male political elites) to further excoriate negotiated material identities and call for the restrained republican simplicity that came to dominate the style of nineteenth-century masculinity as well as men's clothing.

Anglo-American elites charted a new relationship to clothing and masculine identity in the second half of the eighteenth century. Clothing challenged and refashioned masculine selfhood, producing "conflict, anxiety and tension in men," while at the same time these elites came to internalize a certain level of surveillance of themselves and other men as fundamental to power and manly control.[51] Male elites were

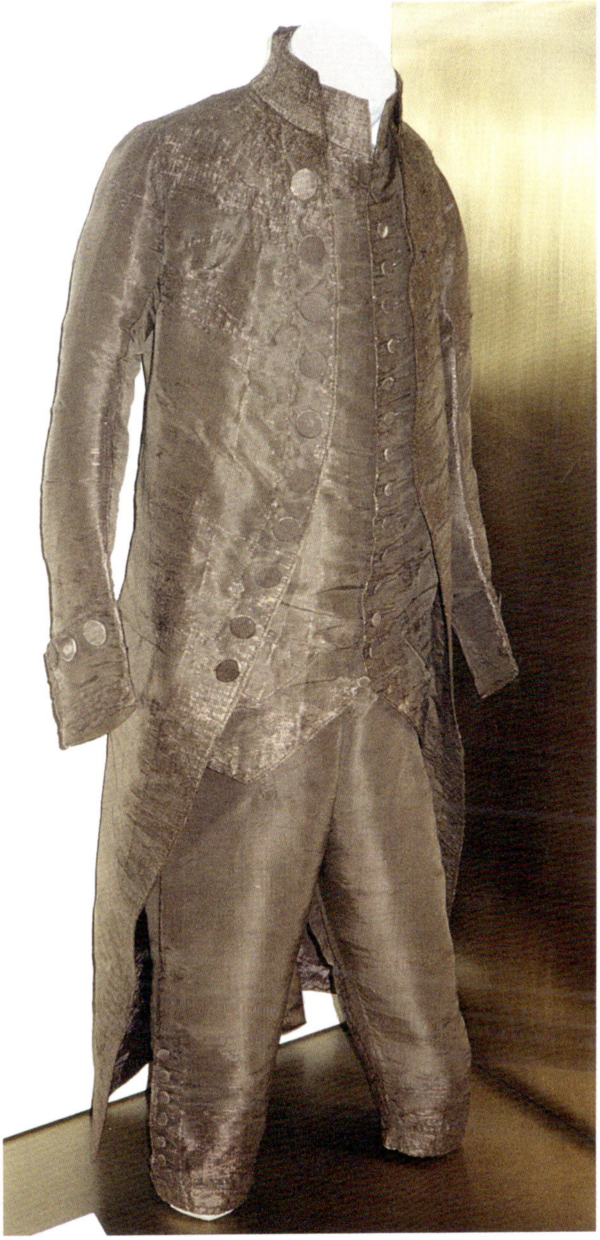

57. Silk coat, vest, and breeches, 1789; coat length, 47 in. (119.4 cm), vest length, 30 in. (76.2 cm), breeches length, 27 in. (68.6 cm). Courtesy of Morristown National Historical Park. After going to great lengths to procure an American-made suit for his inauguration, Washington selected this imported silk three-piece suit for the ball and other social events following his swearing-in. The suit is a rich cream color, possibly fashionable "buff," with tight-fitting sleeves and narrow cuffs embellished with flat metal buttons, popular in England during the 1780s.

influenced both by conflicted personal experiences with dress and by a postwar political and economic climate that stigmatized fashion for men as unpatriotic and effeminate. As more women were pulled into the fashion marketplace, men were pressured to alter and defend their participation amid new levels of scrutiny. They did not renounce dress as they had renounced their allegiance to king and Parliament, but instead they forged a masculine idiom of material selfhood that balanced the political imperatives of republicanism with their own physical and emotional values.

1. George Washington to Henry Knox, 29 Jan. 1789, in *The Papers of George Washington*, ed. Dorothy Twohig, Presidential Series (Charlottesville: Univ. Press of Virginia, 1987), 1:260–61. Washington directed enslaved African-American spinners and weavers at his Mount Vernon plantation and knew firsthand what an uneven appearance "stained" cloth—dyed by a pad after it was carded, spun, and woven—presented as opposed to wool dyed in the fleece—"in grain"—which imparted a more even color less likely to run or fade.
2. T. H. Breen, "'Baubles of Britain': The American and Consumer Revolutions of the Eighteenth Century," *Past and Present* 119 (May 1988): 73–104.
3. Ireland experienced a movement for economic and cultural nationalism very similar to America's in the second half of the eighteenth century, and "Buy Irish" campaigns attempted to decrease dependence on British manufacturing by developing partisan symbols such as shamrocks, in shades of green, blue, and orange, to signify nationalist loyalties; see Sarah Foster, "Buying Irish: Consumer Nationalism in Eighteenth-Century Dublin," *History Today* 47 (1997): 44–51.
4. Catherine Haulman, "The Empire's New Clothes: The Politics of Fashion in Eighteenth-Century British America," (PhD diss., Cornell Univ., 2002), 2; Breen, "'Baubles of Britain.'"
5. Henry Knox to George Washington, 12 Feb. 1789, in *Papers of George Washington*, 1:291.
6. Henry Knox to George Washington, 16 Feb. 1789, in *Papers of George Washington*, 1:316.
7. Henry Knox to George Washington, 19 Feb. 1789, in *Papers of George Washington*, 1:322.
8. Daniel Hinsdale to George Washington, 23 March 1789, in *Papers of George Washington*, 1:433; Henry Knox to George Washington, 27 March 1789, in *Papers of George Washington*, 1:450–51; George Washington to Daniel Hinsdale, 8 April 1789, in *Papers of George Washington*, 2:41; George Washington to Henry Knox, 10 April 1789, in *Papers of George Washington*, 2:45.
9. "Advantages of Good Breeding," *Columbian Magazine*, Sept. 1787, 637.
10. Elite men in Britain faced a similar balancing act throughout much of the eighteenth century, though the revolution in America politicized the situation there differently. See Philip Carter, *Men and the Emergence of Polite Society, Britain, 1660–1800* (London: Longman, 2001); G. J. Barker-Benfield, *The Culture of Sensibility: Sex and Society in Eighteenth-Century Britain* (Chicago: Univ. of Chicago Press, 1992); and Tim Hitchcock and Michele Cohen, eds., *English Masculinities, 1660–1800* (London: Longman, 1999).
11. T. H. Breen, *The Marketplace of Revolution: How Consumer Politics Shaped American Independence* (New York: Oxford Univ. Press, 2004); Richard L. Bushman, *The Refinement of America: Persons, Houses, Cities* (New York: Random House, 1993); Michael Zakim, *Ready-Made Democracy: A History of Men's Dress in the American Republic, 1760–1860* (Chicago: Univ. of Chicago Press, 2003). However, none of these works explore the issue of gender. Scholars of Europe have been more attentive to the way gender informed material culture; see especially Christopher Breward, *The Hidden Consumer: Masculinities, Fashion, and City Life, 1860–1914* (New York: St. Martin's Press, 1999); Victoria de Grazia and Ellen Furlough, eds., *The Sex of Things: Gender and Consumption in Historical Perspective* (Berkeley: Univ. of California Press, 1996); David Kuchta, *The Three-Piece Suit and Modern Masculinity: England, 1550–1850* (Berkeley: Univ. of California Press, 2002); Richard Wrigley, *The Politics of Appearances: Representations of Dress in Revolutionary France* (New York: Berg, 2002); Moira Donald

and Linda Harcombe, eds., *Gender and Material Culture in Historical Perspective* (New York: St. Martin's Press, 2000); Susan Fillin-Yeh, ed., *Dandies: Fashion and Finesse in Art and Culture* (New York: New York Univ. Press, 2001); and Peter McNeil, "That Doubtful Gender: Macaroni Dress and Male Sexualities," *Fashion Theory* 3, no. 4 (1999): 411–48. For scholarship on the history of gender and material culture in America, see Karen Halttunen, *Confidence Men and Painted Women: A Study of Middle-Class Culture in America, 1830–1870* (New Haven and London: Yale Univ. Press, 1982); Catherine E. Kelly, *In the New England Fashion: Refashioning Women's Lives in The Nineteenth Century* (Ithaca, NY: Cornell Univ. Press, 1999); Laurel Thatcher Ulrich, *The Age of Homespun: Objects and Stories in the Creation of an American Myth* (New York: Alfred A. Knopf, 2001); Haulman, "Empire's New Clothes"; and Mark Swiencicki, "Consuming Brotherhood: Men's Culture, Style, and Recreation as Consumer Culture, 1880–1930," *Journal of Social History* 31, no. 4 (1998): 773–808.

12. The profusion of criticism of male fashionability nicely supports Christopher Breward's argument that "the insistence on the un-manliness of the whole clothing business in general, actually positioned men right at the centre of a debate concerning fashion and modern life while apparently denying their participation in its wider cultural ramifications"; Breward, *Hidden Consumer*, 2. For an eighteenth-century perspective on men's involvement in fashion, see "Male Coquetry," *The American Museum*, Sept. 1789, and "The Progress of a Countryman," *Columbian Magazine*, March 1787.
13. J. C. Flugel, *The Psychology of Clothes* (London: Hogarth Press and the Institute of Psycho-analysis, 1966); Philippe Perrot, *Fashioning the Bourgeoisie: A History of Clothing in the Nineteenth Century* (Princeton: Princeton Univ. Press, 1994).
14. Among recent scholars who have challenged the renunciation argument, see Breward, *Hidden Consumer*; Wrigley, *Politics of Appearances*; and Kuchta, *Three-Piece Suit*.
15. See especially Samuel Eliot Morison, *Harison Gray Otis: The Urbane Federalist* (Boston: Houghton Mifflin, 1969).
16. For work on women's engagement with consumerism and their use of material culture for social, economic, and political power, see Catherine Allgor, *Parlor Politics: In Which the Ladies of Washington Help Build a City and a Government* (Charlottesville: Univ. of Virginia Press, 2000). See also Haulman, "Empire's New Clothes"; Breen, *Marketplace of Revolution*; Helen Bradley Foster, *New Raiments of Self: African American Clothing in the Antebellum South* (New York: Oxford Univ. Press, 1997); Laurel Thatcher Ulrich, "Wheels, Looms, and the Gender Division of Labor in Eighteenth-Century New England," *William and Mary Quarterly*, 3rd ser., 55, no. 1 (Jan. 1998): 3–38; Ulrich, *Age of Homespun*, especially chap. 5; Amanda Vickery, *The Gentleman's Daughter: Women's Lives in Georgian England* (New Haven and London: Yale Univ. Press, 1998), especially chaps. 4, 5, 6; Elizabeth Kowaleski-Wallace, *Consuming Subjects: Women, Shopping, and Business in the Eighteenth Century* (New York: Columbia Univ. Press, 1997).
17. John Adams, diary entry, Jan. 1759, in *Adams Family Papers: An Electronic Archive* (vol. 2, Oct. 1758–9 April 1759), Massachusetts Historical Society, http://www.masshist.org/digitaladams/.
18. Benjamin Franklin, *The Autobiography of Benjamin Franklin*, ed. Louis P. Masur (Boston: Bedford Boooks, 1993), 88.
19. *Pennsylvania Gazette*, 22 Feb. 1739, 1 and 15 Nov. 1750; see also Hannah Benner Roach, "Benjamin Franklin Slept Here," *Pennsylvania Magazine of History and Biography* 84, no. 1 (Jan. 1960): 127–58.
20. Julian P. Boyd, ed., *The Papers of Thomas Jefferson* (Princeton: Princeton Univ. Press, 1950–), 1:3–5, 11; see also David Waldstreicher, "Why Thomas Jefferson and African Americans Wore Their Politics on Their Sleeves: Dress and Mobilization between American Revolutions," in *Beyond the Founders: New Approaches to the Political History of the Early American Republic*, ed. Jeffrey L. Pasley, Andrew W. Robertson, and David Waldstreicher (Chapel Hill: Univ. of North Carolina Press, 2004), 79–106, especially 82.
21. On similar posturing in Britain, see Carter, *Men and the Emergence of Polite Society*, chap. 2, and Barker-Benfield, *Culture of Sensibility*, chap. 2.
22. On the influence of Whig philosophy and opposition politics in America, see Bernard Bailyn, *The Ideological Origins of the American Revolution* (Cambridge, MA: Harvard Univ. Press, 1967).
23. John Adams to Abigail Smith, 20 April 1763, in *Adams Family Papers: An Electronic Archive*.
24. John Adams, diary entry, 14 Jan. 1766, in *Adams Family Papers: An Electronic Archive* (vol. 12, 30 Dec. 1765–20 Jan. 1766).

25. Boyd, *Papers of Thomas Jefferson,* 1:44; see also Waldstreicher, "Why Thomas Jefferson," 82.
26. Jefferson was a state official when the Virginia nonimportation resolutions of 1770 were adopted. One article resolved "that we the subscribers, as well by our own example as all other legal ways and means in our power, will promote and encourage industry and frugality, and discourage all manner of luxury and extravagance." Boyd, *Papers of Thomas Jefferson,* 1:44.
27. John Adams to Abigail Adams, 1 Sept. 1777, in *Adams Family Papers: An Electronic Archive.*
28. John Adams to Abigail Adams, 12 April 1778, in *Adams Family Papers: An Electronic Archive.*
29. Waldstreicher, "Why Thomas Jefferson," 82.
30. John Adams to Abigail Adams, 13 Feb. 1779, and Abigail Adams to John Adams, 1 May 1780, in *Adams Family Papers: An Electronic Archive.*
31. Linda Baumgarten, *What Clothes Reveal: The Language of Clothing in Colonial and Federal America* (Williamsburg, VA: Colonial Williamsburg Foundation, 2002), 98. Differences between silk and cotton velvet were explored in conversation with textile curator Linda Eaton, Winterthur Museum, fall 2005.
32. Baumgarten, *What Clothes Reveal,* 98.
33. See Kuchta, *Three-Piece Suit,* 163.
34. *Pennsylvania Gazette,* 29 Aug. 1787 and 9 July 1788.
35. Joseph Lyman, *A sermon preached . . . May 30, 1787. Being the day of general election* (Boston: Adams and Nourse, 1787), 43.
36. Joanne Freeman, *Affairs of Honor: National Politics in the New Republic* (New Haven and London: Yale Univ. Press, 2001), 3.
37. *Pennsylvania Gazette,* 29 Aug. 1787; see also Stuart Bruchey, *The Roots of American Economic Growth, 1607–1861* (New York: Harper and Row, 1965), 66, 69.
38. Benjamin Huntington to Anne Huntington, 8 Sept. 1783, and Anne Huntington to Benjamin Huntington, 28 July 1788, in *The Huntington Letters,* ed. W. D. Mccrackan (New York: Appleton Press, 1905), 56, 66.
39. Kenneth R. Bowling and Helen E. Veit, eds., *The Diary of William Maclay and Other Notes on Senate Debates* (Baltimore: Johns Hopkins Univ. Press, 1988), 274; on Maclay's political insecurities, see Freeman, *Affairs of Honor,* 86.
40. Bowling and Veit, *Diary of William Maclay,* 275.
41. Henry Adams, *History of the United States of America during the Administration of Thomas Jefferson* (1889–91), cited in Waldstreicher, "Why Thomas Jefferson," 98.
42. Beverly Lemire, *Fashion's Favourite: The Cotton Trade and the Consumer in Britain, 1660–1800* (Oxford: Oxford Univ. Press, 1991), 7.
43. On Washington's and Jefferson's purchase of livery for their slaves, see Baumgarten, *What Clothes Reveal,* 128, and Freeman, *Affairs of Honor,* 47–48.
44. The term is French for a young, elegant beau with pretentious and affected manners; see the poet Gérard de Nerval, "Cet homme semblait avoir toute la politesse importune, tout le bavardage fatigant d'un petit-maître français de la vieille école," *News and Fantasies,* 1855, 39.
45. Thomas Dwight to Hannah Dwight, 31 Jan. 1796 and 31 Jan. 1799, Dwight-Howard Papers, Massachusetts Historical Society, Boston.
46. *The Philadelphiad or, New Pictures of the City* (Philadelphia, 1784), 10.
47. "A Dialogue in the purgatory of the Maccaronies," *Columbian Magazine,* July 1789.
48. "Dialogue in the purgatory."
49. Cited by Zakim, *Ready-Made Democracy,* 25.
50. *Pennsylvania Gazette,* 15 April 1789; eyewitnesses confirm that Washington was indeed wearing the dark brown suit from Connecticut. William Maclay wrote in his diary, "Washington was dressed in deep brown, with metal buttons, with an eagle on them, white stockings, a bag and sword"; Bowling and Veit, *Diary of William Maclay,* 11–13.
51. Herbert Sussman, *Victorian Masculinities: Manhood and Masculine Poetics in Victorian Literature and Art* (New York: Cambridge Univ. Press, 1995), 8.

The Laboring-Class Domestic Sphere in Eighteenth-Century British Social Thought

Jonathan White

THIS ESSAY TRACES the emergence and development of ideas about laboring-class domestic spheres in eighteenth-century England. Examining published pamphlet literature across the eighteenth century, I show how the laboring-class home and its familial relations came into public view and became an object of knowledge for propertied Englishmen. This was largely due to the rise of a new perspective on the political economy of the nation, a perspective that emerged in line with the needs and demands of a particular section of the middling sorts and the emergent British bourgeoisie, and that focused for the first time on the need to widen and deepen domestic consumption. This fixed attention on the previously hidden domestic lives of the laboring classes. Perceiving a need to encourage the consumption of new domestic manufactures in particular, the middling class and bourgeoisie accorded a new level of consumer agency to laboring people, which they then sought to regulate and shape through ideological hegemony and practical reforms. In their writings, the representatives of these groups devolved onto the laboring classes notions of industriousness, economy, and decency, as well as gendered notions of the division of household labor and divisions of desire that reflected their own values and economic needs.

During the first half of the eighteenth century, these groups were broadly confident that history was on their side, and they sought to remove all barriers to further commercial development in the face of entrenched landed property and oligarchic mercantile and financial capital. While not hegemonic in any strong sense, their social and political strength and their ideology were effective enough to force the dominant social groups to adapt their own ideologies. The essay ends by indicating that by the later eighteenth century, the developing contradictions in British society were such as to bring to an end what we might call the "heroic" phase of this strand of progressive capitalist ideology. With this, the conviction that the laboring-class domestic sphere and its social relations and practices were being, or could be, reformed by greater market participation subsided for the time being.

THE RISE OF A NEW POLITICAL ECONOMY AND DISCOVERY OF THE LABORING-CLASS HOME

In the early eighteenth century, the commanding heights of British economic life were controlled by the nexus of financiers, merchants, established industrial capitalists, and aristocratic landowners that formed the social basis of Whig oligarchic rule.[1] From their lofty and removed social vantage points, these groups barely registered the lives—particularly the domestic lives—of the mass of the people. Predominantly concerned with the value and price of British exports, and armed with their primitive labor theory of value, the representatives of these groups were chiefly interested in driving down the wage bill in vital export industries and securing the maximum possible labor time from their recalcitrant workforces.[2] In 1693, for example, the East India Company magnate Josiah Child wrote of the poor that "in a cheap year they will not work above two days in a Week; their humour being such, that they will not provide for a hard time, but just work so much and no more as may maintain them in that mean condition to which they have become accustomed."[3] This basic position remained fundamental to the large Whig-supporting mercantile and industrial interests throughout the first half of the eighteenth century. For such writers, the consumer habits and domestic lives of the poor were of interest only inasmuch as their actions detracted from the extraction of surplus value from their labor. To the extent that this position was based on experience, it reflected the perspective of the capitalist clothiers in the strategically vital and increasingly export-oriented wool industry. Their experiences and needs were themselves shaped by the particularly hierarchical industrial and social relationships characteristic of the wool industry in the West Country and East Anglia, reliant as it was on increasingly subordinated and wage-dependent semi-peasant workers imbued with their own specific work and consumer cultures.[4]

However, the burgeoning foreign commerce of the period helped to stimulate new domestic trades and manufactures. The late seventeenth and early eighteenth centuries saw the growth of trades in a range of semi-luxury consumer goods such as metalware, earthenware, printed linens and cottons, and, of course, books, pamphlets, prints, and newspapers. These newer industries and trades were often dependent on working people with high levels of skill and independence, working in conditions of artisan production very different from those that oppressed the weavers of the wool-manufacturing districts. In addition, crucially, these highly skilled and relatively affluent producers increasingly formed part of the growing domestic market for the very consumer goods they manufactured.[5] Consequently, the representatives of these new industries and trades took a very different view of the function and value of their workers from that of the large merchant capitalists, financiers, and landowners who dominated Britain's political-economic formation. These small- and medium-sized capitalists and their print-culture representatives were also often men with strong backgrounds in the popular politics of radical dissent. Drawing on older, radical Puritan ideas of liberty that had sought to devolve power through the social order, and applying them to the growing economic infrastructure of the domestic market economy, writers such as Nicholas Barbon, Thomas Tryon, Henry Martyn, and John Cary argued that the poor were, in fact, full of potential. The proliferation of new skilled manufactures showed that the poor could be industrious and highly dexterous producers. Equally, these writers pointed to the developing tastes for new consumer goods among sections of the laboring people, goods such as cotton, tea, furniture, and earthenware. The laboring people, they suggested, constituted an increasingly significant market. If laborers could be encouraged to consume more, the writers argued, this would reflect back onto their work, making them more diligent in pursuit of civilized pleasures. They would then receive higher wages, with which they could purchase even more goods. Commerce, the writers suggested, could do the work of godly reform, animating and civilizing workers while enriching and refining the social whole.[6]

By the 1720s, these ideas can be said to have become an established and coherent body of social thought. In his grand celebration of British trade, titled *A Plan of the English Commerce* and published in 1728, Daniel Defoe wrote that it was the meaner people, "the Manufacturers and Shopkeepers, even the poor," that supported the wealth of the nation. He added that "tis upon the Gain they make either by their Labour or their Industry in Trade, and upon their inconceivable numbers that the Home Consumption of our own produce, and of the produce of foreign Nations imported here, is so exceeding great and that our trade is raised up to such a prodigy of magnitude."[7] As attention turned ever more toward the domestic market, so it began to delve increasingly into the domestic lives and material conditions of the laboring people.

In his *Plan*, Defoe pointed to the consumer tastes and material lives of the laboring classes as an index of their economic importance, bringing the mundane details of their everyday existence into imaginative proximity with his readers. One had only to look, he claimed, to see that in England, because of its commerce and its manufactures, the people "eat well and they drink well; for their eating of Flesh Meat, such as Beef, Mutton, Bacon, etc., in Proportion to their Circumstances, 'tis to a Fault, nay even to a Profusion." As for their drink, he claimed, "tis generally stout strong Beer, not to take notice of the Quantity, which is sometimes a little too much, or good Table Beer for their ordinary Diet." Defoe then moved his roving eye into the laboring family's home: "for the rest, we see their Houses and Lodgings tolerably furnished, at least stuff'd with useful and necessary Household Goods; even those we call Poor people, Journeymen, working and Pains-taking people do thus; they lye warm, live in Plenty and (need) know no Want."[8]

As writers like Defoe began to focus on the domestic lives of the poor, pointing to their prosperity or urging the need to increase their consumption, so their ideological armory began to develop in two related directions. First, the laboring-class family became an object of scientific inquiry, and progressive writers began to apply the tools of political arithmetic to the poor. The original political arithmeticians had transformed ideas developed for the management and governance of landed families' estates into a set of concepts for determining the distribution of national wealth and power, reflecting the emergence of the idea of a systemic economy.[9] The new political economists further developed these ideas by translating them down through the social order and domesticating them. The idea of economy was reshaped to fit their vision of a civil society composed of a multitude of household economies.

A key development here was the idea that it was possible to produce budgets of laboring-class domestic economies to establish the realities and potentials of their household-based consumer practices. In 1734, the merchant economist Jacob Vanderlint produced almost certainly the first budget for what he called a laboring family of the middling sort, showing the effects of excises on necessary commodities and using it to establish the exact value of laboring people's potential as consumers, a potential that he claimed was being stifled by taxation.[10] Eighteen years later, the radical projector Joseph Massie developed the same idea into a comprehensive survey of the effects of wartime taxation on families of all ranks. Calculating the "Income and Expences" of all ranks, Massie produced a set of tables that differentiated between the various trades and strata of the laboring people, as well as embraced the middling and propertied classes.[11] And in 1757, Josiah Tucker, an enthusiastic advocate of the new political economy, further extended this concern to ascertain the actual facts of laboring-class lives. Tucker suggested that scientifically minded tourists might assist their country by comparing the level of economic developments across and within nations. One way of measuring this, he suggested, was to look closely at the houses of the people:

> Let the traveller . . . Inquire into the state of living in Cities and Towns: viz; Whether the Inhabitants in general occupy separate Dwelling-houses, or whether many Families are crowded into one. . . . If a Family is to be pent up in a Room or two, the Quantity of Household Goods cannot be great:

> and yet, were a National Inventory to be taken in every Country, the Greatest Riches of a State will always be found to consist in Household Goods.[12]

The laboring-class domestic interior was emerging as an object of scientific knowledge, as an accounting unit through which money and goods passed as they circulated through society, enriching household and society in the process.

The second crucial development was the emergence of the idea that the laboring people could be brought, progressively, to civilization through commerce. It was argued that contact with more refined consumer goods, through higher wages, could do the work of reform. The evidence that laboring people could be led toward the consumption of fine clothes, new furnishings, and a range of domestic goods, such as cutlery and earthenware, suggested that they, as much as the other ranks of society, could be civilized through the regulated expression of new levels of need. By the 1750s in particular, progressive writers, representing the new trades and industries, argued that the consumption of refined consumer goods would encourage laboring people to further levels of industriousness by enlarging their desires for comfort and decency. Thus, it was argued, higher wages would enable greater popular access to consumer goods, and merely coming into contact with such commodities might begin the work of reform. In 1752, a pamphleteer named Richard Parrott, who passionately advocated greater investment in the emerging high-skill industries and drew heavily on the philosopher David Hume's works, urged that the poor should receive decent wages, suggesting that

> a suitable Degree of Encouragement and Honour might give the Ambition of the Vulgar a better Turn, and excite them to excel each other in Clothes and Household Ornaments. The proper Effect of Wealth ought to be Refinement; higher Degrees of Humanity and Virtue with more agreeable Manners. Vices themselves are refined away by Politeness the Attendant of Opulence.[13]

Thus, making the poor more "polite" required them to enjoy more of the fruits of their industry in the form of consumer goods—and not just any consumer goods, but ones that engaged the consumer's feelings as well as increased the family's stock. If English workers could be enticed away from drink by decent wages and widely available consumer goods, it was argued, they might be made more like the French, who spent their money on clothing and adorning their houses. "He that lays out his Money on Dress and decent Furniture," Parrott argued, "has a permanent Reward, ever in his Sight to make him pleased with the past Labour, encourage his future Industry and excite the emulation of his Neighbour."[14] For these writers, moral and economic improvement advanced together. Redirecting consumer desires into "permanent rewards" not only enriched the family but further circulated wealth through the domestic economy. "Cloaths and Furniture make not only the enduring Riches of a Family," Parrott insisted, "but contribute much to the public Honour and Strength," providing "Employment to infinite Numbers, and those the most valuable and industrious Members of Society, the Clothier, Weaver, Threadman, Sempstress, Woolcomber, Joiner and the other numberless trades depending on Dress and Household Furniture."[15]

With the emphasis on dress and the furnishings of a household, Parrott was here delineating the components of properly managed consumer agency for the laboring classes. Dress and "decent" furnishings constituted physical embodiments of labor, permanent rewards that could animate greater effort and improvement. The idea of decency is here functioning in much the same manner as that of taste for the middling ranks and aristocracy. Although it was unimaginable for any eighteenth-century commentators to accredit the laboring classes with the capacity for taste, these progressive writers had to address the question of how laboring people were expected to discriminate in an expanding market.

For the aristocracy and the bourgeoisie, the contested and historically developing notion of taste did much of this work, acting both to constitute an emerging aesthetic realm, supposedly above the mundane world of economic need, and, at the same time, to mark out criteria by which hierarchies might be established within an economic world that was in fact suffused with goods embodying and appealing to the feelings and ideas from which the supposedly abstract realm of the aesthetic was being forged. The concept of decency appears to have functioned in a similar manner. It assisted in mediating increasingly inadequate distinctions between luxury and necessity, enabling consumption on the grounds of capacious notions of comfort and convenience that engaged at some level with the realm of feeling.[16] But decency also policed consumption by enclosing consumer autonomy and the exercise of what was, in practice, a form of taste, within notions of moral and political-economic "fitness." As Parrott had argued, decent dress and furnishings were, at least in part, those whose consumption stimulated domestic trade. In terms of particular commodities, the boundaries of decency were always contested, not least because laboring people's actual tastes developed through cultural superstructures that arose out of quite different social foundations from those of the middling writers and readerships of the mid-century. The perceived practical failure of laboring people to demonstrate sufficient decency in their consumer choices perplexed the reform-minded writers of the mid-century. They responded by devolving onto laboring people their own notions of the household economy and the gender division of labor in the household.

WOMEN, DOMESTIC ECONOMY, AND DECENCY IN THE LABORING-CLASS HOME

As the household became the site for the proper expression of consumer desires and affective relations, and as middling ideals of domestic economy and domestic relations were devolved onto laboring-class families, so poor workingwomen's lives assumed a higher level of ideological visibility and significance.

All political economists ignored women's waged work. In this, progressive writers were no different. However, their notions of the gender division of labor and the gendered division of desire did illuminate women's roles in reproducing the household in unpaid labor and domestic consumption. Just as women and femininity were becoming more integral to the understanding of the desires and feelings that animated commerce and civilization, so the devolution of consumer agency onto laboring women gave new import to housewifery and the reproduction of the household.[17] Women who were tasked with reproducing a household that was supposed to be on a developmental trajectory toward civilization through decent consumption were seen to perform a more important role than had their forebears. Correspondingly, they were held more responsible for failures.

These developments and tensions were manifestly apparent in a series of practical policy debates during the 1740s and 1750s. During a period of intense interest in social reform, particularly in the wake of the Peace of Aix-la-Chapelle in 1748, progressive reformers weighed in on debates over the reform of the tax system and the poor laws. They also attempted to use the law to steer the poor away from what they saw as dangerous habits, such as a taste for gin and tea, and toward goods that expressed industriousness and decency. The home became a site in which women's success or failure to demonstrate economy and decency could be depicted in ever more graphic and visual terms.[18]

During the 1744–45 debates on the taxation of the tea trade, some reformers attempted to argue that any reforms to the excise system must try to price the poor out of the market. The laboring-class taste for tea was attacked as a foolish fashion that wasted money and diverted women from the proper and decent reproduction of the laboring-class domestic economy. In 1744, John Newball complained that the tea-drinking wife neglected her family, failing to educate the children, or to teach them spinning, sewing, knitting, and housewifery, and choosing instead to visit her neighbors to drink tea.[19] In similar terms, one year later, the apothecary Simon Mason argued that tea-drinking women undermined the economic worth and credit of the family as a whole: "These poor Creatures, to be fashionable, and imitate their Superiors, are neglecting their Spinning, Knitting and spending what their Husbands are labouring hard for," while, at home, "their Children are in Rags, gnawing at a brown Crust, while these gossips are conversing over the affairs of the whole Town."[20]

Eight years later, the Reverend Thomas Alcock, a fairly radical would-be reformer of the poor laws, identified several "new Species of Expence" that had arisen since the reign of Queen Elizabeth and greatly contributed to the miseries of the poor. This included tobacco, snuff, tea, spirits, and "the wearing of Ribands, Ruffles, Silks, and other slight foreign Things." Items like snuff might be inexpensive, he noted, but "tho' these Things are bought by small Quantities, and the Money is laid out by Pence and Half-pence, and seemingly is not felt," yet, he argued, "if an Account was kept of the sum thus yearly expended, it would appear no small Matter; it would appear much too great for the Person that expends it." Women, were, of course, seen as the prime offenders in every case. Alcock instead urged that the poor should wear good "English Woollens or Worsteds."[21]

The importance of decency in the domestic sphere was most clearly asserted during progressive reformers' attacks on the taste for gin, occasioned by the debate around the proposed reform of the spirits trade in 1750–52. For these reformers, gin was seen to be peculiarly dangerous because it supposedly killed desire. Gin was characterized as addictive, engendering a desperate need that bypassed reason and replaced genuine feeling and affection with an ersatz and compulsive pleasure.[22] The novelist Eliza Haywood, at the forefront of calls for women to assume control of the home, published a volume urging them to renounce their taste for spirits. Women's desire for power, she argued, achieved legitimate expression in the sphere of the household. Gin's peculiar capacity to destroy human rational faculties made it enormously dangerous to the women who drank it, reducing their ability to exercise effective economy. This was especially crucial in the case of the poor, for "where little is got," she argued, "the more Economy is needful to make it go further." Thus, she warned, "if the Woman idles away her time, the man might as well Play too, her gossipings will get the better of his Activity and the Sisterhood of Tipplers will consume more than he ever could."[23] Haywood then pointed to the home as an index of the dire economic consequences of women's moral failing: "When you see the Kitchen in disorder, the Children half Naked and the House in a universal Litter, your Indignation will rise at the Thought of what Occasions it." She assured her readers, "You will, from that moment, look upon a Dram Glass, as a more dangerous Instrument than a Blunderbuss."[24]

Just as material improvement engendered moral development, so material impoverishment generated affective decay. As one writer expressed it, the true pleasures to be gained from domestic decency and familial relationships were replaced by "the Enjoyment of their delightful Companion, the Gin Bottle." This ersatz pleasure entailed the material and moral neglect of the family's children.

These could be easily recognized, the author claimed, as they would be "half naked, tho' in the coldest weather," and "half starved for want of proper Nourishment," while their "tender mothers," to "stop their little gaping mouths . . . will pour down a spoonful of their own delightful Cordial."[25]

Gin-drinking women were depicted as little better than animals, their civilization literally stripped away. The accoutrements of decency, sartorial and domestic, were pawned to pay for gin, leaving poor families in a state of increasingly desperate barbarism. "Household Economy, so requisite in a poor man's family, has not the least Appearance," wrote one author in 1751. "Cast your Eyes around the Room and take Notice of its Furniture," he entreated. "What can you see that is not offensive, or carries not the marks of Misery and Wretchedness?" He claimed, "It will be much, if there is any Thing worth Two-Pence in the whole Apartment, either in Cloaths, Linnen or Woollen."[26] Josiah Tucker made the same point, bidding his readers to take notice of "the Rags and Nakedness of these miserable Objects, their want of proper Change, washing, etc.—the shocking scenes of Nastiness and Poverty in the places they herd together in, often without so much as a Bed to lie on, never with what is decent or convenient."[27] For Isaac Maddox, the bishop of Worcester and a keen economic and moral reformer himself, the gin drinker's spiral of material and moral degradation had serious economic consequences:

> Look in upon the dwelling of a regular industrious workman of the like Occupation of the slaves of Gin; How many Trades have been employed to provide Cloaths and furnish a homely, but decent and cleanly Habitation for himself, his Wife and healthy Children, while the noisome and filthy abode of gin drinkers, if they have any settled abode at all, shall be void of every decent thing or even necessary.[28]

In these writings of the 1750s, it is notable that the focus on the home was at once empirical and highly sentimental. These descriptions were designed to bring the middle-class or aristocratic reader into imagined and horrified proximity to shocking scenes of distress and misery, in the name of generating a reforming zeal. Where, at a political-economic level, the household appeared almost solely in the form of an accounting unit, here, at the level of particular reforms, empirical observation of the home was overlaid with an emphasis on stirring the imagination with highly visual language.

By the 1750s, therefore, descriptions of the laboring-class home and family had become a conventional part of reforming literature and an object of empirical study and imaginative evocation in social thought. However, the 1750s also saw other social groups beginning to use these conventions, adapting them to their very different visions of society.

In 1755, the Manchester high Tory cleric John Clayton wrote and published a pamphlet with the somewhat misleading title *Friendly Advice to the Poor.* Writing in the mode of long-established conservative ideologies, Clayton scourged the poor, in fairly traditional terms, for their disorderly conduct. But he also made free use of the idea of the laboring-class domestic sphere. In Clayton's hands, domestic economy and decency became a standard of conduct that demarcated the respectable propertied classes from their poor neighbors. The poor, he argued, were characterized by "an abject Mind, which entails their miseries upon them," and a "mean and sordid Spirit, which prevents all Attempts at bettering their Condition."[29] Clayton complained, "Their whole aim is only to live, and their Want of Economy so palpable, that their Money is generally spent before it is received and the Week's Wages forestalled by the current expenses."[30]

Clayton deployed the imaginative tour of the laboring-class homes to stimulate moral outrage and disgust, making the presence of tea sets and the absence of the more appropriate decencies of civilized domestic life operate as signifiers of bad management by laboring-class women. "It is no uncommon thing," he assured his readers, "to see a Cottage, nasty even to a Degree of Infection, amply furnished with all the foolish Utensils pertaining to this Junketing and Riot," while "the most necessary Goods for the Comfort and Conveniences of Life are miserably wanting."[31] In Clayton's hands, the conventions used to describe gin drinkers' homes were generalized as the habitual traits of a degraded and barbaric class. Where progressives such as Tucker, Maddox, and Parrott had seen the domestic sphere as the locus for the expression of developing consumer desires regulated by expansive notions of comfort and convenience, Clayton refashioned it into a place where the poor might do no more than demonstrate a minimal level of self-sufficiency and remain off the poor rates. Economy was not so much a way of sharing in the growing prosperity of the whole as an updated form of deference expressed through economic calculation.

The idea that exploring the laboring-class domestic economy was a way of measuring and evoking working people's lack of self-mastery was also adapted and developed by representatives of the established large industrial interests in the West Country and East Anglia. In 1758, William Temple, a clothier and amateur political economist, wrote a short book titled *A Vindication of Commerce and the Arts.* Resolutely progressive in his view of commerce, Temple nonetheless shared his particular class fraction's contempt for the impoverished weavers and spinners of the western counties, who desperately clung to the remnants of their independence and customary culture, and he generalized his views of these workers across the entire class.[32] "Nothing but necessity produces industry," Temple argued, "and nothing but an economy which the mass of mankind will never practise can prevent poverty, want and distress." He added, "There is no making provision for numerous families, sickness, old age, frosts, floods, rains, wars, want of employment fires, dearths and other distressing accidents but by economy." Yet he argued that "not one in a thousand is possessed of this economy but live, as Mr Locke observes . . . hand to mouth."[33] Temple, like Clayton, used his supposed familiarity with the material and moral lives of the poor to stimulate revulsion against their degradation. "If a labourer can procure by his high wages or plenty, all the necessaries of life; and have a residuum," Temple argued, "he would expend the same either in gin, rum, brandy or strong beer; luxurize on great heaps of fat beef or bacon, and eat perhaps until he spewed; and having gorged and gotten dead drunk, lie down like a pig and snore till he was fresh."[34] There was no room for decency and the development of civilization here.

SOCIAL CRISIS AND THE LABORING-CLASS DOMESTIC SPHERE

From the 1760s onward, a growing social, economic, and political crisis helped to expose further the fragility of laboring-class domestic economies and decisively shifted the context in which they were observed and discussed. The growing waves of industrial and social unrest that swept British society between 1756 and the end of the century were symptomatic of the broader social transformations affecting working people's lives. Class divisions sharpened throughout British society. In the older industrial regions, the impoverishment of the proto-industrial workforce continued apace while, even in the new industries, with their skilled artisan workforces, increasingly complex divisions of labor made workers more dependent on merchant capital and unstable international markets. These tendencies intersected with the effects of the long-term development of capitalist food markets, dependent on and helping to accelerate the separation of British workers from the land, a process that in turn made them more vulnerable to wage and price fluctuations.[35]

This crisis increasingly divided the rising middling classes, eroding the social basis of the alternative political economy and weakening the progressive case for the unproblematic advance of universal prosperity. The growing crisis also fueled an ideological reaction among those interests that represented the large capitalist and propertied interests that dominated economic life. The representatives of these sections of the propertied classes further developed the themes and conventions that we saw emerging with Clayton and Temple, turning the use of the laboring-class domestic sphere to their more punitive ends.

In the face of the gathering social crisis, progressives became increasingly divided between those who maintained a political economic optimism concerning the market's ability to deliver a better standard of living than ever before (if not strict justice), and those who enjoined their contemporaries to police the market in order to defend the standard of living of the mass of the people. For moderate progressives, the political economy of the jurisprudential power of the market, theorized in its highest form by Adam Smith, offered the best hope for the mass of the people. Joseph Priestley, for example, pointed to the domestic comforts that commerce had only recently brought to the people. The poor might clamor for relief, but a quick glance around a domestic interior sufficed to demonstrate the legacy of progress: linen clothing, chimneys, glass windows, candles, paper, tea, and sugar—all had been brought by a free and extensive commerce.[36] Arthur Young, the enthusiastic projector of British agriculture, found himself similarly compelled to defend commercial modernity from the clamors of the laboring people. Between 1767 and 1771, in the wake of serious industrial and social unrest, Young produced his vast surveys of the "general economy" of the northern and southern counties of England. In these, he enormously extended the work that projectors such as Massie had undertaken, producing calculations of the prices of provisions, the costs of implements, and the wages of labor in every region of England. Young sought to demonstrate that the recent riots had no real basis in actual poverty. Such actions were instead the consequence of the permeation of luxurious wants and unstable desires through the social order, themselves an unfortunate symptom of the generally rising national prosperity.[37] This tendency toward the more rigorous and scientific collection of empirical data on the incomes and expenditures of the poor culminated in the far grander projects of the Reverend David Davies and, in particular, Frederick Eden, who compiled volumes of budgets from across the country during the 1780s and 1790s, marking the beginning of the large-scale social surveys of the nineteenth century.[38]

Other progressives remained more wedded to the idea that laboring people possessed rights in a commercial society. However, as they generally accepted the fundamental tenets of political economy and broadly accepted the sovereignty of Adam Smith's system over what was becoming more clearly defined as an economic field, their arguments gradually ceded this ground, moving instead toward moral injunctions to police the market.[39] Whereas earlier, such writers came close to arguing for the greater distribution of economic power through land reform, higher wages, and consumer spending, now they turned toward the more defensive idea that laboring people possessed a *moral* right to a fair wage: "the fruits of their industry." But since all progressive writers, of whatever hue, were careful to avoid establishing this as a property right, their calls for justice for the poor were forced ever further inward to draw on the resources of the heart.

This movement pushed progressive writers even further toward launching their appeals for ameliorative reforms from within the realm of feeling. In attempting to transcend imaginatively, if not actually, the realities of class divergence and bring the poor into a sympathetic relationship with their readers, these writers appealed to realms of experience and made use of techniques that were being developed in the sentimental novels and paintings so popular in the period.[40] In the hands of such writers, the laboring-class domestic sphere became an increasingly fraught emotional space.

One of the most interesting examples of this is John Scott's *Observations on the Present State of the Parochial and Vagrant Poor*, published in 1773. Scott, a Quaker and a well-known poet and antislavery campaigner, attacked parish workhouses and houses of industry for removing the poor from their homes and breaking up their families. In so doing, he invited his readers to sympathize with laboring-class families and to imagine that the poor existed in the same domestic and affective regimes as themselves. Laboring people too, he noted, valued their homes:

> Attachment to one's situation is the natural consequence of long continued residence and this foible seems to operate equally through all ranks of society: the cottager is as fond of his cottage as the tradesman is his shop, or the gentleman his villa. There is often a secret wish not easily accounted for, to resign the last breath of life on the same spot where it was received; there is often as unaccountable an affection for some particular convenience of habitation.

While he admitted that such things might be "of little importance in reality," Scott insisted that "they are of much in idea; and in idea, exist many of our sublimest pains and pleasures."[41]

Scott injected a far greater emotional content into the relations of the laboring-class family than had previously been allowed. Placing unemployed men in workhouses, he argued, caused what we would recognize as immense psychic damage. Once the members of a family were separated, "the tender connexion is broken; one is committed to the workhouse, and the other is left to pine in artificial widowhood," he argued. "The unfortunate parent, in that season of debility when the officious cares of filial affection are most requisite for the alleviation of those painful infirmities common to the greatest and the meanest mortals, is ravished from the arms of his dutiful and assiduous offspring, and transferred to the management of those whom interest is continually stimulating to oppression."[42]

For all its emotional and rhetorical sophistication, however, Scott's pamphlet is also notably defensive in tone and ambition. Unlike Defoe, Vanderlint, or even

Tucker, Scott could no longer assume that a freely operating commerce would naturally tend toward the greater economic emancipation and prosperity of the people. Instead, he attempted to utilize developing imaginative emotional resources to win support for ameliorative reforms.

By the late eighteenth century, then, the laboring-class domestic sphere had become an established site for public ideological contestation in assessing the condition of the laboring classes. For conservatives and entrenched economic interests far removed from the material lives of the mass of the people, the laboring classes' domestic spheres were a social space in which it could be demonstrated that the entire class was prodigal, lazy, sordid, and uncivilized, or where it could be proved that they enjoyed greater material prosperity than their forebears. For the middling progressives who had first brought the domestic lives of the poor into discursive visibility during the early eighteenth century, the laboring-class domestic sphere had become a site in which the most that could be imagined was the fighting of defensive battles to win specific social reforms or elicit charitable sentiments. It was certainly no longer a site in which the forward march of commercial societies and the inevitable devolution of material prosperity through the social order could be demonstrated and advocated.

In this essay, I have tried to suggest that the middle of the eighteenth century saw a section of an emerging capitalist class attempting to reinterpret and reshape the political economy of the nation to suit its own sectional interest in creating a vibrant home market. In imagining this market and its agents, this section attempted to devolve onto the laboring classes its own ideas of consumer agency, of the gender division of labor and desire in the domestic economy, and of the taste that allowed consumers to discriminate in the widening market economy of eighteenth-century England. I have also suggested that this effort ran aground on the realities of widening class divisions that underpinned the formation of the market economy. Although the idea that the laboring classes might be known, understood, and controlled through the illumination of their domestic lives survived to form part of nineteenth-century social thought, the peculiar optimism that had driven this discovery subsided as consumerist ideas came to provide a less plausible account of the realities of British society. This was not the last time such bodies of ideas have surfaced in British history, however. Indeed, it might be suggested that such ideas have reappeared in different forms during expansive phases of capitalist development, to be replaced as expansion has repeatedly foundered on the internal contradictions particular to this economic system. Perhaps the last point to be made here is to suggest that if historians are to understand the movement of ideas and analyze cultural change better, they need to look to theories that allow them to relate these to the political-economic conditions and social formations of the period.

1. For the classic analysis of this development, with examination of its implications for class relations in early-eighteenth-century England, see E. P. Thompson, *Whigs and Hunters: The Origin of the Black Act* (Harmondsworth, UK: Allen Lane, 1975).
2. This was the perspective that Edgar S. Furniss noted, generalizing it across the whole of the eighteenth century as part of a "mercantilist" mental framework. My work is aimed in part at closer examination of the historical record to uncover a more complex, conflictual, developmental, and materialist history of ideas. See Furniss, *The Position of the Labourer in a System of Nationalism: A Study in the Labour Theories of the Later English Mercantilists* (New York: Houghton Mifflin, 1920).
3. Josiah Child, *A New Discourse of Trade, Wherein is Recommended Several Weighty Points Relating to Companies of Merchanting* (London: J. Everingham, 1693), 19.
4. Maxine Berg, Pat Hudson, and Michael Sonenscher, eds., *Manufacture in Town and Country before the Factory* (Cambridge: Cambridge Univ. Press, 1983), 5–8; Julia De Lacy Mann, *The Cloth Industry in the West of England: 1640–1880* (Oxford: Clarendon Press, 1971), 18–36, 89–119; Mann, "Clothiers and Weavers in Wiltshire during the Eighteenth Century," in *Studies in the Industrial Revolution*, ed. L. S. Pressnell (London: Athlone Press, 1960), 66–96; David Rollison, *The Local Origins of Modern Society: Gloucestershire, 1500–1800* (London: Routledge, 1992), 32–43; A. F. J. Brown, *Essex at Work, 1700–1815* (Chelmsford, UK: Essex County Council, 1969), 3–6. For examples of the ideological position outlined above, see John Pollexfen, *A Discourse of Trade and Coyn* (London: Printed for Brabazon Aylmer, 1697), 80; Charles King, *The British Merchant: Or, Commerce Preserved, In three Volumes. By Mr. Charles King, Chamber Keeper to the Treasury, and late of London Merchant* (London: Printed by J. Darby, 1721), 1–9; and Joshua Gee, *The Trade and Navigation of Great Britain Considered*, 2nd ed. (London: Printed by Sam Buckley, 1730), 29–31.
5. Maxine Berg, "Small-Producer Capitalism in Eighteenth-Century England," *Business History* 35 (1993): 5–6, 23–24; Berg, *The Age of Manufactures, 1700–1820: Industry, Innovation and Work in Britain* (London: Routledge, 1994), 211–12, 219–21, 255–79. For artisan consumption of new goods, see the suggestive evidence of craftsmen's inventories in Lorna Weatherill, *Consumer Behaviour and Material Culture in Britain, 1660–1760*, 2nd ed. (London: Routledge, 1996), 184–85.
6. See, for example, Nicholas Barbon, *An Apology for the Builder: Or, A Discourse Shewing the Cause and Effects of the Increase of Building* (London: Printed by Cave Pullen, 1685), 5, 32–33. See also Barbon, *A Discourse of Trade* (London: Printed by Tho. Milbourn for the author, 1690); Anon., *A Discourse of the Necessity of Encouraging Mechanick Industry* (London: Printed for R. Chiswell, 1690), 2–3, 25–27; Thomas Tryon, *England's Grandeur, And Way to get Wealth: Or, Promotion of Trade made Easy and Lands Advanced, by Thomas Tryon, Merchant of London* (London: Sold by J. Harris at the Harrow and G. Conyers, 1699), 7–8; Henry Martyn, *Considerations on the East India Trade* (London: Printed for A and V Churchill, 1701); John Cary, *An Essay Towards Regulating the Trade and Employing the Poor of this Kingdom. The Second Editions, Whereunto is added An Essay Towards Paying off the Publick Debts* (London: T. Goodwin & E. Symon, 1717), 97–99, 111–12.
7. Daniel Defoe, *A Plan of the English Commerce* (London: Charles Rivington, 1728), reprinted in *The Political and Economic Writings of Daniel Defoe*, ed. W. R. Owens and P. N. Furbank (London: Pickering & Chatto, 2000), 7:177. See also Defoe, *A Brief State of the Inland or Home Trade of England; and of the Oppression in Suffers and the Dangers which Threaten it from the Invasion of Hawkers, Pedlars and Clandestine Traders of all Sorts* (London: Printed for Tho. Warner, 1730).
8. Defoe, *Plan of the English Commerce*, 177.
9. For a discussion of this, see Keith Tribe, *Land, Labour and Economic Discourse* (London: Routledge and Kegan Paul, 1978), 80–109.
10. Jacob Vanderlint, *Money Answers all Things: Or, An Essay to Make Money Sufficiently Plentiful Amongst all Ranks of People* (London: Printed for T. Cox, 1734), 75.
11. Joseph Massie, *Calculation of Taxes for a Family of Each Rank, Degree or Class: For One Year* (London: Thomas Payne, 1756). See also Massie, *A Plan for the Establishment of Charity Houses for Exposed or Deserted Women and Girls, and for Penitent Prostitutes* (London, 1758), 105. Here, Massie generalized from a "typical" laboring class, constructing a table that estimated "the Annual income and Expences of a Manufacturer, his Wife, and Children." Not simply taxable commodities, but all the commodities that he judged

constituted the "expences" of the poor, were aligned against the estimated earnings of a family who worked "300 days a year" and brought in £30. Among these he reckoned "Grocery wares and medicines," "Woollen cloathing," "Linen cloth," "shoes," "coals, candles, soap," and "repairs of utensils."

12. Josiah Tucker, *Instructions for Travellers* (London: privately printed, 1757), 60–61.
13. [Richard Parrott], *Reflections on Various Subjects Relating to Arts and Commerce, Particularly the Consequences of Admitting Foreign Artists on Easier Terms* (London: George Woodfall, 1752), 70–72. For similar statements during the 1750s, see Anon., *The Fisheries Revived: Or, Great Britain's Hidden Treasures Discovered* (London: Printed for J. Robinson and J. Millan, 1750), 46–47, and J. G., *An Appeal to Facts Regarding the Home Trade and Inland Manufactures of Great Britain and Ireland* (London: George Woodfall, 1751), 10–11, 37–38. See also two of the entrants to Lord Townshend's famous essay competition of 1756, an abortive attempt to stimulate interest in commerce at Cambridge University: [William Weston], *A Dissertation on the following Question: in what Manner do trade and Civil Liberty support and assist each other?* (London: Printed for R. and J. Dodsley, and sold by M. Cooper, 1756), 11, and [Benjamin Newton], *Another Dissertation on the Mutual Support of Trade and Civil Liberty* (London: Printed for T. Payne, 1756), 13–15.
14. [Parrott], *Reflections on Various Subjects*, 70–72.
15. [Parrott], *Reflections on Various Subjects*, 70–71.
16. The classic work on the sociological functioning of taste is, of course, Pierre Bourdieu, *Distinction: A Social Critique of the Judgment of Taste*, trans. Richard Nice (Cambridge, MA: Harvard Univ. Press, 1984). The development of taste in relation to the formation of the aesthetic is far less well understood, but see a useful discussion in Robert W. Jones, *Gender and the Formation of Taste in Eighteenth-Century Britain: The Analysis of Beauty* (Cambridge: Cambridge Univ. Press, 1998). For work on the notion of comfort in the eighteenth century, see John E. Crowley, *The Invention of Comfort: Sensibilities and Design in Early Modern Britain and America* (Baltimore: Johns Hopkins Univ. Press, 2001), 111–201.
17. For the relationship between women, femininity, taste, and beauty in eighteenth-century thought, see Jones, *Gender and the Formation of Taste*, 37–78.
18. Nicholas Rogers, "Confronting the Crime Wave: The Debate over Social Reform and Regulation, 1749–1753," in *Stilling the Grumbling Hive: The Response to Social and Economic Problems in England, 1689–1750*, ed. Lee Davison, Tim Hitchcock, Tim Keirn, and Robert B. Shoemaker (Stroud, UK: Alan Sutton, 1992), 77–98. See also Richard T. Connors, "Pelham, Parliament and Public Policy, 1746–1754" (DPhil thesis, Cambridge Univ., 1993).
19. John Newball, *A Scheme to prevent the Running of Wool unmanufactur'd* (Stamford: Printed by F. Howgrave, 1744), 59.
20. Simon Mason, *The Good and Bad Effects of Tea Consider'd* (London: Printed for M. Cooper, 1745), 41–42.
21. Thomas Alcock, *Observations on the Defects of the Poor Laws and on the causes and consequences of the Great increase and Burden of the Poor. with a Proposal for redressing these Grievances. In a letter to a Member of Parliament* (London: R. Baldwin, 1752), 48, 45–46.
22. Jonathan White, "'The Slow Sure Poyson': Representing Gin and Its Drinkers in Eighteenth-Century England, 1736–1751," *Journal of British Studies* 42, no. 1 (2003): 35–64. See also Peter Clark, "The Mother Gin Controversy in the Early Eighteenth Century," *Transactions of the Royal Historical Society*, ser. 5, 38 (1988): 63–98, and Jessica Warner, *Craze: Gin and Debauchery in an Age of Reason* (London: Profile, 2003), 181–208.
23. Eliza Haywood, *A Present for Women Addicted to Drinking. Adapted to all the different Stations of Life, from a Lady of Quality to a Common Servant* (London: Owen, 1750), 22–25.
24. Haywood, *A Present for Women Addicted to Drinking*, 34–35.
25. Anon., *A Dissertation on Mr Hogarth's Six Prints, Lately Publish'd viz. Gin lane, Beer Street and the Four Stages of Cruelty* (London: Dickinson, 1751), 15–16.
26. Anon., *Dissertation on Mr Hogarth's Six Prints*, 17, 26.
27. Josiah Tucker, *An Impartial Inquiry into the benefits and damages arising to the Nation from the present very great use of Low-Priced Spirituous Liquors* (London: Trye, 1751), 30.
28. Isaac Maddox, Bishop of Worcester, *The Expediency of Preventive Wisdom, A Sermon Preached before the Right Honourable the Lord Mayor, The Aldermen and Governors of the Severall Hospitals of the City of Lon-*

don, at St. Bridget's Church on Easter Monday, 1750 (London: Printed by H. Woodfall, 1750), ix–x. See also Tucker, *Impartial Inquiry*, 28–30.

29. John Clayton, *Friendly Advice to the Poor, Written and Published at the Request of the Late and Present Officers of the Town of Manchester* (Manchester: Printed by J. Harrop, 1755), 4.
30. Clayton, *Friendly Advice to the Poor*, 24–25.
31. Clayton, *Friendly Advice to the Poor*, 19, 22–23.
32. Temple was known to Josiah Tucker, with whom he shared a progressive view of commerce. However, Temple's view of laboring people, unlike Tucker's, was dominated by the hierarchical structures of the West Country's wool industry, about which he had written at length earlier in life. Tucker himself appears to have felt uneasy with Temple's virulent views, writing to Lord Kames that Temple had "immense erudition in his way," and "understands the principles of commerce extremely well," but "pushes some of them too far." See Alexander Fraser Tytler, *Memoirs of the Life and Works of the Honourable Henry Home of Kames*, 2 vols. (Edinburgh: Printed for W. Creech, 1807), 1:6.
33. William Temple, *A Vindication of Commerce and the Arts: Proving that they are the Source of the Greatness, Power, Riches and Populousness of a State* (London: J. Nourse, 1758), 28–29.
34. Temple, *Vindication*, 31.
35. For this, see Douglas Hay and Nicholas Rogers, *Eighteenth-Century English Society: Shuttles and Swords* (Oxford: Oxford Univ. Press, 1997), 84–113, 188–208. See also R. W. Malcolmson, *Life and Labour in England, 1700–1780* (London: Hutchinson, 1981), 136–60, and Andrew Charlesworth, ed., *An Atlas of Rural Protest in Britain, 1548–1900* (London: Croom Helm, 1983), 86–88, 111–13.
36. Joseph Priestley, *Lectures on History and General Policy; to which is prefixed an Essay on a Course of Liberal Education for Civil and Active Life*, 3rd ed. (Birmingham and London: Printed by Pearson and Rollason, for J. Johnson, 1788), 280–81, 383–84.
37. Arthur Young, *Six Weeks Tour through the Southern Counties* (London: W. Nicoll, 1768); Arthur Young, *A Six Month Tour through the North of England* (London: W. Strahan, 1770).
38. See David Davies, *The Case of the Labourers in Husbandry* (London: G. & J. Robinson, 1795), and Frederick Eden, *The State of the Poor*, 2 vols. (London, 1797).
39. See, for example, [John Hustler], *The Occasion of Dearness of Provisions, and the distresses of the Poor: With Proposals for Remedying the Calamity. By a Manufacturer* (London: W. Owen, 1767), 18–19; Francis Moore, *Considerations on the Exorbitant Price of Provisions, setting forth the Pernicious Effects which a real Scarcity of the Necessaries of Life, must Eventually have upon the Commerce, Population, and Power of Great Britain* (London: T. Cadell, 1773); and Anon., *A View of Real Grievances with Remedies Proposed for Redressing them; Humbly submitted to the Consideration of the Legislature* (London: Printed for the author, and sold by Dodsley, Millan, Baldwin, [etc.], 1772).
40. See, for example, Janet Todd, *Sensibility: An Introduction* (London: Methuen, 1986); G. J. Barker-Benfield, *The Culture of Sensibility: Sex and Society in Eighteenth-Century Britain* (Chicago: Univ. of Chicago Press, 1992); and Michael Rosenthal, *The Art of Thomas Gainsborough: A Little Business for the Eye* (New Haven and London: Yale Univ. Press, 1999), chap. 9. For a particularly fine analysis of sentimentalism, see Michael Bell, *Sentimentalism, Ethics and the Culture of Feeling* (Basingstoke, UK: Macmillan, 2000).
41. John Scott, *Observations on the Present State of the Parochial and Vagrant Poor* (London: Printed for Edward and Charles Dilly, 1773), 25, 46–47.
42. Scott, *Observations*, 48.

People

A Family Affair: The Design and Decoration of 321 South Fourth Street, Philadelphia

Amy H. Henderson

Between 1785 and 1790, a family, living on opposites sides of the Atlantic Ocean, managed to design, construct, and decorate a grand town house together. Henry Hill and his wife, Ann Meredith Hill, built the house (fig. 58)—which still stands today—in the Old Society Hill neighborhood of Philadelphia, while one of Hill's sisters, Mary Lamar, supplied ideas, materials, and furnishings from the West End of London.[1] The collaboration between the Hills and Lamar on 321 South Fourth Street offers new evidence that in the eighteenth century, the responsibilities as well as the pleasures of architectural design and interior decoration were increasingly shared between men and women.[2] From the middle of this century, in fact, women participated to an ever greater degree in building and furnishing their domestic environment and frequently worked alongside men—brothers, fathers, and husbands—to create elegant homes capable of expressing the genteel character of the entire family.[3] The focus of this essay is on Mary Lamar, who, living near the heart of fashionable London, was exceptionally well positioned to assist her brother and sister-in-law in their architectural endeavors by serving, first, as their arbiter of cosmopolitan taste and, second, as their purchasing agent.

An exploration of 321 South Fourth Street also offers insight into the ways in which men and women spread notions of taste and culture around the Atlantic rim and collectively used their homes to negotiate a communal identity in the wake of the American Revolution. To understand the significance of material culture in the last quarter of the eighteenth century in the lives of people like the Hills and Lamar, I turn to historian David Shields's use of *sensus communis.* He borrows the term from the Earl of Shaftesbury's *Characteristics of Men, Manners, Opinions, Times* (1711) to describe how elite eighteenth-century Americans formed a communal identity and created social cohesion through specific manners, speech acts, and writing.[4] I contend that architectural design functioned in the same way, offering like-minded individuals a visual language they could use to institute a *sensus communis*, or a community of interest.[5] In Federal Philadelphia, as in Georgian London, an individual's social status was increasingly dependent on merit and

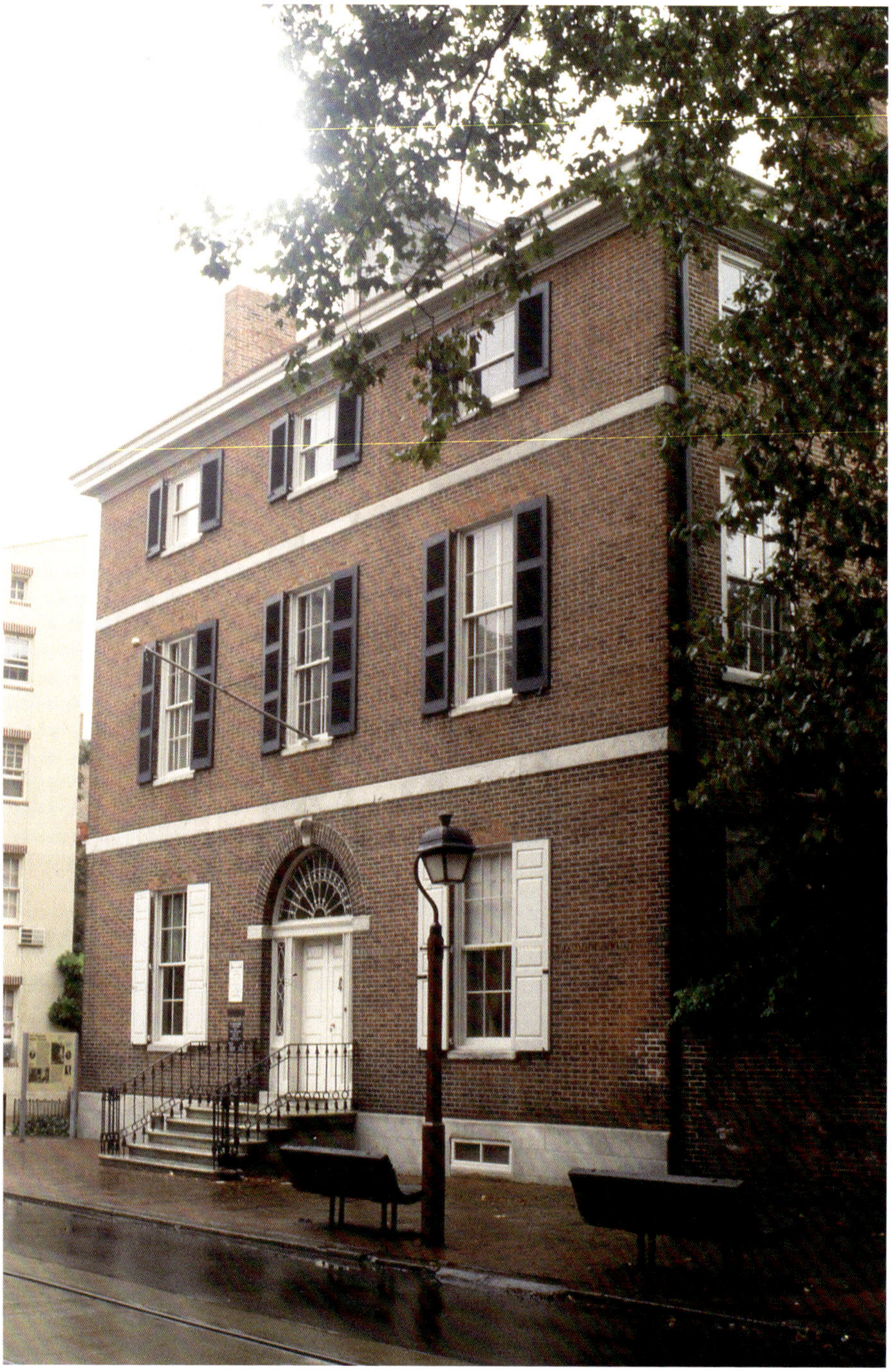

58. Facade, Henry and Ann Hill house (Hill-Physick-Keith House), 321 South Fourth Street, Philadelphia, c. 1786–88. Photo: Bernard L. Herman.

material display instead of on family lineage or birth. Consequently, "taste" in the fine and decorative arts functioned as a powerful indicator of one's gentility and thus membership in elite society. To build and decorate a home with the same taste as one's neighbor was to announce a shared appreciation for a particular style and, subsequently, a social connection to that family.[6]

When the Hills decided to construct a new town house, they instinctively turned to Lamar to help them build and decorate their home. With her knowledge of London fashions, Lamar gave them access to the latest neoclassical style and, by extension, the cultural authority of Europe. Although the architecture of the Adam brothers and their followers had been popular in London for close to two decades, this style was just beginning to filter into Philadelphia in the early 1780s. By providing the Hills with the costly materials and neoclassical furnishings that only the wealthiest and most discriminating Americans could afford, Lamar empowered them to exhibit their ties to the select families included in a *sensus communis.*

The Hills embarked on their house project at a critical moment in the new nation's history. Philadelphians were literally rebuilding their city—and their society—following the Revolution. In 1784, when the Hills purchased the land for their new home, they and their neighbors were forced to respond not only to the mess and destruction left behind by occupying British forces and the chaos unleashed by street rioting and violence during the war, but also to a breakdown in the traditional social order that had governed colonial Pennsylvania. New families—who had profited financially and politically during the Revolution—emerged to fill the vacuum created by the loyalists and pacifist Quakers who had departed entirely or retreated from the political scene.[7] As a result of this shift in society, it became imperative for elite families such as the Hills to define themselves in relation to their fellow citizens. In this context, the facade of an imposing house such as 321 South Fourth Street became both a defense against the confusion of an evolving society and a proclamation of the family's place within that society. And from the inside of the house, the ownership, and perhaps more importantly the proper use, of such furnishings as mahogany sofas or marble mantels continued to express the ideals of gentility begun on the front steps. Both the exterior and interior of the home distinguished the Hills—and, by association, Lamar—from the vast majority of American society. The story that unfolds through Lamar's surviving correspondence and the house itself is of one family's attempt to navigate the architectural, as well as social, landscape of the transatlantic world.

For years, Henry Hill had employed his sister as his proxy in London, augmenting his provincial ideas about taste with her more sophisticated ones derived from experience in the cultural center of the British Empire. Therefore, Henry and Ann knew they could rely on Mary and her husband, Thomas, to guide them through the monumental process of creating a home. The Hills and Lamars were successful Madeira wine merchants who rose to social prominence within the mercantile communities in Philadelphia and London during the 1760s and early 1770s.[8] Around 1769, the Lamars permanently moved to London from the island of Madeira to manage the London branch of the family wine house, Lamar, Hill, Bisset and Co.[9] From this period, the Lamars served both the business and personal interests of the Hills, for example, sending the Hills a phaeton in 1770 shortly after the couple were married and supplying Ann with fashionable clothing and jewelry.[10] As Claire Walsh explores in her essay in this volume, proxy shopping could be a personal method of acquiring goods from afar. Unlike correspondence shopping, which was often performed by tradesmen or business associates hired as agents, and thus fraught with accusations of mismanagement,[11] proxy shopping was the province of trusted friends and relatives. Those relations who acted as proxies were valued for their knowledge of taste and the retail market as well as their ability to purchase goods as though choosing for their own homes. Eventually, the Hills commissioned Mary to fulfill orders not just for themselves, but also for a wide circle of their friends. With demonstrated skills in this arena, Lamar was an asset to her relations in Philadelphia; she carefully dispatched sets of dinner and dessert china, silver candlesticks, bed and window curtains, and wallpaper for a network of wealthy families that included the Hills, Clymers, Merediths, Powels, and Dickinsons.[12]

Mary Lamar was by no means unusual in her role as a proxy. Individuals living in large, metropolitan cities were expected to provide their families back home with news about the latest fashions as well as goods; London was the cultural center of choice for elite Philadelphians, before and after the Revolution, when it came to small and large household items. Indeed, Lamar's good friend Anne Allen Penn of Philadelphia similarly shopped for the Mifflin, Ross, and Bordley families when she lived in London.[13] Lamar, like Penn, was an avid shopper and seemed to relish visiting the different tradesmen, comparing prices and styles, and consulting with her friends in London—whom she called connoisseurs—on what were the handsomest decorations. On more than one occasion, Lamar made a point to reassure her brother that she derived great pleasure from these shopping sprees and would gladly oblige him and his friends with all of their future commissions.[14]

It is hard to attribute the exact source of Lamar's pleasure, whether it was simply the thrill of the chase, so to speak, or the knowledge that she was dutifully fulfilling a familial obligation (either personal or professional). Perhaps, too, she derived enjoyment from the opportunity to shop for high-priced architectural elements and furnishings that often fell outside a woman's daily shopping purview of foodstuffs, clothing, and small decorative items.[15] Whatever was the cause, by the time the Hills were ready to begin building 321 South Fourth Street, Lamar had positioned herself as a connoisseur of the London marketplace and enthusiastically agreed to step in as their mentor.

Lamar advised the Hills and filled most of their ornament and furniture commissions while living in the parish of St. Marylebone. Her residence in this area undoubtedly contributed to her growth as an arbiter of taste. Between 1774 and 1792, the Lamars rented several houses, first in Newman Street and then a few blocks west in Welbeck Street.[16] In the latter half of the eighteenth century, the five parishes of Kensington, Chelsea, Paddington, St. Pancras, and St. Marylebone, in the increasingly desirable West End, were among the fastest growing in London.[17] St. Marylebone in particular became one of the most attractive places to live, surpassing older parishes in central London, such as Covent Garden, in prestige. Although the Lamars resided just north of Oxford Street, and thus on the edge of the most fashionable neighborhoods, they lived close enough to the newly developed and outfitted terrace houses to experience firsthand the influence of such architects and craftsmen as the Adam brothers, Thomas Chippendale, George Seddon, and Josiah Wedgwood. Just by strolling along the homes in Grosvenor Square, Lamar presumably cultivated an appreciation for the architectural details and interior decorations of the reigning neoclassical style.

Before the Hills began construction in 1786, they consulted Lamar and her growing knowledge of London architecture. She responded to one of Henry's inquiries:

> I shall be pleased to hear or see your and Mrs. Hill's design for the House you propose building, if you inherit my Dear Father's Mechanical genius, as some of his descendents do, I darsay building would be a great amazement to you. I shall take the liberty of sending some particulars of the present taste here. In the first place Stone hall and Staire Case with Iron rails, the windows from the ceiling down to the floor with Iron rails before each window like those at madeira only projecting as much further as will bring them to a half circle painted green or white. . . . This fashion is I think confined to one story in the best apartments and on the front of the House. But I think it will be better to send you the plan of a House in the Modern Style, not grand but Elegant and Convenient. That seems by your letter to Mr. Lamar to be your design.[18]

Lamar's understanding of modern styles and her ability to articulate architectural details may have been enhanced through reading the new periodical literature designed for women. *The Lady's Magazine or Entertaining Companion for the Fair Sex* was one such resource with advice on style through textile fashion.[19] If Lamar indeed sent the Hills a "plan," she also may have had access to such design books as William Pain's *The Practical House Carpenter* (1784) or James Miller's *The Country Gentleman's Architect, in a great variety of New Designs* (1787), which offered information on the design and planning of an assortment of house types.[20]

Ultimately, Lamar's greatest resource would have been her ability to observe domestic architecture and interiors in her daily rounds visiting acquaintance, family, and friends. Not only was Lamar familiar with the four London residences in which she and her husband successively lived, but she also enjoyed access to those inhabited by her sister Sarah Hill Dillwyn, at 128 Wapping, New Stairs, and her brother-in-law Robert Bisset, at 6 New Inn, Wyck Street.[21] These houses were in the older parts of the City of London and did not necessarily represent the recent fashions of the West End, though they might have been remodeled. Regardless of their level of fashion, however, the buildings did allow Lamar to investigate and compare a range of architectural designs. In addition to visiting her relatives, Lamar mentioned socializing with a number of Americans living in St. Marylebone, including the painter Benjamin West, who lived across the street from her in Newman Street; John and Abigail Adams, who resided at 9 Grosvenor Square when Adams represented the United States as minister plenipotentiary to the Court of St. James; and William and Anne Bingham, the Hills' friends from Philadelphia, when they rented 30 Harley Street in Cavendish Square.

Lamar was a tremendous asset to the Hills in planning their house mainly because she was in the right place at the right time and was genuinely interested in architecture and domestic furnishings. Using her knowledge from a variety of sources, she directed her brother and sister-in-law on those elements that were particularly prone to changes in fashion, such as the materials for an entry stair and hall, window proportions, and decorative details on the facade. Through her correspondence alone, Lamar was able to develop and transmit a cosmopolitan decorative and architectural language that conveyed London ideas of what was fashionable, elegant, and serviceable.

Unfortunately, there are no extant records to confirm who actually designed 321 South Fourth Street. The Hills may have designed it entirely themselves, hired a local master builder to create a floor plan, or followed the plan Lamar said she would send.[22] Because of several secondary references to Ann Hill's involvement in planning—let alone paying for—the new house, it seems plausible that she played a significant, albeit undocumented, role in its layout.[23] In the spring of 1787, the house plan was finalized and Hill's nephew in Madeira, Richard Lamar Bisset, wrote to him:

> It is some time since I have received the plan of your house—it is everything that is neat and may well be called—*simplex munditiis.* Monday at two there

goes a vessel direct to England, and the only one since the time I received the plan, by which I shall forward it to my aunt.[24]

When completed, 321 South Fourth Street was one of the largest freestanding, brick town houses in Philadelphia and among the city's earliest examples of neoclassical domestic architecture—appropriately called *simplex munditiis*, meaning "simple elegance." As neoclassicism was just gaining popularity in the city, there were few local examples of the style before 1786, when William and Anne Bingham erected their Mansion House on South Third Street.[25] In this early period, craftsmen generally created Adam-style houses by adding neoclassical decorative elements to traditional Palladian, or Colonial, house types.[26] Although craftsmen would build houses with both structural and decorative elements in the neoclassical style within the decade,[27] the Hills were following the newest fashion in 1786 when they chose to build a Colonial house type with neoclassical embellishments.

Two rooms wide and two rooms deep with a central, flagged-marble hallway, the Hills' house is almost a perfect cube, forty-eight feet square. According to an insurance survey conducted in 1815, there were three parlors and a kitchen on the ground floor, five rooms on the second floor, and five rooms on the third floor (figs. 59, 60). A flight of common winding stairs led to a one-room garret under a hipped roof. Between the northeast and northwest rooms were two separate flights of stairs; one had a mahogany handrail and scroll and connected the first to the second and third stories, and the second was a common winding stair that joined all four floors and the cellar. North of the house was a one-story brick building in two parts, ten feet by thirty feet with a flat roof, used as a scullery, and "adjoining and communicating" to the east of the house a three-story brick building sixteen feet by twenty-two feet, used as a second kitchen and washroom.[28] Finally, an open two-story piazza connected the house and the second kitchen to a two-story brick stable seventy-five feet east of Fourth Street.[29]

An unusual aspect of the house that is not mentioned in the 1815 survey is the difference in the floor levels between the northeast quarter and the rest of the house. On the ground floor, the kitchen is a few feet lower and has a lower ceiling than the three parlors. In fact, three full stories rise above the kitchen, while only two stories rise above the other ground-floor rooms. In the northeast quarter, the floor directly above the kitchen is a mezzanine and has no level access to the second floor.[30] Only on the uppermost story of the house do the floors of the two sections level out again. Since the lower ceiling proportions are continued on all four stories, it seems likely that the Hills intended the northeast quarter of the house to be a separate servants' quarter.[31] The end result of such a structural arrangement

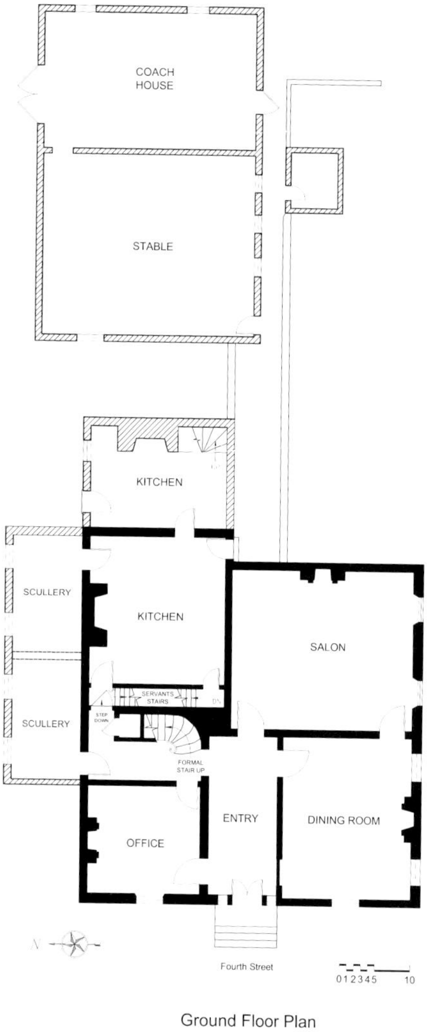

59. Plan of the ground floor, Hill-Physick-Keith House, c. 1789, with conjectural locations of the scullery, second kitchen, and stable based on an 1815 insurance survey, nineteenth-century engravings, and historical photographs. Drawing: Jeroen van den Hurk, after architectural drawings by George C. Roberts for the Society of the Preservation of Historic Landmarks (1965–66). Philadelphia Historical Commission, Philadelphia.

was the clear segregation of public and private space throughout the house. Furthermore, by setting the main staircase in a side hall, the Hills closed off access to the floors above and turned the three first-floor parlors into their primary public rooms. From notations in Hill's receipt books, it is possible to conclude that he used the small northwest parlor as either an informal receiving room or an office, the southwest parlor as a dining room, and the large southeast parlor as a formal entertaining room.[32] Although public and private spaces in both London and Philadelphia houses were traditionally arranged along the front and back of the building, the Hills chose to designate the ground floor for the public display of

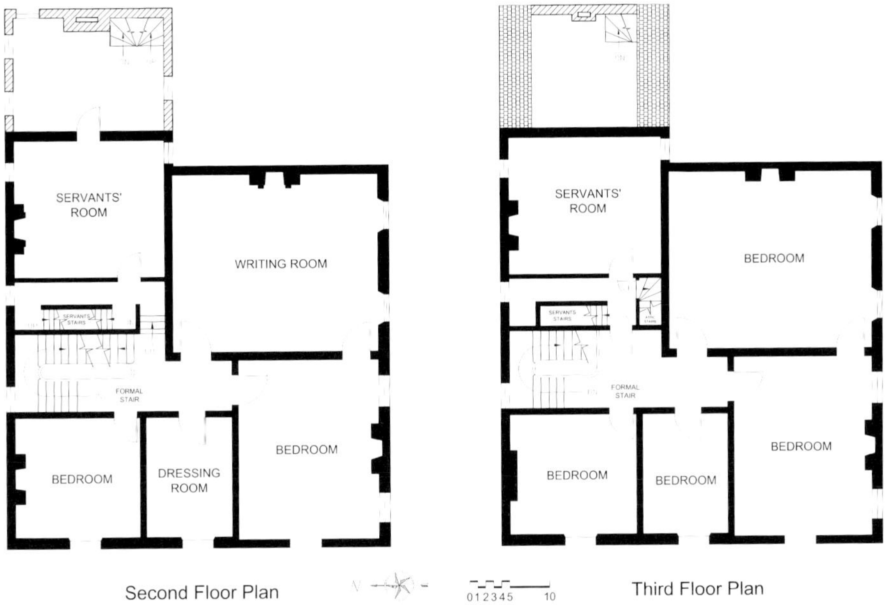

60. Plan of the second and third floors, Hill-Physick-Keith House, c. 1789, with conjectural location of the three-story kitchen addition based on an 1815 insurance survey, nineteenth-century engravings, and historical photographs. Drawing: Jeroen van den Hurk, after architectural drawings by George C. Roberts for the Society of the Preservation of Historic Landmarks (1965–66). Philadelphia Historical Commission, Philadelphia.

their taste and to reserve the upper floors for private use. However unusual this internal organization of space, it apparently appealed to the visitors who commented that the house was indeed a "model of convenience."[33]

Once the Hills had determined the size and layout of their house, they asked Lamar to acquire an assortment of architectural ornaments and furnishings to render their Colonial house neoclassical, and thus fashionable, in style. Lamar's documented contributions in this area include the fan and sidelights, marble chimneypieces, and parlor furnishings. The fanlight, still installed in its original position above the front door, was one of the first ornaments Lamar purchased for 321 South Fourth Street (fig. 61). The Hills received the wirework in one piece by May 1787 and seemed pleased with the style and craftsmanship.[34] Similarities in design suggest that Lamar ordered the wirework for both fan and side windows from the British designer and inventor James Keir in Gerrard Street, Soho.[35] Unlike earlier designers who built fanlights out of cast lead, Keir used cast iron for the structural ribs and cast brass for the ornaments, to provide a stronger foundation for the glass. This added strength allowed for larger panes of glass, making Keir's "Eldorado" fanlights lighter and more decorative.[36]

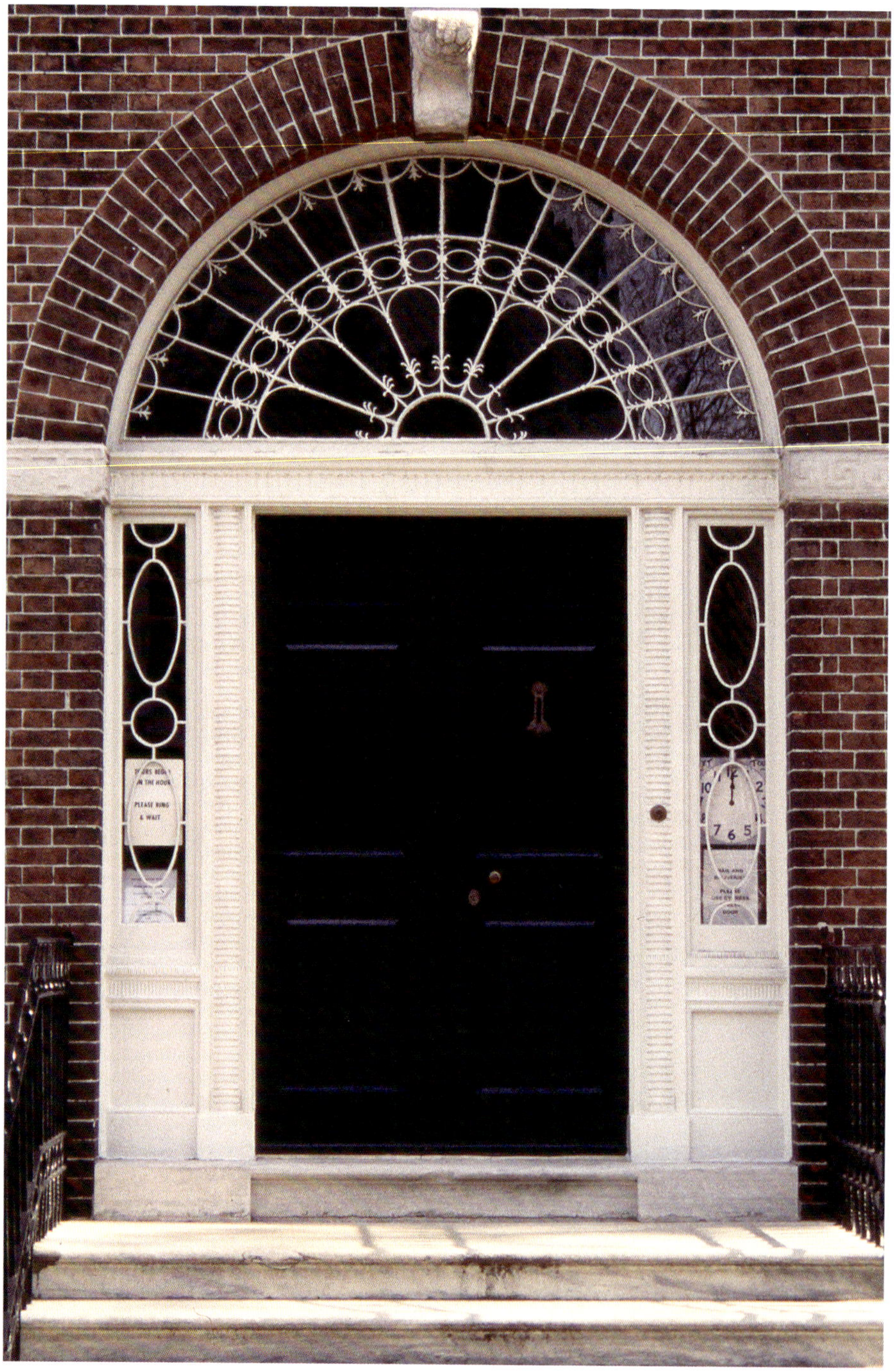

61. "Eldorado" fan and sidelights, attributed to James Keir, c. 1787, Hill-Physick-Keith House, Philadelphia. Photo: Amy H. Henderson.

Fanlights became popular fixtures in London town houses around 1765 and were increasingly installed in neighborhoods such as Welbeck Street. The fanlight design that Lamar selected from Keir's studio, with its delicate spokes springing from the central arch, an oval chain intertwined with rosettes and acanthus leaves in the double ring, and festoons in the outer arch, is characteristic of the Adam style. A fanlight of this size and elegance was extremely rare in Philadelphia in the 1780s, leading Hill's brother-in-law George Dillwyn to pun:

> Happy the Man with such a Treasure,
> Whose greatest Pain's his greatest Pleasure;
> Stoics who do not fear the Devil,
> Assure us Pain is not an Evil,
> They boast a Negative at best
> But thou with Panes are truly blest.
> What strange delusion must possess his pate
> When bliss increases as his pains are great!
> On read[in]g the foregoing by G.D.[37]

Despite such teasing, one can assume the Hills were delighted with windows that visually linked their town house to the terrace houses in the West End of London. Furthermore, by choosing to commission a fanlight that signified the cosmopolitan style as well as innovation of London designers, Lamar gave Philadelphians on the outside of the house a sample of the elegance to come on the inside.

After shipping off the fanlight, Lamar turned her attention to the chimneypieces for 321 South Fourth Street. Wealthy Philadelphia merchants in this period typically installed carved wooden mantels, though, increasingly, many elite families were beginning to import at least one marble chimneypiece for a principal room.[38] The Hills' friends Samuel and Elizabeth Powel, for example, had a plain marble mantel imported and installed in their house as early as 1770, and in the 1780s they advised another couple in their circle, Bishop William and Mary Harrison White, to do the same.[39] In 1786, Mary White was supervising the construction of her new house at 309 Walnut Street and informed her husband, who was then in London, that Mr. Powel recommended she "should have some of the chimneys measured and the dimensions sent you for marble . . . he tells me you will save near one-half by bringing it with you."[40] The Hills probably realized, as did the Whites, that, in the mid-1780s, it was impossible to find craftsmen in Philadelphia capable of producing marble mantels in the neoclassical style. Consequently, they followed the lead of their friends and requested that Lamar commission the mantels for them.

The Hills and Lamar were able to discuss with each other the style and cost of the mantels by using the Whites' recent purchase as a reference point. In an undated letter, probably from the summer of 1787, Lamar offered her brother and sister-in-law a tutorial on shopping for mantels. "As a chimney-piece and slab," she wrote,

> a handsome white marble, which is the fashion for a best room, and looks beautiful, cannot be got under £40 or £50. By what you say of Mr. [William] White's, it cannot be such as I mean, which is entirely marble without any wood. His I imagine is only a plain slip of wood in front; such, here, are only put in bed and back rooms; the best dining parlours of late have also entire marble pieces.[41]

Evidently swayed by her judgment in this matter, the Hills agreed to the additional cost and let Lamar order two fully carved mantels for their ground-floor parlor and dining room.

Before Lamar could complete the mantel commission, Ann Hill passed away.[42] The occurrence of her death inspired Lamar to acquire only the very best mantels for her grieving brother. By early 1788, she informed Hill that work on his mantels was under way, and she was optimistic they would be sent later that spring. She continued:

> If I am not Mistaken they will be as well if not better executed than any thing of the kind that has hitherto been sent to America[.] The design is my own thought and I flatter myself will meet your aprobation and that you will not think them too costly. . . . [Thomas Lamar and Robert Bisset] think I must have exceeded your intention but as I pleaded our dear departed Mrs. H. as well as yourself had left it to me they gave it up when I could not think of sending any if not elegant.[43]

Over a year later, she paid John Bacon the Elder £90 for two marble chimneypieces that her brother-in-law Robert Bisset noted were "noble and elegantly executed."[44] The first mantel, most likely intended for the Hills' parlor, has fluted engaged pilasters and an entablature with inlaid stone (fig. 63). A cherub astride a dolphin—reminiscent of the sea god Palaemon, a personification of safety—decorates the central tablet (fig. 62), while female figures, representing Peace and Liberty, adorn the trusses. One relative, Susanna Emlen, recorded that the iconography was intended to convey "the present prosperous state of America,"[45] presumably a reference to a longed-for stability upon the cessation of war. Less ornate, the second mantel was probably installed in the adjoining dining room; a suspended portrait medallion graces the central tablet, while the trusses are decorated with figures of children (fig. 64).[46]

Lamar contracted a master craftsman when she employed John Bacon, who, in the late 1780s, was at the height of a prolific career and popular with both the aristocracy and an urban mercantile elite. Bacon's early training included modeling figures in porcelain for Josiah Wedgwood and designing bas-reliefs for Mrs. Coade's Artificial Stone. In 1768, his interest in the fine arts led him to the Royal Academy Schools in London in order to develop his skills as a sculptor. During the 1770s and 1780s, although Bacon continued to design for companies such as Wedgwood and Coade, he also received many important chimneypiece, monument, and portrait commissions, such as the *Bust of King George III*, which established his reputation as a sculptor.[47] Between the 1760s and 1790s, Bacon fulfilled several chimneypiece commissions, including one for an anteroom at Fonthill Abbey in 1790 and another for Daylesford, Warren Hastings's house in Gloucestershire, in 1793.[48] Between his work for Mrs. Coade's Stone and his own shop, Bacon contributed greatly to the spread of neoclassical design; indeed, in addition to his receiving many commissions from the West Indies, Bacon's work was prominently displayed on the facade of the Binghams' Mansion House in Philadelphia, in narrative plaques of Coade Stone.[49]

Lamar explicitly states in her letter to Hill that the "design" of the mantels is her "own thought," raising questions about how she worked with Bacon to devise the two chimneypieces. It is certainly possible that Bacon employed marketing techniques similar to those of Wedgwood, encouraging customers to visit a showroom or workshop and select from patterns on display. Between 1783 and 1799, Bacon occupied commodious premises in Newman Street, not far from the Lamars' home. One can imagine Lamar viewing illustrations or sample carvings and selecting from an assortment of Bacon's favorite motifs: allegorical and elegantly draped female figures from classical mythology.[50] The end result of their collaboration was a pair of carved marble mantels more elaborate and sophisticated than any made in Philadelphia in the 1780s; indeed, Susanna Emlen remarked of the parlor mantel: "The chimney piece was beautiful. . . . I admired it more than anything of the kind I ever saw in this country but it had one defect which we plain [Quaker] people should think a very considerable one—it was quite too nice, ever to be used."[51] With Bacon's considerable talents, Lamar transported the language of classicism—a shared code within their elite mercantile community that alluded to the family's education and refinement—directly into the Hills' home.

Even before the Hills finished erecting the walls of their new house, they began to plan with Lamar the interior furnishings for the principal rooms. When Lamar asked Hill to send a plan of the house in 1786, she was interested in the physical

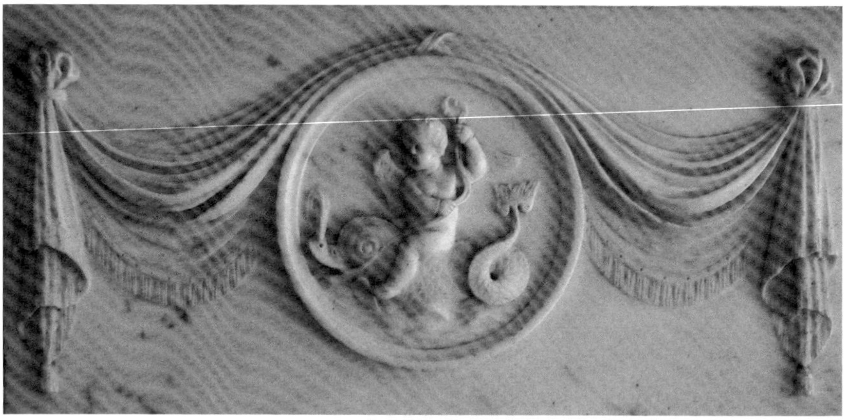

62. White marble mantel with verde inlay (detail of central tablet), attributed to John Bacon the Elder, c. 1789, Hill-Physick-Keith House, Philadelphia. Photo: Amy H. Henderson.

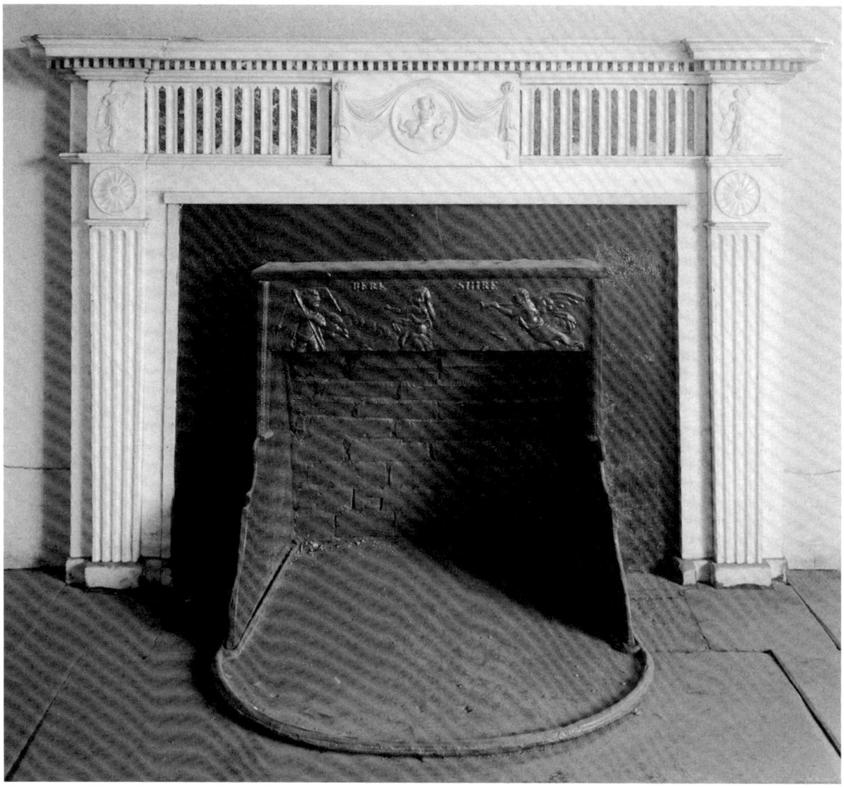

63. White marble mantel with verde inlay, attributed to John Bacon the Elder, c. 1789, Hill-Physick-Keith House, Philadelphia. Courtesy Library of Congress, Prints and Photographs Division, Historic American Buildings Survey (HABS, PA-1334-5). Photo: Cervin Robinson, 1959.

layout as well as the size and possible function of each room, so that she could suggest the most appropriate chairs, tables, carpets, mirrors, lighting devices, and wallpaper. The following letter from Lamar, quoted at length, reveals not only the many objects the Hills needed to consider purchasing, but also her extensive involvement in this phase of the project:

> I have given the plan &c. of the house to the upholsterer who is to draw me some plans, when I shall strive to fix on something that is handsome, and as cheap as possible. . . . I have some thoughts of sending only one large handsome glass for the best room, if that is the best room in the front; there being but two windows, one large glass will do with handsome girandoles or something more fashionable. . . .

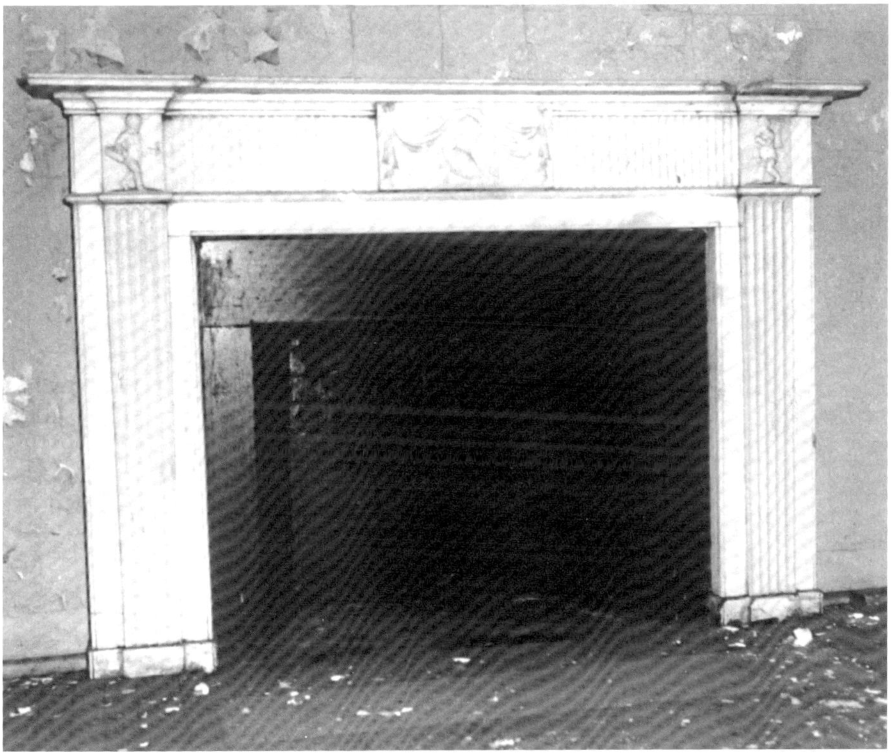

64. White marble mantel, attributed to John Bacon the Elder, c. 1789, Hill-Physick-Keith House, Philadelphia. Courtesy Library of Congress, Prints and Photographs Division, Historic American Buildings Survey (HABS, PA-1334 FN-242, photo 1362-9). Photo: Philadelphia Historical Commission, City of Philadelphia Official Photographer, Room 728, City Hall, Philadelphia.

You say nothing of chairs. I shall strive to make the upholsterer give some plans, when, if you want any you can choose. I think the best for America are cane seats with hair cushions covered with silk, which may be taken off in summer; the sofas made in the same manner.

A best room furnished in the present style and plainest taste is nothing more than two sofas, twelve or more chairs, a marble half circular table under glass or glasses, glass lustres on the slabs to hold four lights, the lowest price of which will be twelve or fourteen guineas the pair, or in place of them, silver or plated branches for three candles; or, in place of the marble slabs, inlaid wood, which are very pretty and come cheaper.

Neither tea or card tables stand in the best room, but are brought in when wanted; in the back room or common sitting room, one or two sofas according to the size of the room; chairs the same as in the best; a small breakfast table, one or two card tables, a double half oval under the glass, or in lieu, the tea or card tables. The Indian counterpanes make very pretty curtains for a back room or best bed room; as one counterpane of the largest size makes a window curtain, they come much cheaper than a good English cotton; some time ago they were to be got for three guineas apiece; but are not to be met with now; they make beautiful beds lined with white, and white clothes and testers.[52]

An experienced decorator and shopper, Lamar held definite ideas on how a fashionable town house should look, feel, and presumably be used. Unfortunately, the remainder of this letter is missing, leaving historians to speculate if Lamar offered advice on room use as well as aesthetics. What is clear, however, is that Lamar provided the Hills—through word and then object—with the stage set for a polite, sociable salon. Large gilt mirrors, Indian counterpane curtains, and sofas formed the backdrop, while smaller tea, card, and breakfast tables and an assortment of lightweight chairs could be moved and adjusted to accommodate a variety of social functions. Taken together, Lamar's furnishing suggestions affirm the room's use as a space for sociability—the entertainment of friends and family through the enactment of pleasing, polite behavior.[53]

Shortly after receiving the Hills' floor plan, Lamar hired an upholsterer named Kennet (perhaps Robert Kennett of 67 New Bond Street) to create this unified ensemble of furnishings.[54] In the fall of 1787, Lamar wrote her brother:

The inclosed are drawings I have procured for your own privite guide, both with regard to the expense and fashion of furnishing a house in the plainest State of elegance not but the expense may be much reduced . . . compared to what is specified in the enclosed, the first by having nothing more than is ab[s]olutely decent[.] The last in the plainness of the Carving gilding & other ornaments. besides decreesing the Glasses cornices &.c for the inferior rooms[.] [T]he inclosed is therefore to give you an Idea of how a house of the size of yours would be furnished in this place, by opinion neither Extravagant or eoconimical.[55]

As with the mantels, it is difficult to determine the extent of Lamar's ideas and influence on the project compared to Kennet's contribution. Two years after sending Kennet's plans, Lamar wrote that "every thing [is] in the newest fashion and as plain as things of that sort can be Made with tast[e] which is entirly my own and I flatter myself will please on that acc.o."[56] In the eighteenth century, the upholsterer was often considered the ultimate tastemaker, or at least the "chief agent" on whose judgment most patrons relied for suggestions in the use of different materials, styles in furniture and ornamentation, and acceptable levels of workmanship.[57] Patrons routinely paid the upholsterer proportionally more than any other craftsman to design the interior of the house, for the upholsterer could act as the middleman, hiring the cabinetmakers, carvers, and woolen drapers to work together.

One wonders how Lamar worked with Kennet to choose furniture in the latest taste. Did she in fact recommend the colors and textile patterns for the Hills' sofas and chairs—or perhaps even draft furniture designs, as did Georgiana Darcy in Jane Austen's *Pride and Prejudice*?[58] Designing small pieces of furniture was then considered, along with music, needlework, and drawing, an acceptable accomplishment for Georgian women. In describing one of the Hills' tables, Lamar wrote:

Your pier Tables are the first of the sort ever made in England or any where else and Superior in beauty to any I ever saw they have been so much admired that I am not a little vain that the thought was my own as well as the figur[e]s that are represented on them.[59]

Unfortunately, Lamar does not reveal more about what these figures looked like (presumably in composition ornament), or even how Kennet may have translated her "thought" into a pier table. Her comments suggest, however, the tremendous influence women consumers had on craftsmen. Lamar herself was evidently more than just a middleman for her brother; not only did she hire a fanlight maker, sculptor, and upholsterer to fulfill his commissions, but she also carefully oversaw the craftsmen's design decisions.

After three years of correspondence, Lamar was ready to ship the Hills' furniture to Philadelphia in the fall of 1789. It is impossible to know exactly how and where the now-widowed Hill used his furnishings, since no inventory of the house survives, yet he seems to have commissioned exactly what Lamar recommended and probably arranged his rooms under her direction. The furnishings ranged in size from a sofa to a pillow and included the two pier tables, "carv'd & gilt," supposedly designed by Lamar; ten gilt chairs and two gilt armchairs; twelve calico covers for chairs; two large looking glasses with gilt frames; three gilt window cornices; one iron register stove; a set of shovel, tongs, and poker; one steel hearth fender; three yellow and two green silk and worsted damask window curtains with line and tassels; and eleven hanging papers. A few months later, Lamar sent Hill's last commission: a carpet.[60]

When the Lamars discharged the Hills' furniture bills, they paid a total of £622 10s.—an exorbitant amount for an American to spend on furnishings. In the last quarter of the eighteenth century, one might spend between £200 and £300 to furnish a class three or four house (roughly 350 square feet) in the West End of London, or between £2,000 and £3,000 to outfit a much larger country villa.[61] However, when compared with other wealthy Philadelphia merchant families, who spent on average £300 sterling to furnish an entire house, the Hills' expenditures indeed seem high; moreover, they spent £622 to furnish just their principal parlor.[62] Although the furnishings that Lamar procured were, according to her opinion, "neither Extravagant or eoconimical," they certainly required a considerable outlay of money. Henry and Ann Hill's level of expenditure greatly surpassed what many of their contemporaries were spending on household furniture and was presumably intended to demonstrate Lamar's cosmopolitan taste and, by extension, the Hills' own elite status in Philadelphia society.

The most important contribution that Lamar was able to make to her brother and sister in law's house was undoubtedly in exporting her "taste." According to the descriptions in her letters, she sent it by way of the chimneypieces, pier tables, curtains, china, lamps, rugs, and pattern books. Regardless of the form it took, taste is exactly what the Hills willingly paid so much money to obtain for their Philadelphia house. Lamar developed a sense of style and honed her "sensitivities to the qualities of persons and things"—a key requirement of taste—by keenly observing how other wealthy British and American mercantile families lived in the West End of London.[63] She was thus an asset to both the Hills and their network of relations, because she was able to absorb, and then export, what historian Maurie McInnis calls the "nuanced language of goods, deportment, and taste."[64]

Lamar was by no means an arbiter of taste on the level of someone like Elizabeth Montagu, "Queen of the Bluestockings." Renowned for her discernment in literature and the decorative arts, Montagu was actively involved in shaping her architectural environment and commissioned both Robert Adam and James Stuart for house projects.[65] Women such as Montagu and her friend Elizabeth Vesey consciously arranged their parlor settings in an attempt to direct and influence how visitors at their literary gatherings interacted with one another.[66] Lamar never ran in these aristocratic trendsetting circles of the 1780s, nor did she necessarily, like Montagu, set fashions within her more modest community of acquaintance in London. Yet her interest in material objects and how to display them was akin to Montagu's: she appreciated furnishings for their potential to define a space and set the tone of social gatherings.

The location of chairs placed around the room (whether in intimate twos and threes or a large semicircle), as well as the quantity and method of illumination during an evening card party, contributed not only to the level of formality but also to the guests' sense of comfort and enjoyment; such details inevitably structured how individuals related to one another and to the host. Moreover, beautiful and unique furnishings invited observation—as demonstrated by Susanna Emlen—and facilitated the flow of polite conversation. Although Lamar received no financial gain from her involvement in the Hills' house, she was amply rewarded with the opportunity to demonstrate her sensitivities to beautiful objects and how they functioned within various social situations. For Lamar, taste was the ability to judge the subtleties of fashion, a defining characteristic of social refinement and gentility; by sharing ideas and goods with her family and their network of friends, she was herself able to perform in the polite society of their elite transatlantic merchant world.

That the Hills and Lamar succeeded on some level in creating the kind of home that would communicate the ideals of gentility is attested to by how their friends reacted to the finished product. They commended the architecture, furnishings, and even Henry Hill's performance as host as being "charming," "elegant," "beautiful," "convenient," "genteel," and "polite."[67] Through size, organization, and interior embellishments, Henry, Ann, and Mary constructed a house that was distinctive, and in their minds distinguished, within the architectural landscape of the city. Indeed, 321 South Fourth Street shared a grandeur and cosmopolitan neoclassical language with such a select number of other town houses built before 1800 that it truly became exceptional.[68]

One wonders, however, how the Hills' house may have been viewed by people outside their *sensus communis*, people who did not share either their access to or appreciation for expensive British imports. As Linzy Brekke's essay in this volume demonstrates, goods imported from Europe—and specifically Great Britain—continued to have ambiguous political significance after the Revolution. Brekke relates how George Washington's patriotism and even virtue were questioned when it was believed his inaugural suit was of foreign-made, instead of American-made, cloth.

We can only speculate how such Americans would have reacted to the Hills' house, which proclaimed on a much more massive scale an admiration for British style, innovation, and materials from the moment one approached the threshold.

The fact that the Hills consciously and strategically looked to Lamar's taste, which by its very location was based on the customs and material culture of London, reflects the transitional nature of national society in the early republic. Freed from the nonimportation restrictions that Americans imposed on themselves during the war years, people like the Hills could once again choose whether or not to buy British manufactures. Because of the nascent state of the country's industries, of course, many of the finer things in life—silk or porcelain, for example—were simply available only from Europe in the 1780s. Yet the Hills and their friends who made up their community of interest invariably had a choice when it came to outfitting their houses with tables and chairs or silver tea services; those goods could be acquired locally, yet they nonetheless returned to London with the aide of their proxy shoppers to visit the showrooms of a James Keir, John Bacon, or Robert Kennet.

Although Americans had severed political ties with Great Britain in their contest for independence, they did not necessarily sever their cultural ties; those families with the financial resources and a belief in the civilizing influence of gentility continued to view London as the arbiter of taste and refinement. And where some Philadelphians would have decried a love of luxury and servile dependence on Great Britain when they viewed the Hills' parlor furnishings, others would have seen beauty and respected the family's discernment. In many ways, these three individuals turned designing and decorating domestic space into a social act intended to manifest rank in an international merchant society. According to David Shields, "a social rite served as a semiotic case—a frame that presented certain signs of rank, place, profession, politeness, talent, and beauty to mark those in power."[69] Together, then, the Hills and Lamar used their exclusive access to high-style London design—in their minds the epitome of beauty and politeness—to claim their places within the *sensus communis* and assume leading roles in defining the elite material culture and manners of the new nation.

This essay is based on Amy H. Henderson, "321 South Fourth Street: An Expression of Eighteenth-Century Taste" (master's thesis, Univ. of Delaware, 1999). A Robert Lee Gill Fellowship from the Henry Francis du Pont Winterthur Museum supported the research of this revision. The author would like to thank Bernard L. Herman for his continued guidance on this project. Many thanks are also due to Damie Stillman, Ritchie Garrison, Gretchen Buggeln, and Rebecca Martin for their insightful comments on this material, and to Jeroen van den Hurk for providing new floor plans for the Hill-Physick-Keith House. This essay is dedicated to John H. Fuson, who encouraged me to rediscover the lives and material world of such people as Henry Hill and Mary Lamar.

1. Henry and Ann Hill's house is located at 321 South Fourth Street, between Spruce and Pine streets. Operated today by The Philadelphia Society for the Preservation of Landmarks, it is known as the Hill-Physick-Keith House.
2. Only in recent years have historians of architecture and material culture begun to reevaluate women's agency in the design and decoration of their homes. Often obscured by the laws of coverture and surviving written records, women as designers of their material world have predominantly been overlooked. For further elaboration of the challenges facing historians in determining what roles women held in shopping and provisioning for the home, see the introduction and Ann Smart Martin's essay in this volume. For evidence of women's involvement in architecture and design, see, for example, Neil McKendrick, "Josiah Wedgwood and the Commercialization of the Potteries," in *The Birth of a Consumer Society: The Commercialization of Eighteenth-Century England*, ed. Neil McKendrick, John Brewer, and J. H. Plumb (Bloomington: Indiana Univ. Press, 1982), 100–145; Charles Saumarez Smith, *Eighteenth-Century Decoration: Design and the Domestic Interior in England* (London: Weidenfeld and Nicholson, 1993), 233–36; Amanda Vickery, *The Gentleman's Daughter: Women's Lives in Georgian England* (New Haven and London: Yale Univ. Press, 1998); and Henry Glassie, *Material Culture* (Bloomington: Indiana Univ. Press, 1999), 82–84.
3. Studies of women and architecture in the eighteenth century tend to focus on aristocratic and gentry women. For examples of such studies in Great Britain, see Stella Tillyard, *Aristocrats: Caroline, Emily, Louisa, and Sarah Lennox, 1740–1832* (New York: Farrar, Straus and Giroux, 1994); Dana Arnold, ed., *The Georgian Country House: Architecture, Landscape and Society* (Stroud, UK: Sutton, 1998), chap. 5; Rosemary Baird, *Mistress of the House: Great Ladies and Grand Houses, 1670–1830* (London: Weidenfeld and Nicolson, 2003); and John Cornforth, *Early Georgian Interiors* (New Haven and London: Yale Univ. Press, 2004), chap. 6.
4. David S. Shields, *Civil Tongues and Polite Letters in British America* (Chapel Hill: Univ. of North Carolina Press, 1997), xviii; Anthony Ashley Cooper, third Earl of Shaftesbury, *Characteristics of Men, Manners, Opinions, Times* (London: John Darby, 1711).
5. Although Lamar did not live in the same physical community as the Hills, she entered into their community of interest by sharing her opinions about culture and fashions with her relations in Philadelphia. John Brewer, *The Pleasures of the Imagination: English Culture in the Eighteenth Century* (London: HarperCollins, 1997), 93–94.
6. My use of taste as an agent of social distinction in the American context is informed by Bernard L. Herman's essay in this volume as well as his recent publication, *Town House: Architecture and Material Life in the Early American City, 1780–1830* (Chapel Hill: Univ. of North Carolina Press, 2005); see also David L. Barquist, "The Meaning of Taste for Wealthy Philadelphians, 1750–1800" (master's thesis, Univ. of Delaware, 1981); J. Thomas Savage and Robert A. Leath, "Buying British: Merchants, Taste, and Charleston Consumerism," in *In Pursuit of Refinement: Charlestonians Abroad, 1740–1860*, ed. Maurie McInnis and Angela Mack (Charleston, SC: Gibbes Museum of Art, 1999), 55–64; Richard L. Bushman, *The Refinement of America: Persons, Houses, Cities* (New York: Vintage Books, 1993); Barquist, "'The Honours of a Court' or 'the Severity of Virtue': Household Furnishings and Cultural Aspirations in Philadelphia," in *Shaping a National Culture: The Philadelphia Experience, 1750–1800*, ed. Catherine E. Hutchins (Winterthur, DE: Henry Francis du Pont Winterthur Museum, 1994), 313–34; Shields, *Civil Tongues*; and McInnis, *The Politics of Taste in Antebellum Charleston* (Chapel Hill: Univ. of North Carolina Press, 2005).
7. Steve Rosswurm, "Class Relations, Political Economy, and Society in Philadelphia," in Hutchins, *Shaping a National Culture*, 55; Richard G. Miller, *Philadelphia—The Federalist City: A Study of Urban Politics, 1789–1801* (Port Washington, NY: Kennikat Press, 1976), chap. 2.
8. Stephen Brobeck, "Changes in the Composition and Structure of Philadelphia Elite Groups, 1756–1790" (PhD diss., Univ. of Pennsylvania, 1973), 353–59; Thomas M. Doerflinger, *A Vigorous Spirit of Enterprise: Merchants and Economic Development in Revolutionary Philadelphia* (New York: W. W. Norton, 1986), 15–16; David W. Maxey, "Madeira, Quakerism, and Rebellion: Reviving Henry Hill," *Quaker History* 93 (Fall 2004): 47–75.
9. John Jay Smith, ed., *The Letters of Dr. Richard Hill and his Children, or The History of a Family as Told by Themselves* (Philadelphia: privately printed for the descendants, 1854), x. For an in-depth account of Lamar,

Hill, Bisset and Co., see David Hancock, *Oceans of Wine, Empires of Commerce: Madeira and the Self-Organization of the Emerging Atlantic Economy, 1640–1815* (forthcoming).

10. Thomas Lamar to Henry Hill, 26 Dec. 1772, Edward Wanton Smith Collection, George Dillwyn Papers, Haverford College Quaker Collection, Haverford, Pennsylvania (hereafter E. W. Smith Collection), Additions, 1971, box 5, 51.

11. George Washington offers a famous example of this mismanagement, as he contended with overpriced, broken, and poorly selected goods throughout the 1750s and 1760s. See, for example, Washington to Robert Cary and Co., 28 Sept. 1760, in *The Writings of George Washington*, ed. John C. Fitzpatrick, 39 vols. (Washington, DC: U.S. Government Printing Office, 1931–44), 2:350. For the relationship between American consumers and British merchants in general, see T. H. Breen, "An Empire of Goods: The Anglicization of Colonial America, 1690–1776," *Journal of British Studies* 25, no. 4 (Oct. 1986): 467–99; and Breen, *The Marketplace of Revolution: How Consumer Politics Shaped American Independence* (Oxford: Oxford Univ. Press, 2004).

12. In addition to purchasing goods for her five sisters living in Philadelphia, Lamar shopped for Ann Hill's sister and brother-in-law, Elizabeth Meredith and George Clymer; Ann's brother and sister-in-law, Samuel Meredith and Margaret Cadwalader; and the Hills' friends Samuel and Elizabeth Willing Powel and John and Mary Norris Dickinson. For examples of the purchases, see Mary Lamar to Henry Hill, 20 Feb. 1784, John Jay Smith Papers, Library Company Collection, 9:40, Historical Society of Pennsylvania, Philadelphia (hereafter Smith Papers); Mary Lamar to Henry Hill, 6 Feb. 1785, Smith Papers, 9:103.

13. For examples of Anne Penn's activities as a proxy, see Letters of Anne Allen Penn, 1788–1812, Shippen Family Papers, vol. 33, Historical Society of Pennsylvania (hereafter HSP), and John F. Mifflin Letter Book, 1788–1802, Penn Papers, HSP. For a sketch of John and Anne Allen Penn's furnishings, see Marie G. Kimball, "The Furnishings of Governor Penn's Town House," *Magazine Antiques* 19, no. 5 (May 1931): 374–78; Kimball, "The Furnishings of Lansdowne, Governor Penn's Country Estate," *Magazine Antiques* 19, no. 6 (June 1931): 450–55.

14. Mary Lamar to Henry Hill, 20 Feb. 1784, Smith Papers, 9:40; Lamar to Hill, 11 Aug. 1786, Smith Papers, 9:240.

15. For women's daily provisioning responsibilities, see Claire Walsh's essay in this volume and Vickery, *Gentleman's Daughter*, chap. 5.

16. During their residence in the city, the Lamars lived in at least four town houses: Bedford-row, Holborn (1769–73); 78 Newman Street (1774–88); 74 Newman Street (1788); and 29 Welbeck Street (1789–92). Number 29 Welbeck Street still stands today, though 74 and 78 Newman Street have been destroyed. Rate Books, 1789–1792, St. Marylebone, Wimpole Ward, microfilm reel 23, City of Westminster Archives Center, London; *Kent's London Directory*, 1769 through 1794; *Lowndes Directories*, 1772 through 1787; *A Compleate Guide*, 1768 through 1777.

17. Damie Stillman, *English Neo-Classical Architecture*, 2 vols. (London: A. Zwemmer, 1988), 1:175.

18. Mary Lamar to Henry Hill, 27 July 1786, E. W. Smith Collection, box 2.

19. Saumarez Smith, *Eighteenth-Century Decoration*, 234.

20. Saumarez Smith, *Eighteenth-Century Decoration*, 392, n. 12.

21. Dillwyn temporarily resided in London when accompanying her husband, George, on his Quaker mission. Sarah Dillwyn to Margaret Morris, July 1784, in Smith, *Letters of Dr. Richard Hill*, 249. The survival of either residence is unknown.

22. Neither the drawing Hill sent to London nor the illustrations Lamar sent to Philadelphia are known to survive.

23. In addition to Lamar's attributing the design of the house to both Henry and Ann in her letter of 27 July 1786, two other individuals remarked on Ann's extensive involvement. Hill's sister Hannah Moore wrote that "our H [Henry Hill] is prevailed on to build a house in town. . . . he let me know that it was not his doings, he sayd he could be content to live in the little house they had but that he s[houl]d never have peace if he did not do it, that the lott was b[ough]t with her money, that there was a pretty handsome sum of hers on the way from Nova Scotia & that it must be layd out that way; she's as busy as any undertaker & says she'll take all trouble off him. I thought she had entirely given up all these thoughts, as I heard noth-

ing for so long a time on the subject, & she seemd so quiet and content in their little box, but like an experienced general [she] lay by till forces could be collected." Hannah Moore to Sarah Dillwyn, 24 June 1786, Thomas Stewardson Letters, 1759–1844, HSP. I thank David Maxey for sharing this reference with me. And Sarah Logan Fisher noted in her journal that Ann Hill had planned the house "chiefly to her own taste, & anxiously wished to have accomplished" due to the illness that led to her untimely death. Sarah Logan Fisher, 12 Dec. 1787, Sarah Logan Fisher Journal, 1776–1796, 16:77, HSP (hereafter Fisher Journal).

24. Richard Lamar Bisset to Henry Hill, 1 May 1787, E. W. Smith Collection, Additions, box 1.

25. William and Anne Bingham erected Mansion House on South Third Street, between Spruce and Walnut streets. They hired British architect John Plaw to draw a replica of the Duke of Manchester's London town house (today known as Hertford House, home of the Wallace Collection). The house measured one hundred feet wide and sixty feet deep and, with three stories, was approximately eighteen thousand square feet; it was the largest freestanding house in the city in the 1780s. Like the Hills, the Binghams imported many of the building materials from London, including composition ornament by Mrs. Coade's Manufactory. The house was destroyed by fire in 1847. See Robert C. Alberts, *The Golden Voyage: The Life and Times of William Bingham, 1752–1804* (Boston: Houghton Mifflin, 1969), 158; Allison Kelly, *Mrs. Coade's Stone* (Upton-upon-Severn, UK: The Self Publishing Association, 1990), 287–90; and Damie Stillman, "City Living, Federal Style," in *Everyday Life in the Early Republic*, ed. Catherine E. Hutchins (Winterthur, DE: Henry Francis du Pont Winterthur Museum, 1994), 140–43.

26. Fully articulated neoclassical houses built in Philadelphia after 1786 adhered more closely to the ideals set forth by the Adam brothers and their followers. The Binghams' Mansion House and William Hamilton's The Woodlands, remodeled c. 1788–89, for example, had an assortment of irregularly shaped rooms (circular, oval, square, rectangular), projecting bays, polygonal ends, and floor-to-ceiling bay windows.

27. Sterling M. Boyd, "The Adam Style in America: 1770–1820" (PhD diss., Princeton Univ., 1966), 170–71.

28. Philip Justus, Mutual Assurance Company Policy no. 3670, 15 July 1815, typescript, Philadelphia Historical Commission, Philadelphia (hereafter PHC).

29. Jas. A. Campbell, Mutual Assurance Company Policy no. 11286, 3 Aug. 1868, typescript, PHC.

30. To reach the rest of the second floor from the northeast quarter's second floor (above the mezzanine), one must descend three stairs.

31. For an elaboration on this unusual allocation of servants' space and access to natural light, see Henderson, "321 South Fourth Street," 30–31, and Neil Burton, "The Later Eighteenth-Century Great House" (paper presented at the proceedings of a conference under the joint directorship of Edward Chaney and Malcolm Airs, Department for Continuing Education, Oxford Univ., 10–12 Jan. 1997), 37, 42.

32. Entries, 6 Jan. 1789 and 26 Dec. 1789, Hill Receipt Book, 1788–1793, Smith Papers; 31 Dec. 1795 and 19 June 1797, Hill Receipt Book, 1793–1802, Smith Papers.

33. Sarah Logan Fisher, 12 Dec. 1787, Fisher Journal; Susanna Dillwyn Emlen to William Dillwyn, 23 Oct. 1792, Dillwyn Correspondence, Library Company Collection, HSP (hereafter Dillwyn Correspondence).

34. The fanlight was sent to Philadelphia sometime before March 1787. Robert Bisset to Henry Hill, 4 March 1787, Smith Papers, 10:4.

35. John Sambrook identified the Hills' fanlight as the product of James Keir's factory. Sambrook to Amy Henderson, 9 Oct. 1998.

36. Keir's were known as "Eldorado" fanlights because their ornaments were generally made of a gold-colored alloy and believed not to rust. Alexander Stuart Gray and John Sambrook, *Fanlights* (Washington, DC: American Institute of Architects Press, 1990), 24–25.

37. George Dillwyn, "Wrote extempore by P.D.L . . . y on the Governors appearing much pleased with some new fashion'd large Panes of Glass he had got for his new House," in *Milcah Martha Moore's Book: A Commonplace Book from Revolutionary America*, ed. Catherine La Courrey Blecki and Karin Wulf (University Park, PA: Pennsylvania State Univ. Press, 1997), 190.

38. See, for example, the carved wooden mantels that Samuel and Elizabeth Powel installed in the first-floor front room of their house at 244 South Third Street, now in the collection of the Philadelphia Museum of Art. George B. Tatum notes that several Virginia families imported marble mantels, including William

Byrd II at Westover, George Mason at Gunston Hall, and George Washington at Mount Vernon; Tatum, *Philadelphia Georgian: The City House of Samuel Powel and Some of Its 18th-Century Neighbors* (Middletown, CT: Wesleyan Univ. Press, 1976), 76.

39. Samuel Powel recorded in his ledger that he paid Gideon Villeneuf 17s. 6d. on 18 Aug. 1770, "for freight of a chimney-piece." The exact size and degree of ornamentation on the marble mantel is unknown. Tatum, *Philadelphia Georgian*, 76.

40. Mary Harrison White to Bishop William White, 27 Nov. 1786, reprinted in *Descendants of Col. Thomas White of Maryland, brought down from 1877 to about March 1, 1932*, by William White (Philadelphia, 1932), 165.

41. Mary Lamar to Henry Hill, n.d., in Smith, *Letters of Dr. Richard Hill*, 197.

42. Ann Hill died 11 Dec. 1787. Mary Lamar to Henry Hill, 19 Feb. 1788, in Smith, *Letters of Dr. Richard Hill*, 265.

43. Mary Lamar to Henry Hill, 23 Feb. 1788, Smith Papers, 10:32.

44. Robert Bisset to Mary Lamar, 15 April 1789, Smith Papers, 10:73. Bisset refers to "Bacon the statuary," who is presumably John Bacon the Elder (1740–1799); see Rupert Gunnis, *Dictionary of British Sculptors, 1660–1851*, 2nd ed. (London: Abbey Library, 1968); Margaret Whinney, *Sculpture in Britain, 1530 to 1830* (Baltimore: Penguin Books, 1964).

45. Susanna Dillwyn Emlen to William Dillwyn, 23 Oct. 1792, Dillwyn Correspondence.

46. Each mantel was partially destroyed by vandals in the mid-twentieth century and required extensive conservation. In the 1960s, Regius Milione resculpted all four of the truss figures as well as the central tablet in the dining-room mantel. George Roberts to Wm. H. Watts & Co., 23 Dec. 1965, George B. Roberts Papers, file 2, 1965 correspondence, Hill-Physick-Keith House, HSP. Illustrated here are the only known photographs of the mantels prior to damage.

47. Gunnis, *Dictionary of British Sculptors*, 24–25.

48. Gunnis, *Dictionary of British Sculptors*, 27.

49. Whinney, *Sculpture in Britain*, 168; Kelly, *Mrs. Coade's Stone*, 287–90.

50. Whinney, *Sculpture in Britain*, 168.

51. Susanna Dillwyn Emlen to William Dillwyn, 23 Oct. 1792, Dillwyn Correspondence.

52. Mary Lamar to Henry Hill, n.d., in Smith, *Letters of Dr. Richard Hill*, 197.

53. For an excellent analysis of the role of decorative arts and pleasure, see Mimi Hellman, "Furniture, Sociability, and the Work of Leisure in Eighteenth-Century France," *Eighteenth-Century Studies* 32, no. 4 (1999): 415–45.

54. Robert Kennett, upholder and cabinetmaker, was listed at 67 New Bond Street between 1779 and 1796; Sir Ambrose Heal, *The London Furniture Makers: From the Restoration to the Victorian Era, 1660–1840* (London: B. T. Batsford, 1953), 99.

55. Mary Lamar to Henry Hill, Sept. 1787, Smith Papers, 10:22.

56. Mary Lamar to Henry Hill, 1 July 1789, Smith Papers, 10:78.

57. Richard Campbell, *The London Tradesman* (London: T. Gardner, 1747), 155–77, excerpted in *The Tyranny of Taste: The Politics of Architecture and Design in Britain, 1550–1960*, by Jules Lubbock (New Haven and London: Yale Univ. Press, 1995), 14.

58. Mimi Hellman notes that in eighteenth-century France, the design of furniture often resulted from a collaboration between architect, patron, *ornemaniste*, upholsterer, furniture maker, or dealer. Hellman, "Furniture, Sociability, and the Work of Leisure," 418. Georgiana Darcy drafted "a beautiful little design for a table"; Jane Austen, *Pride and Prejudice*, 1813; repr. in *Jane Austen: The Complete Novels* (New York: Gramercy Books, 1981), 200.

59. Mary Lamar to Henry Hill, 2 Aug. 1789, Smith Papers, 10:91.

60. Lading bill from the ship *Pigou*, 27 Sept. 1789, Henry Hill Folder, Philadelphia Society for the Preservation of Landmarks; Mary Lamar to Henry Hill, n.d. (but before 30 Jan. 1790), Smith Papers, 10:116. Unfortunately, the current whereabouts of the Hills' personal furnishings are unknown.

61. Lubbock, *Tyranny of Taste*, 10.

62. A study of inventory records in the last quarter of the eighteenth century revealed that twenty-three merchants out of a group of eighty-five owned furniture worth £501 in Pennsylvania currency, which was approximately £300 sterling. Doerflinger, *Vigorous Spirit of Enterprise*, 26, n. 14.

63. Shields, *Civil Tongues*, 39.

64. McInnis, *Politics of Taste*, 279.

65. Adam redesigned parts of her home in Hill Street, Mayfair (1766), and Stuart designed and built a new, neoclassical house for Montagu in Portman Square (1775–81). Reginald Blunt, ed., *Mrs. Montagu, "Queen of the Blues": Her Letters and Friendships from 1762 to 1800*, 2 vols. (Boston: Houghton Mifflin, 1923): 1:8, 9, 152.

66. For Montagu's description of an evening at Vesey's, see Montagu to Vesey, Hill Street, London, 13 Nov. 1788, reprinted in Blunt, *Mrs. Montagu*, 58. For the role of furniture as a facilitator of social interaction, see Saumarez Smith, *Eighteenth-Century Decoration*, 233–34, and Baird, *Mistress of the House*, 70–71.

67. Sarah Logan Fisher, 12 Dec. 1787, Fisher Journal; Susanna Dillwyn Emlen to George Dillwyn, 23 Oct. 1792, Dillwyn Correspondence.

68. Comparable town houses that participated in a neoclassical dialogue with 321 South Fourth Street include William and Ann Bingham's Mansion House (1786); Robert and Mary Morris's house on Chestnut Street, called "Morris's Folly" (1796); John and Clementina Ross's house at 22 Pine Street (1789); and George and Martha Washington's presidential mansion at 190 High Street (1768, 1782).

69. Shields, *Civil Tongues*, 143–44.

Leading the Fashion: The Material Culture of London's *Beau Monde*

Hannah Greig

THE CHARACTERIZATION OF London's *beau monde* as matchless masters of fashion is a compelling feature of eighteenth-century commentary. Whether celebrated or despised, the representation of this metropolitan set as the "world of fashion" was commonplace in both pictures and print. Commentators debated the precise criteria for access, but they concurred that members of the *beau monde* were best defined as the "people of fashion" whose material goods, social practices, and cultural preferences were without question "quite the fashion."[1] The linkage between the *beau monde* and fashionability was conspicuous, but what did the accolade of fashion mean, and how was it won?

This essay investigates the interrelationship between fashion and the eighteenth-century elite *beau monde*. Neither the culture of the *beau monde* nor the contemporary concept of fashion has been examined in detail within current historical scholarship. However, as this essay demonstrates, interrogating both can shed new light on status configurations in eighteenth-century England. It might be presumed that, by allowing arrivistes to purchase the required "fashion" symbols, fashionability was a democratizing force challenging traditional social hierarchies. In fact, a study of the practices of the *beau monde* demonstrates how an exclusive elite retained status during a period of considerable sociopolitical change, and that displays of fashion played a major role in its success. The practices of the *beau monde* and eighteenth-century conceptions of fashion were so intertwined that one cannot be brought into focus without a study of the other. On the one hand, then, this essay is concerned with revealing contemporary perceptions of fashion through a case study of the *beau monde*. On the other hand, it is equally concerned with using contemporary definitions and expressions of fashion to understand better the priorities and experiences of the elite *beau monde*.

The fashion process has long preoccupied social theorists. Canonical theoretical studies, such as Roland Barthes's *The Fashion System*, portray fashion as the product of "modernity," a system enabled by capitalism and "mass media" and driven onward by the insatiable desires of the consumer.[2] Other sociological analyses take a longer historical view to compare "premodern" and "modern" experiences of fashion, but they do so in order to track the rhythm of stylistic change and to develop a definitive model of the fashion "cycle."[3] The quest in this literature for an overarching theory overlooks the possibility that alternative interpretations of fashion operated in different historical periods and in different social and cultural contexts.

Within eighteenth-century studies, sociability, politeness, consumption, and luxury have all engrossed historians' attention.[4] The contemporary concept of fashion, however, has been comparatively neglected. Dress history chronicles eighteenth-century clothing, and important surveys by scholars such as Anne Buck and Aileen Ribeiro recount with impressive detail the clothes worn by the Georgian rich and poor.[5] Yet the focus of these studies is restricted to personal attire and does not extend to a history of ideas that wrestles with the meaning of fashion per se.

Despite the absence of an appropriate conceptual framework, social historians of the eighteenth century routinely refer to fashion when analyzing consumer choices and tastes. For example, in his study of contemporary purchasing power, Roy Porter explains that "people did not merely acquire more household goods. Fashions changed, and they invested in furnishings and ornaments which were lighter, more comfortable, more elegant or just simply newer."[6] When used in this way, the implicit (but untested) belief is that fashion as a concept operated, then as now, as a quality solely associated with modishness and the latest style.

By contrast, contemporary usage of the term "fashion" suggests that its meanings were specific to the eighteenth century. From the 1690s onward, a particular etymological connection between "fashion" and the elite *beau monde* can be identified. Indeed, the increased use of terms such as "*beau monde*," as well as "politeness" and "gentility," attests to the new ways in which the social hierarchy was conceptualized by contemporaries in the late seventeenth and early eighteenth centuries.[7] Title, wealth, and family name remained powerful indicators of privilege in many situations. Increasingly, however, social status was also determined by additional criteria more attuned to the requirements of complex, urban communities. "Fashion" was one of the key concepts and status categories to emerge in this environment, and the newly defined *beau monde* became its keeper.

Also described as a "brilliant vortex,"[8] the *beau monde* incorporated the most privileged, prominent characters of eighteenth-century London and was directly associated with the power-brokering political elite.[9] Paradoxically, though, their very prominence has led to their exclusion from social-historical methodologies rooted in the study of non-elite groups. Derived from within this disciplinary tradition, the more recent history of eighteenth-century consumption has retained a marked predilection for the poorer and middling sorts. The existence of a particular elite culture of the *beau monde* is recognized in this literature, but it is only ever cast as the ostentatious "other" against which the middle class rose to sober greatness. Leonore Davidoff and Catherine Hall, for example, expose a shameless late-eighteenth-century "aristocracy" whose leadership qualities of "lavish display and consumption" provided "patent lessons for the middling ranks."[10] Similarly, for Marjorie Morgan, London's fashionable society was the gross exemplar of privilege that respectable professionals opposed.[11]

The drama of middle-class restraint winning out over aristocratic vice is seductive, and it underpins innumerable studies of the eighteenth and nineteenth centuries. However, this narrative rests almost entirely on caricatured portrayals of the *beau monde*'s penchant for the expensive and luxurious. These clichéd representations are taken as evidence of one-dimensional status displays that prioritized wealth and show above all else. Such readings are problematically reductive and seem to presuppose that only the possessions of non-elite groups can have complicated, multiple meanings. Very little attention has been paid to how the elite actually selected goods, or their significance and meanings to members of the *beau monde*.

By considering the material practices of the *beau monde* in detail, it is possible both to develop a more sophisticated understanding of the contemporary concept of fashion and to gain a more detailed appreciation of elite status displays. That lavish spending was not the sum of elite consumer behavior is readily conveyed in contemporary correspondence. This essay uses letters detailing the behavior of members of London's *beau monde* to chart their relationship to a range of goods: from the fixtures and fittings of their homes to the sparkling accessories and elaborate clothes of their wardrobes.[12] These missives reveal the *beau monde* to have been painstaking, not foolhardy, in their consumer choices. They agonized over the smallest detail of dress, anxiously deliberated over appropriate furnishings, and endlessly debated the finer points of consumer choices.

From these sources, it is possible to recover the interpretation and application of particular objects by members of the *beau monde*. In doing so, it becomes clear that it was not only the material characteristics of luxury goods that contributed to their fashionable value. Instead, it was the access to social networks that they communicated that determined their fashionability—criteria that were unpurchasable and inimitable. It was the life of an object after acquisition (its application and use) that warranted its attribution to fashion in the eighteenth century, not necessarily its allure at the point of sale.

"*Beau monde*" was used from the 1690s onward in a range of ways and a multitude of commentaries.[13] Nevertheless, recurring themes are apparent within the rhetoric, which enable the historian to establish the key features of this social group. In particular, the metropolitan nature of the *beau monde* was routinely expressed: the "people of fashion" were designated as those who set the tone of the town. The social community imagined by "town" incorporated those who were free from the daily grind of city professional life, and it included the politicians of Westminster rather than the financiers of St. Paul's. It also defined a specific urban space, delineating those on the west side of the notorious east-west divide, in an enclave from the Strand to Hyde Park, rather than City of London streets from Cheapside to Fleet Street. James Gillray parodies this gulf between London's town and city, positioning the lady of "Cheapside" against her "St James's" counterpart in his 1794 caricature *Following the Fashion* (fig. 65).[14] The divide is similarly made clear in *The Man of Pleasure's Pocket-Book* for 1780, which claimed the *beau monde* "is never to be met with on the eastern side of Temple bar, where the tar of Thames Street and the tallow of Blow-Bladder-Street contaminate the air."[15]

A clear sense of the *beau monde*, and its shadowy membership criteria, can be teased from the correspondence of those either excluded from participation or lobbying for access. Gertrude Savile's emotional diary entries in the 1720s, for instance, disclose her frustration at her inability to infiltrate the ranks of the *beau monde*. The unmarried sister of an affluent baronet and member of Parliament, Savile was related to the famous politician George Savile, first Viscount Halifax, and associated with figures such as the fourth Earl of Chesterfield, Lady Castlemaine, the Duchess of Rutland, and Lady Oxford. In addition, the family owned a vast and lucrative estate in Yorkshire. Thus, Gertrude Savile was theoretically well positioned within the eighteenth-century social hierarchy. Yet access to London's *beau monde* still eluded her. "There was no coming out of my brother's family redy cutt and dry'd a fine woman," she confessed in her diary in September 1721, "it was not possible to be made aqquented with the World . . . [or] be made fitt to converse with the Beau-Mond."[16] Six years later, Savile decided to end her unsuccessful bid for acceptance within fashionable society. A diary entry of 6 November 1727 is saturated with her anguished sense of failure:

> What should I do any more in publick. No! I'll strive no more against the Stream. The World was not for me nor I for the World. I have but two things to choose. One, to show myself a disagreeable and ridiculous figure . . . the other to hide myself and let people invent what they please for reasons for my perticularity. The latter I must choose, I can no longer support the first.[17]

As Savile found to her cost, membership was not determined by rank or wealth. "People of fashion it appears do not earn their designation by reason of birth or

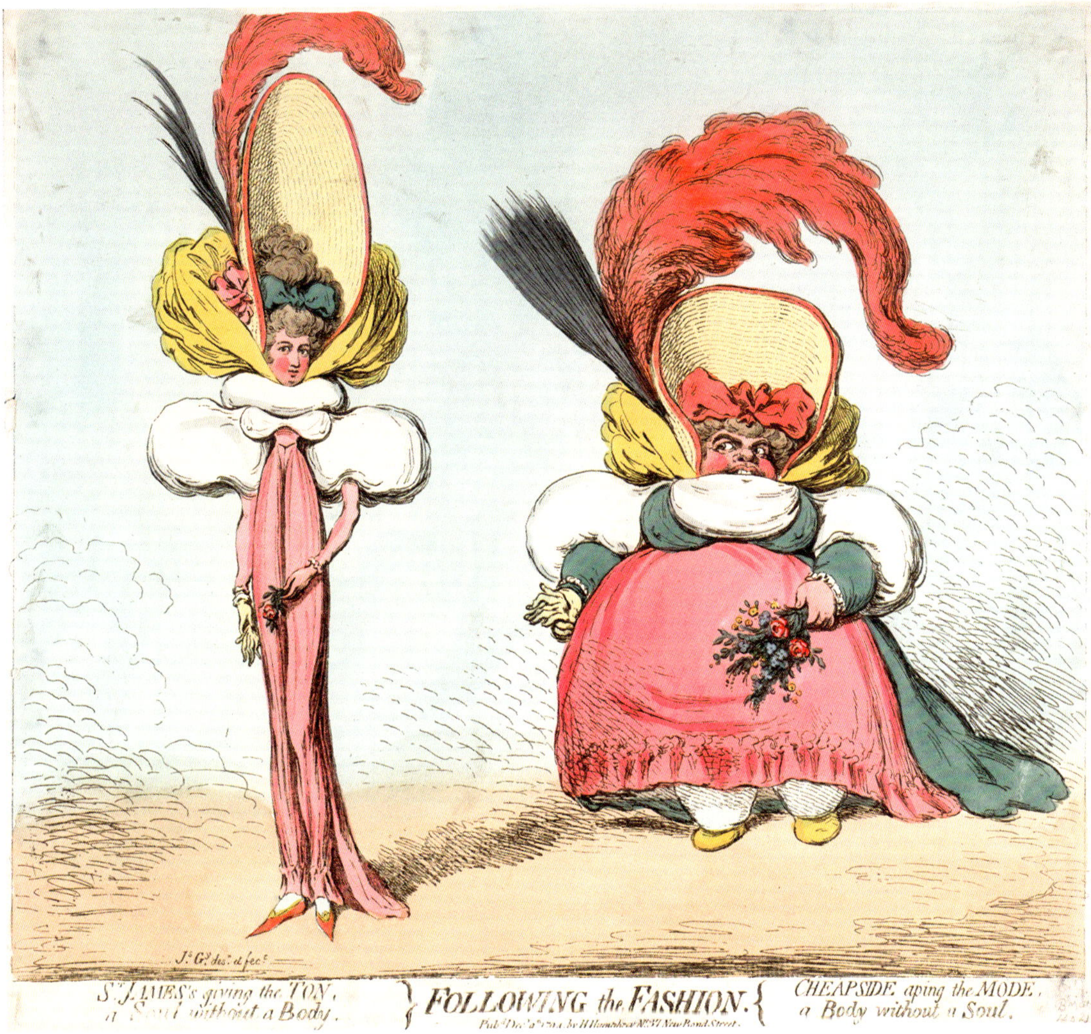

65. James Gillray, *Following the Fashion*, etching with hand color (1794), 12⅞ x 15⅝ in. (32.7 x 39.7 cm), trimmed sheet. Courtesy of The Lewis Walpole Library, Yale University.

fortune," reflected Lord Chesterfield in 1755, "but through a certain je ne scay quoy which other people of fashion acknowledge."[18]

In 1711, the Earl and Countess of Strafford were also struggling aspirants to a fashionable life. The daughter of a wealthy shipbuilder, the countess had a hefty dowry but no inherited title. Her alliance with Thomas Wentworth, formerly Lord Raby and newly created Earl of Strafford, catapulted her into the peerage, but their joint access to the metropolitan *beau monde* was not a given.[19] The Wentworth family was precariously positioned in the new order ushered in by the Glorious Revolution of 1688–89. The Earl of Strafford's mother, Isabella Lady Wentworth, had formerly been a lady of the bedchamber to James II's queen. Her husband was a nephew of the royalist first Earl of Strafford, who was chief adviser to Charles I and was executed in 1641. Such associations were treated with suspicion in the early eighteenth century, when the ruling political elite sought to defend the Whig-engineered succession of William III and Mary, the reorganization of the relationship between Crown and Parliament, and the looming shift to a Hanoverian dynasty.

With the financial backing of his marriage, however, Thomas Wentworth, Earl of Strafford, sought to enhance his family's status and gain a foothold in the newly configured sociopolitical landscape of early-eighteenth-century London. The Straffords initially met with some success. Appointed ambassador to The Hague in 1711, the earl enjoyed an important political profile, and his wife was entertained at the social resorts and houses of elite London. But their success was short-lived. An attempt to impeach the earl in 1715 forced his retreat to the family's Yorkshire seat. Testifying to the scale of the disgrace is the lack of surviving correspondence after this date until the earl's death in 1739. Nevertheless, the letters written by the countess to the earl prior to this provide a rare illumination of the strategies deployed to infiltrate the *beau monde* and attain a fashionable status.

The Straffords' initial London experiences reveal that a broad array of material goods was included in fashion's armory. For the newly wed couple, establishing a suitable marital home in London was crucial to their bid for a metropolitan profile, and their letters are replete with references to fixtures, fittings, furnishings, and a multitude of other household matters. They plumped for an impressive house in the eminently exclusive St. James's Square, an area of London favored by the *beau monde* throughout the century.[20] Soon after their wedding, the earl left town to fulfill diplomatic duties in The Hague while Anne, Countess of Strafford, shouldered the responsibility for furnishing their new residence.

The redecoration of their new house took over a year to complete, and the suite of rooms on the first floor—the "best" bedroom, drawing room, and dining room—was the primary focus of the countess's efforts. Selecting goods made from expensive materials, and incorporating the family crest on most objects, she did not shy away from flashy shows of rank and wealth. However, her correspondence with her husband also reveals that her choices were determined by concerns that extended beyond such blunt assertions of status. Significantly, the countess's letters communicate the great care taken to decorate their home according to "the fashion," with the aim of warranting their inclusion in the *beau monde*. At the same time, she proved equally adept at identifying those who made inappropriate choices in their material display. Writing to her husband in December 1712, the countess confidently reported,

I wonder Mr Marshall can talk of his great living here, for they had a very indifferent Lodging in St James's Street & the house was kept the Nastiest I ever see a House . . . & she sat in the first room with the Cole fire and Tallow candles which I know was made a great jest on.[21]

The Marshalls had failed to make the grade on a number of counts. A house in St. James's Street put them alongside—but not within—the most fashionable London locale of St. James's Square. Moreover, their use of smoky tallow candles and a coal fire, rather than the more expensive wax and wood, exposed their ignorance of the material world of London's elite.

Far from the spontaneous, excessive consumption shown in caricatures, the countess favored slow, strategic decision making. She routinely used her presence in London and her carefully gleaned observations of the fashionable world to explain her decorative choices to the earl, as well as to negotiate and demand their conformity to the *beau monde*'s apparently shared material culture. In 1712, for example, she claimed that "the round sconces you speak of for Chimneys are quite out of fashion for there is a sort they now make for Chimneys of a particular pattern which if you'll have I can give directions"[22] (fig. 66). The countess's letters go on to reveal that, for her, the fashion in furnishings was determined not from discussions with designers, reference to pattern books, or visits to suppliers. Instead, she closely observed the styles favored by other members of the *beau monde*, then sought to display her own urban networks by replicating them.

When commissioning new silver lighting equipment, she turned first to the advice of her new neighbor the Countess of Portland. "I see Lady Portland yesterday who told me Lord Portland had some Sconces now made the handsomest she ever see & she will borrow won of them for me to show Mr Shales [the Straffords' household steward]."[23] However, the Countess of Strafford did not rely on a single source; she extended her search further. Updating her husband, she reported that

now the Queen has had some new [sconces] made which I see & they are very handsom they are looking glass in the midle & silver round about & the Seat for the Candle are Silver. . . . I was last week to see the Duke of Marlboroughs house which is extremely fine, they have great Branches for the midle of the rooms in imitation of Plate in wood silver'd or Gilded over & they look very well, now if you have not won of Silver I should think won of them for the midle of our great dining room would doe very well for there must be won of some sort or other.[24]

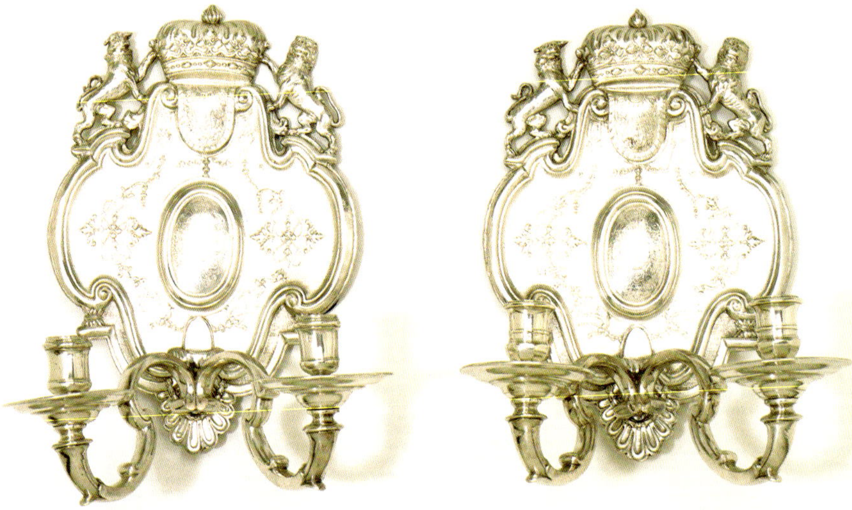

66. Engraved silver sconces, engraved by John Boddington, hallmarked 1710–11. V&A Images / Victoria and Albert Museum. Made for William Herbert, second Marquess of Powis (1667–1745), these sconces are engraved with his arms and completed in the same year as those commissioned by the Straffords.

It was not only during her hunt for sconces that the countess investigated the currency of particular styles among other elite figures. When commissioning other furnishings, her letters are similarly packed with comparisons. For example, when the Earl of Strafford sent her two japanned cabinets in 1712, she had frames made by "the man who did them at Montague House and at the Duke of Marlboroughs which are by much the neatest I ever see."[25] The countess also bought matching tables "done by the same man [for] he has don all for the Dutchess of Marlborough, the Dutchess of Montagu and now is doing for Lady Massam." And when trying to convince her husband to commission a very handsome "dish of plates and covers," she assured him that "they are very much used, the Duke of Somerset has won, Lord Hallifax, the Duke of Kent, Lord Portland and a great many more just made."[26]

The Countess of Strafford's campaign for urban status says much about the meaning of fashionability and also about the nature of the *beau monde*. To begin with, historians have strained to link stylistic change to political allegiance, fixing particular aesthetic preferences to particular political agendas.[27] While this does not deny the potential for material displays to convey politicized identities, it is striking that the Countess of Strafford's role models of fashionability crossed political and court-related divisions. The Marlboroughs, for example, were major political power brokers in the early eighteenth century. Formerly the court favorite, the Duchess of Marlborough was estranged from the monarch at the time of the Countess of Strafford's visit, had left her court post as groom of the stole, and was effectively presiding over an opposition court at Marlborough House. A staunch supporter of the Marlboroughs, the Whig Lord Halifax was similarly out of favor with the queen. Lady Masham (referred to as "Massam" by the Countess of Strafford) had usurped the Duchess of Marlborough as the queen's confidant, and the Duchess of Somerset had replaced her as the groom of the stole. In their political conduct, the Straffords backed the court Tories and opposed the Marlboroughs.[28] The Countess of Strafford's letters describe the "spleen and mallis" with which she was met by the Duchess of Marlborough and her daughter, the Duchess of Montagu. She accepted invitations only to assemblies that Lady Masham hosted, never attending those at Marlborough House.[29] Though shunning their company, the countess was nonetheless happy to include the Marlboroughs and their allies in her search for the signifiers of fashion.

That the Countess of Strafford's quest for fashionability also encompassed Queen Anne and her court constitutes a further characteristic of the eighteenth-century *beau monde*. It is widely accepted that the influence of the royal court was in abeyance after the Glorious Revolution and was weighed down by successive financial and political constraints over the following century. Elite authority and cultural leadership flourished, it has been presumed, precisely because of the court's decline and stagnation.[30] However, the Countess of Strafford's attentiveness to courtly style is suggestive of a more complicated pattern than current historiography allows. The often-unchallenged social and cultural authority of earlier royal courts was a thing of the past, but the court remained an influential and powerful arena. For London's *beau monde*, attendance at court and a familiarity with court etiquette were essential. Far from being the arbiter of their social status, though, the court had become just one of a number of spheres in which a fashionable identity was cultivated.

Besides the Countess of Strafford's search for sconces, this reformed relationship with the court was played out through dress. Descriptions of clothing and recommendations for dress styles, fabrics, colors, and trimmings are abundant in accounts of the *beau monde*, with court dress standing out as a particular preoccupation. Despite being worn infrequently and often purchased new each year, court dress was one of the most expensive items in any *beau monde* wardrobe (fig. 67). The Countess of Strafford confessed in 1712 that "indeed it cost me a great deal of mony," and she quoted £100 as the cost of trimmings and velvet. Other sets of accounts illuminate similar expenditure on court dresses. In 1752, Elizabeth, Duchess of Hamilton, spent just over £100 on silks and trimmings for a court dress.[31] Lady Louisa Stuart

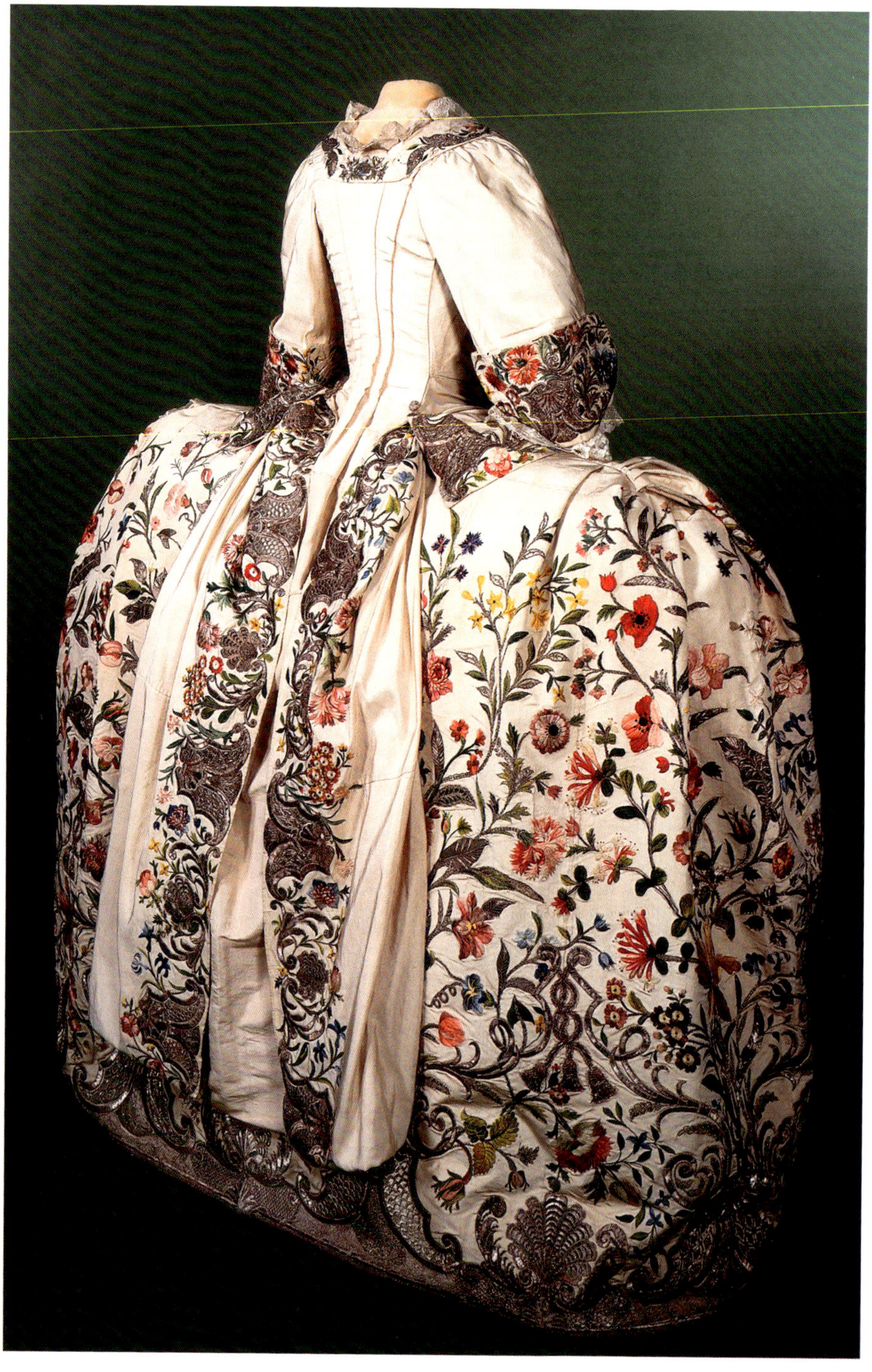

67. Silk embroidered court dress, 1740–45. V&A Images / Victoria and Albert Museum.

maintained that a court dress for "a Birthday" could easily cost three times as much as a regular ball dress, citing £70 for the former and £24 for the latter.[32]

Planning attire for a court celebration was a lengthy process. Anne, Countess of Strafford, began preparations four months in advance, commissioning her husband to get some suitable material from Holland. In the meantime, she scoured London for a "Gold Trimming which everybody will allow to be the finest they ever see."[33] The most important accessories were the jewels that would adorn herself and her outfit. In December 1711, the countess anxiously requested that her husband "send me over the Diamonds for the Tops of the earrings & the won diamond that is the same of my ring."[34] For the mantua itself, the countess decided she would "have all Lady Wentworths diamonds," which she designed "to put in Loops all round the edge of ye manto & upon the Sleeves & some in my hare"—a plan that took her and her sister-in-law Lady Betty Wentworth two days to complete.[35] Their effort paid off. Just before the celebrations, the earl's mother reassured him that "there will not be one there at court will make a better show than y[ou]r d[ea]r Spous."[36] After the event, the countess unblushingly confessed to her brilliant splendor, "'twas allowed I had the most jewells of anybody there & the Queen told me I was very fine"[37] (figs. 68, 69).

The significance of jewelry is equally pronounced in other descriptions. In 1712, the Countess of Strafford described Lady Pawlet's appearance at a wedding, noting that she "was in all her fine true Lover Knots of Diamonds set in as much Silver as would make a pare of Candlesticks."[38] In February 1742, Horace Walpole described a masquerade with "five hundred persons" and "all the jewels of London."[39] At another masquerade, in 1773, Catherine Stapleton emphasized the "profusion of Pearl and Diamonds" when describing the appearance of Lady Chatham's niece.[40]

Why, then, were jewels privileged in this way? Contemporary portraiture suggests the scintillating show they guaranteed. For example, arrays of gems were carefully depicted in Allan Ramsay's portrait of Queen Charlotte (fig. 70). Undoubtedly, whether passed down through generations or purchased new, they symbolized lineage or wealth or both. However, contemporary descriptions also reveal that when worn by the *beau monde*, jewels conveyed more specific meanings linked to assessments of urban status.

The origin of jewels was crucial. For her court spectacle, the Countess of Strafford wore her own diamonds and also those belonging to her new mother-in-law, Lady Wentworth. Commenting on a later court function of 1725, Mary Thynne of Longleat, Wiltshire, set out in detail the various aspects of the court dresses worn:

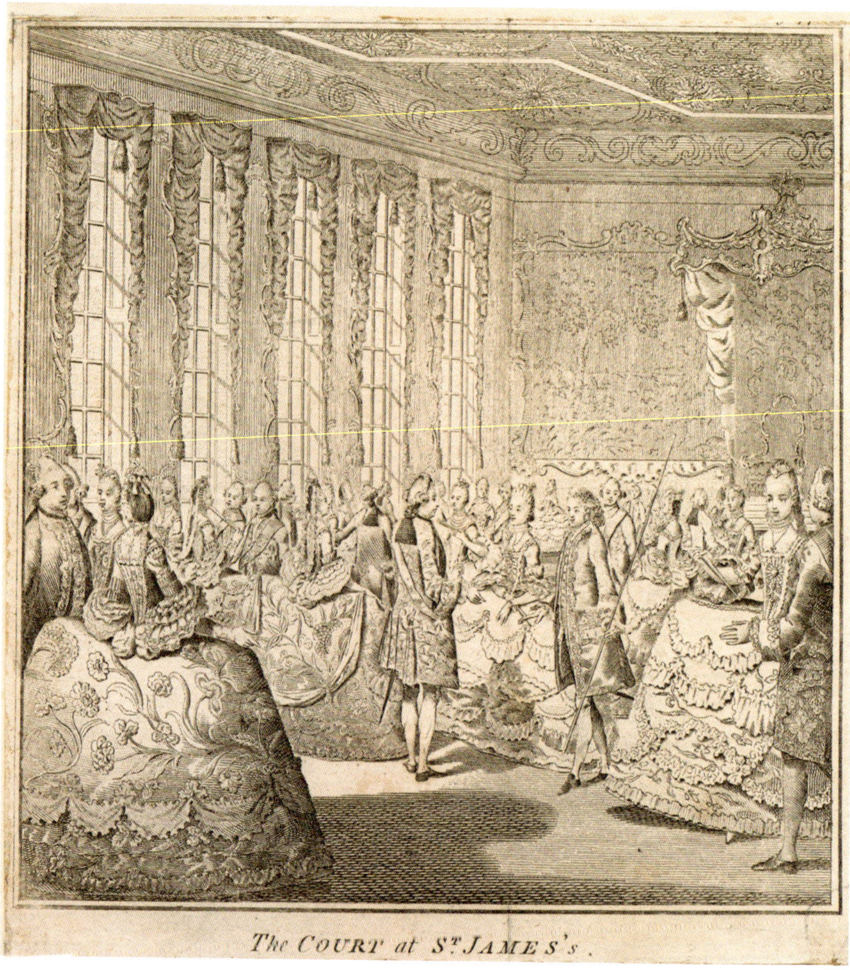

68. Artist unknown, *The Court at St. James's*, etching and engraving (1766), 6¼ x 6 in. (15.8 x 15.2 cm), sheet. Courtesy of The Lewis Walpole Library, Yale University.

My Lady Weymouth had on a gold stuff embroidered with green, and green and gold small knots, and a head of three pounds a yard and her diamond earrings and pearl necklace. Lady Carteret had a blue satin embroidered with gold and silks and blue and silver small knots and a head of four pounds a yard, and her own diamond necklace and Lady Weymouth's cross and a pair of three-dropped earrings borrowed of the jeweller and a buckle that the dowager C gave her since she came to town; . . . Lady Worsley had a pink coloured flowered satin. . . . She had her own upper stones set transparent and three drops and string of the jewelers and my cross and her own buckles

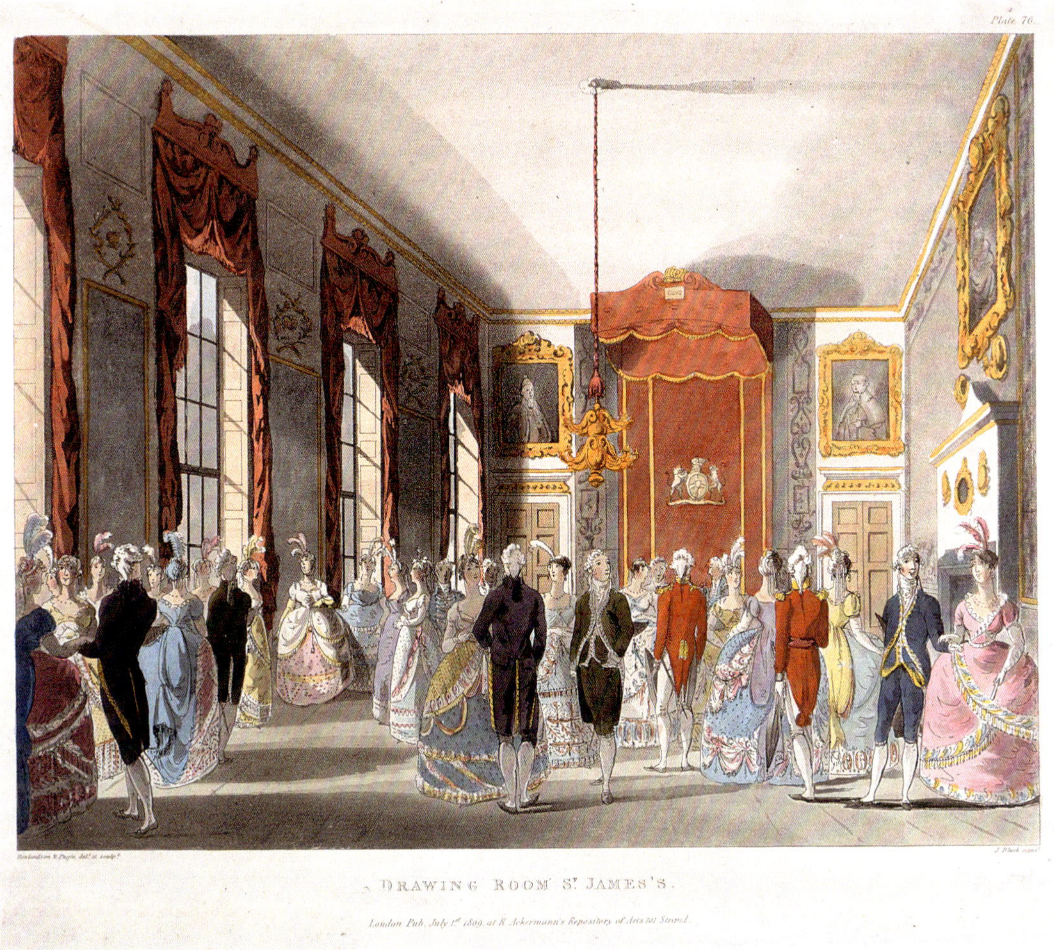

69. John Bluck, *Drawing Room, St. James's*, aquatint hand colored (1809), 7⅞ x 10¼ in. (20 x 26 cm). Yale Center for British Art, Paul Mellon Collection. Photo: Richard Caspole, Yale Center for British Art.

> and pink and silver small knots. . . . My sister had a cherry and silver of forty shillings a yard and a head of 47 shillings a yard and cherry and silver small knots; and three-dropped earrings and cross and her [loops] made a bunch of five diamonds for her hair and girdle buckle.[41]

As well as recording the cost of the materials used in the dresses, this description charts the movement of sets of jewelry between different figures. That Mary Thynne listed the origin of the jewelry implies that she interpreted the attributed relationships as part of the display.

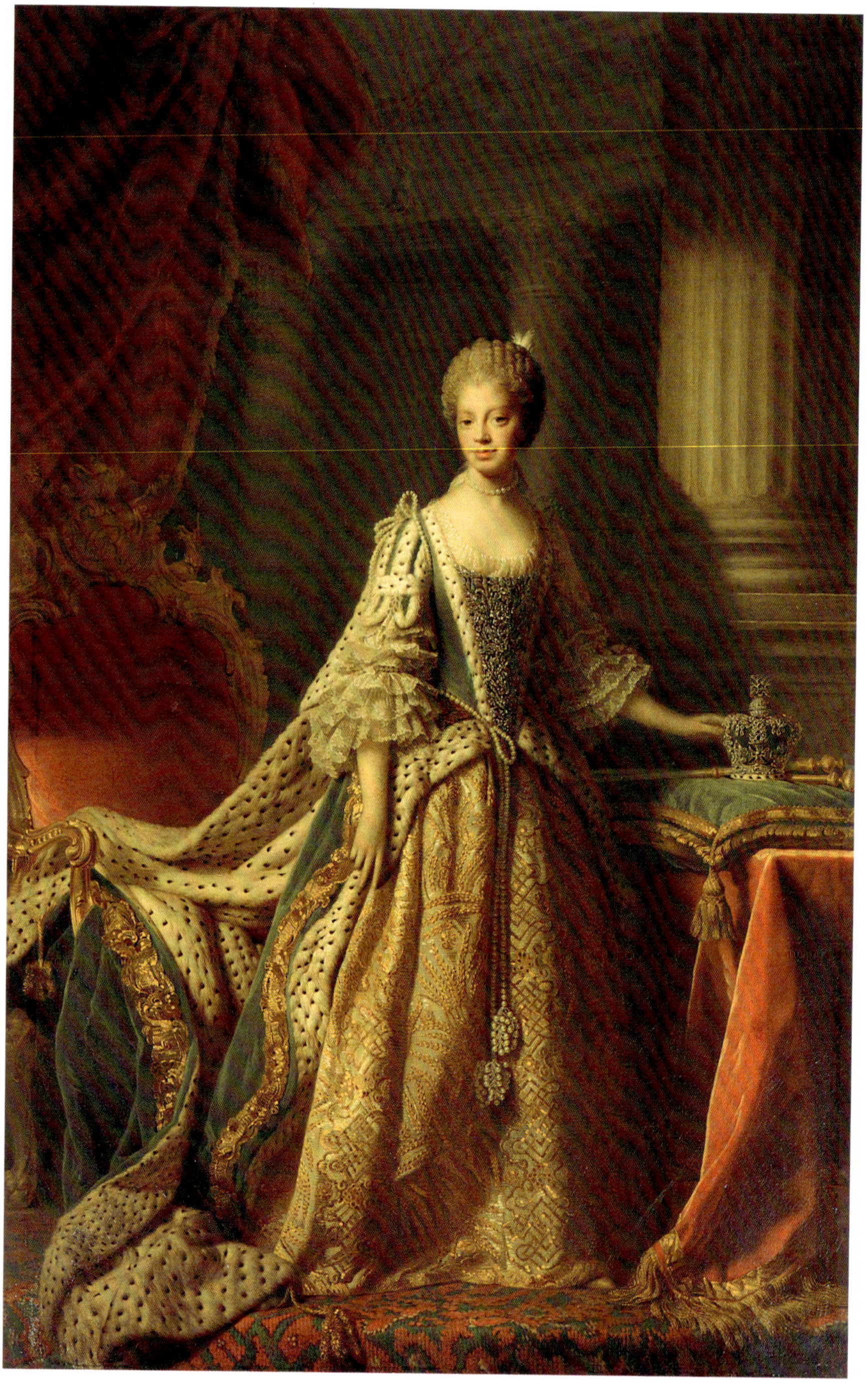

70. Allan Ramsay, *Queen Charlotte*, oil on canvas (1761–62), 98 x 63½ in. (248.9 x 161.3 cm). The Royal Collection © 2006, Her Majesty Queen Elizabeth II.

The gift and loan of jewels appears as common practice within the *beau monde*. Precious gems circulated between family members and among fashionable acquaintances, and their associations were advertised when the item was worn.[42] The display of an item given or lent by a fashionable figure broadcast the wearer's fashionable contacts. The Duchess of Marlborough's strategic distribution of her jewelry, for instance, testifies to its potential to represent networks. The Countess of Strafford reported in 1712 that, on leaving town, the Duchess of Marlborough had "given a great many of her dear friends Diamond rings," eventually giving away "in jewells to the value of 6000£" with "none of her Whigg Friends but she had given Jewels of considerable value."[43] In 1716, Lady Cowper indicated that it was an obligation to display connections, rather than a desire for tinseled adornment, that motivated her to wear Madame Gouvernet's emerald necklace to a court birthday: "I accepted rather because it was offered me, and I was afraid of disobliging her, than to make myself fine (for I don't care one Farthing for setting myself out)."[44] Regardless of whether Lady Cowper was accurately relaying her motivations or trying to excuse her excess, the implication that connections were revealed when jewels sparkled is unmistakable.

The importance of confirming networks through dress and accoutrements continued throughout the century. The marking out of membership of the *beau monde* in this way is suggested in Lady Louisa Stuart's descriptions of the celebrations following George III's recovery from ill health. Men attending a Windsor ball were required to appear in the "Kings Hunt" uniform. Ladies wore deep blue dresses trimmed with scarlet and gold, with diamond buckles, which "by the Queens direction [were] to be from Mrs Beauvais only." White's Club also had a celebration ball with a uniform of "white sattin body and petticoat, with a white and gold belt and white and gold bands around the arm," a cap with a "white satin with 'God save the King' upon it in gold spangles, and four very high feathers on the other side." This dress had to be bought from "one of three milliners whom their Graces of Rutland, Gordon and Chatham" appointed.[45] Not only would considerable capital have been required to keep up with these displays, but also a knowledge of the correct colors was necessary, as was information from the patronesses regarding the use of specific milliners.

The relationship this suggests between leading figures in the *beau monde* and certain retailers was certainly significant. However, the fount of fashion information was clearly the patroness, not the producer. This is confirmed by the experiences of those excluded from the *beau monde* who, rather than receiving instructions from such patronesses, relied on retailers for details of what constituted "the fashion." That they could not penetrate the core of fashionability is made plain by the frequently faulty intelligence they received. For example, appearing at court in 1781, Mary

Grantham (eldest daughter of Jemima, Marchioness Grey) was rather shocked to discover that there "were chiefly plain satins trimmed with gauze and foils . . . but there were not so many of those Silks as Mr King [a supplier] had represented as being bespoke."[46] Thus, while no official sumptuary laws were in place in eighteenth-century Britain, the *beau monde* constructed an exclusive identity through dress, using insider knowledge and accessories to convey membership and consolidate networks. The cost of dress placed this fashionable identity beyond the reach of most, but their strategic display of the networks constituted a further level of exclusivity that could never be purchased over the counter.

From the 1740s, dictionaries attempted to elucidate the complex contemporary application of the term "fashion." Suggestively, those listing "*beau monde*" defined it as the "world of fashion" and interpreted "fashion" as indicative of "rank, state or dignity."[47] A study of elite practices certainly reveals that fashion functioned as a powerful determinant of social status and identity. For the *beau monde*, however, fashionability was not achieved through modish trendsetting. The circulation of mass-produced goods did not fuel it, and the mass of the population would never attain it. Suppliers, capitalizing on a thriving economy and burgeoning marketplace, did not dictate it. Moreover, though often expressed by expensive goods, fashionability was not gained by financial show alone. Instead, it was the currency that underpinned elite networks and alliances, and the substance of group identity. Fashion was a reformulation of rank, as well as a fiercely defended expression of the *beau monde*'s self-proclaimed superiority.

The interrelationship of the *beau monde* and fashion, and the concomitant association between fashion, elite identity, and status, has far-reaching implications for existing historical models. Scholars of the eighteenth century often allude to the potential of goods to challenge social hierarchies, and they revere the period as one of democratizing material change. Classic interpretations of consumption practices advocated a "trickle-down" or emulative model, in which trends were established at the top of the hierarchy and then, as living standards rose or producers circulated cheap imitations, aped by aspirants and gradually passed down the social chain.[48] More recently, this formula has been widely discredited by historians who, emphasizing the multiple meanings of possessions, have insisted that goods can be purchased and used for reasons other than mechanical emulation. All the same, material goods continue to be interpreted as important agents in the "rise" of the middling sort in the eighteenth century. Daniel Roche's study of clothing in *ancien régime* France positions material practices at the heart of the French Revolution, arguing that clothing was used to erode long-standing hierarchies.[49] In British history, the supposedly luxurious and excessive displays of the eighteenth-century elite are portrayed as a red flag to the virtuous middle-class bull, rousing the beast into action. In his important synthesis of eighteenth-century culture, Paul Langford argues that it was material possessions that enabled the newly propertied classes to renegotiate the established hierarchy. In Langford's thesis, accumulated assets empowered new groups:

> Propertied people trailed their possessions before the gaze, fascinated, awed, resentful, of the unpropertied people. . . . They also flaunted them in the face of their own kind, anxiously measuring them against the visible assets of their competitors.[50]

As we have seen, however, these analyses do not accommodate the realities of fashion within the *beau monde*. In 1778, and with tongue firmly in cheek, Lady Mary Grey maintained that fashionability was simple. "If your cap is but in the fashion," she claimed, "then you may be as much or as little of a goose as you please."[51] A study of the material practices of the *beau monde* demonstrates that obtaining goods "in the fashion" was considerably more difficult than might be presumed.

Fashion, in this sense, must also be read as a creative response to the changing conditions of elite existence. To begin with, the *beau monde* was itself a new development. The internal ordering of the peerage, the meaning of titles, and the balance of power between elite and court had all been recast in the turbulent years of the late seventeenth and early eighteenth centuries. The rapid growth of urban spaces had challenged the preeminence of the country seat and called for alternative parades of status in different spheres. Demonstrations of social position through land ownership, wealth, rural paternalism, hospitality, and service to the Crown were no longer sufficient. An annual Parliament, established for the first time in the 1690s, bolstered the role of the metropolis as an alternative forum for status configuration. New indicators of privilege and new sociocultural qualities were required, and the *beau monde* comprised those adept at surviving in this new environment.

The status of fashion as the *lingua franca* of this new territory is made clear by the striking linkage between the *beau monde* and fashionability. A study of the relationship between the two brings the nature of eighteenth-century elite urban life into focus. Fashion cut a new path through the arenas of elite authority. It retained the sociocultural significance of the court—for example, through the prioritization of court dress and reference to courtly style. At the same, however, it limited the reach and power of the monarchy in ways consonant with the new realities of parliamentary and constitutional rule. The Crown no longer dictated fashion. Rather, fashionability lay in the gift of the *beau monde*, for whom the court was only one of a range of important spheres of operation.[52] Like "politeness," fashion could transcend potentially dangerous political schisms, while simultaneously distinguishing the elite who held political power (whether in government or opposition) from a broader urban group who did not. This nexus of fashion and the *beau monde* in the eighteenth century countered the anonymizing tendencies of urban life by distinguishing groupings of readily identifiable personages and stigmatizing interlopers. Contemporaries defined this grouping as the *beau monde*, and the *beau monde* in turn defined a particular construction of fashion.

My thanks to Penelope Corfield, Inge Daniels, Frances Harris, Miles Ogborn, Giorgio Riello, John Styles, and Susan Whyman for their valuable comments and assistance with my research on the *beau monde*. I am particularly indebted to Amanda Vickery for her inspiring supervision of my doctorate and ongoing support. I am grateful to the British Library and the Bedfordshire and Luton Archives and Records Service for permission to consult and quote from their manuscripts.

1. Published commentary on the *beau monde* throughout the century was prolific, varied in its forms and wide-ranging in its conclusions. See, for example, George Farquhar, *The Constant Couple: Or a Trip to the Jubilee* (London: Printed for Ralph Smith and Bennet Banbury, 1700), especially 19; *The Beau Monde or the Pleasures of St James's a New Ballad* (1730); *A View of the Beau Monde, or Memoirs of a Celebrated Coquetilla* (London: Printed for A. Dodd . . . and J. Jolyffe . . . , 1731); Lord Chesterfield's analysis of a fashionable identity in *The World by Adam Fitz-Adam* (pseud.), no. 151 (London, 20 Nov. 1755); and *The Man of Pleasure's Pocket-Book or the Bon Vivant's Vade Mecum for the year 1780, being the Universal Companion in Every Line of Taste, Gallantry and Haut Ton* (London: Printed for S. Bladon . . . , 1780), especially 144–46. From the mid-eighteenth century, dictionaries also offered definitions of the term "*beau monde*"; see, for example, Henry Fox, *A New Dictionary in French and English* (London: Printed for J. Nourse, and S. Hooper, 1769), and *A Dictionary of the English Language*, 4th ed. (London: W. Peacock, 1794).
2. Roland Barthes, *The Fashion System*, trans. Matthew Ward and Richard Howard (London: Jonathan Cape, 1985). The association between "fashion" and "modernity" is challenged by Jennifer Craik, *The Face of Fashion: Cultural Studies in Fashion* (London: Routledge, 1993), especially 5–10.
3. Alfred Louis Kroeber and Jane Richardson, *Three Centuries of Women's Dress Fashions: A Quantitative Analysis* (Berkeley: Univ. of California Press, 1940).
4. John Sekora, *Luxury: The Concept in Western Thought, Eden to Smollett* (Baltimore and London: Johns Hopkins Univ. Press, 1977); Ann Bermingham and John Brewer, eds., *The Consumption of Culture, 1600–1800: Image, Object, Text* (London: Routledge, 1995); John Brewer, *The Pleasures of the Imagination: English Culture in the Eighteenth Century* (London: HarperCollins, 1997); Paul Langford, *A Polite and Commercial People: England 1727–1783* (Oxford: Oxford Univ. Press, 1998); Maxine Berg and Helen Clifford, eds., *Consumers and Luxury: Consumer Culture in Europe, 1650–1850* (Manchester: Manchester Univ. Press, 1999); Susan E. Whyman, *Sociability and Power in Late-Stuart England: The Cultural World of the Verneys, 1660–1720* (Oxford: Oxford Univ. Press, 1999).
5. Anne Buck, *Dress in Eighteenth-Century England* (London: B. T. Batsford, 1979); Aileen Ribeiro, *The Art of Dress: Fashion in England and France, 1750–1820* (New Haven and London: Yale Univ. Press, 1995). For a French comparison, see Daniel Roche, *The Culture of Clothing: Dress and Fashion in the Ancien Régime*, trans. Jean Birrell (Cambridge: Cambridge Univ. Press, 1994). The most recent studies offer new cultural approaches; see David Kuchta, *The Three-Piece Suit and Modern Masculinity: England 1550–1850* (London and Berkeley: Univ. of California Press, 2002), and Susan Vincent, *Dressing the Elite: Clothes in Early Modern England* (Oxford: Berg, 2003).

6. Roy Porter, *English Society in the Eighteenth Century* (London: Penguin Books, 1990), 219. Historians often cited fashion as a key force behind social emulation, in the demand-led economic model presented in work by Neil McKendrick and others; see Neil McKendrick, John Brewer, and J. H. Plumb, eds., *The Birth of a Consumer Society: The Commercialization of Eighteenth-Century England* (London: Europa Publications, 1982). These studies were strongly influenced by Thorstein Veblen's *Theory of the Leisure Class: An Economic Study in the Evolution of Institutions* (New York: Macmillan, 1899). More recently, historians have voiced increasing suspicions of emulation as a sole motivation for consumption and discredited some of McKendrick's findings. See, for example, Maxine Berg, "New Commodities, Luxuries and Their Consumers in Eighteenth-Century England,' in Berg and Clifford, *Consumers and Luxury*, 63–69.
7. Penelope J. Corfield, "Class by Name and Number in Eighteenth-Century Britain," *History* 72 (1987): 38–61.
8. *Man of Pleasure's Pocket Book*, 146.
9. Hannah Greig, "The Beau Monde and Fashionable Life in Eighteenth-Century London, c. 1688–1800" (PhD thesis, Royal Holloway, Univ. of London, 2003).
10. Leonore Davidoff and Catherine Hall, *Family Fortunes: Men and Women of the English Middle Class, 1780–1850*, rev. ed. (2002), 21–22.
11. Marjorie Morgan, *Manners, Morals and Class in England, 1774–1858* (London: Macmillan, 1994), 56.
12. Susan Vincent's important new study of early-modern elite dress uses personal narratives to rethink the role of clothing in contemporary culture; see Vincent, *Dressing the Elite*, especially 79 and 8, 47–48.
13. The earliest use found by the author is in Langbaine Gerard, *An Account of the English Dramatick Poets* (Oxford: Printed by L. L. for G. West and H. Clements, 1691), 406, which noted that the death of Katherine Philips was "to the regret of all the beau monde in general." I am grateful to Brian Cowan for this reference. In 1705, Lord Raby, later Earl of Strafford, referred to the "beau monde" when describing the London society based abroad. James J. Cartwright, ed., *The Wentworth Papers, 1705–1739: Selected from the Private and Family Correspondence of Thomas Wentworth* (London: Wyman, 1883), 137. The *Oxford English Dictionary* defines "beau monde" as "fashionable world" and cites its common usage between 1714 and 1823.
14. This juxtaposition appears in another anonymous print of the same year, *St James's St Giles's* (1794), Lewis Walpole Library Digital Collection, 794.1.0.4.
15. *Man of Pleasure's Pocket Book*, 146.
16. Gertrude Savile, diary entry, Sept. 1721, in *Secret Comment: The Diaries of Gertrude Savile, 1721–1757*, ed. A. Saville (Kingsbridge, UK: Kingsbridge History Society, 1997), 32.
17. Savile, diary entry, 6 Nov. 1727, in Saville, *Secret Comment.*
18. Lord Chesterfield, *The World by Adam Fitz-Adam* (pseud.), no. 151 (London: Printed for R. and J. Dodsley, 20 Nov. 1755), 51.
19. Thomas Wentworth, the third son of Sir William Wentworth, inherited the title of Lord Raby on his father's death; after completing a series of successful diplomatic missions, he was later made Earl of Strafford. Cartwright, *Wentworth Papers*, introduction.
20. Greig, "Beau Monde," 98 and appendix 2, "Fashionable Residences Database."
21. Countess of Strafford to the Earl of Strafford, 8 April 1712, British Library (hereafter BL), Add. MSS 22226, fol. 135.
22. Countess of Strafford to the Earl of Strafford, 23 July 1712, BL, Add MSS 22226, fol. 181.
23. Countess of Strafford to the Earl of Strafford, 15 Aug. 1712, BL, Add. MSS 22226, fol. 195. The reference is to Henry Bentinck, second Earl of Portland, and his wife, Elizabeth Noel. The Earl of Portland had succeeded his father in 1709, and he was soon to be elevated to a dukedom (1715).
24. Countess of Strafford to the Earl of Strafford, 29 Aug. 1712, BL, Add. MSS 22226, fol. 203.
25. Countess of Strafford to the Earl of Strafford, 26 Dec. 1712, BL, Add. MSS 22226, fol. 254.
26. Countess of Strafford to the Earl of Strafford, 19 Sept. 1712, BL, Add. MSS 22226, fol. 220.
27. This is especially the case in studies of the rococo and Palladian aesthetic. The richly molded and gilded interior of Norfolk House from the 1750s, for example, has been interpreted as an architectural expression of political opposition (and alliance with the estranged Frederick, Prince of Wales), challenging the Palladianism

favored by Lord Burlington and other court favorites. D. Fitzgerald, "The Norfolk House Music Room," *V&A Museum Bulletin* 2, no. 1 (Jan. 1966): 48.

28. To ascribe political labels to contemporaries is problematic. Throughout the eighteenth century, contemporaries used a whole range of terms, particularly "independence," to describe their political persuasions. However, "whig" is the label the Countess of Strafford herself applies to the Marlboroughs, and she distinguishes them from her own "tory" allegiance. Consequently, these labels have been retained here. For further details on the multiplicity of political factions between 1688 and 1800, see John Brewer, *Party Ideology and Popular Politics at the Accession of George III* (Cambridge: Cambridge Univ. Press, 1976); Tim Harris, *Party Politics under the Late Stuarts: Party Conflict in a Divided Society, 1660–1715* (London: Longman, 1993); and John W. Derry, *Politics in the Age of Fox, Pitt and Liverpool: Continuity and Transformation* (Basingstoke, UK: Palgrave Macmillan, 2001).

29. For details of her encounter with the Duchess of Marlborough and daughter, see Countess of Strafford to the Earl of Strafford, 4 Dec. 1711, BL, Add. MSS 22226, fol. 39; for references to her acquaintance with the Duchess of Somerset, see Countess of Strafford to the Earl of Strafford, 20 Nov. 1711, BL, Add. MSS 22226, fol. 25; and for Lady Masham, see Countess of Strafford to the Earl of Strafford, n.d., BL, Add. MSS 22226, fol. 48.

30. George Macauley Trevelyan, *English Social History: A Survey of Six Centuries, Chaucer to Queen Victoria* (London: Longmans, Green, and Co., 1944), 338. Trevelyan's scathing pronouncement on eighteenth-century court life as "occasions of proverbial dullness" has often been taken as the final word on court culture in the period and is often quoted. See, for example, John Beattie, "The Court of George I and English Politics 1717–1720," *English Historical Review* 81 (Jan. 1966): 26, and R. O. Bucholz, *The Augustan Court: Queen Anne and the Decline of Court Culture* (Stanford: Stanford Univ. Press, 1993), 34. Evidence for the numbingly dull routine of court life seems readily available in the letters, diaries, and memoirs of contemporary courtiers such as Fanny Burney and Lord Hervey. The extent to which these can be taken as the sum of court culture, however, is questionable. Despite such complaints, the eighteenth-century court remained a central resort for those in London for the season. A recent exhibition of George III and Queen Charlotte's significant patronage of the arts argued for a repositioning of the court in the history of art and material culture. See Jane Roberts, ed., *George III and Queen Charlotte: Patronage, Collecting and Court Taste* (London: Royal Collection, 2004). Practices such as these need to be distinguished from the notorious boredom of the domestic routine.

31. By comparison, the Duke of Hamilton spent £195 on a new, fully fitted sedan chair in the same year (the chair itself cost £74, with the "rich deep mantua silk festoon" and trimmings coming to £102 before the additional expense of glass and labor); accounts of the Duke and Duchess of Hamilton, National Register of Archives, Scotland, NRA(S) 2177, bundle 426, no. 532. Although average incomes are difficult to calculate, the cost of the court dress is incredible in comparison to many assessments. Grandees commanded substantial annual incomes. Roy Porter suggests that the average for members of the peerage was £5,000 to £8,000 a year, compared to the £400 per annum paid to a country parson, the £12–15 per annum wage of schoolteachers and curates, and the £3 salary of a maid; Porter, *English Society*, 59, 68, 77, 87. For a contemporary view of average wages, see Gebhardt Friedrich August Wendeborn, *A View of England Towards the Close of the Eighteenth Century* (Dublin: Printed by W. Sleater, for P. Wogan, 1791), 12–15. Wendeborn defines "gentlemen" as those with an annual income of £500 or more and estimates that there were ten thousand men of such a status—but also twenty thousand younger brothers without such fortunes.

32. Lady Louisa Stuart to Lady Portalington, 30 March 1789, in *The Letters of Lady Louisa Stuart*, ed. R. Brimley Johnson (London: John Lane, 1926), 96.

33. Countess of Strafford to the Earl of Strafford, 8 Jan. 1711/12, BL, Add. MSS 22226, fol. 65; Countess of Strafford to the Earl of Strafford, 29 Jan. 1711/12, BL, Add. MSS 22226, fol. 79.

34. Countess of Strafford to the Earl of Strafford, 11 Dec. 1711, BL, Add. MSS 22226, fol. 42.

35. Countess of Strafford to the Earl of Strafford, 8 Jan. 1711/12, BL, Add. MSS 22226, fol. 65.

36. Countess Wentworth to the Earl of Strafford, 2 Feb. 1711/12, BL Add. MSS 22225, fol. 223.

37. Countess of Strafford to the Earl of Strafford, 8 Feb. 1711/12, BL, Add. MSS 22226, fol. 290.

38. Countess of Strafford to the Earl of Strafford, 19 Dec. 1712, BL, Add. MSS 22226, fol. 247.

39. Horace Walpole to Sir Horace Mann, 18 Feb. 1742, in *The Yale Edition of Horace Walpole's Correspondence*, ed. Wilmarth Sheldon Lewis (New Haven: Yale Univ. Press, 1937–83), 17:338.

40. Catherine Stapleton to Lady Chatham, Feb. 1773, in *So Dearly Loved, So Much Admired: Letters to Hester Pitt Lady Chatham from her Relations and Friends, 1744–1801*, ed. Vere Birdwood (London: HMSO Books, 1994), 189.

41. Mary Thynne to an unknown recipient, [15 Feb.?] 1715, in *The Gentle Hertford: Her Life and Letters*, ed. Helen Sard Hughes (New York: Macmillan, 1940), 13.

42. The Strafford correspondence reveals that over an eighteen-month period in 1711–12, the family's diamonds were worn in rings, buckles, buckles, earrings, and necklaces by the Countess of Strafford, her husband, and her sister-in-law Lady Betty Wentworth.

43. Countess of Strafford to the Earl of Strafford, 9 Jan. 1712/13, BL, Add. MSS 22226, fol. 263; Countess of Strafford to the Earl of Strafford, 3 Feb. 1712/13, BL, Add. MSS 22226, fol. 285.

44. Mary, Lady Cowper, diary entry, 16 Feb. 1716, in *Diary of Mary, Countess Cowper: Lady of the Bedchamber to the Princess of Wales 1714–1720*, ed. Hon. Spencer Cowper (London: Printed for John Murray, 1864), 76.

45. Lady Louisa Stuart to Lady Portalington, 30 April 1789, in Johnson, *Lady Louisa Stuart*, 100.

46. Mary Grantham (née Grey) to her sister, 20 Jan. 1781, Wrest Park Papers, Bedfordshire and Luton Archives and Records Service (hereafter Wrest Park Papers), L30/11/240/13.

47. Daniel Fenning, *The Royal English Dictionary; or a Treasury of the English Language* (London: Printed for S. Crowder, 1761).

48. Neil McKendrick, "The Commercialisation of Fashion," in McKendrick, Brewer, and Plumb, *Birth of a Consumer Society*, 34–99. For a review of subsequent historiographical developments challenging McKendrick's thesis, see Berg, "New Commodities," 63–69.

49. Roche, *Culture of Clothing*, 6. Pierre Bourdieu has countered the theory of emulation with an alternative system whereby each class seeks to distinguish itself from others through the distinctions of their lifestyle and material goods; see Pierre Bourdieu, *Distinction: A Social Critique of the Judgment of Taste*, trans. Richard Nice (Cambridge, MA: Harvard Univ. Press, 1984), 1–7.

50. Paul Langford, *Public Life and the Propertied Englishman, 1689–1798* (Oxford: Clarendon Press, 1991), 9.

51. Lady Mary Grey to Amabel, Lady Polwarth, 17 Dec. 1774, Wrest Park Papers, L30/123/31.

52. This is not to deny that other social groups might set a trend or favor different designs. Rather, this essay is concerned with establishing how "fashion" was formulated when attributed to the *beau monde*, who were—unlike other social groups—defined by their claim to fashionability.

Patrilineal Portraiture? Gender and Genealogy in the Eighteenth-Century English Country House

Kate Retford

Over the last few decades, as part of a broader concern with the life of the image subsequent to production, many art historians have studied the display of paintings and concomitant issues of space and spectatorship.[1] Those working on eighteenth-century visual culture have shown particular interest in the location, hanging, and framing of works of art and in how those factors affected audience perception. As Marcia Pointon has pointed out, "Knowing when and where objects were seen, and in relation to which other artefacts they were apprehended, allows the historian to begin to grasp their specific historical meanings."[2] The implementation of this principle has had a number of fruitful outcomes. The seminal show *Art on the Line*, at the Courtauld Institute of Art a few years ago, provided detailed insights into the impact that Royal Academy exhibitions had on artists, patrons, and the viewing public at large.[3] More importantly for the current study, the work of scholars such as Pointon and Shearer West has emphasized how the spaces of the country house determined aspects of the production of portraits, encouraging artists to create works that could hang in harmony with ancestral portraits, and controlled the way in which those images functioned, promoting messages of power, dynasty, and political affiliation.[4]

Elsewhere, I have also been concerned with showing how the display of portraits within the eighteenth-century country house determined their content; affecting poses, costumes, compositions, and size.[5] This essay demonstrates that that environment also enabled the production of meanings that were, to a large extent, impossible to countenance in other artistic domains. An important component of recent research into gender and art in eighteenth-century Britain has been concerned with the predominance of patriarchy in family portraits.[6] For example, in Arthur Devis's *Robert Gwillym of Atherton with His Family* of about 1745–47 (fig. 71), the paterfamilias makes an expansive gesture that encompasses the full extent of his property. That property constitutes not only Atherton Hall, Herefordshire, and its grounds, but also his nuclear family, composed of his wife and their children, and his household family, indicated by the steward who

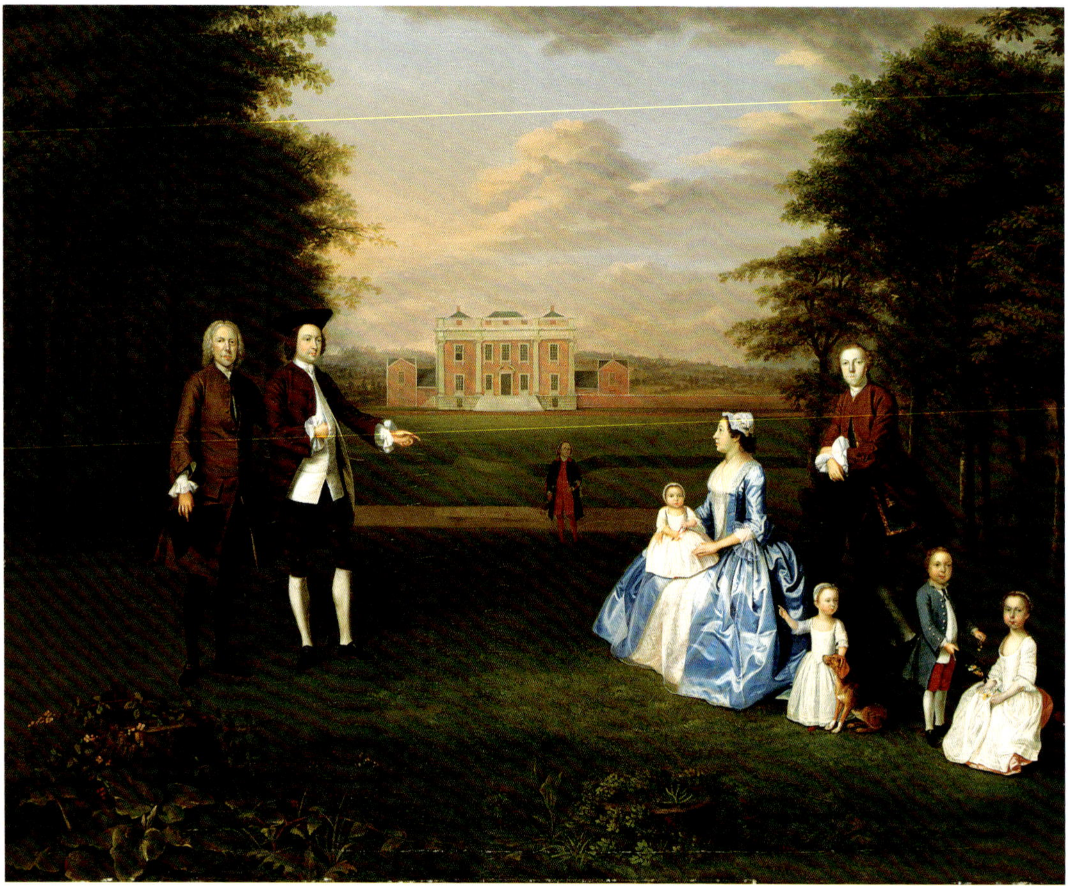

71. Arthur Devis, *Robert Gwillym of Atherton with His Family*, oil on canvas (c. 1745–47), 40 x 50 in. (101.6 x 127 cm). Yale Center for British Art, Paul Mellon Collection. Photo: Richard Caspole, Yale Center for British Art.

advances across the lawn. Nothing in this visual display of social and economic status could give the viewer any clue that the hall had only come into the family when Robert married the heiress Elizabeth Atherton the previous decade. Such paintings rigorously had to define the hierarchy of the household, establishing the paterfamilias as an authority figure. They had to show men gesturing to their estates and dependents, usually depicted higher in the picture plane than other members of their families, and frequently in a particular relationship with their eldest sons to show the process of descent. They could not reveal the reality that wives often played a vital role in enhancing the status, wealth, and social position of the family. Only on very rare occasions were such female contributions acknowledged within the conventions of eighteenth-century family portraiture, and even then they were indicated with considerable subtlety. At Temple Newsam in Yorkshire, companion portraits by Benjamin Wilson depict Charles, ninth Viscount Irwin, and his wife, Frances (figs. 72, 73). While he is shown in the outfit of the polite gentleman, she is garbed in the dress of a shepherdess. It was not unusual for a woman to be depicted in such a pastoral guise, but in this case it would have prompted the informed viewer to reflect on the fact that Frances was the daughter of Samuel Shepheard, a highly successful Cambridgeshire politician and landowner who had made her his heiress with a fortune of £60,000.[7]

The family group and pendant portrait, then, had to emphasize the proper structures of patriarchy. If such images had explicitly acknowledged a wife's role in the aggrandizement of her husband's family, it would have undermined his position. Turning to the family portrait collection, it would seem, on first inspection, to be as patriarchal, if not more so. Many members of the gentry and aristocracy grouped, adapted, framed, and inscribed images of their forebears to present tidy dynastic lines that progressed from father to son through the generations. If lacking particular links in their visual displays of primogeniture, they ordered copies of paintings of ancestors not in their possession or commissioned entirely fabricated portraits from contemporary artists, suitably antiquated in style, costume, and pose.[8] The resultant effect of such efforts was not lost on the numerous tourists who duly admired artistic manifestations of great dynasties.[9] When John Loveday, an Oxford student, visited Belvoir Castle in Leicestershire in 1735, for example, he marveled at the impressive ranks of portraits on display: "In the Gallery are Lengths of the Peers of this House beginning with the first Earl of Rutland and continued without any interruption to the present Duke."[10] Four decades later, Samuel Curwen, an American loyalist, was similarly impressed with the family portraits at Longleat in Wiltshire, describing them as "all or most at full length, continued down from the first Sir John to the present Lord."[11] As is indicated by both these accounts, family portrait collections were always located in the country, rather than the town.[12] It was the country house that demonstrated a family's dynastic heritage, longevity, and inherited wealth, particularly as many members of the elite only leased their residences in London.[13] It was the country seat that provided the basis for the political power exercised in town, and the images of military heroes, politicians, and statesmen displayed there testified to the roots of affiliations apparent in more transient party politics.[14] More prosaically, it was the country residence that usually provided the sheer space needed to contain any substantial collection of ancestral portraits.[15]

However, while such collections were clearly dominated by principles of patrilineage and patriarchy, they could also record the important connections, titles, land, and wealth transferred into the family through marital unions. In contrast

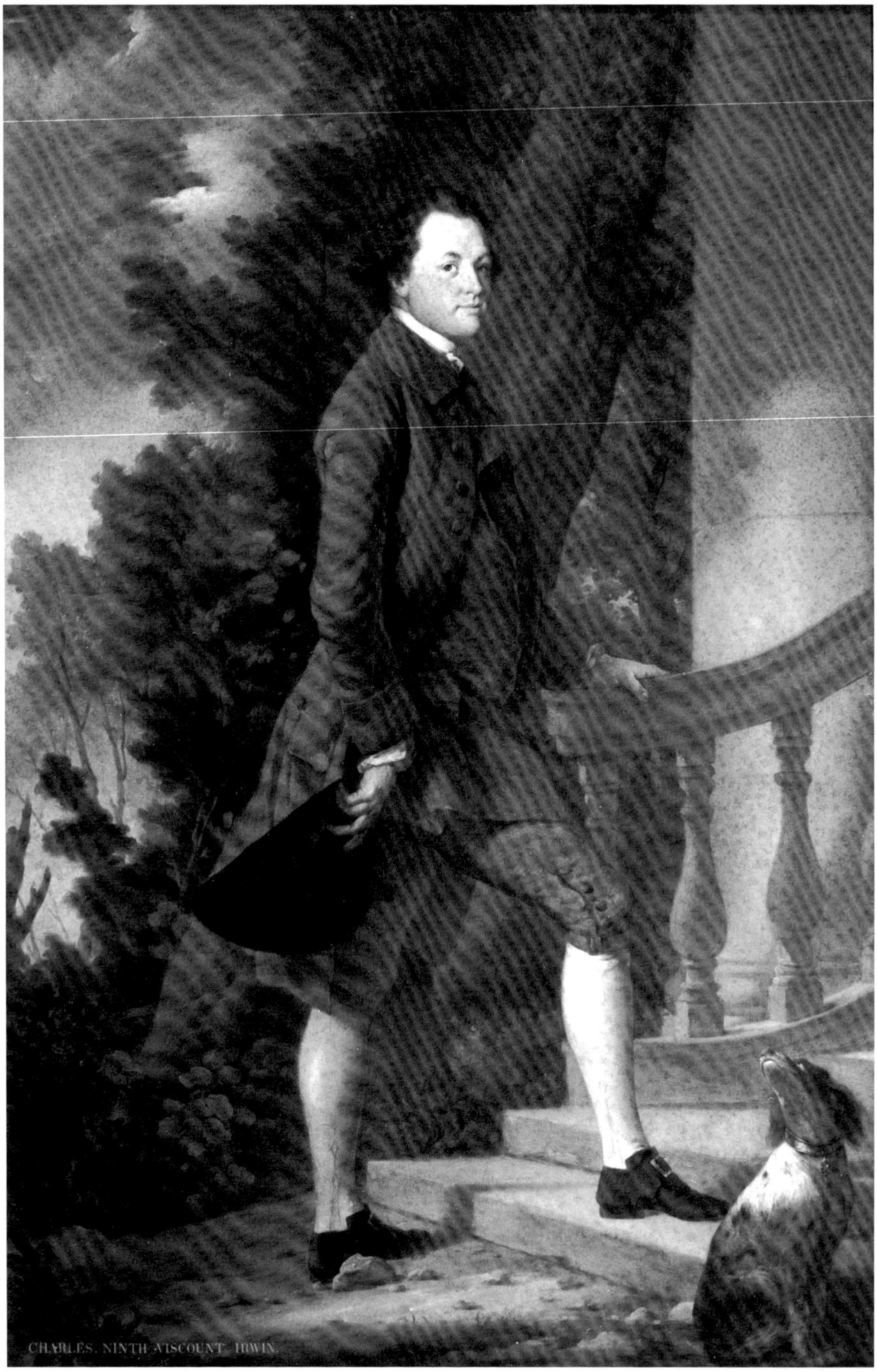

72. Benjamin Wilson, *Charles, 9th Viscount Irwin* (1727–1778), oil on canvas (n.d.), $98\frac{1}{8}$ x $57\frac{1}{8}$ in. (249 x 145 cm). Leeds Museums & Galleries (Temple Newsam). Photo: Photographic Survey, Courtauld Institute of Art.

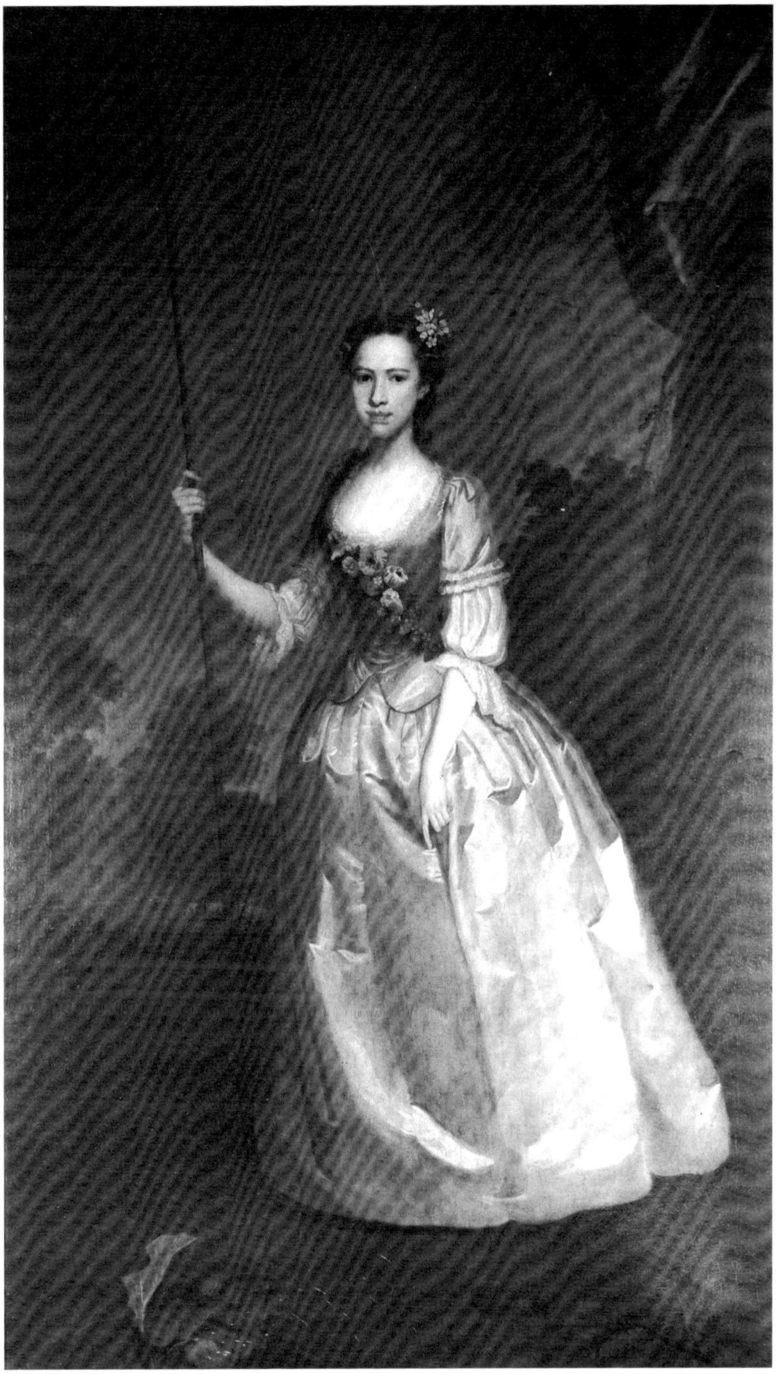

73. Benjamin Wilson, *Frances, Viscountess Irwin* (1734–1807), oil on canvas (n.d.), 80 x 47⅛ in. (203 x 119.5 cm). Private collection. Photo: Photographic Survey, Courtauld Institute of Art.

to the group or pendant portrait, the more complex dynamics, larger scale, and carefully controlled context and display of a family's portrait collection provided a space in which a wife's contributions could be shown alongside the overarching message of patrilineage. The inclusion of images of a wife's family, ancestors, and benefactors in her husband's house provided a satisfactory means of acknowledging her role in the complex processes by which a dynasty was enhanced. Certainly a wife's history would be yoked to that of her spouse, visually incorporated into the overall display of her husband's ancestry. Yet it would also retain a distinct identity. For example, the Herbert family benefited greatly when Henry, tenth Earl of Pembroke, married Elizabeth Spencer, daughter of the third Duke of Marlborough, in 1756. This was a prestigious match that raised their standing and so was duly commemorated in their collection at Wilton, their Wiltshire mansion. As well as displaying paintings of Elizabeth's parents by Jean-Baptiste Van Loo, Henry commissioned a half-length portrait of her father from Sir Joshua Reynolds the year after their marriage.[16]

The rest of this essay focuses on the role that some women, particularly Henrietta Cavendish, Countess of Oxford, played in the creation of such pictorial records, being actively engaged in providing a lasting record of their own heritage. As women clearly played a major part in the construction and manipulation of the domestic environment—which is amply documented in other essays in this volume—so they could own, bequeath, gift, and exploit images as well as being subject to the often constricting parameters of female representation.[17] In 1828, Elizabeth Herbert, then Duchess Dowager of Pembroke, bequeathed two more Reynolds portraits of members of her family to the collection at Wilton. One depicted her elder brother, George Spencer, fourth Duke of Marlborough, while the other represented her younger brother, Charles Spencer. Indeed, as another version of the portrait of the fourth duke was also on display in Blenheim, the Spencers' family seat in Oxfordshire, the image created a direct pictorial connection between the two houses that echoed the dynastic link created by the marriage of Elizabeth and Henry.[18] When such women were transplanted into other houses through wedlock, the images of their own family that they commissioned or brought with them created a web of complex pictorial cross-references that spread through great houses across the country.

As the union of two elite families is enshrined within the collection at Wilton, so the display of portraits at Rousham in Oxfordshire commemorates the marriage of Sir Charles Cottrell-Dormer and Jane Adelmare Caesar. Many of the paintings relating to Jane's family were concentrated in the rococo drawing room, created in 1764 (fig. 74). At one end of the room, a full-length portrait of Sir Julius Adelmare Caesar, her most notable forebear, hangs opposite a portrait of Queen Elizabeth I,

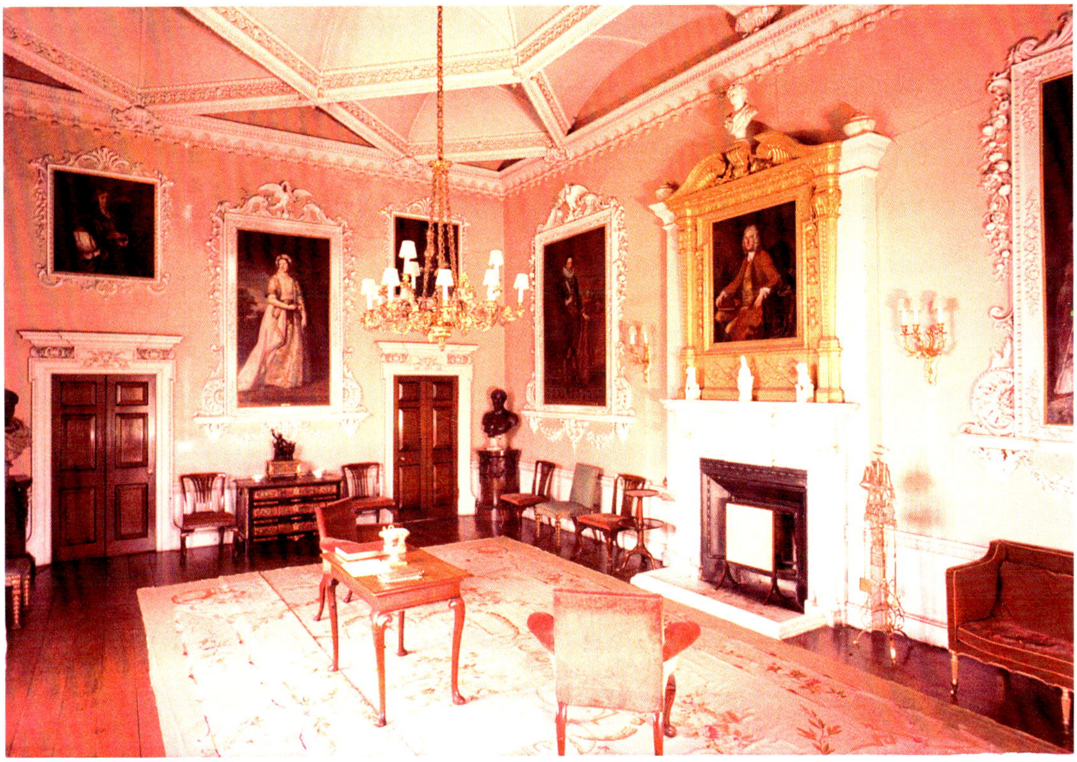

74. Drawing room at Rousham, Oxfordshire. © Rousham House.

to whom he acted as medical adviser. An inscription on this latter canvas proudly commemorates the fact that the painting had been a personal gift to the family. Both these images were altered to fit the display. The portrait of Sir Julius was extended from a head-and-shoulders canvas, while that of Elizabeth was slightly enlarged so that they would match in size and, together with other images in the room, create an impressive series of full-length canvases. In addition, Thomas Roberts of Oxford was paid £266 1s. 6d. to provide stuccowork frames for the doorcases and all the pictures in the room.[19] These matching surrounds serve a number of purposes. They create visual harmony between the disparate canvases and help to incorporate them into a coherent decorative scheme. They also suggest stability, setting ties of family, friendship, and patronage in plaster, as well as making it difficult for future generations to alter the display.[20]

Unfortunately, there is no documentation as to the respective roles of husband and wife in creating this hang. However, in other cases, we have much more information regarding the role of elite women in the formation of such displays.

While Holland House at Kensington, then a village adjoining London, was all but destroyed by bombing in World War II, there is considerable evidence as to the appearance of the portrait gallery in the eighteenth century.[21] The hang constituted a carefully organized visual demonstration of the union of families created by the marriage of the wealthy politician Henry Fox (later Lord Holland) and Caroline Lennox, daughter of Charles Lennox, second Duke of Richmond.[22] Henry's coat of arms was shown over the north door on the east wall, leading into the rest of the house, while that of his wife was placed over the south door, opening onto the terrace (fig. 75).[23] This heraldic display not only reflected the conventions of shields, in which the husband's arms are always on the left, but also provided the starting point for the organization of the room. Images of Henry's relatives were grouped in the north end, while those of Caroline were shown to the south. Together, they provided a display of the various connections of the Fox and Lennox families. Both sets of parents were included, as were the couple's offspring, their various siblings,

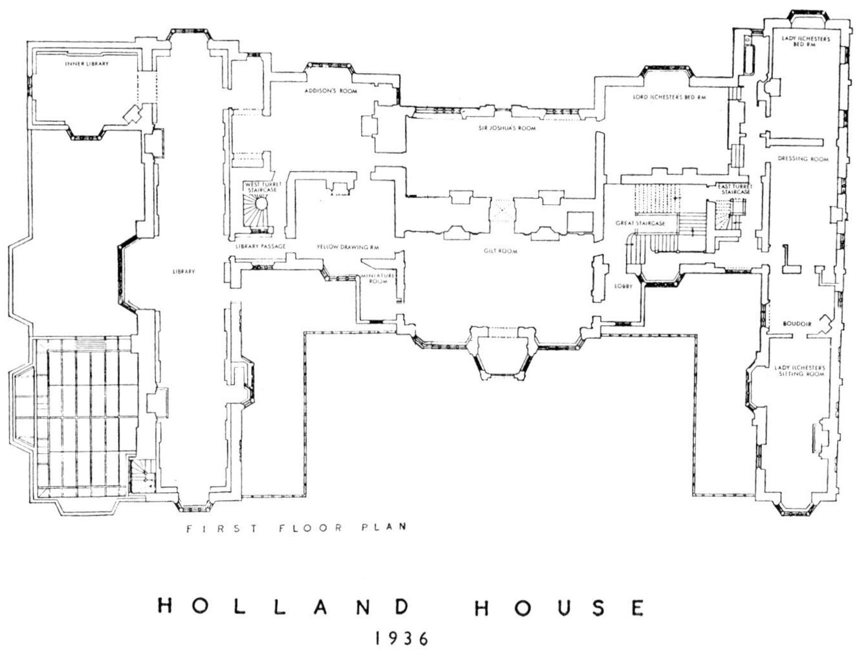

75. Second-floor (British first-floor) plan of Holland House, Kensington, from *Holland House in Kensington*, by Derek Hudson (London: P. Davies, 1967). James Marshall and Marie-Louise Osborn Collection, Beinecke Rare Book and Manuscript Library, Yale University. The long gallery is labeled as the library in this twentieth-century plan, in which north is at the top.

and the families of those siblings.[24] Some pictures were already at hand. Many others were commissioned especially for the scheme, relatives being repeatedly urged to visit the studios of artists such as Reynolds and Allan Ramsay when in town in order to sit for their portraits.

Although the room gave equal spatial weighting to the lines of both husband and wife, the only two ancestral portraits on display demonstrated Caroline's heritage. Her dynastic line began when the relationship between Charles II and Louise de Kéroualle, Duchess of Portsmouth, resulted in the birth in 1672 of a son, who was given the title Duke of Richmond and Lennox. The creation of the Lennox dynasty, the title, and the connection with the monarchy were signified in the gallery by the inclusion of images of Charles and his mistress, inlaid and surrounded with small mirrors for added decorative and symbolic emphasis.[25] The continuation of that dynasty was also acknowledged in the display of paintings of the first duke by Sir Godfrey Kneller, the second by Van Loo, and a portrait of Caroline's brother, the third Duke of Richmond, painted while on a visit to Florence, part of a grand tour. Henry, meanwhile, was of significantly lesser stock. As Horace Walpole noted on the occasion of his marriage to Caroline: "His father was a footman; her great-grandfather a king."[26] Indeed, presented with a suitor lacking title and property, her parents had initially forbidden the match, forcing the couple to elope in 1744. Reflecting his inferior status, the earliest representations of his family in the Holland House gallery were paintings by Kneller of his parents.

Until quite recent work by scholars such as Stella Tillyard and Rosemary Baird, the building, decoration, and amalgamation of portraits in the gallery were presented as the accomplishments of Henry Fox. In 1820, Thomas Faulkner noted, "The first Lord Holland fitted up this room as a picture gallery for family portraits," while Derek Hudson's account of 1967 similarly claimed that it was Henry who had built up the collection.[27] As well as reflecting assumption and convention, such statements also often depend on account books that inevitably link the purchase of items such as portraits to male patrons. For example, we know that Reynolds sent a bill of £120 to Henry Fox for his triple portrait of Lady Sarah Lennox, Lady Susan Fox-Strangways, and Charles Fox.[28] Examination of correspondence is often the only way to ascertain the female agency that can underlie such economic realities. Caroline's letters to her sister Emily, Marchioness of Kildare, reveal that it was Caroline who was largely responsible for the new commissions for the Holland House gallery. She chivied relations to sit for chosen artists, stipulated which formats should be employed for which portraits, and decided on their final arrangement in "my Gallery."[29] The fact that the collection was very much Caroline's project was reflected in the central location of her portrait by Ramsay between the two doors (fig. 76).

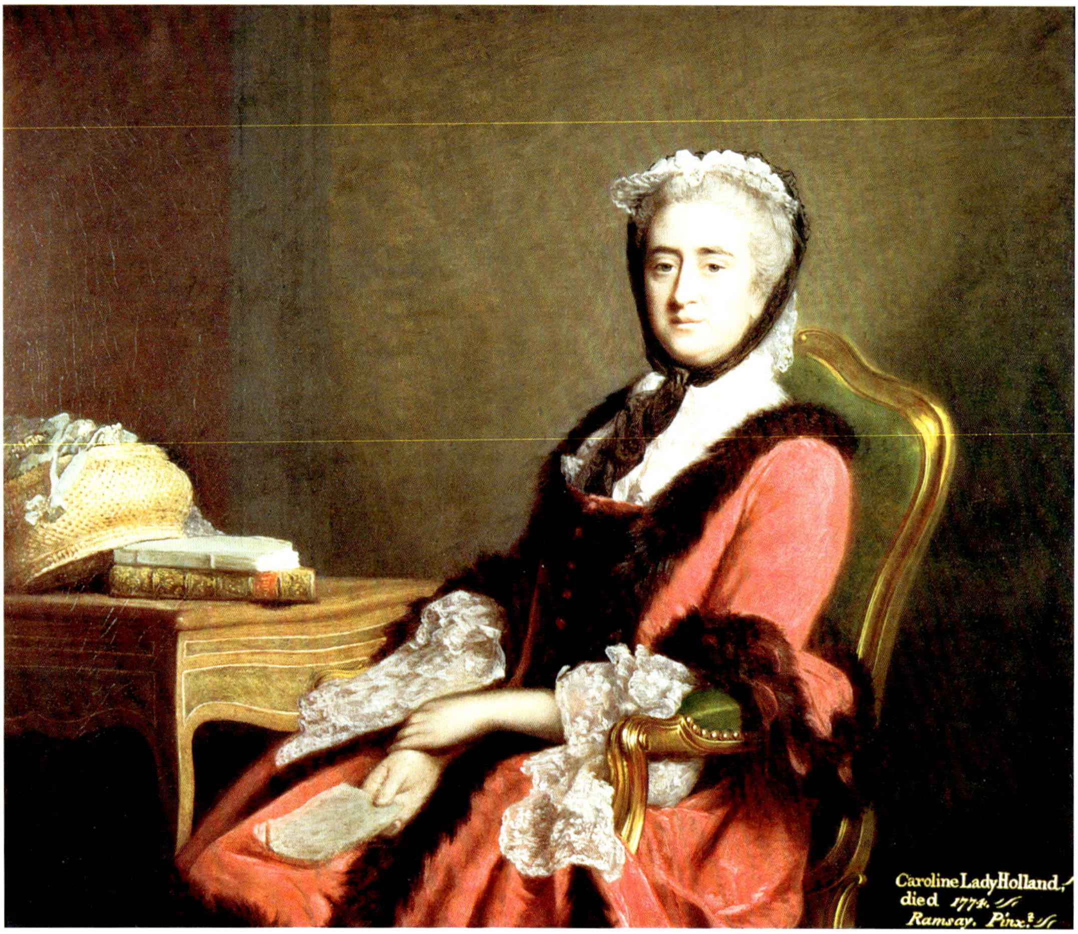

76. Allan Ramsay, *Lady Caroline Fox, Baroness Holland*, oil on canvas (1766), 40 x 48 in. (101.6 x 121.9 cm). Private collection. The Bridgeman Art Library International.

It is unsurprising that one of the most remarkable examples of an elite lady constructing a pictorial testament to her own family concerns a wealthy widow. After the death of her husband, Edward Harley, second Earl of Oxford, Henrietta Cavendish spent much of her time and a considerable sum of money on renovating Welbeck Abbey in Nottinghamshire (fig. 77) and amalgamating, organizing, cataloguing, and inscribing more than two hundred portraits that recorded both her and her husband's family lines.[30] However, those depicting her own ancestors outweighed those that represented the earl's forebears. As Horace Walpole informed the artist and writer Richard Bentley after a visit to Welbeck in 1756, her collection primarily commemorated "all the great families from which she descended, and which centred in her."[31] Indeed, the countess's family was far more impressive than that of her husband and could be traced back to Sir William Cavendish and his wife, Bess of Hardwick, later Countess of Shrewsbury. It was their son, Sir Charles Cavendish, who had purchased the estate at Welbeck. The line had descended neatly through the proper route of primogeniture until the son of Henry Cavendish, second Duke of Newcastle, had failed to produce an heir. The Cavendish estates had then passed to Lady Margaret, Henrietta's mother, and her husband, John Holles, Earl of Clare. They also failed to produce a male heir; after years of legal wrangling to prevent all the estates from going to the earl's nephew, Thomas Pelham, Henrietta acquired the Cavendish properties of Bolsover Castle, Derbyshire, and Welbeck. She also inherited the family name, as it was a stipulation of the second Duke of Newcastle in his will that all his heirs should be called Cavendish.[32] Henrietta was clearly very proud of this heritage and keen to publicize it. In 1752, for example, she provided both financial assistance and a number of prints for Arthur Collins's

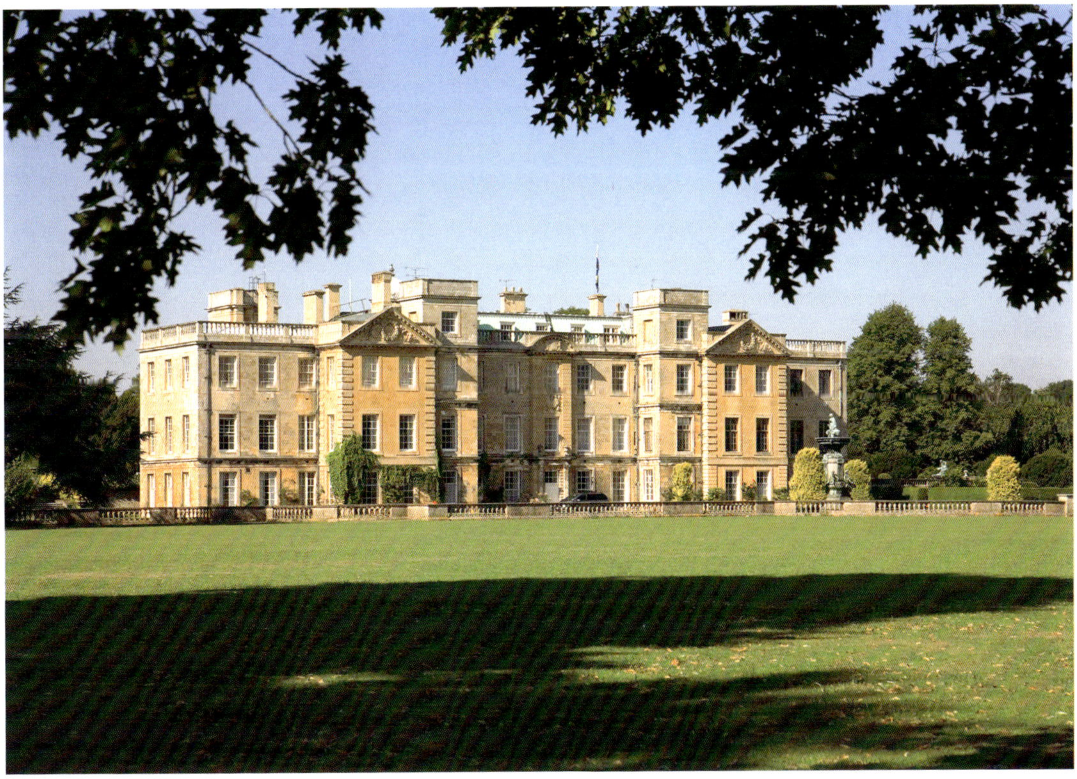

77. Exterior view of Welbeck Abbey, Nottinghamshire. Photo: John Hammond.

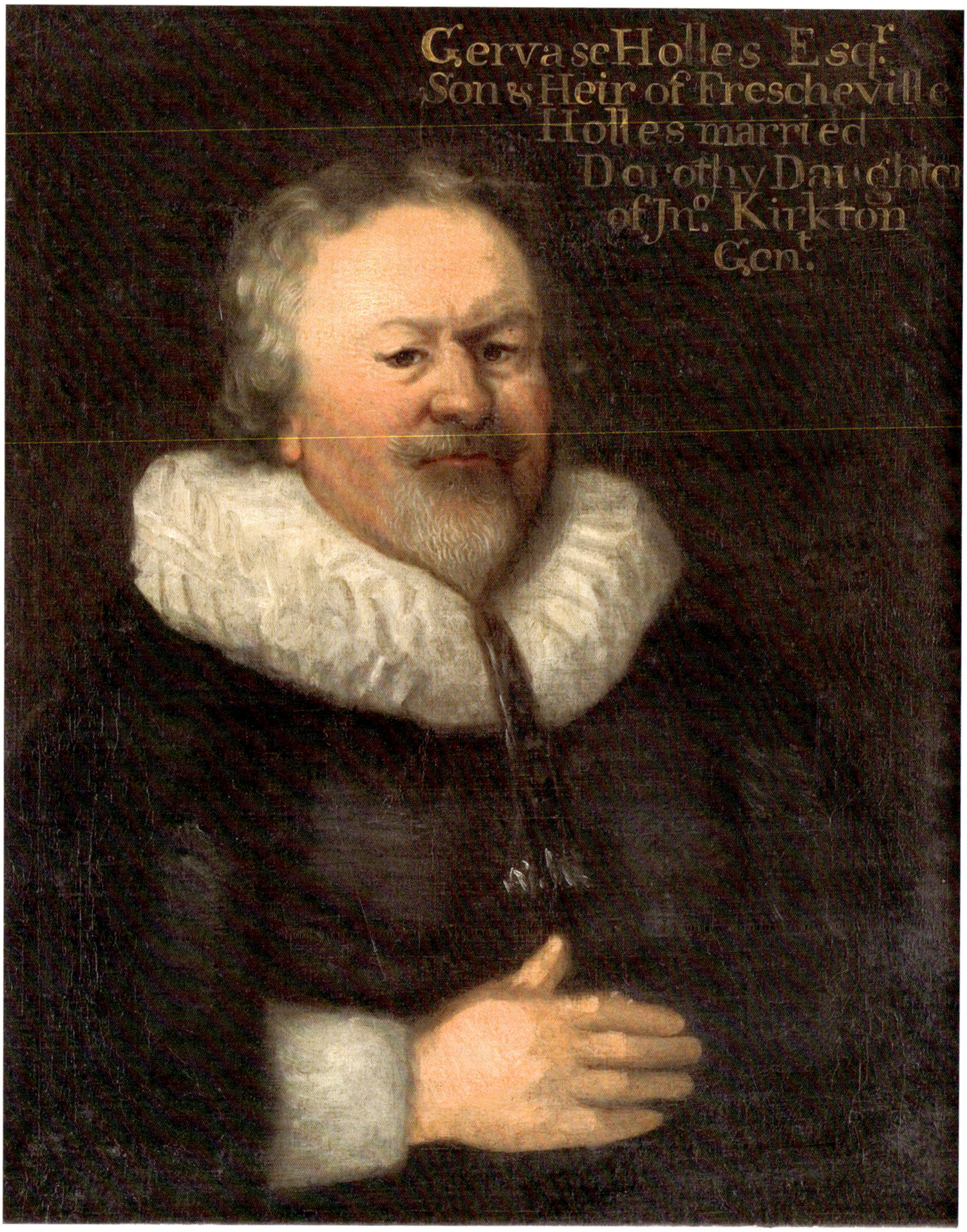

78. Artist unknown, *Man Traditionally Identified as Gervase Holles* (1607–1674/75), oil on canvas (n.d.), 30 x 25 in. (76.2 x 63.5 cm). Welbeck Abbey, Nottinghamshire. Photo: John Hammond.

complete history of the Cavendish family, copies of which were then distributed among various relations.[33]

When Henrietta's husband died in 1741, she commissioned George Vertue to make a catalogue of all the paintings "in his several Houses - London - Marybon. his Library & - those from Wimpole & Clerkenwell house." According to Vertue's account, while a considerable number of these images were sold at auction the following year, "all the family pictures of the Cavendishes, Holles^s, Pierponts, Harleys etc., noblemen Ladys and Gentlemen any ways related my Lady reserved for her own use not to be sold."[34] Many of these were then moved to Welbeck.[35] She also transferred some paintings from her own property at Bolsover to the abbey and commissioned a number of new portraits, including pendants of her son-in-law and daughter, the Duke and Duchess of Portland.[36] All these portraits were then carefully arranged, grouped together in rooms according to various factors including size, the gender of the sitters, and, most notably, the branch of her family tree to which those sitters belonged. Although the eighteenth-century portrait collection still sometimes centered on the long gallery, as at Holland House, there were no hard-and-fast rules; portraits were displayed in various rooms, particularly halls, drawing rooms, and dining rooms. Indeed, at Welbeck, Henrietta had to utilize almost every space to accommodate her vast collection. She placed a number of paintings of the Harleys, her husband's ancestors, in one bedchamber. While most of these were head-and-shoulders portraits, slightly larger images of the same dynasty were grouped in the south drawing room. Early-seventeenth-century paintings of members of the Holles line, from which Henrietta's father was descended, were arranged in a dressing room (fig. 78). Meanwhile, she reserved the largest images in her collection, particularly those representing the Cavendish dynasty of which she was clearly most proud, for the great drawing room, the grand saloon, and the great dining room. The hang contrived in the first of these spaces is especially interesting, as it consisted entirely of three-quarter- and full length portraits of women, including her grandmother, her great-aunt, her mother, and two of her aunts. This display of female ancestors was completed by her own image by Sir Godfrey Kneller (fig. 79). The grand saloon was much more conventionally patrilineal, based predominantly around full-length formal portraits of male members of the Cavendish and Holles lines depicted in robes of state, with a particular emphasis on the Order of the Garter. The dining room was adorned with a mixture of paintings of male and female forebears, all at three-quarter length and mostly depicting sitters from the Cavendish line, beginning with images of its founders, Sir William Cavendish and Bess of Hardwick.

Henrietta's extensive display at Welbeck thus constituted a complex pictorial family tree, in which the corridors between rooms acted as branches linking

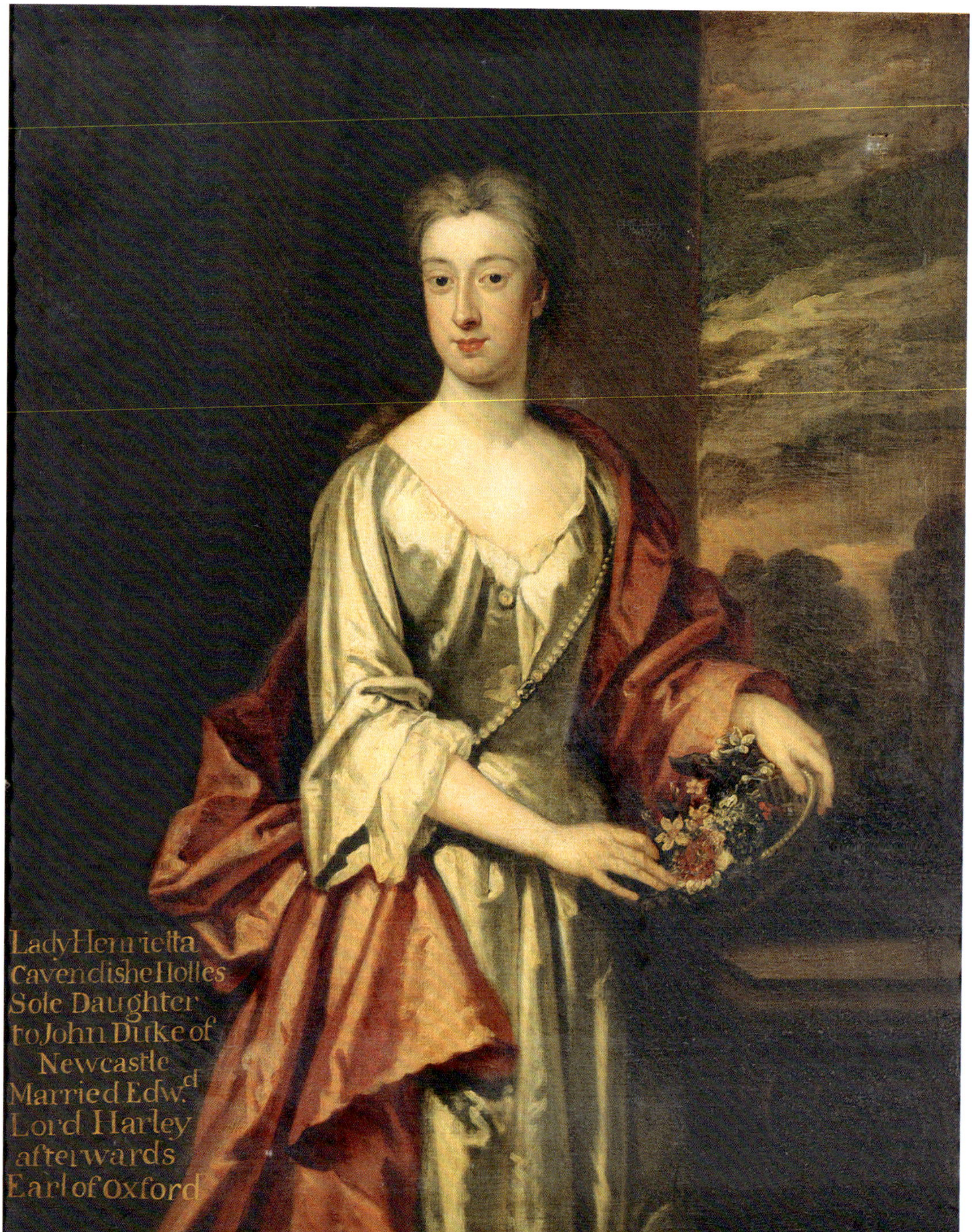

79. Sir Godfrey Kneller, *Henrietta Cavendish Holles, Countess of Oxford*, oil on canvas (1716), 50 x 40 in. (127 x 101.6 cm). Welbeck Abbey, Nottinghamshire. Photo: John Hammond.

various groups. The allocation of particular portraits to particular rooms is revealing. Although Henrietta did not follow the oft-quoted advice of William Salmon, proffered in his *Polygraphice* in 1678, her display did echo his broad principle that portraits should be arranged in more or less public rooms according to the identity and status of the sitters.[37] As a more private space, the withdrawing chamber was deemed suitable for images of women, while male portraits complemented the formal environment of the grand saloon. The most important rooms of the house emphasized the primary line of Henrietta's family, the Cavendishes, while images of early members of the Holles family, a rather uninspiring collection of paintings, were relegated to a dressing room. The context within which these portraits were displayed was as carefully contrived as their arrangement, designed to work with the images to strengthen and confirm their message of illustrious dynasty. When she informed Lady Mary Wortley Montagu that the new dining room was to "be Hung wth whole length [*sic*] Pictures in Cedar Frames," Henrietta noted at the same time that "ye Ceiling is to be Painted wth ye Armes of my family & ye Marriages into it in proper Colours" and that she had commissioned "a Gothick Chimney Peice Designed partly from a fine one at Bolsover" for this room (fig. 80).[38] The reference to a fireplace in the star chamber at the little keep at Bolsover further emphasized Henrietta's inheritance and created a unity between her estates.[39] This particular fitting is also characteristic of the furnishings at Welbeck in its adornment with heraldic devices and family crests. The overmantel contains Henrietta's arms, while the pillars and hearth are decorated with the coiled snake of the Cavendishes and the rose-and-sun badge of the Ogle line. Account books and receipts relating to Welbeck record numerous payments to craftsmen for decorating rooms at the abbey with such devices: carving, gilding, stuccoing, and painting the "roses and glory" of the Ogles, the stags' heads and snakes of the Cavendishes, and various family coats of arms.[40] Indeed, Benjamin Hague, one of the painters employed, was responsible not only for painting the arms in the Gothic hall but also for "Copeying ye Armes ought of ye Book & going to Derby to examine those armes upon ye monument of Elizabeth Hardwick & likewise at Hardwick house."[41]

In addition to amalgamating and grouping the portraits of her and her husband's families, the countess ordered craftsmen to blacken and gild a large number of new frames, suggesting a desire to create a visual harmony among the collection.[42] Most importantly, she had the pictures inscribed by Hague and another painter named George Machin. In October 1748, Hague presented her with a bill for having "[written] 11 Dozn & 8 of Letters upon ye Picktures at 6d—Dozen."[43] Such adornment was intended to assert ownership and status, to ensure that no confusion could arise over the identities of the sitters in the future, and to convey

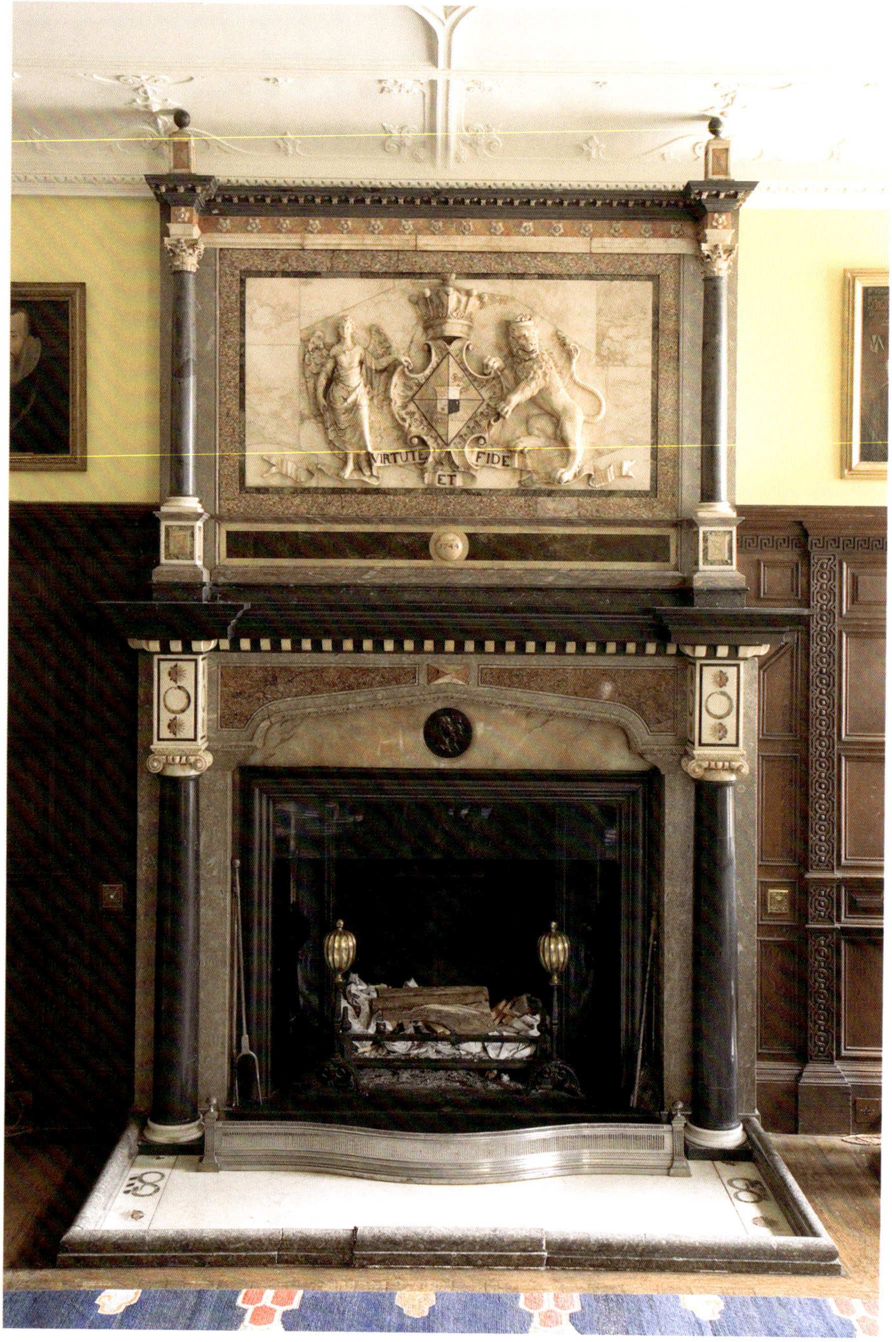

80. Chimneypiece in the present entrance hall (formerly the dining room) at Welbeck Abbey, Nottinghamshire, 1744. Photo: John Hammond.

biographical information to spectators. The inscriptions also provided a certain visual unity, both in their uniform yellow script and in their repetitive phrasing, in an otherwise rather disparate and motley collection of images. They enabled a certain amount of cross-referencing, encouraging the viewer to move between pictures and develop a sense of their relationships. For example, a painting in the dressing room identified as "Gervase Holles Esqr Son & Heir of Frescheville" (see fig. 78) would have prompted the interested spectator to turn to a nearby image inscribed with the name of that individual's father. It was also these texts that, as Mrs. Delany noted, rendered the pictures "historical," revealing the Countess of Oxford's essentially antiquarian, documentary approach to the display of her collection.[44]

Significantly, Hague and Machin were neither specialists in the task of lettering nor artists supplementing commissions with more mundane work on the side. Rather, both painted these inscriptions in between coating walls, charging Henrietta for their primary service by the yard. This serves to reinforce the accumulative impression that such ancestral portraits were not primarily seen as works of art, having aesthetic value. Instead, they were predominantly biographical documents, objects whose value lay in their signification to such a degree that their material form could be treated with minimal respect.[45] Indeed, it can be argued that a family's most notable and valuable works of art, their finest old masters, were more likely to be contained in their London town house. The dukes of Montagu displayed their rarest and most expensive works at Montagu House in Whitehall; Norfolk House in St James's Square contained the richest treasures of the dukes of Norfolk; and Devonshire House in Piccadilly seems to have taken precedence over Chatsworth, Derbyshire, at this date as a repository of the treasures owned by the dukes of Devonshire.[46] Although a schematic divide, the association of antiquarianism with the country seat and aestheticism with the town house does have a ring of truth. Certainly, if a family portrait was by Sir Peter Lely or Sir Anthony Van Dyck, the name of the painter would be deemed worthy of record. However, this was arguably a bonus, adding to the authority of the portrait's biographical message and to the status and importance of the sitter. Thus, Henrietta's full-length Van Dyck portrait of the Earl of Strafford was inscribed with no fewer than 109 words, stating, "An Original drawn by Vandike" before going on to cover a large portion of that "Original" with details of the sitter's date of birth, wives, children, and the circumstances of his death (fig. 81).

The inscriptions at Welbeck thus convey much more than mere identification. Many inform the viewer of a link between a particular sitter and either the family of the countess or that of her deceased husband, especially when that link is potentially unclear. When Mrs. Delany visited Welbeck in 1756, she noted that "the vast number of family pictures" bore not only the names of their sitters, but also "an

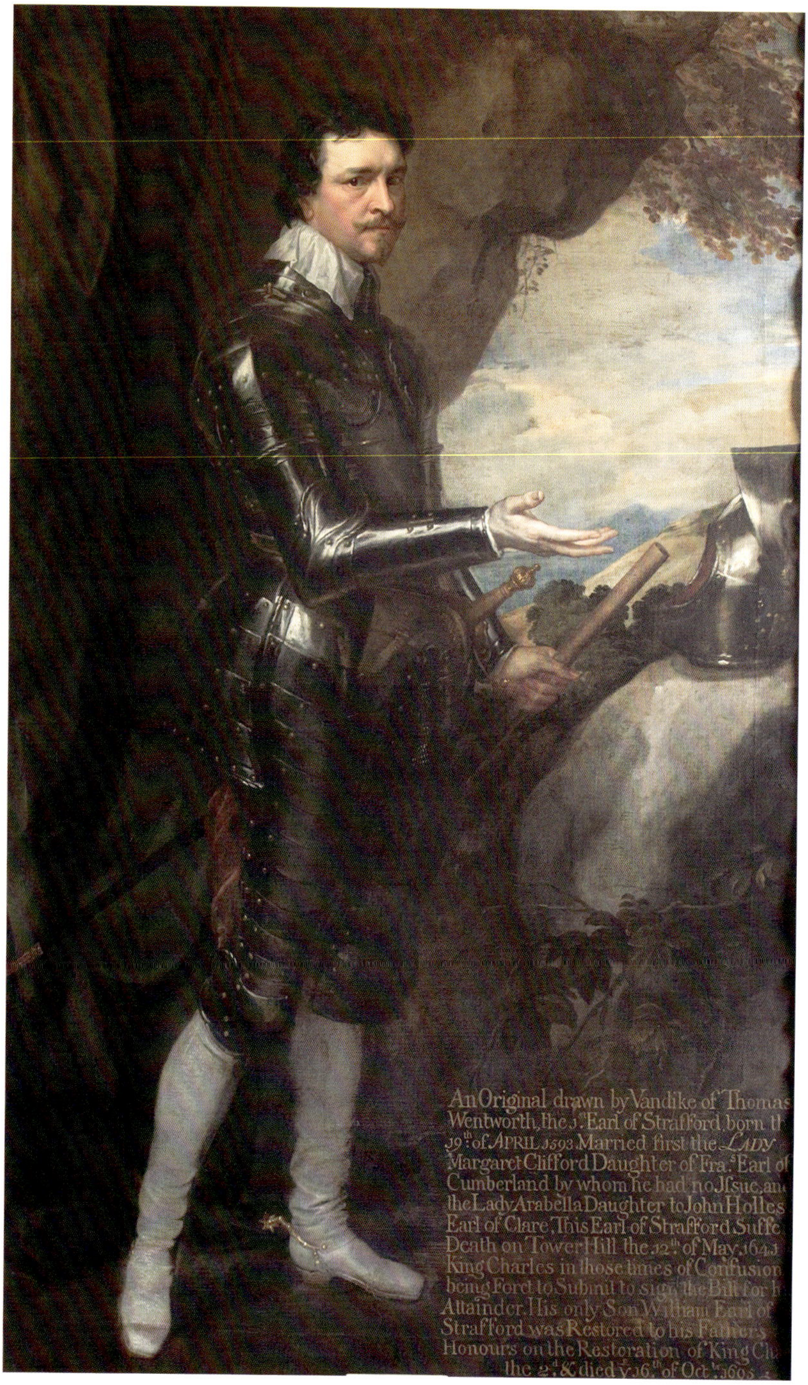

81. Sir Anthony Van Dyck, *Thomas Wentworth, Earl of Strafford* (1593–1641), oil on canvas (n.d.), 87 x 53 in. (221 x 134.6 cm). Welbeck Abbey, Nottinghamshire. Photo: John Hammond.

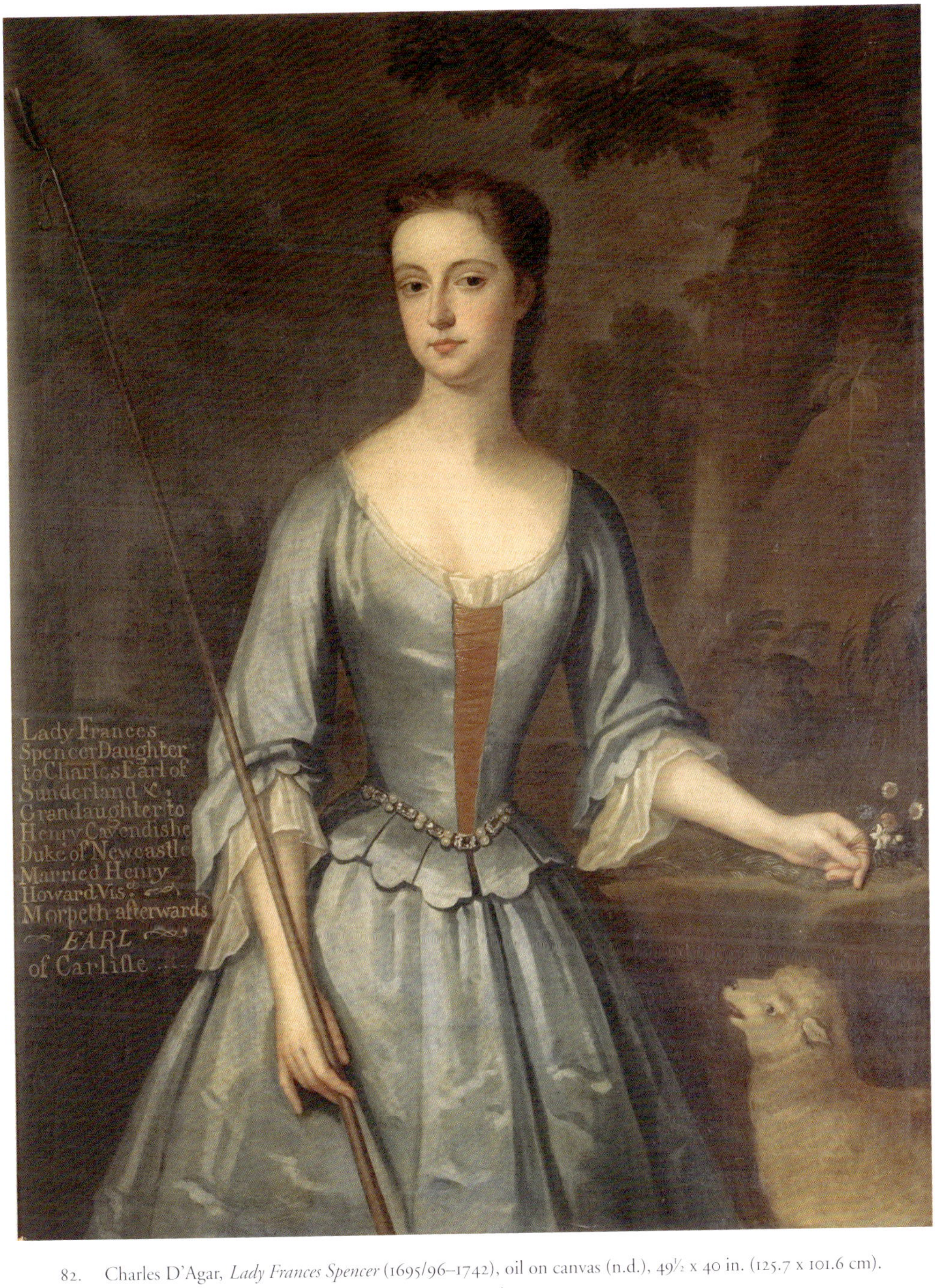

82. Charles D'Agar, *Lady Frances Spencer* (1695/96–1742), oil on canvas (n.d.), 49½ x 40 in. (125.7 x 101.6 cm). Welbeck Abbey, Nottinghamshire. Photo: John Hammond.

account of the families they married into."[47] Such explanation was particularly important in the case of women depicted in the collection who had married into other families and thus assumed other names. For example, when a viewer came across a painting of Lady Frances Spencer by Charles D'Agar in the dining room, he or she might have been unclear as to the purpose of the portrait's presence (fig. 82). However, on reading the inscription, it would have become apparent that Frances merited a place in the collection as "Grandaughter to Henry Cavendishe Duke of Newcastle." These texts were also exploited in order to convey details of heroism and great deeds, matching the demonstration of ancestry with a demonstration of that ancestry's merit. The inscription on an image of Jane Cavendish informs the viewer that she was the daughter of William, first Duke of Newcastle, and had "kept Garrison for her Father at Welbeck against ye Parliament ARMY" (fig. 83).

It is unsurprising to find that some of these inscriptions are far from accurate. There seems to have been a considerable mix-up over the Holles portraits in the dressing room. Richard W. Goulding argued that the costume and apparent age of the sitters in two images inscribed with the name of Gervase Holles the Antiquary (see fig. 78) would suggest that they are much more likely to be depictions of his father, Frescheville. Conversely, another portrait in that room presented by Henrietta as an image of Frescheville can more convincingly be identified as a representation of Gervase.[48] While these particular errors are likely to have been accidental, it seems reasonable to suggest that on other occasions, given Henrietta's clear obsession with exhibiting as many identified images of her family as possible, the mistakes may have something more willful about them. Some portraits appear to have been labeled on the basis of scanty or possibly nonexistent evidence as to the identity of the sitter. For example, the figure in a portrait putatively identified as "The first Sr Charles Cavendishe" wears a costume that postdates his death in 1617 and is much more likely to represent his son (fig. 84). The absence of other images of the named individual in the collection may well have prompted this misidentification, not so much an act of self-delusion as a subordination of the picture to the genealogical intent of the overall display.[49]

Henrietta's efforts were not just concerned with the past. Such work was to consolidate a legacy that would become the heritage of future generations. The countess's stated intent was "to incline my family to reside at ye only Habitable Seat of my Ancesters, it being my oppinion ye Estate reduced, will still bear maintaining one House upon it."[50] She was very concerned that her daughter's family should approve of her endeavors, informing her grandson that "your Father Mother & your selfe, liking Welbeck & the Improvements I have made & going on with, as fast as the Time & other Circumstances will permit, is a just reason for an Inducement to go on with them."[51] She was always keen for her descendants to

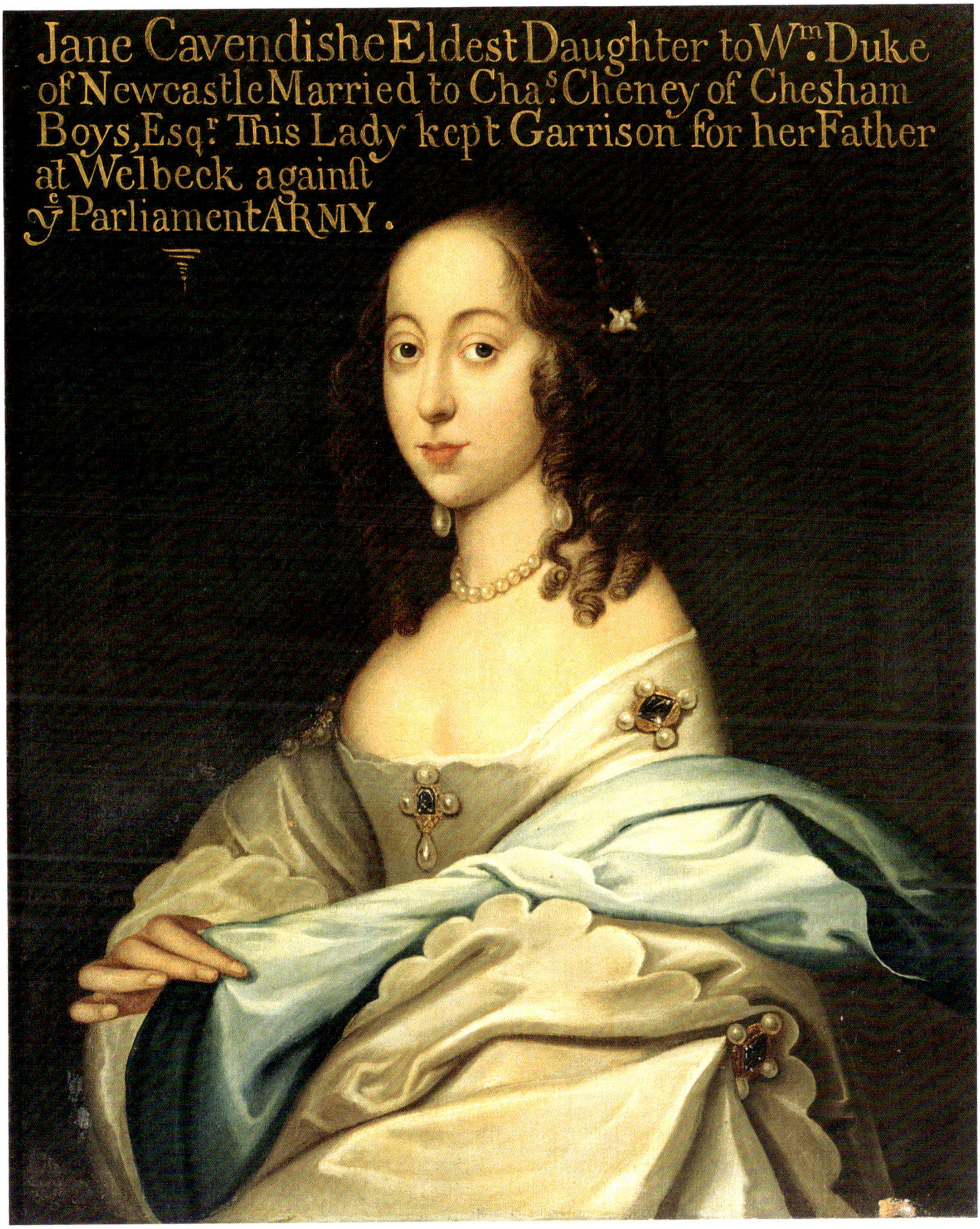

83. Artist unknown, *Lady Jane Cavendish* (1621–1669), oil on canvas (n.d.), 30 x 25 in. (76.2 x 63.5 cm). Welbeck Abbey, Nottinghamshire. Photo: John Hammond.

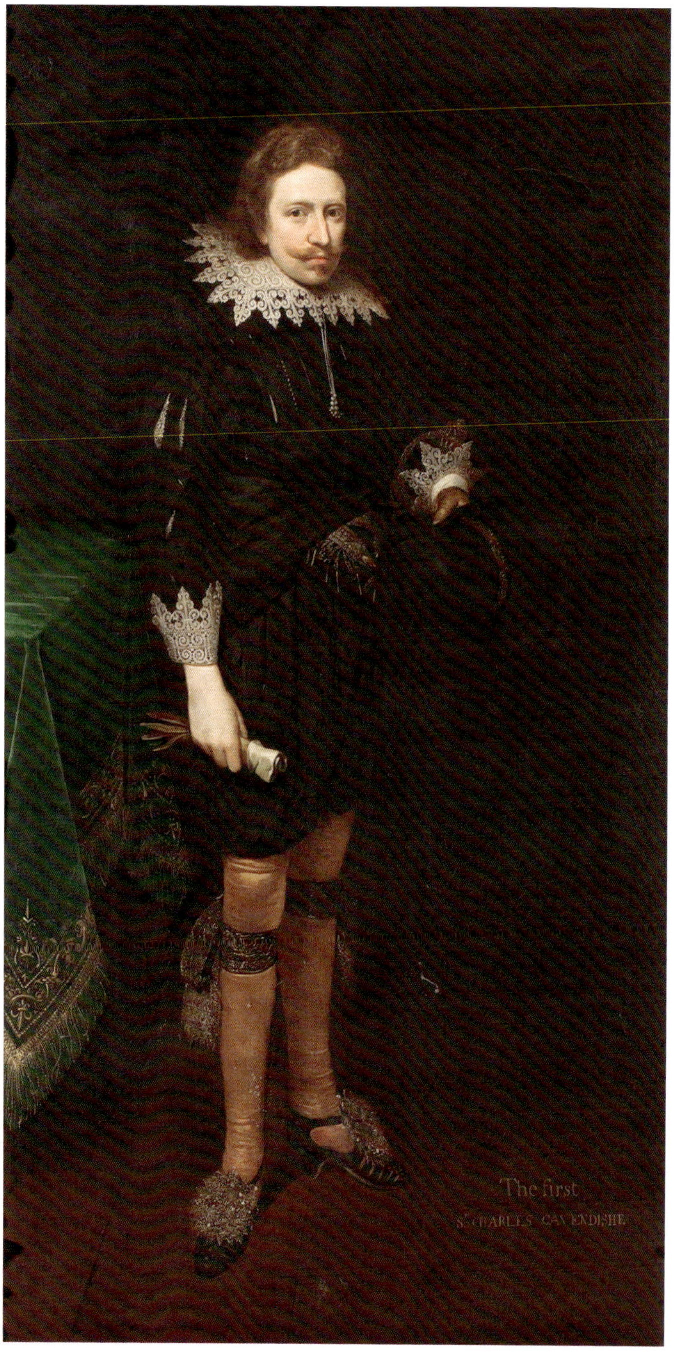

84. Paul van Somer, *Man Traditionally Identified as Sir Charles Cavendish* (1553–1617), oil on canvas (n.d.), 84 x 47½ in. (213.4 x 120.7 cm). Welbeck Abbey, Nottinghamshire. Photo: John Hammond.

travel to Nottinghamshire to visit both her and the house; in her letters, she constantly expresses her impatience for their next visit.[52] Ultimately, her wish that her successors live at the abbey was fulfilled as her grandson, once the third Duke of Portland, moved the main family seat from Bulstrode to Welbeck.

However, Henrietta's developments caused interest in a much wider circle than her kin. Despite her constantly professed desire to live in retirement, she had a large number of visitors at Welbeck while the work was being executed.[53] Some of these were close personal acquaintances whom she personally entertained, including the Duke of Kingston and the Duke and Duchess of Norfolk.[54] Others were more tangential acquaintances or complete strangers, visiting the house and its contents out of pure curiosity. On 1 August 1752, Henrietta wrote to her grandson from Cavendish Lodge at Clipstone, ten miles from Welbeck, informing him that just before she had left there the previous day, "came six [or] seven Visiters at the Manor, & Mis Clifford with them to see Welbeck, I sent for Mis Clifford up stairs. . . . I saw none of the others nor heard their Names, & left them in the House & came away."[55] Such a scenario was entirely typical of visits to country houses in this era, while town houses seem to have been less widely accessible.[56] Although important guests would have been personally entertained by the family, many others would turn up, either speculatively or with letters of introduction, and be shown around the house and its contents by a servant, most frequently the housekeeper. In the most popular destinations, such as Blenheim and Kedleston Hall in Derbyshire, tickets were sold and guidebooks and catalogues produced for the benefit of such tourists.[57]

Some of the visitors to Welbeck praised Henrietta's work; for example, "Lord Galaway & some others last Thursday comended all the Gothick Parts & execution of them."[58] Others were much less favorably impressed—and she recorded the fact with some bitterness, referring to her project as what "y[e] Generality of y[e] World calls part of my foly" and writing to her grandson, "I assure you, Your Pappa, your Mamma & Your Aprobation of My Intended Improvements, makes the few impertinent seekers to find faults, affects me as little as their Directions deserve."[59] These critics included Mrs. Delany, who found the countess's display rather too ostentatious, writing that "everything displays the antiquity of the noble race from whence the owners are descended, and the walls are covered with family portraits, but there is a *glare of grandeur*."[60] Walpole may have relished the antiquarian profusion, but his words acknowledge the effect of excess: "It is impossible to describe the bales of Cavendishes, Harleys, Holleses, Veres, and Ogles: every chamber is tapestried with them; nay, and with ten thousand other fat morsels; all their histories inscribed."[61] Certainly, one needed to illustrate one's heritage. Visitors were impressed by evidence of ancestral descent, took pleasure from seeing images of historical figures, and enjoyed comparing likenesses to those viewed in other houses.[62] Antiquarianism had become part of polite culture.[63] However, Henrietta had overdone it. Her resolve to include an image of every member of the family, no matter how remotely related, and to record in great detail their connection with either her line or that of her husband was too much. It went beyond the limits of necessity and acceptability and into the realms of excess, revealing an expenditure of time and money that breached the boundaries of decorum.

The rules by which the Countess of Oxford was operating were not the same as those that governed the judgments of many visitors. For her, antiquarianism and familial pride were the sole considerations; all else was subject to her intent to present a complete, detailed account of her family's history. For viewers such as Mrs. Delany, the degree to which that intent surpassed all other imperatives, primarily those of taste and decorum, made the visual glut of genealogical heritage somewhat repellent. In addition, the problematic nature of Henrietta's excessive preoccupation with lineage and pride can only have been heightened by her gender. Indeed, it seems arguable that Henrietta's desire to trace every branch of her family tree conveyed a certain defensiveness. While Henrietta's mother had contested her husband's bequest of Welbeck and other Cavendish estates to Thomas Pelham, the dispute had only been resolved a year after her death by Henrietta herself.[64] The considerable effort, not to mention the funds, that Henrietta had invested in securing her inheritance could only have increased her desire to provide a visual, material testament to the family through which it had descended. Paradoxically, however, that collection must simultaneously have drawn attention to the fact that the Cavendish line had failed to follow the ideal route of direct succession in two generations and was soon to pass through her daughter in the absence of a male heir.[65]

As the work of Henrietta, Countess of Oxford, at Welbeck Abbey amply demonstrates, the family portrait collection provided an environment in which women could demonstrate their own heritage alongside testaments to the ancestry of their spouses. In some cases, such as those of Lady Jane Cottrell-Dormer and Caroline Fox, Lady Holland, they appear to have echoed masculine narratives of patrilineage, emphasizing and investing in patriarchy and their paternal heritage. In that of Henrietta, the pictorial narrative she created embraced both direct and indirect succession, together with those dynasties to which she was connected through her maternal ancestry. The heraldic device at Welbeck that most clearly rivals those associated with the Cavendish line is that of the Ogles, a Northumberland clan with whom the family had become connected through the marriage of Sir Charles Cavendish. The country house as a space in which women's contributions to their husband's lines could be recorded is in notable contrast to family group and pendant portraits. As we have seen, these had to reflect the more dominant ideology and legal reality that, to employ the Marquess of Halifax's terms, a woman was "transplanted" or "grafted" into another family on the occasion of her marriage.[66]

The family portrait collection thus counters what Susan Staves has identified as a tendency on the part of historians to distinguish between the interests of the family and the interests of women, viewing wives as individuals either bringing assets to or acting as drains on an estate rather than as integral to a family's collective endeavor.[67] Similarly, Judith Lewis has rightly observed that "if the ruling principle of coverture regarded married women as nothing but vessels for the transmission of male property rights, the actual conditions of their lives were often quite different. Contemporaries regarded women as real kinfolk."[68] Certainly, Henrietta's mother was subject to property laws that meant her husband could bequeath her ancestral property outside her family. Yet Henrietta could fight to regain that property and then own it outright for her lifetime on the death of her husband. In fact, Henrietta was a custodian rather than an owner, but then the principles of strict settlement placed elite men in the same position. The countess's possession of Welbeck Abbey and its contents after Edward's death relied on his generous will, and her work was primarily concerned with adapting and displaying objects that were merely passing through her hands. Yet this situation was one that affected the elite as a whole, regardless of gender.

Henrietta had to deal with the heirlooms that had been passed down to her. She had no choice over her ownership of those possessions, and even if they had not been secured as the future property of her grandson, her potential ability to alienate them was severely restricted by well-established aristocratic culture. As John Styles notes in his essay in this volume, the history of consumption has been dominated by the notion of people exercising taste, selecting from an ever-expanding world of goods according to ever-more-complex wants and desires. However, the heirloom denied the processes of selection, channeling and delimiting the exercise of taste into and within the bounds of management, arrangement, and display.[69] Equally, the heirloom stands outside the realm of the commodity and thereby demands as much investigation as has been accorded to the gift as an object that resists the parameters of exchange value. Indeed, many of the portraits at Welbeck would also have been of minimal use value if it were not for the identity of their sitters. It was the names and lives recorded in those numerous and lengthy inscriptions that made them such valuable objects. Nevertheless, they still possessed this value only for Henrietta, her family, and her descendants. This was explicitly acknowledged by Nicolas Courtney, who had gained a number of Holles portraits through marriage. He sent three of these, including a half-length portrait of Gervase Holles, to William Wenman, Edward Harley's agent, in 1714, declaring, "I Will put noe price on ye Pictures, neither does I think them valuable to Strangers."[70] Similarly, when Sarah, Duchess of Marlborough, visited the third Duke of Bedford at Woburn Abbey in 1732, she thought the portraits only "valuable as they belong to the family and in antique dresses."[71] Indeed, if an ancestral portrait moved into what Arjun Appadurai has dubbed "a commodity situation" in the course of its life cycle—sold or auctioned off, its symbolic value spurned in favor of any material value it might have—it was generally met with disapprobation.[72] It was the duty of aristocrats, whether male or female, to maintain, consolidate, and continue their family's collections, creating displays that would inspire future generations and buttress the claims of those generations to heritage and respectability. It was their responsibility to retain and display the identity of portraits in order that their utility to the family might continue.

Many thanks to John Styles, Amanda Vickery, Michael Hatt, and all the other contributors for their feedback on earlier drafts of this essay. Thanks also to Derek Adlam, Karen Hearn, Lucy Worsley, and the participants at the "Function and Its Relation to the Conception and Reception of Portraiture in the Eighteenth Century" session at the Association of Art Historians annual conference, April 2005.

1. This is one aspect of a wider emphasis on patterns of consumption. See, for example, Marcia Pointon, "Portrait Painting as a Business Enterprise in London in the 1780s," *Art History* 7 (1984): 187–205; Iain Pears, *The Discovery of Painting: The Growth of Interest in the Arts in England, 1680–1768* (New Haven and London: Yale Univ. Press, 1988); David Solkin, *Painting for Money: Visual Arts and the Public Sphere in Eighteenth-Century England* (New Haven and London: Yale Univ. Press, 1993); and Louise Lippincott, "Expanding on Portraiture: The Market, the Public and the Hierarchy of Genres in Eighteenth-Century Britain," in *The Consumption of Culture, 1600–1800: Image, Object, Text*, ed. Ann Bermingham and John Brewer (London: Routledge, 1995), 75–88.
2. Marcia Pointon, *Hanging the Head: Portraiture and Social Formation in Eighteenth Century England* (New Haven and London: Yale Univ. Press, 1993), 13.
3. David Solkin, ed., *Art on the Line: The Royal Academy Exhibitions at Somerset House, 1780–1836*, exh. cat. (New Haven and London: Yale Univ. Press, 2001).
4. Pointon, *Hanging the Head*, sec. 1, pt. 1, and Shearer West, "Patronage and Power: The Role of the Portrait in Eighteenth-Century England," in *Culture, Politics and Society in Britain, 1660–1800*, ed. Jeremy Black and Jeremy Gregory (Manchester and New York: Manchester Univ. Press, 1991), 131–53; see also Andrew Moore, "Hanging the Family Portraits," in *Family and Friends: A Regional Survey of British Portraiture*, by Andrew Moore and Charlotte Crawley (London: HMSO, 1992), 31–38, and Karen Stanworth, "Picturing a Personal History: The Case of Edward Onslow," *Art History* 16, no. 3 (1993): 408–23.
5. Kate Retford, "Reynolds's Portrait of Mrs Theresa Parker: A Case Study in Context," *British Art Journal* 4, no. 3 (2003): 80–86; Retford, "Sensibility and Genealogy in the Eighteenth-Century Family Portrait: The Collection at Kedleston Hall," *The Historical Journal* 46, no. 3 (2003): 533–60; Retford, *The Art of Domestic Life: Family Portraiture in Eighteenth-Century England* (New Haven and London: Yale Univ. Press, 2006), chap. 5.
6. Richard Leppert, *Music and Image: Domesticity, Ideology and Socio-cultural Formation in Eighteenth-*

Century England (Cambridge: Cambridge Univ. Press, 1988); Pointon, *Hanging the Head*, chap. 6; Shearer West, "The Public Nature of Private Life: The Conversation Piece and the Fragmented Family," *British Journal for Eighteenth-Century Studies* 18, no. 2 (1995): 152–71.

7. For a discussion of the Benjamin Wilson portraits, see James Lomax, "Family Faces: An Anthology of Temple Newsam Portraits," *Leeds Arts Calendar* 113 (1994): 32–33. See also Shearer West's discussions of Thomas Bardwell's *Broke and Bowes Families* (1740) in her "Public Nature of Private Life," 157–59, and "Framing Hegemony: Economics, Luxury and Family Continuity in the Country House Portrait," in *The Rhetoric of the Frame: Essays on the Boundaries of the Artwork*, ed. Paul Duro (Cambridge: Cambridge Univ. Press, 1996), 63–78. For a relevant consideration of Thomas Gainsborough's *Mr and Mrs Andrews* (1748/49), see Gillian Rose, "Looking at Landscape: The Uneasy Pleasures of Power," in *Feminism and Geography: The Limits of Geographical Knowledge* (Cambridge: Polity Press, 1993), 86–112, especially 91–93. This is a response to John Berger's analysis in *Ways of Seeing* (Harmondsworth, UK: Penguin, 1972), 106–8.

8. For such display of and fabrication of portraits, see John Martin Robinson, "Ancestral Piety," in *The British Face: A View of Portraiture 1625–1850* (London: P & D Colnaghi, 1986), 11–13, and Moore, "Hanging the Family Portraits."

9. See Esther Moir, *The Discovery of Britain: The English Tourists, 1540–1840* (London: Routledge & K. Paul, 1964), chap. 6; Adrian Tinniswood, *A History of Country House Visiting: Five Centuries of Tourism and Taste* (Oxford: Basil Blackwell, 1989); and Ian Ousby, *The Englishman's England: Taste, Travel and the Rise of Tourism* (Cambridge: Cambridge Univ. Press, 1990). Peter Mandler points out that such tourism was restricted to the polite classes at this date and did not become truly popular until the following century; see Mandler, *The Fall and Rise of the Stately Home* (New Haven and London: Yale Univ. Press, 1997): prelude and chap. 2.

10. Sarah Markham, *John Loveday of Caversham 1711–1789: The Life and Tours of an Eighteenth-Century Onlooker* (Wilton, UK: Michael Russell, 1984), 200.

11. Samuel Curwen, 2 Oct. 1776, in *The Journal of Samuel Curwen, Loyalist*, ed. Andrew Oliver, 2 vols. (Cambridge, MA: Harvard Univ. Press, 1972), 1:240.

12. There has been some, though by no means extensive, debate on how art collections were carved up between a family's residences. See Francis Haskell, "The British as Collectors," in *The Treasure Houses of Britain: Five Hundred Years of Private Patronage and Art Collecting*, ed. Gervase Jackson-Stops, exh. cat. (New Haven and London: Yale Univ. Press, 1985), 50–59; Francis Russell, "The Hanging and Display of Pictures, 1700–1850," in *The Fashioning and Functioning of the British Country House*, by Gervase Jackson-Stops and others, exh. cat. (Washington, DC: National Gallery of Art, 1989), 133–53; M. H. Port, "West End Palaces: The Aristocratic Town House in London, 1730–1830," *The London Journal* 20, no. 1 (1995): 17–46; Giles Waterfield, "The Town House as Gallery of Art," *The London Journal* 20, no. 1 (1995): 47–66; and Port, "Town House and Country House: Their Interaction," in *The Georgian Country House: Architecture, Landscape and Society*, ed. Dana Arnold (Stroud, UK: Sutton, 1998), 117–38.

13. This is discussed at length in Port, "West End Palaces," 24–37. See also Port, "Town House and Country House," 125.

14. Paintings in town houses often had to support the owner's political-party roles and the entertaining that came with them. For an analysis of the second Marquess of Rockingham's collection at 4 Grosvenor Square, see Douglas Fordham, "Raising Standards: Art and Imperial Politics in London, 1745–1776" (PhD diss., Yale Univ., 2003), chap. 4.

15. Waterfield, "Town House as Gallery of Art," 51.

16. The Van Loo portraits are cited in George Richardson, *Aedes Pembrochianae: A New Account and Description of the Statues, Bustos, Relievos, Paintings, Medals, and other Antiquities and Curiosities in Wilton-House*, 10th ed. (Salisbury, UK: Wilton-House, H. Coward, 1784), 116, and Wiltshire and Swindon Record Office 2057/H5/11, draft inventories of paintings, etc., c. 1800. The Reynolds portrait is cited in James Kennedy, *A New Description of the Pictures, Statues, Bustos, Basso-Relievos and other Curiosities in the Earl of Pembroke's House, at Wilton*, 9th ed. (Salisbury, UK: Printed by E. Easton, for Henry Coward, 1779), 59. For further details, see David Mannings and Martin Postle, *Sir Joshua Reynolds: A Complete Catalogue of His Paintings* (New Haven and London: Yale Univ. Press, 2000), 423.

17. Marcia Pointon, *Strategies for Showing: Women, Possession and Representation in English Visual Culture, 1665–1800* (Oxford: Oxford Univ. Press, 1997), chap. 1.

18. Mannings and Postle, *Sir Joshua Reynolds*, 423–24; Sidney, sixteenth Earl of Pembroke, *A Catalogue of the Paintings and Drawings in the Collection at Wilton House* (London and New York: Phaidon, 1968), 31–32.

19. For Rousham and the drawing room, see Christopher Hussey, "Rousham, Oxfordshire," *Country Life* 99 (17 May 1946): 900–903; and *Country Life* 99 (24 May 1946): 946–49.

20. West, "Framing Hegemony," 70–71.

21. For accounts of the gallery, see Stella Tillyard, *Aristocrats: Caroline, Emily, Louisa and Sarah Lennox, 1740–1832* (London: Vintage, 1995), 128, 149–52, 155, and Rosemary Baird, *Mistress of the House: Great Ladies and Grand Houses, 1670–1830* (London: Weidenfeld and Nicolson, 2003), 108–10. For discussions of the house more generally, see the Earl of Ilchester, *The Home of the Hollands, 1605–1820* (London: J. Murray, 1937), and Derek Hudson, *Holland House in Kensington* (London: P. Davies, 1967).

22. My account of the hang is based on Thomas Faulkner, *History and Antiquities of Kensington* (London: Printed by D. Jaques, for T. Egerton [etc.], 1820), chap. 4, especially 106–9, and Brian Fitzgerald, ed., *Correspondence of Emily, Duchess of Leinster, 1731–1814*, vol. 1, *Letters of Emily, Duchess of Leinster; James, First Duke of Leinster; Caroline Fox, Lady Holland* (Dublin: Stationery Office, 1949).

23. Faulkner, *History and Antiquities of Kensington*, 107.

24. For the pictures included, see Tillyard, *Aristocrats*, 149–50, and Baird, *Mistress of the House*, 109–10.

25. Faulkner, *History and Antiquities of Kensington*, 107.

26. Horace Walpole to Horace Mann, 29 May 1744, in *Horace Walpole's Correspondence*, ed. W. S. Lewis, W. H. Smith, and G. L. Lam, 48 vols. (London: Oxford Univ. Press, 1937–83), 18:450.

27. Faulkner, *History and Antiquities of Kensington*, 106; Hudson, *Holland House*, 27.

28. Mannings and Postle, *Sir Joshua Reynolds*, 204.

29. Lady Holland to the Marchioness of Kildare, 9 June 1766, in Fitzgerald, *Correspondence of Emily, Duchess of Leinster*, 452. For examples, see Lady Holland to the Marchioness of Kildare, 5 Sept. 1762 and 11 Sept. 1763, in Fitzgerald, *Correspondence of Emily, Duchess of Leinster*, 338, 388. For more complete details, see Kate Retford, "'A Sort of Sex in Souls': Gender and the Marital Portrait in Eighteenth-Century England," *British Journal for Eighteenth-Century Studies* 27, no. 1 (2004): 99–120.

30. For Henrietta Cavendish and Welbeck Abbey, see A. S. Turberville, *A History of Welbeck Abbey and Its Owners*, 2 vols. (London: Faber and Faber, 1938), 1:393–400, and Peter Smith, "Lady Oxford's Alterations at Welbeck Abbey, 1741–55," *The Georgian Group Journal* 11 (2001): 133–68. For the portraits, see William Bentinck, sixth Duke of Portland, *Catalogue of the Pictures belonging to his Grace the Duke of Portland, at Welbeck Abbey and in London* (London: Chiswick Press, 1894), and especially Richard W. Goulding, *Catalogue of the Pictures belonging to his Grace the Duke of Portland*, rev. by C. K. Adams (Cambridge: Cambridge Univ. Press, 1936). The earlier catalogue specifies original room location, while the later volume identifies which inscriptions were executed on the orders of Henrietta. Unfortunately, I have been unable to locate a recorded 1831 copy of a catalogue made in 1747, probably by George Vertue. I am most grateful to Derek Adlam at Welbeck for all his advice and assistance and to Lucy Worsley for allowing me to read her article, "Female Architectural Patronage in the Eighteenth Century and the Case of Henrietta Cavendish Holles Harley," *Architectural History* 48 (2005): 139–62, prior to publication.

31. Horace Walpole to Richard Bentley, Aug. 1756, in Lewis, Smith, and Lam, *Horace Walpole's Correspondence*, 35:271.

32. Worsley, "Female Architectural Patronage," 145. In 1713, a family servant had informed Henrietta that "yor Honrs Father had told me your surname was Cavendyshe and found great fault wth me for writing yr Honrs Name Henrietta Holles in an Assessment of the Poll Tax some years agoe"; John Cossen to Henrietta Cavendish, 26 July 1713, British Library (hereafter BL), Add. MSS 70431.

33. Arthur Collins, *Historical Collections of the Noble Families of Cavendishe, Holles, Vere, Harley and Ogle* (London: Printed for Edward Withers, 1752), v. See also Henrietta Cavendish to her grandson the Marquis of Titchfield, 13 Jan. 1752, Nottingham University Archive (hereafter NUA), PwF 4756, and John Peyto Verney, 14th Baron Willoughby de Broke, to Henrietta Cavendish, 7 May 1754, BL, Add. MSS 70431.

34. George Vertue, BL, Add. MSS 23093, fol. 26.

35. Goulding, *Catalogue*, no. 430; George Vertue, BL, Add. MSS 23069, fol. 39, and Add. MSS 23072, fol. 73. Some pictures had been transferred earlier. See accounts of Isaac Hobart, steward, Nottinghamshire Record Office (hereafter NRO), DD5P 1/1. He records a payment of 3s. to Ignatius Stanley and a helper to "hang up the first parcel of pictures wch were brought fro Wimpole."

36. For the portraits transferred from Bolsover, see Goulding, *Catalogue*, nos. 264, 350, 358, 494. The countess paid Thomas Hudson a total of £84 for the pendants of the Duke and Duchess of Portland in the mid-1740s. See entries for 22 June 1744, 13 July 1744, and 20 June 1745, "Disbursements for the Right Honble the Countess of Oxford," 1738–49, NRO, DD5P 7/2/2.

37. William Salmon, *Polygraphice* (London: Printed by Robert White, for John Crumpe, and sold by Charles Passenger, 1678), 160. He specifies that royal and noble portraits should be hung in the dining room, "other draughts of the life, of Persons of Honour, intimate or special friends, and acquaintance" be placed in the withdrawing room, and portraits of wives and children in the bedroom. This repeats almost verbatim the advice given in William Sanderson, *Graphice: The Use of the Pen and Pensil, or the most Excellent Art of Painting* (London: Printed for R. Crofts, 1658), 24–25.

38. Henrietta Cavendish to Lady Mary Wortley Montagu, 7 June 1744, BL, Add. MSS 70432.

39. Smith, "Lady Oxford's Alterations at Welbeck Abbey," 145–46.

40. See, for example, NRO, DD5P 6/25/21, DD5P 6/23/1–3, DD5P 6/26/14, DD5P 6/28/3, DD5P 6/19/7, and DD5P 6/29/17.

41. Bill from Benjamin Hague, paid 27 Jan. 1752, NRO, DD5P 6/29/20.

42. See, for example, NRO, DD5P 6/26/14 and DD5P 6/21/5.

43. Bill from Benjamin Hague, paid 10 Nov. 1750, NRO, DD5P 6/26/14, and bill from George Machin, n.d., NRO, DD5P 6/21/5. For a consideration of the process of "monumenting portraits," see Morris R. Brownell, *The Prime Minister of Taste: A Portrait of Horace Walpole* (New Haven and London: Yale Univ. Press, 2001), 109–11. Thanks to Lucy Peltz for this reference.

44. Mrs. Delany to Mrs. Dewes, 19 Sept. 1756, in *The Autobiography and Correspondence of Mary Granville, Mrs Delany*, ed. Lady Llanover, 6 vols. (London: Richard Bentley, 1861–62): 3:443. For women's involvement in antiquarianism, see Lucy Peltz, "The Extra-Illustration of London: The Gendered Spaces and Practices of Antiquarianism in the Late Eighteenth Century," in *Producing the Past: Aspects of Antiquarian Culture and Practice, 1700–1850*, ed. Martin Myrone and Lucy Peltz (Aldershot, UK: Ashgate, 1999), 115–34.

45. In this, they were similar to engraved portraits published in series or used for the purposes of extra-illustration. See Pointon, *Hanging the Head*, 53–62, and Lucy Peltz, "The Pleasure of the Book: Extra-Illustration, an Eighteenth-Century Fashion," *Things* 8 (1998): 7–31.

46. Russell, "Hanging and Display of Pictures," 134, 136, 139, 147; Port, "West End Palaces," 37–39; Waterfield, "Town House as Gallery of Art"; Port, "Town House and Country House," 130–31. However, Francis Haskell argues that there was a trend between the 1730s and 1760s for members of the aristocracy to move their collections out of their town residences and into the country, citing the examples of Lord Burlington, Sir Andrew Fountaine, and Sir Robert Walpole; see Haskell, "British as Collectors," 51–52.

47. Mrs. Delany to Mrs. Dewes, 19 Sept. 1756, in Llanover, *Mrs Delany*, 3:443.

48. Goulding, *Catalogue*, nos. 4, 464, 491.

49. This new identification was first suggested by Sir Oliver Millar to Karen Hearn, who subsequently confirmed it and will publish it in her forthcoming essay titled "William Cavendish, 1st Duke of Newcastle, and the Fine Arts." Many thanks to Karen Hearn for her help with this matter. See also Goulding, *Catalogue*, no. 191, a portrait identified as "Alice Daughter of John Parker of Cavendishe married to Thos Cavendishe Mother of Sr Wm Cavendishe of Chatsworth."

50. Henrietta Cavendish to Lady Mary Wortley Montagu, 7 June 1744, BL, Add. MSS 70432.

51. Henrietta Cavendish to the Marquis of Titchfield, 22 Dec. 1750, NUA, PwF 4749. See also Henrietta Cavendish to the Marquis of Titchfield, 2 June 1750 and 28 July 1753, PwF 4746 and PwF 4767.

52. See, for example, Henrietta Cavendish to the Marquis of Titchfield, 5 Aug. 1749, 6 May 1751, and 1 Aug. 1752, NUA, PwF 4744, PwF 4752, and PwF 4761.

53. See, for example, Henrietta Cavendish to Lady Mary Wortley Montagu, 17 Sept. 1743, 17 Jan. 1747, and 21 Jan. 1747, BL, Add. MSS 70432.
54. See, for example, Henrietta Cavendish to the Marquis of Titchfield, 28 Oct. 1752, 13 June 1752, and 25 Nov. 1752, NUA, PwF 4764, PwF 4759, and PwF 4765.
55. Henrietta Cavendish to the Marquis of Titchfield, 1 Aug. 1752, NUA, PwF 4761.
56. Waterfield, "Town House as Gallery of Art," 55.
57. For accounts of visits to Kedleston, see Oliver, *Journal of Samuel Curwen*, 1:353; James Plumptre, "Tour into Derbyshire" (1793), Cambridge University Library, Add. MSS 5804, fols. 8–12. For Blenheim, see the Reverend William Mavor, *A New Description of Blenheim, the Seat of His Grace the Duke of Marlborough. To Which Is Prefixed, Blenheim, a Poem* (London: T. Cadell, 1789), and *The Oxford University and City Guide, to which is added a Description of Blenheim and Nuneham* (Oxford: Munday & Slatter, 1818), 154–73.
58. Henrietta Cavendish to the Marquis of Titchfield, 2 Oct. 1751, NUA, PwF 4755.
59. Henrietta Cavendish to Lady Mary Wortley Montagu, 7 June 1744, BL, Add. MSS 70432; Henrietta Cavendish to the Marquis of Titchfield, 24 Oct. 1753, NUA, PwF 4768.
60. Mrs. Delany to Mrs. Dewes, 7 Sept. 1756, in Llanover, *Mrs Delany*, 3:438.
61. Horace Walpole to Richard Bentley, Aug. 1756, in Lewis, Smith, and Lam, *Horace Walpole's Correspondence*, 35:270.
62. John Cornforth, *Early Georgian Interiors* (New Haven and London: Yale Univ. Press, 2004), 226.
63. Myrone and Peltz, *Producing the Past.*
64. Will of John Holles, fourth Earl of Clare and Duke of Newcastle, dated 29 Aug. 1707, probate dated 6 July 1717, NUA, PL C 3/2/16.
65. Henrietta had given birth to a son in Oct. 1725, but he died soon after birth. See NUA, PL C 1/496, PL C 2/137, PL C 2/138, and PL C 2/141.
66. George Savile, Marquess of Halifax, "The Lady's New Year's Gift; or, Advice to a Daughter" (1688), repr. in *Halifax: Complete Works*, ed. J. P. Kenyon (Harmondsworth, UK: Penguin, 1969), 288, 286.
67. Susan Staves, *Married Women's Separate Property in England, 1660–1833* (Cambridge, MA, and London: Harvard Univ. Press, 1990), 203.
68. Judith S. Lewis, *Sacred to Female Patriotism: Gender, Class and Politics in Late Georgian Britain* (London and New York: Routledge, 2003), 12.
69. Henry Glassie argues that the collector's alteration and recontextualization of objects should be seen as a creative process in its own right; see Glassie, *Material Culture* (Bloomington: Indiana Univ. Press, 1999), 82–85. However, he is discussing objects, such as cars, that have been actively chosen by their owner.
70. Nicolas Courtney to William Wenman, 24 May 1714, quoted in Goulding, *Catalogue*, no. 488.
71. Sarah, Duchess of Marlborough, to Diana, Duchess of Bedford, 4 July 1732, in *Letters of a Grandmother, 1732–1735*, ed. Gladys Scott Thomson (London: J. Cape, 1943), 36.
72. Arjun Appadurai, "Introduction: Commodities and the Politics of Value," in *The Social Life of Things: Commodities in Cultural Perspective*, ed. Arjun Appadurai (Cambridge: Cambridge Univ. Press, 1997), 13. Igor Kopytoff similarly discusses the principle that certain things, including humans and works of art, fall outside the logic of the consumer marketplace; see Kopytoff, "The Cultural Biography of Things: Commoditization as Process," in Appadurai, *Social Life of Things*, 64–91. For views on the sale of family portraits, see, for example, *The Oracle* (1796), quoted in *Artists and Their Friends in England, 1700–1799*, by William T. Whitley, 2 vols. (London and Boston: Medici Society, 1928), 2:198, and Richard Brinsley Sheridan, *The School for Scandal* (1777), repr. in *The School for Scandal and Other Plays*, ed. Eric Rump (Harmondsworth, UK: Penguin Books, 1988), 239, 242.

Notes on Contributors

Linzy Brekke is an Assistant Professor of History at Stonehill College in Massachusetts. Her work focuses on fashion and consumer culture in the early American republic.

Hannah Greig is a Junior Research Fellow at Balliol College, Oxford, and was previously a Postdoctoral Research Fellow at the AHRC Centre for the Study of the Domestic Interior. She recently wrote "Eighteenth-Century English Interiors in Image and Text," in *Imagined Interiors: Representing the Domestic Interior since the Renaissance*, ed. J. Aynsley and C. Grant (2006), and is completing a book on eighteenth-century elite identities based on her 2003 University of London doctoral dissertation, "The Beau Monde and Fashionable Life in Eighteenth-Century London, 1688–1800."

Ellen Hartigan-O'Connor is an Assistant Professor of History at San Jose State University. She is currently completing a book on women's economic networks in Revolutionary-era American port cities.

Amy H. Henderson is a doctoral candidate in art history at the University of Delaware. Her dissertation, "Furnishing the Republican Court: Building and Decorating Philadelphia Homes, 1790–1800," explores the material worlds of early American elites.

Bernard L. Herman is the Edward and Elizabeth Goodman Rosenberg Professor of Art History at the University of Delaware, where he also serves on the faculty of the Center for Material Culture Studies, the Winterthur Program in Early American Culture, and the Center for Historic Architecture and Design. He is the author of numerous books, including *The Stolen House* (1992), *Everyday Architecture of the Mid-Atlantic: Looking at Buildings and Landscapes* (with Gabrielle M. Lanier, 1997), and *Town House: Architecture and Material Life in the Early American City, 1780–1830* (2005). He is currently working on a book on the first-period buildings (c. 1680–1740) of the Delaware Valley and Philadelphia region.

Karen Lipsedge is a Lecturer in Media and Cultural Studies and English Literature at Kingston University. Her research focuses on the representation of the domestic interior in eighteenth-century British novels, and she recently wrote "Representations of the Domestic Parlour in Samuel Richardson's *Clarissa,*" in *Eighteenth-Century Fiction* 17, no. 3 (2005).

Ann Smart Martin is Chipstone Professor of American Decorative Arts at the University of Wisconsin–Madison, where she administers the interdisciplinary Certificate in Material Culture. She is the author of *Buying into the World of Goods: Early Consumers in the Virginia Backcountry* (2006).

Kate Retford is a Lecturer in Eighteenth- and Early-Nineteenth-Century Art History in the School of History of Art, Film, and Visual Media at Birkbeck, University of London. She has written a number of articles on eighteenth-century English portraiture and has just published *The Art of Domestic Life: Family Portraiture in Eighteenth-Century England* (2006).

Robert Blair St. George is a Professor of History at the University of Pennsylvania. A past Guggenheim Foundation Fellow, he has published *The Wrought Covenant* (1979), *Material Life in America* (1988), *Conversing by Signs* (1998), and *Possible Pasts* (2000).

John Styles is Research Professor in History at the University of Hertfordshire and was an Associate Director of the AHRC Centre for the Study of the Domestic Interior from 2001 to 2004. He coauthored *Design and the Decorative Arts: Britain 1500 to 1900* (2001) and is completing a book about the clothes worn by ordinary people in eighteenth-century England.

Amanda Vickery is Reader in the History of Women and Gender at Royal Holloway, University of London, and was an Associate Director of the AHRC Centre for the Study of the Domestic Interior from 2001 to 2006. Her first book, *The Gentleman's Daughter: Women's Lives in Georgian England* (1998), won the Whitfield, Wolfson, and Longman–History Today prizes. She is now writing a study of gender and the domestic interior in eighteenth-century England.

Claire Walsh is an Associate Lecturer for the Open University in the East of England Region. She has written extensively on seventeenth- and eighteenth-century shops and shopping, including "Social Meaning and Social Space in the Shopping Galleries of Early-Modern London," in *A Nation of Shopkeepers: A History of Retailing in Britain, 1550–2000*, ed. John Benson and Laura Ugolini (2003). She is completing a monograph on shops and shopping in early-modern England, c. 1660–1800.

Jonathan White completed a PhD dissertation, "Luxury and Labour: Ideas of Labouring-Class Consumption in Eighteenth-Century England," at the University of Warwick in 2001. It is being rewritten as a book with the provisional title *The Fruits of Industry: Capitalist Ideology and the Labouring Classes.* He now works for the University and College Union, the higher-education trade union in Britain.

Index

Illustrations are indicated by page numbers in italics.